Universal Critical Acclaim for *Gideon's Spies*

"Tells it like it was—and like it is."
> —Meir Amit, former director general of Mossad

"Gripping and compulsively readable."
> —*Sunday Express* (UK)

"Gordon Thomas has a grasp of history. . . . This is one of the few books to have captured the true nature of the Israeli government and the thought process of the Israeli power elite. . . . This book is a must for any student of modern Middle Eastern history."
> —Ari Ben-Menashe, former adviser on intelligence to Prime Minister Yitzhak Shamir and the Israeli government

"Thomas provides readers with a good sense of how the Mossad trains its agents. Fun read."
> —*Kirkus Reviews*

"A fascinating look at a spy organization that has remained off-limits to most journalists. Some of the incredible episodes Gordon Thomas writes about seem like they belong in fiction, and yet this is a first-rate nonfiction account."
> —Mary Fischer, *GQ* magazine

"Gordon Thomas has kept his head above the orchestrated campaigns of disinformation and produced a document about the Mossad that is as balanced and as truthful as can be arranged. This book is neither a vilification nor a condemnation of the Mossad. Thomas clearly understood Israel's dilemmas when he put together this fine work."
> —Barry Chamish, coeditor of *Israel Today Intelligence Review* and author of *Who Murdered Yitzhak Rabin?*

"A thought-provoking and compelling book."
> —David Pitt, *Booklist*

"Gordon Thomas digs deeply into the secrets of the Israeli intelligence service as a result of being given *exclusive* access."
> —*Soldier* magazine (UK)

"Rich in detail . . . powerful in the writing."

—*El Pais* (Spain)

"Fascinating from beginning to end."

—*Japan Times* (Japan)

"A story crying out to be filmed! All-action, great characters."

—*Hollywood Reporter*

"Great revelations. The author of this acclaimed history of Mossad has done it again."

—*Drudge Report*

"Here is real insider stuff, written by an acknowledged expert. It is shocking and absorbing; rich and powerful. Go buy it!"

—All American Radio, Washington, DC

"Gordon Thomas has written a major work on the history of the Israeli secret service, Mossad."

—*Ireland on Sunday* (Ireland)

"Using eyewitness accounts from directors, agents, and even assassins, Thomas goes where few writers have gone before—inside the Mossad, Israel's ruthless, super-secretive intelligence agency."

—*Maxim*

"This is essential reading for anyone concerned with the Middle East and world affairs."

—*Al-Wasat* (Saudi Arabia)

"Thomas meticulously documents the shadowy world of spies and covert operations. Espionage buffs will love every page."

—*Booklist*

"What he says is always ominous—but never judgmental. That is what makes this book one of the most trusted on the world of secret intelligence."

—*European* (Spain)

Also by Gordon Thomas

Nonfiction

Fiction

GIDEON'S SPIES

The Secret History of the Mossad

Seventh Edition, Revised and Updated

GORDON THOMAS

THOMAS DUNNE BOOKS
ST. MARTIN'S GRIFFIN
NEW YORK

THOMAS DUNNE BOOKS.
An imprint of St. Martin's Press.

www.thomasdunnebooks.com
www.stmartins.com

Design by Maureen Troy

Library of Congress Cataloging-in-Publication Data

Thomas, Gordon, 1933–
    Gideon's spies : the secret history of the Mossad / Gordon Thomas.—7th ed.
        p. cm.
    Includes bibliographical references and index.
    ISBN 978-1-250-05640-5 (trade paperback)
    ISBN 978-1-4668-6658-4 (e-book)
    1. Israel. Mosad le-modi'in ve-tafkidim meyuhadim.   2. Intelligence service—Israel—History.   3. Israel—Politics and government.   I. Title.
    UB251.I78T49   2009
    327.125694—dc22   2008042893

Seventh Edition: March 2015

10 9 8 7 6 5 4 3 2 1

CONTENTS

CONTENTS

Acknowledgments

ISRAEL

Meir Amit
Juval Aviv
Ari Ben-Menashe
Barry Chamish
Eli Cohen
Jaakov Cohen
Meir Dagan
Alex Doron
Ran Edelist
Raphael Eitan
Efraim Halevy

Isser Harel
Wafa'a Ali Ildris
David Kimche
Michael Koubi
Amiran Levine
Ariel Merari
Reuven Merhav
Yoel Ben Porat
Uri Saguy
Zvi Spielman

and those who still cannot be named

ELSEWHERE

Mohamed al-Fayed
Ehud Barak
Alice Baya'a
John A. Belton
Richard Brenneke
Sean Carberry
Ahmad Chalabi
Sebastian Cody
David Dastych
Art Dworken
Heather Florence
Ted Gunderson
William Hamilton
Cheryl Hanin Bentov
Amanda Harris
Barbara Honegger
Diana Johnson
Emery Kabongo
Gile Kepel
Otto Kormek
Zahir Kzeibati
Emer Lenehan

Lewis Libby
John Magee
Paul Marcinkus
John McNamara
Laurie Meyer
Muhamed Mugraby
Daniel Nagier
John Parsley
Samir Saddoui
Samira Shabander
Christopher Story
Susannah Tarbush
Michael Tauck
Elizabeth Tomlinson
Richard Tomlinson
Jacques Vergès
Colin Wallace
Russell Warren-Howe
Catherine Whittaker
Stuart Winter
Marcus Wolff
David Yallop

each in their own way played their part

AND LAST BUT NOT LEAST

William Buckley
William Casey
Joachim Kraner
Edith—of course

} among them they
inspired the idea

MOSSAD DIRECTORS GENERAL

1951–1952	REUVEN SHILOAH
1952–1963	ISSER HAREL
1963–1968	MEIR AMIT
1968–1974	ZVI ZAMIR
1974–1982	YITZHAK HOFI
1982–1990	NAHUM ADMONI
1990–1996	SHABTAI SHAVIT
1996–1998	DANNY YATOM
1998–2002	EFRAIM HALEVY
2002–2010	MEIR DAGAN
2011–	TAMIR PARDO

GLOSSARY

Active measures	Operations to influence or otherwise affect other nations' policies
AFR	Automatic fingerprint recognition
ANC	African National Congress
ANO	Abu Nidal Organization
AI	Artificial intelligence
AL	Specialist unit operating under deep cover in the United States
Aman	Israeli military intelligence
ASU	Active service terrorist unit
AWACS	Airborne warning and control aircraft
Babbler	Counterbugging device
Backstopping	Fake identification papers
Base	Permanent station in foreign country
Bat leveyha	Female assistant agent
Better world	Euphemism for killing enemy agent; similarly, to "send a person on vacation" means to injure him/her—the extent of the injury depends on whether the "vacation" is to be brief or long
Bioleverage	Euphemism for blackmail—literally, the use of derogatory information to coerce someone
Blind dating	Meeting place chosen by a contact to meet his controller
Blow-back	Fake stories fed to foreign news media
BND	Bundesnachrichtendienst, German Federal Intelligence Service, concerned with both foreign and domestic intelligence
Bodel	A courier
Bug	Electronic device for hearing and recording
Burn	An agent deliberately sacrificed in order to protect a more valuable spy
BW	Biological weapons
Case death	Operation that fails for no obvious reason
Case officer	In charge of field agents
CAT	Computer-aided tomography
Chamfering	Technique for opening sealed mail
CIA	Central Intelligence Agency
CIO	Central Imagery Office

CIS	Commonwealth of Independent States
Cold approach	Attempt to recruit a foreign national
Comint	Acronym for communications intelligence
Cover	Identity assumed by intelligence officer when abroad
Cultivation	Establishing rapport with a source of information
CW	Chemical weapons
Daylight	Highest form of alert
DCI	Director of Central Intelligence Agency
DEA	Drug Enforcement Administration
DI	Directorate of Intelligence
DIA	Defense Intelligence Agency
Diamond	Communications unit
DO	Directorate of Operations
Dry cleaning	Various techniques to avoid surveillance
ECM	Electronic countermeasures
EDP	Electronic data processing
Elint	Electronic intelligence intercepted from radar, satellites
Exfiltrate	Removing an agent from hostile country
FACES	Facial Analysis Comparison and Elimination System
False flagging	Recruiting a person who believes he or she will be working for another country or interest
Fumigate	Sweeping an area for electronic bugs
Go-away	Prearranged signal not to make contact at previously arranged rendezvous
Grinder	Debriefing room, also used to interrogate suspects
Honey trap	Sexual entrapment for intelligence purposes
Humint	Intelligence gathered by agents in the field
IDA	Intelligence database
IED	Improvised explosive device
IFF	Identification, friend or foe
II	Image identification
Institute	Formal name of Mossad—Institute for Intelligence and Special Operations; originally called Institute for Coordination

GLOSSARY

IR	Infrared
ISA	Intelligence support activity
JIC	Joint Intelligence Center
Jumper	Agent working overseas on short-term assignment
Katsa	Case officer
Kidon	Operative specializing in assassination
LAKAM	Intelligence agency gathering scientific data
LAP	Department of Psychological Warfare
Legend	Bogus biography for *katsa*
Light cover	*Katsa* working under diplomatic cover
Loot	Intelligence gathered from operations
Mabuah	A non-Jewish informer
Measles	Assassination that appears to stem from natural causes
Meluckha	Recruiting department
Memune	Title given to director general of Mossad
Mishlashim	Dead-letter box; a secure place for an agent to receive or drop off information
Music box	Radio transmitter
Naka	Writing system
Neviot	Surveillance specialist
NHITC	National Human Intelligence Tasking Center
NIC	National Intelligence Center
NSA	National Security Agency
NSTL	National security threat list
OAU	Organization of African Unity
PFLP	Popular Front for the Liberation of Palestine
PLF	Palestine Liberation Front
PLO	Palestine Liberation Organization
Photint	Photographic intelligence
PROD	Technique for retrieving photographs from optical disc
Radint	Radar intelligence
RAF	Red Army Faction (Germany)

GLOSSARY

Reg-sig   Recognition signal for *katsa* to make contact with field agent in public place

Safanim   Unit to target PLO

Sayanim   Volunteer Jewish helpers who live outside at Israel (singular: sayan)

Safe house   Apartment or house used for secret meetings or as an operations base

Sleeper   *Katsa*/agent to be called upon in only the most dire circumstances

Slick   Hiding place for documents

Target   Intelligence assignment

Teud   Forged document

Telint   Telemetry intelligence

Walk-in   Person who volunteers to serve

Wash   Recycling of a valid passport obtained by theft or purchased

Yaholomin   Special communications unit

BRIEF ARABIC GLOSSARY

Ayatollah	Title in the hierarchy of the Shiite clergy
Dawa	Propagation of the faith; also a call to Islam
Deobandi	School of doctors of Islamic law founded in 1867 to preach against British domination in India
Fatwa	Legal opinion based on the holy texts of Islam; usually ratified by senior clerics
Fedayeen	Men ready to sacrifice themselves for a sacred cause; most recently applied to suicide bombers
Fiqh	Unchallengeable Muslim law
Haj	Pilgrimage to Mecca to be attained by every devout Muslim once in a lifetime
Harb	War, especially when waged in the land of infidels
Hegira	Flight of the Prophet in September 622 from Mecca to Medina, signifying the establishing of Islam
Hezbollah	Party of God, prominent in Israel and Lebanon
Hudud	Punishments in religious law, Sharia, such as the stoning of a woman guilty of adultery, beheading for a crime, etc.
Imam	A mosque's director of prayer and the authority on all matters of religious regulation
Intifada	Uprisings; usually applied to the two Palestinian uprisings of 1987 and 2000
Jihad	Holy war to propagate Islamic faith and overthrow infidels
Madrassa	Religious school where Islamic law is taught
Mujahideen	(singular: mujahed) Jihad fighters
Pasdaran	Members of the Iranian Revolutionary Guards
Shebab	Arab youth
Takir	Excommunication from the Islamic faith
Taliban	Graduates of a religious school
Ulema	Doctors of Islamic law
Wahhabism	Founded by Ibn Abu al-Wahhab (1703–92); puritan doctrine still dominating Saudi Arabia

OTHER INTELLIGENCE SERVICES

ISRAEL

IDF
Responsible for coordinating all intelligence for the General Staff of the Israeli Defense Forces. From time to time gives Mossad specific tasks.

Aman
Intelligence branch of the IDF with specific responsibility for gathering military, geographic, and economic intelligence. Its prime focus remains the activities of Israel's Arab neighbors in the new millennium.

AFI
Intelligence branch of Israel's air force. Specializes in gathering signals intelligence and aerial reconnaissance. By the year 2001, the latter will be largely replaced by satellite, leaving AFI's role to provide conventional air support intelligence.

BP
Paramilitary-style border police in Israeli-occupied territories. Limited intelligence-gathering role.

NI
Naval intelligence unit of all Israeli seaborne forces. Work includes monitoring Israel's coasts and updating foreign naval resources.

GSS
Also known as Shin Bet or Shabak. Responsible for internal security and defense of Israeli installations abroad such as embassies, consulates, and important Israeli organizations.

RPPC
Research and Political Planning Center advises prime minister of the day and his policymakers on long-term strategy.

UNITED STATES OF AMERICA

CIA
Conducts covert operations, provides intelligence analysis for the incumbent president. Forbidden by executive order from conducting assassinations.

DIA
Coordinates all military intelligence for the Joint Chiefs of Staff.

INR	State Department's small intelligence and research department (1999 staff approximately 500). Reports only to incumbent secretary of state.
NIO	Based in the Pentagon, the National Imagery Office controls all U.S. satellite intelligence gathering. Constantly "tasked" by the CIA and DIA.
NRO	Pentagon-based. Works closely with NIO and has specific responsibility for all satellite hardware and deployment.
NSA	Operates from Fort George G. Meade, Maryland. Over the years its "spy in the sky" image has given the National Security Agency a glamour once only the prerogative of the CIA. Specializes in signals intelligence, cryptography. Works closely with NIO on satellite intelligence gathering.

United Kingdom

GCHQ	Its 7,000 (approx. 1999) staff acts as Britain's "invisible eye in outer space." Formally known as Government Communications Headquarters, it monitors and decodes radio, telex, fax, and e-mail traffic in and out of the United Kingdom. Regularly "tasked" by Britain's two main intelligence services.
MI6	Also known as the Secret Intelligence Service. Staff of under 2,000 (1999) plans, carries out, and analyzes worldwide clandestine operations and intelligence gathering.
MI5	2,000 staff (1999). Britain's prime internal counter-espionage service. Specializes in monitoring all designated subversives in the country and conducts surveillance on a large number of foreign diplomats and embassies, including those of Israel.

Russia

GRU	Glavnoye Razvedyvatelnoye Upravlenie provides Kremlin with military intelligence. Staffed with the best of the former Soviet Union's intelligence services. Equipped with satellite surveillance.
FCS	Renamed the Federal Counterintelligence Service, it is really the old KGB updated. Staff of 142,000 (1999). Focuses on border movement control,

internal counterintelligence, surveillance of all foreign diplomats, many journalists, and business people. Has a powerful secret police division with units in every major city in Russia.

SVR   Sluzhba Vneshnie Razvedaki runs worldwide, multi-layered intelligence-gathering operation. Specialist units gather political, industrial, and commercial intelligence. Conducts covert operations, including assassinations.

CHINA

ILD   Harmless-sounding International Liaison Department, the organization engages in a wide range of covert activities. Prime target is the United States.

MID   Military Intelligence Department reports to the General Staff of the People's Liberation Army. Brief includes updating all foreign military capabilities (especially the United States) and conducting satellite reconnaissance. Staff are attached to every PRC embassy and consulate.

MSS   Founded in 1983, the Ministry of State Security is responsible for all counterespionage within China. Has a fearsome reputation.

STD   Based in the Ministry of Defense, the large Science and Technology Department has two prime functions: to collate all signals traffic from the Chinese navy and overseas embassies; to target primarily U.S. firms working at the cutting edge of military and civilian technology.

NCNA   Nominally a news agency reporting on Chinese affairs. Has long been a cover for all other Chinese intelligence agencies engaged in clandestine activities.

FRANCE

DAS   Miniscule (staff of under 50 in 1999). Focuses on assessing long-term defense planning work by other nations.

DPSD   Direction du Production et de la Sécurité de la Défense. Responsible for gathering military intelligence abroad.

DRM   At the coal-face of French satellite intelligence program. Divided into five subdirectorates. Reports directly to prime minister of the day.

DST   The Directorate for Surveillance of the Territory is the largest and most powerful of France's intelligence agencies. Has several thousand employees. Operates both internally and overseas. Wide-ranging responsibilities include surveillance of all foreign embassies in Paris and conducting a large number of clandestine operations. Reports directly to incumbent minister of the interior.

DGSE   Direction Générale de la Sécurité Exterieure. Brief is to gather industrial and economic intelligence, penetrate terrorist organizations, and conduct old-fashioned spying.

SGDN   Reporting to the incumbent prime minister, the Secrétariat Général de la Défense Nationale provides an overview of military intelligence developments in countries of interest to France.

JAPAN

NAICHO   Part of Cabinet Research Office. Has a large budget to analyze defense policies of all major nations of interest to Japan.

MITI   Responsible for gathering commercial and economic data worldwide.

PSIA   The Public Security Investigation Agency concentrates on counterterrorism and counterespionage. Primarily operates internally but increasingly by 1999 had developed a global approach.

GIDEON'S
SPIES

CHAPTER 1

BEYOND THE LOOKING GLASS

When the red light blinked on the bedside telephone, a sophisticated recording device was automatically activated in the Paris apartment near the Pompidou Center in the lively Fourth Arrondissement. The light had been wired in by an Israeli communications technician who had flown from Tel Aviv to install the recorder, intended to allay any suspicions neighbors would have about the phone ringing at ungodly hours. The technician was one of the *yaholomin*, a member of a Mossad unit that dealt with secure communications in the safe houses of Israel's secret intelligence agency.

The one in Paris was like all the others. It had a bombproof front door and window glass which, like the panes in the White House, could deflect scanners. There were scores of such apartments in all the major cities in the world, either purchased outright or rented on long leases. Many were left unoccupied for lengthy periods, ready for the time they would be needed for an operation.

One had been conducted from the Paris apartment since June 1997, when Monsieur Maurice had arrived. He spoke fluent French with a slight Central European accent. Over the years his neighbors had encountered others like him: men, and occasionally women, who arrived without warning, spent weeks or months among them, then one day were gone. Like his predecessors, Maurice had politely discouraged interest in himself or his work.

Maurice was a *katsa*, a Mossad field agent.

Physically he was nondescript; it had been said that even on an empty street he would pass virtually unnoticed. He had been recruited in what was still a halcyon time for Mossad, when its legend remained largely intact. His potential was spotted during Israel's compulsory military service, when, after boot camp, he had been drafted into air force intelligence. An aptitude for languages (he knew French, English, and German) had been noted, along with other qualities: he was good at filling gaps in a case study and drawing fact out of speculation, and he knew the limits of informed conjecture. Above all, he was a natural manipulator of people: he could persuade, cajole, and, if all else failed, threaten.

Since graduating from the Mossad training school in 1982, he had worked in Europe, South Africa, and the Far East. At various times he had done so under the guise of a businessman, a travel writer, and a salesman. He had used a number of names and biographies drawn from the library of aliases maintained by Mossad. Now he was Maurice, once more a businessman.

During his various postings he had heard of the purges back in "the Institute," the name its staff used for Mossad: corrosive rumors of disgraced and ruined careers, of changes at the top, and each incoming Mossad director with his own priorities. None of them had stemmed the loss of morale within the service.

This had increased with the appointment of Benjamin Netanyahu as Israel's youngest prime minister. A man with a proven intelligence background, he was supposed to know how things worked on the inside; when to listen, how far to go. Instead, from the outset, Netanyahu had astonished seasoned intelligence officers by dabbling in operational details.

At first this was put down to unnecessary zeal, a new broom showing he was ready to look into every closet to make sure there were no secrets he should know. But matters had become alarming when not only the prime minister but his wife, Sara, wanted to peer behind the looking glass into Israel's intelligence world. She had invited senior Mossad officers to call on her at home and answer her questions, claiming she was following the example of Hillary Clinton's interest in the CIA.

The featureless corridors of Mossad's headquarters building in Tel Aviv had echoed with the scandalized whispers of how Sara Netanyahu had demanded to see psychological profiles of world leaders she and her husband would be entertaining or visiting. She had especially asked for details about President Bill Clinton's sexual activities. She had also asked to review dossiers on Israel's ambassadors whose embassies they would be staying in during overseas trips, expressing an interest in the cleanliness of their kitchens and how many times the bedding was changed in the guest suites.

Bemused by her requests, Mossad officers had explained to the prime minister's wife that obtaining such information was not in their intelligence-gathering remit.

Some of the veterans had been removed from the mainstream of intelligence and given responsibility for small operations that required little more than creating paperwork which went virtually unread. Realizing their careers were stagnating, they had resigned, and were now scattered across the length of Israel, keeping themselves occupied with reading, mostly history, trying to come to terms with the fact that they were also yesterday's people.

All this had made Maurice glad to be out of Tel Aviv and back in the field.

The operation that had brought him to Paris had provided another chance to show he was a methodical and careful agent, one able to deliver what was expected. In this case the task was relatively simple: there was no real physical danger, only the risk of embarrassment should the French authorities discover what he was doing and quietly deport him. The Israeli ambassador knew Maurice was in Paris but had not been told why. That was standard operational procedure: if things went wrong, the envoy could plead ignorance.

Maurice's task was to recruit an informer. This was known in the esoteric language of Mossad as a "cold approach," suborning a foreign national. After two months of patient work, Maurice believed he was now close to succeeding.

His target was Henri Paul, assistant chief of the city's Ritz Hotel, who also acted as chauffeur to its celebrity guests.

One had been Jonathan Aitken, a minister in Britain's last Conservative government. Aitken had held special responsibility for coordinating arms sales and had built up a raft of contacts with Middle Eastern weapons dealers. This had led to *World in Action*, a TV investigative program, and the *Guardian* newspaper publishing highly damaging reports about Aitken's ties to men not normally found in the company of government ministers. Aitken had sued for libel. The case had come to hinge on who had paid Aitken's hotel account when he had stayed at the Ritz to meet some of his Arab contacts. In court, Aitken had sworn on oath that his wife had settled the account.

Through a third-party source, Mossad had tipped off investigators acting for the defendants that Mrs. Aitken had not been in Paris. The case had collapsed. Mossad, which had long regarded Aitken's activities as a threat to Israel, had effectively destroyed him.

In 1999, after facing a lengthy criminal trial in London, Aitken was found guilty of perjury and given a prison sentence. By then his wife had left him, and a man who walked the corridors of power for many years faced a bleak future.

Understanding, if not sympathy, came from an unlikely source, Ari Ben-Menashe (see chapter 8). He had once experienced the rigors of a New York prison after his own fall from grace as intelligence coordinator for Prime Minister Yitzhak Shamir. The position had given Ben-Menashe a rare insight into how Mossad and Israel's other intelligence services operated. He regarded Aitken as "a man consumed by his own belief that he could outwit anyone. He did for years. But his mistake was to underestimate Mossad. They don't take prisoners."

Unlike Jonathan Aitken, whose life after prison holds little prospects, Ben-Menashe has made a spectacular recovery. By 1999 he had a well-established intelligence-gathering company based in Montreal, Canada. It numbers among clients several African countries as well as some in Europe. Multinationals also seek his services, having assured themselves their anonymity will be protected by Ben-Menashe.

His staff includes several former Canadian secret intelligence service officers and others who had worked for similar Israeli and European organizations. The company provides a wide range of economic, industrial, and protection services. The staff know their way around the arms dealers and well understand the rules of negotiating with kidnappers. There is not a city in the world where they are without contacts, many of them nurtured by Ben-Menashe from his days as a serious player in the Israeli intelligence world. He and his associates constantly update themselves on shifting political alliances and can often foresee which Third World government will fall—and who will replace it. Small and compact, Ben-Menashe's company is in many ways modeled on Mossad, "moving," Ben-Menashe cheerfully admits, "like thieves in the night. That's the way it has to be in our business." And it pays well.

Equipped with a new Canadian citizenship, he has found himself once more working with "the princes and kings of this world . . . the famous and those who use their fortunes to buy better protection. For them all knowledge is power and part of my job is to provide that essential information."

In London he is a favored guest at the Savoy. In Paris it is the Ritz that greets him with deference.

In no time Ben-Menashe discovered that the hotel remained a meeting place for Middle Eastern arms brokers and their European contacts. He checked with Mossad colleagues. From them he learned just how important the hotel had become in Mossad's overall strategy. Ben-Menashe, a natural-born acquirer of information—"long ago I learned that nothing I hear goes to waste"—decided he would watch how matters developed. It was a decision that would eventually directly involve him in the fate of Diana, Princess of Wales, and her lover, Dodi al-Fayed, the playboy son of the Ritz's owner, the mega-wealthy Mohamed al-Fayed.

Mossad had decided to have an informer in the Ritz who would be able to report on activities. It had set about the task by first obtaining the hotel's staff list; this had been done by hacking into the Ritz computer system. No one at the hotel's senior management level appeared to be a likely prospect; junior staff did not have the overall accessibility to guests for the task required. But Henri Paul's responsibility for security meant every area of the Ritz was open to him. His passkey could access a guest's safe-deposit box. There would be no questions asked if he wanted a copy of a person's hotel bill, no raised eyebrows if he asked to see the hotel's telephone log to obtain details of calls made by arms dealers and their contacts. He could know which woman a dealer had discreetly hired for a contact. As chauffeur to VIPs, Paul would be in a good position to overhear their conversations, witness their behavior, see where they went, whom they met.

The next stage had been to create a psycho-profile of Paul. Over several weeks information on his background had been unearthed by one of the resident *katsas* in Paris. Using a number of covers including an insurance company employee and a telephone salesman, the *katsa* had learned that Paul was a bachelor in no permanent relationship, lived in a low-rent apartment, and drove a black Mini but liked fast cars and racing the motorcycle of which he was part owner. Hotel staff had spoken of his liking a drink. There had been hints that, from time to time, he had used the services of an expensive hooker who also serviced some of the hotel's guests.

The information had been evaluated by a Mossad psychologist. He had concluded that there was an inherent vulnerability about Henri Paul. The psychologist had recommended that steadily increasing pressure, linked with the promise of substantial monetary reward to finance Paul's social life, could be the best way to recruit him. The operation could be a lengthy one, requiring considerable patience and skill. Rather than make further use of the resident *katsa*, Maurice would be sent to Paris.

As in any such Mossad operation, Maurice had followed well-tried guidelines. First, over several visits, he had familiarized himself with the Ritz and its environs. He had quickly identified Henri Paul, a muscular man with a certain swagger in his walk, who made it apparent that he sought approval from no one.

Maurice had observed the curious relationship Paul had with the paparazzi who staked out the front of the Ritz, ready to snatch photographs of the more newsworthy rich and famous guests. From time to time Paul would order the photographers to leave, and usually they would do so, circling the block on their motorcycles before returning. During those short trips, Paul would sometimes emerge from the hotel's staff entrance and engage the paparazzi in friendly banter as they passed.

At night, Maurice had observed Paul drinking with several of the paparazzi in one of the bars around the Ritz he patronized with other staff after work.

In progress reports to Tel Aviv, Maurice had described Paul's ability to drink considerable amounts of alcohol yet appear stone-cold sober. Maurice also confirmed that Paul's suitability for the role of informer overrode his personal habits: he appeared to have the essential access and a position of high trust.

At some point in his discreet surveillance, Maurice discovered how Paul was betraying that trust. He was receiving money from the paparazzi for providing details of guest movements, enabling the photographers to be in a position to snatch pictures of the celebrities.

The exchange of information for cash took place either in one of the bars or in the narrow rue Cambon, where the Ritz staff entrance was situated.

By mid-August that exchange had focused on the expected arrival at the Ritz of Diana, Princess of Wales, and her new lover, Dodi al-Fayed, the son of the hotel's owner. They would stay in the fabled Imperial Suite.

All the Ritz staff were under strict instructions to keep details about Diana's arrival secret under penalty of instant dismissal. Despite this, Paul had continued to risk his career by providing details of the forthcoming visit to several paparazzi. From each he had received further sums of money.

Maurice saw that Paul had also begun to drink more heavily and had overheard Ritz staff complain that the assistant security chief had become even more of a martinet: he had recently fired a floor maid he had caught stealing a bar of soap from a guest bedroom. Several of the hotel's employees said that Paul was also taking pills and wondered if they were to help control his mood swings. Everyone agreed Paul had become more unpredictable: one moment he would be good-humored; the next he would display barely controlled anger over some imagined slight. Maurice decided the time had come to make his move.

The first contact was in Harry's Bar in the rue Daunou. When Paul came in, Maurice was already sipping a cocktail. The Mossad *katsa* smoothly struck up a conversation, and the security man accepted a drink after Maurice mentioned that friends of his had stayed at the Ritz. Maurice added they had been surprised how many other guests had been wealthy Arabs.

If it had been a shot in the dark, it produced a staggering result. Paul replied that many of the Arabs were rude and arrogant and expected him to jump when they raised a finger. Worst were the the Saudis. Maurice mentioned he had heard that Jewish guests were just as difficult. Paul would have none of it. He insisted that Jews were excellent guests.

On that promising note, the evening ended with an arrangement to meet again in a few days, over dinner at a restaurant near the Ritz. During the meal Paul confirmed, under Maurice's well-timed questions, much of what the *katsa* knew. The hotel security chief spoke of his passion for fast cars and his liking for piloting a small aircraft. But it was difficult to enjoy those habits on his salary.

That may well have been the moment Maurice began to exert pressure. Finding money was always a problem for such hobbies, but not an insoluble one. Almost certainly that perked Paul's interest.

What followed then developed a rhythm of its own: Maurice laying down the bait and Paul all too eager to take it. The hook in place, Maurice would then have begun to reel in the line with the skills he had acquired at the Mossad training school.

At some point Maurice would have planted the idea he might be able to help, perhaps mentioning he worked for a company that was forever looking for ways to update its database and would pay good money to those who could help do so. This was a favorite opening gambit for Mossad recruiters on a cold-approach operation. From there it would be a small step to tell Paul that many of the Ritz guests no doubt possessed the kind of information that would interest the company.

Paul, perhaps uneasy at the turn of the conversation, may have balked. Maurice would have then moved to the next stage, saying that of course while he understood Paul's reservations, they did come as a surprise to him. After all, it was common knowledge that Paul already took payment for information from the paparazzi. So why turn away the chance to make some real money?

Looking back, Ari Ben-Menashe would judge the operation at this stage as developed along classic lines. "From my personal knowledge there is no one better than Maurice [his name for this one operation], at this. A cold-approach operation requires a real finesse. Move too quickly and the fish is off the hook. Take too long and suspicion is soon coupled with fear. Recruiting is an art all by itself and a European like Henri Paul is very different from hooking an Arab on the West Bank or Gaza Strip."

Maurice's undoubted skill at delivering his proposition and accompanying revelations of how much he knew of Paul's background would have been delivered with a combination of worldliness and persuasion, with the essential undertow of pressure. It would also have had an effect on Paul.

Even if he had not asked, he may well have realized that the man seated across from him at the dinner table was an intelligence officer or at least a recruiter for a service.

That may well be the reason for his response. According to an Israeli intelligence source who has a certain knowledge of the matter: "Henri Paul came straight out with it: Was he being asked to spy? If so, what was the deal? Just like that. No hedging or bullshit. Just what was the deal—and whom would he really be working for? That would have been the point when Maurice would have had to decide. Did he tell Paul he would be working for Mossad? There is no standard operational procedure for something like this. Every target is different. But Henri Paul was on the hook."

If so, Maurice may well have told Paul what would be required of him: obtaining information on guests, perhaps even bugging their suites, and noting whom they entertained. There would have been discussions about payment, accompanied by an offer to open an account in a Swiss bank or, if need be, to pay Paul in cash. Maurice would have given the impression that such matters were not a problem. At that point he may even have revealed that Paul would be working for Mossad. All this would be standard for the successful conclusion of a cold-approach operation.

Paul was very probably scared at what he was asked to do. It was not a question of his loyalty to the Ritz; like other members of the staff, he worked for the hotel because of the relatively high salary and the perks. Paul was understandably frightened he was getting in over his head and could well end up in prison if he was found spying on the hotel's guests.

Yet if he went to the police what would they do? Maybe they already knew that he was going to be propositioned. If he turned down the proposition, what then? If the hotel management learned he had already betrayed that most precious of all assets the Ritz offered—confidentiality—by informing the paparazzi, he could be fired, even prosecuted.

For Henri Paul in those last days of August 1997, there seemed no way out. He continued to drink, to take pills, to sleep restlessly, to bully junior staff. He was a man teetering close to the edge.

Maurice maintained the pressure. He often managed to be in a bar where Paul was drinking off duty. The *katsa*'s very presence could only have been a further reminder to the security chief of what he was being pressured to do. Maurice continued to visit the Ritz, sipping an aperitif in one of the hotel bars, lunching in its restaurant, taking afternoon coffee in a lounge. To Henri Paul it would have seemed as if Maurice had become a personal shadow. That would have only further increased the pressure on him, reminding him that there was no way out.

Compounding the pressure was the forthcoming visit of Princess Diana and Dodi al-Fayed. Paul had been put in charge of their security while they were in the hotel, with particular responsibility for keeping away the paparazzi. At the same time the photographers were calling him on his cell phone seeking information about the visit; he was being offered large sums of money to provide details. The temptation to accept was another pressure. Everywhere he turned, there seemed to be pressure.

Though he managed to conceal it, Henri Paul was unraveling mentally. He was taking antidepressants, sleeping pills, and pep pills to get him through the day. This combination of drugs could only have furthered the strain on his ability to make reasoned judgments.

Later, Ben-Menashe felt if he had been running the operation, "that would have been when I would have pulled out. Henri Paul might well have been able to conceal from most people his mental state, but to an experienced operative like Maurice, trained to a high degree in making such observations, the evidence of deterioration would have been all too obvious. Almost certainly, Maurice would have told the man in charge in Tel Aviv, Danny Yatom, he should pull the plug . . . let it go. But for reasons only Yatom knows, he did not. Yatom was barely a year in the hot seat. He wanted to make a name for himself. Vanity, like arrogance, is one of the great dangers in intelligence work. Yatom has plenty of both and that's okay—except when it gets in the way of reality. And the reality was Mossad should have pulled out."

It did not. Yatom's consuming need to have his own man inside the Ritz drove him. But other events that no one could have foreseen were moving to their own climax.

The blinking light—signaling an incoming telephone call—which awoke Maurice was timed by the recorder at 1:58 A.M. on Sunday, August 31, 1997. The caller worked in the Paris gendarmerie accident unit and had been recruited by Mossad some years before; its computers classified him as a mabuah, a non-Jewish informer. On the totem pole of Maurice's Parisian contacts, his caller was somewhere near the bottom.

Nevertheless, the man's news about a traffic accident stunned Maurice. It had occurred less than an hour before, when a Mercedes sedan had struck a reinforced concrete pillar on the westbound roadway of the underpass beneath the place de l'Alma, a notorious accident spot in the city.

The dead were Diana, Princess of Wales, whose two sons are in line to become king of England; Dodi al-Fayed, son of Mohamed, the Egyptian-born owner of Harrods of Knightsbridge, the "Royal" store; and Henri Paul. The couple's bodyguard had been critically injured.

Hours after the accident Maurice flew back to Tel Aviv, leaving in his wake questions that would remain unanswered.

What part had his pressure played in the accident? Had Henri Paul lost control of the Mercedes, causing it to smash into the thirteenth concrete pillar of the underpass beneath the place de l'Alma, because he could see no way of extricating himself from the clutches of Mossad? Was that pressure linked to the high level of prescribed drugs found in his bloodstream? When he had left the Ritz with his three passengers, had his mind continued to vacillate over what he should do about the pressure? Was he not only responsible for a terrible road accident but also the victim of a ruthless intelligence agency?

Questions would continue to fester in the mind of Mohamed al-Fayed. In February 1998, he publicly announced: "It was no accident. I am convinced of that in my heart of hearts. The truth cannot remain hidden forever."

Five months later, the British network ITV screened a documentary that claimed Henri Paul had close links to French intelligence. He had none. The program also hinted that an unnamed intelligence agency had been involved in the deaths; there were dark hints that the agency had acted because the British establishment feared Diana's love for Dodi could have "political repercussions" because he was an Egyptian.

To this day Mossad's involvement with Henri Paul has remained a well-kept secret—the way the service has always intended it should remain. Mossad acted at the behest of no one outside Israel. Indeed, few outside the service still have any idea of Mossad's part in the death of the then most famous woman in the world.

Mohamed al-Fayed, prompted by what he saw as a campaign of vilification in the English media, has continued to claim that unnamed security services had been ranged against his son and Diana. In July 1998 two *Time* magazine journalists published a book that included the suggestion that Henri Paul could have had some connection with French intelligence. Neither al-Fayed or the journalists offered any conclusive proof that Henri Paul was an intelligence agent or even an informer—and none of them came near to identifying Mossad's involvement with him.

In July 1998, Mohamed al-Fayed asked a number of questions in a letter he sent to every one of Britain's members of Parliament, urging them to raise the questions in the House of Commons. He claimed that "there is a force at work to stifle the answers I want." His behavior was seen as the reaction of a grieving father lashing out in every direction. The questions deserve repeating, not because they shed any light on the role Mossad played in the closing weeks of Henri Paul's life, but because they show how the entire tragedy has gained a momentum that only the true facts can stop.

Al-Fayed wrote of a "plot" to get rid of Diana and his son and attempted to link all kinds of disparate events with his questions:

"Why did it take one hour and forty minutes to get the princess to hospital? Why have some of the photographers failed to give up some of the pictures they shot? Why was there a break-in that night at the London home of a photographer who handles paparazzi pictures? Why have all the closed-circuit television cameras in that part of Paris produced not one frame of videotape? Why were the speed cameras on the route out of film, and the traffic cameras not switched on? Why was the scene of the crash not preserved but reopened to traffic after a few hours? Who was the person in the press group outside the Ritz who was equipped like a news photographer? Who were the two unidentified men mingling in the crowd who later sat in the Ritz bar? They ordered in English, watching and listening in a marked way?"

Mossad had no interest in the relationship between Diana and Dodi. Their sole concern was to recruit Henri Paul as their informer in the Ritz. Regarding the mysterious news photographer: in the past Mossad has allowed its agents to pose as journalists. It may well have been Maurice keeping watch outside the hotel. The two unidentified men in the hotel bar may have had some connection to Mossad. It would no doubt comfort Mohamed al-Fayed if that were true.

By 1999, Mohamed al-Fayed's belief in a "plot" had hardened to what he saw as "a full-blown criminal conspiracy." He insisted it had been manufactured by MI5 and MI6, and French intelligence with Mossad "manipulating in the background." To those who would listen, and they were steadily declining in number, he would name a London newspaper editor as well as a close friend of Diana as both having "direct links" to Britain's intelligence services.

The reasons why these services had become involved in the "conspiracy" were clear-cut in Mohamed's mind. "A decision had been made by the Establishment, and at the very top, that Diana must not be allowed to marry a Muslim. Then the future king of England, Prince William, would have an Arab as his stepfather and another as his grandfather. There was also a real fear that I would provide the money to allow Diana to become a rival to the Queen of England. The Establishment would do anything to end my son's relationship with the one woman he had ever truly loved."

Facts were never produced to support an allegation which, if proven, would surely accelerate the end of the royal family in Britain and perhaps pave the way to a crisis of confidence that could even sweep away a government.

Nevertheless, al-Fayed authorized his spokesman, Laurie Meyer, a former anchorman with one of Rupert Murdoch's television networks, to state to the media: "Mohamed firmly believes Di and Dodi were murdered by agents loyal to the British Crown and that other agencies were deeply involved in the crime. He further believes there is deep-seated racism within the Establishment."

To confirm that murder most foul had taken place, al-Fayed had employed the skills of a former senior Scotland Yard detective, John Mac-Namara. By early 1999 the soft-spoken investigator was scouring the world for evidence. Along the way, in Geneva, Switzerland, he met a former MI6 officer, Richard Tomlinson, who claimed he had seen documents at MI6 headquarters on the bank of the River Thames. Tomlinson insisted they described "a plan to murder the Serbian leader, Slobodan Milošević—a plan that has unsettling parallels to the way Di and Dodi died. The MI6 document stated that the 'accident' should happen in a tunnel where the chance of fatal injury is high. The weapon of choice the document recommended was a high-powered laser beam that could be used to temporarily blind the driver of the target vehicle."

Despite all his efforts, MacNamara has been unable to find any independent evidence to support Tomlinson's claims—and efforts to obtain the MI6 document totally failed.

Then came news, reluctantly confirmed, that the United States

National Security Agency, NSA, had some 1,050 pages of documents on the couple. Al-Fayed launched an immediate court battle in Washington to obtain the documents.

"The more he is blocked, the greater is his determination," said the loyal Meyer. But, like others, he is not holding his breath. "It could take years to work its way through the system."

Part of the reason, I had discovered, was that Diana and Dodi had been under surveillance by ECHELON, one of NSA's most sensitive and ultrasecret surveillance systems. This global electronic network is of truly astounding proportions. It links satellites to a series of high-speed parallel computers. The system enables NSA and those it allows to share information—Britain is one—to intercept and decode virtually every electronic communication in the world—in real time. Searching for key words it has been fed, ECHELON can identify and segregate messages of interest to its users.

Following her divorce from Prince Charles, Diana had launched her campaign to abolish land mines. She was blunt, outspoken, and quickly gathered support that was not welcomed by the Clinton administration or in London and other European capitals. She was seen as a meddler, someone who did not understand what she was talking about.

"The reality was that the land mine manufacturing industry provided thousands of jobs. No one wanted to see the mines used—but no one wanted people put out of work because Diana had a bee in her bonnet," one Washington source told me; perhaps understandably he insisted on not being named in return for this insight.

The arrival of Dodi in Diana's life automatically meant he became part of ECHELON's collection activities. Unknown to them, their every telephone conversation, however intimate, was silently gathered up by ECHELON's satellites.

By 1997, Mohamed al-Fayed's name had also been added to the global computer search. ECHELON may well have been the first outside his family circle to know of his hope that his son would marry a princess of the line—and then later his claim that on the eve of their deaths he had planned to announce their engagement.

There is much in the NSA documents that may still cause further surprise—and provide proof, through Diana's own words, that she had indeed planned to marry her lover.

I only became aware of ECHELON's role shortly before publication of the original edition of this book in March 1999. It was then that

I also became aware of just how far the deaths of his son and Diana had continued to consume Mohamed al-Fayed. It was a jolting experience to be exposed to such uncontrolled grief and his anger and belief in a conspiracy that fed it.

On a March afternoon I met Mohamed al-Fayed in the privacy of his private salon on the fifth floor of Harrods. Guarding its approaches were his personal bodyguards. Al-Fayed told me they "are all former SAS soldiers, totally loyal to me. I pay them well. They make sure I live. I have been threatened so many times. My car is bulletproof."

These revelations, delivered in a tense low voice, came as he entered the salon. I was not sure whether I should take his outburst as a warning or a reassurance I was safe to tell him anything he wanted to know.

He did not waste time in telling me what that was: access to all my Mossad contacts. "You give me the names. They give me the information I want. I give you one million pounds in whatever currency you want. No need to pay tax. I will take care of everything."

I had been warned that there is still an element of a souk trader in al-Fayed. For the next twenty minutes he launched into a diatribe that I was not quite prepared for. He attacked the Queen and Prince Philip and well-known figures he called "Establishment whores and pimps." He reserved his greatest venom for the intelligence service, branding them "killers."

Picking up my book, which had been marked and annotated in the margin, he said again: "Mossad are the people who can tell me the truth. Bring them to me and I will make you a very happy man." Before I could respond, he launched an attack on Henri Paul: "I trusted him, *really* trusted him. I would have done anything for him because Dodi liked him. My son, like me, was too trusting. That was one of the reasons Diana loved him, wanted him to be her husband, a father to her children. But they didn't want it. The Queen and her husband, her lackeys, that awful brother of hers, Earl Spencer . . . none of them wanted it. None of them wanted a Wog in the family. You know what Wog is? A Wily Oriental Gentleman. Only they didn't see that Dodi *was* a gentleman. They smeared his character when he was alive. They continue to do so now he is dead. Yet all Diana needed was what she told me she needed: someone she could trust after all she had gone through . . ."

Those words do not convey the intensity of his delivery, the profanities he used, the wild hand gestures and, above all, the painful torment on his face. Mohamed al-Fayed was a man in pain. I could only listen as he continued to unburden himself.

"Did you know Diana was almost certainly pregnant . . . maybe eight weeks . . . and that Dodi, my son, was the father? Did you know that at the hospital in Paris, after her death, they removed many of her organs and that she came home to London as a mummy? Did you know that when we last met she told me how much she loved Dodi and how happy they were together?"

I said I did not know any of those things. For a long moment Mohamed al-Fayed sat there, tears close, his face working, lost in some inner world.

Then he said: "Tell me who can help me to find out all the truth about who arranged for my son and his beloved Diana to die?"

I told him I had in mind two people. One was Victor Ostrovsky (see chapter 10, "A Dangerous Liaison," pp. 192–94, 208–10). The other was Ari Ben-Menashe.

"Find them. Bring them to me," commanded Mohamed al-Fayed. At that moment there was more than a hint of an imperious pharaoh about him.

It took me a week to locate them. Ostrovsky was living in Arizona; he would only speak with me through an intermediary, a journalist who works for an Arab news magazine. In the end Ostrovsky had a short discussion with John MacNamara that led nowhere.

Ari Ben-Menashe had just returned from Africa when I spoke to him in Montreal. I told him about my meeting with al-Fayed. Ben-Menashe said "it is not altogether crazy what he says. That much I know already. There was a definite intelligence presence around Diana and Dodi in that last day in Paris."

He agreed to meet Mohamed al-Fayed in London the following week, early April.

Ben-Menashe's account of that meeting echoes what Mohamed al-Fayed had told me at our meeting. Ben-Menashe, a fastidious, unfailingly polite man, had been frankly shocked at the emotive language al-Fayed had used to attack members of the royal family. Nevertheless, he had agreed to make further inquiries in Tel Aviv to see how much more Mossad would be prepared to add to the material I had already published in the original edition of this book.

Ten days later he met with al-Fayed in his Harrods salon and told him that a number of intelligence services "might well have a case to answer." Ben-Menashe added he would be happy to put his own staff to work on building such a case and suggested a retainer fee of $750,000 a year plus expenses to be agreed mutually.

Meantime, independent of Ben-Menashe, I had continued to make my own inquiries to establish the role ECHELON had played in the last days of Diana and Dodi's lives.

I discovered through sources in Washington and elsewhere that the couple had continued to be under surveillance during the week they had spent cruising off the Emerald Coast of Sardinia on the *Jonikal*, the 60-meter yacht owned by Mohamed al-Fayed. ECHELON had also tracked the posse of paparazzi that had chased them in speedboats, on motorcycles, in cars. Time and again the *Jonikal* had evaded its pursuers. But ECHELON's computers picked up Diana's chagrin at being hunted. Conversations between her and Dodi, between the couple and their bodyguard, Trevor Rees-Jones, recorded by ECHELON, all reflect her tense mood. On that Friday night, August 28th 1997, she told Dodi she wanted to go to Paris "as soon as possible."

Within hours, arrangements had been finalized. A Gulfstream-IV was ordered to fly to Sardinia's private airport the following day. Tomas Muzzu, an elderly Sardinian with many years experience of driving celebrities around the island, was retained to drive the couple to the airport.

Muzzu's account of the conversation in the car is striking confirmation to what an ECHELON satellite had scooped up.

"They spoke in English, very loving words. From time to time Dodi, who spoke good Italian, spoke to me. Then he switched back to English. I do not speak that language very well, but my impression was of a couple very much in love and making plans for their future."

My sources insist that a portion of the ECHELON tapes show the couple talking of marriage and the life they planned together. Dodi continuously reassured her that he would ensure their privacy by enlisting the services of the al-Fayed protection team.

The private jet left Sardinia after the pilot made an urgent call to European air traffic control center in Brussels to give him a priority takeoff slot.

During the two-hour flight to Le Bourget airport ten miles north of Paris, the aircraft's occupants were monitored by ECHELON, the conversations of Di and Dodi once more uplifted to a satellite and then downloaded to computers at Fort Meade in Maryland.

While my source could offer no "smoking gun" proof, he was, "in my own mind," convinced that "relevant parts" of the conversation were relayed to GCHQ, Britain's communications center. "From there they would find their way up through the Whitehall network. By then anything Diana said, any decision she made, would have been of prime interest to certain people in authority."

I put all this to Ari Ben-Menashe. His response was gratifying but frustrating. "You're very close to being on the button. How close I can't tell you." Ben-Menashe's position was simple. He was hoping to sign a lucrative contract with Mohamed al-Fayed. Any information would have to go to him first.

In the end, the contract would not materialize. Al-Fayed wanted first to see what "evidence" Ben-Menashe could show him before agreeing to pay.

Ben-Menashe, more used to dealing with governments than "a man with the manner of a souk trader," found himself handling "a number of somewhat hysterical telephone calls from MacNamara insisting I should show him documents. This was very surprising for a man who should have had some experience of how the security services work from his own days at Scotland Yard. I had to tell him that Mossad doesn't hand out documents willy-nilly. I had to explain to him, much as you do to a new copper on the beat, the facts of life in the intelligence community."

Thwarted, al-Fayed refused to retreat into silence. His spokesman, Laurie Meyer, found himself waging new battles with the media, which, with increasing force, challenged al-Fayed's view of an "Establishment plot to murder my son and his future bride."

Watching from a distance, Ari Ben-Menashe felt that al-Fayed "was his own worst enemy. From all the inquiries I had made, at no expense to him, the sort of preliminary investigation I made before assigning my company to any such work, it was clear that the royal family as such has no case to answer. It may well be that privately they would not have wished Diana to marry Dodi. But that is a long way from saying they wanted the young couple murdered. That said, I did turn up some hard evidence that does point to the involvement of security services around the time of their deaths. There are serious questions to be asked and answered. But al-Fayed will not get answers the way he continues to behave. Fundamentally he does not understand the mentality of those he is trying to convince. And worse, he is surrounded by lackeys, 'yes men' who tell him what he wants to hear."

Early in May 1999, John MacNamara flew to Geneva, Switzerland, to meet Richard Tomlinson, a former staff officer with MI6. For four years Tomlinson, who had once been tipped to be a high-flier in British intelligence, had run a relentless campaign against his former employers. Originally recruited at Cambridge University by an MI6 "talent spotter," Tomlinson had been abruptly sacked in the spring of 1995 after telling his MI6 personnel officer of his growing emotional difficulties.

In a telephone conversation he told me that "my honesty cost me my job. The 'powers-that-be' decided that despite my impressive results, I lacked a stiff upper lip."

Tomlinson described how he had tried to sue MI6 for unfair dismissal but the British government had successfully stopped his case coming before a court. Then its offer of a payoff—"cash for my silence" was how Tomlinson put it—was withdrawn after an Australian publisher to whom Tomlinson had sent a synopsis of a book about his career with MI6, submitted the document to MI6 to see if publishing would lead to legal action. MI6 moved swiftly. Tomlinson was arrested as he was about to leave Britain and sentenced to two years in jail for breaching the Official Secrets Act.

Released from prison in April 1998, Tomlinson moved first to Paris and then to Switzerland. There he began to use Internet cafés to post highly embarrassing details of MI6 operations. This included revealing a high-level mole in Germany's central bank claiming the man—code-named Orcadia—had betrayed his country's economic secrets to Britain. He also disclosed details of a plot by MI6 to assassinate President Slobodan Milošević of Serbia in 1992.

Then came the moment he moved from being just another disgruntled former spy into the world of Mohamed al-Fayed, already well-peopled with conspiratorial figures.

To the billionaire Tomlinson, by now almost penniless, was, al-Fayed told me, "like a sign from heaven." He encouraged Tomlinson to tell all he knew to the French judge investigating the deaths of Diana and Dodi.

In a sworn affidavit, Tomlinson claimed MI6 was implicated in the couple's deaths. Agents of the service had been in Paris for two weeks prior to their deaths and had held several meetings with Henri Paul, "who was a paid informer of MI6." Later in his affidavit, Tomlinson alleged "Paul had been blinded as he drove through the underpass by a high-powered flash, a technique which is consistent with MI6 methods in other assassinations."

Such allegations brought Tomlinson even deeper into al-Fayed's inner circle. The former agent was now more than "a sign from heaven." He had become, in al-Fayed's words to me, "the man who could unravel the terrible truth of an incident of such magnitude and historical importance."

It was to further encourage Tomlinson to continue with his campaign that MacNamara had flown to Geneva.

Ever since he had arrived in the city, Tomlinson had faced increasing insolvency. He could barely find the rent for his studio apartment. His efforts to raise money by writing travel articles had come to nothing. His efforts to be employed as a private detective had also failed because he feared to travel around Europe in case MI6 agents "snatched me." On the advice of MI6, he had been banned from being admitted to the United States, Australia, and France. Only Switzerland had offered him sanctuary on the grounds that any breach of the Official Secrets Act was "a political crime" and therefore not a subject for extradition.

MI6 sources I have spoken to suggest that MacNamara had gone to see Tomlinson with a view to resolving the former spy's financial plight. More certain is that shortly afterward Tomlinson had sufficient funds to launch what he called "my nuclear option." Using a sophisticated Microsoft program he had installed in his state-of-the-art computer, Tomlinson began to publish on his specially created and very expensive Web site the names of over one hundred serving MI6 officers—including twelve he said had been involved in a plot to kill Diana and Dodi.

There was no clear-cut, smoking-gun evidence offered against any of those agents. But within hours their names had been flashed around the world.

A stunned MI6 desperately tried to close down the Web site, but no sooner had they managed to close one than another opened. In London the Foreign Office admitted the breach of security was the most serious since the Cold War—"and the lives of some MI6 agents and their contacts have been put at risk." Certainly those named as working in

Iran, Iraq, Lebanon, and other Middle East countries had to be urgently withdrawn.

But neither Tomlinson nor Mohamed al-Fayed could have calculated one effect. So grave was the overall breach of security that the claim that a handful of MI6 agents had been involved in a plot against Diana went virtually unnoticed. It was dismissed as being part of al-Fayed's obsession.

In June 1999 matters took a more serious turn when al-Fayed's Harrods Web site published the name of a senior MI6 officer. The Web site alleged that the agent, who was then serving in the Balkans, had orchestrated "a vicious campaign" to smear al-Fayed and "destroy his reputation."

Britain's Ministry of Defence took the unusual step of publicly warning that publication had endangered the agent and his contacts in Kosovo and Serbia.

The agent's identity had been revealed alongside the site's online book where thousands of visitors have left messages commemorating the deaths of Diana and Dodi.

Laurie Meyer, the Harrods spokesman, promised to have the agent's name removed—"obviously it is an error."

Reports then surfaced in Germany's mass-circulation *Bild* that Richard Tomlinson had evidence that Henri Paul had installed a bugging device in the Imperial Suite at the Ritz Hotel and had obtained tapes of the "last intimate moments" of Diana and Dodi. Shortly before Paul drove them to their death, the couple had spent several hours alone in the suite.

The tapes, according to *Bild*, had become the subject of a hunt by MI6 to locate them.

Around this time Earl Spencer, Diana's brother, decided to intervene. He told American television audiences that at best "the romance my sister had with Dodi al-Fayed was no more than a summer fling. She had absolutely no intention to marry him."

Mohamed al-Fayed pointed out, with some justification, that the relationship between Spencer and Diana was hardly close at the time of her death.

None of this was any surprise to Ari Ben-Menashe. He had continued to follow the never-ending saga of al-Fayed's attempts "to prove his fixation that the Queen and Prince Philip organized a plot to kill Diana."

The highly experienced Israeli intelligence officer felt that, "in throwing in his lot with Richard Tomlinson, al-Fayed had lost the plot. He is now reduced to running to the tabloids. Yet I know for a fact that if he had gone about matters properly and organized a serious investigation he would have turned up some very surprising results. There *is* something very strange about the deaths of Diana and Dodi. No doubt about it. There was a case to investigate. But the trail has been muddied by al-Fayed himself. It may not even be his fault. He is surrounded by people who tell him to look here, not *there*. For some of them, keeping the whole thing going is a sort of pension for them. They know that every new, half-baked theory they come up with will encourage al-Fayed to spend more of his money in pursuing it. Along the way he tramples out of sight what evidence there may have been to uncover."

A hint of what that could be came in late June 1999 when it emerged that the mysterious white Fiat Uno seen zigzagging away from the scene of the death crash of Diana and Dodi was destroyed in a car crusher. In moments the Uno, from which traces of paint scrapes had been found in the tunnel, had been reduced to a block of scrap metal.

The claim was contained in a secret Mossad investigation that began within hours of the fatal crash. It had been launched by Mossad's then director general, Danny Yatom. He had been concerned that Mossad's determined attempts to recruit Henri Paul could lead to accusations that this had played a part in Diana's death.

The investigation focused on a period that covered the two weeks before the accident—or what al-Fayed still calls "the appearance of an accident to cover up murder"—and the days afterward.

Mossad investigators discovered that as well as the agency's own presence in Paris prior to the death of the couple, there was a four-man MI6 team in the city. They were based at the British embassy for the first week, but later moved into a rented apartment—"an MI6 safe house"—near the Ritz. One of the team checked into the hotel itself four days before the death of Dodi and Diana.

The Mossad report reveals that around August 14–15 1997, a CIA team also arrived in the city. The team had been tracking Diana for some time, keeping tabs on her attacks on land mine manufacturers, many of which are U.S.-based.

The CIA reports form part of the 1,051 documents Mohamed al-Fayed has unsuccessfully battled through the American courts to obtain copies of. The U.S. Justice Department has claimed the documents contained material "sensitive to national security."

The Mossad report suggests that sensitivity could refer to why Britain had asked the United States to help in monitoring Diana.

"Britain saw her as a loose cannon," insisted al-Fayed. "In fact she was a woman of great courage who was ready to confront the land mines issue."

The Mossad investigation details how the various intelligence services hurriedly left Paris after the deaths of Diana and Dodi.

Mossad's report contains a detailed timetable of Dodi and Diana's last hours. It is partly based on firsthand observations by Maurice and his contacts. Other information came from Mossad's "back channel" contacts with agents in the French capital, from MI6, the CIA, and French intelligence.

"I have been told by a former senior Israeli intelligence officer that all those services had a vested interest in Diana and Dodi," Mohamed al-Fayed has insisted.

Mossad's account of the final moments of the lives of Diana and Dodi begins at 11:45 P.M. Saturday, August 29, 1997, when Henri Paul was put in charge of the operation to whisk them away from the Ritz Hotel.

Mohamed al-Fayed still remembers vividly the instruction he had telephoned to Paul.

"I told him he must drive carefully, that he must never forget he had the life of the mother of the future king of England and my beloved son in his hands. I trusted him never to forget that. God knows, how I trusted him. God only knows now why I did."

The next Mossad entry is 11:50 P.M. In the Ritz bar Trevor Rees-Jones, who was there to body-guard Diana and Dodi, was in a huddle with other security men from the hotel staff and Henri Paul, discussing the route he would use.

Paul was very bullish. He said the hotel would provide two Range Rovers to act as decoys for the waiting paparazzi. That would give him enough time to get away. Rees-Jones is reported to have said the plan "sounds good to me."

00:15 A.M. Sunday, August 30. In the hotel lobby Henri Paul was using his cell phone to mobilize the two decoy vehicles.

00:19 A.M. The two decoy vehicles roared out of the Place Vendome that fronts the Ritz. Paparazzi give chase.

00:20 A.M. At the hotel's rear entrance Paul arrived with the Mercedes. He was seen by one of the eyewitnesses that Mossad subsequently interviewed as "drumming his fingers nervously on the steering wheel."

00:21 A.M. At the top of the Rue Cambon, a Mossad agent kept watch. He would later report that "a white Fiat Uno passed the top of the street."

The Mossad report states that in the car were two intelligence officers from the French security service, DST. The DST—more formally known as the Directorate for Surveillance of the Territory—is the largest and most powerful of France's intelligence agencies. With several thousand employees, it operates both internally and overseas. Its wide-ranging responsibilities include surveillance of all foreign embassies in Paris and conducting a number of clandestine operations. It reports to the incumbent minister of the interior.

00:22 A.M. The white Fiat Uno passed through traffic lights in the Place de la Concorde. Henri Paul's Mercedes is forced to temporarily stop at the lights.

00:23 A.M. The Mercedes approaches the Alma tunnel. Henri Paul would most certainly have seen the white Uno ahead of him.

00:24 A.M. The Mercedes, traveling at high speed, passed over the dip at the tunnel entrance. In the back seat Diana and Dodi would have experienced for a split second a sensation not unlike that of a plunging roller-coaster.

Seconds later there came a thunderous noise inside the tunnel. A roaring screeching of metal, a reverberating, crumping sound that seemed to go on and on.

Henri Paul and Dodi were dead. Diana was dying.

Moments later, according to the Mossad report, the white Uno had driven into a side street off the avenue Montaigne. Waiting there was a van, its ramp lowered. The Uno drove up the ramp. The van's doors closed.

Hours later the Uno was gripped in the claws of the crusher. In moments it became a piece of crushed metal, devoid of any identification.

There, at the time of writing, the matter rests. Can Tomlinson produce anything new? Could Ben-Menashe have found evidence that would finally satisfy al-Fayed's belief in a conspiracy? Was Diana really pregnant at the time of her death? Had Mohamed al-Fayed become so blinded by grief mingled with anger that he was ready to make this thesis fit the facts?

These questions will be revisited well into this new century. But they may never be answered fully enough to satisfy Mohamed al-Fayed or convince all those who believe him a dangerously misguided man who is using vast sums of money to nail down a truth that may, just may, be best kept under lock and key by all those directly involved.

Some of Maurice's colleagues have increasingly felt that the attempt to entrap Henri Paul was additional proof that Mossad has lurched a little further out of control, carrying out reckless international operations without taking into account the potential long-term consequences for itself, for Israel, for peace in the Middle East, and, ultimately, for the relationship with the Jewish state's oldest and closest ally, the United States of America. Several officers claimed that since Benjamin Netanyahu became prime minister in 1996, matters have worsened.

A veteran member of the Israeli intelligence community has said: "People are seeing those who work for Mossad are often thugs masquerading as patriots. That is bad for us [and] for morale, and, in the end, will have a bad effect on Mossad's relationship with other services."

Another experienced Israeli intelligence officer was equally blunt: "Netanyahu behaves as if Mossad is part of his own version of the Court of King Arthur; something new every day or the knights of his own Round Table get bored. That's why things have gone very wrong with Mossad. There's a need to ring the alarm bell before it's too late."

The first lesson I learned during a quarter of a century of writing about secret intelligence is that deception and disinformation are its stock-in-trade, along with subversion, corruption, blackmail, and, sometimes, assassination. Agents are trained to lie and to use and abuse friendships. They are the very opposite of the dictum that gentlemen do not read each other's mail.

I first encountered their behavior while investigating many of the great spy scandals of the cold war: the betrayal of America's atomic bomb secrets by Klaus Fuchs, and the compromising of Britain's MI5 and MI6 by Guy Burgess, Donald Maclean, and Kim Philby. Each made treachery and duplicity his byword. I also was one of the first writers to gain access to the CIA's obsession with mind control, a preoccupation the Agency was forced to confirm ten years after my book on the subject,

Journey into Madness, appeared. Denial is the black art all intelligence services long ago perfected.

Nevertheless, in getting to the truth, I was greatly helped by two professional intelligence officers: Joachim Kraner, my late father-in-law, who ran an MI6 network in Dresden in the post–World War II years, and Bill Buckley, who was station chief of the CIA in Beirut. Physically they were similar: tall, lean, and trim, with chins ready to confront trouble halfway. Their eyes revealed little—except to say if you weren't part of the answer, you had to be part of the problem. Intellectually formidable, their criticism of the agencies they served was at times astringent.

Both constantly reminded me that a great deal can be heard from what Bill called "murmurs in the mush": a deadly skirmish fought in an alley with no name; the collective hold-your-breath when an agent or network is blown; a covert operation that could have undone years of overt political bridge building; a snippet of mundane information that completed a particular intelligence jigsaw. Joachim added that "sometimes a few words, casually offered, could often throw a new light on something."

Proud of being members of what they called "the second oldest profession," both not only were my friends, but convinced me that secret intelligence is the key to fully understanding international relations, global politics, and diplomacy—and, of course, terrorism. Through them I made contacts in a number of military and civilian intelligence agencies: Germany's BND and France's DGSE; the CIA; Canadian and British services.

Joachim died in retirement; Bill was murdered by Islamic fundamentalists who kidnapped him in Beirut and triggered the Western hostage crisis in that city.

I also met members of Israel's intelligence community who first helped me by filling in the background of Mehmet Ali Agca, the Turkish fanatic who attempted to assassinate Pope John Paul in St. Peter's Square, Rome, in May 1981. Those contacts were arranged by Simon Wiesenthal, the renowned Nazi hunter and an invaluable Mossad "source" for over forty years. Because of his fame and reputation, Wiesenthal long found doors readily open, especially in Washington.

It was in that city in March 1986 that I learned a little more of the tangled relationship between the intelligence communities of the United States and Israel. I was there to interview William Casey, then the director of the Central Intelligence Agency, as ongoing research for my book *Journey into Madness*, which deals in part with the death of Bill Buckley.

Despite his customized suit, Casey was a shambling figure. His jowled face was pale and the rims of his eyes were red as we sat in a Washington club; he looked like someone whose ectoplasm was running out after five years of directing the CIA.

Over a Perrier he confirmed the conditions for our meeting. No notes, no tape recordings; anything he said would be purely background. He then produced a sheet of plain paper on which were typed his biographical details. He had been born in New York on March 13, 1913, and graduated from St. John's University in 1937 with a law degree. Commissioned into the U.S. Naval Reserve in 1943, within months he had transferred to the Office of Strategic Services, the forerunner of the CIA. In 1944 he became chief of the OSS Special Intelligence Branch in Europe. Next came the chairmanship of the Securities and Exchange Commission (1971–73); then, in quick succession, he was undersecretary of state for economic affairs (1973–74); president and chairman of the Export-Import Bank of the United States (1974–76); and a member of the president's Foreign Intelligence Advisory Board (1976–77). In 1980 he became campaign manager for Ronald Reagan's successful bid for the presidency. A year later, on January 28, 1981, Reagan appointed him DCI, the thirteenth man to hold the single most powerful office in the U.S. intelligence community.

In response to my remark that he appeared to have been a pair of safe hands in a number of posts, Casey sipped more water and mumbled he "didn't want to get into the personal side of things."

He put the paper back into his pocket and sat, watchful and waiting for my first question: what could he tell me about Bill Buckley, who, almost two years earlier to the day—on Friday, March 16, 1984—had been kidnapped in Beirut and was now dead. I wanted to know what efforts the CIA had made to try to save Bill's life. I had spent time in the Middle East, including Israel, trying to piece together the background.

"You speak to Admoni or any of his people?" Casey interrupted.

In 1982, Nahum Admoni had become head of Mossad. On Tel Aviv's embassy cocktail circuit, he had a hard-nosed reputation. Casey characterized Admoni as "a Jew who'd want to win a pissing contest on a rainy night in Gdansk." More certain, Admoni had been born in Jerusalem in 1929, the son of middle-class Polish immigrants. Educated at the city's Rehavia Gymnasium, he developed linguistic skills that had earned him a lieutenant's stripes as an intelligence officer in the 1948 War of Independence.

"Admoni can listen in half a dozen languages" was Casey's judgment.

Later, Admoni had studied international relations at Berkeley and taught the subject at the Mossad training school on the outskirts of Tel Aviv. He'd also worked undercover in Ethiopia, in Paris, and in Washington, where Admoni had linked closely with Casey's predecessors, Richard Helms and William Colby. These postings had helped hone Admoni into a soft-spoken intelligence bureaucrat who, when he became Mossad's chief, in Casey's words, "ran a tight ship. Socially gregarious, he has as keen an eye for women as for what's best for Israel."

Casey's thumbnail sketch was of an operative who, he said, had "climbed through the ranks because of his skills at avoiding his superiors' 'corns.'"

His next words came in the same mumbling undertone.

"Nobody can surprise like someone you took to be friendly disposed. By the time we realized Admoni was going to do nothing, Bill Buckley was dead. Remember what it was like at the time over there? There had been the massacre of almost a thousand Palestinians in those two Beirut refugee camps. The Lebanese Christian forces did the killings; the Jews looked on in a kind of reversal of the Bible. Fact is, Admoni was in bed with that thug, Gemayel."

Bashir Gemayel was head of the Phalangists and later became president of Lebanon.

"We ran Gemayel as well, but I never trusted the bastard. And Admoni worked with Gemayel all the time Buckley was being tortured. We had no idea where exactly in Beirut Bill was held. We asked Admoni to find out. He said no problem. We waited and waited. Sent our best men to Tel Aviv to work with Mossad. We said money was not a problem. Admoni kept saying okay, understood."

Casey sipped more water, locked in his own time capsule. His next words came out flat, like a jury foreman handing down a verdict.

"Next thing Admoni was selling us a bill of goods that the PLO were behind the kidnapping. We knew the Israelis were always ready to blame Yasser Arafat for anything, and our people did not buy at first. But Admoni was very plausible. He made a good case. By the time we figured it wasn't Arafat, it was long over for Buckley. What we didn't know was that Mossad had also been playing real dirty pool—supplying the Hezbollah with arms to kill the Christians while at the same time giving the Christians more guns to kill the Palestinians."

Casey's less-than-full glimpse of what the CIA now believed had happened to Bill Buckley—that Mossad had deliberately done nothing to save him in the hope the PLO could be blamed, so frustrating Arafat's hopes of gaining sympathy in Washington—provided a chilling insight into the relationship between two intelligence services supposedly friendly with each other.

Casey had shown there was another side to the ties between the United States and Israel other than fund-raising and other manifestations of American-Jewish solidarity that has turned the Jewish state into a regional superpower out of a fear of the Arab enemy.

Before we parted, Casey had a final thought: "A nation creates the intelligence community it needs. America relies on technical expertise because we are concerned to discover, rather than secretly rule. The Israelis operate differently. Mossad, in particular, equates its actions with the country's survival."

This attitude has long made Mossad immune to close scrutiny. But, during two years of research for this book, a series of mistakes—scandals in some cases—has forced the service into Israel's public consciousness. Questions have been asked, and, if the answers are rarely volunteered, gaps have begun to appear in the protective body armor Mossad has worn against that outside world.

I spoke to more than a hundred persons either directly employed by, or working indirectly for, Israeli and other intelligence services. The interviews were spread over two and a half years. Many of the key people in Mossad agreed to be taped. Those recordings run to eighty hours and are transcribed to some 5,800 pages. There are also some fifteen foolscap notebooks filled with contemporaneous notes. This material will, as with previous books of mine, find its place in the research section of a university library. Several of those I spoke to urged I should focus on recent events; the past should only be used to illustrate events that are relevant to Mossad's role at the cutting edge of the current frontiers of espionage and intelligence gathering. Many interviews were with participants who had not been questioned before; often no amount of probing could produce a comfortingly simple explanation for the way they or others behaved. Many were surprisingly frank, though not all agreed to be fully identified. In the case of serving Mossad personnel, they are prevented by Israeli law from voluntarily allowing their names to be published. Some of the non-Israeli sources asked, and received, a guarantee of anonymity.

On the organization charts newspapers try to piece together and publish, many sources remain among the empty spaces. They still take their anonymity seriously and some wish to be known in these pages by an alias or only a first name: it does not make their testimony less valid. Their personal motives for breaking silence may be many: a need to secure their own place in history; a desire to justify their actions; the anecdotage of old men; even perhaps expiation. The same can be said for those who agreed to be identified.

Perhaps the best motive of all that drove them to break silence was a real and genuine fear that an organization they had served with pride was increasingly endangered from within—and that the only way to save it was to reveal what it had achieved in the past and what it is doing today. To understand both requires knowing how and why it was created.

CHAPTER 2

BEFORE THE BEGINNING

Since dawn, the faithful had come to the most sacred wall in the world, the only remaining relic of Herod the Great's Second Temple in Jerusalem, the Wailing Wall. The young and the old, the lean and the fat, the bearded and the balding: all had made their way through the narrow streets or from outside the city walls.

Office clerks walked alongside shepherds from the hills beyond Jerusalem; newly bar mitzvahed youths proudly marched with men in the winter of their years. Teachers from the city's religious shuls were shoulder to shoulder with shopkeepers who had made the journey from a distance away, from Haifa, Tel Aviv, and the villages around the Sea of Galilee.

Uniformly dressed in black, each carried a prayer book and stood before the towering wall to recite portions of scripture.

Down the centuries, Jews had done that. But this Friday Sabbath in September 1929 was different. Rabbis had urged as many men as possible to be united in public prayer and to show their determination to their right to do so. It was intended not only as an expression of their faith, but also as a visible symbol of their Zionism—and a reminder to the Arab population, which vastly outnumbered them, that they would not be cowed.

For months there had been persistent rumors that the Muslim population was once more becoming increasingly angry over what they saw as Zionist expansion. These fears had started with the 1917 Balfour Declaration and its commitment to a formal Jewish homeland in Palestine. To Arabs who lived there and could trace their ancestry back to the Prophet, this was an outrage. Land that they had farmed for many centuries would be threatened, perhaps even taken from them by the Zionists and their British protectors, who had arrived at the end of the Great War to place Palestine under a Mandate. The British had ruled as they did in other parts of the empire, trying to please both sides. It was a recipe for disaster. Tensions between Jews and Arabs had increased. There had been skirmishes and bloodletting, often over where the Jews wanted to build their synagogues and religious shuls. But the Jews were stubbornly determined to exercise their "prayer rights" at the Wailing Wall in Jerusalem. For them it was part of the core of their faith.

By noon, the hour of the shema prayer, there were close to a thousand reading aloud the ancient words of scripture before the yellow sandstone wall. The rise and fall of their voices had its own soothing cadence.

Then, with stunning swiftness, missiles—stones, broken bottles, and tins filled with rubble—rained down on them. The assault had been launched by Arabs from vantage points around the Wailing Wall. The first crack of gunfire rattled, a ragged volley of musket shots from Muslim marksmen. Jews fell and were dragged away by their fleeing neighbors. Miraculously, no one was killed, though the injured numbered scores.

That night the leaders of the Yishuv, the Jewish community in Palestine, met. They quickly realized that their carefully planned demonstration had lacked one essential: foreknowledge of an Arab onslaught.

One of those present at the meeting spoke for them all: "We need to remember scripture. From King David onward, our people have depended on good intelligence."

Over cups of Turkish coffee and sweet pastries were sown the seeds for what would one day become the most formidable intelligence service in the modern world: Mossad. But its creation was still almost a quarter of a century away. All that the Yishuv leaders could suggest as a first practical step on that warm September night was to pool what money they could spare and call upon their neighbors to do the same. The cash would be used to bribe Arabs who were still tolerant toward Jews and who would provide advance warning of further attacks.

In the meantime Jews would continue to exert their right to pray at the Wailing Wall. They would not depend on the British for protection, but would be defended by the Haganah, the newly formed Jewish militia. In the months to come a combination of prior warning and the presence of the militia faced down Arab attacks. Relative calm between Arab and Jew was restored for the next five years.

In that period the Jews continued to secretly expand their intelligence gathering. It had no formal name or leadership. Arabs were recruited on an ad hoc basis: peddlers who worked in Jerusalem's Arab Quarter and shoeshine boys who burnished the boots of Mandate officers were put on the payroll, along with students from the city's prestigious Arab Rouda College, teachers, and businessmen. Any Jew could recruit an Arab spy; the only condition was the information was shared. Slowly but surely the Yishuv obtained important information not only about Arabs but about British intentions.

The coming to power of Hitler in 1933 marked the start of the exodus of German Jews to Palestine. By 1936 over three hundred thousand had made the long journey across Europe; many were destitute by the time they reached the Holy Land. Somehow food and accommodations were found for them by the Yishuv. Within months Jews made up over a third of the population. The Arabs reacted as they had before: from the minarets of a hundred mosques came the cries of the mullahs to drive the Zionists back into the sea.

In every Arab *mafafeth*, the meeting house where local Arab councilmen met, came the same raised voices of angry protests: We must stop the Jews from taking our land; we must stop the British giving them arms and training them.

In turn the Jews protested that the opposite was true, that the British were encouraging the Arabs to steal back land lawfully paid for.

The British continued to try to placate both sides—and failed. In 1936 sporadic fighting flared into full-scale Arab revolt against both the British and the Jews. The British ruthlessly suppressed the rebellion. But the Jews realized it would only be a matter of time before the Arabs struck with renewed fury.

Throughout the land young Jews rushed to join the Haganah. They became the core of a formidable secret army: physically hardened, crack shots, and as cunning as the desert foxes in the Negev.

The network of Arab informers was extended. A Haganah political department was set up to spread dissension through disinformation. Men who later became legends in the Israeli intelligence community learned their skills in that formative period before the start of World War II. The Haganah—the word means "defense" in Hebrew—became the best informed of all the forces in the Holy Land.

World War II brought a renewed uneasy peace to Palestine. Jews and Arabs sensed the grim future they would both face if the Nazis won. The first details of what was happening in the death camps of Europe had reached the Yishuv.

David Ben-Gurion and Yitzhak Rabin were among those who attended a meeting in Haifa in 1942. There was consensus that the survivors of the Holocaust must be brought to their spiritual home, Eretz Israel. No one could estimate how many there would be, but everyone agreed the arrival of the refugees would rekindle confrontation with the Arabs—and this time the British would openly side against the Jews. Britain had steadfastly said it would refuse to admit the survivors into Palestine after Hitler was defeated, on the grounds it would create a population imbalance.

Ben-Gurion's urging for an upgrade of the Haganah's intelligence capacity was fully endorsed by the meeting. More informers would be recruited. A counterintelligence unit would be formed to uncover Jews who were collaborating with the British and unearth "Jewish communists and dissenters in our midst." The new unit was known as Rigul Hegdi and was commanded by a former French foreign legionnaire working under cover as a traveling salesman.

Soon he was turning up Jewish women who consorted with officers of the Mandate; shopkeepers who traded with the British; café owners who entertained them. In the dead of night the culprits were brought before Haganah drumhead courts-martial; the guilty were either sentenced to be severely beaten or were executed in the Judaean hills by a single bullet in the back of the head. It was a precursor to the ruthlessness Mossad would later display.

By 1945 the Haganah included a unit responsible for procuring arms. Soon caches of Italian and German weapons captured in North Africa after the defeat of Rommel were being smuggled by Jewish soldiers serving with the Allies across the Egyptian Sinai Desert into Palestine. The arms came by ramshackle trucks and camel caravans and were stored in caves in the Wilderness where the Devil had tried to tempt Jesus. One hiding place was close to where the Dead Sea Scrolls were waiting to be discovered.

After the defeat of Japan in August 1945 ended the war, Jews who had served in Allied military intelligence units arrived to provide their expertise for the Haganah. The elements were in place to deal with what Ben-Gurion had forecast—"the war for our independence."

The trigger point he knew would be the *bricha*, the Hebrew name for the unprecedented operation to bring the Holocaust survivors from Europe. First they came in the hundreds, then thousands, then tens of thousands. Many still wore their concentration camp garb; each bore a tattoo with a Nazi identification number. They came by road and rail through the Balkans and then across the Mediterranean to the shores of Israel. Every available ship had been bought or rented by Jewish relief agencies in the United States—often at highly inflated prices: tramp steamers, coasters, landing craft from the beaches of Normandy, riverboats, anything that could float was pressed into service. There had not been an evacuation like it since Dunkirk in 1940.

Waiting for the survivors on the beaches between Haifa and Tel Aviv were some of the very British soldiers who had been ferried back to England from Dunkirk. They were there to carry out their government's order to keep out the Holocaust survivors. There were ugly clashes, but also times when the soldiers, perhaps remembering their own salvation, had looked the other way as a boatload of refugees struggled ashore.

Ben-Gurion decided that such acts of compassion were not enough. The time had come for the Mandate to end. That could only be done by force. By 1946, he had united the disparate Jewish underground movements. Fired by the unquenchable spirit of those who had first set-tled the land, the order was given to launch a guerrilla war against both the British and the Arabs.

Every Jewish commander knew it was a dangerous gamble: fighting on both fronts would stretch their resources to the very limit. The consequences of failure would be dire. Ben-Gurion ordered a no-holds-barred policy. Soon the catalog of atrocities was appalling on all sides. Jews were shot on suspicion of collaborating with the Haganah. British soldiers were gunned down and their barracks bombed. Arab villages were set to the torch. It was medieval in its ferocity.

For the Haganah, intelligence was critical, not least to spread disin-formation to give the impression in British and Arab eyes that the Jews had far more men than they actually could muster. The British found themselves chasing a will-o'-the-wisp enemy. Among the Mandate forces morale began to crumble.

Sensing an opening, the United States tried to broker a deal in the spring of 1946, urging Britain to admit into Palestine one hundred thou-sand Holocaust survivors. The plea was rejected and the bitter fight-ing continued. Finally, in February 1947, Britain agreed to leave Palestine by May 1948. From then on the United Nations would deal with the problems of what would become the State of Israel.

Realizing there must still be a decisive conflict with the Arabs to en-sure the fledgling nation would not be stifled at birth, Ben-Gurion and his commanders knew they must continue to depend on superior in-telligence. Vital data were obtained about Arab morale and military strength. Jewish spies positioned in Cairo and Amman stole the attack plans of the Egyptian and Jordanian armies. When what became known as the War of Independence started, the Israelis achieved spectacular military victories. But it also became clear to Ben-Gurion as the fight-ing continued that eventual victory must be predicated on a clear divi-sion between military and political aspirations. When victory did finally come in 1949, that division had not been properly settled—and that had led to feuding within the Israeli intelligence community over its responsibilities in peacetime.

Rather than dealing with the situation with his usual incisiveness, Ben-Gurion, as Israel's first prime minister, set up five intelligence ser-vices to operate both internally and abroad. The overseas service modeled itself on Britain's and France's security services. Both those services readily agreed to work with the Israelis. Contact was also established with the U.S. Office of Strategic Services (OSS) in Washington through the agency's head of counterintelligence in Italy, James Jesus Angleton. His bonding with Israel's fledgling spies would play a crucial role in the eventual bridge building between the two intelligence communities.

Yet, despite this promising start, Ben-Gurion's dream of an integrated intelligence organization working in harmony died in the birth pangs of a nation itself struggling for a cohesive identity. Muscle flexing remained the order of the day as his ministers and officials fought for power and positions. At every level there were clashes. Who would coordinate an overall intelligence strategy? Who would evaluate raw data? Who would recruit spies? Who should see their reports first? Who would interpret that information for the country's political leaders?

Nowhere was the jockeying more relentless than between the foreign ministry and the defense ministry, both of whom claimed the right to operate abroad. Isser Harel, then a young operative, felt his colleagues "saw intelligence work in a romantic and adventurous light. They pretended to be expert in the ways of the whole world . . . and sought to behave like fictional international spies enjoying their glory as they lived in the shadow of the fine line between law and licentiousness."

Meanwhile people continued to die, killed by Arab terrorists and their bombs and booby traps. The armies of Syria, Egypt, Jordan, and Lebanon still threatened. Behind them, millions more Arabs were ready to raise jihad, holy war. No nation on earth had been born into such a hostile environment as Israel.

For Ben-Gurion there was an almost messianic feeling about the way his people looked to him to protect them, in the way the great leaders of Israel had always done. But he knew he was no prophet, only a hard-bitten street fighter who had won the War of Independence against an Arab enemy with combined forces more than twenty times those at his disposal. There had not been a greater triumph since the boy shepherd David had killed Goliath and routed the Philistines.

Yet the enemy had not gone away. It had become cleverer and even more ruthless. It struck like a thief in the night, killing without compunction before vanishing.

For four long years the rivalry, squabbling, and sniping had gone on at all those meetings Ben-Gurion had chaired to try and resolve matters among the intelligence community. A promising foreign ministry plan to use a French diplomat as a spy in Cairo had been thwarted by the defense ministry. It wanted its own man for the job. The young officer, with no real experience of intelligence work, was caught in weeks by Egyptian security officers. Israeli agents in Europe were discovered to be working in the rampant black market to finance their work because there was an insufficient official budget to pay for their spying activities. Attempts to recruit the moderate Druze forces in Lebanon had ended when rival Israeli intelligence agencies disagreed on how they could be used. Often grandiose schemes were wrecked by mutual suspicion. Naked ambition was everywhere.

Powerful men of the day—Israel's foreign minister, the army chief of staff, and ambassadors—all fought to establish the supremacy of their favorite service over the others. One wanted the focus to be on the collection of economic and political information. Another thought intelligence should concentrate purely on the military strength of the enemy. The ambassador to France insisted intelligence should be run the way the French Resistance had operated in World War II, with every Jew in the land being mobilized. The ambassador to Washington wanted his spies protected by diplomatic cover and "integrated in the routine work of the embassy, so as to place them above suspicion." The Israeli minister to Bucharest wanted his spies to work along the lines of the KGB—and to be as ruthless. Israel's minister in Buenos Aires demanded that agents concentrate on the role of the Catholic church in helping Nazis to settle in Argentina. Ben-Gurion had patiently listened to every proposal.

Finally, on March 2, 1951, he summoned the heads of the five intelligence agencies to his office. He told them that he intended to place Israel's intelligence-gathering activities abroad in a new agency called Ha Mossad le Teum, "the Institute for Coordination." It would have an initial budget of twenty thousand Israeli pounds, of which five thousand pounds would be spent on "special missions, but only with my prior approval." The new agency would draw its personnel from the existing intelligence agencies. In everyday usage the new agency would be called only Mossad.

Mossad "for all administrative and political purposes" would come under the jurisdiction of the foreign ministry. However, it would have on its staff senior officers representing the other organizations within the Israeli intelligence community: Shin Bet, internal security; Aman, military intelligence; air force intelligence; and naval intelligence. The functions of the officers would be to keep Mossad informed of the specific requirements of their "clients." In the event of disagreement over any request, the matter would be referred to the prime minister's office.

In his usual blunt way Ben-Gurion spelled it out. "You will give Mossad your shopping list. Mossad will then go and get the goods. It is not your business to know where they shopped or what they paid for the goods."

Ben-Gurion would act as a one-man oversight committee for the new service. In a memo to its first chief, Reuven Shiloah, the prime minister ordered "Mossad will work under me, will operate according to my instructions and will report to me constantly."

The ground rules had been set.

Twenty-two eventful years after those Jews had sat through the Jerusalem night in September 1929 discussing the vital importance of intelligence to ward off further Arab attacks, their descendants had an intelligence service that would become more formidable than any other in the world.

The birth of Mossad, like that of Israel, was anything but smooth. The service had taken over a spy ring in Iraq that had been operating for some years under the control of the Israel Defense Forces' Political Department. The prime function of the ring was to penetrate the upper echelons of the Iraqi military and run a clandestine immigration network to bring Iraqi Jews out of the country to Israel.

In May 1951, just nine weeks after Ben-Gurion signed the order creating Mossad, Iraqi security agents in Baghdad swooped down on the ring. Two Israeli agents were arrested, along with dozens of Iraqi Jews and Arabs who had been bribed to run the escape network, which extended across the Middle East. Twenty-eight people were charged with espionage. Both agents were condemned to death, seventeen were given life sentences, and the others were freed "as an example of the fairness of Iraqi justice."

Both Mossad agents were subsequently released from an Iraqi jail, where they had been severely tortured, in exchange for a substantial sum of money paid into the Swiss bank account of the Iraqi minister of the interior.

Another debacle swiftly followed. The Political Department's longtime spy in Rome, Theodore Gross, now worked for Mossad under the new setup. In January 1952, Isser Harel, then head of Shin Bet, Israel's internal security service, received "incontrovertible proof" that Gross was a double agent, on the payroll of the Egyptian secret service. Harel decided to fly to Rome, where he persuaded Gross to return with him to Tel Aviv, convincing the traitor that he was about to be given a senior post in Shin Bet. Gross was tried in secret, convicted, and sentenced to fifteen years in jail. He would die in prison.

A crestfallen Reuven Shiloah resigned, a broken man. He was replaced by Harel, who would remain Mossad's chief for eleven years, a tenure never equaled.

Senior staff who welcomed him to Mossad headquarters on that September morning in 1952 could hardly have been impressed with Harel's physical appearance. He was barely four feet eight inches tall, with jug ears, and he spoke Hebrew with a heavy central European accent; his family had emigrated from Latvia in 1930. His clothes looked as if he had slept in them.

His first words to the assembled staff were: "The past is over. There will be no more mistakes. We will go forward together. We talk to no one except ourselves."

That same day he gave an example of what he meant. After lunch he summoned his driver. When the man asked where they were going, he was told the destination was a secret; dismissing the driver, Harel set off by himself at the wheel of the car. He returned with a box of bagels for the staff. But the point had been made. He would ask the questions.

That was the defining moment that endeared Harel to his demoralized staff. He set about energizing them with his own example. He traveled secretly to hostile Arab countries to personally organize Mossad networks. He interviewed every person who wanted to join the service. He looked for those who, like him, had a kibbutz background.

"People like that know our enemy," he told a senior aide who questioned the policy. "The kibbutzniks live close to the Arabs. They have learned not only to think like them—but think faster."

Harel's patience was as legendary as his bursts of anger; his loyalty to his staff became equally renowned. All those outside his closed circle were looked upon with suspicion as "unprincipled opportunists." He had no dealings with persons he saw as "bigots masquerading as nationalists, particularly in religion." Increasingly he showed an open dislike for Orthodox Jews.

There were a number of them in Ben-Gurion's government and they quickly came to resent Isser Harel, then tried to find a way to remove him. But the wily Mossad chief made sure he remained close to another kibbutznik, the prime minister.

It helped that Mossad's record now spoke for itself. Harel's agents had contributed to the success of the Sinai skirmishes against the Egyptians. He had spies in place in every Arab capital, providing a steady stream of priceless information. Another coup came when he traveled to Washington in 1954 to meet Allen Dulles, who had just taken over the CIA. Harel presented the veteran spymaster with a dagger bearing the engraved word of the psalmist: "the Guardian of Israel neither slumbers or sleeps."

Dulles replied: "You can count on me to stay awake with you."

Those words created a partnership between Mossad and the CIA. Dulles arranged for Mossad to have state-of-the-art equipment: listening and tracking devices, remote-operated cameras, and a range of gadgets that Harel admitted he never knew existed. The two men also formed the first intelligence "back channel" between their services, through which they could communicate by secure phone in the case of any emergency. The channel effectively bypassed the normal diplomatic route, to the chagrin of both the State Department and the Israeli foreign ministry. It did nothing to improve Harel's standing in diplomatic circles.

In 1961 Harel masterminded the operation to bring to Israel thousands of Moroccan Jews. A year later the tireless Mossad chief was in southern Sudan assisting pro-Israeli rebels against the regime. That same year he also helped King Haile Selassie of Ethiopia crush an attempted coup: the monarch had been a longtime ally of Israel.

But at home the Orthodox Jews in the cabinet were becoming more vociferous, complaining that Isser Harel had become insufferably autocratic and increasingly indifferent to their religious sensibilities, and that he was a man with his own agenda, perhaps even an aspiration to the highest political office in the land. Ben-Gurion's well-tuned political antenna was up, and relations between him and Harel cooled. Where before he had given Harel a virtual free hand, he now began to demand to be briefed on the smallest details of an operation. Harel resented the tight leash but said nothing. The whispering campaign against him intensified.

In February 1962, the innuendos coalesced over the fate of an eight-year-old boy, Joselle Schumacher. Two years before, the child had been kidnapped from his parents by an ultra-Orthodox sect.

The boy's maternal grandfather, Nahman Shtarkes, was a member of the sect Neturei Karta, the "Guardians of the Walls of Jerusalem." He was suspected of complicity in the kidnapping. Already there had been a huge police hunt for Joselle that had produced no clue as to his whereabouts. Nahman had been briefly imprisoned when he had refused to cooperate with the investigation. Orthodox Jews had turned the old man into a martyr; thousands had paraded with banners proclaiming Ben-Gurion to be no different from the Nazis, imprisoning an old man. Nahman had been released on "health grounds." The protests had continued.

Ben-Gurion's political advisers warned that the matter could lose him the next election. Worse, in the event of another war with the Arabs, some Orthodox groups could actually support them. The embattled prime minister had sent for Harel and ordered Mossad to find the boy. Harel argued it was not a task for the service. In his later words:

"The atmosphere turned to ice. He repeated he was giving me an order. I said I needed at least to read the police file. The prime minister said I had an hour."

The file was large but, as he read it, something stirred deep in Isser Harel—the right of parents to bring up their child without being pressured by extreme religious belief.

Joselle had been born in March 1953 to Arthur and Ida Schumacher. Due to family financial difficulties, Joselle had been sent to live with his grandfather in Jerusalem. The child found himself in a religious enclave, spiritually isolated from the rest of the city. Increasingly Nahman inducted his grandson into the sect's ways. When Joselle's parents visited, Nahman angrily criticized them for what he saw as their own wayward religious attitudes.

The old man belonged to a generation whose faith helped them survive the Holocaust. Nahman's daughter and son-in-law felt their prime role was to create a life for themselves in the young nation. All too often prayer had to take second place.

Tired of Nahman's constant criticism, Joselle's parents said they wanted him back. Nahman objected, arguing that to move him would disrupt Joselle's instruction into a prayer life that would serve him as an adult. There were more angry exchanges. Then, the next time they visited Jerusalem, Joselle had disappeared.

Both Orthodox and secular Jews had seized upon the incident to give full vent to an issue that continued to divide the nation, and was exemplified by Ben-Gurion's Labor Party only being able to survive in office by cobbling together various religious factions in the Knesset. In turn, those groups had obtained further concessions for the strict laws of Orthodoxy. But always they wanted more. Liberal Jews demanded that Joselle must be returned to his family.

Having read the file, Isser Harel told Ben-Gurion he would mobilize Mossad's resources. He put together a team, forty agents strong, to locate Joselle. Many of them were openly opposed to what they saw as a misuse of their skills.

He silenced their criticism with a short speech:

"Although we will be operating outside our normal type of target, this is still a very important case. It is important because of its social and religious background. It is important because the prestige and authority of our government are at stake. It is important because of the human issues which the case involves."

In the first weeks of the investigation the team soon discovered how formidable the investigation would be.

A future head of Shin Bet, then a Mossad agent, grew the curly sidelocks of the ultra-Orthodox and tried to penetrate their ranks. He failed. Another Mossad agent was ordered to maintain surveillance on a Jewish school. He was spotted within days. A third agent tried to infiltrate a group of Hasidic mourners traveling to Jerusalem to bury a relative within the walls of the city. He was quickly unmasked when he failed to utter the right prayers.

Those failures only made Harel more determined. He told his team he was certain the child was no longer in Israel but somewhere in Europe or even farther afield. Harel moved his operations headquarters to a Mossad safe house in Paris. From there he sent men into every Orthodox community in Italy, Austria, France, and Britain. When that produced nothing, he sent the agents to South America and the United States.

The investigation continued to be enlivened with bizarre episodes. Ten Mossad agents joined a Saturday-morning service at a synagogue in the London suburb of Hendon. The furious congregation called the police to arrest the "religious impostors" after their false beards came unstuck during scuffles. The agents were quietly released after the Israeli ambassador intervened with the Home Office. A venerated Orthodox rabbi was invited to Paris on the pretext that a member of a wealthy family wished him to officiate at a circumcision. He was met at the airport by two men dressed in the severe black coats and hats of

Orthodox Jews. They were Mossad agents. Their report had an element of black comedy.

"He was taken to a Pigalle brothel, having no idea what it was. Two prostitutes who had been paid by us suddenly appeared and were all over the rabbi. We took Polaroid photographs and showed them to him and said we would send them to his congregation unless he revealed where the boy was. The rabbi finally convinced us he had no idea and we destroyed the photographs in front of him."

Another rabbi, Shai Freyer, surfaced in Isser Harel's ever-expanding search through the world of Orthodox Jewry. The rabbi was picked up by Mossad agents as he traveled between Paris and Geneva. When they became convinced, after rigorous questioning, that once more this was another dead end, Harel ordered Freyer to be held a prisoner in a Mossad safe house in Switzerland until the search ended. He feared the rabbi would alert the Orthodox community.

Another promising lead appeared. She was Madeleine Frei, the daughter of an aristocratic French family and a heroine of the French Resistance in World War II. Madeleine had saved a large number of Jewish children from deportation to the Nazi death camps. After the war she had converted to Judaism.

Checks revealed she was a regular visitor to Israel, spending her time with members of the Neturei Karta sect, and on several occasions she had met Joselle's grandfather. Her last visit to Israel had been around the time of the boy's abduction. Madeleine had not returned to Israel since then.

In August 1962, Mossad agents tracked her to the outskirts of Paris. When they introduced themselves, she physically attacked them. One of the agents summoned Isser Harel.

He explained to Madeleine "the great wrong" done to Joselle's parents. They had the moral right to bring up their son as they wished. No parents should be denied that right. Madeleine still insisted she knew nothing about Joselle. Harel saw his own men believed her.

He asked for Madeleine's passport. Beneath her photograph was one of her daughter. He asked an agent to bring him a photograph of Joselle. The facial structures of the children in both photographs were almost identical. Harel called Tel Aviv. Within a couple of hours:

"I had everything I needed to know, from details of her love life during her student days to her decision to join the Orthodox move-

ment after renouncing her Catholic faith. I went back to Madeleine and told her, as if I knew everything, that she had dyed Joselle's
hair to disguise him and smuggled the boy out of Israel. She flatly
denied it. I said she must understand that the future of the country she loved was in grave danger, that in the streets of Jerusalem
people she loved were throwing stones at each other. Still she refused to admit anything. I said the boy had a mother who loved
him as much as she loved all those children she had helped in World
War Two."

The reminder worked. Suddenly Madeleine began to explain how
she had traveled by sea to Haifa, a tourist come to see Israel. On the
boat she made friends with a family of new immigrants who had a child
about the age of Joselle. She had led the little girl down the gangplank
at Haifa, and the immigration officer had taken the child as Madeleine's
own. He made a note of this in his records. A week later, under the very
noses of Israeli police, she had boarded a flight to Zurich with her
"daughter." Madeleine had even persuaded Joselle to dress in girl's clothing and have his hair dyed.

For a while Joselle had lived in an Orthodox school in Switzerland
where Rabbi Shai Freyer was a teacher. Following his detention,
Madeleine flew with Joselle to New York, placing him with a family
who were members of the Neturei Karta sect. Harel only had one
more question for her: "Will you give me the name and address of the
family?"

For a long moment there was silence before Madeleine calmly said:
"He is living at 126 Penn Street, Brooklyn, New York. He is known as
Yankale Gertner."

For the first time since their encounter, Harel smiled. "Thank you,
Madeleine. I would like to congratulate you by offering you a job with
Mossad. Your kind of talent could serve Israel well."

Madeleine refused.

Mossad agents flew to New York. Waiting for them was a team of
FBI agents, authorized to cooperate by U.S. Attorney General Robert
Kennedy. He had received a personal request from Ben-Gurion to do
so. The agents traveled to the apartment house at 126 Penn Street. Mrs.
Gertner opened the door. The agents rushed past her. Inside, her husband was praying. Beside him was a pale-faced boy with a yarmulke on
his head and dark side-curls framing his face.

"Hello Joselle. We have come to take you home," one of the Mossad men said gently.

Eight months had passed since Mossad had begun its search. Close to a million U.S. dollars had been spent on the operation.

The safe return of Joselle did nothing to bridge the religious divide within the country. Successive governments would continue to totter and fall at the whim of small ultra-Orthodox groups elected to the Knesset.

Successful though he had been in finding the boy, Isser Harel returned to Israel to face a powerful new critic, General Meir Amit, the newly appointed chief of Aman, military intelligence. Just as Harel had connived against his predecessor, he now found himself on the receiving end of Amit's barbed criticisms over the operation to rescue Joselle.

Amit, a formidable field commander, had become close to Ben-Gurion in the ever-shifting political sands of Israel. He told the prime minister that Harel had "wasted resources," that the whole rescue operation had been the sign of an intelligence chief who had been too long in the job. Forgetting that he had ordered Harel to mount the operation, Ben-Gurion agreed. On March 25, 1963, bruised by many weeks of intensive sniping, Isser Harel, at the age of fifty, resigned. Grown men were close to tears as he shook their hands and walked out of Mossad headquarters. Everyone knew it was the end of an era.

Hours later a tall, spare man with the hawkish good looks of the actor he could once have been strode briskly through its doors: Meir Amit had taken over. No one needed to be told that radical changes were about to happen.

Fifteen minutes after settling himself behind his desk, Mossad's new chief summoned his department heads. They stood in a group before him while he silently eyeballed them. Then, in the brisk voice that had launched countless battleground attacks, he spoke.

There would be no more operations to recover lost children. No undue political interference. He would protect each one of them from external criticism, but nothing could save their jobs if they failed him. He would fight for more money from the defense budget for the latest equipment and backup resources. But that was not a signal to forget the one asset he placed above all others: humint, the art of human intelligence gathering. He wanted that to be Mossad's greatest skill.

His staff found they were working for a man who saw their work as beyond day-to-day operations, but bearing results in years to come. The acquisition of military technology fell into that category.

Shortly after Meir Amit took command, a man who gave his name as Salman had walked into the Israeli embassy in Paris with an astounding proposition. For one million U.S. dollars in cash he could guarantee to provide what was then the world's most secret combat aircraft, the Russian MiG-21. Salman had concluded his astounding offer to an Israeli diplomat with a bizarre request. "Send someone to Baghdad, call this number, and ask for Joseph. And have our million dollars ready."

The diplomat sent his report to the resident *katsa* in the embassy. He had been one of those who had survived the purging that followed Meir Amit's appointment. The *katsa* sent the report to Tel Aviv, together with the phone number Salman had provided.

For days Meir Amit weighed and considered. Salman could be a confidence trickster or a fantasist, or even part of an Iraqi plot to try to entrap a Mossad agent. There was a very real risk that other *katsas* working under deep cover in Iraq would be compromised. But the prospect of getting hold of a MiG-21 was irresistible.

Its fuel capacity, altitude, speed, armaments, and turnaround servicing time had made it the Arab world's premier frontline fighter aircraft. Israel's air force chiefs would cheerfully have given many millions of dollars for just a glimpse of the MiG's blueprint, let alone for the actual plane. Meir Amit "went to bed thinking of it. I woke up thinking of it. I thought of it in the shower, over dinner. I thought about it every spare moment I had. Keeping up with an enemy's advanced weapons system is a priority with any intelligence service. Actually getting your hands on it almost never happens."

The first step was to send an agent to Baghdad. Meir Amit created an alias for him, as English as the name in his passport, George Bacon: "No one would think a Jew would have a name like that." Bacon would travel to Baghdad as the sales manager of a London-based company selling hospital X-ray equipment.

He arrived in Baghdad on an Iraqi Airways flight with several sample boxes of equipment and demonstrated how well he had absorbed his brief by selling several items to hospitals. At the beginning of his second week, Bacon made the call to the number Salman had provided. Bacon's reports to Mossad contained vivid descriptions.

"I used a pay phone in the hotel lobby. The risk the phone was tapped was smaller than making the call from my room. The number was answered at once. A voice asked in Farsi who was speaking. I replied in English, apologizing I must have the wrong number. The voice then asked, also in English, who was speaking. I said I was a friend of Joseph's. Was there someone there by that name? I was told to wait. I thought maybe they were tracing the call, that this was a trap after all. Then a very cultured voice was on the line saying he was Joseph and that he was glad I had called. He then asked if I knew Paris. I thought: Contact!"

Bacon found himself agreeing to a meeting in a Baghdad coffeehouse the following noon. At the appointed hour, a man smilingly introduced himself as Joseph. His face was deeply etched, his hair white. The agent's later report once more captured the surreal atmosphere of the moment:

"Joseph said how very pleased he was to see me, as if I was some long-awaited relative. He then started to talk about the weather and how the quality of service had dropped in cafés like this one. I thought, here I am in the middle of a hostile country whose security service would surely kill me if they had the chance, listening to an old man's ramblings. I decided whoever he was, whatever his connection was with Salman in Paris, Joseph was certainly not an Iraqi counterintelligence officer. That calmed me. I told him my friends were very interested in the merchandise his friend had mentioned. He replied, 'Salman is my nephew who lives in Paris. He is a waiter at a café. All the good waiters have left here.' Joseph then leaned across the table and said, 'You have come about the MiG? I can arrange it for you. But it will cost one million dollars.' Just like that."

Bacon sensed that perhaps, after all, Joseph was more than he appeared. There was a quiet certainty about him. But as he began to question him, the old man shook his head. "Not here. People could be listening."

They arranged to meet again the following day on a park bench along the Tigris River, which flowed through the city. That night Bacon slept very little wondering if, after all, he was being slowly hooked, if not by Iraqi intelligence, then by some very clever con men who were using Joseph as a front.

The next day's meeting revealed a little more of Joseph's background and motives.

He came from a poor Iraqi Jewish family. As a boy he had been employed as a servant by a rich Maronite Christian family in Baghdad. Then, after thirty years of loyal service, he had been abruptly dismissed, wrongly accused of stealing food. He found himself, on his fiftieth birthday, cast out into the streets. Too old to find other work, he existed on a modest pension. He had also decided to seek out his Jewish roots. He discussed his quest with his widowed sister, Manu, whose son, Munir, was a pilot in the Iraqi air force. Manu admitted she too had a strong desire to go to Israel. But how could they possibly do that? Even to mention the idea was to risk imprisonment in Iraq. To leave anyone behind would guarantee the authorities would punish them severely, perhaps even kill them. And where would the money come from? She had sighed and said it was all an impossible dream.

But in Joseph's mind the idea took hold. Over dinner Munir had often told how his commander boasted that Israel would pay a fortune for one of the MiGs he flew, "perhaps even a million U.S. dollars, Uncle Joseph."

The sum had focused Joseph. He could bribe officials, organize an escape route. With that money he could somehow move the entire family out of Iraq. The more he thought about it, the more feasible it became. Munir loved his mother; he would do anything for her—even stealing his plane for a million dollars. And there would be no need for Joseph to have to organize the family's escape. He would let the Israelis do that. Everyone knew they were clever at such things. That was why he had sent Salman to the embassy.

"And now you are here, my friend!" Joseph beamed at Bacon.

"What about Munir? Does he know any of this?"

"Oh, yes. He has agreed to steal the MiG. But he wants half the money down now, then the balance delivered just before he does so."

Bacon was astounded. Everything he had heard sounded both genuine and feasible. But first he had to report to Meir Amit.

In Tel Aviv, the Mossad chief listened for an entire afternoon while Bacon reported every detail.

"Where does Joseph want to be paid?" Meir Amit finally asked.

"Into a Swiss bank. Joseph has a cousin who needs urgent medical treatment not available in Baghdad. The Iraqi authorities will give him permission to go to Switzerland. When he arrives, he expects to have the money already deposited by us."

"A resourceful man, your Joseph," Meir Amit commented wryly. "Once the money is in that account, we'll never get it back."

He put one more question to Bacon. "Why do you trust Joseph?"

Bacon replied. "I trust him because it is the only choice."

Meir Amit authorized half a million U.S. dollars should be deposited in the main branch of Credit Suisse in Geneva. He was gambling more than money. He knew he could not survive if Joseph turned out to be the brilliant fraud some Mossad officers still believed he was.

The time had come to brief Prime Minister Ben-Gurion and his chief of staff, Yitzhak Rabin. Both men green-lighted the operation. Meir Amit had not told them he had taken one more step—withdrawing the entire Mossad network from Iraq.

"If the mission failed, I didn't want anyone's head on the block except my own. I set up five teams. The first team was the communications link between Baghdad and me. They would break radio silence only if there was a crisis. Otherwise I didn't want to hear from them. The second team was to be in Baghdad without anyone knowing. Not Bacon, not the first team, no one. They were there to get Bacon out of the country if there was trouble, and Joseph, too, if possible. The third team was to keep an eye on the family. The fourth team was to liaise with the Kurds who would help in the last stages of getting the family out. Israel was supplying them with arms. The fifth team was to liaise with Washington and Turkey. For the MiG to be flown out of Iraq, it would have to fly over Turkish air space to reach us. Washington, who had bases in northern Turkey, would have to persuade the Turks to cooperate by saying the MiG was going to end up in the United States. I now knew that the Iraqis feared the possibility of a pilot defecting to the West, so they kept fuel tanks only half-full. That was something we could do nothing about."

There were still other problems. Joseph had decided that not only his immediate family but distant cousins should have the opportunity of escaping from the harsh Iraqi regime. In all he wanted forty-three persons to be airlifted to safety.

Meir Amit agreed—only to face a new worry. From Baghdad, Bacon sent a coded message that Munir was having second thoughts. The Mossad chief "sensed what was happening. Munir was first and foremost an Iraqi. Iraq had been good to him. Betraying his country to Israel did not sit well. We were the enemy. All his life he had been taught that. I decided the only way was to convince him the MiG would go straight to America. So I flew to Washington and saw Richard Helms, then DCI [director of the Central Intelligence Agency]. He listened and said no problem. He was always very good like that. He arranged for the U.S. military attaché in Baghdad to meet Munir. The attaché confirmed the plane would be handed over to the United States. He gave Munir a lot of talk about helping America catch up with the Russians. Munir bought it and agreed to go ahead."

The operation now took on a pace of its own. Joseph's relative received his Iraqi exit permit and flew to Geneva. From there he sent a postcard: "The hospital facilities are excellent. I am assured of a total recovery." The message was the signal that the second five hundred thousand dollars had been deposited.

Reassured, Joseph told Bacon the family were ready. On the night before Munir would make his flight, Joseph led them in a convoy of vehicles north, to the cool of the mountains. Iraqi checkpoints did not trouble them; residents moved every summer away from the stifling heat of Baghdad. In the foothills Kurds waited with the Israeli liaison team. They led the family deep into the mountains, where Turkish air force helicopters were waiting. Flying below radar, they crossed back into Turkey.

An Israeli agent made a call to Munir telling him his sister had safely delivered a baby girl. Another coded signal had been safely transmitted.

Next morning, August 15, 1966, at sunup, Munir took off for a practice mission. Clear of the airfield he kicked in the MiG's afterburners and was over the border with Turkey before other Iraqi pilots could be instructed to shoot him down. Escorted by U.S. Air Force Phantoms, Munir landed at a Turkish air base, refueled, and took off again. Through his headphones he heard the message, in plain talk this time. "All your family are safe and on the way to join you."

An hour later the MiG touched down at a military air base in northern Israel.

Mossad had become a serious player on the world stage. Within the Israeli intelligence community the way matters were conducted in the future would be known as "BA"—before Amit—or "AM"—after Meir.

CHAPTER 3

ENGRAVINGS OF GLILOT

Exiting the highway north of Tel Aviv, Meir Amit continued to maintain his speed at a little above the speed limit. Discreetly bucking the system had continued to be part of his life since, almost forty years before, he had masterminded the theft of an Iraqi jet.

He put down blindly refusing to follow the rule book as stemming from his Galilean background: "We are a stubborn lot." He had been born in King Herod's favorite city, Tiberias, close to the shore of the Sea of Galilee, and spent most of his early life on a kibbutz. Long ago all traces of the region's flat accent had been smoothed away by his mother, an elocution teacher. She had also instilled her son's sense of independence, his refusal to tolerate fools, and a barely concealed contempt for city dwellers. Most important of all, she had encouraged his analytical skills and ability to think laterally.

In his long career he had used those qualities to discover an enemy's intention. Often action could not wait for certainty, and motive and deception had been at the center of his work. At times his critics in the Israeli intelligence community had been concerned at what they saw as his imaginative leaps. He had one answer for them all: Read the case file on the stolen MiG.

On this March morning in 1997, as he continued to drive out of Tel Aviv, Meir Amit was officially on the retired list. But no one in Israeli intelligence believed that was the case; his vast knowledge was too valuable to be put in cold storage.

The previous day Meir Amit had returned from Ho Chi Minh City, where he had visited former Vietcong intelligence officers. They had swapped experiences and had found common ground over besting superior opposition: the Vietnamese against the Americans, Israel fighting the Arabs. Meir Amit had made other trips to places where his secret maneuvers had once created havoc: Amman, Cairo, Moscow. No one dared to question the purpose of these visits, just as during his five momentous years as director general of Mossad—1963–68—no one had mounted a successful challenge over his sources or methods.

In that period he had turned humint, human intelligence gathering, into an art form. No other intelligence agency had been able to match his agents on the ground in collecting information. He had placed spies in ever greater numbers in every Arab country, across Europe, down into South America, throughout Africa, and in the United States. His *katsas* had penetrated the Jordanian Mukabarat, the best of the Arab intelligence services, and Syrian military intelligence, the most cruel. They were men of cool nerve and steel resolve that no novelist would have dared to invent.

Soon after he became director general, Meir Amit circulated within the service a memo stolen by an agent from Yasser Arafat's office:

"Mossad has a dossier on each of us. They know our names and addresses. We know there are two photographs with each of our files. One is a copy of how we look without a kaffiyeh and the other wearing one. So the Mossad have no difficulty tracking us down with or without our headdresses."

To create further fear, Meir Amit had recruited an unprecedented number of Arab informers. He worked on the principle that by the law of averages he would discover a sufficient number who would be useful. Bribed Arabs had betrayed PLO gunmen and revealed their arms caches, safe houses, and travel arrangements. For each terrorist killed by Mossad, Meir Amit paid an informer a bonus of one U.S. dollar.

In the run-up to the Six-Day War in 1967, there was either a Mossad *katsa* or an informer inside every Egyptian air base and military headquarters. There were no fewer than three in the General High Command headquarters in Cairo, staff officers who had been persuaded by Meir Amit. How he had done so remained his closely guarded secret: "There are some matters best left that way."

To each informer and agent in place he had given the same instruction: as well as "the big picture," he wanted "the small details. How far did a pilot have to walk from his barracks to the mess for his meals? How long was a staff officer held up in the notorious Cairo traffic jam? Did a key planner have a mistress?" Only he fully understood how such disparate matters would be used.

One *katsa* had managed to get himself a job as a waiter in the officers' mess in a frontline fighter base. Every week he provided details of aircraft readiness and the lifestyle of pilots and technicians. Their drinking habits and sexual pleasures were among the information secretly radioed to Tel Aviv.

Mossad's newly created Department of Psychological Warfare, Loh Amma Psichologit (LAP), worked around the clock preparing files on Egyptian fliers, ground crew, and staff officers: their flying skills, whether they had achieved their rank through ability or influence, who had a drink problem, frequented a brothel, had a predilection for boys.

Well into the night, Meir Amit pored over the files, looking for weaknesses, for men who could be blackmailed into working for him. "It was not a pleasant task but intelligence is often a dirty business."

Egyptian families of servicemen began to receive anonymous letters posted in Cairo giving explicit details of their loved one's behavior. Informers reported back to Tel Aviv details of family rows that led to aircrew going on sick leave. Staff officers had anonymous phone calls giving information about a colleague's private life. A teacher at school was called by a sympathetic-sounding woman to be told that the only reason a pupil was doing badly was because her father, a senior officer, had a secret male lover; the call led to the officer shooting himself. This relentless campaign caused considerable dissension within the Egyptian military and brought great satisfaction to Meir Amit.

By early 1967, it became clear from all the evidence his Egyptian network was producing that the country's leader, Gamal Abdel Nasser, was preparing for war against Israel. More informers were recruited by fair means or foul, helping Mossad to know as much about the Egyptian air force and its military command as did Cairo.

By early May 1967 he was able to give Israel's air force commanders the precise time of day they should launch a knockout strike against the Egyptian air bases. Mossad's analysts had produced a remarkable blueprint of life on all Egyptian air bases.

Between 7:30 A.M. and 7:45 A.M. airfield radar units were at their most vulnerable. In those fifteen minutes the outgoing night staff were tired after their long shift, while their incoming replacements were not yet fully alert, and were often late in taking over due to slow service in the mess halls. Pilots breakfasted between 7:15 A.M. and 7:45 A.M. Afterward they usually walked back to their barracks to collect their flying gear. The average journey took ten minutes. Most fliers spent a further few minutes in the toilets before going to the flight lines. They arrived there around 8:00 A.M., the official start to the day. By then ground crew had begun to roll out aircraft from their hangars to be fueled and armed. For the next fifteen minutes the flight lines were crammed with fuel trucks and ammunition trucks.

A similar detailed itinerary was prepared for the movements of staff officers in the Cairo High Command. The average officer took thirty minutes to drive to work from his house in one of the suburbs. Strategic planners were often not at their desks before 8:15 A.M. They usually spent a further ten minutes settling in, sipping coffee, and gossiping with colleagues. The average staff officer did not properly start studying overnight signals traffic from the fighter bases until close to 8:30 A.M.

Meir Amit told the Israeli air force commander that the time their aircraft must be over their targets should be between 8:00 A.M. and 8:30 A.M. In those thirty minutes they would be able to pulverize enemy bases, knowing that the Cairo High Command would be without many of its key personnel to direct the fight back.

On June 5, 1967, Israel's air force struck at precisely 8:01 A.M. with deadly effect, sweeping in low over the Sinai to bomb and strafe at will.

In moments the sky turned reddish black with the flames from burning fuel trucks and exploding ammunition and aircraft.

In Tel Aviv, Meir Amit sat looking out of his office window toward the south, knowing his intelligence analysts had virtually settled the outcome of the war. It was one of the most stunning examples of his extraordinary skills—and even more remarkable given the numerical size of Mossad.

From the time he took over, Meir Amit had resisted attempts to turn Mossad into a version of the CIA or KGB. Those services between them employed hundreds of thousands of analysts, scientists, strategists, and planners to support their field agents. The Iraqis and Iranians had an estimated ten thousand field agents; even the Cuban DGI possessed close to a thousand spies in the field.

But Meir Amit had insisted that Mossad's permanent total staff would number little more than twelve hundred. Each would be hand-picked and have multiple skills: a scientist must be able to work in the field should the need arise; a *katsa* must be able to use his specialist skills to train others.

To them all he would be the memune, which roughly translates from Hebrew as "first among equals." With the title came unfettered access to the prime minister of the day and the annual ritual of presenting his budget for the Israeli cabinet to rubber-stamp.

Long before the Six-Day War he had established Mossad's ability to strike mortal terror into Israel's enemies, penetrating their ranks, vacuuming up their secrets, and killing them with chilling efficiency. He had soon made Mossad mythic in stature.

Much of that success came from the rules he laid down for selecting *katsas*, the field agents who, ultimately, were at the cutting edge of Mossad's success. He fully understood the deep and complex motives that allowed them, upon selection, to shake his hand, the gesture that acknowledged they were now his to command as he wished.

While much else had changed in Mossad, Meir Amit knew on that March morning in 1997 that his recruiting criteria had remained intact:

No *katsa* is accepted into Mossad who is primarily motivated by money. The overly zealous Zionist has no place in this work. It gets in the way of a clear understanding of what the job is all about. It is one that calls for calm, clear, farsighted judgment and a balanced outlook. People want to join Mossad for all kinds of reasons. There is the so-called glamour. Some like the idea of adventure. Some think joining will enhance their status, small people who want to be big. A few want the secret power they believe being in Mossad would give them. None of these are acceptable reasons for joining.

And always, always, you must ensure your man in the field knows he has your total support. That you will look out for his family, make sure his kids are happy. At the same time you must protect him. If his wife starts to wonder if he has another woman reassure her he has not. If he has, don't tell her. If she goes off the rails, bring her back on the straight and narrow. Don't tell her husband. You want nothing to distract him. The job of a good spymaster is to treat his people as family. Make them feel he is always there for them, day, night, no matter what the time. This is how you buy loyalty, make your *katsa* do what you want. And in the end what you want is important.

Each *katsa* underwent three years of intensive training, including being subjected to severe physical violence under interrogation. He, or she, became proficient in the use of Mossad's weapon of choice—the .22-caliber Beretta.

The first *katsas* stationed outside the Arab countries were in the United States, Britain, France, and Germany. In the United States there were permanent *katsas* in New York and Washington. The New York *katsa* had special responsibility for penetrating all UN diplomatic missions and the city's many ethnic groups. The Washington *katsa* had a similar job, with the additional responsibility of "monitoring" the White House.

Other *katsas* operated in areas of current tensions, returning home when a mission ended.

Meir Amit also considerably expanded the organization to include a Collections Department responsible for intelligence-gathering operations abroad and a Political Action and Liaison Department, working with so-called friendly foreign intelligence services, mostly the CIA and Britain's MI6. The Research Department had fifteen sections or "desks" targeting Arab states. The United States, Canada, Latin America, Britain, Europe, and the Soviet Union all had their separate desks. This infrastructure would, over the years, expand to include China, South Africa, and the Vatican. But essentially Mossad would remain the same small organization.

A day did not pass without the arrival of a fresh sheaf of news stories from overseas stations. These were circulated throughout the drab gray high-rise building on King Saul Boulevard. In Meir Amit's view, "If it made someone walk a little taller, that was no bad thing. And, of course, it made our enemies that much more fearful."

Mossad's *katsas* were coldly efficient and cunning beyond belief—and prepared to fight fire with fire. Operatives incited disturbances designed to create mutual distrust among Arab states, planted black counterpropaganda, and recruited informers, implementing Meir Amit's philosophy: "Divided, we rule." In all they did, his men set new standards for cold-blooded professionalism, moving like thieves in the night, leaving a trail of death and destruction. No one was safe from their retaliation.

A mission completed they returned to be debriefed in Meir Amit's corner-window office overlooking the broad thoroughfare named after Israel's Old Testament warlord. From his office he personally ran two spies whose bravery would remain without equal in the annals of Mossad. Recalling their contributions, his voice became tentative, the occasional smile one of apologetic self-protection, as he began by recounting biographical details.

Eli Cohen was born in Alexandria, Egypt, on December 16, 1924. Like his parents, he was a devout Orthodox Jew. In December 1956 he was among Jews expelled from Egypt after the Suez crisis. He arrived in Haifa and felt himself a stranger in his new land. In 1957 he was recruited into Israeli military counterintelligence, but his work as an analyst bored him. He began to inquire how he could join Mossad, but was rejected. Meir Amit recalled, "We heard that our rejection had deeply offended Eli Cohen. He resigned from the army and married an Iraqi woman named Nadia."

For two years Cohen led an uneventful life as a filing clerk in a Tel Aviv insurance office. Unknown to him, his background had surfaced in a trawl through Mossad's "reject files" by Meir Amit, who was looking for a "certain kind of agent for a very special job." Finding no one suitable in the "active" files, he had gone to the "rejects." Cohen seemed the only possibility. He was put under surveillance. The weekly reports by Mossad's recruiting office described his fastidious habits and devotion to his wife and young family. He was hardworking, quick on the uptake, and worked well under pressure. Finally he was told that Mossad had decided he was "suitable" after all.

Eli began an intensive six-month course at the Mossad training school. Sabotage experts taught him how to make explosives and time bombs from the simplest of ingredients. He learned unarmed combat and became a first-class marksman and an accomplished burglar. He discovered the mysteries of encoding and decoding, how to work a radio set, use invisible inks, and hide messages. He constantly impressed his instructors with his skills. His phenomenal memory came from memorizing tracts of the Torah as a young man. His graduate report stated he had every quality needed by a *katsa*. Still Meir Amit hesitated.

"I asked myself a hundred times: can Eli do what I want? I always showed him, of course, my confidence was always in place. I never wanted him for a moment to think he would always be one step from the trapdoor which would send him to kingdom come. Yet some of the very best brains in Mossad put everything they knew into him. Finally I decided to run with Eli."

Meir Amit spent weeks creating a cover story for his protégé. They would sit together, studying street maps and photographs of Buenos Aires so that Cohen's new background and name, Kamil Amin Taabes, became totally familiar. The Mossad chief saw how quickly

"Eli learned the language of an exporter-importer to Syria. He memorized the difference between waybills and freight certificates, contracts and guarantees, everything he would need to know. He was like a chameleon, absorbing everything. Before my very eye, Eli Cohen faded and Taabes took over, the Syrian who had never given up a longing to go home to Damascus. Every day Eli became more confident, more certain and keen to prove he could carry off the role. He was like a world champion marathon runner, trained to peak at the start of the race. But he could be running his for years. We had done all we could to show him how to pace his new life, to live the life. The rest was up to him. We all knew that. There was no big good-bye or send-off. He just slipped out of Israel, the way all my spies went."

In the Syrian capital, Cohen quickly established himself in the business community and developed a circle of high-level friends. These included Maazi Zahreddin, nephew of Syria's president.

Zahreddin was a boastful man, eager to show how invincible Syria was. Cohen played to that. In no time he was being given a guided tour of Syria's Golan Heights fortifications. He saw the deep concrete bunkers housing the long-range artillery sent by Russia. He was even permitted to take photographs. Within hours of two hundred T-54 Russian tanks arriving in Syria, Cohen had informed Tel Aviv. He even obtained a complete blueprint of Syria's strategy to cut off northern Israel. The information was priceless.

While Cohen continued to confirm Meir Amit's belief that one field agent was worth a division of soldiers, he eventually began to become reckless. Cohen had always been a soccer fan. The day after a visiting team beat Israel in Tel Aviv, he broke the strict "business only" rule about transmissions. He radioed his operator: "It is about time we learned to be victorious on the soccer field."

Other unauthorized messages were translated: "Please send my wife an anniversary greeting," or "Happy Birthday to my daughter."

Meir Amit was privately furious. But he understood enough of the pressures on the agent to hope Cohen's behavior was "no more than a temporary aberration often found in the best of agents. I tried to get inside his head. Was he desperate and this his way of showing it by dropping his guard? I tried to think like him, knowing I'd rewritten his life. I had to try and weigh a hundred factors. But in the end the only important one was: could Eli still do his job?"

Meir Amit decided that Cohen could.

On a January night in 1965, Eli Cohen waited in his Damascus bedroom ready to transmit. As he tuned his receiver to go, Syrian intelligence officers burst into the apartment. Cohen had been caught by one of the most advanced mobile detection units in the world—supplied by the Russians.

Under interrogation he was forced to send a message to Mossad. The Syrians failed to notice the subtle change of speed and rhythm in the radio transmission. In Tel Aviv, Meir Amit received news Eli had been captured. Two days later, Syria confirmed his capture.

"It was like losing one of your family. You ask yourself the questions you always ask when an agent is lost: Could we have saved him? How was he betrayed? By his own carelessness? By someone close to him? Was he burned-out and we didn't realize it? Did he have some kind of death wish? That, too, happens. Or was it just bad luck? You ask, and go on asking. You never get the answer for certain. But asking can be a way to cope."

At no stage did the Syrians succeed in breaking Eli Cohen—despite the torture he endured before being sentenced to death.

Meir Amit devoted almost all his time trying to save Eli Cohen. While Nadia Cohen launched a worldwide publicity campaign for her husband's life—she approached the pope, the Queen of England, prime ministers, and presidents—Amit worked more secretly. He traveled to Europe to see the heads of French and German intelligence. They could do nothing. He made informal approaches to the Soviet Union. He fought on right until, on May 18, 1965, shortly after 2:00 A.M., a convoy drove out of El Maza Prison in Damascus. In one of the trucks was Eli Cohen.

With him was the eighty-year-old chief rabbi of Syria, Nissim Andabo. Overcome by what was to happen, the rabbi wept openly. Eli Cohen calmed the old man. The convoy reached El Marga Square in the center of Damascus. There Eli recited the Vidui, the Hebrew prayer of a man about to face death: "Almighty God forgive me for all my sins and transgressions."

At 3:35 A.M., watched by thousands of Syrians and in the full glare of television lights, Eli stood on the gallows.

In Tel Aviv, Nadia Cohen watched her husband die and tried to kill herself. She was taken to a hospital and her life was saved.

Next day, in a small private ceremony in his office, Meir Amit paid tribute to Eli Cohen. Then he went back to the business of running his second prized agent.

Wolfgang Lotz, a German Jew, had arrived in Palestine shortly after Hitler came to power. In 1963 Meir Amit had selected him from a short list of candidates for a spying mission to Egypt. While Lotz underwent the same rigorous training as Cohen, once more Meir Amit thought carefully about his agent's cover. Amit decided to make him a riding instructor, an East German refugee who had served in the Afrika Korps in World War II and had returned to Egypt to open an equestrian academy. The job would readily give him access to Cairo's high society, which was built around the city's riding fraternity.

Soon Lotz had developed a circle of clients that included the deputy head of Egyptian military intelligence and the chief of security for the Suez Canal zone. Emulating Cohen, Lotz persuaded his newfound friends to show off Egypt's formidable defenses: its rocket launchpads in Sinai and on the Negev frontier. Lotz also obtained a complete list of Nazi scientists living in Cairo who were working in Egypt's rocket and arms programs. Soon they were systematically executed by Mossad agents.

After two years under cover, Lotz was finally arrested and convicted. The Egyptians, sensing he was too valuable to kill, kept him alive in anticipation he could be traded for Egyptian soldiers captured in a future war with Israel. Once again, Meir Amit was deeply concerned over Lotz's capture.

Meir Amit wrote to Egypt's then president, Gamal Abdel Nasser, asking him to exchange Lotz and his wife in return for Egyptian POWs Israel had captured. Nasser refused. Amit applied psychological pressure.

"I let the Egyptian prisoners know they were all being held because Nasser refused to hand over two Israelis. We allowed them to write home. Their letters made their feelings very clear."

Meir Amit wrote to Nasser again saying Israel would publicly give him all the credit for recovering his POWs and would keep quiet about the return of Lotz and his wife. Nasser still did not agree. So Amit took the matter to the United Nations commander responsible for keeping the peace in the Sinai. The officer flew to Cairo and obtained the assurance that Lotz and his wife would be set free "at some future date."

Meir Amit "understood the coded language. A month later Lotz and his wife left Cairo in complete secrecy for Geneva. A few hours later they were back in my office."

Meir Amit recognized his *katsas* would need support in the field. He created the sayanim, volunteer Jewish helpers. Each sayan was an example of the historical cohesiveness of the world Jewish community. Regardless of allegiance to his or her country, in the final analysis a sayan would recognize a greater loyalty: the mystical one to Israel, and a need to help protect it from its enemies.

Sayanim fulfilled many functions. A car sayan, running a rental agency, provided a *katsa* with a vehicle without the usual documentation. A rental agency sayan offered accommodation. A bank sayan might unlock funds outside normal hours. A sayan physician would give medical assistance—treating a bullet wound for example—without informing the authorities. Sayanim only received expenses for their services.

Between them they collected technical data and all kinds of "overt" intelligence: a rumor at a cocktail party, an item on the radio, a paragraph in a newspaper, a half-finished story at a dinner party. They provided leads for *katsas*. Without its sayanim Mossad could not operate.

Again, Meir Amit's legacy would remain, though vastly expanded. In 1998 there were over four thousand sayanim in Britain, almost four times as many in the United States; while Meir Amit had operated on a tight budget, Mossad, to maintain its worldwide operations, now spent several hundred million dollars a month maintaining its "assets," paying the expenses of sayanim, running safe houses, providing logistics and covering operational costs. He had left them one other reminder of his time as their chief: a language of their own. Its report writing system was known as Naka; "daylight" was the highest form of alert; a kidon was a member of Mossad's assassination team; a neviot was a specialist in surveillance; *yaholomin* was the unit that handled communications to *katsas*; safanim was the one that targeted the PLO; a *balder* was a courier; a *slick* was a secure place for documents; teuds were forgeries.

On that March morning in 1997, as he drove to keep a rendezvous with the past, Meir Amit knew so much had changed in Mossad. Pressured by political demands, most notably from Prime Minister Benjamin Netanyahu, Mossad had become dangerously isolated from the foreign intelligence services Meir Amit had so carefully courted. It was one thing to live by the credo "Israel first, last, and always. Always." It was quite another, as he put it, to be caught "going through the pockets of your friends." The key word was "caught," he added with another bleak smile.

An example had been Mossad's increased penetration of the United States through economic, scientific, and technological espionage. A special unit, code-named Al, Hebrew for "above," prowled through California's Silicon Valley and Boston's Route 128 for high-tech secrets. In a report to the Senate Intelligence Committee, the CIA had identified Israel as one of six foreign countries with "a government-directed, orchestrated, clandestine effort to collect U.S. economic secrets."

The president of Germany's internal intelligence organization, the Bundesamt für Verfassungsschutz (BFV), had recently warned his department heads that Mossad remained a prime threat to steal the republic's latest computer secrets. A similar caution was issued by France's Direction Générale de la Sécurité Exterieure (DGSE) after a Mossad agent had been spotted near the Satellite Imagery Interpretative Center at Creil. Israel had long tried to increase its capability in space to match its nuclear capability on earth. Britain's counterespionage service, MI5, included in its briefing to newly elected prime minister Tony Blair details of Mossad's efforts to obtain sensitive scientific and defense data in the United Kingdom.

Meir Amit did not object, as such, to these adventures, only that they often appeared to have been carried out with a lack of planning and disregard for long-term consequences.

The same applied to how LAP's psychologists conducted their campaigns. In his days the department had built up a global network of media contacts and used them with great skill. A terrorist incident in Europe would produce a call to a news organization contact with "background" that was of sufficient interest to be worked into the story, giving it the spin LAP wanted. The unit also created information for press attachés at Israeli embassies to pass on to a journalist over a drink or dinner, when a "secret" could be quietly shared and a reputation discreetly tarnished.

While the essence of that black propaganda still remained, there was a crucial difference: the choice of a target or victim. It appeared to Meir Amit that the decision was too often predicated on political requirements: a need to divert attention from some self-serving diplomatic maneuver Israel planned to make in the Middle East, or to regain its fluctuating popularity, especially in the United States.

When Trans World Airlines Flight 800 crashed off the southeastern coast of Long Island on July 17, 1996, killing all 230 people on board, LAP began a campaign to suggest the tragedy was masterminded by Iran or Iraq, both Israel's bêtes noires. Thousands of media stories quickly perpetuated the fiction. Almost a year later, after expending some five hundred thousand dollars and ten thousand work hours, the FBI's chief investigator, James K. Kallstrom, ruled out a terrorist bomb or any evidence of a forensic crime. Privately he told colleagues, "If there was a way to nail those bastards in Tel Aviv for time wasting, I sure would like to see it happen. We had to check every item they slipped into the media."

LAP struck again after the bombing of the Atlanta Olympic Games. The fiction was spread that the bomb had "all the signs" of being manufactured by somebody who had learned his skills from the bomb makers of Lebanon's Bekáa Valley. The story took off—and LAP brought the specter of terrorism home to an understandably fearful American public. The only suspect was a hapless security guard at the Games—a man who manifestly had no connection with international terrorism—and when he was cleared, the story died.

Again, Meir Amit understood the importance of reminding the world about terrorism. But the warning "needed to be copper-fastened, something I always insisted upon." The admission was followed by a shrug, as if some inner fire blanket had doused his spark of irritation. Long ago he had learned to hide his feelings and to be vague about details; for years his strength had been in concealment.

In his mind the downward spiral of Mossad had begun when Prime Minister Yitzhak Rabin was assassinated at a peace rally in Tel Aviv in November 1995. Shortly before Rabin was gunned down by a Jewish extremist—a further sign of the deepening malaise Meir Amit saw in Israeli society—Mossad's then director general, Shabtai Shavit, had warned Rabin's staff that there might be an attempt on his life. According to one staffer the possibility was ignored as being too vague "to constitute a definite threat."

Under Meir Amit's command Mossad still had no mandate to operate within Israel, any more than the CIA could do so within the United States. Yet, despite his criticisms, Meir Amit liked to say that Mossad had shared the destiny of Israel. Under his tenure the impact of what it did had often reverberated around the world. Much of that he put down to loyalty, a quality that now seemed to have become passé. People still did their work—as dangerous and dirty as it had always been—but they wondered if they would be held accountable not only to some superior, but to some political figure in the background. That interference could account for the paranoia that regularly surfaced and challenged the concept that Israel is a true democracy.

Beside the highway between the resort of Herzliyya and Tel Aviv is a compound bristling with antennae. This is Mossad's training school. Among the first things a new political officer, a spy, at a foreign embassy in Tel Aviv learns is the location of the dun-colored building. Yet, for an Israeli publication to reveal its existence is still to run the risk of prosecution. In 1996 there was a furious debate within the country's intelligence community about what to do when a Tel Aviv newspaper published the name of Mossad's latest director general, the austere Danny Yatom. There was talk of arresting the offending reporter and his editor. In the end nothing happened when Mossad realized Yatom's name had by then been published worldwide.

Meir Amit was firmly against such exposure: "Naming a serving chief is serious. Spying is a secret business and not a pleasant one. No matter what someone has done, you have to protect him or her from outsiders. You can deal as harshly as you think fit with him or her inside the organization. But to the outside world he or she must remain untouchable and, better yet, unaccountable and unknown."

In his tenure as director general his code name had been Ram. The word had a satisfying Old Testament ring for a boy raised in the unquenchable spirit of the early pioneers at a time when the whole of Arab Palestine was in revolt against both the British Mandate and the Jews. From boyhood he had trained his body hard. Physically slight, Meir Amit became strong and fit, sustained by a belief that this was *his* land. Eretz Israel, the land of Israel. It did not matter that the rest of the world still called it Palestine until 1947, when the United Nations proposed its partition.

The birth of a nation, Israel, was followed by its near annihilation as Arab armies tried to reclaim the land. Six thousand Jews died; no one would ever be certain how many Arabs fell. The sight of so many bodies all but completed the maturing of Meir Amit. What deepened the process was the arrival of the survivors of the Nazi death camps, each bearing a hideous blue tattoo branded into his or her flesh. "The sight was a reminder of the depth of human depravity." From others the words would sound inadequately banal; Meir Amit gave them dignity.

His military career was the biography of a soldier destined for the top: a company commander in the 1948 War of Independence; two years later a brigade commander under Moshe Dayan; then, within five years, army chief of operations, the second-ranking officer of the Israel Defense Forces. An accident—the partial failure of his parachute to open—ended his military career. The Israeli government paid for him to go to Columbia University, where he took a master's degree in business administration. He returned to Israel without a job.

Moshe Dayan proposed Meir Amit should become chief of military intelligence. Despite initial opposition, mostly on the reasonable grounds that he had no intelligence experience, he was appointed: "The one advantage I had was that I had been a battlefield commander and knew the importance of good intelligence to the fighting soldiers." On March

25, 1963, he took over Mossad from Isser Harel. His achievements had become so many they needed a shorthand of their own: the man who introduced Mossad's policy of assassinating its enemies; who set up a secret working relationship with the KGB at the very time millions of Jews were being persecuted; who refined the role of women and the use of sexual entrapment in intelligence work; who approved the penetration of King Hussein's palace shortly before the Hashemite ruler became a CIA spy in the Arab world.

The techniques he created to achieve all that remain in use. But no outsider will ever learn how he first developed them. His jaw muscles tightening, all he would say was: "There are secrets and there are my secrets."

When the time had come when he felt Mossad could benefit from a new hand at the helm, he had departed with no fuss, called his staff together and reminded them that if ever they found being a Jew and working for Mossad created a problem between their personal ethics and the demands of the state, they should resign at once. Then, after a round of handshakes, he was gone.

But no incoming chief of Mossad failed to call upon him for coffee in his office on Jabotinsky Street, in Tel Aviv's pleasant suburb of Ramat Gan. On those occasions, Meir Amit's office door remained firmly closed and the phone switched off.

"My mother always said a trust broken is a friend lost," he explained in English, smiling an old man's wily smile.

Outside his immediate family—a small tribe of children, grandchildren, cousins, kith and kin stretching over generations—few really know Meir Amit. He would have it no other way.

On that March morning in 1997, behind his car wheel, Meir Amit looked surprisingly young, closer to sixty than his actual age of seventy-five. The physique that once enabled him to complete a stress test at an Olympian pace had softened; there was a hint of a belly beneath the well-cut blue blazer. Yet his eyes were still sharp enough to startle and impossible to fathom or penetrate as he drove toward an avenue of eucalyptus trees.

How many times he had made this journey even he could no longer count. But each visit reminded him of an old truth: "that to survive as a Jew still means defending yourself to the death."

The same reminder was on the faces of the soldiers waiting for rides under the trees outside the boot camp at Glilot, north of Tel Aviv. There was a swagger about them, even an insolence; they were doing their compulsory service in the Israel Defense Forces and imbued with the belief they served in the finest army on earth.

Few gave Meir Amit a second glance. To them he was another of the old men who came to remember at a war memorial close to where they waited. Israel is a land of such memorials—over 1,500 in all—raised to the paratroops, the pilots, the tank drivers, and the infantry. The monuments commemorate the dead of five full-scale conventional wars and sixty years of cross-border incursions and antiguerrilla operations. Yet, in a nation that venerates its fallen warriors in a manner not seen since the Romans occupied this land, there is no other monument in Israel, indeed the world, like the one Meir Amit helped to create.

It stands just within the perimeter of the boot camp and consists of several concrete-walled buildings and a mass of sandstone walls assembled in the shape of a human brain. Meir Amit chose that shape because "intelligence is all about the mind, not some bronzed figure striking a heroic pose."

The memorial commemorates so far 557 men and women of Israel's intelligence community, 71 of whom served in the Mossad.

They died in every corner of the world: in the deserts of Iraq, the mountains of Iran, the jungles of South and Central America, the bush of Africa, the streets of Europe. Each, in his or her own way, tried to live by Mossad's motto, "By way of deception, thou shalt do war."

Meir Amit knew many personally; some he had sent to their deaths on missions he conceded were beyond the "cutting edge of acceptable danger, but that is the regrettable unavoidability of this work. One person's death must always be weighed against our nation's security. It has always been so."

The smooth sandstone walls are engraved only with names and the date of death. There are no other clues to the circumstances in which someone died: a public hanging, the fate of all convicted Jewish spies in Arab countries; a murderer's knife thrust in an alley that had no name; the merciful release after months of prison torture. No one will ever know. Even Meir Amit could often only suspect, and he kept those dark thoughts to himself.

The brain-shaped memorial is only part of the memorial complex. Within the concrete buildings is the File Room, holding the personal biographies of the dead agents. Each person's early life and military service are carefully documented; the final secret mission is not. Each agent has his or her memorial day commemorated in a small synagogue.

Beyond the synagogue is an amphitheater where on Intelligence Day families gather to remember their dead. Sometimes Meir Amit addresses them. Afterward they visit the memorial's museum, filled with artifacts: a transmitter in the base of a flatiron; a microphone in a coffeepot; invisible ink in a perfume bottle; the actual tape recorder that secretly recorded the critical conversation between King Hussein of Jordan and President Nasser of Egypt, the precursor to the Six-Day War.

Meir Amit had burnished the stories of the men who used the equipment to the brightness of heroic myth. He would point out the disguise Ya'a Boqa'i wore when he slipped in and out of Jordan until he was captured and executed in Amman in 1949, and the crystal radio Max Binnet and Moshe Marzuk used to run Mossad's most successful network in Egypt before they died painful, lingering deaths in a Cairo prison.

To Meir Amit, they were all "my Gideonites." Gideon was the Old Testament hero who saved Israel against superior enemy forces because he had better intelligence.

Finally, it was time for him to go to the maze, accompanied by the museum's curator. They paused before each engraved name, gave imperceptible little head bows, then moved on. Abruptly it was over. No more dead to respectfully acknowledge—only ample space for more names on the sand-colored tombstone.

For a moment Meir Amit was again lost in reverie. In whispered Hebrew the old Mossad chief said to the curator: "Whatever happens, we must ensure this place lives on."

Apropos of nothing that had gone before, Meir Amit added that on his office wall in Damascus, President Hafez al-Assad of Syria only has one picture, a large photograph of the site of Saladin's victory against the Crusaders in 1187. It had led to the Arab reconquest of Jerusalem.

For Meir Amit, Assad's fondness for the photograph "has a significance for Israel. He sees us the same way Saladin did—someone to be eventually vanquished. There are many who share that aspiration. Some even purport to be our friends. We have to be especially watchful of them. . . ."

He stopped, said his good-bye to the curator, and walked back to his car as if he had already said too much; as if what he had said would further energize the whispers beginning to circulate within the Israeli intelligence community. Another crisis in the nowadays uneasy alliance between Mossad and U.S. intelligence was about to surface—with potentially devastating effects for Israel.

Already caught up in the brewing scandal was one of the most colorful and ruthless operatives who had once served under Meir Amit, a man who had already secured his place in history as the capturer of Adolf Eichmann, yet still liked to play with fire.

CHAPTER 4

THE SPY IN THE IRON MASK

Wealthy residents in the exclusive suburb of Afeka in the north of Tel Aviv were used to seeing Rafael "Rafi" Eitan, a squat, barrel-chested elderly man, myopic and almost totally deaf in his right ear since fighting in Israel's War of Independence, return home with pieces of discarded lavatory piping, used bicycle chains, and other assorted metal junk. Wearing a pair of chain-store trousers and shirt, his face covered with a welder's guard, he fashioned the scrap into surreal sculptures with an acetylene torch.

Some neighbors wondered if it was a means of momentary escape from what he had done. They knew he had killed for his country, not

73

in open battle, but in secret encounters that were part of the ceaseless undercover war Israel waged against the state's enemies. No neighbor knew exactly how many Rafi Eitan had killed, sometimes with his stubby, powerful hands. All he had told them was: "Whenever I killed I needed to see their eyes, the white of their eyes. Then I was very calm, very focused, thinking only of what I had to do. Then I did it. That was it." Accompanying the words was an endearing smile some strong men use when seeking the approval of the weak.

Rafi Eitan had for almost a quarter of a century been Mossad's hands-on deputy director of operations. Not for him a life behind a desk reading reports and sending others to do his bidding. At every opportunity he had gone into the field, traveling the world, jaw thrust forward, driven by a philosophy that he had reduced to one pithy sentence: "If you are not part of the answer, then you are part of the problem."

There had been no one like him for cold-blooded ruthlessness, cunning, an ability to improvise at ferocious speed, an inborn skill at outwitting even the best-laid plan and tirelessly tracking down a quarry. All those qualities had come together in the one operation that had given him lasting fame—the kidnapping of Adolf Eichmann, the Nazi bureaucrat who epitomized the full horror of Hitler's Final Solution.

To his neighbors on Shay Street, Rafi Eitan was a revered figure, the man who had avenged their dead relatives, the onetime guerrilla who had been given the opportunity to remind the world that no living Nazi was safe. They never tired of being invited into his house and listening again to him describe an operation that is still unrivaled in its daring. Surrounded by expensive objets d'art, Rafi Eitan would fold his muscular arms, tilt his square block of a head to one side, and for a moment remain silent, allowing his listeners to carry themselves back in their mind's eye to that time when, against all odds, Israel had been born. Then, in a powerful voice, an actor's voice playing all the parts, missing nothing, he began to tell his trusted friends how he had set about capturing Adolf Eichmann. First he set the scene for one of the most dramatic kidnapping stories of all time.

After World War II, tracking down Nazi war criminals was initially done by Holocaust survivors. They called themselves Nokmin, "Avengers." They didn't bother with legal trials. They just executed any Nazis they found. Rafi Eitan did not know of a single case where they killed the wrong person. Officially in Israel there was little interest in pursuing war criminals. It was a matter of priorities. As a nation Israel was clinging on by its fingertips, still surrounded by hostile Arab states. It was one day at a time. The country was almost broke. There was no spare cash for resolving the evil of the past.

In 1957, Mossad received the electrifying news that Eichmann had been seen in Argentina. Rafi Eitan, already a rising star in Mossad as a result of astute forays against the Arabs, was selected to capture Eichmann and bring him to Israel to stand trial.

He was told the outcome would have a number of significant benefits. It would be an act of divine justice for his people. It would remind the world of the death camps and the need to make sure they never happened again. It would place Mossad at the forefront of the global intelligence community. No other service had dared to attempt such an operation. The risks were equally great. He would be working thousands of miles from home, traveling on forged documentation, relying entirely on his own resources and working in a hostile environment. Argentina was a haven for Nazis. The Mossad team could end up in prison there or even be killed.

For two long years, Rafi Eitan patiently waited while the first tentative sighting was confirmed—that the man living in a middle-class suburb of Buenos Aires under the name of Ricardo Klement was Adolf Eichmann.

When the go order finally came, Rafi Eitan became "ice-cold." He had done all his thinking of what could go wrong. The political, diplomatic, and, for him, the professional repercussions would be enormous. He had also wondered what would happen when, having captured Eichmann, the Argentinian police intervened. "I decided I would strangle Eichmann with my own bare hands. If I was caught, I would argue to the court it had been the biblical eye for an eye."

El Al, the national airline, had specially purchased from the Mossad slush fund a Britannia aircraft for the long flight to Argentina. Rafi Eitan remarked:

"We just sent someone to England to buy one. He handed over the money and we had our plane. Officially the flight to Argentina was to carry an Israeli delegation to attend Argentina's one hundred fiftieth independence day celebrations. None of the delegates knew why we were going with them or that we had constructed a cell in the back of the aircraft to hold Eichmann."

Rafi Eitan and his team arrived in Buenos Aires on May Day 1960.

They moved into one of seven safe houses a Mossad advance man had rented. One had been given the Hebrew code name Maoz, or "Stronghold." The apartment would act as the base for the operation. Another safe house was designated Tira, or "Palace," and was intended as a holding place for Eichmann after his capture. The other houses were in case Eichmann had to be moved under the pressure of an expected police hunt. A dozen cars had also been leased for the operation.

With everything in place, Rafi Eitan's manner became settled and determined. Any doubts of failure had lifted; the prospect of action had replaced the tension of waiting. For three days he and the team conducted a discreet surveillance on how Adolf Eichmann, who had once been chauffeured everywhere in a Mercedes limousine, now traveled by bus and alighted on the corner of Garibaldi Street in a suburb on the outskirts of the city, as punctual as he had once been in signing the consignment orders for the death camps.

On the night of May 10, 1960, Rafi Eitan chose for the snatch a driver and two others to subdue Eichmann once he was in the car. One of the men had been trained to overpower a target on the street. Rafi Eitan would sit beside the driver, "ready to help in any way I could."

The operation was set for the following evening. At 8:00 P.M. on May 11, the team's car drove into Garibaldi Street.

There was no tension. Everyone was long past that. No one spoke. There was nothing to say. Rafi Eitan looked at his watch: 8:03. They drove up and down the empty street. 8:04. Several buses came and went. At 8:05, another bus came. They saw Eichmann alight. To Rafi Eitan, "he looked a little tired, perhaps how he looked after another day of sending my people to the death camps.

"The street was still empty. Behind me I heard our specialist snatchman open the car door. We drove up just behind Eichmann. He was walking quite quickly, as if he wanted to get home for his dinner. I could hear the specialist breathing steadily, the way he had been taught to do in training. He had got the snatch down to twelve seconds. Out of the door, grab him around the neck, drag him back into the car. Out, grab, back."

The car came alongside Eichmann. He half turned, gave a puzzled look at the sight of the specialist coming out of the car. Then the man tripped on a loose shoelace, almost stumbling to the ground. For a moment Rafi Eitan was too stunned to move. He had come halfway across the world to catch the man who had been instrumental in sending six million Jews to their deaths and they were just about to lose him because a shoelace had not been properly tied. Eichmann was starting to walk quickly away. Rafi Eitan leaped from the car.

"I grabbed him by the neck with such force I could see his eyes bulge. A little tighter and I would have choked him to death. The specialist was on his feet holding open the door. I tossed Eichmann onto the backseat. The specialist jumped in, sitting half on top of Eichmann. The whole thing didn't last more than five seconds."

From the front seat Rafi Eitan could smell Eichmann's sour breath as he struggled for air. The specialist worked his jaw up and down. Eichmann grew calmer. He even managed to ask what was the meaning of this outrage.

No one spoke to him. In silence they reached their safe house about three miles away. Rafi Eitan motioned Eichmann to strip naked. He then checked his physical measurements against those from an SS file he had obtained. He was not surprised to see that Eichmann had somehow removed his SS tattoo. But his other measurements all matched the file—the size of his head, the distance from elbow to wrist, from knee to ankle. He had Eichmann chained to a bed. For ten hours he was left in complete silence. Rafi Eitan "wanted to encourage a feeling of hopelessness. Just before dawn, Eichmann was at his lowest mental state. I asked him his name. He gave a Spanish one. I said, no, no, no, your German name. He gave his German alias—the one he had used to flee Germany. I said again, no, no, no, your real name, your SS name. He stretched on the bed as if he wanted to stand to attention and said, loud and clear, 'Adolf Eichmann.' I didn't ask him anything else. I had no need to."

For the next seven days Eichmann and his captors remained closeted in the house. Still no one spoke to Eichmann. He ate, bathed, and went to the lavatory in complete silence. For Rafi Eitan:

"Keeping silent was more than an operational necessity. We did not want to show Eichmann how nervous we all were. That would have given him hope. And hope makes a desperate person dangerous. I needed him to be as helpless as my own people were when he had sent them in trainloads to the death camps."

The decision on how to move him from the safe house to the El Al plane waiting to fly the delegation home was filled with its own black humor. First Eichmann was dressed in the spare El Al flight suit Rafi Eitan had brought from Israel. Then he was induced to drink a bottle of whiskey, leaving him in a drunken stupor.

Rafi Eitan and his team dressed in their own flight suits and liberally sprinkled themselves with whiskey. Thrusting a flight hat on Eichmann's head, and squashing him into the backseat of the car, Rafi Eitan drove to the military air base where the Britannia was waiting, engines running.

At the base gate Argentinian soldiers flagged down the car. In the back Eichmann was snoring. Rafi Eitan recalled:

"The car reeked like a distillery. That was the moment we all earned our Mossad Oscars! We played the drunken Jews who couldn't handle strong Argentinian liquor. The guards were amused and never gave Eichmann a second look."

At five minutes past midnight on May 21, 1960, the Britannia took off with Adolf Eichmann still snoring in his cell in the back of the plane.

After a lengthy trial, Eichmann was found guilty of crimes against humanity. On the day of his execution, May 31, 1962, Rafi Eitan was in the execution chamber at Ramla Prison: "Eichmann looked at me and said, 'Your time will come to follow me, Jew,' and I replied, 'But not today, Adolf, not today.' Next moment the trap opened. Eichmann gave a little choking sound. There was the smell of his bowel moving, then just the sound of the stretched rope. A very satisfying sound."

A special oven had been built to cremate the body. Within hours the ashes were scattered out at sea over a wide area. Ben-Gurion had ordered there must be no trace left to encourage sympathizers to turn Eichmann into a Nazi cult figure. Israel wanted him expunged from the face of the earth. Afterward the oven was dismantled and would never be used again. That evening Rafi Eitan stood on the shore and looked out to sea, feeling totally at peace, "knowing I had finished my assignment. That is always a good feeling."

Mossad's deputy operations chief Rafi Eitan's rolling gait continued to take him across Europe to find and execute Arab terrorists. To do so he used remote-controlled bombs; Mossad's handgun of choice, the Beretta; and where silence was essential, his own bare hands to either garrote a victim with steel wire or deliver a lethal rabbit punch. Always he killed without compunction.

When he returned home he stood for hours at his open-air furnace, wreathed in sparks, totally consumed with bending metal to his will. Then he would be off again, on journeys that often required several plane changes before he reached his final destination. For each journey he chose a different nationality and identity, built around the vast number of stolen or perfectly forged passports Mossad had patiently acquired.

In between killing, his other skill was recruiting more sayanim. He had a routine that played upon the Jewish love for their homeland.

"I would tell them that for two thousand years our people dreamed. That for two thousand years we Jews had prayed for deliverance. In song, in prose, in their hearts, we had kept alive the dream—and the dream kept us alive. Now it had happened. Then I add: to make sure it continues we need people like you."

In cafés along the Paris boulevards, in restaurants on the banks of the Rhine, in Madrid, Brussels, and London's Golders Green he would repeat the poignant words. More often than not, his vision of what it meant to be a Jew today would gain another sayan. To those who hesitated, he deftly mixed the personal and the political, retelling stories of his time in the Haganah with affectionate stories about Ben-Gurion and other leaders. The last resistance would melt away.

Soon he had over a hundred men and women across Europe to do his bidding: lawyers, dentists, schoolteachers, doctors, tailors, shopkeepers, housewives, secretaries. One group he particularly cherished: German Jews who had returned to the land of their Holocaust; Rafi Eitan called them his "survivor spies."

Toiling at the coal-face of Mossad operations, Rafi Eitan was careful to distance himself from the politicking that continued to bedevil the Israeli intelligence community. He knew what was going on, of course, the maneuvering by Aman, military intelligence, and Shin Bet to whittle away some of Mossad's supreme authority. He had heard about the cabals that formed and re-formed, and the "eyes only" reports they sent to the prime minister's office. But under Meir Amit, Mossad had remained rock steady, brushing aside any attempts to undo its prime position.

Then, one day Meir Amit was no longer in command; his brisk stride down the corridors was gone, along with his piercing gaze and the smile that never seemed to reach his lips. Following his departure, colleagues had urged Rafi Eitan to allow them to lobby for him to become Amit's replacement, pointing out that he had the qualifications and commanded loyalty and popularity within Mossad. But before Rafi Eitan could decide, the post went to a Labor Party nominee, the colorless and pedantic Zvi Zamir. Rafi Eitan resigned. He had no quarrel with the new Mossad chief; he simply felt that Mossad would no longer be a place where he would feel "comfortable." Under Meir Amit his brief had been to roam virtually unfettered; he felt that Zamir would do "things only by the book. That was not for me."

Rafi Eitan set himself up as a private consultant, offering his skills to companies who had to beef up their security or to a wealthy individual who needed to have his staff trained on how to protect him against a terrorist attack. But the work soon paled. After a year Rafi Eitan let it be known he was ready to step back into the fast lane of intelligence work.

When Yitzhak Rabin became prime minister in 1974, he appointed the aggressive, hands-on Yitzhak Hofi to run Mossad and made him answerable to the hawkish Ariel Sharon, who was Rabin's adviser on security affairs. Sharon promptly made Rafi Eitan his personal assistant. Hofi found himself working closely with a man who shared his own cutthroat attitude toward intelligence operations.

Three years later, in another reshuffle of government, a new prime minister, Menachem Begin, named Rafi Eitan as his personal adviser on terrorism. Eitan's first act was to organize the assassination of the Palestinian responsible for planning the 1972 Munich Olympics massacre of eleven Israeli athletes. Their actual killers were already dead, each one executed by Mossad.

The first to die had been standing in the lobby of his Rome apartment building when he was shot eleven times at close range—a bullet for each murdered athlete. When the next terrorist to die answered a telephone call in his Paris apartment, his head was blown off by a small bomb planted in the receiver and triggered by remote control. Another terrorist was asleep in a hotel room in Nicosia when it was wrecked by a similar bomb. To create panic among the remaining members of the Black September group who had killed the athletes, Mossad Arab sayanim arranged for their obituaries to appear in local Arab newspapers. Their families received flowers and condolence cards shortly *before* each was killed.

Rafi Eitan set about finding and killing their leader, Ali Hassan Salameh, known throughout the Arab world as the "Red Prince." Since Munich he had flitted from one Arab capital to another, advising terror groups on strategy. Time and again when Rafi Eitan had been set to strike, the Red Prince had moved on. But finally he had settled among the bomb makers of Beirut. Rafi Eitan knew the city well. Nevertheless, he decided to refresh his memory. Posing as a Greek businessman he traveled there. In the next few days he had discovered Salameh's precise whereabouts and movements.

Rafi Eitan returned to Tel Aviv and made his plans. Three Mossad agents who could pass for Arabs crossed into Lebanon and entered the city. One rented a car. The second wired a series of bombs into its chassis, roof, and door panels. The third agent parked the car along the route the Red Prince traveled to his office every morning. Using precise timers Rafi Eitan had provided, the car was set to explode as Salameh passed. It did, blowing him to pieces.

Rafi Eitan had shown he was once more a player in the Israeli intelligence community. But Prime Minister Menachem Begin decided that Rafi Eitan was too valuable to risk on further such adventures. He told his adviser that from now on he must remain in the office and keep a low profile. Recently, John le Carré had used Eitan as a model for the central character who tracks down terrorists in his thriller *The Little Drummer Girl*.

But lending credibility to a novelist's imagination did little to settle Rafi Eitan's perpetual restlessness. He wanted to be where the action was, not stuck behind a desk or attending an endless round of planning meetings. He began to badger Prime Minister Begin to give him something else to do.

After some hesitation—for Rafi Eitan was an excellent adviser on counterterrorism—Begin appointed Rafi Eitan to one of the most sensitive posts in the intelligence community, one that would stretch him intellectually and satisfy his craving for a hands-on job. He was made director of the Bureau of Scientific Liaison, known by its Hebrew acronym, LAKAM.

Created in 1960, it had operated as the defense ministry's spy unit to obtain scientific data "by all means possible." In principle that had meant stealing or bribing people to provide material. From the beginning LAKAM had been hampered by the hostility of Mossad, who saw the unit as the proverbial "new kid on the block." Both Isser Harel and Meir Amit had tried to have LAKAM either closed down or absorbed into Mossad. But Shimon Peres, Israel's deputy defense minister, had stubbornly insisted that the defense ministry needed its own collecting agency. Slowly and laboriously, LAKAM had gone about its business, setting up offices in New York, Washington, Boston, and Los Angeles, all key centers for cutting-edge science. Every week LAKAM staff dutifully shipped boxes of technical journals back to Israel, knowing the FBI was keeping an eye on their activities.

This surveillance increased after 1968, when one of the engineers building the French Mirage IIIC fighter aircraft was discovered to have stolen over two hundred thousand blueprints. He received a four-and-a-half-year prison sentence—having given LAKAM the data to build its own Mirage replicas. Since then LAKAM had enjoyed little other success.

For Rafi Eitan, the memory of the Mirage coup was the deciding factor. What had been achieved before could be achieved again. He would take a now virtually moribund LAKAM and turn it into a force to be reckoned with.

Working out of cramped offices in a Tel Aviv backwater, he told his new staff, awed at now being commanded by such a legendary figure, that what he knew about science he could place in a test tube and still leave plenty of space. But, he added, he was a fast learner.

He immersed himself in the world of science, looking for potential areas to target. He left his home before dawn and often returned close to midnight with bundles of technical papers and read into the small hours; there was little time to relax by sculpting scrap metal. In between the huge amounts of data he absorbed, he reestablished contact with his old service. Mossad now had a new director, Nahum Admoni. Like Rafi Eitan, Admoni had a deep-seated suspicion of U.S. intentions in the Middle East. Outwardly, Washington continued to show an open commitment to Israel, and the CIA had kept open the back-channel contact Isser Harel and Allen Dulles had instigated. But Admoni complained that the information from that source was of little importance.

The Mossad chief was also concerned about reports from Mossad's own *katsas* and well-placed sayanim in Washington. They had discovered discreet meetings between high-ranking State Department officials and Arab leaders close to Yasser Arafat who had discussed ways to pressure Israel to be more accommodating over Palestinian demands. Admoni told Rafi Eitan he now felt he could no longer regard the United States as "a foul weather friend."

This attitude was reinforced in an incident that would shock American belief in its inviolability more than anything since the Vietnam War.

In August 1983, Mossad agents discovered an attack was being planned against the U.S. forces in Beirut, there as UN peacekeepers. The agents had identified a Mercedes truck that would contain half a ton of explosive. Under back-channel arrangements, Mossad should have passed on the information to the CIA. But at a meeting at Mossad headquarters overlooking King Saul Boulevard, staff were informed they were to "make sure our people watch the truck. As far as the Yanks go, we are not here to protect them. They can do their own watching. We start doing too much for the Yanks and we'll be shitting on our own doorstep."

On October 23, 1983, monitored closely by Mossad agents, the truck was driven at full speed into the headquarters of the U.S. Eighth Marine Battalion situated near Beirut Airport. Two hundred forty-one marines died.

The reaction in the upper echelons of Mossad, according to a former officer, Victor Ostrovsky, was, "They wanted to stick their nose into this Lebanon thing, let them pay the price."

That attitude had further encouraged Rafi Eitan to think seriously about targeting the United States. Its scientific community was the most advanced in the world, its military technology without equal. For LAKAM to get its hands on even some of that data would be a tremendous coup. The first hurdle to overcome would be the hardest: finding an informer sufficiently well placed to provide the material.

Using the list of U.S. sayanim he had helped compile during his time with Mossad, he put out the word that he was interested in hearing of anyone in the United States who had a scientific background and was known to be pro-Israeli. For months it produced nothing.

Then, in April 1984, Aviem Sella, a colonel in the Israeli air force who was on a sabbatical to study computer science at New York University, went to a party given by a wealthy Jewish gynecologist on the Upper East Side of Manhattan. Sella was a minor celebrity among the city's Jewish community as the pilot who had led an air attack three years before that had destroyed Iraq's nuclear reactor.

At the party was a diffident young man with a shy smile who seemed ill at ease among the small set of doctors, lawyers, and bankers. He told Sella his name was Jonathan Pollard and that the only reason he had come was to meet him. Embarrassed by such obvious adulation, Sella made polite small talk and was about to move on when Pollard revealed he was not only a committed Zionist, but worked for U.S.

naval intelligence. In no time the astute Sella had learned that Pollard was stationed at the Antiterrorist Alert Center in one of the navy's most secret establishments at Suitland, Maryland. Pollard's duties included monitoring all classified material on global terrorist activities. So important was the work that he had the highest possible U.S. intelligence community security clearance.

Sella could not believe what he was hearing, especially when Pollard began to give specific details about incidents where the U.S. intelligence community was not cooperating with its Israeli counterpart. Sella began to wonder if Pollard was part of a sting operation by the FBI to try to recruit an Israeli.

Yet there was something about the intense Pollard that rang true. That night Sella called Tel Aviv and spoke to his air force intelligence commander. The officer switched the call to the Israeli air force chief of staff. Sella was ordered to develop his contact with Pollard.

They began to meet: at the skating rink at Rockefeller Plaza; in a coffee shop on Forty-eighth Street; in Central Park. Each time Pollard handed over secret documents to confirm the truth of what he said. Sella couriered the material to Tel Aviv, enjoying the frisson of being caught up in an important intelligence operation. He was therefore understandably stunned to be told that Mossad knew all about Pollard, who had actually offered to spy for them two years previously and had been rejected as "unstable." A Mossad *katsa* in New York had also described Pollard as "lonely . . . with an unrealistic view about Israel."

Unwilling to relinquish his role in an operation certainly more exciting than sitting before a classroom computer keyboard, Sella looked around for a way to keep matters alive. During his time in New York he had come to know the science attaché at the Israeli consulate in the city. His name was Yosef Yagur. He was Rafi Eitan's head of all LAKAM operations in the United States.

Sella invited Yagur to dinner with Pollard. Over the meal Pollard repeated that Israel was being denied information to defend itself against Arab terrorists because the United States did not wish to upset its relations with Arab oil producers.

That night, using a secure consulate phone, Yagur telephoned Rafi Eitan. It was in the early hours in Tel Aviv but Eitan was still at work in his study. It was almost dawn when he put down the phone. He was exultant: he had his informer.

For the next three months Yagur and Sella assiduously cultivated Pollard and his future wife, Anne Henderson. They took them to expensive restaurants, Broadway shows, first-night films. Pollard continued to hand over important documentation. Rafi Eitan could only marvel at how good the material was. He decided it was time to meet the source.

In November 1984, Sella and Yagur invited Pollard and Henderson to accompany them on an all-expenses-paid trip to Paris. Yagur told Pollard the vacation was "a small reward for all you are doing for Israel." They all flew first-class and were met by a chauffeured car and driven to the Bristol Hotel. Waiting for them was Rafi Eitan.

By the end of the night Rafi Eitan had finalized all the practical arrangements for Pollard to continue his treachery. No longer would matters continue in their free-and-easy way. Sella would fade from the picture, his role over. Yagur would become Pollard's official handler. A proper delivery system was worked out for documents to be handed over. Pollard would deliver them to the apartment of Irit Erb, a mousy-haired secretary at the Washington embassy. A high-speed Xerox had been installed in her kitchen to copy the material. Pollard's visits would be spaced between those to a number of designated car washes. While Pollard's car was being cleaned, he would hand over documents to Yagur, whose own car would be undergoing a similar process. Concealed beneath the dash was a battery-operated copier. Both Erb's apartment and the car-wash facilities were close to Washington's National Airport, making it easier for Yagur to fly back and forth to New York. From the consulate he transmitted the material by secure fax to Tel Aviv.

Rafi Eitan returned to Tel Aviv to await results. They exceeded his wildest expectations: details of Russian arms deliveries to Syria and other Arab states, including the precise location of SS-21 and SA-5 missiles; maps and satellite photographs of Iraqi, Syrian, and Iranian arsenals, including chemical and biological manufacturing plants.

Rafi Eitan quickly obtained a clear picture of U.S. intelligence-gathering methods, not only in the Middle East, but in South Africa. Pollard had provided reports from CIA operatives which provided a blueprint for the entire U.S. intelligence network within the country. One document contained a detailed account of how South Africa had managed to detonate a nuclear device on September 14, 1979, in the southern end of the Indian Ocean. The Pretoria government had steadfastly denied it had become a nuclear power. Rafi Eitan arranged for

Mossad to pass over copies of all material relating to South Africa to Pretoria, virtually destroying the CIA network. Twelve operatives were forced to hurriedly leave the country.

During the next eleven months, Jonathan Pollard continued to asset-strip U.S. intelligence. Over one thousand highly classified documents, 360 cubic feet of paper, were transmitted to Israel. There Rafi Eitan devoured them before passing over the material to Mossad. The data enabled Nahum Admoni to brief Shimon Peres's coalition government on how to respond to Washington's Middle East policies in a manner previously impossible. One note taker at the Sunday cabinet meetings in Jerusalem claimed that "listening to Admoni was the next best thing to sitting in the Oval Office. We not only knew what was the very latest thinking in Washington on all matters of concern to us, but we had sufficient time to respond before making a decision."

Pollard had become a crucial factor in the mysteries of Israeli policymaking and the intricacies of choosing options. Rafi Eitan authorized an Israeli passport for Pollard in the name of Danny Cohen, as well as a generous monthly stipend. In return he asked Pollard to provide details about the electronic eavesdropping activities of the National Security Agency (NSA) in Israel and the bugging methods used against the Israeli embassy in Washington and its other diplomatic stations within the United States.

Before Pollard could supply the information he was arrested, on November 21, 1985, outside the Israeli embassy in Washington. Hours later Yagur, Sella, and the embassy secretary in Washington had all caught an El Al flight from New York to Tel Aviv before the FBI could stop them. In Israel they disappeared into the protective arms of a grateful intelligence community. Pollard was sentenced to life imprisonment and his wife to five years.

In 1999, Pollard could draw comfort from the tireless way powerful Jewish groups lobbied for his release. The Conference of Major American Jewish Organizations, a consortium of over fifty groups, had launched a sustained campaign to have him set free on the grounds that he had not committed high treason against the United States "because Israel was then and remains today a close ally." Equally influential Jewish religious groups such as the Reform Union of American Hebrew Congregations and the Orthodox Union lent support. The Harvard Law School professor Alan M. Dershowitz, who had been Pollard's attorney, said there was nothing to show the spy had actually compromised "the nation's intelligence-gathering capabilities or betrayed worldwide intelligence data."

Alarmed at what they realized was a skilled public relations campaign orchestrated from Israel, the U.S. intelligence community took an unusual step. They moved out of the shadows into the public domain, setting out the facts of Pollard's treachery. It was both a bold and dangerous decision. It would not only cast a light on sensitive material but also mobilize the evermore powerful Jewish lobby to attack them. They had seen what it had done to others in the frenetic atmosphere of Washington. A reputation could be discreetly tarnished over a late drink at an embassy between acts at the Kennedy Center or over a quiet Georgetown dinner.

Those intelligence men feared that Clinton—"in one of his quixotic moments," a senior CIA officer told me—would free Pollard before he left office if that would ensure Israel entered into a peace settlement and gave Clinton a last foreign policy success. The CIA's director at the time of writing, George Tenet, had warned the president "that Pollard's release will demoralize the intelligence community," Clinton was reported to have merely said: "We'll see, we'll see."

In Tel Aviv, Rafi Eitan has closely followed every move, telling friends that "should the day come when Jonathan makes it to Israel, I'd be happy to have a cup of coffee with him."

Meantime Eitan continued to rejoice at the success of another operation he had also mounted against the United States. It led to Israel's becoming the first nuclear power in the Middle East.

CHAPTER 5

GIDEON'S NUCLEAR SWORD

In the darkness of a Tel Aviv cinema in 1945, Rafi Eitan had watched the birth of the nuclear age over Hiroshima. While all around him young soldiers whistled and cheered at the newsreel footage of the devastated Japanese city, he had only two thoughts. Would Israel ever possess such a weapon? Suppose her Arab neighbors obtained one first?

From time to time down the years the questions had surfaced in his mind. If Egypt had had a nuclear bomb, it would have won the Suez War and there would have been no Six-Day War or Yom Kippur War. Israel would have been a nuclear desert. With a nuclear weapon, Israel would be invincible.

In those days, for an operative whose work was primarily concerned with killing terrorists, such strategic questions were only of academic interest and answering them was the province of others. However, when he took command of LAKAM, he began to seriously consider the matter. He now only had one question: Could he help to provide Israel with a nuclear shield?

Reading long into the night, fueled by the forty vitamin capsules he swallowed each day, he discovered how Israel's politicians and scientists had initially been divided over "going nuclear." In the files were details of angry exchanges within cabinet meetings, the bitter monologues of scientists, and always the overpowering voice of Prime Minister David Ben-Gurion cutting through the anguish, protests, and long-winded arguments.

Trouble had begun in 1956, when France had sent a twenty-four-megawatt reactor to Israel. Ben-Gurion announced its purpose was to provide a "pumping station" to turn the desert into an "agricultural paradise by desalinating a billion cubic gallons of seawater annually." The claim promptly led to the resignation of six of the seven members of the Israeli Atomic Energy Commission, protesting the reactor was actually intended to be the precursor of "political adventurism which will unite the world against us." Israel's leading military strategists supported them. Yigal Allon, a hero of the War of Independence, roundly condemned the "nuclear option"; Yitzhak Rabin, who would soon become the IDF chief of staff, was equally vocal in his protest. Even Ariel Sharon, then Israel's leading hawk, vehemently opposed a nuclear arsenal. "We have the best conventional forces in the region."

Ignoring all opposition, Ben-Gurion gave the order for the reactor to be sited in the Negev Desert, close to the bleak, sand-blown settlement at Dimona. Once a staging post on the camel caravan route between Cairo and Jerusalem, Dimona had long become a place time had passed by. Few maps marked its position in the desert south of Tel Aviv. But from now on no mapmaker would be allowed to pinpoint the location of Israel's first faltering steps into the nuclear age.

Dimona's silver dome—beneath which was the reactor—rose above the desert heat. Kirya le Mehekar Gariny, Dimona's Hebrew name, employed over 2,500 scientists and technicians. They worked within the most fortified plant on earth. The sand around the perimeter fences was continuously checked for signs of intruders. Pilots knew that any aircraft flying within a five-mile air exclusion zone could be shot down.

Engineers had bulldozed an eighty-foot-deep chamber to house the reactor, part of an underground complex known as Machon-Two. At its core was the separating/reprocessing plant that had been labeled "textile machinery" when shipped from France.

By itself the reactor could not provide Israel with a nuclear bomb. To produce one required fissionable material, uranium or plutonium. The handful of nuclear powers had agreed among themselves never to provide as much as a gram of either substance to all those outside their exclusive "club." Imposing though it was, the reactor at Dimona was little more than a showpiece until it received fissionable materials.

Three months after the reactor had been installed, a small nuclear material processing company opened for business in a converted World War II steel plant in the unappealing town of Apollo, Pennsylvania. The company was called the Nuclear Materials and Equipment Corporation, Numec. Its chief executive was Dr. Salman Shapiro.

On LAKAM's computer database of prominent American Jews with a scientific background, Shapiro was also listed as a prominent fund-raiser for Israel. Rafi Eitan knew he had found a potential answer to how to provide the Dimona reactor with fissionable material. He ordered a full check made into the background of Shapiro and every member of the plant staff. The investigation was entrusted to the *katsa* in Washington.

The inquiry launched, Rafi Eitan continued to immerse himself in a story that had switched from the desert heat of Dimona to the cool corridors of the White House.

Among the data the Washington *katsa* had sent was a copy of a memo written on February 20, 1962, by the U.S. Atomic Energy Commission to Shapiro, bluntly warning that the company's "failure to comply with security regulations may be punishable as provided by law, including the Atomic Energy Act of 1954 and by the espionage laws."

The threat increased Rafi Eitan's feeling he may have found a way into the U.S. nuclear industry. Numec appeared to be a company not only with poor security, but also lax bookkeeping and a management that left a great deal to be desired by America's nuclear watchdog. Those very deficiencies made the company an attractive target.

The son of an Orthodox rabbi, Salman Shapiro's brilliance had already carried him far. At Johns Hopkins University he had obtained his doctorate in chemistry by the age of twenty-eight. His capacity for hard work had seen him become an important member of the nuclear research and development laboratory at Westinghouse; the corporation was contracted to the United States Navy to develop submarine reactors. Checks on Shapiro's personal background revealed some of his relatives had been Holocaust victims and Shapiro, in "his typical discreet way," had provided several million dollars for the Technion Institute in Haifa that offered tuition in science and engineering.

In 1957 Shapiro had left Westinghouse and set up Numec. It had twenty-five stockholders, all openly sympathetic to Israel. Shapiro found himself head of a small company in an aggressive cutthroat industry. Nevertheless, Numec had won a number of contracts to recover enriched uranium, a process that usually led to the loss of a quantity of uranium during the salvage operation. There was no way of telling how great or when the loss had taken place. The revelation made Rafi Eitan pop his vitamins with even more satisfaction.

He continued to read how the already uneasy relationship between Israel and the United States over the desire of the Jewish state to become a nuclear power increased when Ben-Gurion traveled to Washington in 1960. At a series of meetings with State Department officials, he was bluntly told that for Israel to possess nuclear weapons would affect the balance of power in the Middle East. In February 1961, President John F. Kennedy wrote to Ben-Gurion suggesting that Dimona should be regularly inspected by the International Atomic Energy Agency.

Alarmed, Ben-Gurion flew to New York to meet with Kennedy at the Waldorf-Astoria Hotel. The Israeli leader was "very worried" about what he saw as "relentless American pressures." But Kennedy was firm: there had to be an inspection. Ben-Gurion gave in with what little grace he could muster. He returned home convinced "a Catholic in the White House is bad news for Israel." The prime minister turned to the one man in Washington he could trust, Abraham Feinberg, a Zionist supporter of Israel's nuclear aspirations.

At one level, the native New Yorker was the most important Jewish fund-raiser for the Democratic Party. Feinberg made no secret of why he had raised many millions: every dollar was to ensure the party backed Israel in Congress. He had also discreetly provided many more additional millions of dollars to create Dimona. The money came in cashier's checks to the Bank of Israel in Tel Aviv, thus avoiding the accountability of the Israeli foreign exchange controls. Ben-Gurion told Feinberg to "sort out the boy. Make the putz understand the reality of life."

Feinberg's method was straightforward political pressure—the kind that had already infuriated Kennedy when he was running for office. Then, Feinberg had bluntly told him: "We are willing to pay your bills if you will let us have control of your Middle East policy." Kennedy had promised to "give Israel every possible break." Feinberg had agreed to provide an initial campaign contribution of five hundred thousand dollars—"with more to come."

Now he used the same direct approach: if President Kennedy continued to insist on an inspection of Dimona, he should "not count on Jewish financial support in the next political election." Powerful support came from an unexpected source. Kennedy's secretary of state, Robert S. McNamara, told Kennedy he could "understand why Israel wants a nuclear bomb."

Nevertheless, Kennedy was resolute and Israel was forced to accept an inspection. The president did at the last minute grant two concessions. In return for access to Dimona, the United States would sell Israel Hawk surface-to-air missiles, then the most advanced defensive weapon in the world. And the inspection need not be carried out by the International Atomic Energy Agency, but by an American-only team—that would have to schedule its visit weeks in advance.

Rafi Eitan relished the detailed account of how the Israelis had duped the American inspectors.

A bogus control center was built over the real one at Dimona, complete with fake control panels and computer-lined gauges that gave a credible impression of measuring the output of a reactor engaged in an irrigation scheme to turn the Negev into lush pastureland. The area containing the "heavy" water smuggled from France and Norway was placed off-limits to the inspectors "for safety reasons." The sheer volume of heavy water would have been proof the reactor was being readied for a very different purpose.

When the Americans arrived, the Israelis were relieved to discover not one spoke Hebrew. It further lessened any possibility of the inspectors uncovering the true intention for Dimona.

The stage was set for Rafi Eitan.

Gaining access to the Numec plant was relatively easy. Israel's embassy in Washington requested permission from the U.S. Atomic Energy

Commission "for a team of our scientists to visit the facility to better understand the concerns expressed by your inspectors on the reprocessing of nuclear waste." The request was granted, even though the FBI was now running a full-scale surveillance operation to discover whether Shapiro had been recruited as an Israeli spy.

He had not—and never would be. Rafi Eitan was satisfied that Shapiro was a genuine patriot, a Zionist who believed in the right of Israel to defend itself. Not only was Shapiro privately wealthy from family money and shrewd stock-market investments, his personal fortune had rapidly increased from the very large profits Numec had already made. Equally, unlike Jonathan Pollard, Shapiro was not a traitor; his love of America was manifest. Rafi Eitan knew that to even attempt to recruit him would be counterproductive. Shapiro would have to remain outside the operation beginning to crystallize in Rafi Eitan's mind.

Nevertheless, some risks were unavoidable. To learn more about Numec, Rafi Eitan had sent two LAKAM operatives to Apollo. They were Avraham Hermoni, whose diplomatic cover at the Israeli embassy in Washington was "scientific counselor," and Jeryham Kafkafi, a *katsa* operating in the United States as a freelance science writer.

Both agents toured the reprocessing plant but were not allowed to photograph it. Shapiro pointed out that would be a breach of Atomic Energy Commission regulations. They had found Shapiro welcoming but, in Hermoni's judgment, "a man run off his feet."

Rafi Eitan decided the time had come for him to go to Apollo. He put together a group of "inspectors." These included two scientists from Dimona with specialized knowledge of reprocessing nuclear waste. Another team member was listed as a director of the "Department of Electronics, University of Tel Aviv, Israel." There was no such post at the campus; the man was a LAKAM security officer whose task would be to try to discover a way of stealing fissionable waste from the plant. Hermoni was included: his job would be to point out the areas of poor security he had discovered during his previous visit. Rafi Eitan was traveling under his own name as a "scientific adviser to the office of the Prime Minister of Israel."

The delegates were approved by the U.S. embassy in Tel Aviv and visas were granted. Rafi Eitan had warned the team they could expect to be under FBI surveillance from the time they landed in New York. But, to his surprise, his experienced eyes saw no evidence of that.

The Israelis' arrival in Apollo coincided with Shapiro's return from another brainstorming tour of American university campuses, where he had been soliciting scientists who were "friendly" to Israel and would agree to go there and "solve its technical and scientific problems." He would underwrite all their expenses and make up any deficit in their salaries.

Rafi Eitan and his team's stay in Apollo was low-key. They took rooms in a motel and spent most of their time at the Numec plant learning the intricacies of converting highly enriched uranium from gaseous uranium hexafluoride. Shapiro explained that Atomic Energy Commission rules meant that Numec would have to pay penalties for any enriched material not accounted for, scaled at $10 a gram, $4,500 a pound.

Rafi Eitan and his spies left Apollo as quietly as they had come.

What followed can only be deduced from FBI reports, and even they leave tantalizing questions as to how much Salman Shapiro may have suspected was behind Rafi Eitan's visit. An FBI report stated that a month after the Israelis had returned home, Numec became a partner with the Israeli government in a business involving what was described as "the pasteurization of food and the sterilization of medical samples by irradiation."

Another FBI report complained that "with a warning notice posted on each container that it contained radioactive material, no one would open or examine them—and no one was prepared to let us do so."

The reason for the refusal was because the Israeli embassy in Washington had made it clear to the State Department that if any attempt was made to inspect the containers, they would place them under diplomatic immunity. The State Department called the Justice Department and warned of the serious diplomatic consequences that would follow any breach of that immunity. All the thwarted FBI agents could do was watch the containers being loaded on to El Al cargo planes at Idlewild Airport.

Despite his best efforts, the CIA station chief in Tel Aviv, John Hadden, said he was unable to "firm up" that the containers were ending up in Dimona. The FBI logged nine shipments in the six months following Rafi Eitan's visit. They noted that the containers arrived at dusk and left before dawn: all were sheathed with lead, needed to transport enriched uranium, and each container was stamped with a pre-addressed stencil in Hebrew giving Haifa as the final destination. On several occasions, agents saw "stovepipes"—storage containers for enriched uranium—being placed in steel cabinets at the Numec loading dock.

Each stovepipe bore a number showing it had come from the company's high-security vaults. But there was still nothing the FBI could do. An FBI memo spoke of "political pressure from State [Department] not to create a diplomatic incident."

After ten months the shipments abruptly stopped. The FBI could only assume that sufficient quantities of fissionable material had by then reached Dimona. During the agency's subsequent interviews, Shapiro denied he had supplied Israel with nuclear bomb-making material. The FBI said their check of company records showed there was a discrepancy in the amount of material reprocessed. Shapiro insisted the "most logical explanation" for any "lost" uranium was that it had seeped into the ground or had been "disposed of into the air." All told, the missing material amounted to one hundred pounds. Shapiro was never charged with any crime.

In the years that followed, Rafi Eitan could be forgiven for thinking how easy it had become to steal fissionable materials after the collapse of the Soviet Union. An incident that took place at Sheremeteyevo Airport in Moscow on August 10, 1994, proved exactly that.

At 12:45 P.M. on that day, Justiano Torres, somberly dressed in a gray business suit bought for this one journey, arrived deliberately late for Lufthansa Flight 3369 to Munich. Physically strong, he still sweated a little under the weight of the new black-leather Delsey suitcase. Torres produced his first-class ticket and smiled at the desk clerk. The smile was captured on a camera secretly installed behind the desk to record his every movement.

Other cameras had secretly filmed him over these past months. Captured on film were his meetings with a disaffected Russian nuclear scientist, Igor Tashanka: their encounters out in the Stalin Hills; their trips on a pleasure steamer on the Moscow River; their dinners at Russian mafia-controlled restaurants; and finally, the meeting where Tashanka passed over the suitcase and in return received an envelope containing $5,000. In every sense, Torres could believe he had struck a wonderful bargain. The suitcase contained fissionable material.

Justiano Torres was a courier for a Colombian drug cartel who had expanded into trafficking in an even deadlier substance. The suitcase contained, in sealed containers, the two hundred grams of plutonium 239 that Tashanka had sold him. It had a street value of $50 million. The plutonium was so lethal that even coming in contact with a microscopic speck would be fatal. The contents of the suitcase were sufficient to make a small nuclear device.

For Uri Saguy, the former head of Israeli military intelligence, the prospect was "every thinking person's nightmare: a bunch of terrorists with their hands on enough fissionable material to devastate Tel Aviv or any other city. In day-to-day intelligence tasking, dealing with a nuclear threat ranks right at the very top."

The Israeli intelligence community had long known that terrorists could manufacture a crude nuclear bomb. An American physics graduate student in the 1970s had carried out and described each one of the processes required. His published work caused huge consternation at Mossad.

Doomsday scenarios were postulated. A bomb could arrive in pieces on board a ship, or be smuggled across a land border and assembled in Israel. The weapon would be detonated by remote control unless impossible demands were met. Would the government stand firm? Mossad's analysts decided that there would be no surrender. This expectation was based on a deep understanding of the terrorist mind at the time: in the 1970s even extreme groups would hesitate to detonate a nuclear bomb because of the political price they would pay. They would become outcasts to even those nations that covertly supported them.

The collapse of Soviet Communism had renewed Mossad's fears. An arena of new uncertainties had been created; no one could say for certain how the new political dimensions within Russia would develop. Already Mossad had discovered Soviet Scud missiles had been exported for hard currency to several Middle East countries. Soviet technicians had helped Algeria build a nuclear reactor. Russia had a large stockpile of biological weapons, including a super-plague germ that could kill millions of people. Supposing even a small portion of it fell into the hands of terrorists? Even a small jar filled with the bug could decimate Tel Aviv. But above all it was the fear Russia would sell off its nuclear arsenal that was the pressing concern. For Uri Saguy that was a threat "no one could ignore."

Mossad psychologists drew up psycho-profiles of Russian scientists likely to provide materials and their motives: there were those who would do it purely for cash, others for complex ideological reasons. The list of Soviet facilities from which materials could be stolen was dauntingly large. Mossad's director general, Shabtai Shavit, sent two *katsas* to Moscow with special orders to infiltrate the scientific community.

One of them was Lila. Born of Jewish parents in Beirut, she had a degree in physics from the Hebrew University in Jerusalem and worked in Mossad's scientific intelligence section. She had witnessed the tentative meetings Torres had with Tashanka and how the deal making progressed.

Lila and her colleague had worked closely with Mossad agents in Germany and elsewhere. The trail had led her to Colombia and back into the Middle East. Other Mossad operatives had observed meetings in Cairo, Damascus, and Baghdad. New leads had opened up: Bosnia appeared to be a possible route for smuggling the plutonium 239 to its final destination—Iraq. But, not for the first time, knowing and proving the complicity of the Saddam regime were difficult.

That was why Torres was being allowed to fly on an unsuspecting commercial airliner with a lethal cargo. The decision to do so had been carefully weighed by the heads of Russian and German intelligence. They had concluded that the risk of the plutonium detonating was "infinitesimal." Permission for Torres to travel had been given by both their respective governments to see if Torres would lead them to the end user for the material. Israel had not been consulted on the matter. The operation was officially only a German-Russian one. In the past, Mossad, on more than one occasion, had been a silent partner where other agencies had claimed the credit.

From her vantage point overlooking the airport departure gates on that August morning, "Lila" knew her role in this case was over. A Mossad agent—code-named Adler—was already positioned in the lobby of the Excelsior Hotel in midtown Munich, where Torres was to make his handover. Another agent—Mort—was at the Munich airport awaiting the arrival of Flight 3369.

A third agent—Ib—sat two seats back from Torres as the plane headed west on its three-hour flight. Across the aisle from Torres sat Viktor Sidorenko, Russian deputy minister for atomic energy. His responsibilities included protecting his country's nuclear arsenal. Russia now had around 130 tons of weapons-grade plutonium, enough to make sixteen thousand atom bombs, each twice the size of the one that destroyed Hiroshima.

Sidorenko had received a number of disturbing reports that detailed lax controls and low morale among the staff of hundreds of Russian institutes and research centers with access to radioactive substances. A few months before, a worker at a nuclear plant in the Urals had been arrested with radioactive uranium pellets in a plastic bag. Over five kilos of uranium had been squirreled away by workmen at another plant near Minsk and hidden in their homes. The thefts had only come to light when a kilo was sold for twenty bottles of vodka. Sidorenko was traveling to Germany to assure Chancellor Helmut Kohl's government that cases like this would never happen again; the Germans were threatening sanctions.

At 5:45 P.M., exactly on time, Flight 3369 landed at Munich's Franz Josef Strauss Airport and taxied to its terminal C stand. Minister Sidorenko was the first to deplane. He was whisked away by a waiting car and driven to a high-security area. There he was told that Tashanka had just been arrested in Moscow.

Torres entered the arrivals area. The presence of heavily armed German police would not have surprised him. Munich had always made a show of its security after the Olympic Games massacre of Israeli athletes. Torres made a telephone call to the Excelsior Hotel, and was connected to room 23. Waiting there was a Spaniard, Javier Arratibel, whose passport described him as an "industrialist." In fact, he was the broker for the plutonium. He called a man he knew only as Julio-O.

The calls had been monitored by German intelligence officers. As Torres strolled to the luggage carousel to collect his suitcase, he was observed from a nearby office by Munich police superintendent Wolfgang Stoephasius and the senior intelligence officer.

Torres picked up his suitcase and walked toward the Nothing to Declare exit. Ib and Mort followed. They could do no more. They had no power of arrest here. Stoephasius emerged from his office. It was the signal for action.

In moments Torres was surrounded and bundled away. The suitcase was taken to a room. Inside waited a white-suited figure with a Geiger counter. With him were bomb-disposal experts. They used a portable X-ray machine to see if the case was wired with explosives. It was not. Neither was there a telltale clicking from the Geiger to indicate a leak of fissionable material. The suitcase was opened. Inside, wrapped in heavy plastic, were the containers of plutonium 239. They were removed and placed in bomb-blast boxes and carried to a waiting armored truck. From there they were taken to Germany's atomic energy complex.

In the Excelsior Hotel, Arratibel was arrested. But the next link in the chain, Julio-O, had slipped across the border into Hungary. The

Hungarian police said they would look for him. But no one was holding his breath in Munich. Hungary was known to be one of the entry points to the West for Russian smugglers.

The Mossad men informed Tel Aviv what had happened.

In Tel Aviv, Mossad's director general, Shabtai Shavit, saw the outcome as another small victory in the endless battle against nuclear terrorism. But he was not alone in wondering how many other suitcases had slipped through, how soon before there would be a nuclear explosion unless impossible demands were met.

A few miles away from where Shavit pondered such questions, Rafi Eitan, the man who had masterminded what the FBI and CIA still believed had been the theft of nuclear material from the Numec reprocessing plant at Apollo, continued to spend his free time carving yet more sculptures from scrap materials. Outwardly he was at peace with the world. Both the Pollard and Apollo operations had faded from memory; when pressed, he said he could not recall the first names of either Pollard or Shapiro. LAKAM had officially been closed down. Rafi Eitan insisted that his work nowadays was very different from what he had done before: he was a director of a small shipping company in Havana where he also had an interest in a company manufacturing agricultural pesticides. He claimed a close relationship with Fidel Castro, "which probably does not please the Americans." He had never set foot in the United States since his trip to Apollo. He said he had no desire to, not least because he suspected he might still be asked "a lot of questions" about Jonathan Pollard and what exactly had happened following his visit to Apollo.

Then, in April 1997, Rafi Eitan's name began to surface in connection with a Mossad spy in Washington whom the FBI identified and code-named Mega.

His own well-placed source within Mossad had told Rafi Eitan that the FBI had begun to explore the role Mega could have had in the way Jonathan Pollard had been run. Had Mega been the source for some of the ultrasecret material Pollard had passed on? The FBI had recently reinterviewed Pollard in prison and he had admitted that even his high security clearance had not been enough to obtain some of the documents his handler, the funereal Yagur, had requested. The FBI knew such documents had a special code word through which they had to be accessed, which changed frequently, sometimes even on a daily basis. Yet Yagur had seemed to know the code within a matter of hours to give to Pollard. Had Mega provided it? Was Mega the second Israeli spy in Washington the FBI had long suspected? How close had he been to Rafi Eitan?

These were the dangerous questions now being asked in Washington that could shatter the relationship between Washington and Tel Aviv.

After the FBI had identified him as the puppet master behind Pollard, Rafi Eitan had accepted that his time in Israeli intelligence was finally over. He had looked forward to ending his days facing no greater risk than being scorched from the blowtorch he wielded when forming his sculptures.

Instinctively he knew that events in Washington posed a threat not only to him—a CIA snatch squad could try to grab him as he came and went from Cuba and bring him to Washington for questioning, and there was no way of telling what would happen then; but the discovery of Mega's existence would also be exercising minds in the upper echelons of the Israeli intelligence community's Va'adat Rashei Hasherutim, the Committee of the Heads of Service, whose primary function is to coordinate all intelligence and security activities at home and abroad.

But even they knew nothing about who Mega was. All they had been told was that he was highly placed in the Clinton administration. Whether the president had inherited him from the Bush government was another carefully guarded secret. Only the incumbent Mossad memune knew how long Mega had been in place.

The committee members did, however, know that the FBI's counterintelligence division finally believed that the lack of action against Mossad was due to the power of the Jewish lobby in Washington, and the reluctance of successive administrations to confront it. Once more that lobby could be called upon to dampen the firestorm building since Mega had first been discovered by the FBI. On February 16, 1997, the National Security Agency (NSA) had provided the FBI with an intercept of a late-night telephone conversation from the Israeli embassy between a Mossad intelligence officer identified only as Dov, and his superior in Tel Aviv, whose name had not been revealed during the short conversation.

Dov had asked "for guidance" as to whether he "should go to Mega" for a copy of a letter written by Warren Christopher, then secretary of state, to PLO chairman Yasser Arafat. The letter contained a set of assurances given to Arafat by Christopher on January 16 about the withdrawal of Israeli troops from the West Bank city of Hebron. Dov was instructed by the voice in Tel Aviv "to forget the letter. This is not something we use Mega for."

The brief conversation had been the first clue the FBI had of the importance of Mega. The code name had not been heard before in its around-the-clock surveillance of the Israeli embassy and its diplomats. Using state-of-the-art computers, the FBI narrowed the urgent search for the identity of Mega to someone who either worked there or had access to a senior official employed by the National Security Council, the body that advises the president on intelligence and defense-related matters. Its office is in the White House, and its members include the vice president and the secretaries of state and defense. The director of Central Intelligence and the chairman of the Joint Chiefs of Staff serve in an advisory role. The permanent staff is headed by the president's national security adviser.

How the Israeli embassy had learned its secure communications channel with Tel Aviv had been breached still remained as closely guarded as the identity of Mega. Like all Israeli missions, the Washington embassy was constantly updated with more sophisticated systems for encryption and burst transmissions: a significant portion of this equipment has been adapted from stolen U.S. blueprints.

On February 27, 1997, a pleasant spring morning in Tel Aviv, the members of the Committee of the Heads of Services drove from their various offices around the city along the broad road called Rehov Shaul Hamaleku to a guarded gate in a high blank wall tipped with barbed wire. All that could be seen of what lay behind the wall were the roofs of buildings. Rising above them was a massive concrete tower visible all over Tel Aviv. At various heights were unsightly clusters of electronic antennae. The tower was the centerpiece of the headquarters of the Israel Defense Forces. The complex is known as the Kirya, which simply means "place."

At a little before 11:00 A.M., the intelligence chiefs used their swipe cards to access a building near the tower. Like most Israeli government offices, the conference room they entered was shabby.

The meeting was chaired by Danny Yatom, who had recently been

appointed as Mossad's latest chief by Prime Minister Benjamin Netanyahu. Yatom had a reputation as a hard-liner, very much in keeping with
Netanyahu. The Tel Aviv rumor mills had it that the new Mossad chief
had "baby-sat" the embattled prime minister when Netanyahu's colorful private life threatened his career. The men around the cedarwood
conference table listened attentively as Yatom outlined the strategy to
be adopted should the "situation" with Mega become a full-blown crisis.

Israel would deliver a strongly worded protest that its Washington
embassy's diplomatic status had been violated by the bugging—a move
that would undoubtedly cause embarrassment to the Clinton administration. Next, sayanim connected to the U.S. media should be instructed to plant stories that Mega was an incorrect decoding of the
Hebrew slang *Elga*, which had long been Mossad-speak for the CIA.
Further, the word Mega was part of one well known to U.S. intelligence. Megawatt was a code name it had until recently used jointly
with Mossad to describe shared intelligence. For good measure sayanim should add that another word, Kilowatt, was used for commonly
shared terrorist data.

But, for the moment, nothing would be done, Yatom concluded.

In March 1997, on receipt of information from Mossad's *katsa* in
Washington, Yatom took action. He sent a *yaholomin* team to Washington to follow up on the *katsa*'s report that President Clinton was
repeatedly indulging in phone-sex calls with a a former White House
aide, Monica Lewinsky. He was making the calls from the Oval
Office to her apartment in the Watergate complex. Knowing that the
White House was totally protected by electronic countermeasures,
the *yaholomin* team focused on Lewinsky's apartment. They began to
intercept explicit phone calls from the president to Lewinsky. The
recordings were couriered by diplomatic bag to Tel Aviv.

On March 27, Clinton once more invited Lewinsky to the Oval
Office and revealed he believed a foreign embassy was taping their conversations. He did not give her any more details, but shortly afterward
the affair ended.

In Tel Aviv, Mossad's strategies pondered how to use the highly embarrassing taped conversations; they were the stuff of blackmail—
though no one suggested any attempt should be made to blackmail the
president of the United States. Some, however, saw the recordings as a
potent weapon to be used if Israel found itself with its back to the wall
in the Middle East and unable to count on Clinton's support.

There was common consensus that the FBI must also be aware of the conversations between Clinton and Lewinsky. Some strategists urged Yatom to use "the backdoor channel" with Washington and let the FBI know Mossad was aware of the president's phone calls: it would be a not-very-subtle way of telling the agency to back off in their continuing hunt for Mega. Other analysts urged a wait-and-see policy, arguing that the information would remain explosive whenever it was released. That view prevailed.

In September 1998, the Starr report was published and Yatom had left office. The report contained a short reference to Clinton warning Lewinsky back in March 1997 that his phone was being bugged by a foreign embassy. Starr had not pursued the matter when Lewinsky had given her testimony before the grand jury about her affair with Clinton. However, the FBI could only have seen the revelations as further evidence of their inability to unmask Mega.

Six months later, March 5th 1999, the *New York Post* published in a cover story the revelations in the original edition of this book. The *Post* story began: "Israel blackmailed President Clinton with phone-tapped tapes of his steamy sex talks with Monica Lewinsky, a blockbuster new book charges. The price Clinton paid for the silence of the Mossad spy agency was calling off an FBI hunt for a top-level Israeli mole."

Within hours of this complete distortion of the facts in the book (which I had carefully checked with sources in Israel), the *Post*'s version had appeared in thousands of newspapers around the world.

The essential point of my story, that public prosecutor Kenneth Starr had not fully pursued his impeachment investigation into Clinton, was lost. Starr had noted in his report that on March 29, 1997: "He [Clinton] told her [Lewinsky] that he suspected that a foreign embassy [he did not specify which one] was taping his telephones. If anyone ever asked about their phone sex, she should say that they knew that their calls were being monitored all day long, and the phone sex was a put-on."

The president's words most strongly indicated he was aware that he had become a potential target for blackmail. By talking to Lewinsky over a public phone network—there is no evidence he had attempted to secure the phone in her apartment—the president had indeed left himself open to interception by foreign eavesdroppers and, even more so, to the powerful microwave vacuum cleaners of the National Security Agency. Given that any incumbent president routinely gets NSA reports, he would also have known that his calls to Monica could well end up on the Washington rumor mills.

A sense of the panic my revelations created in the White House can be seen from its briefing to correspondents by Oval Office spokesmen Barry Toiv and David Leavy. There is a shifting-sands feeling about their responses that the official White House transcript has retained.

Q: Why did the president reportedly tell Monica Lewinsky that he was concerned about his phone conversations being taped?

TOIV: Well, as you know, other than the president's testimony in this case, we really haven't commented on specifics, on other specifics like that and we're not going to start now.

Q: When the president heard about this, was he concerned by it, was he shocked by it? What was his reaction, Mr. Toiv?

TOIV: To be honest, I haven't gotten the president's reaction to the book.

Q: Well, why did he say that to Monica Lewinsky? Why did he warn her?

TOIV: I've already not answered that question. (Laughter). I'm sorry.

Q: I know you've not answered it, but it's very valid, really.

TOIV: Well, again, we're not going to get into commenting on specifics beyond what the president has already testified to.

Q: I don't understand why you think it's legitimate for you not to comment on the president of the United States supposedly saying that he thinks a foreign government is tapping his conversations. For you just to say, no comment.

TOIV: There have been questions about all sorts of comments that have been made or testified to and we have not gone beyond the president's testimony in discussing these and we're not going to do that.

Q: That's because you've said it's unseemly and it's about sex. This is about the national security of the United States and the president supposedly saying that a foreign government is taping his conversations. And you're just going to say sorry, no comment?

TOIV: I am not going to go beyond what he has already testified to.

Q: You're not denying it. You're not denying it.

LEAVY: Obviously, we're not aware of a mole at the White House. But it's the long-standing practice for people who speak at this podium to refer calls to the appropriate authorities who undertake these types of investigations.

Q: Was there any attempt by the president to intervene in any kind of investigation or search for a mole?

LEAVY: No. There is no basis in that allegation whatsoever.

Q: Well, there is a basis for it. There is a sworn testimony that Lewinsky gave that attributes to the president a comment that a foreign embassy was taping—

LEAVY: And Barry just answered that question.

Q: His answer was that he is not going to comment on it. That's not much of an answer. With all due respect.

LEAVY: Let me say two things—noted.

TOIV: I wouldn't go beyond my comments.

LEAVY: Yes, I'm definitely not going to add to Barry's comments. But let me just say this. We take all the necessary precautions to secure the president's communications. There is absolutely no basis for the allegation in the book.

Q: Are you getting that from CIA or FBI, or are you getting it out of just an automatic reflex?

LEAVY: You can take that as authoritative.

Q: I understand that you would have his communications secure. However, if he picks up the phone and calls some ordinary citizen at 2:30 A.M. in the morning at their apartment, what's to say that that person's phone couldn't be tapped? Does your security system prevent that?

LEAVY: There is some very serious allegations in this book, and what I am saying is that there is absolutely no basis for the allegation. So I have to leave it at that.

Not one serious newspaper made any attempt to follow up those revealing responses.

It turned out that Mossad was not the only organization that had taped the sex phone calls. The Republican senator for Arizona, Jon Kyl, a member of the Select Committee on Intelligence, told his local newspaper *The Arizona Republic* that "a U.S. intelligence agency may have taped telephone conversations between President Clinton and Monica Lewinsky. There are different agencies in the government that make it their business to tape certain things for certain reasons, and it was one of those agencies."

Kyl refused to identify to the newspaper who the agency or agencies were: "That's something I absolutely can't get into in any greater detail." Of his sources he said, "By virtue of who they are, they have credibility. You can assume that they are people who at some period in time have been in the employ of the federal government." He went on to compare the existence of the tapes to the "smoking-gun" evidence in the Watergate scandal.

These explosive allegations from a respected politician were never pursued into the public domain.

According to at least one well-placed Israeli intelligence source, Rafi Eitan had received a phone call from Yatom reinforcing the need to stay well clear of the United States for the foreseeable future.

Rafi Eitan did not need to be told how ironic it would be if he fell victim to the very technique that had made him a legend—the kidnapping of Adolf Eichmann. Even worse would be to be quietly killed by one of the methods that had burnished his reputation among men who saw assassination as part of the job.

CHAPTER 6

AVENGERS

On a warm afternoon in mid-October 1995, a technician of Mossad's

internal security division, Autahat Paylut Medienit (APM), used a hand-

operated scanner to check an apartment off Pinsker Street in down-

town Tel Aviv for bugging devices. The apartment was one of several

safe houses Mossad owned around the city. The search was an indica-

tion of the sensitivity of the meeting shortly to take place there. Satis-

fied the apartment was electronically clean, he left.

The apartment's furniture could have come from a garage sale; noth-

ing seemed to match. A few cheaply framed pictures hung on the walls,

views of the Israel tourists liked to visit. Each room had its own separate unlisted telephone. In the kitchen, instead of domestic appliances, were a computer and modem, a shredder, a fax, and, where an oven would be, a safe.

Usually the safe houses were dormitories for trainees from the Mossad school for spies on the outskirts of the city while they learned street craft: how to tail someone or themselves avoid surveillance; how to set up a dead-letter box, or exchange information concealed inside a newspaper. Day and night the streets of Tel Aviv were their proving ground under the watchful eye of instructors. Back in the safe houses, the lessons continued: how to brief a *katsa* going to a target country; how to write special-ink letters or use a computer to create information capable of being transmitted in very short bursts on specified frequencies.

An important part of the seemingly endless hours of training was how to form relationships with innocent, unsuspecting people. Yaakov Cohen, who worked for twenty-five years as a *katsa* under deep cover around the world, believed one reason for his success was lessons learned in those lectures:

"Everyone and anyone became a tool. I could lie to them because truth was not part of my relationship with them. All that mattered was using them for Israel's benefit. From the very beginning, I learned a philosophy: Do what was right for Mossad and for Israel."

Those who could not live by that credo found themselves swiftly dismissed from the service. For David Kimche, regarded as one of Mossad's best operatives:

"It's the old story of many think they are called, few are chosen. In that way we are a little like the Catholic church. Those who remain, develop bonds which will carry them through life. We live by the rule of 'I help you, you help me.' You learn to trust people with your life. No greater trust can ever be given by one person to another."

By the time every man or woman who had access to the safe houses graduated to the next group, that philosophy had been engraved on their minds. They were now *katsas* departing on a mission or returning to be debriefed. Known as "jumpers" because they operated overseas on a short-term basis, they inevitably called the safe houses "jump sites." Too much imaginative description was frowned upon by their superiors.

Finally, the safe houses were used as meeting places for an informer, or to interrogate a suspect who had the potential to be recruited as a "mole." The only indication of their numbers has come from a former Mossad junior officer, Victor Ostrovsky. He claimed in 1991 there were "about 35,000 in the world; 20,000 of these operational and 15,000 sleepers. 'Black' agents are Arabs, while 'white' agents are non-Arabs. 'Warning agents' are strategic agents used to warn of war preparations: a doctor in a Syrian hospital who notices a large new supply of drugs and medicines arriving; a harbor employee who spots increased activity of warships."

Some of these agents had received their first instructions in a safe house like the one that had been meticulously checked for bugs on that October afternoon. Later in the day, a handful of senior members of Israel's intelligence community would meet around the apartment's dining-room table to sanction an assassination that would have the full approval of Prime Minister Yitzhak Rabin.

In the three years he had been in that office, Rabin had attended a growing number of funerals for the victims of terrorist attacks, each time walking behind pallbearers and watching grown men weep as they listened to the committal prayer. With each death he had conducted "a funeral in my own heart." Afterward he had again read the words from the prophet Ezekiel: "And the enemy shall know I am the Lord when I can lay down my vengeance on them."

This was not the first time Rabin's vengeance had been felt; Rabin had himself on more than one occasion participated in an act of revenge. Most notable had been the assassination of Yasser Arafat's deputy, Khalil Al-Wazir, known throughout the Arab world and on Mossad's Honeywell computer as Abu Jihad, the voice of holy war, who lived in Tunisia. In 1988, Rabin had been Israel's defense minister when the decision was taken in the same apartment off Pinsker Street that Abu Jihad must die.

For two months Mossad agents conducted an exhaustive reconnaissance of Abu Jihad's villa in the resort of Sidi Bou Said on the outskirts of Tunis. Access roads, points of entry, fence heights and types, windows, doors, locks, defenses, the routing employed by Abu Jihad's guards: everything was monitored, checked, and checked again.

They watched Abu Jihad's wife play with her children; they came alongside her as she shopped and went to the hairdresser. They listened to her husband's phone calls, bugged their bedroom, listened to their lovemaking. They calculated distances from one room to another, found out what the neighbors did, when they were at home, and logged the makes, colors, and registrations of all the vehicles that came and went from the villa.

The rule for preparing an assassination Meir Amit had laid down all those years ago was constantly in their minds: Think like your target and only stop being him when you pull the trigger.

Satisfied, the team returned to Tel Aviv. For the next month they practiced their deadly mission in and around a Mossad safe house near Haifa that matched the target villa. From the time they would enter Abu Jihad's house, it should take the unit just twenty-two seconds to murder him.

On April 16, 1988, the order was given for the operation to go ahead.

That night several Israeli air force Boeing 707s took off from a military base south of Tel Aviv. One carried Yitzhak Rabin and other high-ranking Israeli officers. Their aircraft was in constant touch by safe radio with the execution team already in position and led by an operative code-named "Sword." The other aircraft was crammed with jamming and monitoring devices. Two more 707s acted as fuel tankers. High above the villa the fleet of aircraft circled, following every move on the ground through a secure radio frequency. A little after midnight on April 17 the airborne officers heard Abu Jihad had returned home in the Mercedes Yasser Arafat had given him as a wedding gift. Prior to that the hit team had set up sensitive listening devices able to hear everything inside the villa.

From his vantage point near the villa, Sword announced into his lip mike that he could hear Abu Jihad climbing the stairs, going to his bedroom, whispering to his wife, tiptoeing to an adjoining bedroom to kiss his sleeping son, before finally going to his study on the ground floor. The details were picked up by the electronic warfare plane—the Israeli version of an American AWACS—and relayed to Rabin's command aircraft. At 12:17 A.M. he ordered: "Go!"

Outside the villa, Abu Jihad's driver was asleep in the Mercedes. One of Sword's men ran forward, pressed a silenced Beretta into his ear, and pulled the trigger. The driver slumped dead across the front seat.

Next, Sword and another member of the hit team laid an explosive charge at the base of the villa's heavy iron front door. A new type of "silent" plastic explosive, it made little sound as it blew the doors clean off their hinges. Inside, two of Abu Jihad's bodyguards were standing in the entrance hall, too stunned by the explosion to move. They, too, were shot dead by silenced weapons.

Running to the study, Sword found Abu Jihad watching video footage of the PLO. As he rose to his feet, Sword shot him twice in the chest. Abu Jihad crashed heavily to the floor. Sword stepped quickly forward and put two more bullets through his forehead.

Leaving the room, he encountered Abu Jihad's wife. She was holding her small son in her arms.

"Get back to your room," Sword ordered in Arabic.

Then he and the team vanished into the night. From the time they had entered the villa to departure had taken them only thirteen seconds—nine vital seconds better than their best practice run.

For the first time, an Israeli assassination met with public criticism. Cabinet minister Ezer Weizman warned that "liquidating individuals will not advance the peace process."

Nevertheless the assassinations continued.

Two months later, South African police were finally forced to reveal a secret that Israel had pressed them to keep: Mossad had executed a Johannesburg businessman, Alan Kidger, who had been supplying high-tech equipment to Iran and Iraq that could be used to manufacture biochemical weapons. Kidger had been found with his arms and legs amputated. Johannesburg's chief police investigator, Colonel Charles Landman, said the killing was a "clear message from the Israeli government through its Mossad."

Six weeks before the execution of Abu Jihad, Mossad had played an important role in another controversial assassination—that of three unarmed members of the IRA shot dead on a Sunday afternoon in Gibraltar by a team of Britain's Special Air Services marksmen.

In previous years, some of their colleagues from British intelligence had been secretly brought to Tel Aviv by Rafi Eitan to witness first-hand how Mossad executed Arab terrorists in the back streets of Beirut and Lebanon's Bekáa Valley.

Four months before the Gibraltar shootings, Mossad agents had begun their own surveillance of Mairead Farrell, Sean Savage, and Daniel McCann in the belief they were once more on a "shopping spree for Arab arms for the IRA."

Mossad's close interest in the activities of the IRA went back to the time when the Thatcher government had, in the utmost secrecy, brought Rafi Eitan to Belfast to brief the security forces on the developing links between the Irish terror groups and the Hezbollah.

"I arrived on a rainy day. It rained every day I was in Ireland. I told the British all we knew. Then I went on a tour of the province, all the way down to the border with the Republic. I was careful not to cross over. Imagine what the Irish government would have said if they'd picked me up! Before I left I arranged for the SAS to come to Israel so they could see something of our methods in handling terrorists."

From those early beginnings a close working relationship developed between the SAS and Mossad. Senior Mossad officers would regularly travel to SAS headquarters in Hereford to brief special forces on operations in the Middle East. On at least one occasion a joint Mossad-SAS unit trailed several high-ranking IRA men from Belfast to Beirut and photographed them in meetings with Hezbollah leaders.

In October 1987, Mossad agents tracked the tramp steamer *Eksund* as it made its way through the Mediterranean with 120 tons of arms, including surface-to-air missiles, rocket-propelled grenade launchers, machine guns, explosives, and detonators. All had been purchased through IRA contacts in Beirut. The *Eksund* was intercepted by the French authorities.

Unable to make headway with the Irish security authorities—at least one Mossad officer still believed this stemmed from Israel's strong opposition to Ireland's peacekeeping role in Lebanon—Mossad used Britain's SAS as a conduit to tip off Dublin about other arms shipments heading for Ireland.

The Mossad agents trailing the IRA commando unit in Spain quickly decided they were not there to meet Arab arms dealers, nor to make contact with ETA, the Basque terrorist group. Nevertheless, the Mossad team continued to dog the footsteps of Spain's International Terrorism Unit, who were also following the Irish trio.

At first there was a keep-your-distance attitude by the Spaniards. This was their operation—the first time they had become seriously involved with both MI5 and the SAS in dealing with the IRA. Understandably, the Spaniards wanted to ensure the glory, if it came, would be theirs. Mossad quickly made it clear that all they wanted to do was help. Relieved, the Spaniards were soon working together with Mossad.

When the Spanish lost track of Mairead Farrell, it was a *katsa* who located her. He discovered that Farrell had hired another car, a white Fiesta, and parked it, loaded with sixty-four kilos of Semtex and thirty-six kilos of shrapnel, in an underground parking lot in Marbella.

The fashionable resort is not only a favorite refuge from the fierce desert sun where a number of Arab notables spend their time dreaming of the day the hated Israel will be overrun; Marbella is only a short distance from the raffish marina of Puerto Banus, where many Arab petrodollar millionaires kept their luxury yachts. Mossad had long feared that the boats traveled the length of the Mediterranean to smuggle explosives and weapons to Arab terrorists. Farrell's car was suspected of being parked for that purpose, ready to be hoisted on board a boat ostensibly bound on a cruise to the Holy Land.

The Mossad team conducted surveillance on the car. They also spotted Farrell at the wheel of another Fiesta, the one she had used to drive McCann and Savage around Spain these past weeks. Two of the Mossad team followed the IRA unit as it drove south toward Puerto Banus. Ten minutes after leaving Marbella, Farrell passed the entrance to the marina and continued on down the coast.

Using their car radio tuned to the police channel, the Mossad *katsa* alerted the Spanish police that the IRA trio were heading toward Gibraltar. The Spanish alerted the British authorities. The SAS team moved into position. Hours later Farrell, McCann, and Savage were shot dead. They were given no warning or chance to surrender. They were executed.

A week later, Stephen Lander, the MI5 officer officially credited with running the operation—and who would later become director general of MI5—telephoned Admoni to thank Mossad for their help with the assassination.

On that October evening in 1995, in the safe house off Pinsker Street, all was ready for the meeting to settle the next assassination.

Selected for execution was the religious head of Islamic Jihad, Fathi Shkaki. Mossad had established that his group had orchestrated the deaths of over twenty Israeli passengers in a bus destroyed the previous January by two suicide bombers outside the small town of Beit Lid.

The incident brought the number of terrorist attacks to over ten thousand in the last quarter century. In that time over four hundred Israelis had been killed and another thousand injured. Many of those responsible for this catalog of death and maiming had themselves been hunted down and killed in what *katsa* Yaakov Cohen, who had himself done his share of revenge taking, would describe as "all those back streets that have no names; where a knife can be more effective at times than a gun; where it's either kill or be killed."

In this pitiless world Shkaki had long been lionized by his people. It was he who had personally granted the bombers of Beit Lid absolution from the inviolable Islamic prohibition against suicide. To do so he had combed the Koran to extrapolate a philosophical assumption that oppression makes the oppressed discover new strengths; in preparing the suicide bombers he had exploited the psychological flaws in unbalanced youngsters who, like the Japanese kamikaze teenagers in World War II, went to their own end on that January day in a state of religious fervor. Afterward, Shkaki had paid for their death notices in Jihad's newspaper and, at Friday prayers, had praised their sacrifice, assuring their families their sons had found a place in heaven.

In the tension of the streets where he operated, it had become a matter of honor for a family to provide a son for Shkaki to sacrifice. Those who died were remembered each day after the muezzin wailed through the crackling loudspeakers to call the faithful to prayer. In the shadowy coolness of the mosques of south Lebanon, their memories were kept alive.

His next recruits chosen, their target selected, Shkaki would hand the youths over to his bomb makers. They were the strategists who could study a photograph of a target and decide upon the quantity of explosive needed. Like ancient alchemists, they worked by experience and instinct, and their language was filled with the words that brought death: "oxidizer," "desensitizer," "plasticines," and "freezing point depressants." These were Shkaki's people. Borrowing a phrase once used by a leader of his hated enemy, Israel, he told them all: "We fight, therefore we exist."

On that October evening when his fate was about to be settled in the Tel Aviv safe house, Shkaki was at home in Damascus with his wife, Fathia. The apartment was strikingly different from the squalor of the refugee camps where he was venerated. Expensive carpets and wall hangings were gifts from the ayatollahs of Iran. A gold-framed photograph of Shkaki with Mu'ammar Gadhafi was a present from the Libyan leader. A coffee service made of silver was a gift from the Syrian president. Shkaki's clothes were far removed from the simple gown he wore on his crusades among the impoverished masses in south Lebanon. At home he wore robes cut from the finest cloth available from London's Savile Row and his feet were shod in custom-made shoes bought in Rome, not the bazaar sandals he wore in public.

Over his favorite meal of couscous, Shkaki reassured his wife he would be safe on his forthcoming trip to Libya to seek further funds from Gadhafi; he hoped to return with one million dollars, the full amount he had requested in a fax to Libya's revolutionary headquarters in Tripoli. As usual the money would be laundered through a Libyan bank in Valletta on the island of Malta. Shkaki planned to spend less than a day on the island before catching the flight home.

News of the stopover in Malta had prompted his two teenage sons to give him their own shopping order: half a dozen shirts each from a Malta store where Shkaki had shopped previously.

Fathia Shkaki would recall: "My husband insisted if the Israelis were planning a move against him, they would have done so by now. The Jews always respond quickly to any incident. But my husband was very certain in his case they would do nothing to make Syria angry."

Until three months before, Shkaki would have correctly judged the mood in Tel Aviv. Early in the summer of 1995, Rabin had turned down a Mossad plan to firebomb Shkaki's apartment in the western suburb of Damascus. Uri Saguy, then chief of military intelligence and effectively Israel's intelligence supremo, who had authority even over Mossad, had told Rabin he detected "a sea change in Damascus. Assad is still on the surface our enemy. But the only way to overcome him is to do the unexpected. And that means giving up the Golan Heights, give it up completely. Move every one of our people out of there. It's a huge price. But it is the only way to get a proper lasting peace."

Rabin had listened. He knew how much the Golan had personally cost Uri Saguy. He had spent most of his military career defending its rugged terrain. He had been wounded four times doing so. Yet he was prepared to put all this behind him to see Israel have real peace.

The prime minister had postponed Mossad's plans to eliminate Shkaki while Saguy continued to explore the reality of his hopes.

They had withered in the heat of the region's summer, and Rabin, who was now a Nobel Peace Prize winner, had ordered Shkaki's execution.

Shabtai Shavit, in his last major operation as Mossad's chief, ordered a "black agent" in Damascus to resume electronic surveillance of Shkaki's apartment. The agent's American equipment was sophisticated enough to override the defense circuit breakers in Shkaki's Russian-built communications system.

Details of Shkaki's forthcoming visit to Libya and Malta were sent to Tel Aviv.

Now, on that October evening in 1995, the heads of Israel's three most powerful intelligence services made their way through the crowds strolling along Pinsker Street. Each one supported the conditions for executing a self-proclaimed enemy of Israel that Meir Amit had so clearly defined when he had been director general:

"There would be no killing of political leaders. They needed to be dealt with politically. There would be no killing of a terrorist's family. If its members got in the way, that was not our problem. Each execution had to be sanctioned by the prime minister of the day. And everything must be done by the book. Minutes kept of the decision taken. Everything neat and tidy. Our actions must not be seen as some act of state-sponsored murder but the ultimate judicial sanction the state could bring. We would be no different from the hangman or any other lawfully appointed executioner."

Since the successful hunting down of the nine terrorists who had killed the Israeli athletes at the Olympic Games in 1972, all subsequent assassinations had broadly observed these conditions. Almost twenty-three years to the day since Meir Amit had first formulated the rules for a state-sponsored killing, his successors headed for the safe house.

The first to arrive was Shabtai Shavit. Colleagues unkindly said he had the manner of a front-desk clerk in one of Tel Aviv's lesser hotels: the same carefully pressed clothes, the handshake that never maintained its grip for long. He had been in the job for three years and gave the impression he never quite knew how long he would remain.

Next came Brigadier General Doran Tamir, chief intelligence officer for the Israel Defense Forces. Nimble and in the prime of his life, everything about him suggested the authority that came from long years of commanding.

Finally Uri Saguy arrived, strolling into the safe house like a warrior god on his way to stardom even more glittering than his position as director of Aman, military intelligence. Soft-voiced and self-deprecating, he continued to provoke controversy among his peers by insisting that beneath its renewed bluster, Syria was still ready to talk peace.

The relationship among the three men was, in Shavit's words, "cautiously cordial."

Said Uri Saguy, "We can hardly compare with each other. As head of Aman, I tasked the other two. There was competition between us but, as long as we were serving the same aim, it's fine."

For two hours they sat around the living-room table and reviewed the plan to have Fathi Shkaki murdered. His execution would be an act of pure vengeance, the biblical "eye for an eye" principle Israelis liked to believe justified such killings. But sometimes Mossad killed a person when he stubbornly refused to provide his skills to support Israel's aspirations. Then, rather than risk those talents falling into the hands of an enemy, he too was ruthlessly terminated.

Dr. Gerald Bull, a Canadian scientist, was the world's greatest expert on barrel ballistics. Israel had made several unsuccessful attempts to buy his expertise. Each time Bull had made clear his distaste for the Jewish state.

Instead he had offered his services to Saddam Hussein to build a supergun capable of launching shells containing nuclear, chemical, or biological warheads from Iraq directly into Israel. The supergun's barrel was 487 feet long, composed of thirty-two tons of steel supplied by British firms to Iraq. Late in 1989 a prototype had been test-fired at a gunnery range at Mosul in northern Iraq. Saddam Hussein had ordered three of the weapons to be built at a cost of $20 million. Bull was retained as a consultant at $1 million. The project was code-named Babylon.

His company, Space Research Corporation (SRC), was registered in Brussels as an armaments design company. From there it had sent out a detailed requirement list to European suppliers, including twenty in Britain, to provide high-technology components.

On February 17, 1990, a *katsa* in Brussels obtained copies of documents setting Babylon's technical goals: the supergun was really going to be an intermediate range ballistics missile launcher. The core of the weapon's launch system would be Scud missiles grouped in clusters of eight to give the warheads a range of 1,500 miles. That would place not only Israel but many European cities in range. Bull believed it would be possible to eventually produce a supergun capable of landing a direct hit on London from Baghdad.

Mossad's director general, Nahum Admoni, sought an immediate meeting with Prime Minister Yitzhak Shamir. A former urban guerrilla leader who had ruthlessly fought the British during the dying weeks of the Mandate, Shamir was the kind of political leader Mossad liked, fully supporting the need to destroy Israel's enemies when it was critical and all else failed. During the 1960s, when Nazi rocket scientists were working with Egypt to provide long-range weapons capable of hitting Israel from across the Sinai Desert, Shamir had been called in by Mossad to provide expertise in planning assassinations. His speciality during the Mandate rule had been devising means to eliminate British soldiers. Shamir had sent former members of his underground forces to kill the German scientists. Some of these assassins later became founding members of the Mossad's kidon unit.

Shamir spent only a short time studying Mossad's file on Bull. The service had done its usual thorough job tracing Bull's career from the time, at the age of twenty-two, he had been awarded a doctorate in physics and gone to work for the Canadian government's Armament and Research Development Establishment. There he had clashed with senior officials, sowing the seeds for what had become a lifelong hatred of bureaucrats. He had set up as a private consultant—"literally a gun for hire," the file observed with a touch of black humor.

His reputation as an armaments inventor was established in 1976 when he designed a 45-caliber howitzer that could shell targets twenty-five miles away; at that time the only comparable weapon NATO possessed had a maximum range of only seventeen miles. But once more Bull fell foul of government attitudes. NATO members were blocked from buying the new gun because the major European weapon producers had effective political lobbies. Bull finally sold the howitzer to South Africa.

He then moved to China, helping the People's Liberation Army develop its missile capability. Bull enhanced the existing Silkworm rockets by giving them a longer range and a greater payload of explosives. Batches of the rockets were then sold by China to Saddam Hussein. Initially Iraq deployed them in the long-running war against neighboring Iran. But a sufficient quantity of Silkworms remained at Iraqi launch sites for Mossad to believe they would eventually be used against Israel.

Meanwhile, Project Babylon was gathering pace. A more advanced prototype had been test-fired. Opponents of the Saddam regime who had been recruited as Mossad informers in Iraq reported that missile nose cones were being designed to hold chemical and biological weapons.

On the afternoon of March 20, 1990, in the prime minister's office, Yitzhak Shamir agreed with Nahum Admoni that Gerald Bull had to die.

Two days after the decision was taken, a two-man kidon team arrived in Brussels. Waiting for them was the *katsa* who had been closely monitoring Bull's activities.

At 6:45 on the evening of March 22, 1990, the three men drove in a hired car to the apartment block where Bull lived. Each kidon carried a handgun in a holster under his jacket.

Twenty minutes later, the sixty-one-year-old Bull answered the chiming doorbell of his luxury apartment. He was shot five times in the head and the neck, the kidons firing their 7.65-mm pistols in turn, leaving Bull dead outside his doorway. Later, Bull's son, Michael, would insist his father had been warned that Mossad would kill him. He could not say who had given the warning or why his father had ignored it.

Once the kidon team was safely back home, Mossad's Department of Psychological Warfare began to feed stories to the media, strongly suggesting that Gerald Bull had died because he had planned to renege on his deal with Saddam Hussein. Now, five years later, the tactics used to execute Bull, a scientist Israel considered as much of a terrorist as Fathi Shkaki, were once more to be implemented on the direct order of another prime minister, Yitzhak Rabin.

On October 24, 1995, two men in their late twenties—code-named Gil and Ran—left Tel Aviv on separate flights; Ran flew to Athens, Gil to Rome. At each airport they collected new British passports handed over by a local sayan. They arrived in Malta on a late-afternoon flight and checked into the Diplomat Hotel overlooking Valletta's harbor.

That evening a motorcycle was delivered to Ran. He told staff he planned to use it to tour the island.

No one at the hotel would recall the two men having any contact. They spent most of their time in their rooms. When one of the bellboys had remarked that Gil's Samsonite case was heavy, Gil had winked and said it was filled with gold bars.

That evening a freighter that had sailed the previous day from the port of Haifa, bound for Italy, radioed the Maltese harbor authorities reporting it had developed engine trouble and, while it was being fixed, the ship would remain hove to off the island. On board the freighter were Shabtai Shavit and a small team of Mossad communication technicians. They established a radio link with Gil, whose suitcase contained a small but powerful radio.

The suitcase's locks had to be opened counterclockwise to deactivate the fuses in the two charges built into the lid. They were designed to explode in the face of anyone who opened the case after turning the keys clockwise. The radio's rhombic antenna, a quarter of a mile of fiber-optic cable, was tightly coiled to form a disk six inches in diameter.

Splitters connected the disk to four dipoles welded to the inside corner of the Samsonite. During the night Gil received a number of radio messages from the boat.

Fathi Shkaki had arrived earlier that day on the Tripoli-Valletta ferry, accompanied by Libyan security men who had stayed on board, their responsibilities over when Shkaki came ashore alone. Before doing so, he had shaved off his beard. He identified himself to Maltese immigration officers as Ibrahim Dawish, showing them his Libyan passport. After checking into the Diplomat Hotel, he spent the next few hours in seafront cafés, sipping endless cups of coffee and nibbling sweet Arabic cakes. He made several telephone calls.

The next morning Shkaki was returning with the promised shirts for his sons, strolling along the seafront, when two men on a motorcycle slowed beside him. One of them shot the Jihad leader at point-blank range six times in the head. Shkaki died instantly. The motorcyclists disappeared. Neither was ever found. But an hour later a fishing boat sailed out of Valletta harbor and dropped anchor in the lee of the freighter. Shortly afterward the captain informed the harbor authorities that the engine malfunction had been temporarily repaired but the ship was returning to Haifa for further repairs.

In Iran, the spiritual home of Shkaki, the mullahs declared a day of national mourning. In Tel Aviv, asked to comment on the death, Prime Minister Yitzhak Rabin said: "I am certainly not sad."

A few days later, on November 4, 1995, Rabin was assassinated at a Tel Aviv peace rally, close to the safe house where his order to execute Shkaki had been prepared. Rabin had died at the hands of a Jewish fanatic, Yigal Amir, who in many ways had the same ruthless qualities the prime minister had so admired in Mossad.

Yitzhak Rabin, the hawk who had become a dove, the powerful political leader who had come to realize the only chance of peace in the Middle East was, as he once misquoted his favorite book, the Bible, "is to turn our swords into ploughshares and till the soil with our Arab neighbors," was murdered by one of his own people because he failed to accept that his Jewish enemies would behave with the same ferocity as his old Arab foes had done—both groups determined to destroy his vision of the future.

In 1998 there were forty-eight members in the Mossad kidon unit, six of them women. All were in their twenties and superbly fit. They lived and worked outside Mossad headquarters in Tel Aviv, based in a restricted area of a military base in the Negev Desert. The facility could be adapted to approximate a street or a building where an assassination was to take place. There were getaway cars and an obstacle course to negotiate.

The instructors included former unit members who supervised practice with a variety of guns, and taught how to conceal bombs, administer a lethal injection in a crowd, and make a killing appear accidental. Kidons reviewed films on successful assassinations—the shooting of President John F. Kennedy, for example—and studied the faces and habits of scores of potential targets stored on their own highly restricted computer and memorized the constantly changing street plans of major cities as well as air and seaport layouts.

The unit worked in teams of four who regularly flew abroad on familiarization trips to London, Paris, Frankfurt, and other European cities. There were also occasional trips to New York, Los Angeles, and Toronto. During all of these outings a team was always accompanied by instructors who assessed their skills in setting up an operation without drawing attention to themselves. Targets were chosen from local sayanim volunteers who were only told they were taking part in a security exercise designed to protect an Israeli-owned facility; a synagogue or bank was usually given as the reason. Volunteers found themselves pounced upon in a quiet street and bundled into a car, or had their homes entered in the middle of the night and awoke to find themselves peering down a gun barrel.

Kidons took these training exercises very seriously, for every team was aware of what was known as the "Lillehammer Fiasco."

In July 1973, at the height of the manhunt for the killers of the Israeli athletes at the Munich Olympics, Mossad received a tip that the "Red Prince" Ali Hassan Salameh, who had planned the operation, was working in the small Norwegian town of Lillehammer as a waiter.

Mossad's then director of operations, Michael Harari, had put together a team not drawn from the kidon unit; its members were scattered across the world chasing the remaining terrorists who had carried out the Munich killings. Harari's team had no field experience, but he was confident his own background as a *katsa* in Europe was sufficient. His team included two women, Sylvia Rafael and Marianne Gladnikoff, and an Algerian, Kemal Bename, who had been a Black September courier before being browbeaten by Harari into becoming a double agent.

The operation had run into disaster from the outset. The arrival of a dozen strangers in Lillehammer, where there had not been a murder for forty years, aroused speculation. The local police began to watch them. Officers were close by when Harari and his team shot dead a Moroccan waiter named Ahmed Bouchiki, who had no connection to terrorism and did not even physically resemble Salameh. Harari and some of his squad managed to escape. But six Mossad operatives were captured, including both women.

They made full confessions, revealing for the first time Mossad's assassination methods and other equally embarrassing details about the service's clandestine activities. The women, together with their male colleagues, were charged with second-degree murder and received jail sentences of five years each.

Returning to Israel, Harari was fired and the entire Mossad undercover network in Europe of safe houses, dead-letter boxes, and secret phone numbers was abandoned.

It would be six years before Ali Hassan Salameh would finally die in the operation masterminded by Rafi Eitan, who said, "Lillehammer was an example of the wrong people for the wrong job. It should never have happened—and must never happen again."

It did.

On July 31, 1997, the day after two Hamas suicide bombers killed 15 and injured another 157 people in a Jerusalem marketplace, Mossad chief Danny Yatom attended a meeting chaired by Prime Minister Benjamin Netanyahu. The prime minister had just come from an emotional press conference at which he had promised that he would never rest until those who planned the suicide bombings were no longer a threat.

Publicly, Netanyahu had appeared calm and resolute, his responses to questions measured and magisterial; Hamas would not escape retribution, but what form that would take was not a matter for discussion. This was the "Bibi" from Netanyahu's days on CNN during the Iraqi war, when he had earned repeated praise for his authoritative assessments of Saddam Hussein's responses and how they were viewed in Israel.

But on that stifling day, away from the cameras and surrounded only by Yatom and other senior intelligence officers and his own political advisers, Netanyahu offered a very different image. He was neither cool nor analytical. Instead, in the crowded conference room adjoining his office, he frequently interrupted to shout he was going to "get those Hamas bastards if it's the last thing I do."

He added, according to one of those present, that "you are here to tell me how this is going to happen. And I don't want to read in the newspapers anything about 'Bibi's' revenge. This is about justice—just retribution."

The agenda had been set.

Yatom, well used to the mercurial mood swings of the prime minister, sat silently across the table as Netanyahu continued to bluster. "I want their heads. I want them dead. I don't care how it's done. I just want it done. And I want it done sooner rather than later."

Tension deepened when Netanyahu demanded that Yatom provide a list of all Hamas leaders and their present whereabouts. No prime minister had ever before asked for sensitive operational details at such an early stage. More than one person in the room thought that "Bibi was sending a signal he was going to be hands-on for this one."

It deepened the unease among some Mossad officers that the service was being forced to come too close to Netanyahu. Perhaps sensing this, Yatom told the prime minister that he would provide the list later. Instead, the Mossad chief suggested that it was "time to look at the practical side of things." Locating the Hamas leaders would be "like searching for individual rats in a Beirut sewer."

Once more Netanyahu erupted. He didn't want excuses; he wanted action. And he wanted it to start "here and now."

After the meeting ended, several intelligence officers were left with the impression that Bibi Netanyahu had crossed the fine line where political expediency ended and operational requirements took over. There could not have been a man in the room who did not realize that Netanyahu badly needed a public relations coup to convince the public the act-tough-on-terrorism policy that had brought him into office was not just empty rhetoric. He had also gone from one scandal to another, each time barely wriggling clear by leaving others to carry the blame. His popularity was at an all-time low. His personal life was all over the press. He badly needed to show he was in charge. To deliver the head of a Hamas leader was one surefire way.

A senior Israeli intelligence officer undoubtedly spoke for many when he said:

"While we all agreed there could be no objection to the principle that to cut off the head kills the snake, it was the time frame which was our concern. All Bibi's talk about 'action now' was pure bullshit. Any operation of that nature requires careful planning. Bibi wanted results as if this was a computer game, or one of those old action-hero movies he likes to watch. But it just doesn't work like that in the real world."

Yatom ordered a full search of every Arab country and sent *katsas* into Gaza and the West Bank to discover more about the whereabouts of the shadowy figures who control Hamas. Throughout August 1997, he was summoned several times to the prime minister's office to report on his progress. There was none. The Israeli intelligence community was rife with accounts of how the prime minister had demanded that Yatom put more men into the field and had begun to hint that if he didn't see results soon, he might have to take "other actions." If Netanyahu had intended this to be a clumsy threat to his Mossad chief, it did not work. Yatom simply said he was "doing everything possible." The unspoken implication was that if the prime minister wanted to fire him, that was his prerogative; but in the public debate that would inevitably follow, there would be questions asked about Netanyahu's own role. But the prime minister continued to press for the death of a Hamas leader—and he wanted it sooner rather than later.

By September 1997, Netanyahu had begun to call Yatom at all hours of the night about progress. The pressurized Mossad chief bowed. He pulled in *katsas* from other stations. For one, "Yatom was rearranging the map as a knee-jerk to Bibi's demands. Yatom is one tough guy. But when it came to push-and-shove, he was just no match for Bibi, who had started to talk about how quickly his brother had helped to put together the raid on Entebbe. The comparison had no meaning. But that's Bibi all over—use anything that can push his case."

On September 9, news reached Tel Aviv that Hamas had struck again, this time seriously wounding two Israeli bodyguards of the cultural attaché at the newly opened Israeli embassy in Amman, the Jordanian capital.

Three days later, shortly before the Friday Sabbath began, Netanyahu requested that Yatom join him for lunch at his home in Jerusalem. The two men sat down to a meal of soup, salad, and a fish course, washed down with beer and bottled water. The prime minister immediately raised the attack in Amman. How could the Hamas gunmen have come close enough to shoot? Why had there been no advance warning? What was the Mossad station in Amman doing about it?

Yatom interrupted Netanyahu in midflow: There was a Hamas leader in Amman named Khalid Meshal who ran the organization's politburo from an office in the city. For weeks Meshal had been traveling through various Arab countries, but Amman station reported that he was back in the city.

Netanyahu was galvanized. "Then go and knock him down!" he said across the table. "That's what you have to do. Knock him down! Send your people in Amman to do that!"

Stung by almost six weeks of relentless pressure from a prime minister who increasingly appeared to have no grasp of the political sensitivity of any intelligence operation, the Mossad chief delivered a sharp lesson. Eyes glinting behind his spectacles, he warned that to launch an attack in Amman would destroy the relationship with Jordan that Netanyahu's predecessor, Yitzhak Rabin, had created. To actually kill Meshal on Jordanian soil would jeopardize Mossad's operations in a country that had yielded a continuous flow of intelligence about Syria, Iraq, and Palestinian extremists. Yatom suggested it would be better to wait until Meshal once more left Amman and then strike.

"Excuses! That's all you give me! Excuses!" Netanyahu was said to have shouted. "I want action. I want it now. The people want action. It's Rosh Hashanah soon!" he added, in a reference to the Jewish New Year. "This will be my gift to them!"

From that moment on, every move that Yatom made would be personally approved by Netanyahu. No other Israeli prime minister had taken such a close personal interest in a state-sponsored act of murder.

Khalid Meshal was forty-one years old, a full-bearded and physically strong man. He lived close to King Hussein's palace and by all accounts was a devoted husband and father of seven children. Cultured and well-spoken, he had remained a little-known figure in the Islamic fundamentalist movement. But the rapidly assembled data that Mossad's Amman station had put together indicated Meshal was the driving force behind the suicide bomb attacks against Israeli civilians.

Details of Meshal's movements had been furnished, together with a photograph the Mossad head of station had surreptitiously taken. With his report was a personal plea that Yatom should once more try to persuade Netanyahu not to go ahead with an assassination in Amman. Such a reckless action would jeopardize two years of important counterespionage work Mossad had done with Jordan's cooperation.

Netanyahu had rejected the plea, saying it sounded like a prediction of failure, something he would not tolerate.

Meantime, an eight-man kidon squad had been preparing: a two-man team would actually carry out the hit in broad daylight; the others would provide backup, including car support. The team would all drive back into Israel, crossing over at the Allenby Bridge near Jerusalem.

Mossad's weapon of choice was unusual, not a gun, but an aerosol filled with a nerve agent. It would be the first time a kidon hit team had used this method of killing, though it had long been perfected by the KGB and other Soviet Bloc intelligence agencies. Russian scientists recently emigrated to Israel had been recruited by Mossad to create a range of deadly toxins, including tabun, sarin, and soman, nerve agents that were all outlawed under international treaties. The substances were intended to produce death that could be instantaneous or lingering; in all cases the victim lost control over his internal organs and suffered pain so excruciating that death itself would be a merciful release. This form of killing had been selected as appropriate for Meshal.

On September 24, 1997, the kidon unit flew into Amman from Athens, Rome, and Paris, where they had been positioned for several days. Some members traveled on French and Italian documents. The hit men had been given Canadian passports in the names of Barry Beads and Sean Kendall. They told staff when they checked into the city's Intercontinental Hotel they were tourists. The other *katsas* bedded down in the Israeli embassy a short distance away.

Beads and Kendall joined them the next day. The two men once more inspected the aerosol. No one knew which nerve agent it contained. The agents speculated that it could induce anything from hallucinations to heart failure before death. They were briefed on the latest movements of Meshal by the station chief.

He had been in London in September 1978 when a Bulgarian defector, Georgi Markov, had been killed by a nerve agent. A passerby had jabbed him in the thigh with the tip of an umbrella. Markov had died an excruciating death caused by ricin, a deadly poison made from the seeds of the castor-oil plant. The passerby had been a KGB agent who had never been caught.

On that optimistic note, Beads and Kendall returned to their hotel shortly before midnight. Each ordered a room service breakfast of coffee, orange juice, and Danish pastries. Next morning, at 9:00 A.M., Beads appeared in the lobby and signed for the first of two rented cars, a blue Toyota. The second, a green Hyundai, arrived shortly afterward and was claimed by Kendall. He told one of the front-desk staff that he and "his friend" were going to explore the south of the country.

At 10:00 A.M. Meshal was being driven by his chauffeur to work; in the back of the car with him were three of his young children, a boy and two girls. Beads followed at a discreet distance in his rented car. Other team members were out on the road in other cars.

As they entered the city's Garden District, the chauffeur informed Meshal that they were being followed. Meshal used the car phone to call in the make and number of Beads's car to Amman police headquarters.

As the rented Toyota drove past, Meshal's children waved at Beads, as they had done to other motorists. The Mossad agent ignored them. Next Kendall's green Hyundai pulled ahead of the chauffeur and both cars disappeared into the traffic.

Moments later an officer at Amman police headquarters called Meshal to say the car was rented to a Canadian tourist. Meshal relaxed and watched his children once more waving at passing motorists, their faces pressed close to the windows. Every morning they took turns riding with their father to work before the chauffeur dropped them off at school.

Shortly before 10:30 A.M. the chauffeur pulled into Wasfi Al-Tal Street, where a crowd had gathered outside the Hamas office, with Kendall and Beads among them. Their presence caused no alarm; curious tourists often came to the office to learn more about Hamas's aspirations.

Meshal quickly kissed his children before leaving the car. Beads stepped forward as if to shake him by the hand. Kendall was at his shoulder, fumbling with a plastic bag.

"Mr. Meshal?" asked Beads pleasantly.

Meshal looked at him uncertainly. At that moment Kendall produced the aerosol and tried to spray its contents into Meshal's left ear.

The Hamas leader recoiled, startled, wiping his lobe.

Kendall made another attempt to spray the substance into Meshal's ear. Around him the crowd was beginning to recover from their surprise, and hands reached out to grab the agents.

"Run!" said Beads in Hebrew.

Followed by Kendall, Beads sprinted to his car, parked a little way up the street. Meshal's chauffeur had seen what was happening and began to reverse back down the street, trying to ram the Toyota.

Meshal was staggering around, moaning. People were trying to support him from falling. Others were shouting for an ambulance.

Beads, with Kendall sprawled beside him and still clutching his half-used aerosol, managed to avoid the chauffeur's car and was accelerating up the street.

Other cars were in pursuit. One of the drivers had a cell phone and was calling for roads in the area to be blocked. The chauffeur was using his car phone to contact police headquarters.

By now backup members of the kidon team had arrived. One of them stopped and waved for Beads to transfer to his car. As the two Mossad men jumped out of the Toyota, another vehicle blocked their path. From it emerged a number of armed men. They forced Beads and Kendall to lie on the ground. Moments later the police arrived. Realizing there was nothing they could now do, the remaining members of the kidon team drove away, eventually making their way undetected back to Israel.

Beads and Kendall were less fortunate. They were taken to Amman central police quarters, where they produced their Canadian passports and insisted they were victims of some "horrendous plot." The arrival of Samih Batihi, the formidable chief of Jordanian counterintelligence, ended the pretense. He told them he knew who they were; he had just gotten off the phone with the Mossad station chief. Later, according to Batihi, the spymaster had "made a clean breast. He said they were his people and Israel would deal directly with the king."

Batihi ordered that the two Mossad agents be locked in separate cells but that they not be harmed in any way.

Meantime, Meshal had been admitted to the intensive care unit at Amman's main hospital. He complained of a persistent "ringing" in his left ear, a "shivery feeling like a shock running through my body," and increasing difficulty with breathing.

The doctors put him on a life-support system.

News of the operation's failure reached Yatom in a secure telephone call from the station chief in the Israeli embassy in Amman. Both men were said to be "beyond rage" at the debacle.

By the time Yatom reached Netanyahu's office, the prime minister had received a telephone call from King Hussein on the hot line installed between the two leaders to deal with a crisis. The flavor of the call came later from an Israeli intelligence officer:

"Hussein had two questions for Bibi. What the fuck did he think he had been playing at? Did he have an antidote for the nerve gas?"

The king said he felt like a man whose best friend had raped his daughter and that if Netanyahu was thinking of denying everything, he had better understand his two agents had made a full confession on video, which was now on its way to Washington for Madeleine Albright, the U.S. secretary of state, to review. Netanyahu sat there hunched over his phone, "as white as anyone caught with his hand in the till."

Netanyahu offered to fly at once to Amman to "explain matters" to the king. Hussein told him not to waste his time. The intelligence officer recalled:

"You could hear the ice crackling on the line from Jordan. Bibi didn't even protest when Hussein told him that he now expected Israel to release Sheikh Ahmed Yassin [the Hamas leader Israel had held in prison for some time], as well as a number of other Palestinian prisoners. The call lasted only a few minutes. It must have been the worst moment in Bibi's political life."

Events now took on their own momentum. Within an hour, an antidote to the nerve gas had been flown to Amman by an Israeli military plane and administered to Meshal. He began to recover and, within a few days, was well enough to stage a press conference in which he ridiculed Mossad. The Amman station chief and Samih Batihi had a short meeting during which they also spoke to Yatom on the phone. The director general fervently promised there would never be another assassination attempt carried out by Mossad on Jordanian soil. Next day Madeleine Albright made two short calls to Netanyahu; she made it clear what she thought of what had happened, her language at times as salty as King Hussein's.

Learning how its passports had been compromised, Canada recalled its ambassador to Israel—a move that fell just short of breaking off diplomatic relations.

When details began to emerge, Netanyahu received a roasting in the Israeli and international press that would have driven other men to resign.

Within a week, Sheikh Yassin was released and returned to a hero's welcome in Gaza. By then Kendall and Beads were back in Israel, minus their Canadian passports. These had been handed over to the Canadian embassy in Amman for "safekeeping."

The two *katsas* never returned to the kidon unit; they were assigned to nonspecific desk duties at Mossad headquarters. As an Israeli intelligence officer said: "That could mean they would be in charge of security in the building's toilets."

But Yatom had become a lame-duck chief. His senior staff felt he had failed to stand up to Netanyahu. Morale within Mossad slumped to a new low. The prime minister's office leaked the view that it "is only a matter of time before Yatom goes."

Yatom tried to stem what one Mossad senior officer likened to "the tidal wave of dejection in which we are drowning." Yatom adopted what he called "his Prussian pose." He tried to browbeat his staff. There were angry confrontations and threats to resign.

In February 1998, it was Yatom himself who resigned in an attempt to head off what he acknowledged was "a near mutiny." Prime Minister Netanyahu did not send his fallen intelligence chief the customary letter of thanks for services rendered.

Yatom left office with the first ripples of a sensation beginning to emerge over the murder of Prime Minister Yitzhak Rabin. A dedicated Israeli investigative reporter, Barry Chamish, had privately gathered medical and ballistics reports and eyewitness accounts from Rabin's bodyguards, his widow, surgeons, and nurses, together with members of the Israeli intelligence community he had spoken to. Much of it was evidence given in closed court.

By 1999 Chamish, at risk to himself, had begun to publish his findings over the Internet. They are an eerie replay of the doubts raised about a lone gunman in the John Kennedy assassination in 1963. Chamish's closely argued conclusions are, if nothing else, intriguing. He has concluded, "The gunman theory, accepted by the Israeli Government's Shamgar Commission into the Rabin assassination, is a cover-up in what was to be a staged, unsuccessful assassination to rekindle Rabin's flagging popularity with the electorate. Yigal Amir had agreed to perform the lone gunman function for his controller or controllers in the Israeli intelligence community.

"Amir fired a blank bullet. And he fired just one shot, not the alleged three. Israeli police lab ballistic tests on a shell casing found at the scene do not match Amir's gun. No blood was seen coming from Rabin. Then there is the mystery of how Rabin's car got lost for eight to twelve minutes on what should have been a forty-five-second drive to hospital on clear streets cordoned off by police for the peace rally Rabin had been attending."

Chamish's most explosive allegation—like all the others he has made, this one has yet to be refuted by any Israeli official in authority—claims: "During that strange drive to hospital by a very experienced chauffeur, Rabin was shot twice by real bullets and they came from the handgun of his own bodyguard Yoram Rubin. His gun disappeared at the hospital and has never been found. Two bullets retrieved from the prime minister's body went missing for eleven hours. Rubin later committed suicide."

Chamish spoke to the three operating room surgeons who fought to save the prime minister's life. The reporter discussed the testimony of police officers who had been present when Amir fired. The officers had all testified that when Yitzhak Rabin was placed in the car, he showed no visible wounds. The surgeons were adamant. When the prime minister finally reached the hospital, he showed clear signs of having sustained a massive chest wound and severe damage to his spinal cord in the lower neck area. The surgeons insisted there was no possible gunshot wound that would have allowed Rabin to leave the attack site showing no evidence of a wound and arrive at the hospital with multiple injuries.

The Shamgar Commission concluded it had found no evidence to confirm those wounds had occurred. Subsequently the doctors have refused to discuss the matter.

Outside Chamish's own investigation, there is independent sworn testimony to support his contention that "what happened is deep and is conspiratorial."

At his arraignment hearing, Amir had told the court: "If I tell the truth, the whole system will collapse. I know enough to destroy this country."

A Shin Bet agent who was close to Amir when he fired at Rabin testified: "I heard a policeman shout to people to calm down. The shot is a blank." His evidence was given in closed court.

Leah Rabin stated at the same hearing that her husband did not stagger and fall after apparently being shot at close range. "He was standing and looking very well." She also insisted she was kept from seeing her husband for a full hour after she had arrived at the hospital and, according to Chamish, was told by a high-ranking intelligence officer that she should "not worry as the whole thing had been staged."

The prime minister's widow has steadfastly refused to make any public comment on this or any aspect of her husband's murder.

Chamish believes she had been scared into silence like seventeen nurses at the hospital where Rabin was admitted on that day. "The plan was evil and brilliant. They persuaded Rabin to let someone take a pot shot at him to help him regain his popularity. That was why he did not wear a bulletproof vest. Amir was carefully selected for his proverbial fifteen minutes of fame. He was a dupe in the hands of his controller or controllers. What he couldn't possibly know was how they would use his blank shot to murder Rabin in his car on the way to hospital."

Barry Chamish does not fit the image of a "conspiracy nut." He is careful in what he writes and overwhelms every piece of evidence with corroborative testimony. He has been slow to rush to judgment and gives the impression there is a great deal more he can say but won't—yet. More certain, Chamish is a man who walks his own path, is beholden to no one and, most important of all, is trusted.

He has posted all the evidence he has so far obtained on the Internet, doing so partly as insurance and partly because he wants to get the truth out. He is also realistic enough to accept it may never surface in a form suitable for a court of law.

CHAPTER 7

THE GENTLEMAN SPY

On a damp spring morning in 1997, David Kimche instructed Arab landscapers how he wanted his garden rearranged in a Tel Aviv suburb. His manner was diffident, the mellifluous voice more suited to a college campus than dealing with manual workers, suggesting Kimche was descended from generations of administrators who had once raised Britain's Union Jack over far-flung lands. The English-born son of middle-class Jews, Kimche's impeccable manners deepened the image of the quintessential Englishman. Expensively tailored clothes emphasized a figure kept trim with regular workouts and a strict diet. Kimche looked twenty years younger than his close to sixty years and there was a boyish quality about him. His every gesture while briefing the gardeners—the flicking away of hair from his forehead, the lengthy pauses, the thoughtful stare—suggested a lifetime spent cloistered on a college campus.

In reality, David Kimche had been what Meir Amit called "one of the intellectual powerhouses" behind many Mossad operations. His reasoning skills had been accompanied by breathtaking nerve, catching even the wariest with some totally unexpected move that had quickly earned the respect of even cynical colleagues. But his very intellectualism had often made them keep their distance; he was too remote and abstract for their earthy ways. Several felt like Rafi Eitan, "that if you said 'good morning' to David, his mind would already be deciding how 'good' it was and how much of the morning was left."

Within Mossad, Kimche was widely regarded as the epitome of the gentleman spy with the cunning of an alley cat. His journey into the Mossad fold began after he left Oxford University with a First in Social Science in 1968. A few months later he was recruited by Mossad, then newly under the command of Meir Amit, who was seeking to introduce into its ranks a sprinkling of university graduates to complement the ruthlessness of men like Rafi Eitan who had learned their skills in the field.

How, where, and by whom Kimche was recruited was something he would forever keep under lock and key. The rumor mills of the Israeli intelligence community offered several scenarios: that he had signed on over a good dinner with a London publisher, a Jew who had long been a sayan; that the proposition came in a rabbi's office in a Golders Green synagogue; that a distant relative had made the first move.

The only certainty is that one spring morning in the early sixties, Kimche walked into Mossad's headquarters building in Tel Aviv, the newest member of the Planning and Strategy Department. To one side was a branch of the Bank of Israel, several business offices, and a café. Uncertain what to do or where to go, Kimche waited in the cavernous lobby. How different it was from the imposing entrance of the CIA he had read about. At Langley the agency proudly proclaimed its existence in marble on the floor with an inlaid sixteen-pointed star on a shield dominated by the head of a bald eagle in profile, accompanied by the words "Central Intelligence Agency of the United States of America." Set in a wall were the words of the apostle John about people being set free by the truth. Beyond the plaque were banks of elevators, guarded by armed guards.

But here, in the somewhat shabby lobby of the building on King Saul Boulevard, were only bank tellers at their stations and people seated on the café's plastic chairs. Not one of them looked remotely likely to be a Mossad employee. In the far corner of the lobby an unmarked door opened and a familiar figure emerged, a consular officer at the Israeli embassy in London who had supplied Kimche's travel documents. Leading Kimche back to the door, he explained that his own diplomatic status protected his real work as a Mossad *katsa* in Britain. At the door he handed Kimche two keys and said that from now on they would be his only means to enter Mossad headquarters. One key opened the door, the second the elevators that rose through Mossad's eight floors. The headquarters was "a building within a building" with its own utilities—power, water, sanitation—separate from the rest of the tower block.

It had become Mossad's headquarters shortly after the end of the Suez War in 1956.

That year, in October, British, French, and Israeli forces had launched a joint invasion of Egypt to recapture the Suez Canal, which Egyptian president Gamal Nasser had nationalized. The invasion had the hallmark of the "gunboat diplomacy" that for so long had dominated the region. The United States had almost no prior warning of an invasion that had turned out to be the last gasp of both British and French domination of the Middle East. Washington had exerted massive diplomatic pressure to stop the fighting, fearing that it would draw the Soviet Union into the conflict on the side of Egypt, creating a superpower confrontation. When the fighting ended on the banks of the Suez Canal, Britain and France found they had been replaced by the United States as the dominating foreign power in the Middle East. But Israel insisted on retaining the land it had captured in the Sinai Desert. Richard Helms, a future director of the CIA, flew to Tel Aviv and was received by senior staff in Mossad's headquarters. They struck Helms "like a bunch of Realtors, proudly pointing out the amenities."

Riding up in the elevator, Kimche's guide explained that the lower floor housed the listening and communications center; on the next floor came the offices of junior staff. Upper floors were given over to analysts, planners, and operations personnel. Research and Development had a floor to itself. On the top floor were the offices of the director general and his senior aides.

Kimche was given space among the planners and strategists. His office was equipped like all the others: a cheap wooden desk, a steel filing cabinet with only one key, a black telephone, and an internal directory stamped "Do Not Remove." A strip of carpet completed the furnishings. The office was painted olive green and offered a fine panoramic view over the city. Thirteen years on, the headquarters showed signs of wear and tear; paint had cracked on some walls and carpeting needed replacing.

But, despite these failings, David Kimche sensed he had arrived at an eventful time. Meir Amit was about to leave, shortly to be followed by Rafi Eitan and other senior Mossad officers.

Kimche soon came to recognize the quirks of colleagues: the analyst who invariably prefaced a judgment with the words "this is a European maneuver, classic as Clausewitz in its way"; the head of department who signaled an action by stuffing black flakes of tobacco into the bowl of his pipe, and when the smoke came out white, he had made a decision; the strategist who always ended a briefing by saying espionage was a continuous education in human frailty. These were all men who had paid their dues and they welcomed Kimche's enthusiasm and his ability to turn a problem on its head. They also sensed he fully understood that solving an enemy's deceptions was as important as perpetuating Mossad's own.

Part of his work included monitoring events in Morocco; there were still a substantial number of Jews living there under the repressive regime of King Hassan. In an attempt to make their lives easier, Meir Amit had established a "working relationship" with the monarch's feared security service, finding common cause in trying to remove Egypt's President Nasser, whose own hatred of Israel was only equaled by what he felt for the king. Nasser saw the monarch as a stumbling block to his dream of establishing a powerful Arab coalition stretching from the Suez Canal to the Atlantic coast of Morocco. The potential threat to Israel of such a coalition had persuaded Meir Amit to train the king's men in counterintelligence and interrogation techniques that stopped little short of sophisticated torture.

Within Morocco, a small but equally ruthless opposition survived, led by Mehdi Ben-Barka. Kimche had charted Ben-Barka's career: the king's loyal tutor; onetime president of Morocco's national consultative assembly, a virtually toothless parliament that merely rubber-stamped Hassan's increasingly oppressive decrees against his people. Finally

Ben-Barka had become the one authentic voice of opposition to Hassan. Time and again Ben-Barka had barely escaped being captured by the king's men. But knowing it was only a matter of time before he was arrested, the charismatic former schoolteacher had fled to Europe. From there he continued to plot the downfall of Hassan.

Twice Ben-Barka's small but efficient resistance movement in Morocco had come close to launching successful bomb plots against the monarch. The enraged Hassan ordered Ben-Barka tried in absentia and sentenced to death, and Ben-Barka responded by ordering fresh attacks against the king.

In May 1965, Hassan asked Mossad to help deal with Ben-Barka. The task of evaluating the request was given to David Kimche. Later that month he traveled on his British passport to London. Ostensibly he was on vacation. In reality he was finalizing his plans. Equipped with a perfectly doctored second British passport provided by a sayan, and with a Moroccan visa, Kimche flew to Rome; he spent a day there sightseeing—a move to make sure he was not being followed—and then traveled on to Morocco.

He was met at Rabat Airport by Muhammed Oufkir, the country's fearsome minister of the interior. That night, over a dinner enlivened by the presence of some of the country's best belly dancers, Oufkir spelled out what the king wanted: Ben-Barka's head. Displaying both a crude sense of humor and an appreciation of Jewish history, Oufkir had added: "After all, your Jewish Salome asked your King Herod for the head of a troublemaker."

Kimche said that while that was indeed correct, it really was not a matter for him. Oufkir would have to come back with him to Israel.

Next day the two men flew to Rome and caught a flight to Tel Aviv. Meir Amit met them in a safe house. He was polite but cautious. He told Kimche he was "not very excited" at the prospect of doing Oufkir's dirty work and insisted our "involvement would be confined to preparatory work."

Unknown to Meir Amit, Oufkir had already made an arrangement with a faction within France's intelligence service, SDECE (predecessor of the DGSE), to murder Ben-Barka if he could be lured out of his fortresslike home in Geneva and across the Swiss border into France. Still reluctant, Meir Amit had insisted that Prime Minister Levi Eshkol must personally sanction Mossad's involvement. The prime minister gave it.

Mossad set to work. A Moroccan-born *katsa* traveled to Geneva and infiltrated Ben-Barka's circle. Over several months, the agent carefully planted the idea that he had access to a sympathetic French millionaire who would like to see King Hassan assassinated and genuine democracy come to Morocco. Kimche had created this fiction. On October 26, 1965, he learned that Ben-Barka, "like the Scarlet Pimpernel of old," was about to travel to Paris.

Mossad's communications center sent a coded message to Oufkir in Morocco. The following day the minister and a small team of Moroccan security men flew to Paris. That night the minister was briefed by the SDECE faction. Concerned he had been excluded from the meeting, the Mossad agent who had accompanied Ben-Barka to the French capital called Kimche on a secure line for instructions. Kimche consulted Meir Amit. Both agreed, in Amit's later words, "that something nasty was cooking and we should stay well clear."

Next evening an SDECE surveillance van was positioned outside when Ben-Barka arrived for dinner at a restaurant in the St. Germain district. He believed he had come to meet the millionaire. After he waited an hour and still no one had showed, Ben-Barka left the restaurant. As he stepped onto the sidewalk, he was grabbed by two SDECE agents and bundled into the van. It was driven to a villa in the Fontenay-le-Vicomte district that the SDECE used from time to time to interrogate its own suspects. Throughout the night, Oufkir supervised Ben-Barka's questioning and torture until, at dawn, the broken man was executed. Oufkir photographed the body before it was buried in the villa's garden. The minister flew home with the film to show the king.

When the corpse was discovered, the outcry in France reached all the way to the president's palace. Charles de Gaulle ordered an unprecedented investigation that led to a massive purging of the SDECE. Its director, anxious to maintain interservice collegiality, struggled to keep Mossad's name out of the affair. But de Gaulle, no friend of Israel, was convinced that Mossad was involved. He told aides that the operation bore the "hallmark of Tel Aviv." Only the Israelis, he had fumed, would show such total disregard for international law. A once-close relationship between Israel and France, established in the 1956 Suez War, was over. De Gaulle promptly ordered that arms supplies to Israel should stop, along with all intelligence cooperation. Meir Amit would "remember the body blows from Paris raining down."

For Kimche, "It was heroic to see the way Meir Amit handled the situation. He could have tried to blame me or the others involved in the operation. Instead he insisted on taking full responsibility. He was a true leader."

Prime Minister Eshkol's government, battered by the reaction from Paris, distanced itself from Mossad's chief. More criticism came from an unexpected source. The more Meir Amit protested that Mossad's role had been "marginal," no more than "supplying a few passports and hiring some cars," the more his predecessor, Isser Harel, insisted the Ben-Barka affair would never have happened in his day. Meir Amit warned the prime minister they would both sink under such sniping. Eshkol responded by setting up a committee of inquiry, headed by the then foreign minister, Golda Meir. The committee concluded Meir Amit should resign, but he refused until Eshkol did the same. Stalemate followed. It was not until a year later that Meir Amit accepted that the death of Ben-Barka was no longer going to trouble him. But it had been a close call.

By then Kimche had other matters to concern him. The Palestinians had secretly trained a commando unit to exploit a security weakness not even Mossad had anticipated: midair aircraft hijacking. Once a plane was seized between destinations, it would be flown to a friendly Arab country. There the passengers would be held for ransom—either for substantial sums of money to buy their freedom, or to be exchanged for Arab prisoners held by Israel. An additional bonus would be the worldwide publicity for the PLO cause.

In July 1968, an El Al flight from Rome was hijacked to Algeria. Mossad was stunned at the simple audacity of the operation. A team of *katsas* flew to Algeria while Kimche and other planners worked almost around the clock to devise a strategy to free the terrified passengers. But any attempt to storm the aircraft was hampered by the presence of the world's media crews covering the story. Kimche recommended playing for time in the hope the story would lose its momentum and the *katsas* could move. But the hijackers had anticipated that and began to issue bloodcurdling threats unless their demands were met: the freeing of Palestinian prisoners in Israeli jails. The Algerian government supported the hijackers. Kimche realized: "We were between the proverbial rock and a hard place." He was one of those who reluctantly recommended the prisoners should be exchanged for passengers, knowing "full well the consequences of such action. It would pave the way for further hijackings. It would ensure the PLO cause would receive from now on maximum coverage. Israel had been put on the defensive. So had Western governments who also had no answer to hijackings. Yet what could we do except to wait grimly for the next hijacking?"

And come they did, each one better prepared than the last. In a short time half a dozen more passenger aircraft were overpowered by hijackers who were not only expert in concealing weapons and placing explosives on board, but had been trained to fly the actual aircraft or know the actual workings of a flight deck crew. In the Libyan Desert, they practiced exchanging fire in the confined area of an airplane cabin, knowing that El Al had now introduced armed guards on its flights— one of the first moves Kimche had recommended. He had also correctly predicted that the hijackers would know the laws of the various countries they would be flying in and out of so that if they were captured, their colleagues could use those laws to obtain their freedom by bargaining or threatening.

Kimche knew that Mossad urgently needed an incident that would enable the service to overcome the hijackers through the two skills for which it was justifiably renowned: cunning and ruthlessness. And, just as the hijackers effectively used publicity, Kimche wanted an operation whose outcome would match the universal praise for Israel that had followed the kidnapping of Adolf Eichmann. The incident Kimche needed must have high drama, considerable risk, and an against-all-the-odds outcome. Those elements would combine to show Mossad leading the fight back.

On June 27, 1976, an Air France plane filled with Jewish passengers, en route to Paris from Tel Aviv, was hijacked after a stopover at Athens Airport, which was notorious for lax security. The hijackers were members of the extreme Wadi Haddad faction and they made two demands: the freeing of forty Palestinians in Israeli jails, together with a further dozen held in European prisons; and the release of two German terrorists arrested in Kenya when they tried to shoot down an El Al jet with a SAM-7 rocket as it took off from Nairobi Airport.

After a stopover in Casablanca, and being refused permission to land in Khartoum, the plane flew to Entebbe in Uganda. From there the hijackers announced the aircraft would be blown up along with all its passengers unless their demands were met. The deadline was June 30.

In Tel Aviv, in closed cabinet sessions, the vaunted public image of "no surrender" to terrorism wilted. Ministers favored freeing Israel's

PLO prisoners. Prime Minister Rabin produced a Shin Bet report to show there was a precedent for releasing convicted criminals. Chief of Staff Mordechai Gur announced he could not recommend military action due to insufficient intelligence from Entebbe. While their anguished deliberations continued, news came from Entebbe that the Jewish passengers had been separated from the others on board—those passengers had been released and were on their way to Paris.

That was the opening Mossad needed. Yitzhak Hofi, Mossad's chief, in what was to be his finest hour, argued powerfully and passionately for a rescue to be mounted. He dusted off the plan Rafi Eitan had used to capture Eichmann. There were similarities: Rafi Eitan and his men had worked far from home in a hostile environment. They had improvised as they went along using bluff—the renowned Jewish chutzpah. It could be done again. Soaked in sweat, his voice hoarse from pleading and arguing, Hofi had stared around the cabinet room.

"If we let our people die, it will open the floodgates. No Jew will be safe anywhere. Hitler would have won a victory from the grave!"

"Very well," Rabin had finally said. "We try."

As well as Kimche, every other strategist and planner in Mossad was mobilized. The first step was to open a safe communication channel between Tel Aviv and Nairobi; Hofi had nursed the unpublicized intelligence link between Mossad and its Kenyan counterpart introduced by Meir Amit. The link started to bear immediate results. Half a dozen *katsas* descended on Nairobi and were installed in a Kenyan intelligence service safe house. They would form the bridgehead for the main assault. Meantime Kimche had overcome another problem. Any rescue mission would require a fuel stop at Nairobi. Working the phone, he obtained Kenya's approval in a matter of hours, granted "on humanitarian grounds."

But there was still the formidable problem of reaching Entebbe. The PLO had established the airport as their own entry point to Uganda, from where the Organization ran its own operation against the pro-Israeli white supremacist regime in South Africa. Idi Amin, Uganda's despotic dictator, had actually given the PLO the residence of the Israeli ambassador as a headquarters after breaking off diplomatic relations with Jerusalem in 1972.

Kimche knew it was essential to know if the PLO was still in the country. Their battle-hardened guerrillas would be a formidable force to overcome in the short time allowed for the actual rescue mission:

the Israeli forces could only be on the ground for minutes, otherwise they ran the risk of a powerful counterattack. Kimche sent two *katsas* from Nairobi by boat across Lake Victoria. They landed near Entebbe and found the PLO headquarters deserted; the Palestinians had recently moved on to Angola.

Then, with the stroke of luck any operation needs, one of the Kenyan security officers who had accompanied the *katsas* discovered that one of his wife's relatives was actually one of the men guarding the hostages. The Kenyan inveigled himself into the airport and was able to see that the hostages were all alive, but he counted fifteen very tense and nervous guards. The information was radioed to Tel Aviv.

Meanwhile, two other *katsas*, both qualified pilots, hired a Cessna and flew from Nairobi, ostensibly to photograph Lake Victoria for a holiday brochure. Their aircraft passed directly over Entebbe Airport, enabling one *katsa* to obtain good photographs of the runway and adjoining buildings. The film was flown to Tel Aviv. There, Kimche recommended yet another strategy to confuse the hijackers.

During several telephone conversations with Amin's palace, Israeli negotiators in Tel Aviv made it clear their government was ready to accept the hijackers' terms. A diplomat in a European consulate in Uganda was used to add credibility to this apparent surrender by being called "in confidence" to see if he could negotiate suitable wording the hijackers would accept. Kimche told the envoy, "It must be something not too demeaning to Israel but also not too impossible for the hijackers to accept." The diplomat hurried to the airport with the news and began to draft suitable words. He was still doing so as Operation Thunderball moved to the final stages.

An unmarked Israeli Boeing 707 to be used as a flying hospital landed at Nairobi Airport, flown by IDF pilots who knew Entebbe Airport. Meantime six Mossad *katsas* had surrounded that airport; each man carried a high-frequency radio and an electronic device that would jam the radar in the control tower. It had never before been tried under combat conditions.

Fifty Israeli paratroopers, under cover of darkness, left the hospital plane and went full speed to Lake Victoria. Inflating their rubber boats, they rowed across the water to wait close to the Ugandan shore, ready to storm into Entebbe Airport. In Tel Aviv, the rescue mission had been rehearsed to perfection; when the time came, a force of C-130 Hercules transporters crossed the Red Sea, headed south, refueled at Nairobi, and then, flying just above the African treetops, swept down on Entebbe Airport.

The radar jammer worked perfectly. The airport authorities were still trying to work out what had happened when the three Hercules transporters and the hospital plane landed. Commandos raced into the building where the hostages were held. By then they were only Jews. All other nationalities had been freed by Amin, enjoying his moment of strutting the world stage. The paratroopers waiting in support were never called into action. They rowed back across the lake and returned to Nairobi. There they would be picked up by another Israeli transporter and flown home.

Within five minutes—two full minutes less than the time allowed—the hostages were free and all the terrorists were killed, along with sixteen Ugandan soldiers guarding the prisoners. The attack force lost one officer, Lieutenant Colonel Yonatan Netanyahu, the elder brother of the future prime minister, Benjamin Netanyahu. He would say that his own hard line against all terrorists came as a result of the death of Yonatan. Three hostages also died.

David Kimche's wish for a headline-making riposte to hijackers had been more than met. The rescue at Entebbe was an episode that, even more than the capture of Adolf Eichmann, came to be seen as Mossad's calling card.

Increasingly, Kimche found himself ever more immersed in Mossad's efforts against the PLO. This deadly struggle was fought beyond the borders of Israel, on the streets of European cities. Kimche was one of the strategists who prepared the ground for Mossad's own assassins, the kidons. They struck in Paris, Munich, Cyprus, and Athens. For Kimche, the killings were remote; he was like the bomber pilot who does not see where the bombs fall. The deaths helped to foster within Mossad a continuing mood of invincibility: the superior information coming from its strategists meant the kidons were always one step ahead of the enemy.

One morning Kimche arrived at work to find his colleagues in a state of near shock. One of their most experienced *katsas* had been assassinated in Madrid by a PLO gunman. The assassin had been a contact the *katsa* was developing in an effort to penetrate the group.

But there was no time to mourn. Every available hand was turned to the task of fighting fire with fire. For Kimche it was a time when "we did not expect to be shown any mercy and showed none in return."

The relentless pressure continued to find new ways to get close to the PLO leadership and discover enough about its inner workings to assassinate its leaders. For Kimche, "cutting off the head was the only way to stop the tail wagging." Yasser Arafat was the first head on the kidon target list.

Another and more serious threat had begun to focus Kimche's mind: the possibility of a second full-scale Arab war, led by Egypt, against Israel. But Mossad was a lone voice within the Israeli intelligence community. Kimche's concerns, echoed by his superiors, were flatly rejected by Aman, military intelligence. Its strategists pointed out that Egypt had just expelled its twenty thousand Soviet military advisers, which should be interpreted as a clear-cut indication that Egypt's president, Anwar Sadat, was looking for a political solution in the Middle East.

Kimche remained unconvinced. From all the information crossing his desk, he grew more certain that Sadat would launch a preemptive strike—simply because Arab demands would be impossible for Israel to accept: Egypt wanted back conquered land and the creation of a Palestinian homeland within Israel. Kimche believed that even if these concessions were granted, the PLO would still continue its murderous campaign to drive Israel to its knees.

Kimche's alarm grew when Sadat replaced his war minister with a more hawkish figure whose first act was to reinforce Egypt's defenses along the Suez Canal. Egyptian commanders were also making regular visits to other Arab capitals to enlist support. Sadat had signed a new arms-purchasing deal with Moscow.

To Kimche the signs were all too ominous: "It was not a question of when war would come, only the day it would start."

But the intelligence chiefs of Aman continued to downplay the warnings coming from Mossad. They told the IDF commanders that, even if war looked like starting, there would be "at least a five-day warning period," more than enough time for Israel's air force to repeat its great success in the Six-Day War.

Kimche countered that most certainly the Arabs would have learned from past mistakes. He found himself branded a member of "a war-obsessed Mossad," an accusation that did not sit well with a man so careful of his every word. All he could do was to continue to assess the Egyptian preparations and try to judge a likely date for an attack.

The broiling heat of that 1973 August in Tel Aviv gave way to a cooler September. The latest reports from Mossad *katsas* on the Sinai side of the Suez Canal showed that Egyptian preparations had gathered momentum. Army engineers were putting the final touches to pontoons for troops and armor to cross the waterway. When Mossad persuaded the Israeli foreign minister to raise the definitely worrying preparations at the United Nations, the Egyptian representative said soothingly, "These activities are routine." To Kimche the words had "the same kind of credibility" as those uttered by the Japanese ambassador in Washington on the eve of the attack on Pearl Harbor.

Yet the Egyptian explanation was accepted by Aman. All the more incredible to Kimche was that by October, wherever his probing eyes settled, there were yet more signs of brewing trouble; Libya had just nationalized Western oil companies; in the oil-producing Gulf states there was talk of cutting off all supplies to the West.

Yet the strategists in Aman continued to lamentably misread the intelligence picture. When Israeli air force jets were attacked by MiGs over Syria—resulting in victory for the IDF due to their pilots' tactical knowledge learned from the MiG stolen from Iraq—the downing of twelve Syrian aircraft was seen by Aman only as further evidence that, if the Arabs ever did go to war, they would be beaten just as soundly.

On the night of October 5–6, Mossad received the most stark evidence yet that hostilities were imminent, perhaps only hours away. Its *katsas* and informers in Egypt were reporting that the Egyptian Military High Command had gone to red alert. The evidence could no longer be ignored.

At 6:00 A.M. Mossad's chief, Zvi Zamir, joined Aman intelligence chiefs in the defense ministry. The building was almost deserted: it was Yom Kippur, the holiest of all Jewish holidays, the day even nonpracticing Jews rested, when all public services, including the state radio, shut down. The radio had always been the means used to mobilize reserves in the event of a national emergency.

Finally driven to action by the incontrovertible evidence Mossad presented, alarm bells began to sound all over Israel that a two-pronged attack—from Syria in the north and Egypt in the south—was about to engulf Israel.

War began at 1:55 P.M. local time while the Israeli cabinet was in emergency session—assured by Aman's strategists that hostilities would still only start at 6:00 P.M. The time turned out to have been pure guesswork.

Never in the history of the Israeli intelligence community had there been such an inglorious failure to predict an event. The mass of impeccable evidence that David Kimche and others had provided had been totally ignored.

After the war ended, with Israel once more snatching victory from the jaws of defeat, there was a massive purging of Aman's upper echelons. Mossad once more ruled supreme over the intelligence community, though there was a key change there too: Zamir was removed as director general on the grounds he had not been sufficiently assertive against his Aman counterpart. His place was taken by Yitzhak Hofi.

Kimche viewed his arrival with mixed feelings. In some ways Hofi was from a similar mold to Meir Amit: the same erect bearing, the same proven battlefield experience, the same incisive manner and total inability to suffer fools at any price. But Hofi was also blunt to the point of rudeness, and the tension between him and Kimche dated from the days they had instructed recruits, between their other duties, at the Mossad training school. Hofi, with his no-nonsense kibbutz mentality, had shown no patience with Kimche's languid intellectualism and his refined English accent when addressing students. But Kimche was not only now a seasoned operative but Hofi's deputy. He had been promoted to deputy director general shortly before Zamir left. Both Hofi and Kimche accepted they must put aside their personal differences to ensure Mossad continued operating with maximum efficiency.

Kimche was given one of the most difficult tasks in Mossad: he was put in charge of the service's "Lebanese account." The country's civil war had begun two years after the Yom Kippur War, and by the time Kimche took charge of "the account," the Lebanese Christians were fighting a losing battle. Just as years before Salman had gone to the Israeli embassy in Paris to initiate the first steps in stealing the Iraqi MiG, so in September 1975 an emissary from the Christians had gone there asking Israel to supply arms to stop them being annihilated. The request ended up on Kimche's desk. He saw an opportunity for Mossad to work its way into "the Lebanese woodwork."

He told Hofi that politically it made sense to "partly support" the Christians against the Muslims who were vowed to destroy Israel. Once more his interpretation was accepted. Israel would give the Christians sufficient arms to deal with the Muslims, but not enough to pose a threat to Israel. Mossad began to ship arms out of Israel into Lebanon. Next Kimche placed Mossad officers within the Christian command. They were ostensibly there to help maximize the use of the weapons. In reality the officers provided Kimche with a continuous flow of intelligence that enabled him to constantly chart the overall progress of the civil war. The information enabled Mossad to launch a number of successful attacks against PLO strongholds in southern Lebanon.

But the service's relationship with the Christians soured in January 1976, when Christian leaders invited in the Syrian army to lend additional support against the pro-Iranian Hezbollah. That group was seen in Damascus as a threat. Within days thousands of battle-hardened Syrian troops were in Lebanon and moving close to its borders with Israel. Too late the Christians found they had, in Kimche's words, "behaved like Little Red Riding Hood, inviting in the wolf."

Once more the Lebanese Christians turned to Mossad for help. But Kimche realized his carefully constructed network to supply arms was insufficient. What was needed was a full-scale Israeli logistical operation. Scores of IDF tanks, antitank missiles, and other weapons were sent to the Christians. Lebanon's civil war began to rage out of control.

Under its cover, Kimche launched his own guerrilla battle against Israel's bête noire, the PLO. Soon that had extended to fighting the Lebanese Shi'ites. Lebanon became a practice ground for Mossad to perfect its tactics, not only in assassinations, but in psychological warfare. It was a halcyon time for the men operating out of the featureless high-rise on King Saul Boulevard.

Inside the building, relations between Kimche and Hofi were deteriorating. There were whispers of violent disagreements over operational matters; that Hofi feared Kimche wanted his job; that Kimche felt he was not properly appreciated for the undoubted contribution he was making. To this day, Kimche will not discuss such matters, only to say he "would never give a rumor respectability by commenting."

On a spring morning in 1980, David Kimche used his unrestricted access card, which had replaced the two keys, to access the headquarters building. Arriving in his office, he was told that Hofi wished to see him at once. Kimche strolled along the corridor to the director general's office, knocked, and entered, closing the door behind him.

What happened there has passed into Mossad legend, a tale of increasingly raised voices, of accusation and counteraccusation. The row lasted for twenty electrifying minutes. Then Kimche came out of the office, tight-lipped. His career in Mossad was finished. But his intelligence activities on behalf of Israel were about to enter a familiar arena, the United States. This time it would not involve the theft of nuclear materials, but the scandal that eventually became known as Irangate.

After a period of considering his future, David Kimche had accepted the director generalship of the Israeli foreign ministry. The post was ideally suited to his ability to think his way into, and out of, a situation. It offered Kimche an opportunity to bring his skills to bear on the international stage far beyond Lebanon.

In the United States the saga of President Nixon and Watergate had moved to an inescapable finale, leaving the CIA tarred with suspicion, the likes of which had not been seen since the death of President Kennedy, as more and more revelations emerged about the Agency's activities during the Nixon years.

Kimche studied every facet of the drama, "absorbing the lessons to be learned from a debacle that should never have happened. The bottom line was that Nixon should never have kept those tapes. Without them he would still probably have been president."

Closer to home, what was happening in Iran, ever a matter of abiding interest to Israel, also occupied him. With Khomeini and his ayatollahs firmly in control, it came as a genuine shock to Kimche to see how badly the CIA and the State Department had failed to correctly judge the situation.

But there was a new president in the White House, Ronald Reagan, who promised a new dawn for the CIA. The Agency, Kimche learned from his own contacts in Washington, would become Reagan's "secret trump" in foreign policy. Heading the CIA was William Casey. Instinctively, Kimche sensed he was no friend of Israel—but someone who could be outmaneuvered should the need arise.

As part of his work, Kimche closely followed CIA operations in Afghanistan and Central America. Many of them struck him as "babe-in-the-wood stuff, old-fashioned intelligence gathering, mingled with some pretty ruthless killing."

Then, once more, Kimche's attention was brought to focus on Iran—and what had happened in Beirut.

A few months after Kimche took up his duties at the foreign ministry, Israel had begun to arm Iran with the tacit support of the United States. Israel had provided the help to weaken the Baghdad regime—part of Jerusalem's long-established tactic of what Kimche called "playing at both ends."

Three years later, two events had affected matters. There had been the car-bomb massacre in Beirut of 241 U.S. Marines and the growing U.S. suspicion that Mossad not only had prior knowledge of the attack, but that Iran's intelligence service had helped to prepare it. Pressure was put on Israel to stop supplying Tehran. It increased with the kidnapping, torture, and subsequent death of William Buckley, the CIA station chief in Beirut. In quick succession, seven other Americans were taken hostage by Iran-backed groups.

For the tough-talking Reagan administration, which had come into office with its promise to crack down on terrorism, the idea of American citizens languishing deep beneath the rubble of Beirut demanded action. But retaliation was out of the question; to bomb Tehran, as Reagan suggested, was ruled out by even his hard-line aides. A rescue mission would also likely fail, said Delta Force chiefs.

There then occurred a conversation between the president and Robert McFarlane, a gung ho former marine who was national security adviser. Kimche was to recall that McFarlane told him that the conversation went like this:

"What do the Iranians need most, Mr. President?"

"You tell me, Bob."

"Weapons to fight Iraq."

"So we give them what they want. And we get back our people in return."

Reagan and McFarlane—against the advice of Casey and other U.S. intelligence chiefs—took the simplistic view that arming Iran would not only result in the mullahs bringing pressure to bear on the Beirut group to free the hostages, but would improve the administration's relations with Tehran. There could also be the added bonus that it was bound to weaken Moscow's position in Iran. The seeds were sown for what became known as Irangate.

Marine colonel Oliver North was put in charge of supplying the arms. North and McFarlane decided to exclude the CIA from their plans. Both were action-oriented men. Their push-and-shove mentality had served them well in Vietnam, and from all they had heard, Israelis were similar men of action. So, in North's words, "it was time to bring Israel into the fold." There was also the personal prospect of visiting the Holy Land; a committed Christian, North relished the thought of treading in the footsteps of Jesus.

Israel's new prime minister, Yitzhak Shamir, decided there was only one person capable of handling the request from Washington for help—and making sure Israel's interests were fully protected. On July 3, 1983, David Kimche flew to meet with McFarlane in the White House. Kimche said he believed the arms-for-hostages deal could work. He asked if the CIA was "actively involved." He was told the Agency was not.

In turn, McFarlane asked Kimche how far Mossad would be involved: "After all," he stated, "they are the guys who do all your secret work overseas." Kimche told him that Yitzhak Rabin, then defense minister, and Shamir had decided to exclude Mossad and leave the entire matter to him. McFarlane said that was fine by him. Kimche had not told him that Mossad's chief, then Nahum Admoni, shared Casey's fears that the arms-for-hostages deal was fraught with operational hazards.

McFarlane drove to Bethesda Naval Hospital to present Kimche's views to Reagan, who was recovering from a colon operation. The president had one question: Could Kimche ensure that Israel would keep the deal secret? A leak could harm U.S. relations with more moderate Arab states already fearful of the growing radicalism of Tehran. Kimche claims that McFarlane reassured Reagan that Israel would "batten down the hatches." The deal was on. Kimche flew back to Israel. Two weeks later Kimche was back in Washington. Over dinner, he laid out his game plan to McFarlane. Kimche was to recall the conversation went like this:

"Do you want the good or bad news first?" Kimche asked McFarlane.

"The good."

"We'll ship the arms for you, using the same routes we used before." McFarlane said "no problem."

Kimche's method would ensure that the United States had no direct contact with Iran, and so the administration's bellicose attitude about being tough on terrorism would not be compromised: the U.S. arms embargo on Iran would be intact and the hostages, when freed, would not have been directly exchanged for weapons.

"And the bad news?" McFarlane prompted.

Kimche said his own well-placed contacts in Iran were uncertain the mullahs could actually manage to procure the release of the Beirut hostages.

"The radicals there are getting beyond Tehran's control," he told his host.

If McFarlane was disappointed, he did not show it. The next day, Secretary of State George Shultz told Reagan, back in the Oval Office, the risks were too high. Supposing the Iranians took the arms and then revealed the deal to embarrass "the Great Satan," as the mullahs called the United States? Wouldn't that draw Iraq further into the Soviet camp? And what about the hostages? They could be even worse off. All morning the arguments continued. By lunchtime Reagan was visibly tired. The decision, when it came, was sudden. The president agreed to support the proposition that the United States would replace all arms Israel sold to Iran. Once more Kimche returned home with a green light. Nevertheless, Shamir insisted that all possible steps should also be taken so that he "could deny any connection with the matter should there be a problem."

To ensure this, Kimche assembled a colorful cast of characters to initiate the operation. There was Adnan Khashoggi, the Saudi petrobillionaire, with a habit of eating caviar by the pound and an eye for the current cover girls; Manacher Thorbanifer, a former agent in the shah's notorious SAVAK secret service who still behaved like a spy, calling meetings for the middle of the night. There was the equally mysterious Yakov Nimrodi, who had run agents for Aman and had once been Israel's military attaché in Iran during the shah's regime. He was invariably accompanied by Al Schwimmer, the closemouthed founder of Israel Aircraft Industries.

Khashoggi brokered a deal that was to be a precursor for all that followed. He would head a consortium that would indemnify the United States if Iran failed to live up to its obligations, and would similarly protect Iran if the arms were not acceptable as specified. For these guarantees the consortium would receive a 10 percent fee from the purchase of all the arms with cash provided by the United States. In return it would also act as a buffer to ensure that plausible deniability would remain intact for both the Iranian and U.S. governments if anything went wrong. Everyone understood that the consortium would essentially be working outside any political control and would first and foremost be driven by the profit motive.

In late August 1985, the first planeload of arms landed in Tehran from

Israel. On September 14, a U.S. hostage, the Reverend Benjamin Weir, was freed in Beirut. As the pace quickened, still more raffish players joined the consortium, including Miles Copeland, a former CIA officer who, on the eve of the shah falling from power in what was soon to be renamed the Islamic Republic of Iran, had sent CIA agents into Tehran souks distributing hundred-dollar bills to anyone who dared shout "Long live the shah!" Other shadowy figures also became involved, such as a former Special Air Services officer who ran a company in London that had once provided nonspecific services to Mossad. Meanwhile, the policymakers in Israel and Washington looked the other way. All that mattered was that the operation had taken off under the noses of an unsuspecting world—at least for the moment.

In all, Iran would receive 128 U.S. tanks; two hundred thousand Katyusha rockets captured in south Lebanon; ten thousand tons of artillery shells of all calibers; three thousand air-to-air missiles; four thousand rifles; and close to fifty million rounds of ammunition.

From Marama Air Force Base in Arizona, over four thousand TOW missiles were airlifted to Guatemala to begin their long journey to Tel Aviv. From Poland and Bulgaria, eight thousand SAM-7 surface-to-air missiles were shipped, together with one hundred thousand AK-47s. China provided hundreds of Silkworm sea-to-sea missiles, armored cars, and amphibious personnel carriers. Sweden provided 105-mm artillery shells, Belgium air-to-air missiles.

The weapons were shipped with certificates showing Israel was the end user. From IDF military bases in the Negev Desert, the consortium arranged for chartered transport aircraft to fly the weapons to Iran. The consortium received a "handling fee" for each consignment, Iran paying the money out of funds in Swiss bank accounts. The sum eventually totaled $7 million. Israel received no financial reward—only the satisfaction of witnessing Iran improve its capability to kill more Iraqis in the long-drawn-out war between both countries. For David Kimche it was a further example of the "divide and rule" policy he strongly advocated.

Nevertheless, his well-honed instincts told him that what had started as "a sweet operation" was now in danger of running out of control. In his view: "The wrong men now had too much power in the consortium."

In creating it, he had again demonstrated Israel's *Realpolitik*: Israel had been ready to help the United States because it recognized it could not survive without Washington's support in other areas. It was also a way to demonstrate that Israel could perform decisively on the world stage and keep matters secret.

But the longer the arms-for-hostages operation continued, Kimche sensed, the greater was the chance of discovery. In December 1985, he told the consortium that he could no longer remain involved in its activities—using the old saw of being overworked at the Ministry of Foreign Affairs.

The consortium thanked him for his help, gave him a farewell dinner in a Tel Aviv hotel, and told him that he was being replaced as the Israeli link by Amiram Nir, who was Peres's gung ho adviser on terrorism. That was the moment, Kimche would later admit, when the arms-for-hostages deal was firmly on the fast track to self-destruction. If anyone could derail it, then Nir was the man. A former journalist, Nir had shown the alarming trait of regarding real-life intelligence as being part of the same world occupied by the James Bond thrillers he so liked. He shared that fatal weakness with men in Mossad who had also decided that journalists could also serve their purpose.

In April 1999, David Kimche showed he had not lost his skills to correctly read the current political situation in the Middle East. Yasser Arafat, the man he had once plotted to murder, "because he was my blood enemy, certain that his demise would be a great victory for Israel," had now, in Kimche's view, become "Israel's best hope for long-term peace. Mr. Arafat is still hardly my idea of a perfect neighbor, but he is the only Palestine leader capable of making concessions to Israel while retaining power and domestic support."

Kimche believed he had found common ground with Arafat. He was convinced the PLO leader had finally come to recognize what Kimche had seen a quarter of a century earlier, "the real threat Islamic fundamentalism posed for the new millennium."

Sitting in his small study looking out over the garden he had seen come to fruition, Kimche was able to deliver a balanced judgment. "I cannot forgive my old enemy for endorsing the murder of my countrymen decades ago. But it would also be unforgivable to deny Arafat—and the Israelis—the chance to end the bloodshed once and for all."

CHAPTER 8

ORA AND THE MONSTER

The cavernous lobby of the Palestine-Meridian Hotel in Baghdad was crowded as usual on that last Friday in April 1988, and the mood was cheerful. Iraq had just won a decisive battle against Iran in the Gulf of Basra and the consensus was that their war was finally drawing to an end after seven bloody years.

One reason for impending Iraqi victory could be attributed to the foreigners who sat in the lobby in their well-tailored blazers and trousers with uniformly knife-edge creases, the permanent smiles of successful salesmen on their faces. They were arms dealers, there to sell their latest weapons, though they rarely used the word, preferring more neutral expressions: "optimum interface," "control systems," "growth capability." Between them, the salesmen represented the arms industries of Europe, the Soviet Union, the United States, and China. The common language of their trade was English, which they spoke in a variety of dialects.

Their Iraqi hosts needed no translation: what they were being offered was a range of bombs, torpedoes, mines, and other destructive gadgetry. The brochures being passed around showed helicopters with cartoonish names—Sea Knight, Chinook, Sea Stallion. One chopper, "Big Mother," could carry a small bridge; another, "the Incredible Machine," could airlift a platoon of troops. Leaflets showed guns that could fire two thousand rounds a minute or hit a moving target in pitch-black darkness with a computer-chip sight. Every and any kind of weapon was for sale.

Their hosts spoke an esoteric jargon the salesmen also understood: "twenty on the day," "thirty at half-and-half minus one": twenty million dollars on day of delivery, or thirty million dollars for a consignment, payable half down, the balance on the day before the weapons were shipped. All payments would be made in U.S. dollars, still the preferred currency in this closed world.

Watching over this ever-shifting bazaar of dealers and clients meeting over mint tea were officers from the Da'lrat Al-Mukhabarat Al-Amah, Iraq's main intelligence organization, controlled by Sabba'a, Saddam Hussein's almost as fearsome half-brother.

Some of the arms dealers had been in the hotel lobby on a very different day seven years before when their stunned hosts had told them that Israel, an enemy even more hated than Iran, had struck a powerful blow against Iraq's military machine.

Since the formation of the Jewish state, a formal state of war had existed between Israel and Iraq. Israel had felt confident its forces could win a conventional war. But in 1977, Mossad discovered the French government, which had provided Israel with its own nuclear capability, had also given Iraq a reactor and "technical assistance." The facility was Al-Tuweitha, north of Baghdad.

The Israeli air force began planning how to bomb the site before it became "hot" with the uranium rods in the reactor core. To destroy it then would cause widespread death and pollution and turn Baghdad and a sizable area of Iraq into an irradiated desert—and earn Israel global condemnation.

For these reasons, Yitzhak Hofi, then Mossad's chief, opposed the raid, arguing an air strike would anyway result in a heavy death toll among the French technicians and would isolate European countries Israel was trying to reassure of its peaceful intentions. Bombing the reactor would also effectively end the delicate maneuvering to persuade Egypt to sign a peace treaty.

He found himself presiding over a divided house. Several of his department chiefs argued that there was no alternative but to neutralize the reactor. Saddam was a ruthless enemy; once he had a nuclear weapon, he would not hesitate to use it against Israel. And since when had Israel worried unduly about winning friends in Europe? America was all that mattered, and the whisper from Washington was that taking out the reactor would result in no more than a slap on the wrist from the administration.

Hofi tried a different tack. He suggested the United States should bring diplomatic pressure to bear on France to stop the export of the reactor. Washington received a curt rebuff from Paris. Israel then chose a more direct route. Hofi dispatched a team of *katsas* to raid the French plant at La Seyne-sur-Mer, near Toulon, where the core for the Iraqi reactor was being built. The core was destroyed by an organization no one had ever heard of previously—the "French Ecological Group." Hofi had personally chosen the name.

While the French began to build a new core, the Iraqis sent Yahya Al-Meshad, a member of its Atomic Energy Commission, to Paris to arrange the shipment of nuclear fuel to Baghdad. Hofi sent a kidon team to assassinate him. While the others patrolled the surrounding streets, two of them used a passkey to enter Al-Meshad's bedroom. They cut his throat and stabbed him through the heart. The room was ransacked to look like robbery. A prostitute in an adjoining room told police she had serviced the scientist hours before his death. Later, entertaining another client, she had heard "unusual movement" in Al-Meshad's room. Hours after she reported this to the police, she was killed in a hit-and-run incident. The car was never found. The kidon team caught an El Al flight back to Tel Aviv.

Despite this further blow Iraq, aided by France, continued with its bid to become a nuclear power. In Tel Aviv, the Israeli air force continued its own preparations while intelligence chiefs wrangled with Hofi over his continued objections. The Mossad chief found a challenge from an unexpected quarter. His deputy, Nahum Admoni, argued destroying the reactor was not essential but would teach "any other Arabs with big ideas a lesson."

By October 1980, the debate preoccupied every cabinet meeting Menachem Begin chaired. Familiar arguments were revisited. Increasingly, Hofi became a lone voice against the attack. Nevertheless he struggled on, producing well-written position papers, knowing he was writing his own professional obituary.

Admoni increasingly made no secret of his contempt for Hofi's position. The two men, who had been close friends, became cold colleagues. Nevertheless, it took a further six months of bitter conflict between the embattled Mossad chief and his senior staff before the General Staff approved the attack on March 15, 1981.

The attack was a tactical masterpiece. Eight F-16 fighter-bombers, escorted by six F-15 fighter-interceptors, flew at sand-dune level across Jordan before streaking toward Iraq. They reached the target at the planned moment, 5:34 P.M. local time, minutes after the French construction staff had left. The death toll was nine. The nuclear plant was reduced to rubble. The aircraft returned unharmed. Hofi's career in Mossad was over. Admoni replaced him.

Now, on that April morning in 1988, the arms dealers in the lobby who, seven years before, had commiserated with their shocked hosts on the Israeli attack—before selling Iraq improved radar systems—would have been stunned to know that in the hotel a Mossad agent was quietly noting their names and what they were selling.

Earlier that Friday, business in the lobby had been briefly interrupted by the arrival of Sabba'a Al-Tikriti, the head of Iraqi secret police, accompanied by his own Praetorian phalanx of bodyguards. Saddam Hussein's half brother strode to the elevator, on his way to a rooftop suite. Waiting there was the tall, buxom prostitute specially flown in from Paris for his pleasure. It was highly paid, high-risk work. Some of the previous whores had simply disappeared after Sabba'a had finished with them.

The security chief left in midafternoon. Shortly afterward, from a suite adjoining the prostitute's, emerged a tall young man dressed in a blue cotton jacket and chinos. He was good-looking in a slightly effete way, with a nervous habit of stroking his mustache or rubbing his face that somehow increased his vulnerability.

His name was Farzad Bazoft. In the details on the hotel registration form—a copy of which had been routinely sent to Sabba'a's ministry—Bazoft had described himself as the "chief foreign correspondent" for *The Observer*, the London-based Sunday national newspaper. The description was inaccurate: only the newspaper's staff reporters on overseas assignments were allowed to call themselves "foreign correspondents." Bazoft was a freelance journalist who, for the past year, had contributed to *The Observer* several stories with Middle Eastern themes. Bazoft had admitted to reporters from other news organizations who were also on this trip to Baghdad that he always passed himself off as *The Observer*'s chief foreign correspondent on trips to cities like Baghdad because it ensured he had the best available hotel room. The harmless fiction was seen as another example of his endearing boyishness.

Unknown to his newspaper colleagues, there was an altogether darker side to Bazoft's personality, one that could possibly jeopardize them if they were ever suspected of being involved in the real reason he was in Baghdad. Bazoft was a Mossad spy.

He had been recruited after he had arrived in London three years before from Tehran, where his increasingly outspoken views on the Khomeini regime had put his life in danger. Like many before him, Bazoft found London alien and English people reserved. He had tried to find a role for himself in the Iranian community in exile, and for a while his considerable knowledge of the current political structure in Tehran made him a welcome guest at their dinner tables. But the sight of the same familiar faces soon palled for the ambitious and restless young man.

Bazoft began to look around for more excitement than dissecting a piece of news from Tehran. He began to establish contacts with Iran's enemy, Iraq. In the mid-1980s there were a large number of Iraqis in London, welcome visitors because Britain saw Iraq not only as a substantial importer of its goods, but also as a nation which, under Saddam Hussein, would subdue the threatening Islamic fundamentalism of the Khomeini regime.

Bazoft found himself "singing for my supper" at Iraqi parties. His new hosts were more relaxed and ready "to let down their hair" than Iranians. In turn they were captivated by his gentle manners and endless witticisms about the ayatollahs of Tehran.

At one party had been an Iraqi businessman, Abu Al-Hibid. He had listened to Bazoft—once more, slightly tipsy by the end of the evening—endlessly proclaiming his abiding ambition to be a reporter and how his heroes were Bob Woodward and Carl Bernstein, who had brought down President Nixon. Bazoft told Abu Al-Hibid he would die happy if he could topple the Ayatollah Khomeini. By now Bazoft was contributing articles to a small-circulation Iranian newspaper for exiles in Britain.

Abu Al-Hibid was the alias for an Iraqi-born *katsa*. In his next report to Tel Aviv, he included a note about Bazoft, his present work, and his aspirations. There was nothing unusual about doing that; hundreds of names every week were forwarded, each to find its place in Mossad's data bank.

But Nahum Admoni was running Mossad and eager to develop his contacts in Iraq. The London *katsa* was instructed to cultivate Bazoft. Over leisurely dinners, Bazoft complained to Al-Hibid that his editor was not making full use of his potential. His host suggested he should try to break into mainstream English journalism. There should be an opening for a reporter with good linguistic skills and knowledge of Iran. Al-Hibid suggested the BBC would be a starting point.

Within the broadcasting organization were several sayanim whose tasks included monitoring forthcoming programs on Israel and keeping an eye on persons recruited for the BBC's Arab-language service. Whether any sayan had a direct role in the employment of Bazoft will never be known for certain, but soon after meeting Al-Hibid, he was hired by the BBC for a research assignment. He did well. Other work followed. Desk editors found they could trust Bazoft to make sense of the intrigues of Tehran.

In Tel Aviv, Admoni decided it was time to make the next move. With Irangate's revelations gathering steam in the United States, the Mossad chief deliberately decided to expose the role in the burgeoning scandal of Yakov Nimrodi, a former Aman operative. He had been a member of the consortium David Kimche had created and had used his own intelligence background to keep Mossad out of what was happening. A wily, fast-talking man, Nimrodi had, as the arms-for-hostages deal began, driven U.S. Secretary of State George Shultz to comment that "Israel's agenda is not the same as ours and an intelligence relationship with Israel concerning Iran might not be one upon which we could fully rely."

When Kimche had pulled out of the consortium, Nimrodi had remained for a while longer. But, as the reverberations from Washington grew louder and more embarrassing for Israel, the former Aman operative disappeared back into the woodwork. Admoni, smarting at the way Nimrodi had treated Mossad, had other plans: he would publicly embarrass Nimrodi and at the same time give Bazoft a career boost that would enable him to better serve Mossad.

Al-Hibid fed sufficient details to the reporter for Bazoft to realize this could be his big break. He took the story to *The Observer*. It was published with references to "a mysterious Israeli, Nimrodi, being implicated in Irangate." Soon Bazoft was a regular contributor to *The Observer*. Finally, a coveted prize for someone who was not on staff, he was given a desk of his own. It meant he would no longer have to pay his own telephone costs to track down a story from home and he would be able to charge entertainment expenses. But Bazoft would still only be paid for what appeared in the paper. It was an incentive for him to find more stories and to push hard for any trip to the Middle East. On those occasions, he would be living on full expenses and, like all reporters, would be able to manipulate them to give himself extra cash above what he had spent and could genuinely reclaim. A shortage of money had always been a problem for Bazoft, something he was careful to hide from his *Observer* colleagues. Certainly none suspected that the reporter who spent hours talking in Farsi on the phone to his contacts was a convicted thief. Bazoft had spent eighteen months in jail after raiding a building society. Passing sentence, the judge had ordered Bazoft should be deported after he was released. Bazoft appealed on the reasonable grounds he would be executed if sent back to Iran. Though the appeal was rejected, he was granted "exceptional leave" to remain in Britain indefinitely. The grounds for such an unusual step have remained locked in a Home Office vault.

Whether Mossad, having spotted Bazoft's potential, used one of its well-placed sayanim in Whitehall to facilitate matters has remained an unresolved question. But the possibility cannot be discounted.

After Bazoft was released from prison, he began to suffer bouts of depression, which he treated with homeopathic medicines. This background had been unearthed by the Mossad *katsa*. Later an English writer, Rupert Alison, a conservative member of Parliament and a recognized expert on intelligence recruiting methods, would say a personality like Bazoft's made him a prime target for Mossad.

A year after they had first met, Al-Hibid recruited Bazoft. How and where this was done has remained unknown. The extra money would have certainly been a consideration for Bazoft, still short of cash. And, for someone who so often viewed life through a dramatic prism, the prospect of living out another of his dreams—to be a spy in the tradition of another foreign correspondent he admired, Philby, who had also once worked for *The Observer*, as a cover for his work as a Soviet spy—could also have been a factor.

More certain, Bazoft began to carve a small reputation for himself; what he lacked in writing style, he made up with solid research. Everything he unearthed on Iran was passed over to the London *katsa*. As well as stories for *The Observer*, Bazoft was also being given assignments by Independent Television News and Mirror Group Newspapers. At the time the foreign editor of the *Daily Mirror* was Nicholas Davies. In his safari-style suit, Davies might have stepped out of the pages of Evelyn Waugh's *Scoop*. He had a reporter's gift for gossip and an ability to hold his drink, and was always ready to buy his round. His north-of-England accent had all but gone: colleagues said he had spent hours perfecting the dulcet tone he now used. Women found appealing his easy good manners and the commanding way he could order dinner and select a good bottle of wine. They loved his been-there-done-that mentality, the way he spoke of faraway places as if they were part of his private fief. Late at night over another drink, he would hint at adventures that cynics said was simply Nick romancing.

Not for a moment did anyone—his colleagues at the *Mirror*, his wide circle of friends outside the newspaper world, even his wife, Janet, an Australian-born actress who had starred in the highly successful BBC television series *Doctor Who*—know that Nahum Admoni had authorized Davies should be recruited.

Davies would always insist that even if he had "been approached," he had never served as a Mossad agent and that his presence in the hotel lobby on that April Friday afternoon was purely as a journalist watching the arms dealers going about their work. He could not later recall what he and Bazoft had spoken about while in the lobby, but said, "I imagine it was about what was going on." He refused to elaborate, a position he would steadfastly maintain.

The pair had traveled to Iraq with a small group of other journalists (among them the author of this book on assignment for the Press Association, Britain's national wire service). On the flight from London,

Davies had regaled the party with ribald stories about Robert Maxwell, who had finally bought Mirror Newspapers. He called him "a sexual monster with a voracious appetite for seducing secretaries on his staff." He made it very clear he was close to Maxwell, though: "Captain Bob is sheer hell to be with, he knows I know too much to sack me." Davies's claim that he personally was fireproof because of what he knew about the tycoon was dismissed by his listeners as hyperbole.

On the flight, Farzad Bazoft was quiet, saying little to the others, confining himself to talking to the flight attendants in Farsi. At Baghdad Airport his language skills helped to ease the translation difficulties with the Iraqi "minders" assigned to the party. In a stage whisper, Davies said they were really security agents. "The dozy buggers wouldn't recognize a spy if he was pointed out," Davies said prophetically.

At the Palestine-Meridian, the man from the *Mirror* informed his traveling companions he was only there because he was "bloody bored with London." But he made it clear he had no intention of following the official itinerary, which included a visit to the Basra battlefield, where the Iraqi army was eager to display the spoils of war after its victory over the Iranian forces. Bazoft said he didn't think the trip south to the gulf would interest his newspaper.

That April Friday evening in 1988, having spent hours in the hotel lobby watching the arms dealers come and go, and sharing several conversations with Davies, Farzad Bazoft ate alone in the hotel coffee shop. He declined an invitation to join other reporters from London, saying he had to "think through my schedule." During the meal he was called to take a telephone call in the lobby. He returned a few minutes later looking pensive. Having ordered dessert, he abruptly left the table, ignoring ribald jokes from some of the reporters that he had a girl stashed away.

He did not return until the next day. He appeared even more tense, saying to, among others, Kim Fletcher—a freelance journalist then working for the *Daily Mail*—that "it's all right for you lot; you're British born and bred. I'm an Iranian. That makes me different." Fletcher was not alone among the English reporters who wondered if this was "Bazoft banging on again about how hard it was to have a background like his."

Bazoft spent most of the day pacing the hotel lobby or in his suite. Twice he left the hotel for short periods. In the lobby he had several conversations with Nicholas Davies, who later said that Bazoft was "like anyone on a story, wondering if he would get what he wanted." For his part, the *Mirror* foreign editor announced he would not be writing anything, "because there is nothing here to interest Captain Bob."

Late that afternoon, Bazoft once more left the hotel. As usual he was followed by an Iraqi minder. But when Bazoft reappeared, he was alone. Reporters heard Bazoft tell Davies he wasn't "going to be followed around like a bitch in heat."

Davies's laughter, however, did little to lighten Bazoft's mood. Once more he went to his suite. When he next appeared in the lobby, he told several reporters that he would not be returning to London with them. "Something's come up," he said in the mysterious voice he liked to use at times.

"It would have to be a good story to keep me here," Fletcher said.

Hours later Bazoft left the hotel. It would be the last any of his companions would see of him until he appeared on a video distributed worldwide by the Iraqi regime seven weeks after his arrest, having confessed to being a Mossad spy.

During that time, Bazoft was on a Mossad mission that would have taxed the skills of a trained *katsa*. He had been ordered to try to discover how advanced were Gerald Bull's plans to provide Iraq with a supergun. That the journalist was given such a task was a clear indicator of how far his controllers were prepared to exploit him. Mossad had also taken its own steps to ensure that, if Bazoft was caught, it would appear he was working for a London-based company, Defence Systems Limited (DSL). When Bazoft was arrested close to one of the supergun test sites, the Iraqi agents also found he had in his possession a number of documents indicating that Bazoft had made several calls from the hotel to the offices of DSL. The company has denied all knowledge of Bazoft, or having any contact with Mossad.

On the videotape, Bazoft's eyes at times stared vacantly, before suddenly blinking rapidly and darting around the room, with its pleasant backdrop of a curtain patterned with flowing tendrils. He looked like a person who believed he was powerless to avoid his annihilation.

Mossad's psychologists in Tel Aviv studied every frame. For them the stages of Bazoft's disintegration followed the same pattern Israeli interrogators had noticed when they extracted confessions from a captured terrorist. First Bazoft would have experienced disbelief, an instinctive denial that what was happening was actually happening to him. Then would have come an overwhelmingly sudden and shattering realization: it *was* happening to him. At that stage, the helpless reporter may have experienced two other reactions: paralyzing fright and a compulsion to talk. This would have been the time he made his confession on the video that he was a Mossad agent.

His monotonous tone suggested he had experienced bouts of exogenous depression while in captivity, a result of being removed from familiar surroundings and having his normal lifestyle totally disrupted. He would have felt continuously tired, and what sleep he was permitted would have left him unrefreshed. That would be when self-accusation was at its most destructive, and his sense of hopelessness maximized. Self-accusation would have gripped him. Like the prisoner in Kafka's *The Trial*, he would have felt "stupid" over the way he had behaved and put others at risk.

On the video, Bazoft's eyes showed signs he had been drugged. Mossad's pharmacologists found it impossible to decide what drugs had been used.

Nahum Admoni knew that such an abject confession as the video contained was the prelude to Bazoft's execution. The Mossad chief ordered his psychological warfare specialists to launch a campaign to deflect embarrassing questions about the service's involvement with Bazoft.

Members of Parliament in Britain soon publicly criticized *The Observer* for sending Bazoft to Iraq. At the same time, trusted reporters were fed stories that Saddam Hussein was viewing videos of every stage of Bazoft's interrogation. It may well have been true. More certain, it was an excuse to remind the world that torture and murder were instruments of state policy in Iraq. Bazoft was hanged in Baghdad in March 1990. His last reported words on the gallows were: "I am not an Israeli spy."

In London, Nicholas Davies read the report on the execution on a Reuters message that came to the *Daily Mirror* foreign desk. As instructed about all stories emanating from the Middle East he judged to be important, Davies took the report up to the office of Robert Maxwell.

Since 1974, the publisher had been the most powerful sayan in Britain. Davies would remember: "Bob read the report without comment," but could not recall "in all honesty" what he had felt about Bazoft's death.

In Tel Aviv, among those who read about the execution was one of the most colorful characters to have served Israel's spymasters, Ari Ben-Menashe. Until then he had never known of the existence of Bazoft.

But typically, that did not stop the mercurial Ben-Menashe feeling a sense of grief that "another good man had been in the wrong place at the wrong time." It was emotional judgments like that which had made the darkly handsome, quick-witted Ben-Menashe such an unlikely candidate for a key position in the Israeli intelligence community. Yet, for ten years, 1977–87, he had held a sensitive post in the External Relations Department (ERD) of the Israel Defense Forces, one of the most powerful and secret organizations in the intelligence community.

ERD had been created in 1974 by then prime minister Yitzhak Rabin. Smarting over the way Israel had been completely surprised by the Syrian-Egyptian onslaught in the Yom Kippur War, he had decided the only way to avert such an intelligence failure occurring again was to have a watchdog to monitor other intelligence services and, at the same time, conduct its own intelligence gathering.

Four branches had been created to operate under the ERD umbrella. The most important was SIM; it provided "special assistance" for the growing number of "liberation movements" in Iran, Iraq, and, to a lesser extent, Syria and Saudi Arabia. The second branch, RESH, handled relationships with friendly intelligence networks. Foremost of those was the South African Bureau of State Security. Mossad had a similar unit called TEVEL, which also had close links with South Africa's intelligence community. The relationship between RESH and TEVEL was often tense because of the inevitable overlapping.

A third ERD department, Foreign Liaison, dealt with Israeli military attachés and other IDF personnel working overseas. The department also monitored the activities of foreign military attachés in Israel. That brought further conflict, this time with Shin Bet, who until then had the sole prerogative to report on such activities. The fourth arm of ERD was called Intelligence Twelve. Set up to liaise with Mossad, this unit had further soured relations with the men on the upper floors of the building on King Saul Boulevard. They felt overall that ERD would diminish their power.

Ben-Menashe had been attached to RESH, with a specific responsibility for the Iranian "account." He arrived at a time when Israel was about to lose its most powerful ally in the region. For over a quarter of a century, the shah of Iran had worked diligently behind the scenes to persuade Israel's Arab neighbors to end their hostility toward the Jewish state. He was still making limited headway, notably with King Hussein of Jordan, when the shah's own Peacock Throne was swept away by Ayatollah Khomeini's Islamic fundamentalist revolution in February 1979. Khomeini promptly handed over the Israeli embassy building in Tehran to the PLO. Equally swiftly, Israel turned to helping the Kurds wage guerrilla war against the new regime. At the same time, Israel continued to supply arms to Tehran for them to use against Iraq. The "kill both sides" policy that David Kimche and others in Mossad advocated was well and truly in force.

Ben-Menashe soon found himself involved in David Kimche's grand design to trade hostages for arms with Iran. Both men traveled together to Washington, where Ben-Menashe claimed he prowled the wide corridors of the White House, met President Reagan, and was on first-name terms with his senior aides.

Charming, and with a devil-may-care attitude, Ben-Menashe was a popular figure at Israeli intelligence community parties, where senior politicians could swap stories with the spymasters to mutual benefit. Few could tell a tale better than Ben-Menashe. By the time Kimche was starting the hostages-for-arms deal, Ben-Menashe had been appointed Prime Minister Yitzhak Shamir's "personal consultant" on intelligence, having told Shamir he knew where "all the bodies were buried." Kimche decided it made Ben-Menashe the ideal choice to work with the one intelligence officer he admired above all others, Rafi Eitan. With the full approval of the prime minister, Ben-Menashe was released from all other duties to work with Eitan. The two men moved to New York in March 1981. Their purpose, Ben-Menashe would recall, was straightforward: "Our friends in Tehran were desperate to have sophisticated electronic equipment for their air force and air and ground defenses. Israel, of course, wanted to help them as much as possible in their war against Iraq."

Traveling on British passports, always a favorite of Mossad, they set up a company in New York's financial district. They quickly recruited a team of fifty brokers who scoured the U.S. electronics industry for suitable equipment. All sales were accompanied by end-user certificates that stated the equipment was to be used only in Israel. Ben-Menashe would recall: "We had packs of certificates which we would fill out and send to Tel Aviv to keep on file in case anyone ever bothered to check."

The equipment was flown to Tel Aviv. There, without going through customs, it was transferred onto aircraft chartered from Guinness Peat in Ireland and flown to Tehran. Guinness Peat, a well-regarded air-charter company, was an obvious choice. The idea of using Irish pilots had also been Rafi Eitan's. He had maintained what he called his "Irish connections. When it comes to a deal, the Irish understand the rules. The only one which matters is to pay on the day."

As the volume of the New York operation increased, it became necessary to have a central holding company to process the billions of dollars involved in the purchasing and selling of arms. The name chosen for the company was ORA, "light" in Hebrew.

In March 1983, Ben-Menashe was told by Rafi Eitan to recruit Nicholas Davies into ORA. How the old spymaster had heard of Davies was almost certainly through Mossad; in turn the service would have been told about Davies by Bazoft, who had done freelance journalist work for the *Mirror* foreign editor. Later that month, Ben-Menashe and Davies met in the lobby of London's Churchill Hotel. By the time they left, Ben-Menashe knew that Davies was "our man." The next day they lunched at Davies's home. Present was Davies's wife, Janet. Ben-Menashe quickly formed the impression that the sophisticated, smooth-talking Davies was afraid of losing her. "That was good. It made him vulnerable."

Davies's role as a consultant to ORA was finally settled over a meeting at the Dan Acadia Hotel on the beachfront north of Tel Aviv. Ben-Menashe remembered: "We agreed he would be our London conduit for arms, our contact man for various Iranian and other deals. His home address would be used on ORA stationery and during the day his direct office phone number—822-3530—would be used by our Iranian contacts."

In return, Davies would receive fees commensurate with his new-found role as a key player in the arms-for-Iran operation. In all, he would receive $1.5 million, deposited in bank accounts in Grand Cayman, Belgium, and Luxembourg. Part of the money went to settle his divorce. Janet received a single payment of $50,000. Davies cleared all his bank debts and bought a four-story house. It became ORA's European headquarters, its phone number—231-0015—another contact for the arms dealers who now had become part of the journalist's life. Through his position as foreign editor, Davies began to visit the United States, Europe, Iran, and Iraq.

Ben-Menashe noted approvingly that "on his travels he introduced himself as a representative of the ORA Group. He would set up a meeting, usually for a weekend, and he would fly to the city concerned, arrange for the number of weapons to be supplied and how payment was to be made."

In 1987, Iran's Ayatollah Ali Akbar Hashemi Rafsanjani received a cable from ORA concerning the sale to Iran of four thousand TOW missiles at a cost of $13,800 each. The cable concluded with the confirmation that "Nicholas Davies is a representative of ORA Limited, with the authority to sign contracts."

It was a champagne time for Ari Ben-Menashe, Nicholas Davies, and the powerful figure who loomed ever larger in the background of unfolding events, Robert Maxwell. But none suspected for a moment the grim truth of the Hollywood cliché Davies liked to quote, "There's no such thing as a free lunch."

CHAPTER 9

SLUSH MONEY, SEX, AND LIES

Matters had looked very different on that morning in late March 1985

when Ari Ben-Menashe had caught the early-morning British Airways

flight from Tel Aviv to London. Eating his kosher airline breakfast, he

reflected that life had never been so good. He was not only making "real

money," but had learned a great deal at the elbow of David Kimche as

they trawled through the Byzantine world of selling arms to Iran. Along

the way, he had also furthered his education in the continuous inter-

play between Israel's politicians and its intelligence chiefs.

For Ben-Menashe, "compared to my former colleagues, the aver-

age arms dealer was a choirboy." He had identified the problem: the aftereffects of Israel's Lebanon adventure, from which it had finally withdrawn, battered and demoralized. Anxious to regain prestige, the politicians gave the intelligence community an even freer hand in how it waged pitiless war against the PLO, whom they saw as the cause of all Israel's problems. The result was a succession of scandals where suspected terrorists and even their families were brutalized and murdered in cold blood. Yitzhak Hofi, the former head of Mossad, had sat on a government commission, set up after intense public pressure, to investigate the brutality. It concluded that intelligence agents had consistently lied to the court about how they obtained confessions: the methods used had too often been gross. The committee had called for "proper procedures" to be followed.

But Ben-Menashe knew the torture had continued: "It was good to be away from such awful matters." He regarded what he was doing, providing arms for Iranians to kill untold numbers of Iraqis, as "different." Nor did the plight of the Beirut hostages, the very reason for his wheeling and dealing, unduly concern him. The bottom line was the money he was making. Even with Kimche's departure, Ben-Menashe still believed the merry-go-round he was riding would only stop when *he* decided—and he would step off a multimillionaire. By his count, ORA's business was now worth "hundreds of millions"—most of it being generated through the house in the London suburb from where Nicholas Davies ran ORA's international operations.

Ben-Menashe knew Davies had continued to amass his own fortune, far in excess of the sixty-five-thousand-pound yearly salary he was paid as foreign editor of the *Daily Mirror;* Davies's commission from ORA was almost always as much in a month. Ben-Menashe didn't mind if the newspaperman took "an extra slice of the cake; it left plenty to go around. It was still champagne time."

Robert Maxwell dispensed it by the magnum from his office on top of the *Mirror* building to his guests. When the BA flight landed, Ben-Menashe would be chauffeured to see the tycoon in a limousine Maxwell would have sent, a further sign, Ben-Menashe felt, of the importance in which Maxwell now held him. In the car with him would be Nahum Admoni, Mossad's director general, traveling on board an El Al flight an hour behind the British Airways jet. Ben-Menashe planned to spend the time waiting at Heathrow Airport for Admoni by reviewing all he had put together on how a powerful press baron had become the most important sayan Mossad had recruited.

Maxwell had volunteered his services at the end of a meeting in Jerusalem with Shimon Peres shortly after Peres had formed a coalition government in 1984. One of Peres's aides would recall the encounter as "the ego meets the megalomaniac. Peres was haughty and autocratic. But Maxwell just drove on, saying things like 'I will pour millions into Israel'; 'I will revitalize the economy.' He was like a man running for office. He was bombastic, interrupted, went off on tangents and told dirty jokes. Peres sat there smiling his Eskimo smile."

Recognizing that Maxwell over the years had developed powerful contacts in Eastern Europe, Peres arranged for Maxwell to see Admoni. The meeting took place in the Presidential Suite of the King David Hotel in Jerusalem, where Maxwell was staying. Maxwell and Admoni found common ground in their central European backgrounds; Maxwell had been born in Czechoslovakia (which had led Peres to utter one of his few remembered jokes, "He's the only bouncing Czech I know with money"). Both men shared a burning commitment to Zionism and a belief Israel had a God-given right to survive. They also enjoyed a passion for food and good wine.

Admoni was keenly interested in Maxwell's view that both the United States and the Soviet Union had a similar desire to achieve global domination, but through significantly different approaches. Russia included international anarchy as part of its strategy, while Washington saw the world in terms of "friends" and "enemies" rather than nations with conflicting ideological interests. Maxwell had offered other insights: the CIA's secret contact with its Chinese counterparts was causing unease in the State Department, which found it could impinge on future diplomatic action and policies.

The tycoon had painted portraits of two men of particular interest to Admoni. Maxwell said that after meeting Ronald Reagan, he came away with the feeling that the president was an eternal optimist who used his charm to conceal a tough politician. Reagan's most dangerous failing was that he was a simplifier and never more so than on the Middle East, where his second or third thought was no better than his original shoot-from-the-hip judgment.

Maxwell had also met William Casey, and judged the CIA director as a man of narrow opinions and no friend of Israel. Casey was running a "can-do" agency with outmoded ideas about the role of intelligence in the current political global arenas. Nowhere, in Maxwell's view, was this more evident than in the way Casey had misread Arab intentions in the Middle East.

These views coincided exactly with those of Nahum Admoni. After the meeting, they drove in Admoni's unmarked car to Mossad headquarters, where the tycoon was given a personally conducted tour of some of the facilities by the director general.

Now, a year later, March 15, 1985, they would meet again.

Not until Admoni and Ben-Menashe entered Maxwell's office suite in Mirror Newspapers headquarters in London's High Holborn did their host announce there would be one other person present to share the bagels, lox, and coffee Maxwell had ordered must be available whenever he was in the building.

Like a conjurer producing a rabbit out of a hat, Maxwell introduced Viktor Chebrikov, vice chairman of the KGB, and one of the most powerful spymasters in the world. With masterful understatement, Ben-Menashe would subsequently admit that "for a KGB leader to be in a British newspaper publisher's office might seem a fanciful notion. But at the time President Gorbachev was on very friendly terms with Prime Minister Margaret Thatcher, so it was acceptable for Chebrikov to be in Britain."

More debatable is what the founder of Thatcherism and its free-trade principles would have made of the agenda for the meeting. Sprawled in Maxwell's hand-tooled leather armchairs, Admoni and Ben-Menashe led the discussion. They wanted to know if "very substantial amounts" of currency were to be transferred to banks in the Soviet Union, could Chebrikov ensure the deposits would be safe? The money was from ORA's profits in the sale of U.S. arms to Iran.

Chebrikov asked how much money was involved.

Ben-Menashe replied, "Four hundred fifty million American dollars. With similar amounts to follow. A billion, maybe more."

Chebrikov looked at Maxwell as if to ensure he had heard correctly. Maxwell nodded enthusiastically. "This is perestroika!" he boomed.

To Ben-Menashe the sheer simplicity of the deal was an added attraction. There would be no galaxy of middlemen chipping away their pieces of commission. There would just be "Maxwell with his connections and Chebrikov, because of the power he wielded. His involvement was a guarantee the Soviets would not steal the funds. It was agreed the initial $450 million would be transferred from Credit Suisse to the Bank of Budapest in Hungary. That bank would disburse the money to other banks in the Soviet bloc."

A flat fee of $8 million would be paid to Robert Maxwell for brokering the deal. Handshakes sealed matters. Maxwell proposed a champagne toast to the future capitalism of Russia. Afterward his guests were flown in the tycoon's helicopter to Heathrow Airport to catch their flights home.

Apart from Nicholas Davies, not one journalist in the *Mirror* building realized a monumental story had just escaped them. Soon another would slip from their grasp as Maxwell betrayed their journalistic skills to try to protect Israel.

At the beginning of his relationship with Mossad, it was agreed that Maxwell was too valuable an asset to be involved with routine intelligence-gathering matters. According to a serving member of the Israeli intelligence community:

"Maxwell was Mossad's high-level Mr. Fixit. He opened the doors to the highest offices. The power of his newspapers meant that presidents and prime ministers were ready to receive him. Because of who he was, they spoke to him as if he was a de facto statesman, never realizing where the information would end up. A lot of what he learned was probably no more than gossip, but no doubt some of it contained real nuggets. Maxwell knew how to ask questions. He had received no training from us, but he would have been given guidelines of areas to probe."

On September 14, 1986, Robert Maxwell called Nahum Admoni on his direct line with devastating news. A freelance Colombian-born journalist, Oscar Guerrero, had approached a Maxwell-owned Sunday tabloid newspaper, the *Sunday Mirror*, with a sensational story—one which would rip aside the carefully constructed veil disguising the true purpose of Dimona. Guerrero claimed to be acting for a former technician who had worked at the nuclear plant. During that time the man had secretly gathered photographic and other evidence to show that Israel was now a major nuclear power, possessing no fewer than one hundred nuclear devices of varying destructive force.

Like all telephone calls to and from the Mossad chief, this one was automatically recorded. That member of the Israeli intelligence community would later claim the tape contained the following exchange:

Admoni: What is the name of this technician?

Maxwell: Vanunu. Mordechai Vanunu.

Admoni: Where is he now?

Maxwell: Sydney, Australia, I think.

Admoni: I will call you back.

Admoni's first call was to Prime Minister Shimon Peres, who ordered every step be taken to "secure the situation." With those words Peres authorized an operation that once more demonstrated the ruthless efficiency of Mossad.

Admoni's staff quickly confirmed Vanunu had worked at Dimona from February 1977 until November 1986. He had been assigned to Machon-Two, one of the most secret of all the plant's ten production units. The windowless concrete building externally resembled a warehouse. But its walls were thick enough to block the most powerful of satellite camera lenses from penetrating. Inside the bunkerlike structure, a system of false walls led to the elevators that descended through six levels to where the nuclear weapons were manufactured.

Vanunu's security clearance was sufficient to gain unchallenged access to every corner of Machon-Two. His special security pass—number 520—coupled with his signature on an Israeli Official Secrets Acts document ensured no one ever challenged him as he went about his duties as a *menahil*, a controller on the night shift.

A stunned Admoni was told that almost certainly for some months, Vanunu somehow had secretly photographed the layout of Machon-Two: the control panels, the glove boxes, the nuclear bomb-building machinery. Evidence suggested he had stored his films in his clothes locker, and smuggled them out of what was supposedly the most secure place in Israel.

Admoni demanded to know how Vanunu had achieved all this—and perhaps more. Supposing he had already shown his material to the CIA? Or the Russians? The British or even the Chinese? The damage would be incalculable. Israel would be exposed as a liar before the world—a liar with the capability of destroying a very large part of it. Who was Vanunu? Whom could he be working for?

Answers were soon forthcoming. Vanunu was a Moroccan Jew, born on October 13, 1954, in Marrakech, where his parents were modest shopkeepers. In 1963, when anti-Semitism, never far from the surface in Morocco, spilled once more into open violence, the family emigrated to Israel, settling in the Negev Desert town of Beersheba.

Mordechai led an uneventful life as a teenager. Along with every other young person, when his time came he was conscripted into the Israeli army. He was already beginning to lose his hair, making him appear older than his nineteen years. He reached the rank of first sergeant in a minesweeping unit stationed on the Golan Heights. After military service he entered Ramat Aviv University in Tel Aviv. Having failed two exams at the end of his first year in a physics-degree course, he left the campus.

In the summer of 1976 he replied to an advertisement for trainee technicians to work at Dimona. After a lengthy interview with the plant's security officer he was accepted for training and sent on an intensive course in physics, chemistry, math, and English. He did sufficiently well to finally enter Dimona as a technician in February 1977.

Vanunu had been made redundant in November 1986. In his security file at Dimona it was noted that he had displayed "left-wing and pro-Arab beliefs." Vanunu left Israel for Australia, arriving in Sydney in May of the following year. Somewhere along his journey, which had followed a well-trodden path by young Israelis through the Far East, Vanunu had renounced his once-strong Jewish faith to become a Christian. The picture emerging from a dozen sources for Admoni to consider was of a physically unprepossessing young man who appeared to be the classic loner: he had made no real friends at Dimona; he had no girlfriends; he spent his time at home reading books on philosophy and politics. Mossad psychologists told Admoni a man like that could be foolhardy, with a warped sense of values and often disillusioned. That kind of personality could be dangerously unpredictable.

In Australia Vanunu had met Oscar Guerrero, a Colombian journalist working in Sydney, while he was painting a church. Soon the garrulous journalist had concocted a bizarre story with which to regale his friends in the raffish King's Cross quarter of Sydney. He claimed he had helped a top Israeli nuclear scientist to defect with details of

Israel's plans to nuke its Arab neighbors and that, one step ahead of Mossad, the scientist was now hiding out in a safe house in a city suburb while Guerrero masterminded what he called "the sale of the scoop of the century."

Vanunu was irritated by such nonsensical claims. Now a committed pacifist, he wanted his story to appear in a serious publication to alert the world to the threat he perceived Israel now posed with its nuclear capability. However, Guerrero had already contacted the Madrid office of *The Sunday Times*, and the London newspaper with a fearless reputation sent a reporter to Sydney to interview Vanunu.

Guerrero's fantasies were swiftly exposed under questioning. The Colombian began to feel he was about to lose control over Vanunu's story. His fears increased when the *Sunday Times* reporter said he would fly Vanunu to London, where his claims could be more fully investigated. The newspaper planned to have the technician questioned by one of Britain's leading nuclear scientists.

Guerrero watched Vanunu and his traveling companion board the flight to London, his misgivings deepening by the minute. He needed advice on how to handle the situation. The only person he could think of was a former member of the Australian Security and Intelligence Service (ASIS). Guerrero told him he had been cheated out of a world-shaking story, and described exactly what Vanunu had smuggled out of Dimona—sixty photographs taken inside Machon-Two, together with maps and drawings. They revealed beyond a doubt that Israel was the sixth most powerful nuclear nation in the world.

Once more Guerrero's luck ran out. He had chosen the wrong man to call. The former ASIS operative contacted his old employer and repeated what Guerrero had told him. There was a close working relationship between Mossad and ASIS. The former provided intelligence on Arab terrorist movements out of the Middle East to the Pacific. ASIS informed the *katsa* attached to the Israeli embassy in Canberra of the call from its former employee. The information was immediately faxed to Admoni. By then more disturbing news had reached him. On his backpacking trip to Australia, Vanunu had stopped over in Nepal and had visited the Soviet embassy in Kathmandu. Had he gone there to show his evidence to Moscow?

It took a Mossad sayan on the staff of the king of Nepal three days to discover that Vanunu's sole purpose in going to the embassy was to inquire about the travel documents he would need to take a vacation in the Soviet Union at some unspecified later date. He had been sent on his way with a pile of brochures.

In the hours that had passed since Vanunu was being flown to London by *The Sunday Times*, Guerrero had tried to make a quick killing—by offering copies of Vanunu's documentation to two Australian newspapers. They had dismissed the material as forgeries.

Growing desperate, Guerrero had set off to London in pursuit of Vanunu. Unable to find him, Guerrero had taken the documents to the *Sunday Mirror*. Included was a photograph of Vanunu taken in Australia. Within hours Nicholas Davies knew they were there. He promptly told Maxwell. The publisher called Admoni. Several hours later, when the Mossad chief again called Maxwell, Admoni received another jolt. *The Sunday Times* was taking Vanunu's story seriously. It was therefore critically important to know what the technician had photographed. It was hoped a damage-limitation response could then be fashioned. The reports from Canberra suggested that Guerrero was clearly motivated by money. If Vanunu was shown to have a similar aspiration, then it might be possible to mount a successful disinformation campaign that *The Sunday Times* had been swindled by two con men.

Once more the indefatigable Ari Ben-Menashe was pressed into service. Admoni ordered him to fly to London to obtain the copies that Guerrero had shown to the *Sunday Mirror*. Ben-Menashe would later recall to the veteran American investigative journalist Seymour Hersh:

"Nicholas Davies had arranged for Guerrero to meet this 'hot' American journalist—me. At the meeting, Guerrero, eager for another sale, displayed some of Vanunu's color photographs. I had no idea if they were significant. They needed to be seen by experts in Israel. I told Guerrero I needed copies. He balked. I said I had to know if they were real if he wanted money and that Nick would vouch for me."

Guerrero handed over several photographs to Ben-Menashe. They were couriered to Tel Aviv.

Their arrival created further consternation. Officials from Dimona identified Machon-Two from the photographs. One of the prints showed the area where nuclear land mines had been manufactured before being sown along the Golan Heights border with Syria. There was no longer any question of being able to destroy Vanunu's credibility. Every nuclear physicist would recognize what the equipment was for.

Prime Minister Peres set up a crisis team to monitor the situation. Some of Mossad's department heads urged that a kidon squad should be sent to London to hunt down Vanunu and kill him. Admoni rejected the idea. *The Sunday Times* would not have the space to publish everything Vanunu told the newspaper; it would require a full-length book to contain all the information to which the technician would have had access. But once the newspaper had finished with Vanunu, the likeliest possibility was he would then be debriefed by MI6 and the CIA, and Israel would face even more problems. It was all the more imperative to learn how Vanunu had carried out his spying activities in Dimona and whether he had worked alone or with others—and if so, whom *they* were working for. The only way to discover all this was to bring Vanunu back to Israel to be interrogated.

Admoni needed a way to flush the technician out of wherever *The Sunday Times* had hidden him. In the open it would be easier to deal with Vanunu, and in the end, if he had to be killed, it would not be the first time Mossad had committed murder on the streets of London. In the hunt for the perpetrators of the massacre of the Israeli athletes at the Munich Olympics, Mossad had killed one of the Black September group in a carefully staged hit-and-run road accident as he walked back to his Bloomsbury hotel.

In London, *The Sunday Times*, realizing Israel would do everything possible to discredit Vanunu, had arranged for him to be questioned by Dr. Frank Barnaby, a nuclear physicist with impeccable credentials who had worked at Britain's nuclear weapons installation at Aldermaston. He concluded that the photographs and documentation were authentic and the technician's detailed recall was accurate.

The Sunday Times then took a fateful step. Its reporter presented the Israeli embassy in London with a summary of all that Vanunu had revealed to them, along with photostats of his passport and the photographs, together with Barnaby's assessment. The intention was to force an admission from the Israeli government. Instead, the embassy dismissed the material as "having no base whatsoever in reality."

In Tel Aviv the photocopies presented to the embassy caused further consternation. For Ben-Menashe:

"The cat was out of the bag. I was still in London when Davies said Maxwell wanted to see me. We met in the same office where I had agreed to pay him $8 million commission for hiding our money behind the

Iron Curtain. Maxwell made it clear he understood what was to be done about the Vanunu story. He said he had already spoken to my boss in Tel Aviv."

As a result of that call, Admoni had finally come up with a way to drive Vanunu into the open.

The next issue of the *Sunday Mirror* contained a large photograph of Mordechai Vanunu, together with a story holding the technician and Oscar Guerrero up to ridicule, calling the Colombian a liar and a cheat, and the claim about Israel's nuclear capability a hoax. The report had been dictated by Maxwell, who had also supervised the prominent positioning of Vanunu's photograph. The first shot had been fired in a major disinformation campaign orchestrated by Mossad's psychological warfare department.

After reading it, Vanunu became agitated to the point where he told his *Sunday Times* "minders"—the reporters who had watched over him since he had been brought to London—that he "wanted to disappear. I don't want anyone to know where I am."

The panic-stricken technician was staying at the latest hotel his minders had chosen, the Mountbatten near Shaftesbury Avenue in Central London.

Following the *Sunday Mirror* publication, sayanim in London were mobilized to find him. Scores of trusted Jewish volunteers had each been given lists of hotels and boarding houses to check. In each call they gave a description of Vanunu from the photograph published in the *Sunday Mirror*, each caller claiming to be a relative checking to see if he had registered.

On Wednesday, September 25, Admoni received news from London that Vanunu had been located. It was time to bring into play the next stage of his plan.

The link between intelligence work and sexual entrapment was as old as spying itself. In the fourth book of Moses, Rahab, a prostitute, saves the lives of two of Joshua's spies from the king of Jericho's counterintelligence people—the first recorded meeting between the world's two oldest professions. One of Rahab's heirs in the love-and-espionage business was Mata Hari, a Dutch seductress who worked for the Germans in World War I and was executed by the French. From the beginning Mossad had recognized the value of sexual entrapment. For Meir Amit:

"It was another weapon. A woman has skills a man simply does not.

She knows how to listen. Pillow talk is not a problem for her. The history of modern intelligence is filled with accounts of women who have used their sex for the good of their country. To say that Israel has not done the same would be foolish. But our women are volunteers, high-minded women who know the risks involved. That takes a special kind of courage. It is not so much a question of sleeping with someone. It is to lead a man to believe you will do so in return for what he has to tell you. That does not begin to describe the great skills that are called into play to achieve that."

Nahum Admoni had handpicked an agent who possessed all those qualities to entice Mordechai Vanunu into Mossad's hands.

Cheryl Ben-Tov was a bat leveyha, one grade below a *katsa*. Born into a wealthy Jewish family in Orlando, Florida, she had seen her parents' marriage end in a bitterly contested divorce. She found solace in religious studies, which led to her spending three months on a kibbutz in Israel. There she became immersed in Jewish history and the Hebrew language. She decided to remain in Israel. At the age of eighteen she met and fell in love with a Sabra, a native-born Israeli, called Ofer Ben-Tov. He worked for Aman as an analyst. A year after they met the couple were married.

Among the wedding guests were several high-ranking members of the Israeli intelligence community, including one from Meluckha, Mossad's recruiting department. During the marriage feast he asked Cheryl the sort of questions any bride might expect. Was she going to go on working? Have a family at once? Caught up in the excitement of the celebrations, Cheryl had said her only plan was to try to find a way to give something back to her country, which had given her so much, referring to Israel as "family." A month after she returned from her honeymoon, she received a call from the wedding guest: he said he had been thinking over what they had spoken about and maybe there was a way for her to help.

They arranged to meet at a café in downtown Tel Aviv. He astonished her by citing with complete accuracy her school grades, her family history, how she had met her husband. Perhaps sensing her anger at having her privacy invaded, he explained that all the information was in her husband's file at Aman.

The recruiter understood that the relationship between himself and a potential recruit could often be tricky; it has been likened to a warlock initiating a neophyte into a secret sect with its special signs, in-cantations, and rites: it is the fellowship of Orpheus without a love of music. After telling Cheryl for whom he worked, the man delivered a set piece. Mossad was always on the lookout for people who wanted to serve their country. At the wedding she had compared Israel to a family. Well, Mossad was like that. Once you were accepted, you were part of its family, protected and nurtured. In return you served the family in any way asked of you. Was she interested?

Cheryl was. She was told she would have to undergo preliminary tests. During the next three months she took a number of written and oral examinations in various safe houses around Tel Aviv. Her high IQ—she consistently registered 140 in these tests—American background, general knowledge, and social skills made her an above-average recruit.

She was told she was suitable for training.

Before that, she had a further session with her recruiter. He told her she was about to enter a world in which she could share her experiences with no one, not even her husband. In such a lonely place, she would feel vulnerable to the corrupting lure of trust. But she must trust no one except her colleagues. She would be tutored in deceit, taught to use methods that violated every sense of decency and honor; she must ac-cept new ways of doing things. She would find some of the acts she would be asked to perform highly unpleasant, but she must always put them in the context of the mission she was on.

The recruiter leaned across the table in the interview room and said there was still time for her to change her mind. There would be no re-criminations; there should be no sense of failure on her part.

Cheryl said she was fully prepared to undergo training.

For the next two years she found herself in a world which, until then, had only been part of her favorite relaxation, going to the movies. She learned how to draw a gun while sitting in a chair, to memorize as many names as possible as they flashed with increasing speed across a small screen. She was shown how to pack her Beretta inside her pants, on the hip, and how to cut a concealed opening in her skirt or dress for easy access to the handgun.

From time to time, other recruits in her class left the training school; such departures were never a subject for discussion. She was sent on practice missions—breaking into an occupied hotel room, stealing documents from an office. Her methods were analyzed for hours by her instructors. She was aroused from her bed in the dead of night and dispatched on more exercises: picking up a tourist in a nightclub, then disengaging herself outside his hotel. Every move she made was observed by her tutors.

She was asked close questions about her sexual experiences. How many men had there been before her husband? Would she sleep with a stranger if her mission demanded? She answered truthfully: there had been no one before her husband; if she was absolutely certain that the success of a mission depended on it, then she would go to bed with a man. It would purely be sex, not love. She learned how to use sex to coerce, seduce, and dominate. She became especially good at that.

She was taught how to kill by firing a full clip of bullets into a target. She learned about the various sects of Islam and how to create a mishlashim, a dead-letter box. A day was spent perfecting a floater, a strip of microfilm attached to the inside of an envelope. Another was devoted to disguising herself by inserting cotton wadding in her cheeks to subtly alter the shape of her face. She learned to steal cars, pose as a drunk, chat up men.

One day she was summoned to the office of the head of the training school. He looked her up and down as if he were doing an inspection, checking off each item on a list in his mind. Finally he said she had passed.

Cheryl Ben-Tov was assigned as a bat leveyha working in Mossad's Kaisrut department, which liaised with Israeli embassies. Her specific role was to provide cover—as a girlfriend or even as a "wife"—for *katsas* on active service. She worked in a number of European cities, passing herself off as an American citizen. She did not sleep with one of her "lovers" or "husbands."

Admoni personally briefed her on the importance of her latest mission: with Vanunu now located, it would be up to her to use her skills to entice him out of Britain. This time her cover would be that of an American tourist traveling alone around Europe after a painful divorce. To give that part of her story credibility, she would make use of details from her own parents' separation. The final part of her story was to have a "sister" living in Rome. Her brief was to get Vanunu there.

On Tuesday, September 23, 1986, Cheryl Ben-Tov joined a team of nine Mossad *katsas* already in London. They were under the command of Mossad's director of operations, Beni Zeevi, a dour man with the stained teeth of a chain-smoker.

The *katsas* were staying in hotels between Oxford Street and the Strand. Two were registered in the Regent Palace. Cheryl Ben-Tov was registered as Cindy Johnson in the Strand Palace, staying in room 320. Zeevi had rented a room at the Mountbatten, close to the one Vanunu occupied, 105.

He may well have been among the first to observe the mood changes in the technician. Increasingly Vanunu was showing signs of strain. London was an alien environment for someone brought up in the small-town life of Beersheba. And, despite the efforts of his companions, he was lonely and hungry for female companionship, for a woman to sleep with. Mossad's psychologists had predicted that possibility.

On Wednesday, September 24, Vanunu insisted that his *Sunday Times* minders should allow him to go out alone. They reluctantly agreed. However, a reporter discreetly followed him into Leicester Square. There he saw Vanunu begin to talk to a woman. The newspaper would subsequently describe her as "in her mid-twenties, about five feet eight inches, plump, with bleached blond hair, thick lips, a brown trilby-style hat, brown tweed trouser suit, high heels and probably Jewish."

After a while they parted. Back in the hotel Vanunu confirmed to his minder he had met "an American girl called Cindy." He said he planned to meet her again. The reporters were worried. One of them said that Cindy's appearance in Leicester Square might be too much of a coincidence. Vanunu rejected their concerns. Whatever Cindy had said, it had been enough to make him want to plan to spend more time with her—and not in London, but in her "sister's" apartment in Rome.

Beni Zeevi and four other Mossad *katsas* were passengers on the flight on which Cheryl and Vanunu traveled to Rome. The couple took a taxi to an apartment in the old quarter of the city.

Waiting inside were three Mossad *katsas*. They overpowered Vanunu and injected him with a paralyzing drug. Late that night an ambulance arrived and Vanunu was carried on a stretcher out of the building. Neighbors were told by the concerned-looking *katsas* that a relative had fallen ill. Cheryl climbed into the ambulance, which drove off.

The ambulance sped out of Rome and down the coast. At a prearranged point a speedboat was waiting, to which Vanunu was transferred. The craft rendezvoused with a freighter anchored off the coast. Vanunu was taken on board. Beni Zeevi and Cheryl traveled with him. Three days later, in the middle of the night, the freighter docked at the port of Haifa.

Mordechai was soon facing Nahum Admoni's skilled interrogators. It was the prelude to a swift trial and a life sentence in solitary confinement. Cheryl Ben-Tov disappeared back into her secret world.

For more than eleven years Mordechai Vanunu remained in solitary confinement in a cell where Israel intended to keep him into the next century. His living conditions were bleak: poor food and an hour's exercise a day, and he spent his time in prayer and reading. Then, bowing to international pressure, Israel's government agreed in March 1998 that Vanunu could be moved to less restrictive conditions. However, he remained an Amnesty International prisoner of conscience and *The Sunday Times* regularly reminded its readers of his plight. Vanunu received no money for the world-shattering scoop he provided the newspaper. In 1998 he was finally released from solitary but, despite renewed appeals by his lawyers, there seemed little prospect of him being released from prison.

Ten years later, plumper now, her once-styled hair blowing in the Florida sea breeze, Cheryl was back in Orlando, ostensibly on vacation at Walt Disney World with her two young daughters.

Confronted in April 1997 by a *Sunday Times* reporter, she did not deny her role in the kidnapping. Her only concern was that publicity would "harm" her "position" in the United States.

Ari Ben-Menashe fared less well. He had seen many good men come and go, victims of the constant manipulation within the Israeli intelligence community. But he had never thought his day would come.

In 1989 he was arrested in New York and accused of conspiring "with others" to violate the Arms Export Control Act by attempting to sell C-130 military aircraft to Iran. The planes had originally been sold to Israel.

During the preliminary court hearing the government of Israel said it had "no knowledge" of Ben-Menashe. He produced a file of references from his superiors in the Israeli intelligence community. The Israeli government said they were forgeries. Ben-Menashe satisfied the court they were not. The Israeli government then said Ben-Menashe was "a low-level translator" employed "within" the Israeli intelligence community. Ben-Menashe countered that the nub of the case against him—the sale of the aircraft—had been sanctioned by the Israeli and the U.S. governments. He spoke of "hundreds of millions of dollars worth of authorized arms deals to Iran."

In Tel Aviv there was consternation once more. Rafi Eitan and David Kimche were both questioned about how much Ben-Menashe knew and how much damage he could do. The responses could only have been less than reassuring. Rafi Eitan said that Ari Ben-Menashe was in a position to blow wide open the U.S./Israeli arms-to-Iran network whose tentacles had extended everywhere: down to Central and South America, through London, into Australia, across to Africa, deep into Europe.

Waiting for trial in the Metropolitan Correction Center in New York, Ben-Menashe was visited by Israeli government lawyers. They offered him a deal: plead guilty in return for a generous financial settlement that would assure him a good life after he came out of prison. Ben-Menashe decided to tell it how it had been. He had started to do so when suddenly, in November 1990, a federal jury acquitted him of all charges.

A number of his former associates in Israeli intelligence felt that Ben-Menashe had been lucky to escape; they would claim that in his attempts to gain freedom he had used what one Mossad officer called "a scatter-gun approach," by attacking everyone who threatened his freedom. Kimche echoed the fervent hope of many when he later recalled "all we wanted was for him to disappear from our sight. He had set out to damage us, his country and its safety. The man was, and is, a menace."

But Israel had not counted on the revenge Ben-Menashe took. He wrote a book, *Profits of War,* that he hoped would have the same effect Woodward and Bernstein achieved with their Watergate exposé that brought down President Richard Nixon. Ben-Menashe's self-stated intention was clear: "to right the terrible wrongs of the 1980s and help remove from power those who were responsible."

In Tel Aviv there were urgent meetings. The question of buying the manuscript and forever locking it away was discussed. It was pointed out that Ben-Menashe had already refused a very large sum—said to be a million dollars—to stay silent; he was unlikely to have changed his mind. The decision was taken that every sayan in New York publishing must be alerted to use every possible means to stop the book appearing. What success they had is debatable, though the manuscript was submitted to several mainstream publishers before being published by Sheridan Square Press, a small New York house.

Ben-Menashe would describe his book as:

a tale of government by a cabal—how a handful of people in a few intelligence agencies determined the policies of their governments, secretly ran enormous operations without public accountability, abused power and public trust, lied, manipulated the media and deceived the public. Last, but not least, it is a tale of war—a war run not by generals, but by comfortable men in air-conditioned offices who are indifferent to human suffering.

Many saw the book as an outrageous act of atonement by its author; others saw it as an exaggerated version of events, with Ari Ben-Menashe at center stage.

In London, as he had done so many times before, Robert Maxwell hid behind the law, threatening to issue writs against anyone who dared to repeat Ben-Menashe's allegations about him. No English publisher was prepared to defy the tycoon; no newspaper was ready to use its investigative skills to substantiate Ben Menashe's claims.

Robert Maxwell, as Ben-Menashe had once firmly believed, remained convinced he was invincible for one simple reason. He had become a thief for Mossad. The more he had plundered for them, the greater had grown his belief he was indispensable to the service.

Again, like Ben-Menashe had once said, Maxwell liked to say on his visits to Israel that he too knew where all the bodies were buried. It was a claim that did not go unnoticed in Mossad.

CHAPTER 10

A DANGEROUS LIAISON

Robert Maxwell, who once fired a reporter who had cheated on his expenses, had been secretly stealing the pension funds of his employees to support Mossad. The wholesale thefts mirrored Mossad's own ruthless cunning and increasing willingness to take high-risk gambles.

Maxwell had personally removed the money through a series of interlinked financial maneuvers which, years later, would leave fraud investigators awed by his skilled duplicity. Maxwell had given mass-scale swindling a whole new dimension, transferring hundreds of thousands of dollars at a time into the special account Mossad maintained at the Bank of Israel in Tel Aviv. The funds had sometimes been laundered through an account the Israeli embassy in London had with Barclays Bank. Other banks Maxwell used for his fraud, unbeknown to them, included Credit Suisse in Geneva, the bank from which Ben-Menashe had transferred $450 million of ORA profits, with Maxwell's connivance. Sometimes the stolen pension funds traveled around the world, touching down at Chemical Bank in New York, Australia's First National Bank, and banks in Hong Kong and Tokyo. Only Robert Maxwell knew the money was purloined and where it was at any given time in its journey. What made matters worse was that he frequently ordered his newspapers to attack "white-collar crime."

Victor Ostrovsky, a Canadian-born Israeli who served as a Mossad case officer from 1984 to 1986, was the first to discover what had been happening:

"Mossad was financing many of its operations in Europe from money stolen from Maxwell's newspaper pension fund. They got their hands on the funds almost as soon as Maxwell made the purchase of the Mirror Newspaper Group with money lent to him by Mossad, together with expert advice he received from its financial analysts. What was sinister about it, aside from the theft, was that anyone in his news organization, traveling anywhere in the Middle East, was automatically suspected of working for Israel, and was only one rumor away from the hangman's noose."

On visits to Israel, Maxwell was feted like a head of state; he was a regular guest of honor at government banquets, and was given the finest accommodations. But Mossad had taken the precaution of being prepared should the proverbial "hand that fed it" suddenly withdraw its largesse. Discovering Maxwell had a strong sexual appetite and, because of his massive size, favored oral sex, Mossad arranged that during the tycoon's visits to Israel he was serviced from one of the stable of prostitutes the service maintained for blackmail purposes. Soon Mossad had acquired a small library of video footage of Maxwell in sexually compromising positions. The bedroom suite of the hotel where he stayed had been rigged with a concealed camera.

Ostrovsky's allegations had surfaced in two personal books that still inflame the entire Israeli intelligence community. *By Way of Deception* and *The Other Side of Deception* tore aside the veil of secrecy about his time in Mossad. He described operational methods and named numerous serving officers, and may well have compromised some of them in a classic exposé by a whistle-blower who believed he had been unfairly treated when he was dismissed from Mossad.

Ironically, the Israeli government had ignored the advice of Maxwell to say nothing about Ostrovsky's claims. In a meeting in Tel Aviv with Prime Minister Yitzhak Shamir, the tycoon cited what happened when the Thatcher government tried to halt publication of a book by a former MI5 officer, Peter Wright. His *Spycatcher* also contained similarly embarrassing details about Britain's security service. Pursuing its campaign to stop publication, the British government had been finally routed in the Australian courts, where Wright's prime publisher was based. *Spycatcher* had become a world best-seller and Britain had looked foolish.

The same fate had befallen the Israeli government. Pressured by serving and former members of Mossad—Meir Amit and Isser Harel had been particularly vocal in demanding action against Ostrovsky—Shamir ordered his attorney general to take legal action to halt the former *katsa*'s first book.

The case also stoked Shamir's virulent anti-Americanism, rooted in a fixed belief that the United States was partially responsible for the Holocaust. There were claims that he believed that President Roosevelt should have come to an "arrangement"—one of Shamir's favorite words—with Hitler to replace Britain, then the dominant power in the Middle East, with the Third Reich. In turn, Hitler would have allowed the Jews to travel to Palestine, and the Holocaust would never have happened.

Nonsensical as the idea was, it had colored Shamir's views of the United States to the point of near hatred. He had personally authorized, "as a gesture of goodwill" (another favorite phrase of Shamir's) to pass on to the Soviet Union a portion of the estimated five hundred thousand pages of documents Jonathan Pollard had stolen. Shamir hoped this would improve Israel's relationship with Moscow. The documents included current U.S. intelligence on Soviet air defenses and the CIA's annual review of the entire Russian capability to make war. One document included satellite photographs, communication intercepts, radar intelligence, and reports from CIA agents in the Soviet Union. When Shamir had been told by Nahum Admoni that the data would almost certainly enable Soviet counterintelligence to discover the spies, he had reportedly shrugged.

At their meeting to discuss what to do about Ostrovsky, Shamir repeated to Robert Maxwell what he had told others: he would do anything to reduce American influence in the world, and was convinced that Washington had encouraged Ostrovsky to publish his books as an act of retaliation.

Shamir asked Maxwell to mobilize his powerful media resources to destroy Ostrovsky's credibility. Maxwell pointed out that before employing him, Mossad would surely have checked his background.

Nevertheless, Ostrovsky became the object of a smear campaign in the Maxwell media, including the Tel Aviv tabloid *Maariv*, which Maxwell had bought. He was attacked as a fantasist, a liar, and, unlike Maxwell, not a true friend of Israel.

Having studied Ostrovsky's books, senior members of the Israeli intelligence community knew much of what he claimed was true.

The New York court refused to accept the Israeli government's argument that Israel's national security was endangered by Ostrovsky's revelations. His book became a best-seller.

Though the first person to publicly identify Robert Maxwell's links to Mossad, Ostrovsky had by no means revealed the full story. Like so much else, it had its roots firmly entangled in the activities of Shamir's old and valued friend, Rafi Eitan.

The two men had known each other since the 1950s, when they had served in Mossad, sharing an equal determination to fight to achieve Israel's place in the world.

Thirty years on, in 1986, it had been Shamir who had stood by Rafi Eitan during the crushing criticism he had faced in the aftermath of the Pollard affair, condemned as the leader "of a group of renegade intelligence officers acting without authorization."

The lie was a desperate attempt by the Israeli government to distance itself from an episode from which the intelligence community had hugely benefited, as had those of the Soviet Union and South Africa. With the full connivance of Israel, both countries had received valuable information about U.S. spying activities.

Nevertheless, with the concurrent unraveling of his role in the arms-to-Iran scandal, Rafi Eitan was professionally severely damaged. Though deeply hurt and angry at the way his own peers had singled him out for blame, the old spymaster had remained stoically silent in public; and for those trusted friends who had once sat in his living room and listened enthralled to his account of the capture of Adolf Eichmann, he had a new story to tell: how Israel turned on its own.

Increasingly fewer people rang Rafi Eitan's doorbell on Shay Street, or joined him in admiring his latest creations fashioned from scrap metal. For hours he would stand alone before his furnace brandishing his fiery torch, his mind filled no longer purely with anger over the way he had been treated, but with plans to find a way not only to "get back into the game," but also to make himself some "real money." His decision to continue to help his country despite the ignominy poured on him contained a touching simplicity: "Patriotism is not a fashionable word anymore. I am a patriot. I believe in my country. Right or wrong, I will fight anyone who threatens it or its people."

That had been the wellspring for a scheme he had secretly nurtured during the height of his involvement in Irangate. Like so many of Rafi Eitan's plans, this one required him to use his undoubted talent to exploit the original idea of someone else. It would be a plan that would eventually find him no longer remembered only as the man who captured Adolf Eichmann, but as someone who became a close associate of Robert Maxwell.

In 1967, communications expert William Hamilton returned to the United States from Vietnam, where he had devised a network of electronic listening posts to monitor the Vietcong as its forces moved through the jungle. Hamilton was offered a job with the National Security Agency. His first task had been to create a computerized Vietnamese-English dictionary that proved to be a powerful aid to translating Vietcong messages and interrogating prisoners.

It was an era when the revolution in electronic communications—satellite technology and microcircuitry—was changing the face of intelligence gathering: faster and more secure encryption and better imagery were coming online at increasing speed. Computers grew smaller and faster; more sophisticated sensors were able to separate thousands of conversations; photographic spectrum analysis lifted from millions of dots only the ones that were of interest; microchips made it possible to hear a whisper a hundred meters away; infrared lenses let one see in the black of night.

The fiber-optic sinews of a new society had contributed to operational intelligence: to amass and correlate data on a scale far beyond human capability offered a powerful tool in searching for a pattern and a modus operandi in terrorist actions. Work had started on the computer-driven Facial-Analysis Comparison and Elimination System (FACES) that would revolutionize the system of identifying a person from photographs. Based on forty-nine characteristics, each categorized on a 1 to 4 scale, FACES could make 15 million binary yes/no decisions in a *second*. Interlinked computers did simultaneous searches to eventually make a staggering 40 million binary decisions a second. Computers themselves had begun to reduce in size but retained a memory that contained the equivalent information of a five-hundred-page reference book.

Still working for the NSA, Hamilton saw an opening in this ever-expanding market; he would create a software program to interface with data banks in other computer systems. Its application in intelligence work would mean that the owner of the program would be able to interdict most other systems without their users being aware. A patriotic man, Hamilton intended his first client for the system would be the United States government.

Just as NASA had given the country an unassailable lead in space technology, so William Hamilton was confident he would do the same for the U.S. intelligence community. Encouraged by the NSA, the inventor worked sixteen-hour days, seven days a week. Obsessive and secretive, he was the quintessential researcher; the NSA was full of them.

After three years, Hamilton was close to producing the ultimate surveillance tool—a program that could track the movements of literally untold numbers of people in any part of the world. President Reagan's warning to terrorists, "You can run, but you can't hide," was about to come true.

Hamilton resigned from the NSA and purchased a small company called Inslaw. The company's stated function was to crosscheck court actions and discover if there was common background to litigants, witnesses and their families, even their attorneys—anyone involved or becoming involved in an action. Hamilton called the system Promis. By 1981, he had developed it to the point where he could copyright the software and turn Inslaw into a small, profit-making company. The future looked promising.

The NSA protested that he had made use of the agency's own research facilities to produce the program. Hamilton hotly rejected the allegation but offered to lease Promis to the Justice Department on a straightforward basis: each time the program was used, Inslaw would receive a fee. The proposed deal itself was unremarkable; Justice, like any government department, had hundreds of contractors providing services. Unknown to Hamilton, Justice had sent a copy of Hamilton's program to the NSA for "evaluation."

The reasons this was done would remain unclear. Hamilton had already demonstrated to Justice that the Promis program could do what he claimed: electronically probe into the lives of people in a way never before possible. For Justice and its investigative arm, the FBI, Promis offered a powerful tool to fight the Mafia's money-laundering and other criminal activities. Overnight it could also revolutionize the DEA's fight against the Colombian drug barons. To the CIA, Promis could become a weapon every bit as effective as a spy satellite. The possibilities seemed endless.

In the meantime, one of those characters the world of international wheeling and dealing regularly produces had heard about Promis. Earl Brian had been California's secretary of health during Reagan's time as state governor. Largely because Brian spoke Farsi, Reagan had encouraged him to put together a Medicare plan for the Iranian government. It was one of those quixotic ideas the future president of the United States loved: a version of Medicare would show Iran a positive side of America and at the same time improve the United States' image in the region. In a memorable phrase to Brian, the governor said, "If Medicare works in California, it can work anywhere."

During his visits to Tehran, Brian had come to the attention of Rafi Eitan, who was then one of the helmsmen steering the arms-for-hostages deal ever closer to the rocks. He invited Brian to Israel. They immediately struck up a rapport. Brian was captivated by his host's account of capturing Eichmann; Rafi Eitan was equally fascinated by his guest's description of California life in the fast lane.

Rafi Eitan soon realized that Brian could not widen his own circle of contacts in Iran and privately thought Reagan's idea for a Medicare program in Iran was "just about the craziest thing I had heard for a long time." Over the years the two men had stayed in touch; Rafi Eitan had even found time to send Brian a postcard from Apollo, Pennsylvania, where he was checking out the Numec plant. It contained the message, "This is a good place to be—from." Brian had kept Rafi Eitan informed about Promis.

In 1990 Brian arrived in Tel Aviv. He was more than weary from his long flight; the paleness on his face came from anger that the Justice

Department was using a version of the Promis program to track money-laundering and other criminal activities.

Rafi Eitan's instincts told him that his old friend could not have arrived at a more opportune time. Once more conflict had flared between Mossad and the other members of the Israeli intelligence community. The cause was a new Arab uprising, the Intifada. Promis could be an effective weapon to counter its activities.

The revolution had spread with remarkable speed, stunning the Israelis and galvanizing the Palestinians in the West Bank and Gaza Strip. The more people the Israeli army arrested, shot, beat, and uprooted from their homes, the swifter the Intifada spread. There was something close to grudging understanding outside Israel when a young Arab boy used a hang glider to evade Israel's sophisticated border defenses with Lebanon and land in scrubland close to the small northern town of Kiryat Shmona. In a few minutes the youth killed six heavily armed Israeli soldiers and wounded seven more before he was shot dead.

The incident became enshrined in Palestinian minds; within the Israeli intelligence community there was furious finger-pointing. Shin Bet blamed Aman; both blamed Mossad for its failure to provide advance warning from Lebanon. Worse followed. Six dangerous terrorists escaped from the maximum-security jail in Gaza. Mossad blamed Shin Bet. That agency said the escape plot had been organized from outside the country—which made Mossad culpable.

Almost daily, Israeli soldiers and civilians were shot dead in the streets of Jerusalem, Tel Aviv, and Haifa. Desperate to regain authority, Defense Minister Yitzhak Rabin announced he was implementing a policy of "force, might and beatings," but it had little effect.

Beset by deepening interservice strife, the Israeli intelligence community was unable to agree on a coordinated policy to deal with mass Arab resistance on a scale not seen since the War of Independence. An added thorn was the criticism from the United States over the growing evidence on TV screens of the brutal methods deployed by Israeli soldiers. For the first time U.S. networks, normally friendly to Israel, began to screen footage which, for sheer brutality, matched what had happened in Beijing's Tiananmen Square. Two Israeli soldiers were filmed relentlessly smashing a rock against the arm of a Palestinian youth; an IDF patrol was caught on camera beating a pregnant Palestinian mother; children in Hebron were shown having IDF rifle butts smashed against their bodies for throwing stones.

The Intifada coalesced to form the United National Leadership of the Uprising. Every Arab community was postered with instructions in Arabic on how to stage strikes, close shops, boycott Israeli goods, refuse to recognize the civil administration. It was reminiscent of the resistance in the last days of the German occupation of France in World War II.

Desperate to reestablish Mossad's preeminent role among the intelligence community, Nahum Admoni took action. On February 14, 1988, a kidon team was sent to the Cypriot port of Limassol. They planted a powerful bomb on the chassis of a Volkswagen Golf. It belonged to one of the leaders of the Intifada, Muhammad Tamimi. With him were two senior PLO officers. They had met with Libyan officials who had handed over $1 million to continue bankrolling the Intifada. All three men were killed in the massive explosion that rocked the entire port.

The following day, Mossad struck again—planting a limpet mine on the hull of the *Soi Phayne*, a passenger ship the PLO had just bought for an intended public relations exercise. With the world's press on board, the ship would have sailed to Haifa as a poignant reminder of the Palestinians' "right to return" to their homeland—and a more pointed reminder of the Jewish boats, immortalized by the *Exodus*, which, forty years before, had defied the British navy to bring the survivors of the Holocaust to Israel, also under their "right to return." The *Soi Phayne* was destroyed.

The operations had done nothing to daunt Arab determination. At every turn guerrillas were able to outsmart the Israelis, whose only response seemed to be violence and more violence. The world watched as Israel not only failed to stop the Intifada but also lost the propaganda war. Commentators made the comparison that here was a modern-day David-versus-Goliath conflict, with the IDF cast in the role of the Philistine giant.

Yasser Arafat used the Intifada as an opportunity to regain control over his dispossessed people. Around the world his voice cracked with fury on radio and television that what was happening was the direct result of Israel's policy of stealing Arab land. He urged every Arab to rally in support. One day Arafat was in Kuwait urging Hamas, the terrorist group backed by Iran, to provide its deadly skills. The next he was in Lebanon, meeting with the leaders of Islamic Jihad. Arafat was achieving what had, only a short time before, seemed impossible— uniting Arabs of all persuasions in a common cause. To them all he was "Mr. Palestine" or "Chairman."

Mossad was constantly flummoxed by Arafat's strategies as he flitted between Arab capitals. It had little or no warning where he would turn up, or whom he would next rally to his side.

All this and more Rafi Eitan explained to his houseguest, Earl Brian. In turn Brian described how Promis worked. In his view, there was still work to be done to bring the program up to speed. Rafi Eitan realized that Promis could then have an impact on the Intifada. For a start, the system could lock on to computers in the PLO's seventeen offices scattered around the world to see where Arafat was going and what he could be planning. Rafi Eitan put aside his foraging for scrap metal and focused on how to exploit the brave new world Promis offered.

No longer, for instance, would it be necessary to rely solely on human intelligence to understand the mind-set of a terrorist. With Promis it would be possible to know exactly when and where he would strike. Promis could track a terrorist's every step.

To achieve such a breakthrough would once more undoubtedly make him a powerful figure in the Israeli intelligence community. But the wounds inflicted on him by his former peers had gone deep. He had been turned out into the cold with little more than a modest pension. He was getting on in years; his first obligation was to his family, whom, through his work, he had been forced to neglect for long periods. Promis offered an opportunity to make amends; handled properly, it could make his fortune. However, for all his brilliance, Rafi Eitan was no computer genius; his skills in that area extended to little more than switching on his modem. But his years at LAKAM had given him access to all the experts he would need.

When Earl Brian returned to the United States, Rafi Eitan put together a small team of former LAKAM programmers. They deconstructed the Promis disc and rearranged its various components, then added several elements of their own. There was no way for anyone to be able to claim ownership of what Promis had become. Rafi Eitan decided to keep the original name because it was "a good marketing tool to explain what the system was."

Intelligence operatives, untrained in computer technology beyond knowing which keys to tap, would be able to access information and judgments far more comprehensive than they could ever carry in their own heads. A Promis disc could fit a laptop computer and choose from a myriad of alternatives the one that made most sense. It would eliminate the need for deductive reasoning because there were too many correct but irrelevant matters to simultaneously take into account for human reasoning alone to suffice. Promis could be programmed to eliminate all superfluous lines of inquiry and amass and correlate data at a speed and scale beyond human capability.

But before it could be sold, according to Ben-Menashe, Rafi Eitan needed to add one further element. Ben-Menashe later claimed he was asked to organize the insertion of a "trapdoor," a built-in chip that, unknown to any purchaser, would allow Rafi Eitan to know what information was being sought.

Ben-Menashe knew someone who could create a trapdoor that even the most sophisticated scanners would be unable to detect. The man ran a small computer research and development company in Northern California. He and Ben-Menashe had been schoolboy friends, and for five thousand dollars he agreed to produce the microchip. It was, Ben-Menashe admitted, cheap at the price. The next stage would be to test the system.

Jordan was selected as the site, not only because it bordered on Israel, but because it had become a haven for the leaders of the Intifada. From the desert kingdom, they directed the Arab street mobs on the West Bank and Gaza to launch further attacks inside Israel. After an atrocity, PLO terrorists would slip across the border into Jordan, doing so often with the connivance of the Jordanian army.

Consequently, long before the Intifada, Jordan had become a proving ground for Mossad to develop its electronic skills. In the 1970s, Mossad technicians had tapped into the computer IBM had sold to the country's military intelligence service. The information gained had supplemented that provided by the deep-cover *katsa* Rafi Eitan had placed inside King Hussein's palace. Promis would offer much more.

To sell it directly to Jordan was impossible because normal business links between both countries were still some years away. Instead, Earl Brian's company, Hadron, made the deal. When the company's computer experts installed the program in Amman's military headquarters, they discovered the Jordanians had a French-designed system to track the movements of PLO leaders. Promis was secretly wired into the

French system. In Tel Aviv, Rafi Eitan soon saw results as the trapdoor showed which PLO leaders the Jordanians were tracking.

The next stage was to prepare the sales pitch for Promis. Yasser Arafat was selected as the ideal example. The PLO chairman was renowned for being security-conscious; he constantly changed his plans, never slept in the same bed two nights in succession, altered his mealtimes at the last moment.

Whenever Arafat moved, the details were entered on a secure PLO computer. But Promis could hack into its defenses to discover what aliases and false passports he was using. Promis could obtain his phone bills and check the numbers called. It would then crosscheck those with other calls made from those numbers. In that way, Promis would have a "picture" of Arafat's communications.

On a trip he would inform the local security authorities of his presence, and steps would be taken to provide protection. Promis could obtain the details by interdicting police computers. Wherever he went, Yasser Arafat would be unable to hide from Promis.

·Rafi Eitan realized that neither Earl Brian nor his company had the resources to market Promis globally. That would require someone with superb international contacts, boundless energy, and proven negotiating skills. There was only one man Rafi Eitan knew who had those requirements: Robert Maxwell.

Maxwell needed little convincing and, in his usual ebullient manner when there was a deal to be profited from, said he had a computer company through which to sell Promis. Degem Computers Limited was based in Tel Aviv and was already playing a useful role in Mossad's activities. Maxwell had allowed Mossad operatives, posing as Degem employees, to use the company's suboffices in Central and South America. Now Maxwell saw an opportunity not only to make a healthy profit from marketing Promis through Degem, but to further establish his own importance to Mossad and ultimately Israel.

On recent visits to Israel he had begun to display disturbing traits. Maxwell told Admoni he should start employing psychics to read the minds of Mossad's enemies. He began to suggest targets for elimination. He wanted to meet kidons and inspect their training camps. All these requests were firmly but politely parried by the Mossad chief. But within Mossad, questions began to be asked about Maxwell. Was his behavior only that of a megalomaniac throwing about his weight? Or was it a precursor of something else? Could the time eventually come when, despite all he had done for Israel, Robert Maxwell became sufficiently mentally unstable and unpredictable to create a problem?

But there was no doubting Maxwell was a brilliant marketeer of Promis—or, as far as Mossad was concerned, of the effectiveness of the system. The service had been the first to obtain the program and it had been a valuable tool in its campaign against the Intifada. Many of its leaders had left Jordan for safer hideouts in Europe after several had been assassinated in Jordan by kidons.

A spectacular success came when an Intifada commander who had moved to Rome called a Beirut number that Mossad's computers already had listed as the home of a known bomb maker. The Rome caller wanted to meet the bomb maker in Athens. Mossad used Promis to check all the travel offices in Rome and Beirut for the travel arrangements of both men. In Beirut, further checks revealed the bomber had ordered the local utility companies to suspend supplies to his home. A further search by Promis of the local PLO computers also showed the bomber had switched flights at the last moment. It did not save him. He was killed by a car bomb on the way to Beirut airport. Shortly afterward, in Rome, the Intifada commander was killed in a hit-and-run accident.

Meantime, Mossad was using Promis to read the secret intelligence of a number of services. In Guatemala, it uncovered the close ties between the country's security forces and drug traffickers and their outlets in the United States. Names were passed on to the DEA and FBI by Mossad.

In South Africa, a *katsa* in the Israeli embassy used Promis to track the country's banned revolutionary organization and their contacts with Middle Eastern groups. In Washington, Mossad specialists at the Israeli embassy used Promis to penetrate the communications of other diplomatic missions and U.S. government departments. The same was happening in London and other European capitals. The system had continued to yield valuable information for Mossad. By 1989, over $500 million worth of Promis programs had been sold to Britain, Australia, South Korea, and Canada. The figure would have been even bigger but for the CIA marketing its own version to intelligence agencies. In Britain, Promis was used by MI5 in Northern Ireland to track terrorists and the movements of political leaders like Gerry Adams.

Maxwell had also managed to sell the system to the Polish intelligence service, the UB. In return the Poles, according to Ben-Menashe, allowed Mossad to steal a Russian MiG-29. The operation was a reminder of the theft of the earlier version of the MiG from Iraq. A Polish general in charge of the UB office in Gdansk, in return for $1 million paid into a Citibank account in New York, had arranged for the aircraft to be written off as no longer airworthy, though the plane had only recently arrived from its Russian aircraft factory. The fighter was dismantled, placed in crates marked "Agricultural Machinery," and flown to Tel Aviv. There the plane was reassembled and test-flown by the Israeli air force, enabling its pilots to counter the MiG-29s in service with Syria.

It was weeks before the theft was discovered by Moscow during a routine inventory of aircraft supplied to Warsaw Pact countries. A strong protest was made by Moscow to Israel—backed by the threat to stop the exodus of Jews from the Soviet Union. The Israeli government, its air force having discovered all the MiG's secrets, apologized profusely for the "mistaken zeal of officers acting unofficially" and promptly returned the aircraft. By then the UB general had joined his dollar fortune in the United States. Washington had agreed to give him a new identity in return for the USAF being allowed to conduct its own inspection of the MiG.

Shortly afterward Robert Maxwell flew to Moscow. Officially he was there to interview Mikhail Gorbachev. In reality he had come to sell Promis to the KGB. Through its secret trapdoor microchip, it gave Israel unique access to Soviet military intelligence, making Mossad one of the best-briefed services on Russian intentions.

From Moscow Maxwell flew to Tel Aviv. As usual he was received like a potentate, excused all airport formalities, and welcomed by an official greeter from the Foreign Office.

Maxwell treated him the way he did all his staff, insisting the official carry his bags and sit beside the driver. Maxwell also demanded to know where his motorcycle escort was, and when told it was not available, he threatened to call the prime minister's office to have the greeter fired. At every traffic stop, Maxwell harangued the hapless official, and he continued to do so all the way to his hotel suite. Waiting was Maxwell's favorite prostitute. He sent her running; there were far more pressing matters than satisfying his sexual needs.

In London Robert Maxwell's newspaper empire was in grave financial trouble. Soon, without a substantial injection of capital, it would have to cease operations. But, in the City of London, where he had previously always found funding, there was a reluctance to go on providing it. Hard-nosed financiers who had met Maxwell sensed that behind his bluster and bully-boy tactics was a man who was losing the financial acumen that in the past had allowed them to forgive so much. In those days he had raged and threatened at the slightest challenge. Bankers had curbed their anger and caved in to his demands. But they would no longer do so. In the Bank of England and other financial institutions in the City, the word was that Maxwell was no longer a safe bet.

Their information was partially based on confidential reports from Israel that Maxwell was being pressed by his original Israeli investors to repay them the money that had helped him to acquire the Mirror Group. The time limit on repayments had long gone and the demands from the Israelis had become more insistent. Trying to fend them off, Maxwell had promised them a higher return on their money if they waited. The Israelis were not satisfied: they wanted their money back now. This was why Maxwell had come to Tel Aviv: he hoped to cajole them into granting him another extension. The signs were not good. During the flight, he had received several angry phone calls from the investors, threatening to place the matter before the City of London regulatory body.

There was a further matter for Maxwell to be concerned over. He had stolen some of the very substantial profits from ORA that he had been entrusted to hide in Soviet Bloc banks. He had used the money to try to prop up the Mirror Group. Maxwell had already stolen all he could from the staff pension fund, and the ORA money would not stretch very far.

And, unlike the Israeli investors, once that theft was uncovered, he would find himself confronting some very hard men, among them Rafi Eitan. Maxwell knew enough about the former Mossad operative to realize that would not be a pleasant experience.

From his hotel suite, Maxwell began to strategize. His share of the profits from Degem's marketing of Promis would not be able to stem the crisis. Neither would profits from *Maariv*, the Israeli tabloid modeled on his flagship *Daily Mirror*. But there was one possibility, the Tel Aviv–based Cytex Corporation he owned, which manufactured high-tech printing equipment. If Cytex could be sold quickly, the money could go some way to solving matters.

Maxwell ordered Cytex's senior executive, the son of Prime Minister

Yitzhak Shamir, to his suite. The executive had bad news: a quick sale was unlikely. Cytex, while holding its own, faced increasing competition. This was not the time to take it to the market. To sell would also throw skilled people out of work at a time when unemployment was a serious problem in Israel.

The reaction provoked a furious outburst from Maxwell as his last hope of rescue faded. Tactically he made an error in lambasting the prime minister's son, who now told his father that Maxwell was in serious financial trouble. The prime minister, aware of the tycoon's links to Mossad, informed Nahum Admoni. He called a meeting of senior staff to see how to deal with what had become a problem.

Later it emerged that several options were discussed.

Mossad could ask the prime minister to use his own considerable influence with the Israeli investors not only to wait a while longer for their money, but to mobilize their own resources and contacts to find money to bail out Maxwell. This was rejected on the grounds that Maxwell had managed to upset Shamir with his cavalier attitude. Everyone knew that Shamir had a strong sense of self-preservation and would now wish to distance himself from Maxwell.

Another option was for Mossad to approach its highly placed sayanim in the City of London and urge them to support a rescue package for Mossad. At the same time Mossad-friendly journalists in Britain could be encouraged to write supportive stories about the troubled tycoon.

Again those suggestions were discounted. Reports Admoni had received from London suggested that many of the sayanim would welcome the end of Maxwell and that few journalists outside Mirror newspapers would dream of writing favorable stories about a tycoon who had spent years threatening the media.

The final option was for Mossad to break off all contact with Maxwell. There was a risk there: Maxwell, on the evidence of his present unpredictable state of mind, could well use his newspapers to actually attack Mossad. Given the access he had been given, that could have the most serious consequences.

On that somber note, the meeting concluded that Admoni would see Maxwell and remind him of his responsibility to both Mossad and Israel. That night the two men met over dinner in Maxwell's hotel suite. What transpired between them would remain a secret. But hours later, Robert Maxwell left Tel Aviv in his private plane. It would be the last time, it would turn out, that anyone in Israel would see him alive.

Back in London, Maxwell, against all the odds, seemed to be succeeding in holding on to his newspaper group. He was likened to an African whirling dervish as he went from one meeting to another seeking financial support. From time to time he called Mossad to speak to Admoni, always informing the director general's secretary that the "little Czech" was on the line. The sobriquet had been bestowed on Maxwell after he had been recruited. What was said in those calls would remain unknown.

But a clue would later emerge from the former *katsa*, Victor Ostrovsky. He believed Maxwell was insisting it was payback time; that the huge sum of money he had stolen from the *Mirror* pension fund should now be returned to him. At the same time, Maxwell also proposed that Mossad should, on his behalf, lobby for Mordechai Vanunu to be freed and handed over to him. Maxwell would then fly the technician to London and personally interview him for the *Daily Mirror*. The story would be Vanunu's "act of atonement," written in a way that would show Israel's compassion. With the chutzpah characteristic of so many of his actions, Maxwell added it would be a huge circulation booster for the *Mirror* and would unlock those doors still closed to him in the City of London.

Ostrovsky was not alone in believing that the preposterous plan finally convinced Mossad that Robert Maxwell had become a dangerous loose cannon.

On September 30, 1991, further evidence of Maxwell's bizarre behavior came when he telephoned Admoni. This time there was no disguising the threat in Maxwell's words. His financial affairs had once more taken a turn for the worse, and he was being investigated in Parliament and the British media, so long held at bay by his posse of high-priced lawyers and their quiver of writs. Maxwell then said that unless Mossad arranged to immediately return all the stolen *Mirror* pension fund money, he could not be sure if he would be able to keep secret Admoni's meeting with Vladimir Kryuchkov, the former head of the KGB. Kryuchkov was now in a Moscow prison awaiting trial for his role in an abortive coup to oust Mikhail Gorbachev. A key element of the plot had been a meeting Kryuchkov had on Maxwell's yacht in the Adriatic shortly before the coup was launched.

Mossad had promised that Israel would use its influence with the United States and key European countries to diplomatically recognize the new regime in Moscow. In return, Kryuchkov would arrange for all Soviet Jews to be released and sent to Israel. The discussion had come to nothing. But revealing it could seriously harm Israel's credibility with the existing Russian regime and with the United States.

That was the moment, Victor Ostrovsky would write, when "a small meeting of right-wingers at Mossad headquarters resulted in a consensus to terminate Maxwell."

If Ostrovsky's claim is true—and it has never been formally denied by Israel—then it was unthinkable that the group was acting without the highest sanction and perhaps even with the tacit knowledge of Israel's prime minister, Yitzhak Shamir, the man who had once had his own share of killing Mossad's enemies.

The matter for Mossad could only have become more urgent with the publication of a book by the veteran American investigative reporter Seymour M. Hersh, *The Samson Option: Israel, America and the Bomb*, which dealt with Israel's emergence as a nuclear power. News of the book had caught Mossad totally by surprise and copies were rushed to Tel Aviv. Well researched, it could nevertheless still have been effectively dealt with by saying nothing; the painful lesson of the mistake of confronting Ostrovsky's publisher (also the publisher of this book) had been absorbed. But there was one problem: Hersh had identified Maxwell's links to Mossad. Those ties mostly involved the Mirror Group's handling of the Vanunu story and the relationship between Nick Davies, ORA, and Ari Ben-Menashe. Predictably, Maxwell had taken refuge behind a battery of lawyers, issuing writs against Hersh and his London publishers. But, for the first time, he met his match. Hersh, a Pulitzer Prize winner, refused to be cowed. In Parliament, more pointed questions were asked about Maxwell's links to Mossad. Old suspicions surfaced. MPs demanded to know, under parliamentary privilege, how much Maxwell knew about Mossad's operations in Britain. For Victor Ostrovsky, "the ground was starting to burn under Maxwell's feet."

Ostrovsky would claim that the carefully prepared Mossad plan to kill Maxwell hinged on being able to persuade him to keep a rendezvous where Mossad could strike. It had a striking similarity to the plot that had led to the death of Mehdi Ben-Barka in Paris.

On October 29, 1991, Maxwell received a call from a *katsa* at the Israeli embassy in Madrid. Maxwell was asked to come to Spain the next day, and, according to Ostrovsky, "his caller promised that things would be worked out so there was no need to panic." Maxwell was told to fly to Gibraltar and board his yacht, the *Lady Ghislaine*, and order the crew to set sail for the Canary Islands "and wait there for a message."

Robert Maxwell agreed to do as instructed.

On October 30, four Israelis arrived in the Moroccan port of Rabat. They said they were tourists on a deep-sea fishing vacation and hired an oceangoing motor yacht. They set off toward the Canary Islands.

On October 31, after Maxwell reached the port of Santa Cruz on the island of Tenerife, he dined alone in the Hotel Mency. After dinner a man briefly joined him. Who he was and what they spoke about remain part of the mystery of the last days of Robert Maxwell. Shortly afterward, Maxwell returned to his yacht and ordered it back to sea. For the next thirty-six hours, the *Lady Ghislaine* sailed between the islands, keeping well clear of land, cruising at various speeds. Maxwell had told the captain he was deciding where to go next. The crew could not recall Maxwell showing such indecision.

In what it claimed was a "world exclusive," headlined "How and why Robert Maxwell was murdered," Britain's *Business Age* magazine subsequently claimed that a two-man hit team crossed in a dinghy during the night from a motor yacht that had shadowed the *Lady Ghislaine*. Boarding the yacht, they found Maxwell on the afterdeck. The men overpowered him before he could call for help. Then, "one assassin injected a bubble of air into Maxwell's neck via his jugular vein. It took just a few moments for Maxwell to die."

The magazine concluded the body was dropped overboard and the assassins returned to their yacht. It would be sixteen hours before Maxwell was recovered—enough time for a needle prick to recede beyond detection as a result of water immersion and the skin being nibbled by fish.

More certain, on the night of November 4–5, Mossad's problems with Maxwell were laid to rest in the cold swell of the Atlantic. The subsequent police investigation and the Spanish autopsy left unanswered questions. Why were only two of the yacht's eleven-man crew awake? Normally five shared the night watch. To whom did Maxwell send a number of fax messages during those hours? What became of the copies? Why did the crew take so long to establish Maxwell was not on board? Why did they delay raising the alarm for a further seventy minutes? To this day no convincing answers have emerged.

Three Spanish pathologists were assigned to perform the autopsy. They wanted the vital organs and tissue to be sent to Madrid for further tests. Before this could be done, the Maxwell family intervened, ordering the body embalmed and flown forthwith to Israel for burial. The Spanish authorities, unusually, did not object.

Who or what had persuaded the family to suddenly act as it did?

On November 10, 1991, Maxwell's funeral took place on the Mount of Olives in Jerusalem, the resting place for the nation's most revered heroes. It had all the trappings of a state occasion, attended by the country's government and opposition leaders. No fewer than six serving and former heads of the Israeli intelligence community listened as Prime Minister Shamir eulogized: "He has done more for Israel than can today be said."

Those who stood among the mourners included a man dressed in a somber black suit and shirt, relieved only at the throat by his Roman collar. Born into a Lebanese Christian family, he was a wraithlike figure—barely five feet tall and weighing little over a hundred pounds. But Father Ibrahim was no ordinary priest. He worked for the Vatican's Secretariat of State.

His discreet presence at the funeral was not so much to mark the earthly passing of Robert Maxwell, but to acknowledge the still-secret ties developing between the Holy See and Israel. It was a perfect example of Meir Amit's dictum that intelligence cooperation knows no limits.

CHAPTER 11

Unholy Alliances

From the beginning, successive Israeli prime ministers had been fascinated by the concept of the pope as an absolute ruler elected for life, a leader not held accountable to any judiciary or legislative control. Using a pyramidic and monarchical structure, the supreme pontiff wielded extraordinary influence to shape the economic, political, and ideological outlook of not only the Catholic faithful but the world at large. David Ben-Gurion once growled: "Never mind that nonsense about how many divisions does the pope have—just look at how many people he can summon to his aid."

For Mossad, the appeal was the sheer secrecy with which the Vatican operated. It was a well-defined mechanism, strictly enforced, and it cloaked everything the Holy See did. Often months passed before the first hints emerged of papal involvement in some diplomatic initiative; even then the full story rarely surfaced. Each Mossad chief wondered how to penetrate the veil. But various attempts by both the government of Israel and Mossad to establish a good working relationship with the Vatican had been politely but firmly rejected.

The reality was that within the Holy See's Secretariat of State—the equivalent of a secular foreign office—there existed a powerful anti-Israeli faction. These soutaned monsignors would invariably refer to the West Bank and the Gaza Strip as "occupied territories" and the Golan Heights as having been "annexed" from Syria. In the evenings, they would drive out of their tiny city-state to the apartments of wealthy Arabs on Rome's Via Condotti, or join them for cocktails in the Piazza Navona, dispassionately listening to dreams of removing Israel from the face of the earth.

The priests were careful what they said; they believed the Jewish state had its agents everywhere, watching, listening, perhaps even recording and photographing. One of the first warnings a newcomer to the Secretariat received was to be aware of being "spied or enveigled upon, especially by agents from countries the Vatican firmly refuses to diplomatically recognize." Israel was high on that list. Upon his election in 1978, Pope John Paul II had reaffirmed it would remain there; only well into his pontificate would he finally agree to grant full diplomatic status to Israel.

The information the pope received about Israel continued to be influenced by contacts his priest-diplomats made with Arabs. Their forays into Rome were followed by the monsignors returning to the third floor of the Apostolic Palace, the overcrowded, artificially lit, and poorly ventilated headquarters of the papal diplomatic service. Known as the Extraordinary Affairs Section, it was responsible for implementing the foreign policy of the Holy See. Its twenty "desks" dealt with almost as much paperwork as other major foreign ministries, a measure of the Vatican's ever expanding worldwide diplomatic interests.

The Middle East desk was housed in cubbyhole offices overlooking the San Damaso Courtyard, a magnificent piazza in the heart of the great palace. One of the first papers the desk presented to the new Polish pontiff was a closely argued case for Jerusalem to have international status and be patrolled by United Nations forces with the Vatican having responsibility for all the city's Christian shrines. News of the proposal reached Tel Aviv early in 1979, having been photocopied from a document passed by a monsignor to a wealthy Lebanese Christian living in Rome. The man's staff included a Mossad sayan. The prospect of internationalizing Jerusalem angered Prime Minister Menachem Begin, who ordered Mossad's chief, Yitzhak Hofi, to redouble his efforts to establish contact with the Vatican.

Both knew what had happened the last time Mossad tried to do that under cover of a state visit by Begin's predecessor, the redoubtable Golda Meir.

Late in 1972, Golda Meir finally received a response from Pope Paul VI that he would be prepared to receive her in a short private audience. In December of that year she told cabinet members at their weekly session who had wondered if the meeting would produce anything worthwhile that she was fascinated by the "Marxist structuralism of the papacy. First it has financial power which is almost unprecedented. Then it operates without political parties or trade unions. The whole apparatus is organized for control. The Roman Curia controls the bishops, the bishops control the clergy, the clergy control the laity. With its multitude of secretariats, commissions and structures, it is a system tailor-made for spying and informing!"

The date for the papal audience was set for the morning of January 15, 1973; Golda Meir was informed she would have precisely thirty-five minutes with the pontiff; at the end they would exchange gifts. There was no specific agenda for the meeting but Golda Meir hoped to persuade the pope to visit Israel. The official reason would be for him to celebrate Mass for the hundred thousand or so Christian Arabs in the country. But she also knew his presence would give the country a huge boost on the international stage.

For security reasons there would be no prior announcement about the meeting. At the end of her visit to a conference of international socialists in Paris, Golda Meir would fly on to Rome in her chartered El Al plane. Only on the flight would journalists accompanying her be told she was going to the Vatican.

Zvi Zamir, Mossad's chief, flew to Rome to check security arrangements. The city was a hotbed for terrorist factions from both the Middle East and Europe. Rome had also become an important listening post for Mossad's current preoccupation, locating and killing the perpetrators of the Munich Olympics massacre.

Zamir had based Mark Hessner, one of his ablest *katsas*, in Rome to probe the city's large Arab community. In Milan, another center for terrorist activity, the Mossad chief had stationed Shai Kauly, another experienced *katsa*. After Zamir briefed both men on the forthcoming visit, they accompanied him to the Vatican.

On January 10, 1973, as the three men were chauffeured across Rome to the Vatican, they knew far more about the Holy See's long relationship with another intelligence service than their hosts may have realized.

In 1945, the wartime Office of Strategic Services (OSS)—the forerunner to the CIA—had been welcomed into the Vatican, in the words of James Jesus Angleton, the head of the OSS Rome station, "with open arms." Pope Pius XII and his Curia asked Angleton to help the Church's militant anti-Communist crusade by getting the Italian Christian Democratic Party into power. Angleton, a practicing Catholic, used all the considerable resources at his disposal to bribe, blackmail, and threaten voters to support them. He had been given full access to the Vatican's unparalleled information-gathering service through Italy; every curate and priest reported on the activities of Italian Communists in their parishes. When the Vatican had assessed the information, it was passed to Angleton, who sent it on to Washington.

There it was used to support the now deeply entrenched State Department fear that the Soviet Union presented a real and long-term threat to the West. Angleton was told to do anything that would stop the wartime resistance activists of Italy's Communist Party from taking over. Like the pope, Angleton was haunted by the specter of a worldwide Communist threat that would split the globe into two systems— capitalism and socialism—which could never peacefully coexist. Stalin had himself said no less.

The pope was convinced that the Italian Communists were at the spearhead of a campaign to destroy the Church at every opportunity. The regular meetings between Pius and the pious Angleton became sessions where the bogey of Communism loomed ever larger. The pope urged Angleton to tell the United States it must do all possible to destroy the threat. The pontiff who represented peace on earth became an enthusiastic proponent of U.S. foreign policy which led to the Cold War.

By 1952, the Rome station of what was now the CIA was being run by another devout Catholic, William Colby—who went on to mastermind the CIA's activities in Vietnam. Colby had established a powerful network of informers within the Secretariat of State and every Vatican congregation and tribunal. He used them to help the CIA fight Soviet espionage and subversion across the globe. Priests regularly reported to the Vatican what was happening. In countries like the Philippines, where Communists were trying to make inroads into what had long been a devout Catholic nation, the CIA was able to launch effective counterattacks. The pope saw the violence as necessary and shared the view that if the United States did not perform what he once called "sad, but necessary actions," the world would have to endure decades of further suffering.

In 1960, the CIA achieved another breakthrough when Milan's Cardinal Montini—three years later to become Pope Paul VI—gave the CIA the names of priests in the United States deemed by the Vatican to be still soft on Communism. The Cold War was at its peak; paranoia ran rife in Washington. The FBI hounded the priests, and many left the country, heading for Central and South America. The CIA had a substantial slush fund, called "project money," used to make generous gifts to Catholic charities, schools, and orphanages to pay for the restoration of church buildings the Vatican owned. All-expenses-paid holidays were given to priests and nuns known to be staunchly pro-American. Italian cardinals and bishops received cases of champagne and hampers of gourmet delicacies in a country still recovering from the food shortages of World War II. Successive CIA station chiefs were regarded by the Vatican as being more important than America's ambassadors to Italy.

When John XXIII was elected supreme pontiff in 1958, he stunned the Curia (the Vatican civil service) by saying that the crusade against Communism had largely failed. He ordered the Italian bishops to become "politically neutral." The CIA was frantic when Pope John ordered its free access to the Vatican must stop. The Agency's panic increased when the CIA learned the pope had begun to nurture the seeds of an embryonic Ostpolitik and started a cautious dialogue with Nikita Khrushchev, the Soviet leader. For the CIA's station chief in

Rome, "the Vatican was no longer totally committed to the American system. The Holy See is hostile and we must from now on see its activities in that light."

CIA analysts in Washington prepared exhaustive assessments with such grandiose titles as *The Links between the Vatican and Communism*. In the late spring of 1963, the Rome station reported that the Holy See was to establish full diplomatic relations with Russia. The CIA's director, John McCone, flew to Rome and bulldozed his way into a meeting with Pope John, saying he had come at the insistence of America's first Catholic president, John F. Kennedy. McCone told the pontiff that the Church "must stop this drift toward Communism. It is both dangerous and unacceptable to dicker with the Kremlin. Communism is a Trojan horse as the recent left-wing victories in the Italian national elections indicate. In office the Communists have dismantled many of the policies Catholic parties supported."

For ten full minutes, McCone spoke in this blunt manner without interruption. Silence finally settled over the audience chamber in the Apostolic Palace. For a moment longer the old pope studied his tall, ascetic visitor. Then, speaking softly, John explained that the Church he led had an urgent duty: to end abject poverty and the denial of human rights, to close down the slum dwellings and the shantytowns, to end racism and political oppression. He would talk to anybody who would help him do that—including the Soviets. The only way to meet the challenge of Communism was to confront it with reasoned argument.

McCone, unable to contain his anger any longer—"I had not come to debate"—said the CIA had ample evidence that, while the pope pursued his détente with Moscow, Communism was persecuting priests through the Soviet Bloc, Asia, and South America: Pope John realized that was all the more reason to seek a better relationship with the Soviets. Defeated, McCone returned to Washington convinced that Pope John was "softer on Communism than any of his predecessors."

John's not unexpected death—he had a rapidly progressing cancer—was greeted with relief by McCone and President Kennedy.

When Montini of Milan became Paul VI in late 1963, Washington relaxed. Two days after his inauguration, the pope received Kennedy in private audience. Outside, McCone strolled through the Vatican gardens like a landowner who had returned home after a long absence.

Paul's long pontificate was blighted on the personal front by his declining health and, on the international stage, by the Vietnam War. He came to believe that the escalation President Lyndon Johnson had ordered in 1966 was morally wrong and that the Holy See should be given the role of peacemaker. Three months after Richard Nixon came into the Oval Office, he flew to Rome to meet the pope. The president told him he proposed to increase America's commitment in Vietnam. Once more the CIA found itself out of favor in the Vatican.

All this, Zvi Zamir had learned from his Washington *katsa*. Now, on this brilliantly sunny morning on January 10, 1973, as he and his two colleagues were driven into the Vatican to check the security arrangements for Golda Meir's visit, Zamir hoped it would result in Mossad taking the place of the CIA in the Vatican's long flirtation with the intelligence world.

Waiting for them outside the Apostolic Palace was the head of Vatican security, a tall, pinch-faced man wearing a dark blue suit, the uniform of the Vigili, the Vatican security service. For several hours he had taken them on a tour of the small city-state, checking possible places where an Arab gunman could hide before trying to assassinate Golda Meir. Unknown to the Vatican security chief, Zvi Zamir was also looking for places where Mossad could plant bugging devices once it had established a working relationship with the Holy See. Zamir flew back to Tel Aviv satisfied with the city-state's security presentations. More important, he believed he had detected a softening in the attitude of the Holy See toward Israel.

Even before Zamir had landed in Israel, details of Golda Meir's visit were in the hands of Black September, almost certainly leaked by a pro-Arab priest in the Secretariat of State. For Ali Hassan Salameh, the group's leader, though he was on the run from Mossad after masterminding the Munich atrocity, Golda Meir's visit was an opportunity he could not ignore. He began to plan a missile attack against her plane as it landed at Rome's Leonardo Da Vinci Airport. He hoped to kill not only her, but key government ministers who would be accompanying the prime minister and the senior Mossad men who would also be on board. By the time Israel had recovered from these blows, Salameh hoped, he and his men would be ensconced in the hideout they were negotiating with the Russians to provide.

Since 1968, when a generation born after World War II launched its own war on society—under such disparate names as Italy's Red Brigades,

Germany's Red Army Faction, the Turkish People's Liberation Army, Spain's ETA, and the PLO—the Kremlin had recognized their value in helping to destroy imperialism—and Israel.

Arab terrorists had struck a special chord with the KGB: they were more daring and more successful than most other groups. And they faced a most powerful enemy, Mossad, long a service the KGB both loathed and admired for its sheer ruthlessness. The KGB arranged for selected Arab activists to receive training at the Patrice Lumumba University in Moscow. This was no ordinary campus, but a finishing school for terrorists. They received not only political indoctrination, but also instruction in the latest KGB terrorism target selection and assassination techniques. It was at Patrice Lumumba that Salameh put together the finishing touches to the Munich massacre. After the murderous attack, the surviving members of the group asked Russia to give them sanctuary. But the Soviets were reluctant to do so: the firestorm of fury the Munich attack had generated had made even the Kremlin unwilling to be discovered shielding the killers. They had told Salameh his request for asylum for himself and his men was still being considered.

Nevertheless, the Russians had done nothing to cooperate in the hunt for Black September—and certainly had not revealed that the group had a cache of Soviet missiles hidden in Yugoslavia. These rockets would be used to shoot down Golda Meir's aircraft.

The plan, like all those created by Salameh, was bold and simple. The missiles would be loaded onto a boat at Dubrovnik and taken across the Adriatic to Bari on Italy's east coast. From there they would be brought by road into Rome shortly before Golda Meir's plane arrived. Salameh had also not forgotten the lessons on strategy his KGB instructor at Patrice Lumumba had given: Always make the enemy look the other way. Salameh needed to direct Mossad's vigilance away from Rome in the run-up to the attack.

On December 28, 1972, a Black September unit attacked the Israeli embassy in Bangkok. The PLO flag was hoisted over the building and six Israelis were taken hostage. Soon five hundred Thai police and troops surrounded the building. The terrorists demanded that Israel release thirty-six PLO prisoners, or they would kill the hostages.

In Tel Aviv, a familiar scenario unfolded. The cabinet met in emergency session. There was the usual talk of standing tough or surrendering. It was left to Zvi Zamir to say that getting to Bangkok would require logistical support that was simply not there along a hostile route. And the Israeli embassy was in the center of busy Bangkok. The Thai government would never allow even the possibility of a shoot-out to occur. Then, after only brief negotiations, the terrorists unexpectedly agreed to a Thai offer of safe conduct out of the country in return for freeing the hostages. Hours later the Black September unit was on a flight to Cairo, where they disappeared.

In Tel Aviv, Zamir's relief that no Israelis had died turned to suspicion. Black September was highly trained and motivated and well financed, and had shown they had strategic cunning. They understood the methods and pressure points to bring any government to its knees. So why had they given in so quickly this time? The Bangkok embassy was a perfect target to gain them further publicity and so attract others to their cause. Almost certainly there was nothing random in their choice of target. Everything the group did was part of its concentrated assault on democracy. Within the embassy's compound the terrorists had followed the advice of their guru, Che Guevara, to keep hatred alive. The helpless hostages had been subjected to a tirade of anti-Semitic abuse—but was it all a diversionary tactic? Was another operation somewhere in the world being planned against Israel? Where and when? Zamir was still pondering these questions when he flew with Golda Meir to the Paris conference. From there he continued to search for answers.

In the early hours of January 14, 1973, the break came. A sayan working in Rome's central telephone exchange handled two telephone calls from a pay phone in an apartment block where PLO terrorists sometimes stayed. The first was to Bari, the second to Ostia, the port that served Rome. The calls were made in Arabic, a language the sayan spoke. The caller said that it was time "to deliver the birthday candles for the celebration."

The words convinced Zamir this was a coded order connected to a forthcoming terrorist attack. "Birthday candles" could refer to weapons; the most likely one with a candle connotation was a rocket. And a rocket would be the perfect way to destroy Golda Meir's aircraft.

To warn her would be pointless. She was a women without fear. To alert the Vatican could well lead to the visit being canceled: the last thing the Holy See would want was to be caught up in a terrorist incident, especially one that would involve it having to condemn its Arab friends.

Zamir telephoned Hessner and Kauly, the two *katsas* who originally accompanied him to the Vatican, and moved Kauly from Milan to Rome. Then Zamir, accompanied by the small Mossad team traveling with Golda Meir, took the first flight to the city. Their mood was reflected in Zamir's gallows humor that it could be the city of eternity for Golda Meir.

In Rome, Zamir laid out his fears to the head of DIGOS, the Italian antiterrorist squad. Its officers raided the apartment block from where the calls had been made to Bari and Ostia. A search of one of its apartments turned up a Russian instruction manual for launching a missile. Throughout the night, DIGOS teams, each accompanied by a Mossad *katsa*, carried out a series of raids on other known PLO apartments. But nothing more was found to confirm Zamir's fears. With dawn breaking and Golda Meir's plane due in a few hours, he decided he would concentrate his search in and around the airport.

Shortly after sunrise, Hessner spotted a Fiat van parked in a field close to the flight path. The *katsa* ordered the van driver to step out of the cab. Instead, the back door of the vehicle opened and there was a burst of gunfire. Hessner was unhurt but two terrorists in the back of the van were seriously wounded when he fired back. Hessner set off in foot pursuit of the driver, catching up with him as he tried to hijack a car—driven by Kauly. The two Mossad *katsas* bundled the luckless terrorist into the car and drove off at high speed to where Zamir had his mobile command post, a truck.

The Mossad chief had already received a radio message that the Fiat van contained six rockets. But he still had to know if there were more positioned elsewhere. The van driver was severely beaten before he revealed the whereabouts of the second set of rockets. Zamir suspected he was one of the men who had provided backup for the Munich massacre. Driving at full speed in the truck, Zamir, Hessner, and Kauly, with the now-battered terrorist slumped between them, headed north.

They spotted a van parked on the side of the road. Protruding from its roof were three unmistakable nose caps of missiles. In the distance, descending by the second, was the equally unmissable shape of Golda Meir's 747, the sun illuminating its markings. Without slowing, Zamir used the truck as a battering ram, hitting the van side-on and toppling it onto its side. The two terrorists inside were half-crushed as the missiles fell on them.

Stopping only to toss the senseless driver out onto the road beside the van, Zamir drove off, alerting DIGOS that there had been "an interesting accident they should look into." Zamir had briefly considered killing the terrorists, but he felt their deaths would serve as a serious embarrassment to Golda Meir's audience with the pope.

Meir had the feeling that the weight of the world bore down on the pope's narrow shoulders, threatening to crush his diminutive white-clad figure. At the end of the audience, in reply to her question, Paul said he would visit the Holy Land, and spoke of his pontificate being a pilgrimage. When she asked him about the possibility of Israel establishing formal ties with the Holy See he sighed and said the "time is not yet appropriate." Golda Meir gave him a leather-bound book depicting the Holy Land; he handed her an inscribed copy of *Humanae Vitae*, the encyclical in which he had spelled out the consecration of his pontificate.

On her way out of the Vatican, Golda Meir told Zamir that the Holy See seemed to have a clock different from the rest of the world's.

The Black September terrorists—who had taken part in the Munich massacre of Israel's Olympic athletes—were taken to a hospital and, after they recovered, were allowed to fly to Libya. But within months they would all be dead—killed by Mossad's kidon.

The biblical eye-for-an-eye retribution Golda Meir had authorized met with distaste from Pope Paul, whose entire pontificate was rooted in the power of forgiveness. It also strengthened the Vatican's ties to the PLO, which John Paul II continued following his own election in 1978.

Since then the pope had received Yasser Arafat and senior aides in several lengthy private audiences, during which John Paul had each time reiterated his commitment to actively pursue a search for a Palestinian homeland. The PLO, now based in Tunisia, had a permanent liaison officer attached to the Secretariat of State, and the Holy See had its own envoy, Father Idi Ayad, assigned to the organization.

With his frayed cassock trailing in the desert dust, padre's hat planted squarely above his pinched face, Ayad served with equal devotion pontiff and the PLO, even to having his bedroom wall decorated with framed and signed photographs of John Paul and Yasser Arafat. Ayad had helped Arafat draft a letter in 1980 to the pope that had delighted him: "Please permit me to dream. I am seeing you going to Jerusalem, surrounded by returning Palestinian refugees, carrying olive branches and spreading them at your feet."

Ayad had suggested Arafat and the pontiff should exchange courtesies on their respective holy days: Arafat began to send John Paul a Christmas card, while the pope sent Arafat greetings on the prophet Muhammad's birthday. The tireless priest had also brokered the meeting between the PLO foreign minister and Cardinal Casaroli, the Holy See's secretary of state. Afterward the Middle East desk had been expanded and the papal nuncios, the Holy See's ambassadors, were instructed to persuade governments to which they were accredited to support the PLO's aspirations to nationhood. All these moves had dismayed Israel. Its official contacts were still limited to infrequent visits by a government official who would be granted only a few minutes in the papal presence.

The chilly relationship on both sides stemmed partly from a bizarre incident following the creation of Israel in 1948. The then secretary of state had sent an emissary to Israel's attorney general, Haim Cohen, carrying a request that Israel should restage the trial of Christ and, of course, reverse the original verdict. Once that was done, the Vatican would formally recognize Israel. The importance of such a diplomatic tie was not lost on Cohen. But to achieve it in such a way he had found "capricious almost beyond belief. Such a trial would be pointless and anyway we had more pressing matters to settle—surviving against the onslaughts of our Arab neighbours. Rattling the bones of Christ's biography was very low down on my list of priorities."

After the monsignor was brusquely seen off by Cohen, the Vatican all but turned its back on Israel.

Since then there had been a glimmer of hope only when John Paul's immediate predecessor, the frail Albino Luciano, hinted during his thirty-three days on the Throne of Saint Peter that he would consider establishing diplomatic ties with Israel. His death from a heart attack, allegedly brought about by the responsibility of his high office, had led to the election of Karol Wojtyla. Under his pontificate the Bronze Door of the Apostolic Palace remained all but closed to Israel as the papacy moved even further into international politics, encouraged to do so by its reestablished links with the CIA.

In 1981, William Casey, a devout Catholic, was the CIA director. He had been among the first men the pope received in private audience after being elected. Casey had knelt before the charismatic Polish pope and kissed the Fisherman's Ring on his finger. In every word and gesture, the CIA director was a humble supplicant, not like the bombastic, hard-bitten men his predecessors had been. But Casey shared their and the pope's deep distrust and fear of Communism.

For over an hour the two men discussed issues dear to them. Where should Ostpolitik go now? How would the Polish regime, indeed the whole of the Soviet Bloc, respond to the change in direction the Church must now take? Casey left the audience chamber sure of one thing: John Paul was not a man to seek easy accommodations. That was what made him so charismatic. His clean-cut beliefs were the best possible answer to that tired old question, the one Stalin was supposed to have posed about how many divisions a pope had. John Paul, Casey believed, was a pontiff who single-handedly would prove that faith could be more effective than any force.

Casey returned to Washington to brief President Reagan, who told the CIA director to return to Rome and tell the pope, under a secret arrangement the president approved, that from now on he would be kept fully informed on all aspects of U.S. policy—military, political, and economic.

Every Friday evening the CIA station chief in Rome brought to the Apostolic Palace the latest secrets obtained from satellite surveillance and electronic eavesdropping by CIA field agents. No other foreign leader had access to the intelligence the pope received. It enabled the most political of all modern pontiffs to stamp his distinctive style and authority on both the Church and the secular world. Papal diplomacy, the political core of a highly centralized Vatican bureaucracy, had, more than at any time in its five hundred years of very active history, become deeply involved with international events. As a world leader, this involvement had nearly cost the pope his life when he was almost assassinated in St. Peter's Square on May 13, 1981.

Two years later, on November 15, 1983, a cold winter's night in Rome, John Paul was about to learn the answer to a question that still consumed him: Who had ordered the assassination? Every moment of what had happened had been seared forever into his memory and remained as vivid as the scar tissue from his bullet wounds.

There had been about one hundred thousand people in St. Peter's Square on that Wednesday afternoon, May 13, 1981. They were packed within the three-quarter circle encompassing Bernini's colonnades—284 columns and 88 pilasters, themselves supporting 162 statues of the saints. A fenced-off route indicated the path the popemobile would travel to the platform from which John Paul delivered his weekly address. There was a festive air and some of the onlookers speculated what the pontiff would be doing in the Papal Apartments while they waited.

What went on in the mind of a swarthy young Turk, Mehmet Ali Agca, would not be known. He had arrived in the square in mid-afternoon and worked his way close to the path along which the pope-mobile would trundle. Agca had been a member of a terrorist group based in Turkey that called itself the Gray Wolves. But he had left their ranks and traveled through the Middle Eastern training camps of even more extreme Islamic fundamentalist groups. Now he was almost at the end of his journey. Agca was in St. Peter's Square not to praise but to kill the pope.

At four o'clock John Paul had changed into a freshly pressed pristine white silk cassock. On the advice of the CIA, the garment had been cleverly modified to enable a flak jacket to be worn undetected beneath the garment. On his last visit to the Apostolic Palace, Casey had warned John Paul that "in these crazy times, even the pope was not above attack. I told him we had no hard evidence he was in danger. But John Paul was a very controversial figure and a fanatic could try to kill him."

John Paul had refused to wear the protection. The very idea, he had told his English-language secretary, Monsignor John Magee, went against all his papacy represented.

John Paul descended to the San Damaso Courtyard inside the Apostolic Palace at 4:50 P.M. The Vatican's security chief, Camillo Cibin, ticked off the pontiff's approach on his copy of the minute-by-minute schedule that governed the pope's working day. In the jacket of Cibin's custom-made steel gray suit was a small but powerful cellular phone linking him to Rome police headquarters. But the immediate protection of the pontiff was in the hands of blue-suited Vigili. The Vatican's small but highly trained security force were the sharp eyes behind the ceremonial Swiss Guards already positioned in St. Peter's Square.

Parked in the courtyard was the popemobile, or *campagnola*, with its white-leather padded seat and handrail for the pope to grip during his progress through the vast piazza. Gathered around the vehicle were senior members of his staff. Magee would remember that John Paul was in "unusually good form."

At five o'clock precisely, the popemobile drove out of the courtyard. Ahead, from St. Peter's Square, the cheering began. As the *campagnola* approached the Arch of the Bells, the Vigili were joined by Rome city policemen, who walked ahead and immediately behind the vehicle. As the popemobile emerged into the piazza, the crowd noise rose to a roar. John Paul waved and smiled; his time as an actor in his youth had given him a powerful stage presence.

At two miles an hour, the pope turning from one side to the other, the vehicle moved toward the Egyptian obelisk in the center of the piazza. At exactly 5:15 P.M. the *campagnola* began a second circuit of the square under the watchful eyes of Cibin; the security chief was trotting behind the popemobile. The crowd's cheering was even wilder. Impetuously, John Paul did something that always made Cibin nervous. The pope reached into the crowd and plucked out a child. He hugged and kissed the little girl and then handed her back to her ecstatic mother. It was part of the pontiff's routine. Cibin's concern was that a child would wriggle free of the pope's grasp and fall, creating a nasty accident. But John Paul had dismissed all such concerns.

At 5:17 P.M. he once more reached out to touch the head of another little girl, dressed in communion white. Then he straightened and looked about him, as if wondering who else he might greet. It was his way of personalizing the papacy in even the largest of crowds.

Furthest from his mind at that moment were the dangers he had faced in other crowds. Only three months before—in Pakistan, on February 16, 1983—a bomb had exploded in Karachi's municipal stadium shortly before he began his journey among the faithful. In January 1980 the French secret service had warned of a Communist plot to kill him. It was just one of scores of threats the Vatican had received against the pope's life. All had been investigated as far as was possible. Later Magee said: "In reality we could only sit and wait. Short of enclosing the Holy Father in a bulletproof cage whenever he appeared in public, something he would never agree to, there was not much else we could do."

At 5:18 P.M. the first shot rang out in St. Peter's Square.

John Paul remained upright, his hands still gripping the handrail. Then he started to sway. Mehmet Ali Agca's first bullet had penetrated his stomach, creating multiple wounds in the small intestine, the lower part of the colon, the large intestine, and the mesentery, the tissue that holds the intestine to the abdominal wall. Instinctively, John Paul placed his hand over the entry wound to try to stop the spurting blood. His face increasingly filled with pain and he slowly began to collapse. Only seconds had passed since he had been hit.

Agca's second bullet struck the pontiff in his right hand, which fell uselessly to his side. Bright red blood spurted over his white cassock. A third 9-mm bullet hit John Paul higher up on the right arm.

The *campagnola* driver twisted in his seat, his mouth open, too stunned to speak. Cibin was screaming at him to move. A papal aide shielded the pope with his own body. The vehicle began to lurch forward. The crowd itself was swaying as if buffeted by a giant wind. One shocking sentence rippled outward from the scene of carnage. In a score of different languages came the same disbelieving words, "The pope has been shot."

Cibin and his Vatican security men and city of Rome policemen were waving their guns, shouting orders and counterorders, looking for the gunman. Agca had burst through the crowd, running very fast, holding his gun in his right hand. The crowd continued to open before his waving pistol. Suddenly he tossed the gun away. At the same moment, his legs were cut from beneath him. A Rome police officer had made the arrest. In a moment both men were buried beneath other policemen in a scene that resembled a rugby scrum. Several policemen kicked and punched Agca before he was dragged away to a police van.

The popemobile had continued at an agonizingly slow speed toward the nearest ambulance stationed by the Vatican's Bronze Door. But the ambulance had no oxygen equipment, so the pope was transferred to a second ambulance nearby. Vital moments were lost.

Lights flashing and sirens wailing, the ambulance raced to Rome's Gemelli Hospital, the nearest to the Vatican, completing the journey in a record eight minutes. During the drive the pope uttered no sound of despair or resentment, only words of profound prayer, "Mary, my mother! Mary, my mother!"

At the hospital, he was rushed to a ninth-floor surgical suite that comprised an induction room, an operating room, and a recovery area. Here, at the center of the crisis, there was no panic, no wasted movement or word. All was quiet urgency and tightly controlled discipline. Here the stricken pontiff could have felt the beginning of hope.

His bloodstained cassock, vest, and underpants were expertly cut away, and the bloodstained cross on its solid gold chain was removed. Surgical towels were draped over his nakedness. Gloved hands reached for, fetched, and carried the first of the instruments needed in a struggle the surgical team was only too familiar with.

When he had recovered after almost six hours of surgery, John Paul believed he had been saved by the miraculous intervention of one of the most revered apparitions in the Catholic world, the Virgin of Fatima, whose feast day was the same one as the attempt on his life.

During his long months of recovery, John Paul became increasingly preoccupied with who had ordered him to be assassinated. He tried to read every scrap of evidence that came from police and intelligence agencies as diverse as the CIA, West Germany's BND, and the security services of Turkey and Austria. It was impossible to read it all: there were millions of words of reports, statements, and assessments.

Not one document answered fully John Paul's question: Who had wanted him killed? He was still no wiser when Agca stood trial at the Rome assize court in the last week of July 1981. The brisk three-day hearing cast no light on the gunman's motives. Agca was sentenced to life imprisonment; with good behavior he would be eligible for parole in the year 2009.

Two years after Agca had been convicted, John Paul had finally been promised the answer to the question that still festered in his mind. It would come from a priest he trusted above all others. His title was *Nunzio Apostolico con Incarichi Speciali*. The words offered no real clue that Archbishop Luigi Poggi was the natural heir to the world of secret papal politics, with special responsibility for gathering intelligence from Communist Europe. People in the Vatican simply called him "the pope's spy."

For many months Poggi had been involved in very secret contacts with Mossad. Only recently, when they were sufficiently advanced, had he informed the pope what he had been doing. John Paul had told him to continue. Since then there had been meetings with a Mossad officer in Vienna, Paris, Warsaw, and Sofia, Bulgaria. Both priest and *katsa* wanted to make sure what was on offer, what was expected. After each contact both had gone away to ponder the next move.

A few days before, there had been another meeting, again in Vienna, a city both Poggi and the officer liked as a background for their clandestine contacts.

It was from that meeting that Poggi was returning to the Vatican on that icy November night in 1983. He was bringing with him the answer to the pope's question: Who had ordered Agca to try to murder him?

CHAPTER 12

BLESSED ARE THE SPYMASTERS

One of the massive gates of the Arch of the Bells was already closed—

the prelude to the nightly ritual of locking all the entrances to the Vat-

ican on the stroke of midnight—when the dark blue Fiat limousine

crunched across the cobblestones, its lights picking out the two Swiss

Guards caped against the chill. Behind them stood a Vigili. One of the

guards stepped forward, arm raised half in salute, half in command to

stop. The car was expected and the figure behind the wheel was the

familiar one of a Vatican chauffeur. But after the assassination attempt

on the pope, no one was taking any chances.

The chauffeur had waited an hour at Rome's airport for the flight from Vienna, which had been delayed by bad weather. The guard stepped back after raising his arm in full salute to the passenger in deep shadow on the rear seat. There was no return acknowledgment.

The car drove past the side of St. Peter's Basilica and bounced over the cobblestones of San Damaso Courtyard before stopping outside the main entrance to the Apostolic Palace. The driver jumped out and opened the door for his passenger. Archbishop Luigi Poggi emerged, dressed in severe black, a scarf covering the white flash of his collar. Physically he bore a resemblance to Rafi Eitan: the same powerful shoulders and biceps, the same rolling gait, and eyes that could be as cold as this night.

As usual, Poggi had traveled with a small leather suitcase for his personal effects and a briefcase fitted with a combination lock. He sometimes joked he spent more time dozing in aircraft seats than asleep in his bed in the spacious suite he occupied at the rear of the Apostolic Palace.

Few recent trips matched the importance of what Poggi had finally been told at the meeting in Vienna's old Jewish Quarter. There, in a narrow steep-roofed building a few blocks from Nazi hunter Simon Wiesenthal's offices, the archbishop had listened raptly to a man they had agreed would only be called by his first name—Eli.

Poggi was now well used to such precautions in his dealings with Mossad. None carried security to such lengths as did its operatives. The only personal detail he knew about Eli was that he spoke several languages, and had finally answered the question of who had orchestrated the attempt on John Paul's life.

For his part, Luigi Poggi's own work was so secret that the Annuario Pontificio, the Vatican register that listed the names and duties of all its employees, contained no clue that for over twenty years, the archbishop had developed his own tried and tested and very secret contacts, which reached all the way into the Kremlin, Washington, and the corridors of power in Europe. He had been among the first to learn that Soviet leader Yuri Andropov was dying from chronic hepatitis, a disease of the liver. It was Poggi who had sat in the Russian mission in Geneva, a palatial nineteenth-century mansion stocked with the finest vodka and caviar the archbishop so relished, and learned firsthand that Moscow was prepared to eventually withdraw its nuclear warheads pointing at Europe if Washington would stop playing hardball in the disarmament talks. The news had been given to the CIA station chief at his next Friday-night briefing with the pope. Over two decades, Poggi had provided pontiffs with details that enabled them to better evaluate information from other sources. The archbishop had that ability, rare even among diplomats, to produce a balanced and swift assessment of material from a dozen sources and in almost as many languages, most of which he spoke fluently.

In his next meeting with Eli, Poggi had spoken in the soft voice that was long his trademark, his brown eyes watchful, lips pursed before putting a new question, his composed appearance never changing.

But on that cold winter's night, no doubt physically tired from his travels, he could be forgiven a bounce in his step. Walking into the Apostolic Palace, past the duty Vigili and the Swiss Guards who sprang to attention as he passed, Poggi took the elevator to the Papal Apartments.

The pope's butler showed Poggi into John Paul's study. The room's bookshelves offered clues to the pope's expanding interests. Along with leather-bound Polish editions of the classics and the works of theologians and philosophers were copies of the *International Defence Review* and books with such arresting titles as *The Problems of Military Readiness* and *Military Balance and Surprise Attack*. They reflected the pontiff's unswerving conviction that the main enemy the world still faced in 1983 was Soviet Communism.

John Paul had never lost an opportunity to tell his personal staff that before the new millennium dawned, something "decisive" would sweep the world. To all their questions as to what the event would be, he had refused to amplify, shaking his massive head and saying they must all pray that the Church would not lose more ground to Communism or the secularism sweeping countries like the United States, Germany, and Holland. He insisted his life had been spared in St. Peter's Square to lead the fight back.

Poggi knew that it was this concern, more than any other, which had affected John Paul both mentally and physically. Greetings over, Poggi could not have failed to notice that away from public gaze, John Paul had become more withdrawn. Agca's bullets had not only shattered bone and tissue, but had created emotional scars that had left the pope introspective and at times remote.

Seated with both hands on his knees, the position Poggi always assumed when there was grave news to impart, the archbishop began to unfold a story that had begun in those first weeks after Agca had shot John Paul.

When news of what had happened in St. Peter's Square on the afternoon of May 13, 1981, reached Tel Aviv, the immediate reaction of Mossad's director general, Yitzhak Hofi, was that the shooting had been the work of a crank. Shocking though the incident in Rome had been, it had no direct bearing on Mossad's current concerns.

Israeli Arabs were becoming ever more radical while, at the same time, Jewish extremists—led by members of the Kahane Kach Party— were becoming more violent. A plot had been discovered just in time to stop them blowing up the most holy Muslim shrine in Jerusalem, the Dome of the Rock. The consequences if they had succeeded were too nightmarish to contemplate. The Lebanon war dragged on despite endless U.S. shuttle diplomacy between Damascus, Beirut, and Jerusalem. In the cabinet, Prime Minister Begin led a party eager for a full-scale "final" showdown with the PLO. Killing Yasser Arafat was still a standing order for Mossad; during the very month the pope was shot there were two unsuccessful attempts to assassinate the PLO chairman.

The fact that seemingly every Western intelligence service was investigating the papal shooting also influenced Hofi's decision to keep Mossad from becoming involved. In any event, he eventually expected to learn from one of them the background to the incident.

He was still waiting to be told when he was replaced by Nahum Admoni in September 1982. With his Polish background—his parents had been middle-class immigrants from near Gdansk—Admoni had more than a passing curiosity about the Catholic church. In his time abroad working under cover in the United States and France, he had seen how powerful the Church's influence could be. Rome had helped elect John F. Kennedy, a Catholic, to the White House and, in France, the Church continued to perform an important role in politics.

Once he had settled into office, Admoni sent for Mossad's file on the attempted papal assassination. It contained mostly news clips and a report from a *katsa* stationed in Rome that did not go much further. Unusually, the six security services who had conducted their own inquiries—including interviewing Agca in his high-security cellblock of Rome's Rebibbia Prison—had failed to pool their knowledge. Admoni decided to conduct his own investigation.

William Casey, then director of Central Intelligence, would later say the likeliest reason appeared to be "Mossad sniffing that maybe here was a way into the Vatican. Admoni had to be thinking he could come up with something to trade off with the Holy See."

In the wake of Golda Meir's unsuccessful attempt to establish diplomatic ties with the Vatican, Zvi Zamir had established a permanent Mossad presence in Rome to try to penetrate the Vatican. Working out of a building close to the Israeli embassy, the *katsa* had tried and failed to recruit priest informers. Most of what he learned was gossip overheard in the bars and restaurants frequented by Vatican staff. He achieved little more than enviously watching the CIA's head of Rome station drive into the Vatican for his Friday-night briefings to the pope; these had resumed as soon as John Paul had recuperated from his surgery.

During that convalescence, Agostino Casaroli, cardinal secretary of state, had run the Vatican. The *katsa* had heard that Casaroli had expressed some very blunt sentiments about the shooting: the CIA should have known about Agca and the entire plot. He had sent on the secretary's views to Tel Aviv.

Within the U.S. intelligence community was a prevailing view that Agca had been a trigger for a KGB-inspired plot to kill the pontiff. In a paper stamped "Top Secret" and titled "Agca's Attempt to Kill the Pope: The Case for Soviet Involvement," the argument was made that Moscow had come to fear how the pontiff could ignite the flames of Polish nationalism.

Already by 1981, Solidarity, the country's workers' movement under the leadership of Lech Walesa, was increasingly flexing its industrial muscles, and the authorities were under mounting pressure from Moscow to curb the union's activities.

The pope had urged Walesa to do nothing that would precipitate direct Soviet military intervention. John Paul had urged Poland's dying cardinal, Stefan Wyszinski, to also reassure the country's Communist leaders that the pontiff would not allow Solidarity to overstep the mark. When the union scheduled a general strike, Cardinal Wyszinski prostrated himself before Walesa in his office, grabbed the bemused shipyard worker's trouser leg, and said he would cling on until he died. Walesa called off the strike.

In Tel Aviv, Mossad analysts concluded that the pontiff fully understood the importance of appeasing the Soviets over Poland so as to avoid losing the considerable ground Solidarity had achieved. It seemed increasingly unlikely Moscow would have wanted the pope killed. There was still the possibility that the Soviets had subcontracted the assassination to one of its surrogates. In the past, the Bulgarian secret service had carried out similar missions for the KGB when it was necessary to keep its own involvement hidden. But the analysts thought this time it would be unlikely the KGB would have delegated such an important mission. The Bulgarians would never have conducted the assassination of their own volition.

Nahum Admoni began to explore the CIA's current involvement with the papacy. In between Casey's regular visits to the pope, an important player in the relationship between the Vatican and the CIA was Cardinal John Krol of Philadelphia, who shuttled between the White House and the Apostolic Palace. To Monsignor John Magee, the pope's English-language secretary, Krol was "the Holy Father's extra-special pal. Both came from a similar background, knew the same Polish songs and stories and could joke across the Pope's dining table in a local Polish dialect. The rest of us just sat there and smiled, not understanding a word."

It had been Krol who had accompanied Casey to the CIA director's first audience with John Paul after his convalescence. Later, the cardinal had introduced Casey's deputy, Vernon Walters, to the pontiff. Since then, the list of subjects the CIA officer and the pope discussed ranged from terrorism in the Middle East to the internal politics of the Church and the health of Kremlin leaders. For Richard Allen, a Catholic, who was Ronald Reagan's first national security adviser: "The relationship between the CIA and the pope was one of the great alliances of all time. Reagan had this deep conviction the pope would help him to change the world."

More certain, common goals were established. The president and pontiff had proclaimed their united opposition to abortion. The United States blocked millions of dollars of aid to countries that ran family-planning programs. The pope, through a "purposeful silence," supported U.S. military policies, including supplying NATO with a new generation of cruise missiles. The CIA regularly bugged the phones of bishops and priests in Central America who advocated liberation theology and opposed U.S.-backed forces in Nicaragua and El Salvador; the phone transcripts formed part of the pope's Friday briefing by the Rome CIA station chief. Reagan had also personally authorized Colonel Oliver North, then working for the National Security Council, to make regular and substantial payments to priests the Vatican deemed "loyal" in Central and South America, Africa, and Asia. The money was used to support their often lavish lifestyles and promote the Holy See's opposition to birth control and divorce.

One of the duties of the pope's personal secretary, Monsignor Emery Kabongo, was to keep the list of approved priests updated. Another task was to file the documents provided by the CIA and act as note taker to their clandestine meetings with the pope.

Kabongo had first encountered the Washington spymasters on November 30, 1981, shortly after John Paul returned to work after being shot. After Kabongo joined John Paul for the first prayers of his day— 5:15 A.M. on the longcase clock in the corridor outside the private chapel in the Papal Apartments—the two men had gone to the paneled study to receive CIA deputy director Vernon Walters. Kabongo would recall:

"I took up my usual position in the corner of the room, a notebook on my knee. There was no interpreter present. General Walters asked what language should he use. His Holiness said he would be comfortable with Italian. Walters began by saying he brought greetings from President Reagan. The pope returned the felicitations. Then it was down to business. Walters produced satellite photographs and His Holiness was fascinated to see how clear they were. Walters spoke for over an hour about the CIA's view of the latest Soviet intentions. His Holiness thanked him. At the end of the meeting, Walters produced a number of rosaries and asked the pope to bless them, explaining they were for relations and friends and His Holiness did so."

Intrigued by the pope's ability to switch from temporal to spiritual matters, Admoni used his personal friendship with Secretary of State Alexander Haig—they had met when Admoni worked out of the Israeli embassy in Washington—to obtain a copy of the CIA's psycho-profile of John Paul.

It was a portrait of a man whose religious fervor could be so intense that he would cry out when praying and would often be found on the marble floor of his private chapel, face down, arms extended to form a cross, as still as in death. He could spend hours in that prone position. Yet his anger could be eruptive and fearful to behold; then he would storm and shout. His grasp of geopolitics was formidable and he could be as unflinching as any dictator. John Paul was also not afraid to confront the Curia, the Vatican's civil service, or his long-serving secretary of state, Agostino Casaroli. The profile concluded that John Paul was "highly politicized from his Polish experiences and that he relishes being a player on the world stage."

For Nahum Admoni, one matter was clear: the close and self-serving ties between the CIA and the pope had played a crucial role in John Paul coming to accept the American view that the attempt on his life had been organized by the Kremlin.

Yet, supposing that standpoint could be demonstrated to be wrong? How would the pope react? Would that shatter his faith in the CIA? Make him wary of all intelligence services? And would it allow Mossad—if it could show there was another hand behind the attempted assassination—to finally find a way past the Vatican's Bronze Door and, if not be admitted as a fully fledged secret secular adviser to the papacy, at least be granted a hearing for its information and, in return, hopefully be able to revise the Holy See's attitude to Israel?

Six months later the answer to Admoni's first question—had someone else masterminded the attempted assassination?—was established to his satisfaction.

The plot had been prepared in Tehran with the full approval of Ayatollah Ruholla Khomeini. Killing the pope was intended as the opening move in a jihad, holy war, against the West and what Khomeini saw as its decadent values being approved by the largest Christian Church.

A report prepared for Admoni said: "Khomeini remains the classic example of religious fanaticism. He has cast himself in the role of God-instructor to his people. To maintain that myth, he will need to act increasingly in a manner more dangerous to Israel, the West and the whole world."

Anticipating that Agca could fail, his Iranian controllers had ensured he would be seen as a fanatical loner by leaking details of his background. Mehmet Ali Agca had been born in the remote village of Yesiltepe in eastern Turkey and had been raised in a hotbed of Islamic fundamentalism. At the age of nineteen he joined the Gray Wolves, a pro-Iranian terrorist group responsible for much of the violence in a Turkey clinging to democracy. In February 1979, Agca murdered the editor of an

Istanbul newspaper renowned for its pro-West policies. Arrested, Agca escaped from prison with the help of the Gray Wolves. The next day the newspaper received a chilling letter about the pope's visit to Turkey, then three days away:

"Western imperialists, fearful that Turkey and her sister Islamic nations may become a political, military and economic power in the Middle East, are sending to Turkey at this delicate moment the Commander of the Crusades, John Paul, designated as a religious leader. If this visit is not called off, I will deliberately kill the Commander Pope."

Admoni became convinced the letter had been composed in Tehran: in style and content it was certainly far above the writing skills of the almost illiterate Agca. Mossad's computer search of Khomeini's speeches revealed he had previously referred to the "Commander of the Crusades" and "Commander Pope" in describing John Paul.

In the end the pontiff's visit passed without incident. Agca's name and photograph went on to the computers of a number of intelligence services, though not Mossad's. Otto Kormek, a case officer with the Austrian security service who had been in charge of its inquiries into the papal shooting, felt it was "not necessary to inform Mossad. Israel would be the last place Agca would go."

Mossad's investigation had discovered that after his prison escape, Agca was spirited into Iran, where he spent months in various training camps being indoctrinated. From its own sources in those camps, Mossad had pieced together a picture of Agca's life at that time.

He arose before dawn, his small, red-rimmed eyes set deep in a long face, watchful as the other recruits awoke. The first light of day showed posters on the walls of their hut: photographs of the Ayatollah Khomeini and revolutionary slogans, each designed to fire their fantasies. Songs piped through the huts' loudspeakers reinforced this.

Clad in vest and shorts, Agca was an unprepossessing figure; large hands and feet were all out of proportion to his body with his concave chest, protruding shoulder blades, and skinny arms and legs. The first thing he did each morning, like the other recruits, was to spread his prayer rug and prostrate himself three times, each time touching his forehead to the ground, murmuring the name of Allah, Master of the World, the All-Meaningful and All-Compassionate, the Supreme Sovereign of the Last Judgment. Afterward he began to recite his long list of hatreds, which his instructor had encouraged him to write down. The list had grown long and diverse and included all imperialists, NATO, and those Arab countries that had refused to cut off oil to the West. He especially called upon Allah to destroy the United States, the most powerful nation on earth, and its people, praying that their way of life, their values and customs, the very wellspring of their existence, would be squeezed from them.

Finally only his religious hatreds remained. They were the most virulent, consuming him like a cancer, eating into his brain. He saw all other faiths as threatening to overthrow the one to which he subscribed. His instructors had taught him to reduce that hatred to one instantly recognizable image: a man, dressed in white, living in a huge palace far beyond the mountains. From there he ruled like a caliph of old, issuing decrees and orders many millions obeyed. The man spread his hated message the way his predecessors had done for over nineteen centuries. Supported by pomp and glory, rejoicing in even more titles than Allah, the man was known variously as Servant of the Servants of God, Patriarch of the West, Vicar of Christ on Earth, Bishop of Rome, Sovereign of the State of Vatican City, Supreme Pontiff, His Holiness Pope John Paul the Second.

Mehmet Ali Agca had been promised that, when the time came, he would be given a chance to kill the pope. His instructors drummed into him that it was no coincidence the pope had come to office at almost the same time as their beloved Khomeini delivered Iran from the shah's regime. The "infidel in Rome," as Agca was taught to refer to John Paul, had come to destroy the revolution the ayatollah had proclaimed in the name of the Holy Koran.

There was a grain of truth in the accusation. John Paul had increasingly spoken harshly about Islam and the dangers he believed it contained in its fundamentalist form. Visiting the Olivetti factory at Ivrea, Italy, John Paul had astonished the workers by inserting into his speech an impromptu passage:

"What the Koran teaches people is aggression; what we teach our people is peace. Of course, you always have human nature which distorts whatever message religion is sending. But even though people can be led astray by vices and bad habits, Christianity aspires to peace and love. Islam is a religion that attacks. If you start by teaching aggression to the whole community, you end up pandering to the negative elements in everyone. You know what that leads to: such people will assault us."

In January 1981, Agca had flown to Libya. Initially Mossad had been puzzled by that part of his journey, until an informer in Tripoli discovered that a renegade CIA officer, Frank Terpil, had been in the country at that time. Terpil had been indicted by a grand jury in Washington for supplying arms to Libya, conspiring to assassinate one of Gadhafi's opponents in Cairo, recruiting former U.S. military pilots to fly Libyan aircraft, and Green Berets to run Gadhafi's training camps for terrorists. In Libya he was instructing terrorists how to evade detection by Western security agencies. Terpil had moved on to Beirut—where he had disappeared. Mossad believed he had been murdered when he had outlived his usefulness.

Mossad knew Agca's contact with Terpil had been arranged by Agca's controllers in Tehran and leaked to the KGB after the attempted John Paul assassination, allowing the Russians to claim the plot had been orchestrated by the CIA. Like Mossad, the KGB had an effective psychological warfare department. The fiction about the CIA filled thousands of column inches and many hours of broadcast time. To further muddy the waters, the Tehran mullahs arranged for Agca, after he left Libya in February 1981, to travel to Sofia, Bulgaria, to meet men who told him they were members of the country's secret service: no convincing proof ever emerged they were. Furious at the KGB's attempts to smear the Agency, the CIA countered by claiming the Bulgarians had controlled Agca on behalf of the Kremlin.

For Mossad the situation was perfectly poised to exploit the adage "We divide to rule." Not only would Mossad be able to discredit the CIA with the Vatican, but at long last, by promoting their version of the plot as the correct one, Mossad had found a way to gain the pope's ear. All else would flow from that: its officers could have access to the secretary of state's own formidable information-collecting network; it would enable *katsas* to work with, and if need be, exploit priests and nuns; and, when the opportunity arose, those electronic bugs could finally be planted in all those holy places in the Vatican Zvi Zamir had indicated.

When Mossad's account of Mehmet Ali Agca's odyssey had been fully pieced together in Tel Aviv, Nahum Admoni set out to answer the one question that would make all that happen. Once more a computer search found the solution. One of Rafi Eitan's "survivor spies," a Catholic living in Munich, had described the extraordinary role Luigi Poggi played in the papacy. Nahum Admoni had sent for Eli and told him to make contact with Poggi.

Now, a full two years after Agca had shot the Pope, the archbishop sat far into the night, explaining completely to John Paul what Eli had told him.

A month later, on December 23, 1983, at 4:30 A.M., almost three hours before the lights on the Christmas tree in St. Peter's Square would be switched off for the day, the pope was awoken by his valet.

The bedroom was surprisingly small, its walls still lined with the pastel linen covering his predecessor favored. The wooden floor, gleaming from being polished, was partly covered by a rug woven by Polish nuns. On the wall above the bed, in which four of John Paul's predecessors had lain waiting for death, was a crucifix. On another wall was a fine painting of Our Lady. Both were gifts from Poland. In addition to the pope's valet, those who saw him at this hour—usually one of his administrative priests with news that could not wait—were relieved to see John Paul had regained some of his old vigor and vitality.

As always, the pope began his day by going to his prie-dieu to kneel in private prayer. Afterward he shaved and showered and dressed in the clothes the valet had laid out: a heavy woolen white cassock caped around the shoulders, white clerical shirt, knee-high white stockings, brown shoes, and white skullcap. He was ready to go to see Agca in Rome's Rebibbia Prison.

The meeting was arranged at the pope's request, intended, he said, as "an act of forgiveness." In reality, John Paul wanted to find out if what Mossad had said was true. He was driven to the prison by the very man who was at the wheel of the popemobile in St. Peter's Square when Agca shot him. Accompanied by a Roman police escort, the limousine sped northeastward across the city to the prison. In a backup car was a small group of journalists (they included the author of this book). They had been invited to witness the historical moment when the pope and his assassin came face-to-face.

Two hours later, John Paul was admitted to Rebibbia's maximum-security wing. He walked alone down the corridor to the open door of cell T4, where Agca stood waiting inside. The reporters waited farther up the corridor. With them were prison guards, ready to run to Agca's cell should he make any threatening move to his visitor.

As the pope extended his ring hand, Agca moved to shake it, hesitated, then bent to kiss the Fisherman's Ring. Next he took the pope's hand and placed it briefly against his forehead.

"Lei è Mehmet Ali Agca?" The pope framed the question softly. He had been told Agca had learned Italian in prison.

"Sì." A quick smile accompanied the word, as if Agca was embarrassed to admit who he was.

"Ah, lei abita qui?" John Paul looked around the cell, genuinely interested in the place where his would-be killer might well spend the rest of his life.

"Sì."

John Paul sat on a chair positioned just inside the door. Agca sank onto his bed, clasping and unclasping his hands.

"Come si sente?" The pope's question as to how Agca felt was almost paternal.

"Bene, bene." Suddenly Agca was speaking urgently, volubly, the words coming in a low torrent only the pope could hear.

John Paul's expression grew more pensive. His face was close to Agca's, partially shielding him from the guards and journalists.

Agca whispered into the pope's left ear. The pope gave an almost imperceptible shake of the head. Agca paused, uncertainty on his face. John Paul indicated, with a quick chopping motion of his right hand, that Agca should continue. Both men were so close their heads almost touched. Agca's lips barely moved. On John Paul's face there was a pained look. He closed his eyes, as though it would help him to better concentrate.

Suddenly, Agca stopped in midsentence. John Paul did not open his eyes. Only his lips moved; only Agca could hear the words.

Once more Agca resumed speaking. After a few more minutes, the pope made another little chopping motion of the hand. Agca stopped talking. John Paul placed his left hand to his forehead, as if he wanted to shield his eyes from Agca.

Then John Paul squeezed the younger man's upper arm, almost as if to thank him for what he had said. The exchanges lasted for twenty-one minutes, and then the pope slowly rose to his feet. He held out a hand, encouraging Agca to do the same. The two men stared into each other's eyes. The pope ended this moment of near perfect drama by reaching into a cassock pocket and producing a small white cardboard box bearing the papal crest. He handed it to Agca. Puzzled, Agca turned the box over in his hand.

The pope waited, the gentlest of smiles on his lips. Agca opened the box. Inside was a rosary crafted in silver and mother-of-pearl.

"Ti ringrazio," thanked Agca. "Ti ringrazio."

"Niente. Niente," responded the pope. Then he leaned forward and spoke again words only for Agca.

Then, saying no more, the pontiff walked from the cell.

Later, a Vatican spokesman said, "Ali Agca knows only up to a certain level. On a higher level, he doesn't know anything. If there was a conspiracy, it was done by professionals and professionals don't leave traces. One will never find anything."

Not for the first time, the Vatican had been economical with the truth. Agca had confirmed what Luigi Poggi had been told by Mossad. The plot to kill the pope had been nurtured in Tehran. The knowledge would color John Paul's attitude toward both Islam and Israel. Increasingly, he told his staff that the real coming conflict in the world was not going to be between the East and West, the United States and Russia, but between Islamic fundamentalism and Christianity. In public he was careful to separate Islam, the faith, and Islamic fundamentalism.

In Israel, Mossad's analysts saw the pontiff's new attitude as the first sign that the evidence presented to Poggi had been accepted. But while there was no immediate move made to invite Mossad to contribute to John Paul's understanding of the world, the pope had become convinced of the value of Poggi's dialogue with Eli. In Tel Aviv, Admoni told Eli to remain in contact with Poggi. They continued to meet in various European cities, sometimes at an Israeli embassy, other times in a papal nunciature. Their discussions were wide-ranging, but almost always focused on two issues: the situation in the Middle East and the pope's wish to visit the Holy Land. Linked to this was John Paul's continued effort to find a permanent homeland for the PLO.

Poggi made it clear the pope had both a liking for, and a fascination with, Yasser Arafat. John Paul did not share the views of men like Rafi Eitan, David Kimche, and Uri Saguy, that the PLO leader, in Eitan's words, was a ruthless killer and "a butcher of our women and children, someone I would kill with my own bare hands."

To the pontiff, raised against the background of the heroic Polish resistance against the Nazis, Arafat was an appealing underdog, a charismatic figure continuously able to escape Mossad's various attempts to kill him. Poggi recounted to Eli how Arafat had once told John Paul he had developed a sixth sense—"and some measure of a seventh"—when he was in danger. "A man like that deserves to live," Poggi had said to Eli.

Through such glimpses, Eli obtained a clearer view of the pope's mind-set. But John Paul also paid more than lip service to the historical truth that the Jewish roots of Christianity must never be forgotten, and that anti-Semitism—so rife in his own beloved Poland—must be eradicated.

In May 1984, Poggi invited Eli to the Vatican. The two men talked together for hours in the archbishop's office in the Apostolic Palace. To this day no one knows what they spoke about.

In Israel, this was once more a time of scandal involving the nation's intelligence community. A month before, April 12, four PLO terrorists had hijacked a bus with thirty-five passengers as it headed for the southern town of Ashkelon. The official version of the incident was that Shin Bet agents had stormed the bus, and in the ensuing gunfight, two terrorists were shot dead and the two who had been wounded died on their way to the hospital.

Newspaper reports showed them being led from the bus, visibly not seriously injured. It emerged they had been so severely beaten in the ambulance by Shin Bet officers that both men died. Mossad, although not directly involved, was tarnished by the international condemnation of the incident.

Against this background, Poggi explained to Eli, there could be no question of John Paul establishing diplomatic relations with Israel. Until he did, Eli reiterated, there could be no question of the pope being allowed to visit the Holy Land.

Yet it was a measure of the bridge building they were engaged upon that both men agreed the issue was not dead.

On April 13, 1986, John Paul did something no other pontiff had done. He entered the Synagogue of Rome on Lungotevere dei Cenci, where he was embraced by the city's chief rabbi. Each dressed in his regalia, the two men walked side by side through the silent congregation to the *teva*, the platform from where the Torah is read.

In the back of the congregation sat Eli, who had played his part in bringing about this historic moment. Yet it still did not achieve what Israel wanted—papal diplomatic recognition.

That would only finally come in December 1993, when, despite the continuing objections of the Secretariat hard-liners, diplomatic ties were established.

By then, Nahum Admoni was no longer Mossad's chief. His successor, Shabtai Shavit, continued the delicate process of trying to bring Mossad closer to the Vatican. Part of that maneuvering was to show the pope that both Israel and the PLO at long last had a genuine interest in reaching a settlement, and recognized the common threat of Islamic fundamentalism. Pope John Paul bore the physical scars of the truth of that.

Meanwhile, Mossad had been busy on a continent where the Vatican pinned so many hopes for the future—Africa. From there the Holy See one day expected to see emerge the Church's first black pope. But it was there that Mossad had already shown itself the past master at the black art of playing off one intelligence service against another to secure its own position.

CHAPTER 13

AFRICAN CONNECTIONS

A few blocks from Nairobi's venerable Norfolk Hotel, the Oasis Club

had long been a favorite among Kenya's business community. They

could drink all night in its gloomy interior and take a bar girl to one of

the rooms out back after checking her current medical certificate con-

firmed she was free of venereal disease.

Since 1964, the club had also received other visitors, Chinese in sa-

fari suits, slab-faced Russians, and men whose nationality could have

been of any country around the Mediterranean basin. They were not

there for the cold beer or what the club advertised as "the hottest girls

in all-Africa." These men worked for intelligence services fighting to gain a foothold in central Africa, where once only Britain's MI6 had secretly operated. The newcomers represented the Chinese Secret Intelligence Service (CSIS), the Soviet KGB, and Mossad. Each service had its own agenda, playing one off against the other. No one had become better at this than Mossad.

All told, there were a dozen *katsas* scattered along the equator, operating from Dar es Salaam on the Indian Ocean to Freetown on the shore of the Atlantic. Possessing an impressive number of false passports, young and superbly fit, the operatives, as well as all their normal skills, had acquired the basics of field medicine and surgery to enable them to survive in the bush, where predatory lions and leopards roamed, as well as hostile tribesmen.

Mossad's African adventure had begun shortly after Fidel Castro came to power in Cuba in 1959 and started to export his revolution. His first success began when his surrogate, John Okello, a self-styled "field marshal," was plucked out of the jungle by a Castro recruiter, given a short course in guerrilla warfare in Havana, and told to go and seize the small island of Zanzibar off the East African coast. His sheer height and bulk—he was three hundred pounds—terrified the island's small police force into submission. Okello's ragtag army stamped their brutal authority on a population whose only weapons were the primitive tools they used to harvest the spices that made Zanzibar world famous. The island became Castro's launchpad for penetrating the African mainland. There was a Chinese ethnic population in the port of Dar es Salaam, and their reports home about what was happening came to the notice of the Beijing government. Realizing the opportunity the embryonic revolution offered for China to gain a greater hold on the continent, the CSIS was ordered to establish itself in the region and to provide all possible support for the revolutionaries.

Meantime, Castro had set up a full-scale operation to Cubanize the now burgeoning black liberation movement. The focus was the port of Casablanca on the West African coast. Shiploads of Cuban weapons arrived and on the return voyages to Havana the boats were filled with guerrilla trainees from all over central Africa. Soon the CSIS was helping to select them.

The prospect of thousands of trained and well-armed revolutionaries being within a few hours' striking distance of Israel was alarming to its politicians and intelligence services. But to provoke this guerrilla army when they had offered no direct threat could lead to a confrontation Israel did not want. With its hands already full fighting off the threat from Arab terrorists, to become embroiled in direct action against black revolutionaries was to be avoided. Meir Amit ordered his *katsas* in Africa to keep a close watch but not to become actively involved.

The arrival of the KGB on the scene changed all that. The Russians brought an offer would-be terrorists could not refuse: the opportunity to be trained at the Patrice Lumumba University in Moscow. There they would receive the wisdom of the KGB's best instructors in guerrilla tactics and how to exploit them under the guise of helping the dispossessed, powerless, and unelectable in democratic states. To help sell the idea, the KGB brought along some of the most successful graduates of Patrice Lumumba: Arab terrorists.

Meir Amit reinforced his African *katsas* with kidons. His new orders were to disrupt by all means possible the relations between the Russians and their African hosts and between the KGB and the CSIS; to kill Arab activists when the opportunity arose; and to foster relations with black African revolutionaries by promising them that Israel would assist their movements to progress beyond guerrilla tactics and allow their organizations to achieve political legitimacy. All Israel wanted in return was a guarantee it would not be attacked by these movements.

The Oasis Club had become part of the battle for the hearts and minds of African revolutionaries. The nights were filled with long discussions of how, without publicity, terrorism was a weapon firing only blanks, and of the need to never lose sight of the ultimate goal: freedom and independence. Within the club's stifling atmosphere plots were hatched, deals made, targets identified for execution or destruction. Some victims would be ambushed driving on a dirt road, others killed in their beds. One day it would be a KGB agent, the next a CSIS spy. Each side blamed the other for what Mossad had done.

Back at the Oasis, the nights would continue as before, with new plans being made around the bamboo tables, with the rain rolling off the hills and beating on the tin roof. There was no need to whisper, but old habits died hard.

Meir Amit had briefed his agents on all he had learned of the CSIS. The service had a tradition of espionage extending back over 2,500 years. For centuries it had been a creature of the ruling emperor spying on his subjects. But with the arrival of first Mao and then Deng Xiaoping, China's intelligence gathering, like so much else in the country, had taken a new direction. The CSIS began to expand its networks across the Pacific into the United States, Europe, the Middle East, and finally Africa.

These networks were used for more than espionage purposes: they were major routes for drug running and money laundering. With about half the world's opium grown on the doorstep of the People's Republic, in the Golden Triangle—Thailand, Laos, and Myanmar—the CSIS worked alongside Triad gangs to smuggle drugs into the West. Given Hong Kong's position as one of the world's major centers for money laundering, the CSIS had a perfect cover for concealing China's profits from drug trafficking. That money helped to finance its operations in Africa. Those were, since 1964, ultimately under the control of the CSIS's director general, Qiao Shi. A tall, stooped man with a taste for French cognac and Cuban cigars, he was a chief with hundreds of spies and a budget for bribery and blackmail rivaled only by that of the KGB. The labor camps of central China were filled with those who had dared challenge Qiao. Mossad's psycho-profile described a man whose entire career consisted of adroit, low-key moves.

CSIS activities in Africa were under the local command of Colonel Kao Ling, already a legendary figure in the service, having made his reputation in Nepal and India with his subversive tactics. Based in Zanzibar, Kao Ling had a lavish lifestyle and a succession of nubile young African women as mistresses. He moved across central Africa like a predator, disappearing for weeks at a time. His visits to Nairobi became occasions for wild parties at the Oasis. Sweet-smelling smoke from bundles of joss sticks filled the club. Delicacies imported directly from China were served. The African whores were dressed up in cheongsams; there were indoor fireworks and cabarets flown in from Hong Kong.

Guerrillas who had returned from Cuba were feted before disappearing into the African bush to wage war. One of them had a party trick of drinking a glass of the human blood he drained from executed enemies he had killed.

Meantime, Kao Ling was expanding his operations not only across the width of Africa, but also northward toward Ethiopia, South Yemen, and Egypt. He provided its terrorists with substantial sums of money to launch attacks on Israel. The CSIS regarded Israel as a pawn in the hands of Washington and a legitimate target for what Kao Ling called "my freedom fighters."

Meir Amit decided Mossad should go head-to-head against the CSIS.

First it wrecked a Chinese plot to overthrow the pro-West Hastings Banda regime in Malawi. Next it informed the Kenyan authorities about the full extent of the Chinese network in its midst. Later the Nairobi government would show its gratitude by granting overfly rights for Israeli air force planes to carry out their mission to Entebbe. The Oasis Club was closed down and its Chinese patrons put on planes out of the country, loudly protesting they were only businessmen. They were lucky; several CSIS operatives would remain permanently in Africa, killed by Mossad *katsas* and left out on the savannas for lions and leopards to consume.

The more the Chinese tried to fight back in other African countries, the more ruthless Mossad became. Kidons stalked CSIS operatives wherever they set up shop. In Ghana, a CSIS agent was shot dead as he left a discotheque with his girlfriend. In Mali another died in a car bomb; in Zanzibar, still the jewel in the CSIS crown, a fire consumed an apartment block where CSIS staff lived. On one of his field trips, Kao Ling himself narrowly escaped death when some instinct made him switch cars in Brazzaville in the Congo. The other vehicle exploded minutes later, killing its driver. In Zambia, a CSIS agent was left bound to a tree for lions to consume.

When Kwame Nkrumah, the pro-Chinese ruler of Ghana, was on a state visit to Beijing, Mossad orchestrated the uprising that led to both Nkrumah's overthrow and the destruction of the CSIS infrastructure in the country.

For three years Mossad waged its deadly war of attrition against the CSIS over the length and breadth of Africa. There was no mercy on either side. When a CSIS hit team ambushed a Mossad *katsa* in the Congo, they fed him to crocodiles, filming his last moments in the water and sending the footage to the local Mossad station chief. He retaliated by personally firing a rocket into the building from where the CSIS operated. Three Chinese were killed.

Finally, through an intermediary, President Mobutu of Zaire, the CSIS let Mossad know it had no wish to fight anymore; rather, they shared a common interest in stemming Russian influence on the continent. The approach perfectly suited Mossad's policy toward all superpowers, articulated in Meir Amit's dictum: "Dividing them helps Israel to survive."

While the CSIS and Mossad had battled each other, the KGB had taken further steps to take over Castro's plans to Cubanize Africa. KGB chiefs and the Politburo had met in the Kremlin and agreed that Russia would underwrite the entire Cuban economy. The terms were enough to ensure that a nation of seven million people became in hock to the Soviet Union. In return, Castro agreed to accept that Moscow's brand of Communism rather than Beijing's was the correct one for Africa. He also agreed to receive five thousand advisers who would "instruct" Cuba's own security service, the DGI, on how to operate "correctly" in Africa.

The KGB began to work alongside Cubans throughout black Africa. Within six months every act of terrorism in Africa was controlled by the Russians. From the Middle Eastern camps it had set up to train terrorists, the KGB brought the very best to Africa to wage war against the apartheid regime of South Africa. Terrorists from Europe, Latin America, and Asia were also soon providing their expertise in Angola, Mozambique, and countries bordering South Africa.

According to Meir Amit, "Matters were really heating up below the equator." He realized it could only be a matter of time before these battle-hardened mercenaries would turn their attention to Israel. The offer from the CSIS to collaborate against a common enemy, the KGB and its terrorists, was one the Mossad chief gratefully accepted. The Chinese began to provide details about Arab movements in and out of Africa. Some were killed by the usual Mossad methods of car bombs or explosives placed in hotel rooms. On one occasion, Mossad placed a bomb in the toilet of a mercenary suffering from "Congo stomach," a particularly unpleasant form of dysentery. The lower half of his body was blown to pieces when he pulled the flush in a Khartoum hotel.

Mossad kept its side of the bargain, tipping off the CSIS that Moscow intended to offer a massive financial aid package to one of the poorest countries on earth, Somalia. Beijing promptly doubled the offer. Next Mossad helped China in Sudan, where Moscow had established a bridgehead through President Nimeri's military government. But when the dictator refused to become completely dependent on the Russians, the KGB planned a coup. Mossad informed the CSIS, who told Nimeri. He expelled all Russian diplomats and suspended Soviet Bloc aid schemes.

Having set the two bastions of Communism at each other's throat while at the same time, as Meir Amit later put it, "working our way into the African woodwork," Mossad turned its attention to the one intelligence service in Africa it had come to look upon as a friend: the

Bureau of State Security, BOSS, the most feared arm of South Africa's security apparatus. BOSS matched Mossad in blackmail, sabotage, forgery, kidnapping, prisoner interrogation, psychological warfare, and assassinations. Like Mossad, BOSS had a free hand in how it dealt with its opponents. The two services quickly became bedfellows. Often operating in tandem, they moved through Africa, enjoined by a secret "understanding" between Israel's prime minister, Golda Meir, and the Pretoria regime.

The first result had been the export of uranium ore to Dimona. The shipments were carried on commercial El Al flights from Johannesburg to Tel Aviv, and listed on manifests as agricultural machinery. South African scientists traveled to Dimona and were the only outsiders who knew the true purpose of the facility. When South Africa tested a crude nuclear device on a remote island in the Indian Ocean, Israeli scientists were present to monitor the blast. In 1972, Ezer Weizman, then a senior official in the Israeli defense ministry, met Prime Minister P. W. Botha in Pretoria to ratify a further "understanding." If either country was attacked and required military assistance, the other would come to its aid. Israel supplied the South African army with substantial quantities of U.S.-manufactured arms and in return was granted permission to test the first nuclear devices produced by Dimona at the site in the Indian Ocean.

By then, Mossad had deepened its own relationship with BOSS. While never able to wean the bureau's agents from their brutish methods of interrogation, Mossad instructors introduced them to a range of other methods that had worked in Lebanon and elsewhere: sleep deprivation; hooding; forcing a suspect to stand at a wall for long periods; squeezing genitals; a variety of mental torture ranging from threats to mock executions. Mossad *katsas* traveled with BOSS units into neighboring black African countries on sabotage missions. Kidons showed the South Africans how to carry out killings that left no embarrassing trails. When Mossad offered to locate African National Congress (ANC) leaders living in exile in Britain and Europe for BOSS to kill, the bureau welcomed the idea. The Pretoria government finally vetoed the proposal, fearing it would lose what support it had among die-hard Conservative politicians in London.

Both Mossad and BOSS were driven by an obsessive belief that Africa was lurching leftward toward a revolution that would eventually engulf both their countries. To avoid that happening, any method was permissible. Feeding off each other's fears, both services gave no quarter and shared a self-perpetuating concept that only they knew how to deal with the enemy. Between them, BOSS and Mossad became the two most feared foreign intelligence services in Africa.

This alliance did not sit well with Washington. The CIA feared it could affect its own efforts to maintain a hold on the black continent. The decolonization of Africa in the early 1960s had produced a new interest in Africa within the Agency—and a huge increase in its clandestine activities. An African division was formed, and by 1963, CIA stations had been established in every African nation.

One of the first to serve in Africa was Bill Buckley, later to be kidnapped and murdered by Hezbollah terrorists in Beirut. Buckley would recall, shortly before his capture, "These were really crazy times in Africa with everybody jockeying for position. We were late to the party, and the Mossad looked at us as if we were gate-crashers."

In Washington, the State Department made discreet but determined efforts to reduce Israeli influence in Africa. It leaked details of how several hundred Jews from South Africa had flown north to help Israel during the Suez War. Twenty black African nations broke off diplomatic relations with Jerusalem. Among them was Nigeria. The severance could have been a severe blow to Israel: Nigeria provided over 60 percent of Israel's oil supplies in return for arms that had originally been supplied by the United States to Israel. Despite the diplomatic breach, Prime Minister Yitzhak Shamir agreed to continue secretly arming Nigeria in return for the continued flow of oil. To Buckley it was a "prime example of realpolitik." Another was how Mossad set about shoring up its longtime partner BOSS. In the aftermath of the Israeli invasion of Lebanon in 1982, Mossad found a substantial quantity of documents revealing close links between the PLO and the ANC, long BOSS's bête noire. The incriminating material was turned over to the bureau, enabling its agents to arrest and torture hundreds of ANC members.

The eighties were halcyon days for Mossad's great African safari. As well as playing off the Chinese against the Russians, it made matters difficult for the CIA, MI6, and other European intelligence agencies operating on the continent. Whenever one threatened Mossad's own position, Mossad exposed its activities. In Kenya an MI6 agent was blown. In Zaire, a French network was wrecked. In Tanzania a German intelligence operation was hurriedly aborted after being uncovered by Mossad through a tip to a local reporter.

When terrorist leader Abu Nidal—who had masterminded the assassination of Israel's ambassador to Britain, Shlomo Argov, on June 3, 1982, outside London's Dorchester Hotel—tried to seek shelter in Sudan, Mossad promised the regime Israel would pay one million U.S. dollars for his capture, dead or alive. In the end Nidal fled to the safety of Baghdad.

In a dozen countries, Mossad exploited newfound African nationalism. Among agents who had served in several of those countries was Yaakov Cohen, who would recall: "We gave them an intelligence capability to remain on top of the opposition. In countries like Nigeria, tribal rivalries had led to civil war. Our policy was to work with anyone who would work with us. That enabled us to know everything that was happening in a country. The slightest mood change which could affect Israel was reported back."

Before going to Africa, Cohen had distinguished himself in undercover missions in Egypt and elsewhere. As part of his disguise, Mossad had changed Cohen's physical appearance by arranging for a plastic surgeon to alter his distinctive ethnic feature—his nose. When he returned from the hospital, his own wife barely recognized Cohen and his new nose.

On New Year's Day, 1984, Nahum Admoni's daily intelligence summary contained news of a coup d'état in Nigeria. A military cabal led by Major General Muhammad Buhari had seized power. Prime Minister Shamir's first question was to ask what effect this would have on Israel's oil supplies. No one knew. Throughout the day, urgent efforts were unsuccessfully made to establish contact with the new regime.

On his second day in office, Buhari issued a list of former members of the government accused of a variety of crimes. At its top was Umaru Dikko, the ousted transport minister, charged with embezzling several million U.S. dollars in oil profits from the government treasury. Dikko had fled the country and, despite strenuous efforts to find him, had vanished.

Admoni saw his opening. Traveling on a Canadian passport—another Mossad travel document of choice for undercover missions—he flew to the Nigerian capital, Lagos. Buhari received him late at night. The general listened as Admoni delivered an offer that had the full approval of Rabin. In return for a guarantee of no interruption in oil supplies, Mossad would find Dikko and return him to Nigeria. Buhari had a question: Would Mossad also be able to locate where Dikko had hidden the embezzled money? Admoni said the cash was almost certainly in numbered Swiss bank accounts and would be virtually impossible to trace unless Dikko volunteered to reveal its whereabouts. Buhari smiled for the first time. Once Dikko was back in Nigeria, there would be no problem getting him to talk. Buhari had a final question: Would Mossad agree to work with Nigeria's own security service and, once Dikko was found, take no credit for his capture? Admoni agreed. There were no kudos to be gained for Mossad in an operation that should be simple enough.

Rafi Eitan's "survivor spies" were mobilized throughout Europe. *Katsas* were sent to trawl from Spain to Sweden. Sayanim in a dozen countries were alerted: doctors were told to be on the lookout in case Dikko needed medical attention or even consulted a plastic surgeon to change his appearance; hotel concierges at Dikko's old playgrounds in St.-Moritz and Monte Carlo watched for him. Clerks at car rental agencies from Madrid to Munich were instructed to report if he hired a car; airline agents were asked to call in if he bought a ticket. Sayanim working for all the credit card companies were asked to watch if he used his cards. Waiters memorized Dikko's description, tailors his measurements, and shirtmakers his collar size. Shoemakers from Rome to Paris were given details of Dikko's size-twelve fitting for the customized shoes he wore. In London, Robert Maxwell was asked to probe his high-level contacts among African diplomats in London for any whisper of where Dikko had gone. Like everyone else, he drew a blank.

Nevertheless, Admoni decided that Dikko was hiding out in London—the city had become a haven for Nigerian opponents of the new regime—and he moved his ablest *katsas* to the city. With them came agents from Nigerian security led by Major Muhammad Yusufu. They rented an apartment in the city's Cromwell Road. The *katsas* chose hotels catering to tourists from Africa.

Working separately, the two groups moved among London's sizable Nigerian community. Yusufu's men posed as refugees from the new regime, the *katsas* as sympathetic to black Africans' aspirations to overthrow the regime in South Africa. Gradually they narrowed down the search to West London, to the area around Hyde Park where many wealthy Nigerians lived in exile. They began to comb electoral registers freely available in the area's town halls. Each time they drew a blank.

Then, seven months to the day after Dikko had fled from Lagos, he surfaced. On June 30, 1984, a *katsa* driving down Queensway, a busy thoroughfare off Bayswater Road, spotted a man who fitted the description of Umaru Dikko. He looked older and thinner but there was no mistaking the broad face and the coal black eyes that did not give the *katsa*'s car a second glance.

Spotting a parking place, the *katsa* set off on foot to tail Dikko to a house in nearby Dorchester Terrace. Admoni was immediately informed. He ordered that the only step to be taken for the moment was full-time surveillance of the house. For the first three days of July 1984, two operatives maintained continuous surveillance on Dikko. Meantime the Nigerians used their embassy as a base to prepare a kidnap operation closely modeled on the one Rafi Eitan had used to snatch Adolf Eichmann.

Unusually, a key role had been assigned to an outsider, a much respected doctor, Levi-Arie Shapiro, a consultant anesthetist and director of the intensive care unit at Hasharon Hospital in Tel Aviv. He had been recruited by Alexander Barak, a *katsa* who had appealed to the doctor's patriotism. The doctor agreed to travel to London and spend the thousand dollars Barak had given him to pay for medical equipment, which included anesthetics and an endotracheal tube. He would receive further instructions in London. Shapiro refused to accept a fee for his services, saying he was proud to serve Israel. Another *katsa*, Felix Abithol, had arrived in London on a flight from Amsterdam on July 2. He checked into the Russell Square Hotel. His first instruction to the head of the Nigerian team, Major Yusufu, was to rent a transit van. One of Yusufu's men chose one that was a bright canary yellow color. That may well have been the moment the plan started to unravel.

Late in the evening of July 3, a Nigerian Airways 707 freighter landed at Stansted Airport, thirty miles northeast of London. It had flown from Lagos empty. The pilot informed the airport authorities he had come to collect diplomatic baggage from the London embassy. Traveling with the aircrew were several Nigerian security men who openly identified themselves and said they were there to protect the baggage. Their presence was reported to Scotland Yard's Special Branch. There had been several claims in the past month that the Lagos military regime was threatening exiles in London. The security men were told they must not leave the airport. Apart from visits to the terminal coffee shop, they remained on board the aircraft.

Around midmorning the next day, the canary yellow van drove out of a garage in Notting Hill Gate that had been rented by one of the Nigerians. At the wheel was Yusufu. In the back squatted Dr. Shapiro beside a crate. Crouching with him were Barak and Abithol. At noon out at Stansted, the 707 captain filed a departure time for Lagos of three o'clock that afternoon. The flight manifest listed the cargo as two crates of "documentation" for the Ministry of External Affairs in Lagos. The paperwork claimed diplomatic immunity for both containers.

Shortly before noon, the van drove through traffic and parked outside the house in Dorchester Terrace. Soon afterward, Umaru Dikko emerged on his way to meet a friend for lunch at a nearby restaurant. Watching from a window was his private secretary, Elizabeth Hayes. As she turned away, the back door of the van burst open and "two dark-skinned men grabbed Mr. Dikko and forced him into the back of the van. He just managed to scream something before they jumped in after him and the van was driven away at high speed."

Recovering, the secretary dialed emergency—999. Within minutes police were on the scene, closely followed by Commander William Hucklesby of Scotland Yard's Anti-Terrorist Squad. He suspected what had happened. Every port and airport was alerted. For Hucklesby, the situation had its own special difficulties. If Dikko had been kidnapped by the Nigerian regime, that could present tricky political questions. The Foreign Office was alerted, as was Downing Street. Hucklesby was ordered to take what action he thought appropriate.

Shortly before 3:00 P.M. the van arrived at Stansted's freight terminal. Yusufu waved a Nigerian diplomatic passport at airport customs officers. They watched the two crates being loaded on board the aircraft. One of the officers, Charles Morrow, would recall: "There was something about one of the containers that was just not right. Then I heard noise coming from one. I thought, sod this. Diplomatic immunity or not, I needed to see inside."

The cases were taken off the plane and brought to a hangar despite Yusufu's furious protest that they were protected by diplomatic privilege. In the first crate, Umaru Dikko was discovered tied and unconscious from an anesthetic. Sitting beside him was Dr. Shapiro, a syringe in his hand ready to increase Dikko's drug intake. There was an endotracheal tube in Dikko's throat to stop him from choking on his own vomit. In the other container crouched Barak and Abithol.

At their trial, both agents stuck stoically to the fiction that they were mercenaries acting on behalf of a group of Nigerian businessmen who wanted to return Dikko to face trial. One of Britain's most eminent and expensive lawyers, George Carmen, QC, had been retained for their defense. In his closing speech he told the court, "Perhaps the most plausible explanation is that the Israeli intelligence service was never far removed from the entire operation."

The prosecution offered no evidence to implicate Mossad. It was left to the judge to do so in his summing-up. He told the jury, "The finger of involvement almost certainly points to Mossad."

Barak received a fourteen-year sentence, Dr. Shapiro and Abithol ten years apiece. Yusufu was given twelve years' imprisonment. All were subsequently released after remission for good conduct and quietly deported to Israel. As it had for others before them who had served Mossad well, the service made sure they would remain out of the limelight and not have to answer such troubling questions as to whether Dr. Shapiro, who had so flagrantly broken his Hippocratic oath, still practiced medicine—and for whom.

Nahum Admoni was told by MI5 that if there was a further lapse, Mossad would be treated as an unfriendly service. By then the Mossad chief was planning yet another operation designed to remind Britain of who the real enemies were—and at the same time gain sympathy for Israel.

CHAPTER 14

THE CHAMBERMAID'S BOMB

On a cloudless morning in February 1986, two Israeli air force fighter aircraft swooped down on a Libyan-registered Learjet flying from Tripoli to Damascus. The civilian plane was in international airspace, thirty thousand feet over the Mediterranean and about to begin its descent into Syrian airspace. On board were delegates returning from a conference of Palestinian and other radical groups that Mu'ammar Gadhafi had convened to discuss new steps to achieve the Libyan leader's burning obsession to see Israel driven from the face of the earth.

The sight of the fighters taking up stations on either side of the Learjet created near panic among its fourteen passengers, and for good reason. Four months before, on Tuesday, October 1, 1985, Israeli F-15 fighter-bombers had destroyed the headquarters of the Palestinian Liberation Organization southeast of Tunis, flying a round-trip of almost three thousand miles, which had involved air-to-air refueling and the kind of precise intelligence that always sent a collective shiver throughout the Arab world.

That raid was a direct response to the murder by PLO gunmen of three middle-aged Israeli tourists as they sat aboard their yacht in the Cypriot port of Larnaca only days before, basking in the sunshine of late summer. The killings had occurred on Yom Kippur and, for many Israelis, the slaughter rekindled memories of the onset of the war on the Day of Atonement when the nation itself had been caught as unaware as the tourists.

Despite having endured almost four decades of terrorism, the murders caused widespread horror and fear among Israelis: the tourists had been held for some time on board their boat and allowed to write down their final thoughts before they were killed. First to die was the woman, fatally shot in the stomach. Her two male companions were made to throw her overboard. Then one after another, they were shot at point-blank range in the back of the head.

In the black propaganda war that had long been a feature of the intelligence war between the PLO and Israel, the former claimed that the three victims were Mossad agents on a mission. So well did the PLO plant the story that several European newspapers identified the woman as one of the agents caught in the Lillehammer affair in 1973. That woman was still alive and had long given up her Mossad activities.

Since then the Arab press had been full of dire warnings that Israel would retaliate. Many of the stories had been planted by Mossad's psychological warfare department to fray still further the nerves of millions of Arabs.

The passengers in the Learjet, who only a few hours before had chanted for the destruction of Israel at the Libyan conference, saw the grim faces of their enemy peering at them. One of the fighters waggled its wings, the follow-me signal recognized the world over by pilots. To reinforce the message, an Israeli pointed a gloved hand straight ahead and then downward toward Galilee. The women on board the jet began to wail; some of the men started to pray. Others stared ahead fatalistically. They all knew this had always been a possibility; the accursed infidels had the capability to reach out and snatch them from the sky.

One of the Israeli aircraft fired a short warning burst from its cannon, warning the Learjet's captain not to contemplate radioing for help from the Syrian air force—only minutes' flying time away. The passengers' fear increased. Were they, too, about to suffer the same fate that had befallen one of the authentic heroes of the Arab world?

Just a month before the Tunis air raid, an Israeli naval patrol boat with Mossad agents on board had stopped a small ship called *Opportunity* on its regular shuttle between Beirut and Larnaca. From the bilges they had dragged out Faisal Abu Sharah, a terrorist with blood on his hands. He had been bundled on board the patrol boat, the prelude to ruthless interrogation in Israel, followed by a quick trial and a long term in jail. The swiftness and audacity of the operation had yet again enhanced the image of invincibility Israel presented to the Arab world.

Such incidents were not uncommon. Working closely with Israel's small but highly trained navy, Mossad had since then intercepted several boats and removed passengers suspected of terrorist activities. Not only Israel's long Mediterranean coast called for vigilance; the Red Sea also presented a constant vulnerability. A Mossad agent in Yemen had been the source for an operation that had thwarted a PLO plot to sail a fishing boat up the Red Sea to the Israeli resort of Elat and detonate its cargo of explosives close to the shore, lined with hotels. An Israeli gunboat had intercepted the fishing boat and overpowered its two suicide bombers before they could detonate the cargo.

As the Learjet descended toward northern Israel, the passengers also feared this was a further retaliation for what had happened when another of their heroes, Abu Al-Abbas, had, only a few months before, on October 2, 1985, taken over the Italian cruise liner *Achille Lauro* in what was the most spectacular act of maritime piracy the world could recall. Al-Abbas had murdered one of the passengers, Leon Klinghoffer, an American Jew in a wheelchair, by throwing him into the sea.

The crime had become a floating diplomatic incident that had embroiled an outraged Israel and the United States, Egypt, Italy, Syria, Cyprus, Tunisia, and the stateless PLO; for days the crisis had drifted around the Mediterranean, gathering publicity for the hijackers and revealing the self-interest which, in the Middle East, governed attitudes toward terrorism. The hijacking of a cruise liner that was bringing much-needed foreign tourists and hard currency to Israel, followed by the murder of a passenger, provoked a wave of indecision. The murder had technically taken place on Italian soil, the Genoa-registered *Achille Lauro*. But Italy was highly vulnerable to terrorism and wished to see a quiet end to the incident. The United States wanted justice for its murdered citizen. Across the nation appeared stickers proclaiming, "Don't get mad, get even." Finally the hijackers, having held the world's headlines for several days, surrendered to the Egyptian authorities, who then allowed them to leave the country—to the fury of Israel.

More than one of the Learjet's passengers wondered whether they would now be held in some Israeli jail in an act of revenge. With the fighters still flying almost wingtip to wingtip, the executive jet landed at a military airfield in northern Galilee. A waiting team of Aman interrogators had been told by Mossad that on board were two of the most wanted terrorists in the world, the notorious Abu Nidal and the equally infamous Ahmed Jibril. Instead the interrogators found themselves questioning a bunch of badly frightened Arabs, none of whose names appeared on Israel's computers. The Learjet was allowed to depart with its passengers.

Israel would insist that the prospect of catching terrorists was the only reason for intercepting the aircraft. But within Mossad was a mood that no opportunity should be lost to create fear and panic in Arab minds. The Aman interrogators had some satisfaction in knowing that the passengers would further the image of an all-powerful Israel.

The head of Aman, Ehud Barak, believed the operation was yet another example of Mossad shooting from the hip, and he made his feeling very clear to Nahum Admoni.

Never a person to suffer a mistake or a rebuke lightly, the Mossad chief set about devising an operation that would not only put an end to the mocking of Mossad on Arab radio stations for being reduced to forcing down an unarmed civilian plane, but one that would also end the sniping within Israel's own intelligence community that the service he commanded should next time be very sure before it made a fool of them all.

So began an operation which, among much else, would ruin the life of a pregnant Irish chambermaid and send her Arab lover to prison to serve one of the longest sentences given by a British court; cause huge embarrassment to German chancellor Helmut Kohl and French prime minister Jacques Chirac; once more reveal Robert Maxwell in full manipulative fury; cause Syria to be exiled from the world's diplomatic table; and force all those Arab radio stations that had so gleefully ridiculed Mossad to change their tune.

Like all operations, there were moments of high tensions and periods of patient waiting. It had its quota of human despair, useful anger, and betrayal, but for men like Nahum Admoni, such a plot was the very substance of his life. It went with asking himself the same questions over and over again. Could it work? Would other people actually believe that it had been like that? And, of course, would the real truth remain buried forever?

More certain, Mossad had enlisted the very different skills of two men for the operation. One was a *katsa* who had served in Britain under the alias of Tov Levy. The other was a Palestinian informer, code-named Abu. The Palestinian had been recruited after being discovered by Mossad stealing from a PLO fund he had been administering in a village on the Israeli-Jordanian border. Playing on his fear that the crime could be revealed through an anonymous tip to the village head, resulting in Abu's death, Mossad had dragooned him to leave for London. He had been provided with fake documents stating he was a businessman and given living expenses commensurate with his role as a high-flying big spender. His assigned controller was Tov Levy.

In every way Abu fit the classic definition by Uzi Mahnaimi, a former member of the Israeli intelligence community, of what an agent should be: "You spend hours with him, days even; you teach him everything he needs to know, you go through his courses with him, help him, socialize with him, look at his family photographs, you know the names and ages of his children. But the agent is not a human being; you must never think of him as one. The agent is just a weapon, a means to an end, like a Kalashnikov—that is all. If you have to send him to the hanging tree, don't even think about it. The agent is always a cipher, never a person."

Abu had played his part to perfection and had become a familiar figure around the gambling tables of Mayfair. Given his success, his sexual appetites and bouts of drinking were tolerated. Moving in the haunts of arms dealers and wealthy PLO supporters, Abu picked up information that enabled Mossad to strike against its enemies. Fifteen PLO men were killed by Mossad over a few weeks as a result of Abu's information.

Some of his meetings with Tov Levy had taken place in the bars and restaurants of the Hilton Hotel on Park Lane. Working there was an Irish woman from Dublin, Ann-Marie Murphy.

Like many others, she had been tempted across the Irish Sea by the lure of making good money in London. All she had been able to get was a chambermaid's job. The pay was low, the hours long. Ann-Marie's little free time was spent in bars in the Shepherds Bush district, long a refuge for Irish expatriates. She joined in the rebel songs and made a glass of Guinness last. Then it was back to her lonely room, ready for another long day of changing bedsheets, scouring lavatory bowls, and leaving each hotel room sparkling in the prescribed Hilton manner. Her career was going nowhere.

Shortly before Christmas, 1985, close to tears at the thought of having to spend it alone in a city so different from the carefree Dublin she longed for, Ann-Marie met a dark-skinned Arab who was handsome in her eyes. In his silk suit and flashy tie he also exuded affluence. When he smiled at her, she smiled back. His name was Nezar Hindawi, and he was a distant cousin of Abu. Hindawi was thirty-five years old, though he lied about that to Ann-Marie, lopping three years from his age to make him the same as her, thirty-two. He would go on lying to a trusting, naive woman.

They had met in a bar close to the BBC Theatre in Shepherds Bush Green. She had never been to this pub before and was surprised to find Hindawi among the ruddy-faced building-site navvies whose accents echoed every county in Ireland. But Hindawi seemed to know many of the drinkers, joining in their rough humor and standing a round when it was his turn.

For weeks, Hindawi had been coming to the bar hoping to make contact with the IRA. Abu had asked him to do so, though typically his cousin had not explained why. Hindawi's few attempts to discuss the political situation in Ireland had been brushed aside by men more interested in sinking pints. Whatever scheme Abu was concocting would remain a secret as far as Hindawi was concerned. The arrival of Ann-Marie had also given him something else to think about.

Captivated by his good manners and charm, Ann-Marie soon found herself laughing at Hindawi's stories about his life in the Middle East. To a woman who had never traveled farther than London, he made it sound like an Arabian Nights fantasy. Hindawi drove her home that night, kissed her on both cheeks, and left. Ann-Marie wondered if the giddy feeling she experienced was the first stage of falling in love. The following day he took her to lunch at a Syrian restaurant and introduced her to the delights of Arabic cooking. Tipsy from a fine Lebanese wine, she put up only token resistance when he took her back to his apartment. That afternoon they made love. Until then Ann-Marie had been a virgin. Raised in the strong Irish Catholic tradition opposed to contraception, she had taken no precautions.

In February 1986, she found she was pregnant. She told Hindawi. He smiled reassurance; he would take care of everything. Alarmed, Ann-Marie said she would never agree to an abortion. He told her the idea had never crossed his mind. In truth he was panic-stricken at the prospect of having to marry a woman he regarded as beneath his social class. He also feared she would go to the authorities and complain. With little understanding of how indifferently officialdom would view such matters, he thought his permission to stay in Britain would be revoked, resulting in his being deported as an undesirable alien. Hindawi turned to the only source of help he knew, his cousin Abu.

Abu had his own problems, having lost a good deal of money gambling. He bluntly told Hindawi he couldn't loan him the money Hindawi had decided he would offer Ann-Marie to return to Dublin, have the baby, and place it out for adoption. She had told him that was common in Ireland.

Next day Abu met Tov Levy. Over dinner the *katsa* told Abu he needed to do something to cause the British government to close down the Syrian embassy in London and order out its staff, long suspected of being involved in terrorist activities. Levy said he needed a "hook" that would achieve that. Could Abu tell him about anyone, anything, that might be useful? Abu mentioned he had a cousin with an Irish girlfriend who was pregnant in London.

The plot began to coalesce after the aftershocks rocking the Israeli intelligence community from the disclosures tumbling out of Washington about the arms-for-hostages deal with Iran. Israel's tough image for dealing with terrorism had taken a pounding. There was anger within Mossad that the Reagan administration had allowed matters to go so badly wrong as to allow Israel's role in Irangate to surface.

The revelations had made it that much more difficult to maintain even the minimum support of cautiously friendly neighbors like Egypt and Jordan at a time when they were both finally growing tired of the PLO and the histrionics of Yasser Arafat. Increasingly the PLO leader had become a political captive of his own extremists. No Marxist himself, he found himself cornered into spouting their rhetoric, calling for "the liquidation of the Zionist entity politically, culturally, and militarily."

The vituperation did nothing to improve his position among the various breakaway factions of the PLO. To them, Arafat was the man who had been forced to make a humiliating withdrawal from Beirut under cover of UN protection from the watchful eye of the Israelis. Some fifteen thousand Palestinian fighters had boarded boats for Tunis. Others had deserted Arafat on the promise of support from Syria and had become even more militant against both him and Israel from their new bases outside Damascus.

Yet for Mossad, Arafat remained the key obstacle to peace. Killing him was still a priority; at the Mossad target range the silhouettes were all of Arafat. Until he was dead, he would continue to be held ultimately responsible for all the acts of savagery committed by the disparate Palestinian groups in Syria.

Then two incidents happened which, momentarily at least, moved the focus from Arafat, and ultimately settled the plot in which Abu was to become a key figure.

A growing problem Syria had with the PLO factions under its wing was the need to satisfy their constant demands for action. As one of the world's prime exponents of state-sponsored terrorism, Syria was more than prepared to finance any operation that did not further blight its own already seriously tarnished image. Many of the schemes the PLO factions placed before Syrian intelligence were too risky for the Syrians to endorse. One had been to poison Israel's water supply. Another was to send an Arab suicide bomber, posing as an Orthodox Jew, to blow himself up at the Wailing Wall in Jerusalem. Either was guaranteed to draw draconian retaliation from Israel.

Then came an audacious plot that Syrian intelligence recognized could not only work, but would strike a telling blow at the very heart of Israel's military supremacy. The first step had been to buy a ship. After several weeks of searching ports around the Mediterranean, a

Panama-registered merchantman, *Atavarius*, was purchased and sailed to the port of Algiers.

A week after it arrived, a detachment of Palestinian commandos arrived from Damascus on a Syrian air force transport plane. With them they brought a small arsenal of weapons: machine guns, antitank weapons, and boxes of Kalashnikov rifles so beloved of terrorists. That night, under cover of darkness, the commandos and arms were placed on board the *Atavarius.*

At daybreak the ship set sail, its captain having told the port authorities he was bound for Greece to undergo an engine overhaul. The commandos were belowdecks. But their arrival had not gone unnoticed. A Mossad informer employed in the harbormaster's office had become sufficiently suspicious to inform the *katsa* stationed in the city. He sent a message to Tel Aviv.

Its arrival triggered a "condition yellow" alert that was sent to the entire Mossad network stationed around the Mediterranean. Memories were still fresh of the unsuccessful attempt to blow up the seafront at Elat, and it was assumed this could be a similar attack, only this time against Haifa. The busy port on the Mediterranean seaboard was an obvious target. Two naval gunboats were stationed offshore ready to deal with any attempt by the *Atavarius* to enter the harbor that was Israel's main trading sea link with the world.

The *Atavarius*'s destination was the beaches north of Tel Aviv. In a plan that could have been plucked from a Hollywood movie, the *Atavarius* would lower the commandos into rubber boats, which they would row ashore. Then they would fight their way into Tel Aviv to their target, the Kirya, the fortresslike headquarters of the Israel Defense Forces, whose tower dominated the skyline and would serve as a beacon for the commandos. The plan depended on total surprise and the ruthless courage the Israelis had themselves made a byword.

The attack had been set for Israel's Independence Day celebrations, when a carnival mood would prevail, and the Kirya, according to Syrian intelligence, would have fewer men than usual guarding it. The commandos did not expect to escape with their lives, but they had been chosen for the mission because they had all shown the same mentality as the Beirut suicide bombers.

Meantime, they could relax and enjoy the short cruise that took them past Tunisia to their next landfall, the island of Sicily. No one on board probably paid any attention to the fishing trawler wallowing in the swell as the *Atavarius* passed. The boat contained sophisticated electronic equipment capable of monitoring radio conversations on board the merchantman. A short transmission in Arabic announced that the ship was on schedule. One of the trawler's two-man crew, both Mossad sayanim, radioed the news to Tel Aviv. For the next twenty-four hours, the *Atavarius* was shadowed by other Mossad-operated vessels as it passed Crete and then the island of Cyprus.

A fast motor yacht crossed its path. It, too, was equipped with detection gear, including a powerful camera concealed in the side of the wheelhouse. On deck were two young women, sunbathing. They were cousins of the Cypriot sayan who owned the yacht and were being used as bait to attract interest from those on board the *Atavarius*. As the yacht cruised alongside, several of the commandos appeared at the deck rail, shouting and smiling at the women. In the wheelhouse, the sayan activated the camera to photograph the gesticulating men. His part in the surveillance over, he raced back to Cyprus. In his home the film was developed, and the prints were wired to Tel Aviv. Mossad's computers identified three of the faces as known Arab terrorists. Condition yellow moved to red.

Prime Minister Shimon Peres ordered that the *Atavarius* be attacked. A plan to bomb it was considered and rejected. An air attack might be mistaken by Egypt as part of a preemptive strike; though diplomatic relations between Israel and its neighbor had survived a number of incidents, there was considerable tension and suspicion in Cairo about Tel Aviv's activities. Peres agreed that the attack should be seaborne.

Six Israeli navy gunboats were fueled and armed with rockets. On board were units of the IDF Special Forces and Mossad operatives who were to interrogate any of the commandos taken alive. The gunboats set off in the early hours for Haifa, heading west out into the Mediterranean. They raced through the waters in stern-to-prow formation, so as to reduce the possibility of detection by radar on board the *Atavarius*. The Israelis had timed their attack to be launched with the rising sun immediately behind them.

At a little after 6:30 A.M., the *Atavarius* was sighted. In a textbook maneuver, the gunboats fanned out, attacking the merchantman from both sides, raking the hull and decks with rockets. On deck the commandos fired back. But their heavy armaments were still crated below, and their automatic rifles were no match for the superior firepower of the Israelis. In minutes the *Atavarius* was on fire and its crew and commandos began to abandon ship. Some were shot as they plunged into the sea.

In all, twenty crew and commandos were killed. Their bodies were all recovered. Eight survivors were taken prisoner. Before the gunboats raced back to Israel, they sank the *Atavarius* with rockets whose nose cones were filled with extra-powerful explosives.

The bodies of the dead were unceremoniously buried in the Negev Desert. The prisoners were tried in secret and sentenced to lengthy terms of imprisonment. During their interrogation, they had totally implicated Syria as the guiding force behind the incident. But, rather than launch an attack on its neighbor, the Israeli government, acting on the advice of Mossad, kept the incident secret. Mossad's psychologists had predicted that the disappearance of the ship and its crew and passengers would become the subject of intense and increasingly fearful speculation among the Syrian-based PLO groups. Mossad also warned Prime Minister Peres that the one thing he could be certain of was that the terrorists, knowing their operation had failed, would be eager to regain face with their Syrian benefactors.

Meanwhile, the Palestinians continued to fulminate against Arafat and applaud the deadly war being waged against him by his onetime associate, Abu Nidal. Long deemed terrorism's "grand master of the unexpected," Nidal had fallen out with Arafat over tactics.

Arafat was slowly coming around to the idea that a movement that had nothing at its disposal but terrorism would ultimately fail; it needed a political program and a sense of diplomacy. Arafat had been trying to demonstrate that in his recent public statements, earning encouragement from Washington to continue on this new path. In Israel, Arafat's words were seen as a sham. For Abu Nidal they were nothing but a betrayal of all he personally stood for—naked, unadulterated terrorism.

For months, Nidal had been biding his time. When he heard about the failure of the *Atavarius* mission and the way the ship had subsequently disappeared from the face of the earth, he decided the time had come to remind Israel he was still around. With the full connivance of his protectors in Syrian intelligence, Abu Nidal struck with horrific effect. At the Rome and Vienna airports in December 1985, his gunmen opened fire on helpless Christmas travelers. In as many seconds nineteen passengers, among them five Americans, were slaughtered at the El Al check-in counters at both airports. How had those terrorists been able to move unhampered around Italian police to reach their targets? Where were El Al's own security men?

While answers to these urgent questions were being sought, Mossad's strategists were also looking at other areas. Though Britain had joined in the total condemnation of the attacks, the country still maintained full diplomatic ties with Syria—despite Mossad having furnished MI5 with ample evidence of Damascus's role in state-sponsored terrorism. It was not enough for the prime minister, Margaret Thatcher, to deliver forceful denunciations in Parliament of terrorism. There was a need for more direct action. However, in the past MI5 had reminded Mossad that even Israel had from time to time shown expedient self-interest, and accepted the need to trade with its sworn enemies. There had been its decision to free over a thousand Palestinian detainees—many convicted terrorists—only months before the Rome and Vienna airport massacres, in exchange for three Israeli soldiers held in Lebanon.

But now Mossad was determined to strike a telling blow to force Britain to sever all diplomatic ties with Damascus by closing down its London embassy, long regarded by Mossad as one of the core missions in Europe for plotting against Israel. Central to the plot would be Abu, the cousin of Nezar Hindawi.

After his dinner with Tov Levy, Abu sought out Hindawi, apologizing for his previous indifference about Ann-Marie. Of course he would help, but first he needed to have some answers. Was she going to keep the baby? Was she still pressing him to marry her? Did Nezar really love the girl? They came from different cultures and mixed marriages rarely worked.

Hindawi replied if he had ever loved Ann-Marie, he did not now. She had become shrewish and weepy, asking all the time what was going to happen. He certainly did not want to marry the chambermaid.

Abu gave his cousin ten thousand dollars—money enough, he said, for Hindawi to be rid of Ann-Marie and continue to live a bachelor's life in London. The money had been provided by Mossad. In return Hindawi would have to do something for the cause they both believed in: the overthrow of Israel.

On the evening of April 12, 1986, Hindawi visited Ann-Marie in her rooming house in the Kilburn area of London. He brought flowers and a bottle of champagne, purchased with some of the money Abu had provided. He told Ann-Marie he loved her and wanted to keep the baby. The news brought tears to her eyes. Suddenly her world seemed a far better place.

Hindawi said there was one final hurdle to clear. Ann-Marie must get the blessing of his parents for them to marry. It was an Arabic tradition no dutiful son could flout. She must fly to the Arab village in Israel where his family lived. He painted a picture of their lifestyle having changed little since Christ had walked the earth. To a girl educated by nuns and for whom Mass had been an important part of her life, the imagery was final confirmation that she was making the right decision in marrying her lover. He and his family might not be Christians, but that did not matter; they came from the land of her Lord. In her eyes that made them God-fearing people. Nevertheless, Ann-Marie hesitated. She couldn't just walk out of her job. And where would she get the money to pay the airfare? And for such an important meeting, she would need new clothes. Hindawi stilled her concerns by producing from his pocket a bundle of notes. He told her it was more than enough for her to buy a new wardrobe. With another flourish, Hindawi produced an El Al ticket for a flight on April 17, five days away. He had bought it that afternoon.

Ann-Marie laughed. "You were sure I would go?"

"As sure as I am of my love for you," Hindawi replied.

He promised that once she returned to London they would be married. The next few days passed in a whirl for the pregnant chambermaid. She quit her job and visited the Irish embassy in London to collect a new passport. She shopped for maternity dresses. Every night she made love to Hindawi. Each morning, over a leisurely breakfast, she planned their future together. They would live in Ireland, in a little cottage by the sea. Their baby would be christened Sean if it was a boy. Sinead if a girl.

On the day of Ann-Marie's departure, Hindawi told her he had arranged for her to collect a "gift" for his parents from a "friend" who was one of the cleaners on the air side of the airport.

Ari Ben-Menashe, who subsequently claimed to have detailed knowledge of the plot, insisted that "because Hindawi didn't want to risk her being stopped for having too much carry-on luggage he had arranged for his friend to pass her the bag when she entered the El Al departure lounge."

Her gullibility in not asking any questions about the "gift" was the reaction of a woman head over heels in love and completely trusting her lover. She was the perfect patsy in the accelerating plot.

In the taxi to the airport, Hindawi was the loving, concerned father-to-be. Would she make sure to do her breathing exercises during the long flight? She must drink plenty of water and sit in an aisle seat to avoid developing the cramps she had started to complain of. Ann-Marie had laughingly shushed him: "Holy be to God, you'd think I was flying to the moon!"

She had lingered at the door to the flight departure area, not wishing to be separated from him, promising to phone from Tel Aviv, saying she would love his parents like her own. He kissed her one last time, then gently pushed her into the line making its way toward the immigration-control desk.

Watching her until she was out of sight, Hindawi continued to follow the instructions given to him by Abu and boarded a Syrian Arab Airlines bus for the ride back into London. Meantime, the unsuspecting Ann-Marie had safely passed through passport control and UK security checks. Next she made her way to the high-security area reserved for the El Al flight. Shin Bet–trained agents carefully questioned her and inspected her hand baggage. She was assigned a seat and motioned through to the final departure lounge to join the other 355 passengers.

According to Ari Ben-Menashe, she was handed the "gift" for Hindawi's parents by a man dressed in the blue coveralls of an airport cleaner. The man disappeared as mysteriously as he had appeared. Ben-Menashe would write: "Within seconds, Ann-Marie was asked to submit to a search. The El Al security people found plastic explosives in a false bottom in the bag."

The explosives consisted of over three pounds of Semtex. Ann-Marie sobbed out her story to waiting Special Branch and MI5 officers. It was the tale of an ill-starred woman not only crossed in love but double-crossed by her partner. The officers concentrated on establishing Hindawi's contacts with Syria after they realized Ann-Marie had been an innocent dupe.

As the airlines bus entered London, Hindawi ordered the driver to divert to the Syrian embassy. When the driver protested, Hindawi said he had the "authority" to do so. At the embassy, he asked consular officials to grant him political asylum. He told them he feared the British police were about to arrest him because he had tried to blow up an El Al plane for the "cause." The astonished officials handed Hindawi over to two embassy security men. They asked him to remain in an embassy staff apartment after they questioned him. They might well have been suspicious that this was some sort of trap to embarrass Syria. If so, those fears would only have deepened when Hindawi left the apartment shortly after.

Hindawi had gone in search of Abu. Failing to find him, he checked into the London Visitors' Hotel in the Notting Hill district, where he was arrested shortly afterward.

The BBC broadcast news of how the police had foiled the plot. The details were unusually precise: the Czech-made Semtex had been concealed in the false bottom of Ann-Marie's bag and was primed to explode at thirty-nine thousand feet.

For Ben-Menashe, the operation had swiftly moved to a satisfying conclusion. "Margaret Thatcher closed down the Syrian embassy. Hindawi was jailed for forty-five years. Ann-Marie went home to Ireland where she gave birth to a daughter." Abu returned to Israel, his role over.

After Hindawi's trial, Robert Maxwell unleashed the *Daily Mirror*: "The bastard got what he deserved," screamed an editorial. "Ambassador of Death," shrieked a headline on the day of the expulsion of Syria's ambassador to the Court of St. James's. "Get Out, You Syrian Swine," screamed another. Ari Ben-Menashe would be the first to claim that Mossad had pulled off a "brilliant coup which cast Syria into the political wilderness."

But there were intriguing questions behind that clear-cut sentiment. Had Ann-Marie Murphy really been handed a working bomb, or had it been part of an elaborate scam? Was the man in blue coveralls—Hindawi's supposed "friend"—a security officer? How much foreknowledge of the plot did MI5 have? And would it not have been unthinkable for Mossad and Britain's security services to actually allow Semtex to be taken on board an airliner when there was even the remotest chance the bomb could have detonated on the ground? Such an explosion would certainly have devastated a sizable area of the world's busiest airport at a time when thousands of people would have been in the area. Had the real brilliance of the coup been that Mossad had achieved the diplomatic castration of Syria at no risk at all to El Al and Heathrow by using a harmless substance resembling Semtex? To all such questions, Prime Minister Shimon Peres would only intone: "What happened is usually known to those who should know and whoever does not know should continue not knowing."

From Britain's high-security jail at Whitmoor, Hindawi has continued to protest he was a victim of a classic Mossad sting operation. White-haired and no longer slim, he says he expects to die in prison. He refers to Ann-Marie only as "that woman." In 1998, she lives in Dublin raising their daughter, who, she is thankful, does not look like her lover. She never speaks of Hindawi.

There is one puzzling footnote to the story. Two weeks after Hindawi was sentenced to a prison sentence that would see him incarcerated well into the twenty-first century, Arnaud de Borchgrave, the respected editor of the *Washington Times*, placed his tape recorder on the desk of France's prime minister, Jacques Chirac, in Paris. De Borchgrave was in Europe to attend the European Community foreign ministers' meeting in London, and the interview with Chirac was to obtain a briefing on the French position. The interview had moved along predictable lines, with Chirac making it clear that France and Germany had been dragooned into a show of loyalty to the British government, which was proving to be increasingly intransigent over Common Market policies. De Borchgrave raised the question of France's own relationship in another area. The editor wanted to know what stage Chirac's negotiations had reached with Syria to end the spate of terrorist bombs in Paris, and of France's efforts to free the eight foreign hostages held by the Hezbollah in Lebanon. The prime minister paused and looked across his desk, seemingly oblivious of the recorder. He then said that the German chancellor, Helmut Kohl, and foreign minister, Hans-Dietrich Genscher, had both told him that the Syrian government was not involved in Hindawi's plan to blow up the El Al airliner; that the plot "was engineered by Mossad, the Israeli Secret Service."

The resulting diplomatic furor nearly ruined Chirac's career. He found himself being attacked on one side by his own president, François Mitterand, and on the other fending off furious telephone calls from Helmut Kohl demanding he must retract. Chirac did what politicians often do. He said he had been misquoted. In London, Scotland Yard said the matter had been fully dealt with by the courts and there was no need for further comment. In Paris, the office of Jacques Chirac—in 1997 president of France—said he had no recall of the interview with the *Washington Times*.

Soon another sting would leave Mossad with a further stain on its reputation.

CHAPTER 15

THE EXPENDABLE CARTOONIST

Nahum Admoni's demise as director general of Mossad began on a July

afternoon in 1986, the result of an incident on one of those Bonn streets

built in the post–World War II building boom in Germany. Forty years

later the street had become a mature avenue with small but well-kept

front gardens and maids' quarters in the rear. Security systems were

discreetly hidden behind wrought-iron gates and the lower windows

were mullioned, the result of using bottle glass.

No one saw the person who left a plastic carrier bag in the telephone

booth at the end of the street. A police patrol car spotted it and stopped

to investigate. The bag contained eight freshly minted blank British passports. The immediate reaction of the local office of the Bundeskriminal Amt (BKA), the equivalent of the FBI, was that the passports were for one of the terrorist groups who had brought terrorism to the streets of Europe with a series of violent and brutal bombings and kidnappings.

Representing causes and minorities from all corners of the world, they were determined to force their way to a role in setting the agenda for international policy. They had found ready support from the radical student politics that had swept Britain and the Continent. Since 1968, when Leila Khaled, a young Palestinian woman revolutionary, hijacked a jet plane to London and was promptly released because the British government feared further attacks, naive students had chanted the agitprop slogans of the PLO. Those middle-class young radicals had a romanticized view of the PLO as "freedom fighters" who, instead of taking drugs, took the lives of the bourgeoisie, and instead of holding sit-ins, held hostages.

The BKA assumed that the passports had been left by a student acting as a courier for a terrorist group. The list of groups was dauntingly long, ranging from the IRA or Germany's own Red Army Faction to foreign groups like the INFS, Islamic National Front of Sudan; the ELN, the National Liberation Army of Colombia; the MDRA, the Angola Liberation Movement; or the LTTE, the Tamil Tigers. These and many more had cells or cadres through the Federal Republic. Any one of them could be planning to use the passports to attack one of the British military bases in Germany or travel to Britain and stage an outrage there.

Despite being Western Europe's leading former imperial power, initially Britain had only encountered continued terrorism at the hands of the IRA. But its intelligence services had warned it was only a matter of time before other foreign groups, allowed to operate against their own countries from London, would drag Britain into their machinations. A foretaste of what could happen came when a group opposed to the Tehran regime took over the Iranian embassy in 1980. When negotiations failed, the Thatcher government sent in the SAS, who killed the terrorists. That well-publicized action had led to a sudden decline in Middle Eastern plots hatched in London. Instead, Paris had become the battleground for bloody internal conflicts between various foreign organizations, most notably Yasser Arafat's PLO and Abu Nidal and his gunmen. Mossad had also done its share of killing Arab enemies on the streets of the French capital.

The BKA believed the passports found in the Bonn telephone kiosk were the precursor of more slaughter. The agency called in the Bundesnachrichtendienst (BND), the republic's equivalent of the CIA, who informed the MI6 liaison officer attached to BND headquarters in Pullach, in southern Germany. In London, MI6 established that the passports were expert forgeries. That ruled out the IRA and most other terrorist groups. They did not have the capability to produce such high-quality documents. Suspicion switched to the KGB; their forgers were among the best in the business. But the Russians were known to have a stockpile of passports and certainly it was not their style to use a phone booth as a pickup point. The South African security service, BOSS, was also ruled out. It had virtually stopped operating in Europe, and false British passports were hardly needed in the unsophisticated African countries where BOSS now concentrated its activities. MI6 turned to the only other intelligence service who could make good use of the passports—Mossad.

Arie Regev, an attaché at the Israeli embassy in London who was also the resident *katsa*, was invited to meet a senior MI6 officer to discuss the matter. Regev said he knew nothing about the passports but agreed to raise the matter with Tel Aviv. Back came the swift response from Nahum Admoni: the passports had nothing to do with Mossad. He suggested that they could be the work of the East Germans; Mossad had recently discovered that the Stasi, the East German security service, was not above selling fake passports to Jews desperate to travel to Israel, in return for hard currency. Admoni knew the passports had been created by Mossad forgers—and were intended to be used by *katsas* working under cover in Europe and to enable them to more easily enter and leave Britain.

Despite an "understanding" with MI5 that Rafi Eitan had originally helped hammer out, in which Mossad agreed it would keep MI5 informed of all operations inside Britain, the agency was secretly running an agent in England in the hope it would lead to a double triumph for Mossad: killing the commander of the PLO's elite Special Forces unit—Force 17—and ending Yasser Arafat's increasing success in establishing a relationship with the Thatcher government.

In London, no longer was Arafat's name synonymous with terrorism. Mrs. Thatcher had slowly become convinced that he could bring about a just and lasting peace in the Middle East that would both recognize the legitimate rights of the Palestinian people and assure the security of Israel. Jewish leaders were more skeptical. They argued it was only terrorism that had brought the PLO to the stage at which it was now, and that the organization would continue to use the threat of more terrorist actions unless all its demands were met. Not for the first time, London was unmoved by Tel Aviv's protestations. Mossad continued to regard Britain as a country which, despite the outcome of the Iranian embassy siege, was becoming too ready to support the Palestinian cause. There was already concern within Mossad over the way the PLO had managed to cozy up to the CIA.

Contacts between the United States and the PLO would later be precisely dated by former secretary of state Henry Kissinger. He would reveal in his memoirs, *Years of Upheaval,* that six weeks after the U.S. ambassador to Sudan was shot dead in Khartoum by Black September gunmen, a secret meeting took place, on November 3, 1973, between CIA deputy director Vernon Walters and Yasser Arafat. The outcome was a "nonaggression pact" between the United States and the PLO. Kissinger subsequently wrote: "Attacks on Americans, at least by Arafat's faction of the PLO, ceased."

When he learned of the pact, Yitzhak Hofi fumed that in the long history of expediency, there had never been a worse example. Using his back channel to the CIA, Hofi tried to have Walters cancel the agreement. The CIA deputy director said that was not possible and warned Hofi that Washington would regard it as an "unfriendly act" if news of the pact became public. It was a shot across the bow not to let loose Mossad's Department of Psychological Warfare on friendly journalists.

Hofi's anger became apocalyptic when he discovered whom Arafat had put in charge of administering the PLO end of the pact: Ali Hassan Salameh, the Red Prince, the Black September group leader who had planned the Munich massacre of the Israeli Olympic athletes and the murder of the U.S. ambassador in Khartoum; Salameh, the man whose life would finally end the way it had been lived, in a powerful explosion arranged by Rafi Eitan. But that was still some years away. In 1973, Salameh was a revered figure within the PLO and Arafat had no hesitation about appointing him to liaise with the CIA. What genuinely shocked Mossad was that the CIA had accepted the Red Prince barely a year after the Munich killings and the murder of the U.S. envoy in Khartoum.

Soon Salameh was a regular visitor to CIA headquarters at Langley. Usually accompanied by Vernon Walters, the Red Prince would stride across the Agency's marble-floored entrance, past the guards, and ride in the elevator to the seventh floor, where Walters had his spacious office. Their meetings would be interrupted to join CIA's senior officers in their special dining room. Walters would unfailingly pay for the Red Prince's meal; there was no such thing as a free lunch at Langley.

What passed between Salameh and the CIA has remained secret. Bill Buckley, who later died at the hands of terrorists in Beirut when he was CIA station chief, would claim that "Salameh played a large part in winning the hearts and minds of the U.S. for the PLO. He was charismatic and persuasive and knew when to argue and when to listen. And, in intelligence terms, he was a super informer."

An early example was when Salameh warned the CIA of an Iran-brokered plot to shoot down Kissinger's plane when it next flew into Beirut during the secretary's shuttle for peace. Next, Salameh brokered a deal in which the PLO escorted 263 Westerners in West Beirut to safety during the height of the Lebanese civil war. Shortly afterward, the Red Prince gave the CIA warning of an attempt to assassinate the U.S. ambassador to Lebanon. Then, in yet another meeting with the CIA, the Red Prince wrote and signed a "non-assassination guarantee" for all U.S. diplomats in Lebanon. In Beirut the repeated joke was "It pays to live in the same building as American diplomats because the PLO security is so good."

Yitzhak Hofi, then head of Mossad, had demanded the CIA break off all contacts with the Red Prince. The request was ignored. Around CIA headquarters at Langley, Salameh was increasingly known as "the bad guy who has come good for us." He continued to provide intelligence and operational information that kept the CIA fully briefed on the Middle East and had become its most important asset in the region. When he was finally killed, the CIA was enraged, and its relations with Mossad were cool for a considerable time.

One U.S. ambassador to Lebanon, Hermann Eilts, later said after Salameh's own assassination: "I know that on a good many occasions, in a nonpublic fashion, he was extraordinarily helpful, assisting with security for American citizens and officials. I regard his assassination as a loss."

Now, six years later, the PLO was once more beguiling the government of Margaret Thatcher while its Force 17, under a new leader, continued to kill Israelis. Nahum Admoni decided he would succeed where his predecessors had failed. He would disrupt the PLO's relationship with Britain and, at the same time, kill the Force 17 commander. The success of the operation would turn out to depend on a young Arab who, as a boy, had prayed in his village mosque that Allah would give him the strength to murder as many Jews as possible.

Ismail Sowan's potential had been spotted ten years before. In 1977, when Sowan was still a teenager living in a West Bank village, an Israeli army intelligence officer had interviewed him as part of a routine updating of the IDF's profile of the area.

The Sowan family had settled there in the 1930s, a time when the revolt against the British mandate and the Jews had heated the blood of all Arabs. Everywhere there was violence; bloodshed had begotten bloodshed. Ismail's father had joined the Palestine Arab Party, organizing protests and raising nationalist feeling in his community. At first his fury had been against the British. But when they withdrew from Palestine in 1948, the new Jewish state became a prime target. Ismail's first remembered words were to chant hatred for the Jews.

Throughout his childhood the one word that he heard most often was "injustice." It was force-fed to him at school; it filled the conversations around the family dinner table: the terrible injustice done to his people, his family, himself.

Then, shortly after his fifteenth birthday, he witnessed a brutal attack on a bus filled with Jewish pilgrims on their way to Jerusalem. Women and children had been slaughtered by Arabs. That night Ismail had asked a question that would change forever his thinking: Supposing the Jews were entitled to defend what they had? All else had flowed from that: his steady alienation from the violence of his companions, his belief that Jew and Arab *could* live together, *must* live together. With this came a conviction that if he could do anything to achieve that, he would.

Two years later, barely seventeen, he had sat down and told the IDF intelligence officer what he still felt. The officer had first listened intently, then thoroughly questioned Ismail. How could he have turned his back on all his people's beliefs, which were like a tocsin sounding a single note: that *Arabs* were the wronged ones, that *they* must fight to the death for what *they* believed was right? The officer's questions had been many and Ismail's answers long.

The officer noted that, unlike other young Arabs living under Israeli rule, Sowan had few objections to the stringent security the army imposed. Refreshingly, the slightly built youth with an engaging smile seemed to understand why the Israelis had to do this. All that really concerned him was that the regular army clampdown meant he could not go to school in East Jerusalem to study his favorite subject, science.

Sowan's file made its way through the IDF intelligence community, flagged as someone worth further investigation, finally reaching the desk of a Mossad officer. He passed it over to recruitment.

Ismail Sowan was invited to travel to Tel Aviv, ostensibly to discuss his future education; he had recently applied to go to Jerusalem to study. Ismail was questioned for an entire afternoon. First his interrogator explored Ismail's knowledge of science and was satisfied with the answers. Then the whole Sowan family history was laid bare and Ismail's answers checked against those given to the IDF intelligence officer. Finally, Ismail was told what was on offer. Mossad would pay for his education, provided he came through its training course. He must also understand that if he spoke a word of any of this to anyone, his life would be in danger.

It was a standard warning, given to all Arabs Mossad recruited. But to the idealistic Ismail Sowan, it was the chance he had been waiting for: to bring together Jew and Arab.

Sowan went through all the interview processes in safe houses before being sent to the training school on the outskirts of Tel Aviv. He excelled in a number of subjects, showing a natural aptitude for computer skills and shaking off a tail. Not surprisingly, he scored high in the subjects dealing with Islam, and his paper on the role of the PLO in the Middle East conflict was sufficiently interesting to be shown to Mossad's then chief, Yitzhak Hofi.

On completion of his training, Sowan became a bodel, a courier between headquarters and Israel embassies from where *katsas* operated under diplomatic cover. He began to shuttle around the Mediterranean, regularly visiting Athens, Madrid, and Rome, carrying documents in diplomatic pouches. Occasionally he traveled to Bonn, Paris, and London. The chance to see the world and be paid for it—he was getting five hundred dollars a month—was an exciting feeling for someone barely out of his teens.

What Sowan did not realize was the documents had no importance. They were part of yet another test—to see if he made any attempt to show them to an Arab contact he might have in any of the cities he visited. During each trip Sowan was shadowed by other newly qualified

Israeli-born Mossad officers, practicing their own skills at surveillance. The person Ismail handed over the documents to at some prearranged meeting in a café or hotel lobby was not, as he imagined, an Israeli diplomat, but a Mossad officer.

After weeks of spending his free time abroad strolling around Rome's Pantheon, visiting the Sistine Chapel, and exploring London's Oxford Street, he was ordered to go to Beirut and join the PLO.

Enlisting was easy. He simply walked into a PLO recruiting office in West Beirut. The recruiter was intelligent and extremely well informed in political matters. He spent time exploring Ismail's attitude toward the need for violence and whether Sowan was ready to eschew all previous affiliations—family and friends—in favor of becoming dependent upon the PLO for emotional support. He was told if he was accepted, it would mean a great change in his life: the organization would be his only protection against a hostile world. In return, the PLO would look to him to give unswerving loyalty.

His Mossad controller had prepared Sowan to give the correct responses, and he was sent to a training camp in Libya. There the indoctrination continued. He was taught in a dozen different ways that Israel was out to destroy the PLO, so it first must be destroyed. His tutors preached an acute hostility to everything and everyone outside the PLO. The lessons learned at the Mossad training school about roleplaying were remembered; Sowan had spent many hours absorbing from his Mossad instructors the dynamics of terrorist groups, their likely behavior and tactics. In Libya, he was harangued that a murder was no more than a means to win liberation; a car bomb represented another step toward freedom; a kidnapping was a way to achieve justice. Ismail continued to show the skills Mossad had instilled. He accepted all the PLO training but never let it affect his core belief. He also displayed sufficient persistence, resourcefulness, and physical toughness to be singled out as more than a foot soldier. When he left the training camp, a place was found for him in the PLO operation echelons. Step by step he moved up the chain of command.

He met the organization's leaders, including Yasser Arafat; he traveled to PLO training camps throughout the Middle East. Back in Beirut he learned to live under the Israeli air force raids, avoiding hiding underground because of the risk the building would be bombed and collapse on top of him. But somehow he managed never to miss an appointment with his Mossad controller, who regularly slipped into Lebanon to collect Sowan's latest news.

Always he maintained his cover. When Ali Hassan Salameh was killed, Ismail Sowan led the chanting against the hated Israelis. Each time a PLO sniper shot an IDF soldier, he was among the cheerleaders. In all he said and did he appeared a fiercely committed militant.

In 1984, with Arafat driven out of Lebanon and regrouping in Tunis, the PLO sent Sowan to Paris to learn French. Nahum Admoni, who had by this time replaced Hofi, saw Sowan's transfer as a golden opportunity to have an agent on the inside of the PLO's burgeoning activities in Europe.

Arab ghettos in Paris's Eighteenth and Twentieth Arrondissements had become a haven for terrorists; in the narrow streets where people lived on the edge of legality, there was ready shelter for the gunmen and bomb makers. From here had been launched the attacks on Jewish restaurants, shops, and synagogues. It was in Paris that the first joint communiqué had been signed by various terrorist organizations pledging united support to attack Israeli targets in all Europe.

Mossad had fought back with its renowned ruthlessness. Kidons had entered the Arab enclaves and killed suspected terrorists in their beds. One had his throat cut from ear to ear, another his neck wrung like a chicken. But these were small victories. Mossad knew that the terrorists retained the upper hand, largely because they were so well directed by the PLO. The prospect of having his own man inside the organization's Paris operational headquarters was an exciting one for Admoni.

Within days of arriving in the French capital, Sowan made contact with his case officer, working out of the Israeli embassy at 3, rue Rabelais. He would only ever know him as Adam. They set up regular meeting points in cafés and on the Metro. Usually, Sowan would carry a copy of that day's newspaper in which he had inserted his information. Adam would have a similar copy in which was concealed Sowan's instructions and his monthly salary, now raised to one thousand dollars. In a technique they had both perfected at the Mossad training school, one would bump into the other and offer profuse apologies, and they would go their separate ways, having exchanged newspapers.

By this simple means, Mossad tried to regain the upper hand in a city that had long relished its reputation for offering sanctuary to political extremists—providing they left France alone. Only Mossad had chosen to break that understanding by launching an operation that delivered a blow to French pride that even now, almost twenty years later, France can neither forgive nor forget. The episode began three thousand miles away, at the Mediterranean mouth to the Suez Canal, designed by Ferdinand de Lesseps, the French visionary.

In a few shattering minutes on the afternoon of October 21, 1967, Israel had discovered its vulnerability to modern warfare. One of its flagships, an old World War II British destroyer renamed *Eilat*, on patrol off the Egyptian coast, was hit by three Russian Styx missiles fired from Port Said. Forty-seven Israeli sailors were killed and another 41 seriously injured out of a complement of 197 officers and men. The *Eilat* was sunk. It was not only the biggest sea disaster Israel had ever suffered, but the first time in the long history of naval warfare that a ship had been destroyed by long-range missile attack.

When the immediate magnitude of the calamity passed, Levi Eshkol's government ordered a crash program to provide its navy with a new kind of ship to replace the outdated *Eilat*. In weeks, designers had come up with a gunboat that would be fast, highly maneuverable, and equipped with electronic countermeasures to provide the precious seconds needed to take evasive action against any future missile attack. An order to build seven of the boats was placed with the Chantiers de Construction Mécanique de Normandie, CCM, shipyard in Cherbourg, France.

While they were being constructed, scientists at Dimona were manufacturing the missiles the boats would carry, together with the sophisticated equipment to be fitted once they arrived in Israel.

Matters progressed uneventfully at Cherbourg until President de Gaulle introduced a total French arms embargo after Israel commandos attacked the Beirut airport on December 26, 1968, and destroyed thirteen parked Lebanese aircraft—a reprisal for a Palestinian attack on an El Al Boeing 707 at the Athens airport two days previously. The embargo meant the gunboats would not be handed over to Israel.

The French response ended a decade-long alliance with Israel. It had been forged during the Algerian revolution, which had finally led to the colony's independence from France in 1962, and was partly rooted in a common hostility to Gamal Abdel Nasser's Egypt. During that time, Mossad had supplied intelligence about the anti-French FLN organization, and France had sold Israel arms and frontline Mirage fighter aircraft.

With the loss of Algeria, de Gaulle had quickly restored France's traditional links with other Arab countries, and the PLO was allowed to open an office in Paris. The Beirut airport raid was seen by de Gaulle as a very public slight to his demand that Israel should not carry out what the president called "revenge attacks" against its Arab neighbors.

The French arms embargo effectively meant Israel would no longer have sufficient replacement Mirage aircraft to dominate the Middle East's skies, or be able to effectively defend itself from seaborne attack. Perversely, the embargo came at a time when Israel was grappling with the price of its stunning victory in the Six-Day War. In those few days in 1967, it had brought the West Bank, East Jerusalem, and the Gaza Strip under its control. With the land came almost a million Arabs, the great majority imbued with hatred for their conquerors.

For Meir Amit, the problem Israel faced "could not be overstated. Within our borders were thousands of *mehabelim*—the Hebrew for terrorist—and they had the support of the general Arab population who, at minimum, would give them succor and shelter: my first job was to increase Mossad's targeting and penetration of all Palestinian organizations."

Meir Amit was told by Israel's new prime minister, Golda Meir, to devise a plan to get the completed boats out of France. He would recall: "The first suggestion was we should sail into Cherbourg with sufficient armed sailors and just take the boats and head back for Israel. Moshe Dayan, then minister of defense, sat on that—hard. He correctly pointed out that the international reaction would create huge repercussions and see Israel branded a thief. Whatever we did had to be done legally. We had to come up with a watertight right to sail out of French territorial waters. Once we were on the high seas, it would be a different matter."

The legality of what was to follow would be in the eyes of the beholder. Despite Dayan's insistence on the letter of the law being obeyed, what was contemplated was pure and simple trickery.

By November 1969, Meir Amit had the first stage of Operation Noah's Ark in place. A London-based firm of lawyers had been briefed by Israel's largest shipping company, Maritime Fruit—which freighted produce around the world—to register a new firm named Starboat, after the Star of David. Its principal shareholder was Mila Brenner, a director of Maritime Fruit. The other shareholders were proxies for Meir Amit. The second part of the operation went equally smoothly. For months Admiral Mordechai Limon, the Israeli navy liaison officer at Cherbourg for the gunboat project, had been discussing compensation with the shipyard for breach of contract; each time the French came close to an agreement, Limon had found a new point to argue. On November 10, he informed the shipyard that Israel was once more ready to discuss the matter.

In Tel Aviv, Mila Brenner had contacted one of the most respected shipping magnates in the world, Ole Martin Siem, based in Oslo. He agreed to join the board of Starboat for the specific purpose of purchasing the gunboats.

Limon, with a sleight of hand worthy of a card player, made his move. On November 11, he met with shipyard officials. He listened to their improved offer of compensation and said he was still not satisfied. The officials were astonished; their new offer was a generous one. While they contemplated what to do next, Limon hurried to Paris. Waiting there was Ole Siem. After the two men met, Limon telephoned the shipyard officials to say he would be in touch with them "in a few days." Within the hour, Siem was seated in the office of General Louis Bonte, the French government's arms salesman. Siem said he had heard that there "are some gunboats for sale that can be converted to drill for oil."

Timing his intervention to perfection, Limon at that moment called Bonte to say he was in Paris and was ready to accept a final offer in compensation. The figure he proposed was the one the Cherbourg shipyard officials had offered. Bonte told Limon he was "in negotiation" and would call back. The general then turned to Siem and revealed the offer Limon had agreed to accept but said it was too high for the government to agree to pay. Siem promptly increased Limon's offer by 5 percent. Bonte called back Limon and said his offer was most agreeable. Bonte believed he had made a good deal in ridding France of a thorny problem. Israel would get its compensation and France would have made a 5 percent profit.

He only had two questions for Ole Siem. Were the boats going to Norway? Could Siem guarantee they would not be reexported after their oil-exploration activities? Siem gave an unequivocal guarantee on both counts. Bonte accepted that, to avoid press inquiries about the site of the oil fields—a sensitive commercial matter in an industry renowned for its secrecy—the removal of the boats from Cherbourg would be done discreetly. A departure date was set for Christmas Eve, 1969, when Cherbourg would be celebrating the start of the holiday season.

There was still a month to go—and Meir Amit was only too well aware that that was more than enough time for things to go wrong. There would be a need to provide 120 Israeli sailors to crew the boats for the three-thousand-mile voyage from Cherbourg to Haifa. To send that many men at one time would most certainly alert the French security service. Once more the inventive Meir Amit had the answer.

He decided only two sailors at a time would travel together to cities all over Europe before going on to Cherbourg. The sailors were instructed not to stay in the port's hotels for more than a night before moving to another one. They all traveled on Israeli passports so that, in case they were caught, they could not be charged with possessing forged travel documents. Nevertheless, Meir Amit knew the risks were still high. "It just needed one suspicious French policeman to ask why so many Jews were coming to Cherbourg for Christmas and the whole operation could be blown."

By December 23, the sailors had all arrived in Cherbourg. Scattered around the town, they listened to the incessant carols; some who had been born and raised in Jerusalem joined in the singing.

In Tel Aviv, a relieved Meir Amit watched other problems come and go. The question of providing enough supplies for eight days at sea had been solved by the operation's supply officer visiting every shop in Cherbourg. But whenever shopkeepers pressed on him Christmas *jambon*, he politely refused. A quarter of a million liters of fuel had been smuggled on board in drums and hidden belowdecks. The one great imponderable was the weather. The boats would have to sail across the Bay of Biscay in winter conditions that could sink them. Meir Amit would recall that in Tel Aviv: "What we prayed for was Dunkirk weather. We had sent a meteorologist to Cherbourg and he monitored every forecast out of England, France, in Cherbourg and Spain."

The hours ticked slowly by until finally it was Christmas Eve. The forecast in Cherbourg was for rain gusting out of the southwest. Nevertheless, the order was given to sail at 8:30 that night. By 7:30 P.M. the crews were all on board. But the weather worsened. A new departure time was set for 10:30 P.M. That came and went, halted again by the weather. From Tel Aviv came urgent coded signals: Sail no matter what the conditions.

In Cherbourg, the ranking Israeli naval officer ignored the pressure; for him the lives of his men were more important at that moment. In his command boat, he sat silently watching the meteorologist feverishly studying his weather charts. At midnight the weatherman announced: "The winds will drop and veer northerly in two hours. They will not be so strong and be behind us. We can go."

At exactly 2:30 A.M. on Christmas Day, the boats' engines started and the crafts headed slowly out to sea. Seven days later, on New Year's Day, they sailed into Haifa Harbor.

Among those waiting on the quayside was Meir Amit. For him the New Year could not have had a better start. But he also knew President Charles de Gaulle would never forgive Israel for what had happened.

So it had proven to be the case. When Mossad came hunting Middle Eastern terrorists in Paris and other French cities, its *katsas* were as closely watched as any terrorist by the French security service. Worse, pro-Arab officers in the SDECE often tipped off the PLO that Mossad was about to launch a counterstrike. Too often a terrorist would slip away.

The most notorious of these was Ilich Ramirez Sanchez, whose activities had earned him the nickname "Carlos the Jackal." In Paris, he was the proverbial gun for hire in the service of one of the PLO breakaway groups based in Syria. His exploits had made him an admired figure in the Marxist underground press that flourished in Europe. Women found his playboy habits thrilling—the more so when he seemed able to flit at will in and out of the traps Mossad set to kill him. One day he would be on the Riviera sunning himself with a girl, the next he would be spotted in London with a group of Middle Eastern terrorists, helping them lay their plans against other Arab groups and, of course, Israel. Carlos and they operated without interference from Britain's police and intelligence services on the understanding they would do no harm to British citizens. By the time Mossad was in a position to kill Carlos, he was back on the Continent, or had flown to Damascus, Baghdad, or other Arab countries to stoke up further mischief making.

Keeping track of Carlos long enough for Mossad to be able to assassinate him had become yet another task assigned to Ismail Sowan during his time in Paris.

His overall contribution to the war Mossad waged in France was considerable, allowing its *katsas* and kidons to claim spectacular successes:

a PLO forgery factory producing false documents was firebombed; weapons caches were destroyed; couriers were intercepted and murdered; explosives smuggled in from Eastern Europe were blown up; in a dozen and more ways, Mossad fought fire with fire as a result of the intelligence Sowan provided.

In January 1984, Sowan was told by Adam, his Mossad controller, he was being sent to England, where he would pose as a mature student studying for a science degree. His new task would be to penetrate the PLO in London and discover everything he could about its active service unit, Force 17. It was now run by Abdul-Rahid Mustapha, who was using Britain as a base. Mustapha was on Mossad's assassination list.

Ismail Sowan told the PLO office manager in Paris he had completed his French studies—a French sayan had produced a forged diploma to confirm this in case he was asked for proof, though no one did—and he wished to go to England to continue his quest for an engineering science degree. He even managed to slip in a reminder that the qualification would make him "even more useful when it came to bomb making."

The prospect of adding another bomb maker to the PLO's team of such experts was always welcome, and never more so than in 1984. The PLO leadership needed to show the Palestinians in the West Bank and Gaza Strip that they were not forgotten. Tens of thousands were suffering increasing hardship under Israeli occupation; they could not understand why Yasser Arafat did not do more to help them in a practical way: rhetoric was one thing, action another.

Mossad knew that Arafat was under growing pressure to support the peace overtures that Egypt's president, Hosni Mubarak, had started to make toward Israel. In Syria, the always unpredictable regime had decided to cool its relationship with the various Palestinian factions, and had imprisoned hundreds of its fighters. President Assad wanted to show the Americans he was not the troublemaker the world believed.

That only increased the feeling among the rank-and-file PLO in the camps that they would be cast adrift by the Arab world, shunted from place to place, left to fend for themselves. There was ugly talk of being betrayed by their own leadership. The Israelis continued to exploit this, broadcasting throughout the occupied territories that the PLO had assets of $5 billion, invested all over the world. Arafat had also become the victim of a separate smear campaign, created by Mossad's experts in psychological warfare, which claimed he used some of the money to satisfy his liking for nubile young boys. The rumor was fed into the refugee camps and though not widely believed, it did have some effect. Arafat, in a shrewd move, ordered the seventeen PLO offices to leak a story that he had a healthy appetite for women—which was true.

For the PLO office manager in Paris, the idea that Sowan would use his hoped-for degree to become a bomb maker was indeed welcome news, and sufficient reason to provide Ismail's train fare to England and a week's living expenses. Sowan was also given five hundred pounds by Adam and told he must find a job to pay for his studies in Britain to avoid any suspicion.

Ismail arrived in London on a blustery day in February 1984, traveling on a Jordanian passport provided by Mossad. He had a second Canadian passport concealed in the false bottom of his suitcase. He had been told to use it only if he had to leave Britain in a hurry. Concealed with the passport was Mossad's briefing about Abdul-Rahid Mustapha and the Force 17 he commanded.

The unit had originally been created as Yasser Arafat's personal security force. Its name came from the number of Arafat's telephone extension in the old PLO headquarters in Beirut. At one stage in Lebanon, Force 17 had grown to a ragtag army of over a thousand fighters; one of its units had been the notorious Black September group that had carried out the massacre of the Israeli athletes at the Munich Olympics. Shortly before the PLO was forced to leave Lebanon and resettle in Tunis, Force 17's original commander, Ali Hassan Salameh, was killed by the car bomb arranged by Rafi Eitan. In Tunis, Arafat had faced hard realities. He was not only hunted by Mossad, but had become increasingly threatened by other Arab extremists. Abu Nidal, who claimed he was the authentic voice of the armed struggle, said there could be no victory until Arafat was eliminated. Arafat's response had been to restructure Force 17 into a close-knit unit with a dual purpose: to continue to protect him, and to launch well-prepared attacks against its enemies, beginning with Israel. Mustapha was given command of Force 17. In Tunis, his men were trained by both Chinese and Russian Special Forces in guerrilla warfare. In 1983, Mustapha began to travel to Britain to recruit mercenaries.

London was awash with former SAS men and regular army veterans who had seen service in Northern Ireland and were looking for a new outlet for their killing skills. The pay as PLO instructors was good and many of the mercenaries had a strong anti-Semitic attitude. A number signed on and traveled to Tunisia to work in PLO training camps. Other instructors were drawn from the ranks of former French foreign legionnaires and, at one stage, even included a former CIA officer, Frank Terpil, who would later become briefly involved with Mehmet Ali Agca, the fanatic who shot Pope John Paul II.

For a whole year Mustapha had slipped in and out of Britain without MI5 or the Special Branch even realizing who he was. When Mossad informed them, the only action taken was for an MI5 officer to remind the PLO office in London it would be closed and its staff expelled at the first hint they were engaged in terrorist activity against Britain. But they could continue to fulminate against Israel.

An intriguing sidelight to the propaganda war came when Bassam Abu-Sharif, then Arafat's chief media spokesman, was invited to meet novelist Jeffrey Archer. The PLO man would remember that Archer had explained "how we should develop and manage our media relations, how to organize our political activity, how to set about building contacts with British politicians and mobilize public opinion. I am extremely impressed."

That meeting ensured that Archer's name found its way onto Mossad's computers.

To the furious Israelis it appeared Mustapha was under the protection of the British authorities and that any attempt to deal with him in Britain could have repercussions for Mossad.

Ismail Sowan's task was to try to lead Mustapha into a trap outside the country, preferably in the Middle East, where waiting Mossad kidons could execute him. Sowan had been told by Adam in Paris he would work under the guidance of his Mossad controllers based at the Israeli embassy in London. The first was Arie Regev. The other was Jacob Barad, who looked after Israel's commercial interests. A third London-based *katsa*, not working under diplomatic cover, was Bashar Samara, who would be Sowan's main contact. Samara had asked a sayan employed by a London house-letting agency to rent an apartment for Sowan in the Maida Vale district of the city.

A few days after arriving in London, Sowan set up his first contact with Samara. The couple met beneath the Eros statue in Piccadilly Circus. Each carried a copy of the *Daily Mirror*, newly acquired by Robert

Maxwell. Using the technique of exchanging newspapers that had worked in Paris, Sowan obtained his six hundred pounds first month's salary, together with instructions on how to find office work at the PLO office in London.

Many of those who worked there wanted to be on the cutting edge of the action, such as carrying messages to various PLO cells around Europe, flying to the Organization's Tunis headquarters with particularly important information, and afterward waiting for hours for the chance just to glimpse Arafat. These young, committed revolutionaries had no interest in routine office work, clerking or filing, reading the newspapers, manning the phones. When Sowan volunteered for this work, he was promptly taken on at the London office.

Within a few days he had met Mustapha. Over tiny cups of sweet mint tea, they quickly developed a rapport. Both had a common background of having lived through the Israeli bombardment of Beirut. They had walked the same streets with the same quickness of eye and mind, passed the same gutted buildings pocked with so many holes they looked like latticework. Both had slept in a different bed each night and waited for the dawn when, over the crackling loudspeakers, the muezzin called the faithful to prayer. Each of them had taken his turn on PLO checkpoint duty in Beirut, waving the Palestinian ambulances through, stopping everyone else, and only running for cover when the whine of Israeli aircraft once more filled their ears. They had laughed over the memory of the old Beirut saying, "If you hear the bomb explode, you're still alive." So many memories; the cries of the dead and dying, the wail of the women, their looks of helpless hatred at the sky.

Sowan and Mustapha spent a whole day in communion with their past. Finally, Mustapha asked what Sowan was doing in London. To further his education so as to better serve the PLO, Ismail replied. In turn, he asked Mustapha what had brought him to England.

The question unleashed a flow of revelations. Mustapha described Force 17 exploits: how its commandos had been about to hijack an Israeli aircraft filled with German tourists when Arafat canceled the mission for fear of antagonizing German opinion. But Mustapha had carried the war against Israel into Cyprus and Spain. Ismail knew that everything his companion boasted of would only make Mossad more determined to kill him.

They agreed to meet in a few days at Hyde Park's Speakers' Corner, London's traditional venue for all kinds of opinion to be freely aired.

Ismail Sowan called the special number he had been given if he had urgent news. Bashar Samara answered. They arranged to meet in Regent Street. Strolling among the lunchtime office workers, Sowan reported what Mustapha had told him. Samara said he would be at Speakers' Corner to photograph Mustapha and then tail him wherever he went.

Mustapha did not keep the appointment. It would be weeks before Sowan saw him again. By that time, Ismail had been accepted as a student by a college in Bath, the spa resort. Twice a week he traveled to London to visit the PLO office to carry out his clerking. On one trip, Mustapha was there.

Once more the two men spoke over endless cups of mint tea. From his briefcase, Mustapha produced an illustrated book recording the history of Force 17. He boasted over one hundred thousand copies were to be distributed to Palestinians. Leafing through it, Ismail saw a picture of Mustapha taken in Lebanon. With a flourish, Mustapha signed it and presented the book to Ismail. Once more they arranged to meet, but Mustapha again broke the appointment.

Meanwhile, Sowan had handed over the book to Samara at what became a regular meeting place, the Bath railway station. The *katsa* would travel down on one train and return to London on the next, taking with him anything Sowan had learned at the PLO office and handing over his monthly stipend of six hundred pounds to the informer.

For almost a year their relationship continued in this manner. By then, Sowan had met an English girl named Carmel Greensmith. She agreed to marry him. But on the eve of the ceremony, Sowan had still not settled on a best man.

Making another trip to the PLO office, he again met Mustapha, who, as usual, did not explain where he had been. Mustapha had with him a bundle of tear sheets from the London-published Arab newspaper, *Al-Qabas*. Each page contained a biting cartoon mocking Yasser Arafat. The newspaper was subsidized by the Kuwaiti ruling family, long an enemy of the PLO.

The cartoons were the work of the Arab world's most celebrated political artist, Naji Al-Ali. Based in London, he had waged a one-man war against Arafat, portraying the PLO leader as venal, self-serving, and politically inept. The cartoons had established *Al-Qabas* as the voice of opposition to Arafat.

Mustapha threw the tear sheets on the table and said Al-Ali deserved to die and his Kuwaiti paymasters taught a lesson.

Sowan smiled noncommittally. Mossad welcomed anything that undermined Arafat's position. He also brought up a matter of more immediate personal concern, finding a best man for his wedding. Mustapha immediately offered himself for the role. They embraced each other in Arab fashion. That may well have been the moment when Ismail Sowan wished he could somehow remove himself from the clutches of Mossad.

In Tel Aviv, Nahum Admoni had begun to wonder how long it would be before MI5 discovered the truth about the eight forged British passports left in the telephone booth in Germany in July 1986. Shimon Peres, no admirer of Mossad, was, in the closing months of his coalition government, asking pointed questions. The prime minister was saying the debacle would ruin Israel's relationship with the Thatcher government; that it was better to make a clean breast of the matter, in keeping with the well-known Peres sentiment, "The sooner said, the sooner mended."

Admoni opposed the idea. It could lead to MI5 and the Special Branch beginning an investigation into just what else Mossad was doing in Britain. That could result in Ismail Sowan being expelled; he had proven to be a mine of useful information. Further, to admit the truth about the passports would be to reveal a piece of incompetent bungling by Mossad.

The passports had been intended for the Israeli embassy in Bonn. The job of couriering them from Tel Aviv had been given to a bodel who was new to the job and had never been to Bonn before. He had driven around the city for a while, not wishing to ask directions for fear of drawing attention to himself. Finally he had used the pay phone to call the embassy. An official had berated him for his tardiness. Either through panic or sheer carelessness, the bodel had left the carrier bag in the phone booth. Arriving at the embassy he realized his mistake but, even more panic-stricken, he couldn't remember exactly the location of the street from where he had made the call. Accompanied by the embassy's furious head of security, they had finally found the phone box. The bag was gone. The bodel had been posted to the Negev. But the problem of the passports had continued to trouble Admoni. The Foreign Office, through Britain's Tel Aviv ambassador, was raising the matter with the Israeli government.

One of the passports had been intended for Sowan's use to enable

him to travel more easily between London and Tel Aviv; a British passport meant he would be subjected to fewer checks by immigration at
Heathrow than with his Canadian one.

In the time Sowan had been in London, he had made occasional trips
to Israel to visit his family; it was part of his cover to do so. To them he
was still a PLO activist. He played the role so convincingly that his
elder brother, Ibrahim, finally warned him the Israelis would arrest
him. He jokingly suggested Ismail should preempt matters by offering to work for the Organization. Ismail pretended to be horrified at
the idea and returned to London to continue his work.

Soon matters were taking an unexpected turn. Sowan's new wife had
urged her husband to accept a post as a researcher at Humberside College in Hull. For her it would mean more money to supplement his office work for the PLO. She knew nothing of her husband's relationship
with Mossad, or the six hundred pounds it paid him every month. For
Ismail the move to Hull could be an opportunity to escape the ever-
increasing demands of his Mossad controller.

Like many an informer who had taken the Mossad shekel, Ismail
Sowan had become badly frightened by the risks he faced. After performing his duties as best man, Mustapha had become even friendlier.
He regularly dropped in to see Ismail and his wife, bringing gifts from
the Middle East for the couple. Over dinner, Mustapha told stories of
how he had dealt with the latest enemy of the PLO. Over the months,
he boasted of killing several "traitors to the cause." Sowan had sat
mesmerized, hoping "my heart beat wasn't thumping too loud." He was
becoming equally frightened after his meetings with Samara; the *katsa*
was asking him to access the PLO office computer and photocopy sensitive documents; he was also to try to arrange to go on "holiday" with
Mustapha to Cyprus, where a kidon team would be waiting. So far, Sowan had managed to come up with excuses—he was never able to be
alone in the computer room, or the pressure of his studies meant he
had to forgo holidays—but he had sensed a growing threat behind
Samara's demands. In Hull, he hoped he would be in less contact with
both Mustapha and Samara, and be allowed to have an academic life
without further pressures. Mossad had very different plans for him.

On Friday, March 13, 1987, Mossad's headquarters on King Saul Boulevard buzzed with the rumor that Admoni was expecting an important visitor. Shortly before noon, the MI6 liaison officer was escorted

up to the director general's ninth-floor office. Their meeting was short. Admoni was told that MI6 was satisfied that the forged passports found in Germany were the work of Mossad. A Special Branch officer who had been involved in the operation recalled in June 1997 how "the man from Six just walked in, said 'Good morning,' declined a cup of tea or coffee, and spelled it out. He then nodded and walked out again. It probably took less than a minute for him to deliver the message."

In London, the Foreign Office called in the Israeli ambassador and delivered a strong protest accompanied by a demand that such behavior would not happen again. The only small comfort for Admoni was that no one had mentioned Ismail Sowan.

In the early evening of July 22, 1987, Ismail Sowan turned on the BBC early-evening television news in his Hull apartment. He had not heard from Mossad since April, when Bashar Samara had traveled to Hull for a meeting at the city's railway station and told Sowan to keep a low profile until further notice—unless Mustapha made contact.

Now, the face of the man Mustapha had said deserved to die filled the screen; Naji Al-Ali, the cartoonist, had been shot as he left the offices of *Al-Qabas* in London. The gunman had fired once and disappeared. The bullet had entered through the cartoonist's cheek and lodged in his brain. Sowan's first reaction was that the assailant was not from Mossad or Force 17. Both organizations used the same professional way of killing: several shots in the head and the upper body. This looked like an amateur attack. The TV report said a massive police hunt was under way and that the cartoonist's colleagues were hinting the attack was because of the unnamed "powerful enemies" Naji had made.

Sowan remembered a previous conversation with Mustapha. He became increasingly certain Yasser Arafat had ordered the shooting. He suddenly wondered if he was the only person Mustapha had confided in about the need for the cartoonist to die. Sowan decided it would be best for him and his wife to fly to Tel Aviv. But even as they packed, there was a knock on the front door. Sowan would recall:

"The man had two suitcases. He said Mustapha needed to hide them urgently. When I said I wanted to know what was inside, he just smiled and told me not to worry. 'He who asks no questions is told no lies,' was all he would say. When he was gone, I looked inside the cases. They were full of arms and explosives: enough Semtex to blow up the Tower of London; AK-47s, pistols, detonators, the works."

Ismail called the special Mossad contact number in London. It had been disconnected. He telephoned the Israeli embassy. He was told that Arie Regev and Jacob Barad were not available. He asked to speak to Bashar Samara. The voice at the other end of the phone asked him to wait. A new voice came on the line. When Ismail gave his name, the voice said, "This is a good time for a holiday in the sun." The words were a signal for Sowan to travel to Tel Aviv.

There, in the Sheraton Hotel, he met Jacob Barad and Bashar Samara. He explained what he had done after discovering the contents of the suitcase. They told him to wait while they reported to their superiors. Later that night, Samara returned and told Sowan to fly to London on the next plane. When he arrived he would find everything had been taken care of.

Not suspecting what lay ahead, Sowan flew to London on August 4, 1987. He was arrested by armed Special Branch officers at Heathrow and charged with the murder of Naji Al-Ali. When he protested he was a Mossad agent, the officers laughed at him. Sowan had become as expendable as the cartoonist who had died after two weeks clinging to life in hospital. Sowan would be sacrificed in an attempt to regain favor with the Thatcher government. The presence of the arms cache in Sowan's apartment would destroy any effort he made to claim he was employed by Mossad. The arms had been brought there by a Mossad sayan.

In London, Arie Regev had turned over to MI5—who passed it on to Scotland Yard—all the "evidence" Mossad had "accumulated" of Sowan's "involvement" with terrorism. The file detailed how Mossad had tailed Sowan through the Middle East, Europe, and Britain, never able to obtain enough proof until now. The moment the arms cache had been discovered, Mossad decided, "in the name of common security," to turn in Sowan.

The decision to do so was a grim reminder of Mossad's unwritten law of expediency. A great deal of time and money had been invested by the service in training and supporting Sowan in the field. But when the time came, all that counted for nothing when weighed against the greater need for Mossad to cover its own tracks in Britain. Sowan would be the sacrificial victim, served up to the British as an example of the kind of terrorist Mossad was always warning about. There would be a loss, of course: Sowan had done a good enough job—even if he had failed to deliver all that was asked of him. But the arms cache had been too good an opportunity to miss. It would wreck the PLO's relationship with the Thatcher government and allow Israel to present Yasser Arafat as the double-dealing terrorist Mossad still said he was. And there would always be another Ismail Sowan ready to be seduced by men in Israel who reveled in broken promises.

For a full week Mossad relaxed, convinced that whatever Sowan told his British interrogators could be shrugged off.

But Admoni had not counted on Sowan's desperate efforts to stay out of jail. He gave Special Branch interrogators detailed descriptions of his controllers as well as everything he had been taught by Mossad. The police gradually realized Ismail could be telling the truth. The MI6 liaison officer in Tel Aviv was recalled. He questioned Sowan. Everything he said about Mossad's headquarters and its methods fit what the officer knew. The full extent of Mossad's role began to unravel.

Regev, Barad, and Samara were expelled from Britain. The Israeli embassy in London issued a defiant statement: "We regret that Her Majesty's Government saw fit to take measures of the kind adopted. Israel did not act against British interests. The struggle against terrorism was its one and only motive."

Telling the truth did not save Ismail Sowan. In June 1988, he was sentenced to eleven years' imprisonment for possessing firearms on behalf of a terrorist organization.

Five years after the expulsion of the three *katsas*, which had effectively closed down Mossad's station in Britain, the service was back. By 1998, five *katsas* worked out of the Israeli embassy in Kensington, liaising with MI5 and the Special Branch in targeting Iranian factions in Britain.

Three years previously, in December 1994, Ismail Sowan was released from Full Sutton Prison, handed back his Jordanian passport, and deported on a plane to Amman. The last anyone saw of him he was walking out of the airport carrying the suitcase Mossad had given him all those years ago when he had traveled to London. But its false bottom had been removed.

From the desert kingdom he had a ringside seat at the gathering storm in the Persian Gulf, which was preceded by a change of watch commander on the Mossad bridge. Nahum Admoni's eight years at the helm finally ended on the eve of the Jewish New Year, Rosh Hashanah. Into his place stepped Shabtai Shavit, who inherited a series of failures: the

Pollard affair, Irangate, and, of course, those blank, forged British passports found in that Bonn phone booth, which had heralded the end of Admoni's tenure. But, for his successor, beyond Jordan more than a sandstorm blew. Saddam Hussein had finally decided the time had come to take on the world.

CHAPTER 16

SPIES IN THE SAND

On December 2, 1990, well to the south of Baghdad, a figure in the

dirty robes of a desert dweller lay motionless just below the lip of a wadi.

It was dawn and the sand ice-cold; during the night the temperature

had dropped to well below zero. The man's head was covered with a

sheep's wool *hupta*, a hat that identified him as a tribesman of the Sarami,

the oldest of the Islamic Sufi sects, who roamed the vast Iraqi desert

and whose fanaticism was matched by a code of honor unequaled by

other tribes'. But the man's loyalty lay some six hundred miles to the

west, in Israel; he was a *katsa*.

His clothes came from a Mossad storeroom where garments from all over the world were kept and regularly updated. Most were obtained by sayanim and delivered to local Israeli embassies and sent on to Tel Aviv in diplomatic bags. Other garments were brought out of hostile Arab countries by pro-Israeli visitors. A few were actually made by the wardrobe mistress who presided over the storeroom. Over the years she and her small team of seamstresses had developed a reputation for detail, even using the right sewing cotton for adjustments.

The *katsa*'s code name—Shalom—came from a list of aliases kept on file in the Operations Division; Rafi Eitan had introduced the idea of a list after the Eichmann operation. Shalom Weiss had been one of the best forgers in Mossad before he had joined the team to help capture Adolf Eichmann. Shalom Weiss had died of cancer in 1963 but his name lived on and had been used on several occasions by *katsas*. Only a handful of senior IDF officers, Shabtai Shavit, and Shalom's own section head knew why he was in the desert.

In August 1990, Saddam Hussein had invaded Kuwait, an action that became the precursor to the eventual Gulf War. Iraq's move against Kuwait had been a spectacular intelligence failure for all the West's services; not one had anticipated it would happen. Mossad had tried to verify reports that Saddam had actually stockpiled chemical weapons at secret sites south of Baghdad, which would place the weapons well within range not only of Kuwait City but also cities in Israel.

Within Mossad there remained doubt as to whether Iraq possessed the rockets needed to fire the warheads. Gerald Bull had been removed from the scene, and his supergun, after its initial testing, according to U.S. satellite surveillance, was now in bits. Shavit's analysts suggested that even if Saddam possessed the warheads, there was no certainty they were actually filled with chemicals; he had done that kind of posturing before.

Shabtai Shavit, displaying the caution of a new man in charge, had said that on what he had been told, to raise the alarm could only create needless panic. Shalom had been given the mission to discover the truth. He had carried out several previous operations in Iraq, once going into Baghdad, where he had posed as a Jordanian businessman. In Baghdad there had been sayanim who could have helped him. But here, in the vast, empty desert, he had to depend on his own resources—and the skills his instructors had once more tested.

Shalom had undergone survival training in the Negev Desert, mastering "memory training," how to recognize the target even in a sandstorm; and "self-image protection," how to blend in with his surroundings. He wore his garments day and night to give them a lived-in look. He spent a full day on the shooting range, demonstrating instinctive and rapid-aim firing for close-quarter combat. An hour was spent with a pharmacist learning when to use his emergency medicine in the desert; a morning was devoted to memorizing the maps that would lead him across the sands.

To all his instructors he was identified only by a number; they neither demeaned him nor offered praise. They gave Shalom no clue as to how he was doing; they were like robots. Part of each day was given over to testing his sheer physical stamina with a forced march in the fierce noon heat, carrying a rucksack weighted with rocks. He was constantly on the clock, but no one told him if he was meeting his times. Another test was to haul him out of an ongoing exercise to get his responses to such questions as: "A Bedouin child spots you: do you kill her to preserve your mission?" "You are about to be taken prisoner. Do you surrender or kill yourself?" "You come across a wounded Israeli soldier who has been on another mission: do you stop to help or leave him, knowing he will certainly die?" Shalom's answers were not intended to be definitive: the questions were designed as another way to test his ability to decide under pressure. How long did he take to respond? Was he flustered or confident in making it?

He ate only the food he would live on in the desert: concentrates that he mixed with the brackish water he could expect to find at watering places in the sand. He had attended a one-to-one class with a Mossad psychiatrist on handling stress and how to relax. The doctor also wanted to make sure Shalom still thought for himself, so that he could draw on the right amount of resourcefulness and ruthlessness for the unpredictable situations he would encounter in the field. Aptitude tests determined his present emotional stability and his self-confidence. He was assessed to see if he had developed signs of becoming a "lone wolf," a worrying trait that had ended other promising careers for *katsas*.

A dialect coach sat with him for hours, listening to him repeat the Sufis' patois. Already fluent in Farsi and Arabic, Shalom quickly grasped the dialect of the tribesmen. Every night he was driven to a different part of the Negev to sleep. Burrowing into the ground, he would rest for a short while, never more than dozing, then move to another place to avoid the instructors he knew were hunting him. Discovery would almost certainly mean his mission would be either postponed for further training, or assigned to another *katsa*.

Shalom had escaped detection. On the evening of November 25, 1990, he boarded a CH-536 Sikorsky helicopter of the Israel Defense Forces Central Regional command.

Its crew had also been separately trained for the mission. In another area of the Negev base, they had practiced low-level weaving through an aerial obstacle course in the dark. Turbines had blasted the chopper with sand so that they could improve their techniques for flying through the unstable air currents of the Iraqi desert. The pilot had continuously stayed as close to the ground as he could without crashing. In another exercise, instructors had straddled the landing struts, firing weapons at target silhouettes, while the pilot kept his machine steady. In between, the crew had studied their flight path.

Only their commanding officer, Major General Danny Yatom, knew the route they would fly to the border with Iraq. Yatom had been a member of the elite Sayeret Matkal commando unit, Israel's Green Berets, who in 1972 had successfully stormed a hijacked Belgium airliner at Tel Aviv airport. Other commandos in the operation included Benjamin Netanyahu. The friendship with Israel's future prime minister would lead to Yatom later being given command of Mossad, a position that would also end his relationship with Netanyahu. But that was all in the future.

On that December morning, while Shalom continued to peer out over the rim of the wadi, he had no inkling that the long and dangerous journey that had brought him deep into hostile territory had been decided in a conference room in the Kirya, the Israel Defense Forces headquarters in Tel Aviv.

As well as Yatom, present had been Amnon Shahak, the head of Aman, military intelligence, and Shabtai Shavit. They had convened to discuss the latest information from a deep-penetration informer inside Iran's terrorist network in Europe. The person—only Shavit knew if the informer was a man or a woman—was known by the letter "I." All that Shahak and Yatom would have deduced was that the informer must have access to the fortified complex on the third floor of the Iranian embassy in Bonn, Germany. The complex contained six offices and a communications room. The entire area had been reinforced to withstand a bomb blast and it was permanently manned by twenty Revolutionary Guards, whose task it was to coordinate Iran's terrorist activities in western Europe. They had recently tried to ship a ton of Semtex and electronic detonators out of Lebanon into Spain. The shipment was to replace explosives for a number of pro-Iranian terrorist groups in European countries. On a tip-off from Mossad, Spanish customs had boarded the ship as it sailed into territorial waters.

But by the summer of 1990, Iran was also providing through the Bonn embassy huge cash disbursements to increase the influence of Islamic fundamentalism and terrorism in Europe. The amounts involved were all the more surprising given that Iran had been economically crippled by its eight-year war with Iraq, which had ended in a cease-fire in 1988.

But on that November day in the Kirya's guarded conference room, it was not a new threat from Iran that the double agent had discovered. It was one from Iraq. "I" had obtained a copy of a detailed Iraqi battle plan stolen by Iran's own secret intelligence service from Baghdad military headquarters outlining how Scud missiles would be used to launch chemical and biological weapons against Iran, Kuwait, and Israel.

Uppermost in the mind of each man in the conference room was one question: Could the information be trusted? "I" had proven to be sound in all the previous data he had provided. But, important though the information had been, it paled against what "I" had now sent. Yet was the battle plan part of a plot by Iranian intelligence to drive Israel into launching a preemptive attack against Iraq? Had "I" been unmasked and was he being used by Iran?

Trying to answer that question was also fraught with risk. It would need time to brief a *katsa* to make contact with "I." It might be weeks before that was possible; bringing an informer out of deep cover was a slow and delicate process. And if "I" proved to have remained loyal, his safety could have still been jeopardized. Yet, the consequences of acting on the Iraqi document without checking could be calamitous for Israel. A preemptive strike would certainly lead to an Iraqi retaliation— and could destroy the coalition being laboriously cobbled together in Washington to drive Saddam out of Kuwait. Many of its Arab members were likely to support Iraq against Israel.

The only way to discover the truth about the stolen battle plan had been to send Shalom into Iraq. Skimming above the desert, his helicopter had flown across a strip of Jordan in the deep black of night. Coated with stealth paint, its engine noise muffled, the Sikorsky was virtually undetectable to even the most sophisticated Jordanian radars.

Flying on silent mode so that its rotor blades made almost no sound, the helicopter had reached its dropping point at the Iraqi border.

Shalom had disappeared into the night. Despite all his training, nothing had quite prepared him for that moment: he was on his own; to survive he had to respect his surroundings. A desert was like no other place on earth for surprises. A sandstorm could appear in moments, changing the landscape, burying him alive. One kind of sky meant one thing, another something quite different. He would do his own weather forecasting; he would have to do everything by himself and learn to let his ears adjust to the silence, to remember that the silence of the desert was like no other. And always he must remember that his first mistake could be his last.

Three days after leaving the helicopter, on that cold December dawn, Shalom lay prostrate in the Iraqi wadi. Beneath his *hupta* he wore goggles; their lenses gave the dark landscape a crepuscular definition. The only weapon Shalom carried was one the Sarami would expect to find on him: a hunting knife. He had been taught to kill with that in a number of ways. Whether he would bother to use it against a superior force, he did not know—any more than whether he could turn it on himself. Or simply commit suicide with the lethal pill he carried. Since Eli Cohen's torture and death, a *katsa* operating in Iran, Iraq, Yemen, or Syria had been given the right to kill himself rather than fall into the hands of barbaric interrogators. Meanwhile, Shalom continued to watch and wait.

The nomads in their camps half a mile away beyond the wadi had begun to recite their first prayers of the day. Already the bark of their dogs carried faintly on the wind, but the animals would not venture beyond the camp until the sun was above the horizon: behavioral patterns were among the first lessons Shalom had learned in desert survival.

According to the information he had been given at his briefing, the convoy should appear between the encampment and the hills to his left. To an untutored eye, the track they would travel over was invisible. To Shalom it was as clear as a well-signposted road: the tiny rumplings of sand were created by desert moles burrowing between vehicle tracks.

The sun was high when the convoy finally appeared: a Scud missile launcher and its support vehicle. It was still about half a mile away when it stopped. Shalom began to photograph and time what he saw.

It took the Iraqi crew fifteen minutes to launch the Scud. It rose in an arc and disappeared over the horizon. Minutes later the convoy was moving at speed toward the hills. In a few minutes that Scud could have hit Tel Aviv or any other Israeli city if the launch had not been a practice. Shalom then began the long journey back to Tel Aviv.

Six weeks later, on January 12, 1991, Shalom was among a joint team of Mossad and Aman intelligence officers who sat around the conference table at the United States Joint Special Operations Command, JSOC (its staff called it "jaysock"), at Pope Air Force Base, Georgia. JSOC commanded the Green Berets and the SEALs, and had maintained a close working relationship with Mossad.

After Shalom had returned from Iraq, Shavit had informed General Earl Stiner, operations commander of JSOC, that Saddam was doing more than posturing. The hard-charging general had a folksy style and a salty language the Israelis liked. But in a war room, his Tennessee drawl swiftly gave way to shrewd decisions. As the nation's top commando, he knew the value of good intelligence, and his own experience of the Middle East had convinced him Mossad offered the best.

Since Saddam's incursion into Kuwait, Stiner had regularly communicated with his Israeli contacts. Some of them went back to 1983, when, as a newly promoted brigadier general, he had been secretly sent by the Pentagon to Beirut to report directly to the Joint Chiefs of Staff on how far the United States should become embroiled in the Lebanon war.

Later, he had worked closely with Mossad during the *Achille Lauro* hijacking, swooping down with his Delta Force commandos on an Italian air force base in Sicily where the hijackers had stopped over in an airliner on their way to freedom out of Egypt. Italian troops had stopped Stiner from capturing the hijackers, and there had nearly been a shootout. Thwarted, Stiner had flown in hot pursuit of the airliner in his own military transport, only abandoning the chase when both planes entered Rome's airspace and its air traffic controllers threatened to shoot down the Delta Force aircraft for "air piracy." In 1989 Stiner had been the ground commander for the invasion of Panama, and had been responsible for the swift capture of Manuel Noriega.

Only Joint Chiefs chairman General Colin Powell and General Norman Schwarzkopf, in charge of the coalition forces, knew about Stiner's relationship with Mossad. While Schwarzkopf battled to create a defensive line along the Saudi border to deal with a thrust out of Kuwait by Iraqi forces, Stiner's intelligence officers were working closely with Mossad to form resistance movements inside Iraq to try to topple Saddam.

When Major General Wayne Downing, commander of JSOC, called the meeting to order in the conference room, everyone knew that, as the hours ticked by to the deadline for war set by the United Nations for Tuesday, January 15, 1991, the world was conducting a dialogue with the deaf in Baghdad. Saddam continued to welcome what he predicted would be "the mother of all wars."

Downing began by reminding his listeners that Washington still required Israel to remain out of the war. In return there would be long-term political and economic benefits for doing so.

The immediate response from the Israelis was to produce a set of Shalom's enlarged photographs of the Scud launch. Then came their questions. Supposing Saddam fitted a nuclear warhead to a Scud? Mossad was satisfied Iraq had already built the facilities needed to manufacture a crude device. It also had the capability to fit chemical or biological warheads to its Scuds. Was Israel supposed to wait for that to happen? What was the coalition force's plan to deal with the Scuds before they were launched? Did the Americans have any idea just how many Scuds Saddam had?

One of Downing's intelligence officers said their "best estimate" was about fifty.

"We think Saddam has about five times that number, maybe even five hundred in all," replied Shabtai Shavit.

The stunned silence in the room was broken by Downing's question. Could he pinpoint them? Shavit could not be more specific than to suggest the Scuds were sited in the Iraqi western desert and in the east of the country. The Americans agreed with Downing that "that was a lot of desert to hide them in."

"Then the sooner you start, the better," Shavit said, not bothering to conceal his frustration.

Downing promised to pursue the matter vigorously, and the meeting closed with the repeated reminder that Israel must stay out of the coming conflict—but all the intelligence Mossad and Aman could gather would be welcomed. In the meantime, they could be reassured the United States and its partners would deal with the Scuds. The Israeli team flew home feeling they had gotten the worse end of the deal.

Shortly after 3:00 A.M. on the morning of January 17, 1991—hours after the start of the Desert Storm conflict—seven Scuds hit Tel Aviv and Haifa, destroying 1,587 buildings and injuring forty-seven civilians.

Later that morning Prime Minister Yitzhak Shamir icily asked over a hot line to Washington how many Israelis had to die before President Bush did something. The short call ended with Bush pleading for restraint and Shamir warning that Israel would not remain much longer on the sideline.

Shamir had already ordered Israeli jets to patrol the northern airspace with Iraq. Bush immediately promised that if the aircraft were recalled, he would send "in double quick time" two Patriot antimissile batteries "to further defend your cities," and the coalition forces "will destroy the remaining Scuds in days."

Missiles continued to fall on Israel. On January 22, one landed in the Tel Aviv suburb of Ramat Gan. Ninety-six civilians were injured, several seriously; three died of heart attacks. The sound of the explosions carried to Mossad headquarters. In the Kirya, Amnon Shahak called a direct line number to the National Military Command Center on the second floor of the Pentagon. His call was even shorter than Shamir's; the gist was: do something or Israel will.

Hours later, Downing and his commandos were on their way to Saudi Arabia. Waiting for them in the tiny Iraqi border village of Ar Ar was Shalom. He was dressed in British army fatigues. He never explained, and no one asked, how he had gotten them. The news he brought was electrifying. He could confirm there were four Scud launchers less than thirty minutes' flying time away.

"Let's go!" Downing said. "Let's go fry some butts!"

Chinooks helicoptered the team into the Iraqi desert, together with their specially adapted Land Rover to operate in a terrain that mostly resembled a moonscape. In an hour, they had located the Scud launchers. Over a secure radio the commando leader called up U.S. fighter-bombers armed with cluster munitions and thousand-pound bombs. A hovering Black Hawk helicopter videoed the kills.

Hours later a copy of the tape was being viewed by Shamir in his office in Tel Aviv.

In another telephone call from Bush, the prime minister conceded he had seen enough to keep Israel out of the war. Neither man mentioned the role Mossad had played.

In the remaining days of the Iraqi war, the Scuds killed or injured almost 500 people—including 128 Americans dead or wounded from a missile that landed in Saudi Arabia; over 4,000 Israelis were left homeless.

The aftermath of the Iraqi war saw Mossad and Aman under fierce attack during secret sessions of the Knesset Foreign Affairs and Defense Oversight Intelligence Subcommittee. Both services were roundly condemned for failing to predict the invasion of Kuwait or to provide "sufficient warning" of the Iraqi threat. Leaks from within the committee room spoke of slanging matches involving Amnon Shahak, head of Aman, and Shabtai Shavit, and committee members. After one clash, the Mossad chief had come close to resigning. But all was not lost for the embattled Shavit.

Mossad's Department of Psychological Warfare, LAP, usually called upon to spread disinformation and blacken the character of Israel's enemies with foreign journalists, focused its skills on the local media. Favored reporters were called and told it was not a question of there having been too little intelligence, it was a matter of the Israeli public having grown accustomed to being spoiled in that area.

Familiar truths were trundled out by LAP: no other country proportionate to its size and population analyzed or used as much intelligence as did Israel; no service could match Mossad in understanding the mind-set and intentions of the country's enemies, or equal its record for frustrating the plans of those who had plagued Israel for almost fifty years. It was rousing stuff and found ready space in a media only too grateful to be given "inside track" information.

A rush of articles appeared reminding readers that, despite defense cuts introduced shortly before the Iraqi war, Mossad had continued to manfully battle on in Lebanon, Jordan, Syria, and Iraq. People had been able to read between the lines: Mossad was being hampered because the politicians had mishandled the defense budget. It was a familiar theme, and always guaranteed to work. To a still badly frightened population recovering from the Scud attacks, claims that a lack of funding lay at the root of what they had suffered turned criticism away from Mossad back onto the politicians. Money suddenly became available. Israel, so long dependent on U.S. satellite data, put its own spy satellite program on the fast track. The first priority was to launch a military satellite to specifically monitor Iraq. A new antimissile missile, the Hetz, was put into mass production. Several Patriot batteries were ordered from the United States.

The intelligence subcommittee wilted in the face of the barrage of pro-Mossad publicity. Shavit emerged triumphant—and set about reaffirming Mossad's position. Deep-penetration *katsas* in Iraq were ordered to try to discover how much of Saddam's arsenal of chemical and biological weapons had survived allied bombardment.

They discovered that Iraq still possessed quantities of anthrax, smallpox, the Ebola virus, and chemical nerve agents capable of killing not only every man, woman, and child in Israel, but a sizable proportion of the entire population on earth.

The question that faced Shabtai, the other heads of the Israeli intelligence communities, and Israel's politicians was deciding whether to make public the information. To do so would certainly create fear and panic in Israel, and could provoke other widespread negative effects. The country's tourist industry had been virtually wiped out by the Iraqi war; the Israeli economy was close to rock bottom and new foreign investment was slow in coming. To reveal that Israel was still in range of deadly weapons would hardly attract tourists or money into the country.

Further, the breakup of the Gulf War coalition, whose Arab members had never been less than cool to waging war against fellow Arabs, had resulted in growing sympathy for the undoubted plight of Iraqis. The evidence of mass destruction caused by coalition bombing and the continued suffering of innocent civilians had stoked up powerful emotions elsewhere in the Middle East, and renewed Arab enmity against Israel. Moreover, if Tel Aviv were to publish details of Iraq's still-intact chemical and biological weapons, it would be seen in those pro-Arab Western countries as an attempt by Israel to persuade the United States and Britain to stage new assaults on Iraq.

The issue of going public about Saddam's arsenal was also influenced by the carefully orchestrated secret discussions to bring an end to hostilities between the PLO and Israel. By 1992, these discussions had moved to Norway, and were progressing well, though it would be a full year before an agreement was reached and publicly ratified in October 1993, when Yasser Arafat shook hands with Prime Minister Yitzhak Rabin on the White House lawn, under the benevolent smile of President Clinton. For each man it was a diplomatic triumph.

However, not everyone in Mossad shared the hope that the "land for peace" formula—a Palestinian homeland in exchange for no more fighting—would work. Islamic fundamentalism was on the march, and Israel's neighbors, Jordan, Egypt, and Syria, were being buffeted by the extremist forces of Iran. For the Tehran mullahs, Israel remained a pariah state. Within Mossad, and indeed, for many Israelis, the prospect of a lasting peace with the PLO was an unrealistic dream. Zionist Israel had little wish to accommodate itself with Arabs: everything about their religion and culture was seen by Zionists as inferior to their own beliefs and history; they could not accept that the Oslo accord guaranteed the future of their Promised Land and that both races would live together, if not always happily, at least with respect for each other.

All this was carefully weighed by Shabtai Shavit as he considered the question of whether to publicize Iraq's arsenal. In the end, he decided to keep the information secret so as not to disturb the wave of optimism outside Israel that had followed the Washington accord. Besides, if things went wrong, the information about Iraq's stockpile of deadly poison could still be made public. The image of a ruthless Saddam poised to have one of his agents place a canister of anthrax in the New York subway, or a terrorist dispersing the Ebola virus into the air-conditioning system of a fully laden Boeing 747, so that each passenger became a biological time bomb who could spread the virus to thousands of people before the truth was discovered, were scenarios perfectly suited for Mossad's experts in psychological warfare to exploit whenever the time came to fan public opinion against Iraq.

Two other incidents, the facts of which had been hidden by Mossad, could also cause massive damage and embarrassment to the United States.

On a December evening in 1988, Pan American Airways Flight 103 from London to New York exploded in the air over Lockerbie in Scotland. Within hours, staff at LAP were working the phones to their media contacts, urging them to publicize that here was "incontrovertible proof" that Libya, through its intelligence service, Jamahirya, was culpable. (The author of this book received a call making such a claim from a LAP source hours after the disaster.) Sanctions were swiftly imposed by the West against the Gadhafi regime. The United States and Britain issued indictments against two Libyans, charging them with the destruction of the Pan Am flight. Gadhafi refused to hand over the men for trial.

LAP next accused Syria and Iran of being coplotters in the Lockerbie disaster. The case against the Damascus regime turned on no more than its well-known support for state-sponsored terrorism. With Iran, the accusation was more specific: Pan Am 103 had been destroyed as an act of revenge for the shooting down on July 3, 1988, by the USS *Vincennes* of an Iranian passenger plane in the Persian Gulf, killing 290 people. It had been a tragic error for which the United States had apologized.

LAP then named the Popular Front for the Liberation of Palestine as having conspired to destroy the airline. None of the journalists who widely published this story stopped to think why Libya, accused as the original perpetrator, would have needed to call for help from Syria or Iran, let along a Palestinian group.

According to one British intelligence source, "LAP was on a roll. Lockerbie was the perfect opportunity to remind the world that there existed the terror network that LAP always liked to promote. Lockerbie didn't need that. In fact putting in too many names in the pot was actually counterproductive. We knew only the Libyans were responsible." However, there were facts that did not make Pan Am 103 such an open-and-shut case.

The loss of the airliner had occurred at the time when George Bush was president-elect and his transition team in Washington was updating itself on the current Middle East situation so Bush could "hit the ground running" when he entered the Oval Office.

Bush had been CIA director in 1976–77, a period when Secretary of State Henry Kissinger had largely dictated Washington's pro-Israeli policy. While Bush publicly maintained Reagan's glad-handing toward Israel, his years at the helm of the CIA had convinced him that Reagan had been "too dewy-eyed about Israel." Waiting to become president, Bush needed no reminding how, in 1986, the United States had been forced to cancel a $1.9 billion arms deal with Jordan when the Jewish lobby in Congress had intervened. Bush had told his transition team that as president he would not tolerate interference in the right of "God-fearing Americans to do business with whom and where they wished." This attitude would play its part in the destruction of Pan Am 103.

On board the aircraft as it left London on that December night in 1988 were eight members of the U.S. intelligence community returning from duty in the Middle East. Four of them were CIA field officers, led by Matthew Gannon. Also on board were U.S. Army major Charles McKee and his small team of experts in hostage rescue. They had been in the Middle East to explore the possibility of freeing the Western hostages still held in Beirut. Though the Lockerbie disaster investigation was under the jurisdiction of a Scottish team, CIA agents were on the scene when McKee's still closed and miraculously intact suitcase was located. It was taken away from the scene for a short time by a man believed to be a CIA officer, though he would never be positively identified. Later the suitcase was returned to the Scottish investigation team, who logged its contents under "empty."

No one queried what had happened to McKee's belongings, let alone why he had been traveling with an empty suitcase. But at the time, no one suspected that the CIA officer might have removed from the suitcase data that explained why Pan Am 103 had been destroyed. Gannon's luggage was never accounted for—giving rise to the belief that the actual bomb had been placed in his suitcase. No satisfactory explanation would ever emerge as to how or why a CIA officer was carrying a bomb in his suitcase.

The PBS investigative television program *Frontline* subsequently claimed to have solved the cause of the disaster. Pan Am 103 had begun its journey in Frankfurt, where U.S.-bound passengers from the Middle East transferred on to Flight 103. Among them were Gannon and his CIA team, who had traveled on an Air Malta flight to make the connection. Their baggage was similar to thousands of suitcases that passed through the hands of Frankfurt baggage handlers every day. One of them was in the pay of terrorists. Somewhere in the airport baggage bays the handler had concealed a suitcase already containing the bomb. His instruction was to spot a matching suitcase coming off a connecting flight, and substitute his suitcase, and then let it continue on into the hold of Pan Am 103. It was a plausible theory—but only one of many advanced to explain the bombing.

Understandably desperate to show the destruction of Pan Am 103 had been an act of terrorism for which it could not be culpable, the airline's insurers hired a New York firm of private investigators called Interfor. The company had been founded in 1979 by an Israeli, Yuval Aviv, who had immigrated to the United States the previous year. Aviv claimed to be a former desk officer with Mossad—a claim the service would deny. Nevertheless, Aviv had satisfied the insurers he had the right connections to unearth the truth.

When they received his report, they could only have been stunned. Aviv had concluded that the attack had been planned and executed "by a rogue CIA group, based in Germany, who were providing protection to a drug operation which transported drugs from the Middle East to the U.S. via Frankfurt. The CIA did nothing to break up the operation because the traffickers were also helping them send weapons to Iran as part of the arms-for-hostages negotiations. The method of drug smuggling was quite simple. One person would check a piece of luggage on the flight, and an accomplice working in the baggage area would switch it with a piece of identical luggage containing the narcotics. On the fatal night, a Syrian terrorist, aware of how the drug operation worked, had switched a suitcase with one containing the bomb. His reason was to kill the U.S. intelligence operatives whom Syria had discovered would join the flight."

Aviv's report claimed McKee had learned about the "CIA rogue team," which had worked under the code name of COREA, and that its members also had close ties to another of those mysterious figures who had found his niche on the fringes of the intelligence world. Monzer Al-Kassar had built a reputation as an arms dealer in Europe, including supplying Colonel Oliver North with weapons for him to pass on to the Nicaraguan Contras in 1985–86. Al-Kassar also had links to the Abu Nidal organization, and his family connections were equally dubious. Ali Issa Duba, head of Syrian intelligence, was his brother-in-law, and Al-Kassar's wife was a relative of the Syrian president. Aviv's report claimed Al-Kassar had found in COREA a ready partner for the drug-smuggling operation. This had been going on for several months before the destruction of Pam Am 103. The report further claimed McKee had discovered the scam while pursuing his own contacts in the Middle East underworld in an attempt to find a way to rescue the Beirut hostages. Aviv stated in his report that "McKee planned to bring back to the U.S. proof of the rogue intelligence team's connection to Al-Kassar."

In 1994, Joel Bainerman, the publisher of an Israeli intelligence report and whose analyses have also appeared in *The Wall Street Journal*, *The Christian Science Monitor*, and Britain's *Financial Times*, wrote: "Twenty-four hours before the flight, Mossad tipped off the German BKA that there could be a plan to plant a bomb on flight 103. The BKA passed on their tip to the COREA CIA team working out of Frankfurt who said they would take care of everything."

Pan Am's attorney, Gregory Buhler, subpoenaed the FBI, CIA, FAA, DEA, NSC, and NSA to reveal what they knew, but, he later claimed, "the government quashed the subpoenas on grounds of national security."

Neither the *Frontline* program makers, Yuval Aviv, nor Joel Bainerman had been able to provide satisfactory answers to troubling questions. If there was a cover-up to COREA's activities, how high did it extend within the CIA? Who had authorized it? Had that person or persons ordered the removal of embarrassing data from within McKee's suitcase? Why had the German BKA police agency tipped off the COREA unit? Was it purely by chance? Or had it been motivated by a decision that the activities of COREA had become unacceptably dangerous for others in the CIA? And just what were the "national security grounds" that had led to Pan Am's attorney receiving a blanket refusal for his subpoenas?

Over the years, these questions have surfaced within the closed ranks of various intelligence agencies, and the answers have been kept closely guarded—not least the truth about a final mystery. Why had Mossad sent a London-based *katsa* north to Lockerbie within hours of the downing of Pan Am 103?

So far the service has kept to itself all it knows about the destruction of the flight. There are sources, who ask not to be named because their lives would be endangered, who claim that Mossad is holding on to its knowledge as a trump card should Washington increase its pressure for Mossad to cease its intelligence activities within the United States.

More certain, there was another episode that could turn out equally as embarrassing to the U.S. intelligence community. It concerned the death of Amiram Nir, the man with a taste for James Bond thrillers who had replaced David Kimche as Israel's point man in Irangate.

Amiram Nir was ideally suited to be Prime Minister Shimon Peres's antiterrorism adviser. Exploitive, inquisitive, acquisitive, manipulative, and ruthless, Nir had a raffish charm, a lack of self-restraint, an ability to ridicule, to take imaginative leaps, to break the rules to work against a background of blending fact and fiction. He had been a journalist.

His previous knowledge of intelligence sprang from his work as a reporter with Israeli television, and then from working for the country's largest daily newspaper, *Yediot Aharonot;* it was owned by the Moses dynasty, into which he had married. The publishing empire was everything Robert Maxwell's had never been: the epitome of respectability and securely financed; it treated its employees on the old adage of a fair day's pay for a hard day's work. Nir's marriage not only had made him the husband of one of the wealthiest women in Israel, but had also provided him with ready access to the higher echelons of the country's political hierarchy.

Nevertheless, there was astonishment when he became one of the most important members of Israel's intelligence community in 1984, when Peres appointed him to the ultrasensitive post of his adviser on combating terrorism.

Nir was thirty-four years old, and the only hands-on experience he had had of intelligence work was a short IDF course. Even among his friends, the general consensus was he needed more than rugged good looks for his new job.

Mossad's chief, Nahum Admoni, was the first to react to Nir's appointment: he changed the structure of the Committee of the Heads of Services to exclude Nir from its deliberations. Unperturbed, Nir spent the first weeks in the job speed-reading everything he could lay his hands on. He quickly came to focus on the arms-to-Iran operation that was still ongoing. Sensing a chance to prove himself, Nir persuaded Peres he should take over the role David Kimche had relinquished. With the indefatigable Ari Ben-Menashe as his mentor, Nir found himself also working with Oliver North.

Soon the two men were hand in glove, wheeling and dealing across the globe. Along their travels they created a plan to bring the arms-for-hostages deal to a stunningly successful conclusion. They would fly to Tehran and meet the Iranian leadership and negotiate the release of the hostages.

On May 25, 1986, posing as technicians employed by Aer Lingus, the Irish national airline, Nir and North flew from Tel Aviv to Tehran on an Israeli aircraft painted with Aer Lingus's distinctive shamrock logo. On board were ninety-seven TOW guided missiles and a pallet of Hawk missile spare parts. Nir was traveling on a false U.S. passport. It had been provided by North.

North, ever the evangelizing Christian, had somehow persuaded President Reagan to inscribe a Bible to be presented to Ayatollah Rafsanjani, a devout Muslim. He had also brought a chocolate cake and sets of Colt pistols for their hosts. It was all reminiscent of the days when traders had bartered for land with the Indians on Manhattan.

The first Mossad knew of the mission was when the aircraft entered Iranian airspace. Nahum Admoni's reaction was described as "incandescent rage."

Luckily the Iranians simply ordered the visitors out and used the mission to score a massive propaganda coup against the United States. Reagan was furious. In Tel Aviv, Admoni cursed Nir as "a cowboy." Nevertheless, Nir managed to remain in government service for another ten months, until the sniping from within the intelligence community calling for his removal had grown to a relentless fusillade. In those months the cases of Hindawi, Vanunu, and Sowan crossed his desk, but any contributions he offered on how matters should be handled were icily rejected by Mossad.

No longer welcome in Washington and isolated in Tel Aviv, Amiram Nir resigned as the prime minister's counterterrorism adviser in March 1987. By then his marriage was in trouble, and his circle of friends had shrunk. Ari Ben-Menashe remained one of Nir's few remaining links with his past. Early in 1988 Nir left Israel to live in London.

Then he set up house with a pretty, raven-haired Canadian, Adriana Stanton, a twenty-five-year-old who claimed to be a secretary from Toronto, whom Nir had met on his travels. Several Mossad officers believed she was connected to the CIA, one of the women it used for entrapment operations. In London, Nir acted as the European representative of a Mexican avocado purchasing company, Nucal de Mexico, based in Uruapan. The company controlled a third of the country's avocado export market.

But it was not avocados that brought Ari Ben-Menashe to Nir's door on a rainy November night in 1988. He wanted to know exactly what Nir intended to reveal when he was a major witness in Oliver North's forthcoming trial over his role in the Iran-Contra scandal. Nir made it clear his testimony would be highly embarrassing not only for the Reagan administration, but also to Israel. He intended to show how easy it had been to sidestep all the usual checks and balances to run illegal operations that would also implicate a number of countries, including South Africa and Chile. He added he was planning a book that he believed would make him the greatest whistle-blower in the history of the State of Israel. Ari Ben-Menashe arranged to meet Nir after he had made another visit to Nucal in Mexico. In the meantime, his visitor cautioned Nir to be "careful of that woman!" after Adriana Stanton had left them alone. Ben-Menashe refused to reveal what had prompted the warning except to say, in his all-too-often mysterious manner: "I know her from before and, though Nir didn't know it, Adriana Stanton wasn't her real name."

On November 27, 1988, Nir and Stanton traveled together to Madrid under false names. He called himself "Patrick Weber," the identity he had last assumed on his ill-fated trip to Tehran. Stanton was listed on the Iberia passenger manifest as "Esther Arriya." Why they had chosen aliases for the flight tickets when they both traveled on their real passports—Israeli and Canadian—would never be explained. Another mystery was why they took a flight first to Madrid when there were several scheduled direct ones to Mexico City. Was Nir trying to impress his lover with how easy it was to fool most people most of the time? Or was there already a nagging fear at the back of his mind after Ari Ben-Menashe's visit? Like so much else of what followed, those questions were to remain unanswered.

They arrived in Mexico City on November 28. Waiting at the airport was a man who would never be identified. The three of them traveled on to Uruapan, arriving there in the afternoon. Nir then chartered a T 210 Cessna from the small Aerotaxis de Uruapan.

Once more Nir behaved with strange inconsistency. He rented the aircraft in the name of "Patrick Weber," using a credit card in that name to pay the charges, and arranged with a pilot to fly them to the Nucal processing plant in two days' time. In the local hotel where they shared a room, Nir registered under his own name. The man who had accompanied them from Mexico disappeared as mysteriously as he had appeared.

On November 30, Nir and Stanton turned up at the small Uruapan airport, this time with another man. On the passenger manifest he was listed as Pedro Espionoza Huntado. Whom he worked for would remain yet another mystery. Another would be why, when they came to enter their own names on the manifest, both Nir and Stanton used their real identities. If the pilot noticed the discrepancy between the name Nir had given to charter the Cessna, it passed without comment.

The plane took off in good flying conditions. On board were the pilot, a copilot, and their three passengers. One hundred miles into the flight, the Cessna suddenly developed engine trouble and moments later crashed, killing Nir and the pilot. Stanton was seriously injured, the copilot and Huntado less so. By the time the first rescuer, Pedro Cruchet, arrived on the scene, Huntado had disappeared—another of those figures never to be seen again. How exactly Cruchet came to be first on the scene was yet another twist. He claimed to work for Nucal—but the company's plant was a considerable distance away. He could not explain why he had been so close to the crash site. Asked by police to prove his identity, he pleaded he had lost his ID at a bullfight. It turned out Cruchet was an Argentinian living in Mexico illegally. By the time that had been established he, too, had vanished. At the crash site, Cruchet had recovered and identified Nir's body, and he had accompanied Stanton to the hospital. He was with her when a local reporter called seeking further details.

Joel Bainerman, the publisher of the Israeli political intelligence digest, would claim: "A young woman indicated Cruchet was present. When she went to get him, another woman appeared at the door and told the journalist that Cruchet wasn't there and that she had never heard of him. The second woman reiterated that Stanton's presence on the Cessna was purely a coincidence and that she had no connection with 'the Israeli.' She refused to identify herself other than to say she was in Mexico as a tourist from Argentina."

Stanton added to the mystery. She told crash investigators, according to Israeli journalist Ran Edelist in 1997: "While injured and shocked, she saw Amiram Nir a few meters away, waving and comforting her in a normal voice. 'Everything will be okay. Help is on the way!' She was twice assured in the days following that Nir was alive."

Nir's body was flown back to Israel for burial. Over one thousand mourners attended his funeral and, in his eulogy, Defense Minister Yitzhak Rabin spoke of Nir's "mission to as-yet-unrevealed destinations on secret assignments and of secrets which he kept locked in his heart."

Had Amiram Nir been murdered to make sure he never revealed those secrets? Was it even Nir's body in the coffin? Or had he been killed before the crash? And if so, by whom? In Tel Aviv and Washington, a blanket of silence continues to greet all such questions.

Two days after the crash, Ari Ben-Menashe emerged from a post office in downtown Santiago, Chile. He was accompanied by two of the bodyguards he now felt it important to have to protect him. Suddenly:

"The window I was walking past shattered. Then something smashed into the metal custom-built briefcase I was carrying. The two bodyguards and I dived to the floor, realizing someone was shooting at us."

Stanton was the next to believe her life was in danger. According to Edelist, his intelligence contacts had told him she "became a recluse, underwent plastic surgery, and changed her appearance."

Increasingly, Mossad believed the CIA had murdered Nir. According to Ari Ben-Menashe, "Israeli intelligence has always believed it was a well-executed CIA operation. Nir's death ensured there would be no embarrassment for Reagan and Bush at the trial of Oliver North."

Support for this theory came from a U.S. Navy commander who had accompanied Nir to Tehran on the fruiterer's mission to free the Beirut hostages. The commander's story revolved around his claim that Nir had met with George Bush, then vice president, on July 29, 1986, at the King David Hotel in Jerusalem, to brief him about the ongoing sale of U.S. arms via Israel to Iran. According to the writer Joel Bainerman, "Nir was secretly taping the entire conversation. And this provided him with evidence linking Bush to the arms-for-hostages deal. At the meeting were McKee and Gannon, who would die in the Pan Am flight over Lockerbie."

Bainerman would describe a visit the commander had made to CIA headquarters in Langley, where he had met Oliver North some months before the colonel faced trial. In the writer's words, the commander asked North "what had happened to Nir. North told him that Nir was killed because he threatened to go public with the recording of the Jerusalem meeting."

Journalists who have tried to question North on the matter have been brushed aside. Bush's aides have over the years maintained a similar attitude: anything the former president of the United States has to say on Irangate has already been stated.

In late July 1991, the home of Nir's widow, Judy, was burgled. His recordings and documents were the only items stolen. Police said the break-in was "highly professional." Judy Nir said she was certain the stolen material contained "information that would attack certain people." She refused to be drawn beyond that. The material has never been recovered. The question of who stole it has remained unanswered.

For the next four years, Shabtai Shavit continued to run Mossad, making every effort to keep it out of the headlines and free of the attention of the mythmakers as it continued to pursue its information gathering.

Away from the public gaze, the old jockeying for power within the Israeli intelligence community had lost none of its energy. Politicians who still sat on the oversight subcommittee on intelligence remembered how Shavit had bested them after the Gulf War. Memories are as long in Israel as anywhere else, and the whispering campaign against Shavit had continued: his focus was too narrow; the back channel to the CIA was barely ajar; he wasn't good at delegating; he was too aloof from the rank and file, among whom morale was falling.

Shabtai Shavit chose to ignore the warning signs. Suddenly, on a pleasant spring morning in 1996, he was summoned to the office of Prime Minister Benjamin Netanyahu and told he was being replaced. Shavit made no attempt to argue; he had seen enough of Netanyahu to know that would be pointless. He had only asked one question: Who was his successor?

Netanyahu had replied: Danny Yatom. The day of the Prussian had arrived for Mossad.

CHAPTER 17

BUNGLEGATE

Dawn was breaking on Thursday, January 16, 1998, when the government car pulled away from the white-painted house in an exclusive suburb close to the electrified fence marking the border between Israel and Jordan. In one of those twists of history that abound in Israel, the house stood on grounds where the spies of Gideon, the great Jewish warrior, had prepared their intelligence-gathering missions to enable the Israelis to defeat overwhelmingly superior forces. Now, Danny Yatom was setting off to finalize an operation that could save his career.

Beginning with the debacle on the streets of Amman in July 1997, when a kidon team failed to assassinate the Hamas leader Khalid

325

Meshal, the past seven months had been, Yatom had told friends, "like living on the edge of the block waiting for the ax to fall."

His executioner-in-waiting was Prime Minister Benjamin Netanyahu. Their once-close friendship had soured to the point where not a day passed without snipers in the prime minister's office targeting the Mossad chief with the same whisper: It was only a matter of time before he was sacked. Other men would have resigned. But not Yatom. Proud and imperious, he was prepared to stand on his record. There were so many successful operations he had ordered that no outsider knew about. "It's only the failures that get publicly dumped on my doorstep," he had bitterly told his friends.

They, together with his family, had seen the strain in him: the sleepless nights; the sudden, unexpected bursts of anger, quickly extinguished; the restless pacing; the long silences; all the outward signs of a man under huge strain.

Two years into the job, he still faced pressures no other Mossad director had. Consequently, his own staff was increasingly demoralized, and he could no longer count on their loyalty. The media were circling, sensing he was wounded, but holding back, waiting to see when the one man Yatom had trusted, but no longer, would finally wield the ax. So far Benjamin Netanyahu had only kept an icy distance.

But on this cold February morning, Yatom knew his time was running out. That was why he needed the operation he had nurtured these past weeks to work. It would show the prime minister his spymaster had not lost his skills. But none of this showed on Yatom's face; despite all he had endured, he kept his emotions under lock and key. Seated in a corner of the backseat of the Peugeot, in repose Yatom looked genuinely intimidating in black leather bomber jacket, open-neck shirt, and gray pants. It was how he usually dressed for work; clothes had never interested him.

His receding hair, steel-framed glasses, and thin lips went well with his nickname—the Prussian. He knew he still commanded by something close to fear. Beside him on the seat were the morning newspapers: for once there had been no speculation about his future.

The Peugeot made its swift way down through the hills toward Tel Aviv, the sun reflecting off the burnished bodywork; morning and evening the chauffeur polished the vehicle to mirror perfection. The Peugeot had bulletproof windows, armor-plated bodywork, and antimine flooring. Only the official car of the prime minister had similar protection.

Benjamin Netanyahu had Yatom confirmed in the post of director general of Mossad within minutes of Shabtai Shavit's going. In Yatom's first weeks in office, he had spent at least one evening a week with the prime minister. They had sat over cold beers and olives and put the world to rights, and remembered the times when Yatom had commanded "Bibi" in an IDF commando unit. Afterward Netanyahu had gone on to become Israel's ambassador to the United Nations and then, during the Gulf War, a self-styled expert on international terrorism, even broadcasting with a gas mask over his face in case a Scud should fall nearby. Yatom, for his part, had said how much he relished the role of the outsider who had been given the most important post in the country's intelligence community: the quintessential career soldier, he had served as military attaché to Prime Minister Yitzhak Rabin.

Yatom and Netanyahu had seemed inseparable until two embarrassments had left a seemingly unbridgeable gulf. There had been the bungled affair in Amman. The operation had been ordered by Netanyahu. When the attack failed and Mossad had been caught in the spotlight of the world's media, the prime minister blamed Yatom for the debacle. He had taken the criticism without flinching; privately he had told friends that Netanyahu had "the courage of other people's convictions."

A second and, in many ways, a graver embarrassment surfaced. In October 1997, a senior Mossad officer, Yehuda Gil, was discovered to have invented, for the past twenty years, top secret reports from a nonexistent "agent" in Damascus. Gil had drawn substantial sums from Mossad's slush fund to pay the man, pocketing the money for himself. The scam had only come to light when a Mossad analyst studying the "agent's" latest report that Syria was about to attack Israel had become suspicious. Gil had been confronted by Yatom and made a full confession.

Netanyahu had pounced. In a stormy meeting in the prime minister's office, Yatom had been brutally questioned over the way he ran Mossad. Netanyahu had brushed aside the argument that Gil had successfully carried off his deception under four previous directors. Yatom should have known, Netanyahu had shouted. It was another foul-up. Staff in the prime minister's office could not recall such a dressing-down.

The details had been leaked to the media, causing further embarrassment to Yatom.

How different it had been when he had come into office and his name had been splashed across the world's media. Reporters had called him a safe pair of hands and there had been speculation that he would assume the mantle of the great spymasters of yesteryear—Amit, Hofi, and Admoni—and once more rekindle the fire Shabtai Shavit had deliberately damped down.

The proof was not long in coming. Despite the Oslo accord giving the PLO a homeland—the Gaza Strip and the West Bank—Yatom had increased the number of Arab agents to spy on Yasser Arafat. He had ordered Mossad programmers to develop new software to hack into PLO computers, and create electronic "microbes" to destroy, should the need arise, its communication systems. He had asked scientists in research and development to focus on "infowar" weapons that could insert black propaganda into enemy broadcasting systems. He wanted Mossad to be part of the brave new world where the weapons of the future would be in keyboards that shut down an enemy's ability to mobilize its military forces.

Yatom had returned to Mossad's old stomping ground, Africa: in May 1997, the service had provided important intelligence that had helped rebel forces to topple President Mobutu of Zaire, who for so long had dominated central Africa. Mossad also increased its ties with Nelson Mandela's security service, helping it to target white extremists, many of whom it had previously worked with. Yatom also increased the budget and strength of the special Mossad unit, Al, responsible for stealing the latest U.S. scientific research.

At fifty-one years of age, there was something unstoppable about Danny Yatom; tireless and ruthless, he had the chutzpah of a street fighter. That was typified by his response to the discovery by the FBI in January 1997 of Mega—the high-level Mossad deep-penetration agent within the Clinton administration. He had told the Committee of the Heads of Services, whose role included preparing a fallback position in the event of an operational failure, all that needed to be done was to make sure that the powerful Jewish lobby in the United States countered demands from Arab organizations that the hunt for Mega must be pursued as vigorously as the FBI dealt with spies from other countries. Jewish dinner guests at the White House dinner table—Hollywood stars, attorneys, editors—all lost no opportunity to remind the president of the damage an ill-conceived manhunt would produce—even more if one of his own staff was arrested. In a presidency already besieged by scandal, that could be an opening that could finally destroy Clinton. Six months later, on July 4, 1997, Independence Day in the United States, Yatom had learned that the FBI had quietly downgraded its hunt for Mega.

Then two months later had come the disaster on the streets in Amman, swiftly followed by the scandal of the agent-who-never-was. Danny Yatom had begun to seek a new operation that would reestablish his authority. Now, on that January morning in 1998, he was on his way to put the finishing touches in place.

Planning for the operation had begun a month before, when an Arab informer in southern Lebanon had met his Mossad controller and told him that Abdullah Zein had made a brief visit to Beirut to meet with Hezbollah leaders in the city. Afterward Zein had driven south to see his parents in the small town of Ruman. The occasion had been one for celebration: Zein had not been home for a year. He had shown his relatives photographs of his young Italian wife and their apartment in Europe.

The controller had steeled himself not to rush the informer; the Arab way was to give his information in all its fine detail: how Zein had left his parents' home the next day laden with Arab delicacies and gifts for his wife, how Hezbollah had escorted him all the way to Beirut Airport to catch the flight back to Switzerland.

Was that Zein's final destination? the controller had finally asked. Yes, Bern, in Switzerland. And that was where Zein lived? The informer thought so, but could not be certain.

Nevertheless, it was Mossad's first positive news about Zein since he had left Lebanon to organize Hezbollah's fund-raising activities among wealthy Shi'ite Muslims in Europe. Their money, along with that from Iran, funneled through its embassy in Bonn, paid for Hezbollah's war of attrition against Israel. In the past year, Zein had been variously reported as operating from Paris, Madrid, and Berlin. But each time Yatom had sent someone to check, there had been no trace of the slim thirty-two-year-old with a taste for snappy Italian-cut suits and customized shoes.

Yatom had dispatched a *katsa* to Bern from Brussels, where Mossad had recently transferred its control center for European operators from

Paris. The *katsa* had spent two fruitless days in Bern searching for Zein. He decided to extend his inquiries. He drove south to Liebefeld, a pleasant dormitory town. The *katsa* had last passed through its streets five years before, on his way out of Switzerland after being part of a team that had destroyed metal vats in a bioengineering company near Zurich; the vats were designed to manufacture bacteria and had been ordered by Iran. The team had destroyed the vats with explosive devices. The company had canceled all its contracts with Iran.

In Liebefeld, the *katsa* had shown that good intelligence work often depended on patient footwork. He had walked the streets, looking for anyone who could be from the Middle East. He had checked the phone book for a listing for Zein. He had telephoned house-leasing agencies to see if they had rented or sold a property to anyone of that name. He had called the local hospitals and clinics to see if a patient of that name had been admitted. Each time he had said he was a relative. With still nothing to show for a day's work, the *katsa* had decided to make another sweep of the town, this time in his car.

He had driven for some time through the streets when he spotted a dark-skinned man, wrapped against the night cold, driving a Volvo in the opposite direction. There had been only the briefest of glimpses, but the *katsa* was convinced that the driver was Zein. By the time the *katsa* had found an intersection to turn his car, the Volvo had disappeared. Next evening, the *katsa* was back, this time parked in a position to follow. Shortly afterward, the Volvo appeared. The *katsa* fell in behind. A mile later, the Volvo parked outside an apartment block and the driver emerged and entered the building, 27 Wabersackerstrasse. The *katsa* had no doubt the man was Abdullah Zein.

The *katsa* followed Zein into the apartment block. Beyond the plate-glass door was a small lobby with mailboxes. One of them identified the owner of a third-floor apartment as "Zein." A door off the lobby led to a basement service area. The *katsa* opened the door and went down to the basement. Fixed to a wall was a junction box for all the telephones in the building. Moments later he was back in his rental car.

Next day he leased a safe house half a mile from Wabersackerstrasse. He told the real estate agency he was expecting friends to join him for a skiing holiday.

Danny Yatom had continued planning. He had sent a communications specialist to Liebefeld to examine the junction box. The technician had returned to Tel Aviv with a set of photographs he had taken of the inside of the box. The prints were studied in the research and development department and adjustments made to the devices being prepared. One was a sophisticated bug capable of monitoring all calls in and out of Zein's apartment. The bug would be linked to a miniature recorder capable of storing hours of phone calls. The recorder had a built-in capacity to be electronically emptied by a prearranged signal from the safe house. There the recordings would be transcribed and sent by secure fax to Tel Aviv.

By the first week of February 1998, all the technical plans were in place. Yatom moved to the most crucial part of the operation: choosing the team who would carry it out. The operation had two stages. The first was to gather sufficient evidence to show that Zein continued to be a key player in Hezbollah's activities. The second part was then to kill him.

By mid February 1998 everything was ready.

Shortly before 6:30 A.M. on that Monday, February 16, Yatom's Peugeot entered the parking lot in the basement of Mossad headquarters in Tel Aviv, and he took the elevator to a fourth-floor conference room. Waiting there were two men and two women. Seated around a table, they had already paired off as couples, the role they would assume in Switzerland. Each was in his late twenties, suntanned, and superbly fit-looking. For the past few days they had been up in the snow of northern Israel brushing up on their skiing.

The previous evening, they had been fully briefed on the mission and had selected their cover identities. The men were to pose as successful stock-market traders taking a short break from the trading floor with their girlfriends, but never quite able to put work behind them: that would explain the laptop computer one of them would carry. The laptop had been wired to provide the link between the concealed recorder to be installed in the apartment basement and the safe house. One couple was to monitor the recorder around the clock once it began working. The other pair were from the kidon unit. Their job was to find the best means to kill Zein. They would travel unarmed to Switzerland; their guns would be provided later by the Brussels office.

On the conference table were the listening device and the recorder. Yatom inspected them, saying the gadgets were far more sophisticated than any he had seen before. His final briefing was short. He asked each for the alias he or she had chosen from the list kept in operations. The men had selected Solly Goldberg and Matti Finklestein; the women were Leah Cohen and Rachel Jacobson. Because they were flying directly out of Tel Aviv on an El Al flight, they would travel on Israeli passports. They would resume their aliases in Switzerland, where false passports would be waiting.

All four, in the later words of an Israeli intelligence source, had "earned their stripes." But the truth was that, after the debacle in Jordan, there was a limited selection of agents available for such a mission. The Amman team had been the best Mossad had been able to field, and its members had been able to pass themselves off as Canadians; all had experience operating on the international stage. The quartet chosen for the Swiss mission had only operated in Cairo—a relatively safe Mossad target—and none of them had had firsthand knowledge of working under cover in Switzerland.

That may have accounted for why, according to the London *Sunday Times*, Yatom ended the briefing with a reminder that the Swiss who lived in German-speaking cantons where Liebefeld was situated had a "tendency to call the police if they saw anything improper."

Yatom had shaken their hands and wished them luck, the standard benediction for any team leaving on a mission. The group had picked up their airline tickets and spent the next twenty-four hours in a Mossad safe house in the city.

Next Tuesday morning, February 20, they boarded El Al Flight 347 to Zurich, obediently arriving at Ben-Gurion Airport, as requested by the airline, two hours before takeoff. They joined the lines of passengers, mostly Swiss nationals or Israelis, making their way through the security checks. By 9 A.M., the two couples were in their business-class seats and sipping champagne and discussing their forthcoming holiday. In the hold of the aircraft were their skis.

Waiting for them at Kloten Airport in Zurich was the *katsa* from the Brussels station with a minibus. He had assumed the role of their guide and had adopted the alias of "Ephrahim Rubenstein."

By late afternoon they were installed in the safe house in Liebefeld. The two women cooked dinner and they all settled down to watch television. Early in the evening two rental cars arrived from Zurich, driven by sayanim. They left in the minibus, their role over. At around 1:00 A.M. on Saturday, February 20, the team left the safe house, each couple in a separate car. Rubenstein was in the first car, leading the way to Wabersackerstrasse. Reaching there, the two vehicles parked almost directly opposite the apartment block. There was no light from Zein's apartment. The persons who called themselves Solly Goldberg, Rachel Jacobson, and Ephrahim Rubenstein walked quickly toward the glass door of the building. Rubenstein carried a roll of plastic, Goldberg the laptop, Jacobson a carrier bag containing the listening devices. Meantime, Leah Cohen and Matti Finklestein had enthusiastically begun to act out their lookout role, pretending to be lovers.

Across the street an elderly woman who suffered from insomnia—Swiss police would later insist on referring to her only as Madam X—was once more unable to sleep. From her bedroom window, she stared out at a strange sight. A man—Rubenstein—was draping plastic across the glass door to stop anyone's looking into the apartment block opposite. Behind the sheet, she could see two other figures. Out in the street in a parked car was another shadowy couple. Just as Danny Yatom had warned, what she saw was certainly improper. The woman called the police.

At a little after 2:00 A.M., a BMW squad car arrived in the street, catching Cohen and Finklestein in midembrace. They were ordered to remain in the car. Meantime, police backup had arrived and the trio inside the lobby were asked to explain what they were doing. Goldberg and Jacobson said they had mistaken the building for one where friends lived and Rubenstein insisted he was taking down, not putting up the plastic.

Matters then became farcical. Goldberg and Jacobson asked permission to go to their car and check the address of their friends. No policemen accompanied them. At the same moment, Rubenstein fell to the ground, appearing to have suffered a heart attack. All the policemen gathered around to help and summon medical assistance. No one moved to stop the two cars as they raced out of Wabersackerstrasse into the frosty night. Shortly afterward, the cars stopped to transfer one couple into the other car. The foursome crossed the border into France in the small hours of the morning.

Meanwhile Rubenstein had been taken to the hospital. Doctors said he had not suffered a heart attack. He was taken into custody.

At 4:30 A.M. Tel Aviv time, Yatom was awoken at home by the night watch officer in Mossad headquarters and told what had happened. Not bothering to call his chauffeur, Yatom drove himself to headquarters.

After the Amman fiasco, a plan had been put in place to deal with further such disasters. The first step was for Yatom to call the senior duty officer at the foreign ministry. The officer telephoned the head of the prime minister's office, who informed Benjamin Netanyahu. He called Israel's ambassador to the European community in Brussels, Efraim Halevy. The English-born diplomat had spent nearly thirty years as a senior Mossad officer with responsibility for maintaining good relations with security services of foreign states that had diplomatic relations with Israel. He had also played an important role in patching up relations with Jordan after the bungled operation in Amman.

"Fix this, and you'll be my friend for life," Netanyahu was later quoted as saying to Halevy.

The ambassador had consulted the Filofax he carried everywhere before deciding whom to call first: Jacob Kellerberger, a senior officer at the Swiss foreign ministry. Halevy was at his diplomatic best: there had been a "regrettable incident" involving Mossad. How "regrettable"? Kellerberger had demanded. "Most regrettable," Halevy had replied. The tone had been set, an understanding in the wind. Or so Halevy believed, until Kellerberger telephoned Switzerland's federal prosecutor, Carla del Ponte.

With a jutting lower lip and steel-rimmed spectacles that matched those of Danny Yatom, del Ponte was a figure within the Swiss legal system as formidable as Yatom had once been in the Israeli intelligence community. Her first question set the tone she would maintain: Why had the Liebefeld police not arrested all the Mossad agents? Kellerberger did not know. Del Ponte's next question raised a specter he was all too familiar with: Could the Mossad operatives have had a "Tehran connection"? Since the Gulf War, Israel had repeatedly claimed that several Swiss companies were supplying technology to Iran to produce missiles. Could the operation even be somehow connected with Israel's other preoccupation over what had become known as the "Jewish gold scandal"? Swiss banks had concealed for their own profit huge sums of money deposited in their vaults before World War II by German Jews who later became victims of the Nazis.

Throughout the weekend of February 21–22, her questions continued while Halevy struggled to keep matters quiet.

He had not counted on the forces arraigned against Danny Yatom in Israel. Within Mossad, as news of the incident percolated through the organization, morale plunged even lower. This time Yatom could not blame Netanyahu for what had happened in Liebefeld. The prime minister had known nothing beforehand of the operation. From within the prime minister's office whispers began to reach the Israeli media that Yatom was now doomed. For three more days, Efraim Halevy continued to plead and argue with Kellerberger to keep the incident quiet. But Carla del Ponte would have none of it. On Wednesday, February 25, she called a press conference to denounce Mossad: "What happened was unacceptable and disconcerting between friendly nations."

Within hours, Danny Yatom had resigned. His career was over and Mossad's reputation even more in tatters. In his last moments as director, he surprised staff who had assembled in the Mossad canteen. The cold Prussian image was replaced by an emotional tone: he was sorry to be leaving them at such a time, but he had tried to give them the best possible leadership. They should always remember Mossad was bigger than anyone. He ended by wishing whoever took over his place the very best of luck; he would need it. It was the nearest Yatom came to saying what he thought about a prime minister who continued to believe Mossad could be ultimately controlled from his office. Yatom walked out of the silent canteen. Only when he was in the corridor did the applause start, and it died as swiftly as it began.

A week later Efraim Halevy agreed to take over the service after Benjamin Netanyahu publicly acknowledged, the first time any Israeli prime minister had done so, "that I cannot deny that Mossad's image has been affected by certain failed missions."

Ever the consummate politician, Netanyahu made no mention of the role he had played.

Efraim Halevy became the ninth director general of Mossad on Thursday, March 5, 1998. He broke with tradition and did not summon his senior staff to hear his views on how the service should be run for the next two years. In appointing Halevy, Netanyahu had also announced that, on March 3, 2000, the new deputy director of the service, Amiram Levine, would take over running the service. The news was greeted with some surprise. No other director general had been given a fixed tenure; no other deputy had been assured he would step into the top job.

By 1999, Yatom had found himself a niche in Israel's thriving arms industry. He became a salesman for one of the country's biggest manufacturers of arms; the company not only provides a range of weapons for internal use but has a thriving export industry to Third World countries. Yatom makes regular visits to African countries and South American nations. From time to time he turns up in Washington.

Like Meir Amit, Levine had no previous intelligence experience, but he had commanded with distinction the Israeli army in northern Israel and south Lebanon.

Halevy's first task was to reduce the tremendous tension and resentments inside Mossad that had so seriously damaged its image both within Israel and beyond. In routine congratulatory telephone calls from both the CIA and MI6, the new director had been told those services would prefer to wait and see how he dealt with the crisis within Mossad before wholeheartedly committing their own services to no-secrets-based collaboration. One factor would be how Halevy dealt with the hard-liners in the Israeli government, especially its prime minister.

Would the urbane Halevy, only a year away from his pension and, by many years, the oldest to be given the office, be able to keep Netanyahu at a proper distance? And for all Halevy's undoubted diplomatic skills—he had played a central role in the negotiations that led to the 1994 peace treaty with Jordan—he had been away from the coalface of intelligence for several years. Since his time with Mossad the agency had increasingly shown signs of being out of control as senior officers had tried to stake their own claims for promotion. Most of those middle-aged men remained in office. Could Halevy deal firmly with them? Would the new director have the essential hands-on skills to raise morale? Mingling on the cocktail circuit in Brussels had hardly been the best preparation for the task of leading agents away from the brink of resignation. Critically, Halevy had no personal operational field experience. He had always been a desk man in his previous time with Mossad. And what could he really achieve in two years? Or was he really there to rubber-stamp what Netanyahu wanted done, or, for that matter, what Netanyahu's wife, Sara, wanted done? Speculation continued within the Israeli intelligence community over the part she had played in the removal of Yatom, a man to whom she had never warmed.

Halevy found a way to charm her. He presented Sara with a microchip that Mossad research scientists had developed. It could be implanted under her skin and allow her to be rescued in the unlikely event she ever fell into the hands of terrorists. Using natural body energy, the bleep was linked to one of Israel's new space satellites, enabling a person who wore it to be swiftly tracked to his or her hiding place. No one knows if Sara has had the implant inserted in her body.

But soon there were more pressing matters than beguiling the prime minister's wife. The first major operation Halevy had enthusiastically approved, an attempt to set up a spy base in Cyprus, came disastrously unstuck. Two Mossad agents, posing as teachers on vacation, were swiftly unmasked by the small but efficient Cypriot security service. They raided the apartment the agents had rented and discovered it was filled with high-tech equipment, capable of spying out Cypriot plans to stiffen its defenses against neighboring Turkey.

Halevy sent his deputy to Cyprus to negotiate the release of the two men. He might well have wished he had gone himself. Israel's president, Ezer Weizman, was a close personal friend of the Cypriot president, Biafcos Clerides (in their youth both men had served together in the Royal Air Force). Weizman dispatched his chief of staff to "eat humble pie in Cyprus" and then lambasted Halevy in a manner that even Netanyahu would have hesitated to use against Yatom.

Further public embarrassment followed when, having approved a plan to assassinate Saddam Hussein during a visit to his mistress, it was canceled after details were leaked to an Israeli journalist. Netanyahu learned what had happened when the reporter called his office for comment. Once more the hapless Halevy found himself facing a severe dressing-down.

For weeks the mercurial prime minister avoided all but essential contact with the Mossad chief, until late November 1998. Then the Turkish prime minister, Bulent Ecevit, telephoned Netanyahu and asked if Mossad would help capture Abdullah Ocalan, the Kurdish leader, long designated as a terrorist by other countries. Turkey held him responsible for 30,000 deaths on its soil. For over twenty years Ocalan's Kurdish Workers Party, the PKK, had waged a guerrilla war to get autonomy for Turkey's twelve million Kurds, who have no minority rights such as education or permission to broadcast in their own language.

Ocalan had constantly evaded Turkey's own security service with effortless ease. He was a leader who inspired messianic fervor in his people. Whether a man, woman, or child, they were ready to die for him. To many he was the epitome of the legendary Scarlet Pimpernel; his deeds of derring-do endlessly recited where two or more Kurds met.

There was a raw passion about his speeches, an unnerving defiance in his challenge to Turkey.

That November—after flitting through Moscow—Ocalan turned up in Rome. The Italian government refused to extradite him to Turkey—but also refused his request for political asylum. Earlier Ocalan had been arrested on a German warrant for traveling on a false passport. He was freed when Bonn withdrew its extradition demand for fear of inflaming its large Kurdish communities. That was the moment that Turkish Prime Minister Bulent Ecevit telephoned Netanyahu.

For Israel, a close working relationship with Turkey is an important element in its strategic and diplomatic survival in the region. Netanyahu agreed and ordered Halevy to find Ocalan. It would be a "black" operation—meaning Mossad's own involvement would never surface publicly. If successful, all the credit would go to Turkish intelligence.

The plan was given the code-name "Watchful." It reflected Halevy's own concern to do as little as possible to disturb his own running operation inside Iraq. There, Mossad *katsas* were working alongside Kurdish rebels to destabilize Saddam's regime.

Six Mossad agents were dispatched to Rome. They included a bat leveyha, a woman, and two technicians from Mossad *yaholomin*, its communications unit.

Working out of a Mossad safe house near the Pantheon, the team set up surveillance on Ocalan's apartment close to the Vatican. The woman agent was briefed to try and make contact with him. She followed the well-established guidelines that had been used by another Mossad female agent to entice Mordechai Vanunu to his doom in this same city over a decade before. But a plan to do the same with Ocalan failed when the Kurdish leader suddenly left Italy.

The Mossad team began to scour the Mediterranean basin for him: Spain, Portugal, Tunisia, Morocco, Syria. Ocalan had been to all those countries—only to move on when refused sanctuary. On February 2, 1999, the Kurdish leader was discovered trying to enter Holland. The Dutch government refused him permission to do so. A Dutch security officer at Amsterdam's Schiphol Airport informed the head of the local Mossad station that Ocalan had caught a KLM flight to Nairobi. His Mossad pursuers set off for the Kenyan capital, arriving on Thursday morning, February 5.

Kenya and Israel had developed over the years a close "understanding" on intelligence matters. As part of Mossad's "safari" in Central Africa it had exposed to the Kenyans the activities of other foreign spy networks. In return, Kenya continued to grant Mossad "special status," allowing it to maintain a safe house in the city and providing ready access to Kenya's small but efficient security service.

The Mossad team soon located Ocalan in the Greek embassy compound in Nairobi. From time to time Kurds—whom the team assumed were his bodyguards—came and went from the compound. Every night the head of the Mossad team reported to Tel Aviv. The order was the same: Watch—do nothing. Then the order dramatically changed. By "all means available," Abdullah Ocalan was to be removed from the embassy compound and flown to Turkey.

The order was Halevy's.

Luck played into the team's hands. One of the Kurds came out of the embassy and drove to a bar close to the venerable Norfolk Hotel. In what is a classic Mossad tactic, one of the team "came alongside" the Kurd. With his dark skin and fluent Kurdish patois, the agent passed himself off as a Kurd working in Nairobi. He learned that Ocalan was getting restless. His latest application for political asylum in South Africa had received no response. Other African countries had been similarly loath to grant the Kurdish leader an entry visa.

Mossad's eavesdropping team were using their equipment to monitor all communications in and out of the compound. It was clear that Greece would also refuse Ocalan sanctuary.

The Mossad agent who had met the Kurd in the bar made his move.

He telephoned the Kurd in the embassy compound and asked for "an urgent meeting." Once more they met in the bar. The agent told the Kurd that Ocalan's life was in danger if he remained in the compound. His only hope was to return to join his fellow Kurds, not in Turkey, but in northern Iraq. In its mountain vastness, Ocalan would be safe and could regroup for another day. The plan was something that Ocalan had actually begun to consider—and had been overheard doing so by the Mossad surveillance team. The agent persuaded the Kurd to return to the embassy and try and persuade Ocalan to come out and discuss the proposal.

Simply—and lethally—the trap was set. It was now only a matter of waiting to see how long Ocalan could hold out from taking the bait.

Based on its intercepts of radio traffic from the Greek Foreign Ministry to the compound, the Mossad team knew it was only a matter of days before Ocalan's increasingly reluctant hosts would show him the door. In an "eyes only for ambassador" message, Greek prime minister Costas Simitis had said that Ocalan's continued presence in the compound would trigger "a political and possibly military confrontation" in Greece.

Next morning a Falcon-900 executive jet landed at Nairobi's Wilson Airport. The pilot said he had come to collect a group of businessmen flying to a conference in Athens.

What happened then is still a matter of intense debate. Ocalan's German lawyer later claimed that "based on a misrepresentation of the situation by the Kenyan authorities," Ocalan was "effectively dragged out of the compound." But the Kenyan government and the Greek Embassy in Nairobi strongly denied the charge. The Greeks insisted that the Kurdish leader left the compound against the advice of his hosts.

One thing is certain.

The executive jet took off from Nairobi with Ocalan on board. As the aircraft cleared Kenyan air space the questions began:

Had the Mossad team followed its normal practice and injected Ocalan with an incapacitating drug as he stepped out of the compound? Had they snatched him off the street—as another team had snatched Adolf Eichmann all those years ago in Buenos Aires? Had Kenya turned a blind eye to an action that broke all international laws?

Hours after Ocalan had been incarcerated in a Turkish jail, an exultant Prime Minister Bulent Ecevit appeared on television to speak of an "intelligence triumph . . . a brilliant surveillance operation conducted in Nairobi over a twelve-day period." He made no mention of Mossad. He was sticking to the rules.

For Efraim Halevy the success of the operation was measured against the loss of a spy network in Iraq that had depended so much on Kurdish support. He was not the first Mossad chief to wonder if Prime Minister Benjamin Netanhyahu's readiness to place Mossad in the role of "gun for hire" would have long-term repercussions in the wider business of intelligence gathering.

The success of the operation was undoubtedly muted by another fiasco that Halevy had inherited.

On October 5, 1992, an El Al cargo jet had plunged into an apartment block near Amsterdam's Schiphol Airport, killing forty-three persons and injuring dozens. Since then hundreds of people living in the area had fallen ill. Despite a relentless campaign to conceal that the aircraft had been carrying lethal chemicals—including the components to produce sarin, the deadly nerve agent—the facts had emerged, drawing unwelcome attention to a secret research center in the suburbs of Tel Aviv where scientists had, among much else, produced a range of chemical and biological weapons for Mossad's kidon unit.

Twelve miles southeast of downtown Tel Aviv is the Institute for Biological Research. The plant is at the cutting edge of Israel's multilayered defense system. Within its laboratories and workshops are manufactured a wide range of chemical and biological weapons. The Institute's chemists—some of whom once worked for the Soviet KGB or East German Stasi intelligence service—created the poison used to try and kill Khalid Meshal, the leader of the Hamas Islamic fundamentalist group.

The Institute's current research programs include developing a range of pathogens which would be, according to a secret CIA report for William Cohen, U.S. defense secretary, "ethnic-specific." The CIA report claims that Israeli scientists are "trying to exploit medical advances by identifying distinctive genes carried by some Arabs to create a genetically modified bacterium or virus."

The report concludes that, "still at the early stages, the intention is to exploit the way viruses and certain bacteria can alter the DNA inside their host's living cells." The Institute research mimics work conducted by South African scientists during the apartheid era to create a "pigmentation weapon that will target only black people."

The research was abandoned when Nelson Mandela came to power but at least two of the scientists who worked in the program in South Africa later moved to Israel.

The idea of the Jewish State conducting such research has triggered alarm bells—not least because of the disturbing parallel with genetic experiments conducted by the Nazis. Dedi Zucker, a member of the Israeli Parliament, the Knesset, is on record as saying, "We cannot be allowed to create such weapons."

It was the raw materials for such weapons that the El Al jet was carrying on that October night in 1992 in its 114 tons of cargo that also included Sidewinder missiles and electronics. Most lethal of all were twelve barrels of DMMP, a component of sarin gas. The chemicals had been bought from Solkatronic, the New Jersey-based chemical manufacturer. The company has steadfastly insisted that it had been told by Israel that the chemicals were "to be used for testing gas masks." No such testing is carried out at the Institute for Biological Research.

Founded in 1952 in a small concrete bunker, today the Institute sprawls over ten acres. The fruit trees have long gone, replaced by a high concrete wall topped with sensors. Armed guards patrol the perimeter. Long ago the Institute disappeared from public scrutiny. Its exact address in the suburbs of Nes Ziona has been removed from the Tel Aviv telephone book. Its location is erased from all maps of the area. No aircraft is allowed to overfly the area.

Only Dimona in the Negev Desert is surrounded by more secrecy. In the classified directory of the Israeli Defense Forces, the Institute is only listed as "providing services to the defense ministry." Like Dimona, many of the Institute's research and development laboratories are concealed deep underground. Housed there are the biochemists and genetic scientists with their bottled agents of death: toxins that can create crippling food poisoning and lead to death; the even more virulent Venezuelan equine encephalomyelitis and anthrax.

In other laboratories, reached through air locks, scientists work with a variety of nerve agents: choking agents, blood agents, blister agents. These include tabun, virtually odorless and invisible when dispensed in aerosol or vapor form. Soman, the last of the Nazi nerve gases to be discovered, is also invisible in vapor form but has a slightly fruity odor. The range of blister agents include chlorine, phosgene, and diphosgene which smells of new-mown grass. The blood agents include those with a cyanide base. The blister agents are based upon those first used in World War I.

Outwardly featureless, with few windows in its dun-colored concrete walls, the Institute's interior has state-of-the-art security. Code words and visual identification control access to each area. Guards patrol the corridors. Bombproof sliding doors can only be opened by swipe-cards whose codes are changed every day.

All employees undergo health checks every month. All have been subject to intense screening. Their families have also undergone similar checks.

Within the Institute is a special department that creates lethal toxin weapons for the use of Mossad to carry out its state-approved mandate to kill without trial the enemies of Israel. Over the years at least six workers at the plant have died but the cause of their deaths is protected by Israel's strict military censorship.

The first crack in that security curtain has come from a former Mossad officer, Victor Ostrovsky. He claims that "we all knew that a prisoner brought to the Institute would never get out alive. PLO infiltrators were used as guinea pigs. They could make sure the weapons the scientists were developing worked properly and make them even more efficient."

Israel has so far issued no denial of these allegations.

The start of the NATO spring offensive against Serbia in 1999 gave Halevy an opportunity for Mossad to provide an intelligence input to the nineteen countries that formed the Alliance. Mossad had long-established contacts in the region—out of real concern that the Balkans could eventually become a Muslim enclave, so providing a back door from which to launch terrorist attacks against Israel. It gave Halevy a welcome opportunity to visit NATO headquarters in Brussels and meet his counterparts. He traveled to Washington to see the CIA. Back home he worked a long day, often not taking a day off from one week to the next. In that respect he reminded people of Meir Amit.

In the spring of 1999, Mossad's old *bête noire*, Victor Ostrovsky, surfaced to irritate the service. Carefully leaked reports from the team acting for two Libyans finally charged with the Lockerbie bombing said that Ostrovsky would give evidence for the defense. Given that the former *katsa* had left Mossad well before the incident, it was hard to see what he would have to contribute. Nevertheless, the sight of Ostrovsky in the witness box in the specially convened court in the Hague had, according to one senior Mossad source, deeply angered Halevy. He believed that an "understanding" had developed between Ostrovsky and his former employers that he would do nothing more to embarrass the agency in return for being allowed to live an unfettered life. For a while Halevy considered if there was any legal action he could take to stop Ostrovsky; in the end he was advised there was none.

To achieve all he must do before he leaves the service would continue to be a huge test of Halevy's physical and mental stamina. Aman and Shin Bet had seized upon the trouble in Mossad to boost their own position to be first among equals. Yet no one had suggested that Mossad should not retain its role as Israel's secret eye on the world. Without its skills Israel might well find itself defeated by its enemies in the next century. Iran, Iraq, and Syria were all developing technology that needed to be closely monitored.

In the beginning, the operational style of Mossad had been to do what must be done, but do it secretly. In one of his one-to-one meetings with a staffer, Halevy had said he would like to see the Israeli intelligence community become a united family once more, "with Mossad the uncle no one talks about."

Only time would tell whether that is an unsupportable dream or whether, as many observers fear, the further Mossad is from its last public humiliation, the closer it is to the next.

That came a step closer when, in June 1999, Mossad learned it could be asked to move its European headquarters in Holland following highly embarrassing claims that it has been secretly buying plutonium and other nuclear materials from the Russian Mafia. The allegation had been made by Intel, a small but formidable division of Dutch intelligence.

Intel's investigation had been run out of a deep bunker—ironically built to shelter the Dutch royal family in the event of a Soviet nuclear attack on Amsterdam. The bunker is near the city's Central Railway Station. Intel had established the terminus was journey's end for some of the nuclear materials stolen from Russian weapons labs such as Chelyabinsk-70 in the Ural Mountains and Arzamas-16 in Nizhnii Novgorod, formerly Gorky.

Senior Mossad officers had insisted to Intel that precisely because the deadly materials were stolen, their agents purchased them from the Russian Mafia. It was the only way to stop the material being sold to Islamic and other terror groups.

While conceding that the Mossad claim was plausible, Intel investigators had become convinced that the nuclear materials had also been secretly shipped out of Amsterdam's Schiphol Airport to Israel to boost the country's own nuclear weapons manufacturing plant at Dimona. Already stockpiled there were, by 1999, an estimated two hundred nuclear weapons.

That Mossad had been trafficking with the Russian Mafia rekindled a nuclear nightmare that has never quite gone away. While the chilling cold war doctrine of MAD—mutually assured destruction—had gone, in its place has come a more dangerous scenario where nuclear know-how and materials are on sale. It is capitalism, Wild East style, in which organized crime syndicates and corrupt government officials work in league to create new markets for nuclear materials—a bazaar with some of the world's most dangerous weapons on offer.

Much of the work of tracing the origins of stolen nuclear material is done at the European Trans-Uranium Institute (ETUI) in Karlsruhe, Germany. There, scientists use state-of-the-art equipment to track whether stolen materials have come from a military or civilian source. But they concede "it's like trying to catch a thief who has never been fingerprinted."

To head off undoubtedly awkward questions should Mossad's own fingerprints be found, Halevy made a secret visit to Holland in early June to explain to Intel Mossad's role. Dutch intelligence remained unconvinced.

Halevy returned to Israel to tell its new prime minister, Ehud Barak, that Mossad should be prepared to move its European headquarters in the El Al complex at Schiphol Airport.

Mossad had been based there for the past six years. From second-floor offices in the complex—known at Schiphol as "Little Israel"—eighteen Mossad officers have run European operations. According to one Mossad source, Halevy's position was clear: better Mossad moves than be kicked out of Holland, a fate it suffered in Britain under the Thatcher government.

It was Mossad's decision to run its own operations within a host country without telling Britain that had led to a souring of relations with London. Ironically. If Mossad left Schiphol, it might be to return to Britain. Under the uncritical approval of Prime Minister Tony Blair—Halevy is said to have told Barak—Mossad would find a ready welcome. Blair believes a strong Mossad presence would benefit MI5's efforts to keep track of the many groups from the Middle East who are now based in London.

A deciding factor in a move to Britain would be whether El Al, the Israeli national carrier, also moved its hub from Schiphol to Heathrow. Given El Al's thriving cargo business, the boost to Heathrow would be considerable.

Intel had established that the link between Mossad and the airline is an integral part of the traffic in nuclear materials.

The Dutch agency insists that Mossad would never have begun the dangerous business of buying nuclear materials unless those materials could be safely and secretly transported to Israel.

Former U.S. Assistant Secretary of Defense Graham Allison, now director of Harvard's Center for Science and International Affairs, has observed that "a criminal or terrorist group could even ship a weapon into the United States in places small and light enough to be sent through the postal service."

Implicit in those words is the fact that a highly efficient organization like Mossad, supported by the vast resources Israel puts at its disposal, would have little or no difficulty in smuggling nuclear materials out of Schipol.

Intel's suspicion about such smuggling was first aroused when it was tipped off that the El Al cargo freighter that crashed shortly after take-off from Schiphol in October 1992 was carrying chemicals.

Since then the agency has gathered what an Intel source describes as "at minimum strong circumstantial evidence" that Mossad has also shipped nuclear materials regularly through Schiphol.

A "mule"—a courier—who in return for her cooperation was given a guarantee against prosecution—has told Intel that she had smuggled nuclear materials from the Ukraine across Germany and finally into Holland.

The courier has claimed to Intel that she was met at Amsterdam's Central Station. Shown photographs, the courier picked out the person. It was a Mossad officer Intel knew was based at Schiphol.

In the "old days"—the words are those of Meir Amit—a Mossad operative would never have allowed himself to be so easily identified. Many others within the Israeli intelligence community believed such basic failures in trade craft did not augur well for Mossad as it entered the new millennium.

There has been a change of attitude within Israel that has led to anger and disillusion over Mossad's operational failures. In those "old days" few Israelis had really minded that Mossad's successes often depended on subversion, lying, and killing. All that mattered was that Israel survived.

But with peace, of a sort, edging closer to Israel's borders with its Arab neighbors, increasing questions are being asked about such methods being used in Mossad's continuing role as shield and sword.

Within Mossad itself there is a stubborn feeling that a great institution can only survive by, in the words of Rafi Eitan, "not giving in to every murmur of a new opinion." Equally there is also a feeling, articulated by Ari Ben-Menashe, that if Mossad persists in locking itself into yesterday's goals, it "will be in danger of being smothered, like a medieval knight in his armor left unhorsed and forgotten on the field of battle."

Behind such evocative words lie some hard truths. Fifty years on, Mossad is no longer seen as a derring-do agency, its deeds burnished bright in the consciousness of Israel. Born in those memorable few years in which Israel built a new world for itself, Mossad was one of the guarantors that world would survive. That guarantee is no longer required.

Ari Ben-Menashe put it as well as anybody: "Israel, and the world, should think of Mossad as they would a dose of preventive medicine—to protect against an illness that could be fatal. You only take the medicine when the illness is threatening. You don't take it all the time."

The still unanswered question is whether Mossad will be content to play a role where maturity and moderation must replace the policy of doing hard things for hard reasons.

CHAPTER 18

NEW BEGINNINGS

On September 11, 2002, every available man and woman in Mossad—

apart from those overseas—made his or her way through the feature-

less corridors of their headquarters in midtown Tel Aviv. Outside it was

another of those late summer days, a clear blue sky and the tempera-

ture in the midtwenties Celsius. There had been the same kind of

weather, a year ago to the day, on the northeastern seaboard of the

United States when al-Qaeda's suicide bombers had crashed into the

Twin Towers in New York and the Pentagon. The unprecedented as-

sault had forever changed the perception of terrorism for Mossad

and the world's other intelligence services, who worked, in 2002, in a

$100 billion global industry employing a million people. Mossad's entire staff now numbered 1,500, an increase of 300 over the last decade.

It was not the first anniversary of what had become known as 9/11 that preoccupied those in Mossad headquarters heading for the staff canteen. The sense of foreboding in some, coupled with a frisson of excitement in others, came from a mixture of hope, expectation, and a fear of disappointment.

The question uppermost in their minds was simple: Was the new head of Mossad they were on their way to meet in the headquarters canteen going to continue to run the service as it had been run under Efraim Halevy? If so, morale would inevitably plunge further and there would be more resignations.

Halevy had finally been eased out by Prime Minister Ariel Sharon as memune—Hebrew for "first among equals." In the four years he had been director general, the tension he had inherited—caused by interservice rivalry and backstabbing that had set field agents against analysts and turned planners into plotters—had increased. Mossad, which once prided itself on unity, had become increasingly fractured.

Could the new man heal the rifts? Could he do what Halevy had spectacularly failed to do: lead Mossad into the new millennium and turn it back into a force with which to be reckoned? The men and women making their way to the canteen on that September day agreed that anyone at the helm must be better than Halevy.

In his four-year tenure, there had been marked physical changes in Halevy. There was a grayness to his skin, and his eyes were often red rimmed, the result of disturbed sleep from calls by a Mossad night-duty officer. The lines around Halevy's mouth were more deeply etched. Gone was the sprightly stride that had once heralded his approach down Mossad's corridors; there was now a stiffness in his gait. Sartorially, too, he was no longer the figure he had been: he had lost weight; his jackets hung on him. His voice, still cultured, was without its crispness; his questions were less incisive. Halevy had come to look and sound like a man edging toward retirement. On that September day, he was sixty-six years of age, the oldest director general to have led Mossad.

In many ways the service had become like Halevy. Its forays onto the international stage had been cut back to operations in the cauldron of the Middle East. Senior Mossad officers accompanied Halevy on his regular visits to the CIA at Langley, to MI6 at its new headquarters at Vauxhall Cross in London, and to Pullach in Bavaria, home of Germany's BND.

Visits to other intelligence chiefs were less frequent. But little came from any of these contacts.

The world in the twenty-first century had become far more danger-ous and unstable than ever before. While Mossad had contributed to assessing the technological developments terrorists had acquired, it played no significant part in identifying new roles for the global intel-ligence community on how to counter drugs and economic espionage. Mossad's contribution had been to argue the need to bring back the traditional spy as a complement to the satellites and other exotic sys-tems. The view was often coolly received.

Then, on September 11, 2001, the world and the global intelligence community were shocked into a new reality after the most deadly ter-rorist attack ever known. Yet, stunning as it was, the events of that day had been long in the making: the assault was the climax of the most sophisticated and horrifying scheme masterminded by Osama bin Laden and his jihad group, al-Qaeda.

In the countless millions of words written in newspapers and the ac-cumulating library of books on the subject, one question has remained, until now, unanswered: *How much did Mossad know beforehand of the events leading up to the destruction of the Twin Towers and the partial toppling of the Pentagon?*

A year after the attacks, only a handful of the most senior Mossad officers from the Operations floor in the Mossad headquarters build-ing knew the answers—and then, not all of them.

From the day bin Laden's suicide bombers partly destroyed the World Trade Center in 1993, Mossad had placed him at the top of its own list of most wanted terrorists. Its deep-cover field agents in Yemen, Saudi Arabia, and Afghanistan had all picked up "whispers in the wind" that bin Laden was planning "something big," said one report. Another spoke of a "strong rumor bin Laden is planning a Hiroshima type attack." Still another revealed a flight simulator being used in an al-Qaeda training camp near Kabul. Then came the even more alarming news that bin Laden had been trying to obtain chemical and nuclear weapons.

While Mossad analysts tried, in the words of one (to this author), to "connect the dots," the reports were also passed on through the long-established back channel to the CIA. The Pentagon was asked to eval-uate the threat of an air strike. One of its analysts, Marvin Cetron, wrote, "Coming down the Potomac, you could make a left turn at the Washington Monument and take out the White House."

A full three years before the September attacks, a commission chaired by Vice President Al Gore had produced a report that urged substantially more spending on airport security. Other reports, again based on input from Mossad, followed. All were ignored, first by the Clinton White House and then by Clinton's successor, President George W. Bush. When he protested, Marvin Cetron was told by a Pentagon official, "Look, we can't manage a crisis until it is a crisis." There was a feeling in Washington that Mossad was once more crying wolf, that it had a vested interest in promoting Islamic fundamentalism as a threat because it feared its terrorists and wanted to persuade the United States that it also faced a similar threat.

By the time Efraim Halevy had come into office, dutifully read the files on terrorism threats, and seen the reaction to Mossad's warnings, he had decided that, in the words of one of his senior officers, "there was no point in pushing against a bolted door."

In Washington, the impending debacle of intelligence ignored had led, not for the first time, to a rupture between the FBI and the CIA. Both agencies had concrete evidence that al-Qaeda *was* an increasing threat: one of its operatives had been stopped at the last moment from flying a hijacked plane into the Eiffel Tower in Paris. Credible intelligence had emerged at Langley that bin Laden was planning to launch an air strike against the economic summit in Italy earlier in 2001. But the sense of paralysis and denial, compounded by the growing turf war between the FBI and the CIA, had continued to hold the U.S. intelligence community in its grip.

It would take the events of September 11 to break that hold.

In the aftermath, senior officers at both agencies were publicly attacked for their lack of counterterrorism policies and their failure of coordination and cooperation. There emerged a picture of recalcitrant intelligence bureaucracies, too concerned with issues of political expediency to take risks. The CIA, in particular, had failed to grasp the importance of the rise of Islamic fundamentalism, and the crucial role played by Osama bin Laden and al-Qaeda. From its training camps, thousands of terrorists had graduated to leave their mark on the world stage. First came the destruction in 1998 of the American embassy in Nairobi, Kenya, and Dar es Salaam in Tanzania in which 213 died. Then followed the attack on the American destroyer the USS *Cole* in the port of Aden on October 12, 2000. Both were very public preludes to the September 11 attacks.

After September 11, among the hundreds of questions dominating Washington's collective soul-searching, were: Why had the CIA not had more spies on the ground in Africa and the Middle East? Why had it depended too much on electronic surveillance? And why had it not relied upon what Paul Bremer, the counterterrorism chief for President Reagan, had called "third-country intelligence"?

Everyone knew he meant Mossad.

Since then, Halevy had been bombarded with calls from CIA director George Tenet, himself facing intense criticism. Tenet wanted to know how much more Mossad had known about the impending attack on the Twin Towers and the Pentagon.

Halevy, in his careful, diplomatic way, had pointed out to Tenet that Mossad *had* sent several warnings in the weeks prior to September that an attack was coming. Halevy had then cited "credible chatter" Mossad agents had picked up in Afghanistan, Pakistan, and Yemen. But under mounting pressure from Congress and the White House, Tenet had furiously persisted in challenging Halevy. *How much had Mossad known?*

A serving Mossad officer later described the "hot line from Langley" as superheated. Sometimes there were a dozen calls a day from Tenet. And then there was all the secure-line high-speed signals traffic. There had never been anything like it. Washington was shocked that a bearded man operating out of a cave somewhere in the Middle East had "done more damage to American prestige than Pearl Harbor."

In a tense phone call, one which, though he did not know it, would trigger his own downfall, Halevy had snapped at Tenet. Where was *your* electronic surveillance?

America's National Security Agency is the most secretive and powerful such service in the world. From Fort George G. Meade in Maryland, it casts an electronic ear over the globe. Its supercomputers hum around the clock, hoping to intercept or identify communications between terrorists. Suspects, names, key words, phone numbers, and e-mail addresses are all sucked up by NSA satellites—either circling or geopositioned around the earth—and downloaded to the computers. There the data are coded into "watch lists," then fed into the system that takes the lists on secure lines throughout the U.S. intelligence community.

In theory, everyone who had needed to know would have been aware of who was out there posing a real and present danger to the United States. But the reality had been different.

Few know exactly what NSA costs to run, but it is widely reported to be more than several billion dollars a year. Its massive, powerful data crushers are part of the ECHELON surveillance system, which sifts tens of billions of snippets of information, daily, matching them up.

The one drawback with the system is that it still has language difficulties: it cannot recognize the dialects and patois of some of the eighteen languages of the Middle East and the even greater number in India and Pakistan. Some of the material obtained from there has to be scrutinized by old-fashioned methods—linguists trained to interpret what is being said and, equally important, what might have been left out. In the end, the lists depend on being accurate.

Efraim Halevy knew that was the weakness in the American system: any list was only as good as the analysts who put a person's name on it. And that, he had politely told Tenet in that phone call, was where the Americans had failed.

Tenet was furious. He was wedded to the wonders of electronic surveillance. For him, it was the ultimate billion-dollar instrument of superpower espionage. The sentinels in space, the high-tech spy satellites with exotic-sounding names like Argus, Magnum, and Keyhole, were how Washington—and in many ways Tenet himself as the head of its intelligence community—kept track of the rest of the world. On his own visits to Israel, he had shown Halevy how, out in the icy blackness of outer space, a satellite pointed down on Yasser Arafat's headquarters on the West Bank had picked up his conversations. Halevy, so the story went, had smiled politely. But what had Arafat been saying that justified the expense of all that surveillance? Tenet had shrugged.

Halevy had studied the satellite photo for a moment longer, noting the date. Then he had asked one of his analysts to fetch a report on the same day. It was a detailed account from a Mossad *katsa* of what Arafat had said when the satellite had passed overhead. Halevy had murmured that that was the point of human intelligence. A spy on the ground could judge a conversation in its setting, obtain the finer details that are lost to even the most sophisticated electronic surveillance.

At his next meeting with President George W. Bush, the CIA chief had complained that "the old man in Tel Aviv is outta touch." Bush had discussed the matter with Condoleezza Rice, his closest adviser. She said she would speak to Dick Clarke, who had been President Clinton's counterterrorism "czar." Few people in Washington had worked for longer in the field.

The son of a Boston chocolate factory worker, Clarke was a survivor of the American politico-military establishment. For successive administrations, from President Reagan onward, he had become a source of endless advice. He saw himself as a defender of American values.

Despite his enemies, people listened to him. Privately they may have mocked the way Clarke strove to look like the latest incumbent in the White House—he had even dyed his hair silver when Clinton was in office, so they said—but he was the man who knew the standing of every intelligence chief in the West, and of many in China and Arab countries. He told Rice that Halevy was "past his sell-by date." She told Bush. He called Sharon. It was only a matter of time before Israel's prime minister would find a reason to send Halevy into retirement.

The men and women making their way through Mossad's corridors knew, if not all, then part of this. Some of their colleagues had already left Mossad, either resigning or being driven out by a feeling that there was no real future in the organization. For them it was no longer enough to create situations that sought to draw fact out of surmise, to spend their days applying the art of informed conjecture and dealing in the middle range of probability. Others had stayed on in the hope that one day things would change—that there would, for instance, be no repetition of an operation for which Efraim Halevy would forever be remembered in these corridors.

On May 9, 2001, two young men drove up to the guard post at Volk Field in Wisconsin, one of several air bases the Air National Guard maintains across the country. Volk Field has another claim of interest. Within its perimeter is a small aeronautical museum. Every year from spring until September, a steady stream of visitors comes to inspect the display of aircraft.

The guard asked the men for their IDs, and was surprised when they produced Israeli passports. He could not recall visitors coming from so far. They explained they were "art students" at the "University of Jerusalem."

As with all visitors, the guard noted down their names—Gal Kantor and Tsvi Watermann—then directed them to the museum. Ten minutes later a military police patrol caught them taking photographs of parked fighter planes. The men were arrested but pleaded that they had not known they were committing an offense. The base duty security officer released them with a warning. His report of the incident made its way through the Wisconsin military command structure and on to the Pentagon.

From there it was sent to the FBI. On that May day, the bureau had already received twenty-seven other reports involving Israeli "art students." The reports came from as far apart as Los Angeles and Miami, Denver and Dallas, Seattle and New Orleans.

The details were remarkable in their consistency. Two "art students" in St Louis had been caught "diagramming the inside of a Drug Enforcement Agency building." In another federal building in Dallas, another pair had been stopped doing the same thing. In several cities, other "art students" had shown up at the homes of senior federal officials—men with unlisted addresses, known as "black addresses" in the U.S. intelligence community. In other cities—Phoenix and San Diego were two—the "students" had been found in possession of photographs of federal agents and their unmarked cars. All the reports said that the students had given their address as the "University of Jerusalem" or the "Bezalei Academy of Arts" in the city.

The FBI had asked the State Department to have the United States embassy in Israel run a check. It reported that no "University of Jerusalem" existed. The nearest was the city's Hebrew University, and it had no record of the "students." The Bezalei Academy was genuine. But the dates of birth, passport numbers, and in some cases military registration numbers of the "art students" were not listed on the academy's enrollment list, or lists of those who had attended up to ten years before. While this information was being obtained, FBI agents in Washington had traced the cell phones the mysterious "students" were carrying. All had been purchased by an Israeli diplomat in Washington who had now returned to Israel.

The news caused consternation in FBI headquarters. Robert Mueller, then the bureau's director, called for a meeting with George Tenet. Uppermost in their minds was whether they were facing another spying operation by Mossad. But would an agency that had made its name for unrivaled planning and stealth have mounted one that, on the surface at least, was so amateurish?

Tenet placed a call to Halevy, who denied that any operation was going on.

He was lying. The operation had been his brainchild. Stung by the refusal—and this was months before the September 11 attacks—to take heed of Mossad's warnings that al-Qaeda was a growing threat within the United States, Halevy had decided to test how vigilant were American defenses. Students from their final year at the Mossad training school on the outskirts of Tel Aviv had been selected to go to America. It would not be the first time that Mossad had used its students for this purpose; it gave them valuable field experience, and anything they acquired could be useful to Mossad.

Halevy had chosen to run the operation with only a few Mossad staff involved. Again, it was not uncommon for a director general to do this. But what made it unusual was that the preplanning and cover stories were a disaster waiting to happen. Just as at Lillehammer and on the streets of Amman—both debacles that had cost Halevy's predecessors their jobs—there was an element of recklessness about what the "art students" had been briefed to do that baffled the FBI. Surely, Mossad could not have slipped so far, to be running something like this?

As the FBI began its investigation, the inevitable happened: the news leaked. Soon a number of reporters were trying to pin down the story. Much of their initial reporting was wide of the mark. The "art students" were described as "Middle Easterners" and "speaking Arabic." They were identified as members of an unnamed terrorist group.

Then the Fox News channel entered the arena. It assigned a hardworking reporter, Carl Cameron, to the story. He picked up the first hint that this could be a Mossad-generated operation.

That provoked an immediate response from the vast and powerful Jewish lobby in Washington, whose tentacles reach out across America. The American-Israel Public Affairs Committee (AIPAC) is a leading political lobby, able to penetrate Congress, the intelligence community, and the White House. The Jewish Institute for National Security Affairs (JINSA) has equally powerful connections. The Anti-Defamation League (ADL) and the Committee for Accuracy in Middle East Reporting in America (CAMERA) are strident watchdogs over what the media publish about Israeli affairs.

The moment Cameron went on air on the Fox network to announce he had uncovered "a possible espionage and surveillance operation by Israelis against al-Qaeda operatives in the U.S.," the combined resources of the Jewish lobby directed their fire against him.

But even as they launched their first volley, Cameron was saying in a second report that "many of the Israelis had failed polygraph tests when asked about their alleged surveillance activities in the United States."

In Paris, *Le Monde*, France's newspaper of record, reported that "a vast Israeli spy network had been dismantled in the United States, the largest operation of its kind since 1985 when Jonathan Pollard was caught selling top secrets to Mossad."

With renewed ferocity, the Jewish lobby set to work.

The Israeli embassy predictably reiterated what it said to all such allegations: "No American official or intelligence agency has complained to us about this. The story is nonsense. Israel does not spy on the United States."

The Israel lobby excoriated Carl Cameron for his exposé. Representatives of JINSA, the ADL, and CAMERA argued that the Fox report "cited only unnamed sources and provided no direct evidence." CAMERA's associate director, Alex Safian, said "it was having 'conversations' with representatives of Fox News regarding Cameron's piece."

Safian also questioned Cameron's "motives" in running the story. "I think Fox has always been fair to Israel in its reporting. I think it's just Cameron who has something, personally, about Israel. He was brought up in the Middle East. Maybe that has something to do with it. Maybe he's very sympathetic to the Arab side. One could ask." The implication was that Carl Cameron was a bigot; Safian would later make the same allegation about the entire editorial staff at *Le Monde*.

"I'm speechless," said Cameron when he heard of Safian's statement. "I spent several years in Iran growing up because my father was an archaeologist there. That makes me anti-Israel?" Cameron, the chief Washington correspondent for Fox News, had never before been attacked for "biased" coverage.

Michael Lind, a senior fellow at the New America Foundation—a think tank—and former executive editor of *The National Interest*, a journal, said: "Among foreign service officers, law enforcement, and military, there is an impression that you can't mess with Israel without suffering direct and indirect smears, such as being labeled an Arabist."

While the attacks on Cameron and *Le Monde* were at full throttle, the "art students" were quietly deported to Israel for what the U.S. Immigration and Naturalization Service called "routine visa violations."

No mainstream media outlet asked why the CIA, through its National Counterintelligence Executive, had been involved. Or why the

FBI had established that the "students" had visited no fewer than thirty-six Defense Department facilities.

Finally, as the "students" were flying out on El Al back to Tel Aviv, all traces of Cameron's reporting vanished from the Fox News Internet site. In its place ran a note. "This story no longer exists." A CIA spokesman said: "We've closed the book on it."

Shortly afterward, Halevy's tenure at Mossad came to an end.

There was one other legacy Efraim Halevy would take into retirement: his decision to revisit the deaths of Princess Diana and Dodi al-Fayed. After reading the Mossad file on the incident, he had asked Maurice, the agent who had been involved in trying to recruit Henri Paul—the driver of the car in which the young lovers had died—to prepare a new record of the couple's last day together.

Had it been mere curiosity on Halevy's part? There were rumors that he had met Diana during his time as Israel's ambassador to the European Community. If so, he would not be the first diplomat to come under her spell. But more likely is that Halevy wanted to ensure that there was no new evidence to support the claims that Mossad had been indirectly involved in the deaths.

Maurice, now a desk man at headquarters, had prepared a detailed account of the last day in the life of Diana and Dodi.

Those who have read the account say it does flesh out the detail in the original Mossad report. Mohamed al-Fayed, the father of Dodi, is described as a man with a continuing obsession that Diana was pregnant and that she was the object of surveillance by the CIA, MI6, and French intelligence from the moment she and Dodi flew into Paris. There are transcripts of various phone calls, including one from Diana's former Scotland Yard bodyguard, warning her to "be careful." The evening of August 30, 1997, which the couple spent together in Paris, is carefully time-tabled. Next comes a similar recounting of how, in the first moments of Sunday, August 31, the couple rushed from the Ritz Hotel to try to reach Dodi's apartment a short drive away. Then Maurice had focused on the white Uno. It had been parked close to the Ritz. Other photographers say it belonged to the paparazzo James Anderson. He had made taking photos of Diana his speciality. It had earned him a fortune. But it has been established Anderson was not present on the night in question.

Maurice described the white Uno in hot pursuit of the Mercedes,

Henri Paul at the wheel, Diana and Dodi in the back, as the two cars raced neck and neck into the place de L'Alma underpass, where Diana and Dodi met their deaths.

Later a car of the same make, but recently painted blue, was found in a Paris garage. When the paint was scratched, the car was white underneath. The police did not pursue the matter. Did they already suspect this was not the vehicle they were searching for? If so, why did they not visit the car-crusher facility in the Paris suburb where another white Fiat Uno, hours after the fatal crash, had been reduced to a block of unidentifiable metal? Did they also realize that would be a waste of time?

Maurice noted in his report: "Almost four hours after the crash, James Anderson suddenly flew to Corsica. There was no known professional reason for him to do so. There was no one famous on Corsica to photograph at the time. In May 2000, a burned-out car was found in woodland near Nantes in France. The driver was still inside the car. DNA tests showed the body was that of James Anderson."

And there lies the last mystery, one that will now perhaps never be resolved. Had Anderson gone to Corsica to collect a substantial fee for loaning his white Uno? But to whom? Mossad certainly had no interest in pursuing Diana or Dodi. Could it have been another secret service? Anderson was reputed to have connections to both French and British intelligence. Even if that was true, it is still an unacceptable leap—as Mohamed al-Fayed made—to suggest that Anderson's car had been "borrowed and used to force Henri Paul to lose control over the Mercedes."

But the questions do not stop. Why was the police investigation into Anderson's death so perfunctory? Why had the police neither attempted to find out why he had gone to Corsica nor conducted a detailed investigation into his bank accounts? Like all wealthy men, Anderson kept a number of accounts around Europe. But none of these were checked to see if he had deposited a substantial amount after his trip to Corsica.

More intriguing is the possibility that it was Anderson's death that had concerned Halevy. Had someone in the past tried to recruit him for Mossad? While there may well have been nothing on a Mossad file, it was still a possibility that a *katsa* on an operation had come across the photographer and tried to use him.

Whatever Efraim Halevy had thought of all this he had kept to himself. He was that sort of man. His inability to share some secrets may well have contributed to his downfall. He had arrived quietly in Mossad. He left the same way.

Now, on that eleventh day of September 2002, the staff of Mossad waited for his successor to arrive in the canteen to address them. No one knew what to expect. The tension, one man recalled, was "a living thing."

Meir Dagan waited in the corridor until he was sure there was total silence in the canteen. Long ago, when he had been a military commander briefing his troops, he had learned the importance of making an entrance. Now the tenth memune to take charge of Mossad, he was equally determined to stamp his authority from the outset. Since his appointment, he had studied staff files. He had a prodigious memory, and a face once seen was not forgotten.

At fifty-seven years of age, his own face was a road map of all the recent wars Israel had fought. He had himself crushed the first Intifada in Gaza in 1991. He had led his men from the front in the Yom Kippur War. In Lebanon, he had fought with distinction. In all these places, he had displayed the same regimen to awaken from a combat veteran's light sleep, take a cold shower, and eat a daily breakfast of natural yogurt, toast spread with honey, and strong black coffee. Blunt, proud, and imperious, he was prepared to stand on his record.

The battle-hardened hero of past wars had earned his reputation in Arab capitals as a man to be feared, one who would not hesitate to venture into those alleys that often have no names with no more than a handgun in his pocket. Twice he had been wounded in action; on some days, when the twinge in his knee became too severe, he walked with the help of a walking stick. He disliked doing so; he had an antipathy to any sign of weakness in himself or others. On that September day he had no stick.

In his spare time he was a student of military history and the intelligence lessons to be learned from battles lost and won.

Few knew he was also an accomplished landscape painter (he had already earmarked a corner of his office where he would set up his easel to produce one of his watercolors). Like everything else about him, this fact remained part of his private world. A man of few friends and with a happy domestic life, he came to Mossad with only one aim: to make it the intelligence service it had once been.

Prime Minister Ariel Sharon had taken him out of military command to do so. The two men had been friends from their days together fighting the PLO in Lebanon. Dagan had made an impression in that political quagmire by showing his skill at morale building. That, Sharon had said, was now a priority in Mossad. He had chosen Dagan because in many ways he was cast from the same steely mold as perhaps the greatest leader Mossad had ever had, Meir Amit.

Satisfied that the sense of expectation in the canteen had built sufficiently, Dagan entered the room. Making his way rapidly past the silent staff to the center, he used a chair as a step to stand on a table. For a long moment, he stared down at the faces looking up at him. Then he spoke.

"In Lebanon I witnessed the aftermath of a family feud. A local patriarch's head had been split open, his brain on the floor. Around him lay his wife and some of his children. All dead. Before I could do anything, one of the patriarch's sons scooped up a handful of the patriarch's brain and swallowed it. That is how they do things in family feuds in that place. Eat the brain. Swallow its power."

He paused, letting the impact of his words have their full effect.

"I don't want any of you to have your brains eaten. You eat *their* brains." Dagan emphasized his point by punching a clenched fist into the palm of his other hand.

His words could only have held his listeners in thrall, even though what he said may also have sent a shudder through some of them. Others in the canteen had killed enemies of Israel who could not be brought to trial because they were protected deep within the boundaries of Arab neighbors.

Underpinning Dagan's words was a clear guarantee that from now on he would sanction any operation against those who would "eat their brains." In turn, he would protect Mossad with every means he knew—legal or illegal. That meant he would effectively allow his agents to use proscribed nerve toxins, dumdum bullets, and methods of killing that even the mafia, the former KGB, or China's secret service rarely used. But he was also implicitly reminding them that he would not hesitate to expose them to torture and certain death at the hands of their enemies. No wonder he held them in thrall.

Some of them who had recently graduated from the training school might well have remembered the words long ago articulated by Meir Amit, and which formed part of the schooling lectures on assassination: "Mossad is like the official hangman or the doctor on Death Row who administers the lethal injection. Your actions are all endorsed by the State of Israel. When you kill, you are not breaking the law. You are fulfilling a sentence sanctioned by the prime minister of the day."

Once more Dagan spoke. "I am here to tell you that the old days are back. The dice are ready to roll."

Then he told them about himself. How he was born on a train between Russia and Poland. That he spoke several languages. That he operated on the premise that action could not wait for certainty. He finished with a final punch of his fist into his palm.

It had been a bravura performance. As he jumped down from the table and walked from the canteen, applause followed him all the way to the door.

The time swiftly came when Meir Dagan would show what he meant by eating their enemies' brains. In Mombasa in East Africa, an explosive-laden land cruiser had driven into the reception area of the island's Israeli-owned Paradise Hotel in October 2002. Fifteen people were killed and eighty seriously injured. At almost the same time, two shoulder-fired missiles had nearly downed an Israeli passenger plane bringing tourists back to Tel Aviv from Kenya. Two hundred seventy-five people on board had barely missed a Lockerbie-style death.

Meir Dagan immediately decided that the attacks had been the work of al-Qaeda and that the missiles had come from Iraq's arsenal. Confirmation of this had come from his own deep-cover agents in Baghdad and from the CIA and MI6.

Within hours, Dagan had assembled a team to go to Mombasa. All had local language skills. They could pass for Arabs or for Asian traders on the island. His men not only dressed the part, they looked the part. Their prime task in Mombasa was to find and kill the men behind the three suicide bombers, who had gone to their deaths laughing as they plunged their vehicle into the hotel.

The team would carry a small laboratory of poisons, sealed in vials until the moment came to strike. They had long- and short-bladed knives. Piano wire to strangle. Explosives no bigger than a throat lozenge capable of blowing off a person's head. They would take an arsenal of guns: short-barreled pistols, sniper rifles with a killing range of a mile. Each agent carried several passports to enable him to cross borders in different guises.

And so they flew south in their own plane to Mombasa. Mossad agents from Lagos, Nigeria—from where Israel gets the bulk of its oil—were there to support the team from Tel Aviv. Other *katsas* from South Africa, Rome, Malta, and Cyprus had sped through Africa into the fierce heat of Mombasa.

Dagan's men were polite to officers from the CIA, MI6, and other European services, and paid lip service to the atrocity's having been committed within Kenya's jurisdiction. But for the team, the dead and injured were Israelis. That made it their job.

In Tel Aviv, Dagan waited. He knew his operatives had melted into the region's multiethnic population.

To this day, no one knows for certain what success the Mossad team had. But sources in a number of other intelligence services say it did kill several suspected terrorists and dumped their bodies in crocodile-infested swamps. If so, that would fit into Mossad's way of doing things. The reality of their world is a different one from that of others.

And while his agents carried out their ruthless safari against al-Qaeda, Meir Dagan was immersing himself in the struggle against another, equally fearsome enemy: the suicide bombers who continued to terrorize Israel in the closing weeks of 2002.

The first suicide bomber had struck in Israel on a warm spring day in April 1993. Others soon followed, killing hundreds and wounding thousands. Men, women, and children had died on buses, in shopping malls and cafés, and on the way to school. Each death had one common purpose: to wreck any hope of bringing peace to the region. Most of the bombers had come from a terrorist group known as the Al Aqsa Martyrs' Brigade. For Israelis, it was more feared than Hezbollah and Hamas.

Each potential bomber was recommended to the Martyrs Jihad Committee. So far the combined resources of Israel's intelligence community had failed to locate its members. All that was known was that they communicated important decisions through handwritten notes.

Long before a candidate was approached, careful checks were made into the family background. A critical decision in the selection process was the religious standing of any bomber. The imam, the prayer leader of the mosque where a candidate worshiped, was consulted on how well the person knew the Koran, how regular was his attendance at Friday prayers. There were other preconditions before a person was accepted for martyrdom. No bomber was selected who was the sole wage earner in the family; if two brothers volunteered, only one was chosen.

Having passed those basic requirements, a candidate was invited to meet the Martyrs Jihad Committee. These meetings were often held in public places, like crowded cafés, to reduce the risk of electronic surveillance.

The first meeting focused on a candidate's religious knowledge. Next he was questioned about his political commitment. If his answers were satisfactory, he was placed on the list of suicide bombers. No one knew its size. But it was believed to number hundreds.

Meir Dagan had found the details in Mossad files. But he wanted to know more. And so, in every spare moment, he had dug deeper into the close world of the bombers and the men who prepared them.

The preparations for martyrdom were conducted in a mosque, usually in a back room away from prying eyes. The iman was assisted by a member of the Martyrs' Jihad Committee. They spent up to eight hours a day with a candidate, the time divided between silent prayer and reading portions aloud from the Koran.

An important task at this stage was to give the candidate repeated assurances, that on the Day of Judgment, he or she—for women were eligible to become bombers—would be allowed, upon entering paradise, to choose seventy relatives to also enter; that in heaven a male bomber would have at his disposal seventy-two houris, the celestial virgins who are reputed in Islamic folklore to live there.

These promises were interspersed with checks to see that a bomber's belief in martyrdom never wavered. The imam and his assistant repeated time and again the same exhortation. "You die to achieve Allah's satisfaction. You have been chosen by Allah because he has seen in you all that is good."

The first sign to a bomber that he was about to go to his death came when he was joined by two "advisers" who replaced the assistant. Older men, steeped in Islamic extreme dogma, their task was to ensure that a bomber did not waver in his readiness to die. They focused on the "glory" waiting in paradise of being finally in the presence of Allah, of being allowed to meet the prophet Muhammad.

As the time grew closer to a mission, the bomber was moved to a specially prepared room. Its walls were inscribed with verses from the Koran. Between the verses were painted green birds flying in a purple sky, a reminder that they carry the souls of martyrs to Allah. The indoctrination became more focused. The bomber was told paradise was very close. When the time came, all he must do was press the detonator button to enter the promised world.

For hours the advisers and the human bomb continued to pray and fast together. In between, the practical side of his departure to paradise was taken care of. All of the bomber's earthly debts were settled by the Martyrs' Jihad Committee. He was told his family would become honored members of their community.

There were constant checks to ensure that the bomber showed no signs of fear. Reassured, the advisers then conferred on him the title *al shaheed al hayy*, the living martyr.

In the final stages, the bomber placed a copy of the Koran inside his clothes. Over it went the body suit. A wire to the detonator button was taped to the palm of his right hand.

The advisers escorted the bomber close to the target area. They bade farewell with the promise given to all human bombs: "Allah is with you. Allah will give you success so that he can receive you in paradise."

Later, as the bomber pressed the button, he cried out, *"Allah akbar."* Allah is great. All praise to Allah.

Almost certainly these were the last earthly words Wafa'a Ali Idris spoke.

Meir Dagan had made a close study of the young woman who had chosen to die. She was assured of her place in the pantheon of Islamic martyrdom. She was the first woman suicide bomber to launch herself against unsuspecting Israelis, doing so on a fine spring morning in 2002—the kind of morning that Israelis liked to remind themselves was why they called this troubled land the Promised Land.

On that Sunday morning Wafa'a was close to her thirty-second birthday. Her proudest gift was a signed, framed photo of Yasser Arafat, personally given to her by the chairman of the PLO. She had been a member of his Fatah organization since, as a teenager, she threw her first stones against Israeli soldiers on the West Bank.

At eighteen, she had married a distant cousin who was a blacksmith. Ten years later his mother forced the couple to divorce because Wafa'a had been unable to produce a child.

She joined the Red Crescent Society after the divorce, working as a paramedic for Islam's equivalent of the Red Cross.

"She was in the thick of the fighting. She would help the injured and often carry the badly wounded and dying children," her mother later said with pride. "At the end of a long day in the front line, my daughter would cry in my arms as she recalled the terrible things she witnessed."

Wafa'a's circle of friends started to change. In the back street cafés she sipped coffee with members of Hamas, founded in 1987 during the first Intifada, in which she had participated. She listened to their plans to create an Islamic state. She also began to mix with Hezbollah, an equally extreme group. They filled her mind with more fanaticism.

Israel's Shin Bet—its internal security force—later established that she became involved with Palestinian Islamic Jihad. It was another step into the world of ruthless militancy that now permeated her life. During the month of Ramadan, 2001, she met a recruiter for the Al Aqsa Martyrs' Brigade.

Her mother said, "Wafa'a had finally found what she wanted. A chance to show she was a true daughter of Palestine."

Now, on that Sunday, five months after she had been accepted by the Al Aqsa Martyrs' Brigade, she was ready to die for them.

On the night before, while the streets of Ramallah were filled with young discogoers, an elderly woman delivered a packet to the house where Wafa'a lived with her widowed mother. The packet contained a new bra and panties, along with a customized body suit. It was designed to conceal up to three kilos of high explosives and specially sharpened nails and razor fragments. The suit was designed to fit under Wafa'a's street clothes. It had several pockets deep enough to take sticks of explosives. They would be distributed around her upper torso. Other pockets around her waist were for the nails and razor fragments. There was a separate pouch that extended over the genital area. Later Dr. Ariel Merari, a ranking expert at Tel Aviv University on the techniques of suicide bombers, suggested the pouch was created "because the Israeli security forces never search Arab women in that area of their body."

Wafa'a had never met the person who made the suit. He was said to come from Jenin, the Arab city that would later be destroyed by Israeli forces. To Mossad the man was known as "the Tailor of Death." The intelligence service eventually established that he was a highly skilled craftsman who used a treble stitch to sew the suit. It was made from a cloth sold in Arab shops for making undershirts. The sewing cotton came from a similar source. Mossad technicians decided the tailor probably used an old-fashioned hand-operated Singer sewing machine. Later it would emerge that Wafa'a's suit, like all those worn by male suicide bombers, had been designed so that the distribution of explosives was carefully balanced, and the explosive effect would cover the widest possible area.

Wafa'a may also have received advice on the choice of outer clothing. "We know that some male suicide bombers have worn wigs and been well dressed. This has helped them to gain access to upmarket cafés and restaurants, which have been among their targets," Dr. Merari has said. Wafa'a's mother later recalled that her daughter had laid out her body suit and clean underwear on her bed early on that Sunday morning. Then she had chosen her finest hipster jeans and a loose-fitting blouse to conceal her body suit.

She had been joined by her spiritual adviser—a male member of the Martyrs. They had prayed together. Then he had recited passages from the Koran. He had handed her a copy of the Koran, which she tucked into her back trouser pocket.

To prepare a candidate for death, contacts with the family were reduced to a minimum. This was to reduce any hesitation over severing earthly ties. He or she was constantly reminded of the new life ahead. Only when a candidate was on the eve of martyrdom was time with his or her family allowed. In part this was to test whether or not he or she would weaken in his or her resolve.

Wafa'a, for example, spent her last two days with her mother. Only when she had taken delivery of her underclothes and body suit did she let her mother know what was going to happen. "We prayed together. For Palestine. For my daughter's safe journey to a better world," Wasfiya Ali Idris would recall.

Wasfiya is herself a woman who sees life through the prism of Islamic extremism. Her reading is confined to the Koran, her hero is Yasser Arafat. Her dream was that her daughter was going to her death to help create a Palestinian homeland.

In some respects Wafa'a Ali Idris did not quite fit the profile of a *shaheed*, a Martyr. Until she had been enrolled by the Martyrs, she had not shown any strong religious feelings. "After time with the Martyrs she became a devout follower of all that I had taught her as a child. There was not a day when she did not study the Koran," said Wasfiya.

Her anger against Israel also became a living vibrant force that sustained her during her work as a paramedic. In the year before her death, she had been injured three times by Israeli soldiers as she had tended to Arabs wounded on the streets of Ramallah. Her mother would remember. "At that time my daughter was getting more and more angry. All she was doing was trying to save lives. But the soldiers did not care. Then one day she said to me, 'Mother, I have joined the Martyrs. It is the only way I can serve my people. All those who have died have to be avenged!' I understood her feelings."

To grasp the power of martyrdom for such people, you need go no further than the Ramallah mosque where one of the imams explained (to the author): "First you must understand the meaning of the spirit. It draws us upward while the power of material things tries to hold us back. But when you are filled with a true desire to be a martyr, the material influence recedes. Only if you are a true believer will you begin to understand that. To all nonbelievers it is impossible to comprehend. But for those who have chosen to die, they know they are close to eternity. They have no doubts of the wonderful world that awaits them. Each and every one understands the legitimacy of what they are about to do. They have each made an oath on the Koran to carry out their noble action. It is the oath of jihad. We call it *bayt al ridwan*, named after the Garden of Paradise for the true prophets."

In Ramallah suicide bombers are heroes. There are posters for the "Martyr of the Month." They are celebrated in song and verse. They are remembered in Friday prayers in every mosque in the West Bank and Gaza City.

Sheikh Ahmed Yassin, the spiritual leader of Hamas, said: "Love of martyrdom is something deep inside the heart. But these rewards are not in themselves the goal of the martyr. The only aim of the true believer is to win Allah's satisfaction. That can be done in the simplest and speediest manner by dying in the cause of Allah. And never forget it is Allah who selects the martyrs."

In March 2004, the sheikh was assassinated by an Israeli gunship as he left a mosque in Gaza City. His sermon had contained a familiar refrain: the need for more young men and women to sacrifice themselves.

There is no shortage of volunteers to follow Wafa'a Ali Idris.

Shortly after noon on that Sunday in March 2002, she blew herself up in a crowded Jerusalem street. She killed an eighty-one-year-old man and injured more than one hundred other men, women, and children.

The explosives blew off her head and one arm and left a gaping hole in her abdomen. An hour later the radios in Ramallah proclaimed her to be "a true heroine of our people."

Wafa'a had been manipulated in the name of religious extremism by the dark and dangerous world of Islamic fanaticism, which would ultimately lead to the attacks on the World Trade Center and the Pentagon, and all the other suicide bomber attacks across the Middle East, in Pakistan, and in the Philippines.

Since Wafa'a died, more young women have experienced similar fates. Between them they have killed or injured close to 250 more Israelis.

Their actions are described as "sacred explosions." The act of suicide is forbidden in Islam. But the spin doctors of the Martyrs are well versed in the black art of propaganda.

For families who have allowed their children to be sacrificed, the financial rewards are good. Each family receives a pension for life. While it varies, it is said to be a minimum of twice the income they received before their son or daughter died.

The money comes from Iran. It is laundered through the central banks from Damascus to Athens. From there it is electronically transferred to an account in Cairo. Then it is couriered to Gaza City for distribution by the Jihad Committee.

Meir Dagan made it a priority to trace the final destination of the money in the hope it could lead Mossad to the men who prepared the bombers. But it was a daunting task. The Martyrs operate on a small-cell basis. Often there are no more than two or three persons in a cell. In the closed world of the refugee camps, informers for Israeli intelligence are hard to recruit. Those discovered are executed. For them death can be agonizingly slow, preceded by unspeakable torture. For their families there is the odium of having bred a traitor to Islamic extremism.

But for the suicide bomber there was only glory. In the world they inhabited there was little enough of that. For them death was perhaps all too often a welcome relief.

After Wafa'a died, a leaflet with her photo was circulated throughout the West Bank. It read "We do not have tanks or rockets. But we have something superior—our Islamic human bombs. In place of a nuclear arsenal we are proud of our arsenal of believers."

The one certainty is that other young men and women will blow themselves—and many others—into eternity. Meir Dagan knew that the further Israel was from the last suicide bomber, the nearer it was to the next.

That was the fearful reality of life and death in the Holy Land.

CHAPTER 19

AFTER SADDAM

By January 2003, five months after he had walked from the Mossad headquarters canteen to thunderous applause, Meir Dagan had become a hero to his staff and a man feared by Israel's enemies. Even the most bitter of them acknowledged that Mossad was once more the most effective and ruthless spy service in the Middle East, and beyond. Dagan knew more about the secrets of Arab security services than did the Arab political rulers. Indeed, he had placed new agents in the private offices of senior government officials in Syria, Egypt, Lebanon, and the United Arab Emirates. Under his watchful eye, Mossad had infiltrated with new vigor all sectors of Arab political life, its business communities, and other areas of Muslim society.

In the past four months since taking command, he had studied the sins and mistakes that had led to a collapse of morale in Mossad. He had rectified this by ensuring that those who were responsible were culled from the ranks of Mossad. Replacements had been brought in from the army; some were also recruited from Shin Bet and Israel's other intelligence services. Dagan made it clear that he had chosen them because they would follow his rules—not the rule book. For their part, they had shown they would serve him purely out of the conviction that he was the man they wished to follow.

He worked eighteen-hour days, and longer, at his desk. He sometimes slept on his couch. Life was hard. He came and went like the proverbial thief in the night. He went to Mombasa and places beyond to follow the trail of Osama bin Laden and al-Qaeda. Other intelligence chiefs would not have left their office. But that was not his style. He had always led, from the front.

Dagan had created a plan that he felt would reduce the threat from suicide bombers. Israel should reduce the stranglehold on Yasser Arafat and ease the blockade on the West Bank and the Gaza Strip—after a firm guarantee from the Palestinian authorities that they would deal with the bombers. The plan had gone to the Sharon cabinet, which had rejected it unless Arafat was removed.

Dagan had bided his time. He well understood that the relationship between Ariel Sharon and Arafat was one of personal hatred: there would be no resolution until Arafat was removed. Dagan's intelligence acumen suggested that this might well come from within Palestine. One of his tasks since coming to office had been to foment dissatisfaction among its more susceptible groups, promoting the idea that Arafat was the one remaining obstacle on the road to peace. Propaganda, in all its guises, was a weapon Dagan had used in his days as a military commander.

Mossad's Department of Psychological Warfare, the LAP, had created a mythical "Academy of Terrorism" in Gaza City, where suicide bombers were trained. The story received wide coverage. Many other stories followed that piece of propaganda, and their results were often included in the Overnight Intelligence Summary delivered to Ariel Sharon when he awoke. Dictated by Dagan, the summary shaped the thinking of Sharon for his coming day.

Both men still shared a close relationship and the same ideal for Israel: to ensure that, in Sharon's words, "this little patch of soil, barren and inhospitable, until we Jews turned it into the powerhouse of the region, will never be taken from us."

Over dinner in his home shortly after Dagan had been appointed, the prime minister had shown him a black painted arrowhead in a showcase. It represented the code name—Hetz Shabor—Sharon had chosen for his attack against the Egyptian army in Gaza in the Six-Day War. It had been the start of his career as the most ruthless military commander since Moshe Dayan. Then had come the massacre in the two Lebanon refugee camps in which allegedly up to one thousand men, women, and children had been slaughtered on September 17, 1982 while Sharon's troops did not intervene. Sharon's career seemed to have ground to a halt. But he had entered the political arena and outsmarted Benjamin Netanyahu—no mean feat—to take charge of the Likud Party. It had been a stepping-stone to the premiership he now held.

Over that dinner, Sharon had told Dagan he had chosen him to head Mossad because they both were fearless, hard-driving leaders.

But there was one difference: Sharon was a gambler, ready to take risks, like his visit to the Temple Mount in Jerusalem, which had triggered the Second Intifada and paved the way for the suicide bombers to gain strength. Dagan was not a gambler. He calculated every move.

Weeks into the job, Dagan had taken an El Al flight to London to meet Britain's two intelligence chiefs, Richard Billing Dearlove, head of MI6, the secret intelligence service, and Eliza Manningham-Buller, the director of MI5.

He had studied their backgrounds as thoroughly as when dealing with an enemy. While both the intelligence chiefs were most certainly not that, they did cause him concern. Britain had for years been a hotbed of Islamic terrorism. Both Richard Reid, the so-called shoe bomber who had attempted to destroy an American airliner with explosives packed in his shoes, and Zacharias Moussaoui, identified as the twentieth hijacker of the September 11 attacks, were recruited for their missions in London mosques.

The capital had become the headquarters for extremist Islamic preachers who, through a network of organizations, were dedicated to sowing pure hatred: hatred of Israel, hatred of America, hatred of the

West—hatred of all democracies that valued tolerance and freedom, the very ideal that gave the extremists freedom to operate in Britain.

Despite protests, Britain had continued to give refuge to Islamic fundamentalists wanted for terrorism in other countries. The governments of France, Algeria, Egypt, Jordan, and Saudi Arabia, as well as the United States, had all challenged Britain's refusal to extradite the terrorists. But the British had successfully claimed that to remove them from British protection would result in their "political persecution."

The Islamic preachers who had inducted these individuals into terrorism had hired expensive lawyers to fight extradition. Legal maneuvers had tied up cases for years. Khalid al-Fawwaz, wanted in the United States for his role in the bombing of the U.S. embassy in Nairobi, had successfully used the English courts to ensure that he stayed in the country. His legal costs of sixty thousand dollars had been met out of public funds.

Dressed in one of his custom-tailored black pinstriped suits, a hand-stitched white shirt, and a striped club tie, Dearlove had sat in his office overlooking the Thames River while Meir Dagan set out his case for why the presence of terrorists in Britain must stop.

The Mossad chief knew exactly the right tone to strike with one of the grandees of the intelligence world, commanding a staff of 2,000—of whom 175 were field intelligence officers, spies. Dearlove had a salary of £150,000 a year, many times greater than Dagan earned. The head of MI6 also had enviable perks: a car with an armed driver, and membership in several exclusive London clubs.

Dagan did not begrudge him any of this. He knew Dearlove had earned his perks.

After graduating from Cambridge, Dearlove joined MI6 in 1964. Four years later he was working undercover in Nairobi. From the Kenyan capital he often traveled to South Africa, making contacts with BOSS, then the South African security service. In 1973 he was posted to Prague as deputy head of the MI6 station. In that position he ran an operation to penetrate the Warsaw Pact. Under his guidance several senior pact spies defected to the West.

After a stint in Paris he was posted to Geneva; his cover was that he was a diplomat attached to the United Nations. There he made his first serious contacts with Arab intelligence officers from Iraq, Syria, and Iran.

A year later he turned up in Washington as a senior liaison officer for MI6 with the U.S. intelligence community. In the spring of 1992 he was back in London, charged with the task of supervising MI6's move from its crumbling headquarters in Century House in the run-down suburb of Lambeth to its postmodern £236 million structure in Vauxhall Cross. It is said that by the time the building was opened, Dearlove had personally checked out every room, tested the menus in the canteen, and slept in the beds in the basement dormitory used by staff during a crisis.

His trips to Washington were frequent. He had astonished his counterpart at the CIA, George Tenet, by making it clear that he no longer saw the hunt for Osama bin Laden as a top priority for MI6. Privately Dearlove had been heard to say that "capturing bin Laden, dead or alive, is very much Bush seeking a headline."

Dagan had warmed to Dearlove when the latter said he was no devotee of the American faith in "Sigint"—satellite signals intelligence. He believed spies on the ground were more valuable and trustworthy, that with human intelligence "you get what they see at close up, not from outer space." In a world of encrypted e-mail messages and superenhanced satellite imagery, Dagan found something endearing in that judgment. It mirrored his own views.

Dagan looked forward to his meeting with Eliza Manningham-Buller more than with any other spy chief. The director of MI5 was only the second woman to head the service. With her double chin and a booming laugh, which seemed to come from somewhere in her ample bosom, she was a striking figure.

At fifty-three, four years younger than Dagan, she also earned a salary far greater than he could ever hope to command; indeed, she earned more than her ultimate political master, Prime Minister Tony Blair.

Her crystal-shattering voice went with her upper-class pedigree. She was the daughter of a former lord chancellor of England; one of her two sisters was married to a former deputy keeper of the privy purse to the Queen.

She had attended Oxford, where she'd been known as "Bullying Manner" for her intimidating ways. In 1968, the university's Dramatic

Society pantomime program for *Cinderella* listed "The Honourable Eliza Manningham-Buller" as the Fairy Godmother. Wearing a head-dress of flowers and with her bushy eyebrows trimmed, she came on-stage in a puff of smoke. She twirled and, to a startled Cinderella—and audience—she boomed: "We thought you would be surprised. But have no fear. I am your Fairy Godmother, my dear."

That night an MI5 recruiter—an Oxford don—suggested that Eliza should give up any plans to take up acting and join MI5. She listened carefully, then consulted her father. He said spying was no career for a lady.

Eliza promptly joined MI5 as a transcription typist of tapped tele-phone conversations, mostly those of Soviet Bloc diplomats in London. But soon she displayed a talent for making sense of their guarded talk. She became a counterintelligence officer—a spy catcher.

"Bullying Manner" became "Formidable Manner." She rose rapidly through the structured MI5 hierarchy.

Taller than most of her colleagues, she had an imperious way of looking down her Roman empress nose when someone annoyed her. Rebuke delivered, she strode off down one of the cheerless corridors of MI5 "like a man o'war in full sail," one colleague said. She had worked in Washington, and in those other postings where the streets have no names. She headed the MI5 team that investigated the Lockerbie di-saster and spearheaded MI5's undercover war against the IRA.

In 1997 she became deputy director general of the service. Three years later, she ran MI5.

For both his hosts, Meir Dagan had the same uncompromising mes-sage: London had become a paradise for terrorists, a city that allowed a terrorist to live in a democracy and be able to destroy what the word meant. Because their prime target was still Israel, this had to stop. Da-gan said it politely. But he said it firmly.

He understood, he added, the difficulty Britain faced. It was home to 1.8 million Muslims, the great majority of whom were law-abiding, peaceful citizens. He knew Britain had strong trading ties with Arab nations. But he also understood that extreme Islamic groups had been able to operate deep within the closed Muslim community of Britain. He was ready to put Mossad at the disposal of MI5 and MI6. For that to work he would require permission to increase the number of his agents operating in Britain. Since 1987 the number had been curtailed, after the Thatcher government had complained about Mossad's methods.

Both Dearlove and Manningham-Buller swiftly agreed. Within days, the Mossad agents arrived in London. With them they brought a list of Muslim radicals they feared were preparing to strike at Israeli targets. The Mossad team made it clear that they would operate on their own. And they would deal with any threat to Israel as forcefully as they always had. They could make an assassination look like an accident—or let it serve as a warning to others by not bothering to hide what they had done.

And now, in January 2003, it was an assassination that Meir Dagan knew also preoccupied President George W. Bush and his aides. It was how best to kill Saddam Hussein.

As the drumbeat of impending war with Iraq beat ever louder in Washington, President George W. Bush let it be known to his closest advisers that he was prepared to lift the ban on the CIA assassinating Saddam Hussein. The restraint on the agency killing any leader had been in force since the CIA's inglorious bungling of its attempts to murder Cuba's leader, Fidel Castro, in the 1970s. The executive order was never officially waived, but on the first days of the new year, in the seasonal cold weather of the American capital, the neoconservatives who surrounded the president—men and women who for the most part had advised Bush's father when he had been president—exchanged toasts that Saddam could soon be dead.

Secretary of Defense Donald Rumsfeld argued that the United States had the legal right to assassinate anyone who had been involved "either directly or planning" the September 11 attacks. Saddam had, Rumsfeld claimed, "another strike" against him because he was stockpiling weapons of mass destruction (WMD). Though Secretary of State Colin Powell and CIA director George Tenet and his analysts insisted there was no firm evidence that Saddam was linked to the September attacks or that he had WMDs, Rumsfeld insisted his own sources told a different story.

Mossad's resident *katsa* at the Israeli embassy in Washington had discovered that Rumsfeld's main source was Ahmad Chalabi, who had helped to found the Iraqi National Congress, the self-styled "Iraqi government in waiting" to replace a deposed Saddam.

The floridly handsome Chalabi had been a Mossad informer in Iraq after Saddam seized power in 1979. Chalabi had moved to neighboring Jordan, where he set up the Petra Bank. For a while it had served as a conduit for Mossad to fund black operations in the Middle East. But in 1979 the bank collapsed, owing hundreds of millions of dollars to depositors.

Mossad had managed to withdraw its own modest deposits before the crash. Shortly afterward, the head of Jordan's central bank, Mohammed Said Nabulsi, had accused Chalabi of switching $70 million of the bank's funds into his own Swiss bank accounts.

Chalabi had arrived in Washington at the time George H. W. Bush had been elected as president. Until the first Iraqi war, following Saddam's invasion of Kuwait, Chalabi had seemed to be no more than another of those Middle East lobbyists, in a city filled with them, trying to promote their own interests. But the war changed all that. Using his imposing-sounding Iraqi National Congress, Chalabi found himself readily being welcomed by Bush's neoconservatives. They included future vice president Dick Cheney and future deputy defense secretary Paul Wolfowitz. Through them, he was introduced to Donald Rumsfeld. Common ground was established in their belief Saddam was a menace to peace not only in the Middle East, but possibly the entire world.

Incredibly, Chalabi began to see intelligence reports provided by the Pentagon on Saddam that had been prepared by the CIA and the National Security Agency. At first he confined himself to expressing that some of the intelligence did not fit what his small organization knew from inside Iraq. Gradually those expressions, often made directly to Rumsfeld, became more critical. Chalabi felt the CIA, in particular, was out of touch because it had no agents on the ground in Iraq.

In the late summer of 2002, in the run-up to the first anniversary of the attacks on the Twin Towers and the Pentagon, Rumsfeld ordered the formation of a special secret unit in the Pentagon to "reexamine" information provided by Chalabi and to "reassess" ties between Saddam and al-Qaeda and Iraq's development of WMD.

Ahmad Chalabi, a discredited banker accused of looting his own vaults, had become a prime source for Rumsfeld. CIA chief Tenet, a man who jealously guarded his turf, was furious—to the point that in August 2002 he had threatened to resign. Cheney had poured balm on very troubled waters, and Tenet had stayed in office. But using his own backdoor connections to MI6 director Richard Dearlove, Tenet had briefed the MI6 chief on Chalabi's continued involvement in the upper echelon of the Bush administration.

When he took over Mossad, Dagan had quickly picked up on Chalabi's bizarre role as Rumsfeld's source. From the Mossad file on the banker, it was clear that Chalabi had provided only low-grade intelligence when he had spied for them in Iraq. Now, over a decade since he had left Baghdad, it was unlikely the banker had any real connections within Saddam's regime.

Not for the first time Mossad analysts wondered how matters of importance were being conducted within the Bush administration.

Dagan's own trips to Washington, obligatory for any new director, had filled in the gaps in the reports from the *katsa* in the Israeli embassy in the capital. In meetings with members of the administration—men like Lewis Libby, Cheney's chief of staff, and Elliot Abrams, in charge of Middle East policy at the National Security Council—Dagan had encountered advocates of what they called "muscular democracy." They peppered their conversations with Arabic words like *jihad* and phrases like *Allah akbar wallilahi'l-hamd*. They knew what they meant: "holy war" and "Allah is great to whom we give praise." What baffled them, they told Dagan, was that they could not understand how God could endorse such a terrible massacre as had occurred on September 11.

Dagan was uncomfortable in religious discussion; his faith, like much else in his life, was a private matter. He had tactfully sidestepped the question. Nevertheless, he later told colleagues in Tel Aviv, he was fascinated by the way religion assumed such an importance in the Bush administration.

When President Bush returned to the White House four days after the attacks of September 11, he received a welcome visitor. The evangelist Billy Graham, a longtime friend of the Bush family, had sat with the understandably shaken president and spoken for a long time about the evil of terrorism and the Bible's "righteous wrath" to destroy it.

A scripture passage struck a chord with the president: "Thus saith the Lord. Because the Philistines have dealt by revenge, and have taken vengeance with a despiteful heart; therefore thus saith the Lord

God: Behold I will stretch out my hand upon the Philistines. And they shall know that I *am* the Lord, when I shall lay my vengeance upon them."

The words of the prophet Ezekiel became a leitmotif for George W. Bush, the rallying call for all he would say and do in the months to come for his "War on Terrorism": the justification for his attack on Afghanistan, for his forthcoming war against Iraq. The Iraqi dictator was *his* Philistine.

Ezekiel, that biblical man of iron, had infused Bush with a similar strength.

At the end of the meeting, Graham gave Bush a pocket-sized Bible. The evangelist had taken the time to annotate it, using a marker to highlight all the scripture passages that reinforced the right to use "righteous wrath."

Bush, like Bill Clinton and other past presidents, was not short of Bibles. He had grown up in what he liked to call "God-fearing country"—that great swath of the southern states known as the Bible Belt. No shack, house, or stately mansion is without its Bible. On the Bush Texas ranch, and in his office when he had been state governor, a Bible stood on a table close to the furled flag of the United States. Equipped with the Bible Billy Graham had presented to him, the president had no doubt that God was on his side as he launched his Global War on Terrorism.

The belief was an insight into his thinking. Another came with his admission he wanted bin Laden "dead or alive." Further evidence of his mind-set came when he spoke of "an axis of evil"—Iran, Iraq, and North Korea. The phrase had a strong biblical connotation.

Throughout 2002, for his speeches to Congress and his military commanders, in his folksy weekly radio talks to the nation, and in meetings with world leaders, Bush drew on passages in Graham's leather-bound gift to reinforce the notion that the War on Terrorism had the total approval of God. Holy war—the jihad of Islamic fundamentalism—had taken on a new meaning.

President Bush's insistence that he would conduct a preemptive strike against Iraq was also deeply rooted in the religious faith of the neoconservatives around him.

Against that background of increasing religious fervor, Mossad monitored Washington's progress to try to assassinate Saddam Hussein—a move that could head off an all-out war against Iraq.

In early February 2003, after a telephone conversation between Ariel Sharon and President Bush, Israel's prime minister told Dagan he had offered to allow Mossad to become directly involved in the assassination of Saddam. Bush had accepted.

In Tel Aviv, the operation planning followed a well-tried procedure. First, previous attempts to kill Saddam were examined to understand why they had failed. In the past ten years there had been fifteen separate attacks on the Iraqi leader. They had been sponsored by either Mossad or MI6. Their failure was due to inadequate planning, or enlisting Iraqi assassins who had either been discovered by Saddam's formidable security apparatus, or simply been unable to get close to their target.

Mossad had made one previous attempt itself, in November 1992. Its agents in Iraq had discovered that Saddam was planning to visit one of his several mistresses, who lived near Tikrit. The agents had learned that Saddam intended to arrive around dusk at the woman's home. Next day, he would visit a military base close by before flying back to Baghdad. In the estimated fifteen minutes between leaving the woman's villa and reaching the air base, Saddam could be vulnerable to attack.

Under the personal control of General Amiram Levine, at the time the deputy director of Mossad, the plan to kill Saddam was approved by Israel's then prime minister, Benjamin Netanyahu. Code-named Skah Atad, the assassination team trained for weeks in the Negev Desert.

Details of the operation offer an insight into the thoroughness of the planning. The Mossad kidon team would be supported by forty hand-picked members of Israel's Special Forces Unit 262—burned into Israel's memory as the one that in 1976 rescued the hostages from Entebbe airport in Uganda, where they were being held by terrorists who had hijacked their passenger plane.

Using two Hercules C-130 aircraft, the assassins would fly into Iraq below radar range. On the ground they would divide. The kidon would move to within two hundred meters of the route Saddam would travel from his mistress's villa to the air base. The main group would wait about six miles away, equipped with a special Mossad-developed radar-controlled missile, code-named Midras, Hebrew for "footstep."

The kidon team was to target Saddam and open fire on his car. At the same time one of the assassins was to signal the missile team to fire from the precise coordinates the kidon would provide—and destroy the vehicle.

But Ariel Sharon, then foreign minister, and Defense Minister Yitzhak Mordechai had ordered the operation canceled because the risks of failure were too high.

Now, almost a decade later, supported by Washington, there was no such hesitation in trying to kill Saddam.

Each morning as the creeping gray ended and another day began— the moment Saddam Hussein's mother had taught him was the "first dawn"—a truck drove to one of his palaces, in which the country's self-appointed president for life would have spent another secure night.

The truck contained live lobsters, fresh shrimps, and sides of fresh lamb and beef; all fat had been trimmed from the meat. There was a variety of yogurts and cheeses, and a special favorite of Saddam Hussein's, olives picked from Syria's Golan Heights. He liked to spit out the pips, "the way I will one day spit out the Israelis from their land," he once said to his former chief of intelligence, General Wafic Samarai.

Later, when he fell out of favor, the spymaster had fled for his life, walking for forty hours to escape through the north of Iraq into Turkey. Samarai was lucky. Most of those who crossed Saddam Hussein were killed by methods that surpassed the torture chambers of ancient times. Samarai's input to the plan to kill Saddam was fed into the Mossad computers.

While the sixty-five-year-old Saddam still slept, perhaps in the arms of another young girl selected by his Republican Guards to satisfy his voracious sexual needs, the truck was unloaded.

In each palace were stationed scientists from the country's nuclear arms program. They worked in a restricted area in the basement of a palace. Access to it was only through swipe cards, whose codes changed every day. In the basement was a suite housing a powerful hospital-style X-ray machine. The scientists X-rayed each item of food. They were looking for any sign of whether it had been poisoned or exposed to previous radiation.

When nothing suspicious was detected, the food passed on to further checks. Chefs took a small portion: a morsel of lobster or fish, a sliver of meat, a nibble of cheese, a small spoonful of yogurt. Food that needed cooking was prepared. Then all the items were tastefully arranged for the waiting tasters. They were selected from some of the untold legions of prisoners in Iraq's jails.

Watched by members of Al Himaya, Saddam's personal bodyguards, each prisoner swallowed and displayed his open mouth to the bodyguards. The tasters were then observed for an hour to ensure they had not been poisoned. Next they were taken to a lab to have blood drawn. This was tested to make sure there was no trace of radiation in what they had digested. The prisoners were then taken to a courtyard in the palace and shot—usually with a single bullet to the back of the head.

The gunshots were a signal for Saddam Hussein that his breakfast, and the other meals he would eat during the day, was safe to consume.

This chilling ritual was one of many that governed his life.

Whichever woman shared his bed overnight was dismissed. Her fate, like those of so many others forced to sleep with him, was a matter of conjecture. Alone, Saddam made his way to his private swimming pool. For him a number of laps was an important exercise to strengthen his spinal cord. Some years before he had undergone surgery for a slipped disk. He swam naked, watched only by his bodyguards. From them there were no secrets about his physical infirmities. He had a limp in public he would walk only a few steps before pausing. For a man so muscular in uniform, he had a belt of fatty tissue around his lower abdomen.

Swim over, there was another essential ritual to the start of his day. His barber, who traveled everywhere with him, arrived to trim Saddam's mustache and touch up the black dye in his hair. The chemicals used in the process came from Paris; each bottle had been tested to ensure it contained no lethal agent. His hair uniformly tinted to hide any trace of gray, his nails were then buffed and manicured with a colorless polish.

Then his personal dresser took over. Saddam's uniform was custommade, cut to emphasize the musculature of his body. His biceps and strong thighs were the result of those early teenage years when he went camel racing. His jacket was tailored to disguise the spreading waistline he had failed to halt despite periods of strict dieting.

These vanities were in a man who was irritated by the way his wife of forty years, Sajida, allowed her hennaed hair to be less than perfect and whose body was matronly.

His physical needs attended to, Saddam Hussein was ready for another day. No one could deny his capacity for work. A twelve- to fourteen-hour day of meetings was not unusual. At the end of each session he would take a small nap in a room adjoining the office. Thirty minutes later he could be back at the top of a conference table ready to plunge himself into a new round of discussions.

Each meeting began the same way. Saddam studied an executive summary of the reports that had been prepared. Sometimes he would ask to see the full report for closer examination. No one around the table knew which report would be chosen for scrutiny. If the summary did not match the full report, he would closely question the writers of both. He then displayed a harsh, inquisitorial manner. He was a natural bully.

Every few hours—wherever he was—his closest aides knew they must arrange for him to be near water: a fountain, an indoor waterfall, a flowing stream. Water is a symbol of wealth and power in the desert land of Iraq. In Saddam's personal milieu—his social relations, the customs and culture in which he was raised—water is a prerequisite. In all his personal offices—no one knows how many there were scattered around Baghdad and beyond—there was always the sound of cascading water on a background disc.

It was Saddam's obsession with personal violence that was the most terrifying side to his multifaceted personality. He had become obsessed with the dynamics of creating pain, spending countless hours reviewing the videos of those he had tortured and then executed. The methods of killing ranged from a victim being buried alive, to a specialty Saddam learned from the Taliban: a long nail was driven through a victim's ear into his brain. His torture chambers were reputed to contain effigies made of wood and iron in which a victim was confined. The hollow effigies contained spikes positioned so as to penetrate the victim's body. Strangulation and being buried alive in the desert were fates reserved for those for whom he had decided hanging was too quick.

Saddam's fixation with torture was passed on to his sons when they were still in their preteens. Uday and Qusay were both taken on weekly visits to witness torture and executions in Baghdad prisons.

Yet despite the carapace of evil that surrounded him, Saddam had also been known to weep openly after having condemned a friend, a relative, even his two sons-in-law to death. During the 1979 purge of the Baath Party that gave him power, he stood at the lectern and wept openly as he condemned party members. As each man was taken to his death, the conference hall echoed with his amplified sobbing, picked up by the microphones on the podium. It was a macabre piece of theater.

All these personality traits, and more, had been studied by Mossad before a plan of how to assassinate Saddam Hussein was prepared.

Once more the operation revolved around Saddam's insatiable sexual appetite. A Mossad *katsa* in Baghdad had learned that a new mistress—the wife of a general Saddam had recently had executed for disobeying an order—had been installed in a villa on the bank of the Euphrates River. Saddam had taken to swimming in the river with his bodyguards before visiting her.

The plan was based on one that the CIA had once used to try to kill Fidel Castro. On that occasion, seashells were rigged with explosives and deposited on the seabed off Cuba; the spot was one where Castro liked to go diving. That operation failed because the CIA had not taken into account that strong sea currents would carry the shells out of the area.

The river would present no such problem. The explosives were designed to be detonated by Saddam and his bodyguards surging through the water.

With days to go before the plan was to be implemented, the Baghdad *katsa* sent a coded short-burst transmission to Tel Aviv that the mistress had committed suicide.

Two days later, the second Iraqi war started. Mossad agents in Iraq's western desert, Baghdad, and Basra provided important intelligence that enabled U.S. and British aircraft to launch devastating air attacks. Thousands of Iraqis were killed or injured.

In the run-up to hostilities, Dagan had experienced a familiar pressure. Tenet had started to call several times a day to inquire whether Mossad was able to confirm that Iraq possessed WMD.

Dagan had replied the way he always did: Not yet, but we are still looking. Indeed, the search had become a priority for his deep-cover *katsas* in Iraq. They had worked independently of the United Nations weapons inspectors, who had had a similar lack of success—much to the barely concealed disappointment of President Bush and Prime Minister Tony Blair. The UN Security Council had become a forum for their frustration. Both leaders were now committed to the claim that they had to go to war to protect the world against WMD.

But in Tel Aviv, Mossad analysts told Dagan that no matter how the CIA and Britain's Joint Intelligence Committee (JIC) presented the evidence, there was no "smoking gun" proof that Saddam did have WMD. Nevertheless, Ariel Sharon, committed to Washington's claims, mobilized Israel's civilian population: gas masks were widely distributed; a warning of an impending chemical or biological attack was repeated over the radio. The precautions were widely reported in the United States and Britain, creating a mood that WMD were about to be launched. Propaganda fed fear, fear created more propaganda.

There was talk of a preemptive WMD strike against Israel; or Cyprus, where Britain had a sizable force; or the Persian Gulf, where the U.S. Navy had gathered in strength; or Kuwait, the launch point for the assault on Iraq. With every rumor the fear increased.

But nothing happened. Not a single rocket containing so much as one spore of a nerve agent or a drop of chemical poison was launched. In the history of warfare, there had never been such an anticlimax.

Twenty days after the war started the fighting was over. But another war, in many ways more deadly, had begun. Inside Iraq, a potent mixture of religious hatred, oil, and greed had started to ignite. In the south of the country, the Shias of the marsh Arabs began to lay their claim to be a powerful voice in planning Iraq's future. They had suffered much. Their demands, uttered from the minarets of their mosques, were reinforced by the mullahs of Tehran. They traveled to the Iraqi holy city of Najaf. The first of many confrontations with American forces took place. There was more bloodshed.

In the north of Iraq, the Kurds prepared to grab their moment of independence. That brought them ever closer to conflict with Turkey, which saw an independent Kurdish nation as unacceptable. In central Iraq, the other tribes wanted their views taken into account in the formation of a new Iraq. Saddam's once all-powerful Baath Party could not be ignored. Just as in postwar Germany it had turned out to be impossible to eradicate the Nazi Party completely from the country's bureaucracy, so it turned out to be with Baathism. The party was embedded into the very structure of what Iraq had been, was, and could become. It ran the police, the civil service, the utilities. To sack and arrest every party member was impossible; they were the only hope to get Iraq moving again.

Inevitably, Iraq had descended into lawlessness, which by May 2003 had turned out to be even more frightening than Saddam's reign of terror.

Meantime, the search for the tyrant had become a manhunt once more led by Mossad. Its analysts had created a scenario that owed something to Saddam's own liking for theatrical gesture.

The analysts suggested that Saddam had washed out the expensive black dye from his hair and shaved off his mustache, and was dressed as a peasant. His most likely way out of Baghdad had been through the vast, forbidding, empty spaces of Iraq's eastern desert; this was the ancient contraband route from Afghanistan that first the silk traders and then the drug dealers had used.

In those first postwar weeks, the route had become the favorite one for Iraqis who feared for their lives now that the regime had fallen.

Was Saddam really among them? No one knew. But the feeling grew that he was heading for the mountains of northern Iran. There were suggestions—never supported by real evidence—that from there he would disappear into the hands of two powerful friends he had counted on before, Russia and China. While both officially denied they would grant Saddam sanctuary, Moscow's and Beijing's records of support for Saddam were long. To have Saddam now in their hands would certainly ensure that he would never reveal all the details of the secret deals he had made with both.

To discover his whereabouts, Mossad agents were supported by American spy satellites. Their multicameras produced thousands of close-up images and scooped up even more separate conversations every minute from refugees across the sands. But there was still the old problem of analyzing and interpreting the data. The American intelligence community was still pitifully short of translators. But the hunt went on.

Then, in May 2003, Meir Dagan switched many of the *katsas* trying to track Saddam onto a more important threat for Israel. Despite the vigilance of Shin Bet, two British-born radical bombers had launched a suicide attack on a Tel Aviv club; three were killed and fifty injured. The explosive they used had overcome the most stringent of airport and airline security checks. It was more lethal than Semtex; it could be smuggled undetected from one country to another, from one terrorist cell to another. For the eighty terror groups listed on Mossad's computers, the weapon had once more tipped the scales in favor of the terrorists.

After a week of intensive investigation by chemists in Israel's center for weapons research in a suburb of Tel Aviv, its lethal qualities and country of origin had been discovered. The revelation sent a collective shock wave through the global intelligence community. The Israeli experts concluded that the explosive had been manufactured in the weapons research laboratories of ZDF, one of China's leading military defense contractors.

The first hint China was working on a new type of explosive had come in March 2001, when a top-ranking Chinese defector, Senior Colonel Xu Junping of the People's Liberation Army and one of the nation's leading military strategists, had defected to the United States, where he was personally questioned by CIA director George Tenet. So important was the debriefing that President Bush had authorized Condoleezza Rice to sit in.

Xu detailed the work that was being done to create the explosives in the ZDF laboratories situated some forty miles to the west of Beijing. He also revealed how China had secretly been helping rogue states like Iraq, Iran, and North Korea. Most critical of all, he outlined China's contacts with terror groups through its powerful intelligence services, the Military Intelligence Department (MID) and its Science and Technology Department (STD). Employing some five thousand field agents and defense analysts, both agencies operate globally. They are supported by satellite surveillance and state-of-the-art equipment. Xu told the CIA that part of the work of the two services was to maintain contact with terror groups not only in the Middle East, but also in the Philippines, Cambodia, and Sri Lanka. But what astonished the CIA was Xu's revelations of Chinese intelligence contacts in Colombia with FARC, in Spain with ETA, and in Peru with Shining Path.

Now, two years after Xu's revelation, intelligence services were bracing themselves to confront this latest weapon of choice for terrorists.

Mossad established that the two British suicide bombers had smuggled their explosive in from Jordan. It had arrived there from Pakistan, whose intelligence service has had long and close links to China's.

Mossad agents already knew that in the months before the attacks on the Twin Towers and the Pentagon, it was from Pakistan that Osama bin Laden made three separate visits to Beijing. Each time he was accompanied by China's ambassador to that country and the head of Pakistan's powerful intelligence service, ISI.

He had gone to organize a defense contract for the Taliban worth $1 billion.

"We now believe that during those visits he was apprised of the progress with the new explosives," a senior Mossad source in Tel Aviv told the author. He agreed that there "is a very strong possibility" al-Qaeda had been provided with a quantity of the explosive—a tiny portion of which had been given to the two British suicide bombers. This took terrorism into a new dimension.

It was a judgment that was never far from Dagan's thoughts as he continued to lead Mossad into the new millennium.

The failure to locate Saddam or discover if he was dead had irritated Ariel Sharon, Tony Blair, and George W. Bush. On the surface, they said it did not matter, that Saddam was no longer a threat. But few believed that Bush, in particular, would want to write closure to the war until he was able to announce that his much vaunted need for a regime change in Iraq had been completed with the actual death of Saddam.

But soon it was not the disappearance of a tyrant that came to haunt George Bush and Tony Blair. It was the failure to locate any WMD. Bush ordered in hundreds of CIA agents and scientists to find WMD. They searched and they searched. In London, Tony Blair insisted the weapons were there, that he had been told of eight hundred sites that had still not been checked in the deserts of Iraq.

Increasingly, however, the truth seemed otherwise. Britain's former foreign secretary Robin Cook, who had resigned over the war, and Claire Short, a former cabinet minister in the Blair government, both said Blair had lied to Parliament and to the people of Britain when he said that WMD existed.

By June 2003, Blair was fighting for his credibility and his political future. In Washington, Congress announced there would be a public hearing into the matter. Nobody seriously believed all the truth would finally emerge. But for the moment, there was talk of a scandal that could balloon into another Watergate. Commentators remembered that Bush's own father had won the first Iraqi war, but lost the presidency to Bill Clinton shortly afterward.

In Tel Aviv, Meir Dagan kept Mossad clear of the deepening crises in London and Washington. When calls came from the CIA and MI6 for any assistance he could give, he stuck to the same story: Mossad would go on looking. No more, no less.

In December 2003, the hunt for Saddam finally ended. He was captured, ironically, because of the demands of the one woman he still trusted: Samira Shahbander, the second of his four wives.

On December 11, she had called Saddam from an Internet café in Baalbek, near Beirut; she and Saddam's only surviving son, Ali, had lived under assumed names in Lebanon after leaving Baghdad some months before the war started.

Samira, whose curly blond hair came from the same French hair product company that provided Saddam with his hair dye, was the married woman who first became his mistress and then his wife.

At the start of their courtship, Samira was married to an Iraqi air force pilot. Saddam simply kidnapped him and said he would be set free only if he agreed to divorce Samira. The husband agreed. In return, he was made head of Iraqi Airways—and given a choice from one of Saddam's cast-off mistresses.

Married, Samira became Saddam's favorite, though he took two more wives and scores of mistresses.

The marriage was cemented by the birth of Ali. The child's arrival deepened the hatred of Saddam's elder sons, Uday and Qusay, toward Samira. But by December, both were dead after a shoot-out with U.S. Special Forces.

Earlier, in March 2003, with the coalition forces closing in on Baghdad, Saddam had arranged for Samira and Ali to flee to Lebanon. With her she took $5 million in cash and a trunk of gold bars from the vaults of the Central Bank of Iraq.

She told friends she was going first to France and then to Moscow, claiming Saddam had been secretly promised by Vladimir Putin, Russia's president, that he would give her sanctuary. Instead, she went to a prearranged hideout, a villa in the Beirut suburbs.

It was there that Mossad discovered her in November 2003. Meir Dagan sent a team of surveillance specialists from the service's *yaholomin* unit to follow Samira's every move.

They discovered that the Lebanese government had provided her and Ali with Lebanese passports and new identities. Samira was given the name "Hadija." But Ali, who has the same deep-set eyes as his father, insisted he would keep the family name of Hussein.

The Mossad team noted that Samira had transferred most of her money out of Lebanon to a Credit Suisse bank account in Geneva. In the past, the bank had been a repository for some of Saddam's own fortune.

Early in December 2003, Samira cashed in her gold bars for U.S. dollars with a Beirut money dealer. Then she started to call Saddam.

Supported by Israeli air force surveillance aircraft, the *yaholomin* discovered that the calls were being made from inside Syria, which borders on Iraq. "The calls were affectionate. It was clear there was a close relationship still between them," said a high-ranking Mossad source in Tel Aviv after Saddam had been captured. That one of the most reviled tyrants in the world—a man who had personally ordered the terrible torture of many thousands, including women and children—could speak of love, both fascinated and repelled the Mossad team.

But along with endearments the listeners also heard, through their electronic equipment, that Samira wanted more money.

Time and again, in further calls in December—each made to a different number the *yaholomin* team pinpointed as going to an area in the desolate sands of the Wadi al-Myrah, which is close to the Syrian border with Iraq—Samira repeated her request for money.

The daughter of a wealthy, aristocratic Baghdad family, Samira had never lost her taste for the good life. During their marriage, Saddam had showered her with gifts, including two palaces.

The Israelis knew that across the border in Iraq, U.S. Special Forces were roaming up and down the border looking for Saddam. Other Israeli agents on the Syrian side of the border had heard radio chatter between the units—known as U.S. Combined Joint Special Operations Task Force 121—as they also set about trying to track down Saddam. The force comprised members of Delta Force, the U.S. Rangers, Britain's SAS and Special Boat Service, and the Australian SAS. "For political reasons, we had not been formally invited to join the party," a source close to Meir Dagan said to the author.

Mossad—not for the first time—decided to keep to itself the information it was gleaning from the surveillance of Samira.

Then, on Thursday, December 11, 2003, the *yaholomin* team picked up a conversation between Samira and the man they were now certain was Saddam. He told her he would meet her close to the Syrian border. Details of the meeting were enough to prompt the Israelis finally to alert Washington. As Samira prepared to drive to her assignation, she received a second call. The meeting had been canceled. The call did not come from Saddam.

By then, it later emerged, he was inside his eight-foot-deep hole on the outskirts of Tikrit, his birthplace in Iraq. Samira and Ali heard the news of his capture on the radio. She burst into tears. Ali's reaction is not known.

In Tel Aviv, Mossad analysts—like those of all the major intelligence services—were poring over the video footage that showed the likeness of Saddam the world had never seen before. And as part of their work, the Mossad analysts began to ask intriguing questions. Who were the two unidentified men armed with AK-47 rifles who stood guard over the hole? Were they there to protect Saddam—or kill him if he tried to escape? Why did Saddam not use his pistol to commit suicide—and become the martyr he had long boasted he would be? Was it cowardice that stopped him—or was he expecting to make a deal? Would he reveal the truth not only about weapons of mass destruction, but also about his deal with Russia and China, whose secret support had encouraged him to continue to confront the United States?

His hiding hole had only one opening. It was blocked. He could not have escaped from the hole. Was it in effect a prison? Was he being held there as part of a trade? What use was to be made of the $750,000 in $100 bills found on him? Was that intended for Samira? Or was it a payment for someone who would help him escape? Why did he have no communications equipment? Not even a cell phone was found on him. Did all this indicate that the remnants of his own followers had come to regard him as a spent force, and that they were ready to trade him in for their own freedom? That may explain why he was so talkative and cooperative when his captors dug him out, bringing to an end his thirty-five-year reign of terror in such a dramatic manner.

The answers to those questions formed part of the interrogation that Saddam Hussein was about to undergo.

Hours after he emerged from his hole, Saddam came under the combined scrutiny of U.S. and British intelligence service psychiatrists, psychologists, behavioral scientists, and psychoanalysts. They are known as "the specialists." They studied the video footage of Saddam's medical examination. The search inside his mouth was not only to obtain a DNA swab, but to see if Saddam had a suicide tablet secreted in a back tooth. None was found.

This, the specialists concluded, was further proof that Saddam was not a suicide risk. Nevertheless, he was dressed in a one-piece orange suit. It had fiber buttons that would dissolve if he tried to swallow them. The suit cloth was too strong for tearing to form a makeshift noose to hang himself. His feet were encased in soft fiber shoes that could not be broken.

His cell was constantly monitored by cameras and guards. His every move was noted and used to assess his ability to withstand the interrogation he now faced. In the esoteric language of the specialists, Saddam had not "allowed the loss of his personal boundary to effect his collective ego."

Saddam was no longer the man on the video showing his capture: then he had been bowed down with despair, suddenly aged beyond his sixty-six years, a haunted look in his eyes. The specialists concluded he then felt "stupid" at being caught. That would explain his "compulsive talking" to his soldier captors. It was to disguise his near-paralyzing fear at being dragged out of his hole. "He may well have expected to be shot on the spot," the specialists told the interrogators.

Subsequently, he had undergone a marked psychological shift. His arrogance returned. His eyes were no longer dull or his lips slack from confinement in his hole. There was a swagger about him. All this had helped his interrogators plan how to break him. His interrogation center was rocketproof and guarded by elite U.S. Special Forces. It had a medical facility with doctors constantly on duty.

In the hope of triggering some response, Tariq Aziz, the former deputy Iraqi prime minister, was taken to see Saddam. Aziz was in a prison camp outside Baghdad airport. He was flown by helicopter to confront

Saddam and urge him to talk. Instead, Saddam exploded, calling Aziz a traitor.

By the time interrogators began to question Saddam, his links with the outside world had been totally severed. He had no idea of time or date. There was no such thing as day or night in his world. The normal patterns of waking and sleeping and mealtimes were deliberately disrupted. There would be no physical torture. But he began to receive what was called "the full coercive treatment." The interrogators did not underestimate their challenge.

"Saddam presents a unique challenge. He is a man who saw himself as morally, spiritually, and intellectually superior to the Western world. Coercive treatment would include sitting for hours with a hood over his head to increase his isolation. All the time, the questions would be designed to increase anger in his mind about being betrayed. For someone like Saddam, betrayal would be hard to cope with. Being confronted with Tariq Aziz was part of that. The interrogators would have told Saddam that Aziz was looking out for number one. Saddam could do the same by revealing what he knew—which is a great deal," said Michael Koubi, the interrogator who for years Mossad had used.

"Nothing will rattle Saddam more than knowing facts he believed over years were no longer valid. It will assault his sense of importance and he will think more about lying because he could be caught out," Koubi said to the author. "Part of the interrogation will be to see how Saddam answers in his own language. In Arabic certain words can have very different meanings. If he chooses to use one that is not correct, his interrogators will show they know the right meaning," added Koubi.

After each interrogation—which could last for many hours, with the questions coming and going—Saddam would be assessed by the specialists. They were looking to see how he responded to certain questions. Was he lying? Covering up? Did those eye blinks caught on camera indicate sudden fear? Or was it arrogance or even indifference?

Koubi lives today in Ashkelon, near the Israeli-occupied Gaza Strip. He knew exactly how the interrogators and their support team of specialists were working on Saddam.

"The first thing the interrogators did was to establish their superiority over Saddam. To remove his belief in his self-control. At every stage, they were looking for his weak points. Those would include playing on Saddam's loss of power and the indifference to his family's fate. The interrogators would lie to him. They would force him to keep eye contact as they pressed their questions. When he would try to look away, as he was bound to do, they would continue to stare at him silently. Saddam would not be used to this. It would be unnerving for him to experience such treatment," said Koubi.

From time to time, the interrogators asked questions they knew Saddam could not answer. What was going on in Washington and London in the run-up to the Iraqi war? Where was he on a certain date? When he could not answer, he would be accused of covering up.

"After a while, a question will be slipped in that he can answer. If the interrogators have done their groundwork properly, he will be glad to answer it. Then the questions will move to other questions they want him to answer," said Koubi.

"Another means to break him would be to offer simple inducements. If Saddam answered a series of questions, he would be promised uninterrupted sleep. And possibly a change in his carefully monitored diet. But always the promises would not be quite kept. And followed by more promises that if he continued to cooperate, they would be fulfilled," explained Koubi.

In January 2004, he was visited by an International Red Cross team of doctors. They pronounced he was being fairly treated.

The deadly mind games would continue until the interrogators and specialists were satisfied that no more could be wrung out of Saddam Hussein. Then he would be left to his fate. More, he would know by then, he could not expect.

Meanwhile, Mossad had joined other intelligence services in the hunt for Saddam's missing fortune. By January 2004, Meir Dagan's team of financially trained agents, some of whom had worked in the City of London and Wall Street before joining the service, had established that the Queen of England's banker, Coutts of London, was one of eighteen British banks Saddam Hussein had used to hide his $40 billion fortune over the 1980s.

The bulk of that money was stolen by him from the central bank of Iraq, transferred to banks in the Middle East, and then deposited under false names in the London banks. Later, the money was transferred to banks in Switzerland, Germany, Japan, and Bulgaria.

"Any transfer coming from a London bank was assumed to be legitimate," said Christopher Story, a former financial adviser to British prime minister Margaret Thatcher at the time Saddam was salting away his fortune. Story, the quintessential English gentleman in his pin-striped Savile Row suits and customized shoes, is a recognized authority on the financial duplicity of the Iraqi leader, and his once close relationship with the major banks of the world. A clipped-voiced Englishman, Story edits a respected financial banking journal, the *International Currency Review*. Its subscribers include the World Bank, the U.S. Federal Reserve Bank, and the Bank of England.

Story has amassed documentation showing that Robert Maxwell, the disgraced tycoon who once owned the London *Daily Mirror* newspaper group, arranged for billions of dollars to be laundered through Bulgarian banks to the Bank of New York. It was then owned by Edmund Safra, known as "financier to the mafia." He died in a mysterious fire in his Monaco penthouse in 1999. Maxwell was killed by Mossad agents when he threatened to reveal Israel's intelligence secrets.

"If Saddam gives up all the names of those who helped him, it would cause panic greater than any Wall Street crash. Many still hold high office today. It is impossible that they did not know what was going on with Saddam. He was moving out huge sums of money right up until the eve of war," said Story.

Until now untold, the story of how Saddam Hussein began to amass one of the world's largest private fortunes began when a private jet took off from London to Baghdad in 1982. During the five-hour flight from London, its solitary passenger, financier Tiny Rowland, spooned beluga caviar into his mouth and sipped vintage Krug champagne. That was his regular diet on a business trip in his Learjet. The delicacies had been sent from Baghdad by Saddam Hussein.

This was no ordinary journey on that summer's day in 1982, even for the sixty-eight-year-old financier with a fearsome reputation as a predator in the City of London, on Wall Street, and on the stock markets of Europe. Sitting in his hand-tooled tan leather armchair on board his customized jet, feet resting on a $150-a-square-foot carpet, Roland W. Rowland—the name on his gold-embossed business cards—had indeed come a long way from where he had been born in 1917 in a British prison camp in India.

He was the son of a German trader called Fritz Fuhrop. His mother was the daughter of a pillar of the English Raj who had followed her husband into internment. Following their release after the end of World War I, Rowland's Indian nanny had called him "Tiny." Even though he would grow to be six feet tall, the nickname stuck. Now it was the only link with his past—those days when he had dug latrines for the British army in World War II and later was a porter at Paddington railway station in London.

Those humble beginnings had fed his determination to join the ranks of the rich and powerful. He sold secondhand cars and refrigerators in postwar London. By the time he was thirty, he was a millionaire. He began to trade in gold in South Africa. His fortune grew. He was hired to "sort out" an ailing company called the London and Rhodesia Mining and Land Corporation—Lonrho. Rowland made it the single most powerful trading company in all Africa. His deals in copper, tin, and other metals made him the darling of Lonrho stockholders.

They did not suspect how Rowland had paid off Lord Duncan Sandys, Winston Churchill's son-in-law. Using a secret account in the Cayman Islands, Rowland had given the peer $500,000 for helping to buy the largest gold mine in Ghana. When Duncan Sandys became mired in sexual scandal, the prudish Rowland cut him dead—refusing to send "even a bunch of flowers" to his funeral in 1987. No one, however rich and well connected, was allowed to implicate Tiny Rowland. He treasured his image as the quintessential Englishman. Only in the confines of a small circle of right-wing friends did he reveal his anti-Semitism and contempt for the way Britain was being run.

Already a multimillionaire, Tiny Rowland allowed his hatred for socialism to surface during the British crisis with Rhodesia (now Zimbabwe) over its determination to challenge the Wilson government over self-rule. Sanctions had been introduced against what Prime Minister Harold Wilson called "this pariah state." It later emerged that Rowland broke them. But by then Mrs. Thatcher was in Downing Street and the matter was not pursued.

Tiny looked for new fields to conquer. He bought the *Observer*, a London Sunday newspaper, and tried to use it to support his business interests in Africa. Next he enlisted the notorious Saudi arms dealer Adnan Khashoggi to broker a deal with Colonel Gadhafi to buy the Metropole hotel chain for $150 million.

Rowland's ability to use anybody to further his own interests had earlier led Britain's then prime minister Ted Heath to castigate him as the "unacceptable face of capitalism." Tiny Rowland shrugged that off in the same imperious way he dismissed other financiers who came to him with deals. He preferred to work alone, to share his profits with no one—except his Siamese cats. Every day he fed them the same fine caviar that he ate on his Learjet as it headed for Iraq on that June day in 1982. They had curled up at his feet as he worked at his desk preparing his greatest coup yet—hiding Saddam's fortune.

When Saddam came to power, his pro-West sympathies were welcomed in London and Washington. Their governments, along with those of France and Germany, saw the need to reinforce Iraq's infrastructure against the looming threat posed by Iran. Baghdad became a vast bazaar. Massive bribes to secure contracts were common. They were siphoned into Saddam's accounts. More money flowed there for his cut on deals to build superhighways, hospitals, and schools. If anybody suspected, nobody cared.

Saddam's relationship with Rowland stemmed from the breathtaking theft of the shah of Iran's personal fortune of $3 billion. In 1979, with the ayatollahs about to seize power in Iran, the shah's most trusted aides had held secret meetings with the director of the Central Bank of Iraq. Rowland had acted as the go-between, and on his advice, the shah agreed to transfer his fortune to Baghdad into the Iraqi central bank, beyond the reach of the ayatollahs. Rowland received a "handling fee" of 15 percent.

In a second deal that laid the foundation for Saddam's fortune, the Iraqi tyrant, then barely a year in power, transferred the money out of the central bank in Iraq to his own numbered accounts with Credit Suisse in Switzerland and a Cayman Island bank. Rowland arranged this, pocketing another handling fee. The deposed, and dying, shah ended up in Washington. He asked the U.S. government to help recover his stolen fortune. His plea fell on deaf ears. The road map in the Middle East had once more changed. Washington was openly backing Iraq against Iran.

All this, and more, the Mossad team had established as they hunted for Saddam's fortune in the winter of 2004.

I have spoken to intelligence officers in London, Washington, and Tel Aviv who have described other documents that reveal the extent of the secret network Rowland set up.

One Mossad document shows how Rowland used one of his London banks to provide a facility for Iraqi arms dealer Ibsan Barbouti to lodge $500 million of Saddam's money. From London, Barbouti helped Libya to build a chemical warfare plant. When he suddenly died—widely believed to be a victim of one of Saddam's hit men—the money was transferred from the London bank to the central bank of Libya.

Another document details how Saddam's son Uday went to Geneva in 1998 to "iron out some financial problems" with Swiss banks who were part of the money-laundering network Rowland had created.

On the eve of the second Iraqi war, accompanied by Iraq's finance minister Hikmat Misban al-Azzawi (who died in prison in 2012), Saddam's son Qusay went to Iraq's central bank with a handwritten letter from his father saying he was authorized to remove $1 billion from the vaults. The money was loaded onto a convoy of trucks. U.S. satellite photographs show the convoy heading for the Syrian border. Later, U.S. troops found $656 million in dollar bills stuffed inside 164 aluminum boxes on the grounds of one of Saddam's palaces, along with 100 million euros in an armored car.

By the spring of 2004, the search for Saddam's billions had become the greatest hunt since the post–World War II search for Nazi gold. Mossad, supported by MI6 and the CIA, deployed scores of agents and financial experts to try to discover the vast fortune Rowland's master plan had enabled Saddam to hide around the world.

A Mossad document, signed by Meir Dagan, names more than seventy banks as being included in Saddam's money-laundering trail that electronically sped out of Iraq to London, Europe, through Gibraltar, down to South Africa, across the Pacific to Hong Kong, on to Japan, up into Russia, and back down to the Balkans. But the searchers—spies, bankers, and brokers—trying to follow the trail found that Rowland's built-in safeguards stood the test of time.

"He used surrogates and cutouts, people in the international banking world. Banks in Eastern Europe which serviced the KGB and were used to not asking questions, were also used," confirmed a Mossad source.

In a memo prepared for the FBI shortly before he died in the World Trade Center attack in September 2001, John P. O'Neill, the FBI executive agent in charge in New York, wrote that Saddam's money "was almost certainly being laundered through international criminal corporations run by South American drug cartels and the Russian Mafia." The memo identified Edmund Safra, the billionaire banker who then owned the National Republic Bank in New York, as a "money laundering conduit for the funds."

Investigators had found that others who could have helped them follow along the money trail were also mysteriously dead. One was Janos Pasztor, a Wall Street analyst. He had worked for Rowland. He died on October 15, 2000, of a previously undiagnosed cancer. The week before, his doctor had given him a clean bill of health.

Another conduit through which Saddam's fortune flowed was the Bank of Credit and Commerce International (BCCI). Based in London, the now dissolved bank provided funds for terrorist groups Saddam already supported. It was closed down after City of London regulators discovered its activities.

MI5 has a fat file on another of the middlemen Rowland used. His name was Cyrus Hashemi. Ostensibly an Arab millionaire playboy who would spend $150,000 on the turn of a card at a Mayfair casino and give doormen Rolex watches for parking his Ferrari, Hashemi allowed his BCCI bank accounts to be used to send Saddam's money on down the money trail. The MI5 intelligence file on Hashemi also says that he was trying to broker a better deal for his services. On July 16, 1986, he suddenly collapsed at his Belgravia home and was rushed to a private clinic owned by BCCI. Two days later he was dead.

Scotland Yard's Serious Crimes Squad investigated. They called in forensic pathologist Dr. Ian West. He said, "Hashemi's death was one of the strangest I have investigated." West sent tissue samples to Porton Down, Britain's chemical and biological warfare establishment, for its scientists to decide if Hashemi had been poisoned. The result of their findings remains unknown to this day.

The location of Saddam's billions may also remain undiscovered in the foreseeable future.

In April 2004, the French lawyer Jacques Vergès announced he had been appointed by Saddam's family as lead counsel for his trial. Vergès became famous when he represented the former SS officer Klaus Barbie, who was convicted of "crimes against humanity" in 1987. After acting for the notorious terrorist Carlos the Jackal, now serving a life sentence in Paris, and advising the late Slobodan Milošević.

Vergès has said he expects Saddam's trial to last even longer. "I will present him as a vanquished hero." He plans to call President George W. Bush and his father, the former U.S. president, as witnesses, along with Britain's prime minister Tony Blair and other world leaders. "Arguing why they should appear should take at least a year," said

Vergès, in his seventy-eighth year when he took the case. One of the key elements of his defense will be to show "how very important people took their slice of the action for helping Saddam hide his money. They still hold high office. But not after I finish with them."

Only time will tell if that will lead to the discovery of the tyrant's fortune. More certain is that by then Mossad will have other tyrants to hunt down.

CHAPTER 20

God's Banker, Whistleblower, and Osama bin Laden

On April 22, 2004, on one of those balmy days when Israelis remind themselves that this was why God had chosen their Promised Land, Meir Dagan watched the live transmission on his television in his top-floor office in Mossad headquarters.

The screen showed Mordechai Vanunu, the former nuclear technician who had exposed Israel's atomic arsenal, finally emerging from incarceration in the high-security prison at Ashkelon in southern Israel. He had served eighteen years. One of Dagan's predecessors, Shabtai Shavit, had publicly said that given the chance, he would have had Vanunu assassinated. On the television screen protesters opposed to

Vanunu's release were shouting the same demand: "Kill him! Kill him!" Vanunu responded by raising his clenched hands above his head in a boxer's victory salute. The screams of "Traitor! Traitor!" mingled with the cheers of supporters who had come from all over the world to welcome Vanunu.

There had never been a scene like it, and it was one that Dagan had difficulty understanding. How could a man who had betrayed his country be treated by anyone as a hero? If Vanunu had done it for money, Dagan had said, that he could almost understand and even accept that Vanunu, once a committed Jew, had converted to Christianity. What the Mossad chief could not understand was the *motivation* that had driven Vanunu to expose Israel's prime defense system—the two hundred nuclear weapons that now made it the fourth nuclear power in the world.

Dagan had been part of Israel since its creation; he had played his own part in helping it fight for its place among nations. He believed with passionate conviction that no other people had struggled so much, and for so long, to enlighten others about the moral and spiritual imperatives that govern the ways of mankind. In those long nights when he sat alone in his office reading the incoming traffic from his agents all over the world, his principle article of faith and an inexhaustible wellspring from which he drew his strength was that the State of Israel was the single most important thing in his life.

That was why Vanunu's great betrayal had preoccupied him. During his imprisonment, Vanunu had filled eighty-seven boxes of documents detailing the production of nuclear weapons at Dimona, out in the Negev Desert. They had, of course, been confiscated on the eve of his release. But what he had put out on paper was to Dagan "proof that Vanunu's knowledge is still enormous, far too extensive to let him leave Israel."

That had been one of the conditions accompanying his release; others included that he was not to have contact with foreigners, he would have his Internet and phone calls monitored, and that he would not approach within five hundred meters of any border crossing or foreign diplomatic mission. He would also have a team of surveillance officers close to him day and night.

Vanunu had accepted all the restrictions with a shrug. There had been many other shrugs during Dagan's final effort to understand his mindset. The night before his release, two Mossad interrogators had questioned Vanunu on camera about why he had betrayed Israel. He had shrugged them off and launched a strong attack on Mossad and how he had been tricked into captivity. He had spoken of his "cruel and barbaric treatment in prison which was organized and approved by Mossad."

Now, on the television screen, Vanunu was repeating the same allegations to the cheers of his supporters. To Dagan if "this was a man we had brutalized he looked in very good shape."

As Vanunu was driven away to pray in St. George's Anglican cathedral in Jerusalem, Meir Dagan turned back to other matters. Vanunu was free. But he would never be out of Mossad's grasp.

Like millions of others, Cindy, the Mossad agent who had played a key role in the capture of Vanunu in 1986, saw the news of his release on television. She knew that to many Israelis she was still a heroine, someone who had used her guile for a classic sexual entrapment. To others, she remained a Mata Hari, a calculating seductress who destroyed the life of an idealist who felt he was driven by the higher cause of world peace.

But Cindy (the code name she operated under for Mossad) had little to say publicly after she saw Vanunu emerge from his prison. "It's all in the past. I did my job. End of story," she said (to the author). Just as Vanunu had spent his long years in jail, reliving what he had done and each time concluding "I did the right thing," so Cindy had undoubtedly also tried to come to terms with what she had done.

Today she lives in an expensive home beside a golf course twenty-five minutes outside Orlando. She looks good for her age, the color of her hair helped by hairdressing skills to hide the effects of the Florida sun. Deeply tanned, she favors loose-fitting casuals to hide the spread of early middle age. Her two daughters are now teenagers who attend an exclusive private school and never, in public at least, speak about their mother's past. But friends at the golf club where Cindy enjoys taking lunch say she has developed a real fear that Vanunu or one of his supporters will come and harm her.

Vanunu has denied he has any interest in doing so. "For me, she is just someone who happened. I was young and lonely. She was there. I took her on trust," was how he summed up the fatal mistake that allowed her to entice him to Rome on the promise of sex. Instead, he fell into the hands of Mossad.

In 2004, Cindy—who is listed in local Orlando records as Cheryl Hanin Bentov—is a Realtor, working with her husband and her mother,

Riki Hanin, who lives nearby. All three are active members of their Jewish community. The Israeli newspaper *Yediot Aharonot* claimed that "she left Israel to flee the media and the people who burrowed into her life. This bothered her a lot. She was terrified about journalists who came into her home and asked questions. She felt a need to run. Cheryl wants only one thing: a normal, quiet life. She still has shaky nerves as she tried to bury the past. Even relatives who talked about her found themselves banished from the family. She moves between discretion and paranoia."

If that is true, then it was a high price to pay for becoming Mossad's most infamous seductress.

On Meir Dagan's desk was a report from the New York consulate that there was no need for concern over the much promoted CBS television documentary on the death of Princess Diana. The full role of Mossad was still securely hidden and seemed likely to remain so for the foreseeable future. The documentation (which enabled part of the story to appear in this book) had been sealed in Mossad's archives with a printed warning on the box. "Not to be opened without prior written order of Director General."

Of far more concern to Dagan was another report, this one from the Washington embassy, that once more the Bush administration, like its predecessors, was preparing to block the release of a whistleblower as dangerous to America as Vanunu had been to Israel. He was Jonathan Pollard, who was serving a life sentence in a high-security prison in Bulmer, North Carolina, having been found guilty of being the greatest traitor in the history of the United States. Pollard, unlike Vanunu, had been sentenced to die in jail.

Dagan knew the reason for this harsh sentence was the forty-six-page affidavit Caspar Weinberger, then secretary of defense, had made for Pollard's trial in 1987. It was so secret that it had never been made public. Every attempt to do so had been blocked by federal lawyers in various Washington courts. In April 2004, the affidavit was still classified "Top Secret Sensitive Compartmented Information" (SCI). This is a restriction to protect the most sensitive data in the U.S. intelligence community.

Dagan believed the affidavit contained crucial details about how Promis software—developed by the specialist Inslaw computer company in Washington and later stolen by Mossad—had been adapted to fit into the artificial intelligence on board U.S. nuclear submarines. The resulting capability was known as "over-the-horizon accuracy," enabling a submarine to hit targets far within the then Soviet Union and China. The Promis software could program details of the defenses around a target along with the advanced physics and mathematics needed to ensure a direct hit from huge distances.

Dagan also feared the affidavit outlined how Israel had developed its own over-the-horizon accuracy for three German-built nuclear-powered submarines it had bought, based on what Pollard had stolen. Dagan further suspected the affidavit contained details of joint U.S.-British listening posts on Cyprus and in the Middle East, which Pollard had compromised, and revealed how Pollard had also compromised CIA-MI6 operations in the Soviet Union and the former East Germany.

While this had led to a considerable change in U.S. intelligence, the data in the Weinberger affidavit was deemed to be still so ultrasensitive that its publication would provide valuable information to foreign intelligence services—including Mossad.

So important was Pollard to Israel that Dagan had sent a Mossad lawyer to attend Pollard's first public appearance since he was sentenced. The case was heard in the Washington District Court in September 2003. Pollard looked older than his forty-seven years, his skin paler, his eyes occasionally glancing around the packed courtroom. He wore wire-rimmed spectacles, an embroidered yarmulke, and a green prison overshirt. He had a gray-brown beard and shoulder-length hair, giving him the appearance of an Old Testament prophet. Some forty relatives and supporters packed the small courtroom. They included several rabbis, among them Israel's former chief rabbi, Mordechai Eliahu. His wife, Esther, and his father were also present. Pollard closely followed the legal arguments. The Mossad lawyer, a slim, middle-aged man, sat at the back of the court, taking notes in Hebrew.

The nub of Pollard's case was that he should be allowed to appeal his sentence because his then attorney, Richard Hibney, had failed to file a notice of appeal when the prosecution asked the trial judge, Aubrey Robinson, for a life sentence without parole after "inducing Pollard to plead guilty by promising the State would not ask for life." A further argument centered around the claim that Pollard's then defense team had been refused access to the Weinberger affidavit "because they did not have the requisite security clearance." Pollard's new lawyers told the court they were also "seeking a pardon or sentence commutation" from the Bush administration. That part of the argument was "based on Pollard's rights as an American citizen to due process."

Over the years, Pollard's attorneys had had meetings with Israeli prime ministers Benjamin Netanyahu, Ehud Barak, and Ariel Sharon. They had also met with Mossad intelligence chiefs Nahum Admoni, Shabtai Shavit, Danny Yatom, Efraim Halevy, and more recently, Meir Dagan. There had been a carefully orchestrated campaign in Israel to bombard the U.S. embassy with requests for Pollard's freedom. Top Jewish lawyers had traveled from Israel to meet with equally renowned lawyers in the United States to plan legal moves. No defendant had had such a powerful support system. At every opportunity, the all-powerful Jewish lobby in Washington had battled tirelessly.

The Conference of Presidents of Major Jewish Organizations, a consortium of fifty-five groups, continued to argue in 2004 that whatever Pollard had done could not be called treason "because Israel was and remains a close ally." Further pressure constantly came from many leading Jewish religious organizations. The most vociferous was the powerful Reform Union of American Congregations. Harvard Law School professor Alan M. Dershowitz, who had served as Pollard's lawyer, had said, "There is nothing in Pollard's conviction to suggest that he had compromised the nation's intelligence-gathering capabilities or betrayed world-wide intelligence data."

But Pollard still had an equally powerful opponent: George Tenet, director of the CIA. In 1998, Tenet had said he would resign if Pollard was released. That still remained his position in 2004. Ted Gunderson, a top FBI agent at the time Pollard was arrested, said, "Pollard stole every worthwhile intelligence secret we had. We are still trying to recover from what he did. We had to withdraw dozens of agents in place in the former Soviet Union, in the Middle East, South Africa, and friendly nations like Britain, France, and Germany. The American public just doesn't know the full extent of what he did."

In prison, Pollard divorced his first wife, Anne (who had been sentenced to five years imprisonment for being his accomplice), and converted to Orthodox Judaism. In 1994 he married, in prison, a Toronto schoolteacher named Elaine Zeitz. Esther Pollard, as she was from then on known, became the spearhead of the campaign to have her husband freed. In April 2004, she repeated a familiar theme. "The issue of Jonathan concerns every Jew and every law-abiding citizen. The issues are much bigger than Jonathan and myself. We are writing a page of Jewish history."

An indication of how much more was written on that page of history has surfaced. Ari Ben-Menashe, a former intelligence adviser to the Israeli government who is now a Canadian citizen running a political consultancy in Montreal, strongly opposes Pollard's gaining his freedom. "The still unresolved question is whether Pollard's thefts were also passed to China," said Ben-Menashe. "Much of what Pollard knows is still in his head. A man like that doesn't lose his touch because he is locked away."

But in April 2004, Meir Dagan had learned that the U.S. deputy attorney general, Larry Thompson, had suggested Pollard's freedom should be seen in the context of the "big picture" in the Middle East. It was an argument that did not go unnoticed by Pollard supporters. Recently, 112 out of 120 members of the Knesset, Israel's parliament, signed a petition demanding Pollard's release on "humanitarian grounds. Washington has double standards, releasing dangerous Palestinian prisoners while keeping Pollard incarcerated."

Pollard was granted Israeli citizenship in 1996 to enable the Tel Aviv government to bring further pressure to bear. Two years later, a U.S.-brokered peace accord between Israel and the PLO nearly foundered when the then Israeli prime minister, Benjamin Netanyahu, tried to link the agreement with the release of Pollard. President Clinton held firm, Israel backed off.

A stumbling block to any new move to obtain Pollard's freedom could be a statement Bill Hamilton, president of Inslaw—the creators of the Promis software—made. "Judge Hogan should also be made aware that the FBI office in New Mexico conducted a foreign counterintelligence investigation of Robert Maxwell in 1984 for selling Promis in New Mexico, which is the headquarters for the two main U.S. intelligence agencies on nuclear warfare, the Sandia and Los Alamos National Laboratories. Although the copy of the FBI Investigative Report that Inslaw obtained under the Freedom of Information Act was heavily redacted by the government for national security reasons, the text that is still able to be read reveals that the FBI investigation was based on a complaint from two employees at the Sandia National Laboratory."

Hamilton's claims are said by Gunderson to be "the real smoking gun that will put the whole Pollard business into its proper context." They will also bring Rafi Eitan's latest activities into the spotlight.

By April 2004, Israel's legendary spymaster had made several secret trips to the United States. FBI agents tracking him admitted they were unable to question Eitan, who had been Jonathan Pollard's controller, because he now traveled on an Israeli diplomatic passport. His visits had been to supervise the mobilization of thousands of sayanim—the name comes from the Hebrew for "to help"—many of whom received weapons training during their military service. Others had worked in U.S. military intelligence. A number were currently employed by police forces across the country. They had been briefed by Eitan on how to update the defense systems of Jewish banks, synagogues, religious schools, and other Jewish-owned institutions.

"While their allegiance to their birth country cannot be doubted, each sayan recognizes a greater loyalty: the mystical one to Israel and a need to help protect it from its enemies," Meir Amit, a former Mossad chief, has said. He created the sayanim secret force. Known as Israel's "invisible army," its members are vetted by professional Mossad intelligence officers, *katsas*, before being recruited to protect Israel's many interests in the United States. But the Department of Homeland Security and the FBI have seen it as a vote of no confidence in their ability to protect those interests.

On his trips, Eitan traveled as "adviser on security and counterterrorism" to Israel's prime minister, Ariel Sharon, a longtime friend. In early 2004, Eitan had visited the Los Alamos area, home of America's cutting-edge nuclear technology. In 1985, he had arranged to sell to Los Alamos's Sandia Laboratories a copy of the Israeli version of Promis software. The program's "trapdoor" enabled Israel to learn something of Sandia's work in providing U.S. nuclear submarines with the latest computer technology. Pollard provided further details, which are contained in Caspar Weinberger's still secret affidavit.

By April 2004 the sayanim had been fully mobilized. Eitan made no secret of their role. Quoting Meir Amit, he confirmed (to the author): "Sayanim fulfill many functions. A car sayan, running a rental agency, lets his handler know if any suspicious person has rented a car. A Realtor sayan provides similar information on anyone seeking accommodation. Sayanim also collect technical data and all kinds of overt intelligence. A rumor at a cocktail party, an item on the radio, a paragraph in a newspaper, a story overheard at a dinner party."

It was a sayan in Phoenix, Arizona, who discovered in the spring of 2004 that one of the most notorious figures in the history of the Catholic church, Archbishop Paul Marcinkus, had kept his undertaking never to divulge what he knew about Mossad's role in the disappearance of $200 million. It had been sent to the Polish Solidarity movement by the Vatican Bank when Marcinkus had been its president.

By the early 1980s, Marcinkus was implicated in massive financial scandals and a stunning list of other crimes, including "being involved in arms smuggling, trafficking in stolen gold, counterfeit currencies, and radioactive materials," according to an indictment lodged by the Rome public prosecutor in 1989. The charges were still on the open file in April 2004. Marcinkus was never interviewed or arrested. Pope John Paul II allowed him to remain in the Vatican so that he could be protected under the city's sovereign immunity, which had been granted to the Holy See in 1929 by Benito Mussolini.

Then one night—the date remains one of the Vatican's many secrets—Marcinkus was quietly driven out of the Vatican in a car bearing diplomatic plates. Next day he arrived in Chicago. From there he was flown to Sun City, a satellite town in Phoenix. Close by lived another colorful character, Victor Ostrovsky. The former Mossad officer was a whistleblower. Like Ari Ben-Menashe, Ostrovsky had revealed many of Mossad's secrets in interviews. Both men in 2004 still lived comfortable lives. But Marcinkus, at eighty years of age, was living out his closing years in a modest white-painted cinder-block house close to a country club fairway in Sun City. Unlike the two Mossad officers, he had still kept the silence when he was known as God's banker and a confidant of popes—Paul VI, John Paul I, and John Paul II. The Polish pope, the supreme pontiff to the Catholic world, was the one man, apart from Marcinkus, who could answer the question: What was Mossad's role in the mystery of the missing $200 million?

The mystery can properly be said to have begun when another limousine arrived at the Vatican.

Close to midnight the dark blue limousine, with its diplomatic plates, stopped before the wrought-iron gates of the Arch of the Bells, the gateway to the Apostolic Palace in the Vatican. It was the prelude to a sequence of events that to this day cast a dark shadow over the pontificate of John Paul. Nearly a decade after his death, the answer to questions that will form the final judgment on his long rule is a deeply troubling one for all those who care about the church and what was done in its name.

Did the pope allow himself to be moved from his own personal moral standards to help Solidarity because of his passionate and abiding commitment to Poland? Was he purely an innocent and unsuspecting victim of what was about to transpire once that limousine entered the Vatican?

In the judgment of David Yallop, the English financial investigator long recognized as the bête noire of the secret financial world of the Vatican, John Paul allowed his papacy "to become a triumph for wheeler-dealers and the international financial thieves. The pope also gave his blessing for large quantities of U.S. dollars to have been sent, secretly and illegally, to Solidarity."

Christopher Story, the publisher of the *International Currency Review*, the journal of the banking world, called it "one of the great black hole mysteries of modern-day financing."

Certainly on that April night in 1983 when the Renaissance-costumed Swiss Guard, caped against the cold, stepped forward to salute the Fiat's passenger, it signaled the start of a chain of staggering events. They began at a period John Paul had called "a very dark time in the history of the world." Two years before, the KGB—through its surrogate, the Bulgarian secret service—had tried to assassinate him in St. Peter's Square. To further distance itself, Moscow had allowed a Muslim fanatic, Mehmet Ali Agca, to carry out the attempt. Until his death in April 2005, the pope felt the pain from the shrapnel still in his body. But his defiance of Communism had led to the creation of the Solidarity movement in Poland. In Washington, President Ronald Reagan had called its birth "an inspiration to the free world. We shall support it."

How he did so has remained secret. Now the extraordinary and, at times, bizarre story can be told of how the CIA and the Vatican Bank created that $200 million secret fund for Solidarity. In 1983, the CIA maintained a well-developed slush fund to mount "no-questions-asked black operations" all over the world.

Richard Brenneke, a mild-mannered man with the careful speech pattern of an accountant, was the senior CIA operative in charge of the agency's secret funding for those operations. He worked sixteen-hour days juggling covert funds in and out of Swiss banks, like Credit Suisse in Geneva, and sending them on complex transfers around the banking world. With the full authority of CIA director William Casey, Brenneke had started to use the Vatican Bank for money laundering. Casey had introduced Brenneke to Archbishop Paul Marcinkus. Brenneke had since made a number of visits to Marcinkus's office in a seventeenth-century tower inside the Vatican walls. "On a good day $400 million was laundered," Brenneke recalled. A substantial portion of the money came from the CIA's ultrasecret operations.

"Like other intelligence agencies, the CIA had established backdoor links with the mafia. The CIA, like the Vatican, had a very real fear Italy could fall into the hands of the Communists. The CIA saw the mafia as a bulwark against that happening. Consequently, the CIA took the view that the mafia's activities in Italy were to be tolerated if they helped to ensure that NATO member Italy did not fall into Moscow's hands at the polling booths," said David Yallop (to the author).

By 1983, the CIA had extended its secret links to international crime to include arming Iran and the contras in Nicaragua. Brenneke said: "Money from guns sold to the Iranians was used by the agency to buy drugs in South America. Cocaine was shipped back to the States and sold on to the mafia. That money was then used to buy weapons for the contras in Nicaragua. It got so out of hand I told President Reagan's national security adviser, Don Gregg. I was told to forget it." By then, Brenneke said, he had laundered $10 billion. A considerable portion of the money came from the Gotti mafia family of New York. The Gotti family, like the Gambino and Colombo crime families, were devout Catholics. FBI intercepts show the bosses gave generously to the church. Another mafia chief, Salvatore "Lucky" Luciano, boasted of visiting the Vatican before his death.

"By 1983 the Vatican Bank was being routinely used by the mafia to move money both into and out of Italy. The money came from drugs, prostitution, and a variety of other crimes that the Vatican officially condemned," said Yallop.

Did the $200 million earmarked for Solidarity come from the mafia? Twenty-one years would pass after that Fiat limousine drove on through the Arch of the Bells gateway before those and other questions would be asked.

The solitary passenger on that April night in 1983 was Archbishop Luigi Poggi. He was the pope's diplomatic troubleshooter, a nuncio extraordinary and a seasoned operator in the world of very secret papal politics. Among the direct-line numbers in his briefcase were those of CIA director Casey—a devout Catholic himself—Lech Walesa of Solidarity, and the foreign ministers of half a dozen European nations. The most recent addition to the list was that of Nahum Admoni, then the director general of Mossad. The archbishop and spy chief had met in Paris during the latest journeying around Europe that Poggi had just completed. Poggi knew that with Admoni's Polish background—his parents had been middle-class immigrants to Israel from Gdansk—the spy chief had more than a passing curiosity about the church.

In Warsaw, Poggi had conferred as usual with Cardinal Josef Glemp in his palace. They had spoken in a lead-lined room to overcome the surveillance of Poland's intelligence services. Even so, the two men had spoken in Latin. A clue to what followed is provided by Admoni, who lives today in the United States.

"I soon knew that the Vatican would help Solidarity. I calculated they would do so through Solidarity's Brussels office, a kind of unofficial embassy. A Polish Jew, Jerzy Milewski, good on knocking on doors, was the main fund-raiser."

Boris Solomatin, the KGB *rezident* (station chief) in Rome, would confirm. "We knew all about the secret alliance between the CIA and the Vatican to support Solidarity." Less certain is Solomatin's claim that the KGB had "an important spy in the Vatican." Yet the claim cannot be totally dismissed. The papal nuncio in Ireland, the late Archbishop Gaetano Alibrandi, said in an interview (with the author) following the attempt on the pope's life in May 1981: "The Soviets appeared to have inside information as to the Holy See's position on foreign affairs."

On that April evening in 1983, late though the hour was, the pope's then senior secretary Stanislaw Dzwisz and Marcinkus were waiting to be briefed. Marcinkus had recently been promoted by Pope John Paul to become governor of Vatican City. He was also now in charge of security for all the pontiff's foreign trips.

The pope's former English-language secretary, Monsignor John Magee, now bishop of Clones in Ireland, provided a rare insight into Poggi: "He was imbued with well-founded confidence in his own abilities, his mission in life and his relationship with God."

Settled in Dzwisz's office in the papal secretariat in the Apostolic Palace, Poggi told them that the outgoing United States ambassador to Poland, the soft-spoken Francis J. Meehan, had revealed that the Reagan administration was going to arrange the transfer of $200 million to support Solidarity. The news came at the end of Poggi's twenty-third visit to Warsaw in the past two years. Each time he had stayed with

Cardinal Josef Glemp, primate of Poland, availing himself of the lead-lined room and speaking in Latin. It made no difference. Mossad, Israel's secret intelligence service, had carried out a major coup only two months before Poggi was briefing Marcinkus and Dzwisz.

It had been set up by Nahum Admoni, the spymaster who had dined with Poggi in Paris and discussed church affairs. Then Mossad's director of operations, Rafi Eitan, had smooth-talked the U.S. Department of Justice and the developer of the software it prized above all else in its electronic arsenal to part with a copy. The software was Promis.

Down the years Bill Hamilton, the president of Inslaw, would say of Rafi Eitan and the cool way he stole Promis: "Rafi fooled me. And he fooled a lot of others." Eitan, now in his seventies, admitted (to the author in 2004): "It was quite a coup. Yes, quite a coup."

The Israelis deconstructed Promis and inserted a trapdoor in the software. Dr. Jerzy Milewski, the hardworking Polish Jew responsible for Solidarity's fund-raising, was persuaded by Eitan on a visit to Brussels to accept the doctored software "as a gift from Israel." Mossad had become the first intelligence service to penetrate the heart and soul of Solidarity.

Born and bred in Cicero—the Chicago suburb that was also the birthplace of Al Capone—Paul Marcinkus had acquired many of the gangster's mannerisms, evident in the way he would terrorize a teller in the Vatican Bank or threaten a bishop. Marcinkus also rejoiced in being on what he once claimed was "Moscow's Top Ten list of targets. Next to the pope, I am the man they most want to knock off." But for the Vatican's banker he had some unusual clients: the casino at Monte Carlo, the Beretta firearms company, and a Canadian company that made oral contraceptives. From the day he took over as the bank's president, Marcinkus had increased its investments beyond all expectations. By 1983, on the night he listened to Poggi, the overall bank deposits were worth tens of billions of dollars. Marcinkus had once boasted to Monsignor John Magee, "It is a real gravy train."

The arrival of the CIA as a client was welcomed by Marcinkus, hosting Casey and Brenneke for dinner in the Villa Stritch, where the banker had a three-bedroom apartment. Served by handsome young Romans— youths Marcinkus was known to refer to as "my bodyguards"—the tall, heavyset archbishop learned how the Vatican Bank would act as a conduit for the $200 million for Solidarity. Later, as he and his dinner guests played a round of golf at the Aquastina—Rome's most exclusive golf club, which had gifted Marcinkus a membership—the final details were settled.

The money would leave America from a number of banks, the Bank of America and Citibank among them. Brenneke had devised special codes for all his transactions. These changed on a regular basis. No transactions remained in any of his accounts for more than seventy-two hours. The money for Solidarity would enter the Vatican Bank from the Banco de Panama (the Panamanian national bank), the Standard Bank of South Africa, and Coutts, the Queen's bankers, in London. The money would then be rerouted to Bank Lambert in Brussels. The system was what Brenneke called "SOP"—standard operating procedure. In part, it was designed to deal with what Casey had called "a tricky little problem."

Solidarity was concerned that if it became known it was receiving substantial financial aid from Washington, it could lead the Jaruzelski regime to crack down on the movement—even perhaps arrest its leaders. But that secrecy would later lead to a very public clash between one of President Reagan's key advisers, Professor Richard Pipes, and President Jimmy Carter's national security adviser, Zbigniew Brzezinski.

Pipes was said to have alleged that he knew well that large sums of money had been transferred to Solidarity through several accounts operated by the CIA. There were reports Pipes had challenged Brzezinski that the money had never reached Solidarity—where did it go? It was a question Brzezinski did not answer then, and has not since.

At best, only a small portion of foreign money—which was urgently needed by Solidarity to pay its members a token weekly wage while on strike—was ever received by the Brussels headquarters of Solidarnosc. Elizabeth Wasiutynski, whose parents had served in the NSZ, part of the Polish resistance, became head of Solidarnosc in Brussels. She insisted that money for Solidarnosc came from the AFL-CIO, international trade union organizations, and the National Endowment for Democracy. Further sums came later through an organization called the Stanton Group in the United States. It was donated on behalf of American taxpayers.

"We received no more than two hundred thousand dollars annually.

There was no large or even small amount of money I'm aware of funded to the Solidarnosc leadership from the CIA. Nor is there an echo of any such activity since Poland's independence in 1989. I think the CIA is taking credit for something it did not do," she said. "Had the CIA indeed been involved, we would have had some sort of more fertile ground in Washington."

Sources at the Bank Lambert in Brussels insist it had no record of such a large payment coming into its coffers from the Vatican Bank. So where did it go? Enter now, not for the first time, one of the undisputed grand villains of financial chicanery—Robert Maxwell.

The Israeli-doctored Promis software had been sold to General Wojciech Jaruzelski, Poland's Communist ruler, by Maxwell. It was to be used—and was—against Solidarity and anyone who supported Poland's then fledgling democratic opposition. But during his global sales drive for Promis, Maxwell had, in 1985—when the money transfer to help Solidarity had already taken place—sold Promis to Belgium's counterespionage service, the Sûreté de l'Etat. It gave Mossad a window into Belgium's intelligence operations—including financial operations by Semion Yukovich Mogilevich.

At that time, still operating from his base in Budapest, Hungary, Mogilevich was rapidly establishing himself as a specialist in major financial crime in preparation for stepping into the post-Communist financial world. By 1985, he had offices in Geneva, Nigeria, and the Cayman Islands. He also held an Israeli passport, which Maxwell had arranged. Mogilevich had been introduced by Maxwell to a Swiss banker who ran an investment brokerage in Geneva, and had regular business dealings with the Vatican Bank and Bank Lambert.

Marcinkus already was deeply ensnared in massive financial scams involving the bank, which had led Pope John Paul to agree to reimburse those swindled by Marcinkus's activities. In one of the more remarkable documents publicly issued by any bank, the Vatican stated in May 1984 that "international banks will get back approximately two-thirds of the 600 million dollars they had loaned to the Vatican Bank. Of that some 250 million dollars will be paid by June 30, 1984. This payment is being made by the Vatican on the basis of non-culpability but in recognition of a moral involvement."

By then, Marcinkus was a virtual prisoner inside the Vatican, not daring to step outside its walls for fear of arrest. A mounting number of criminal charges awaited his appearance in court. But Marcinkus still went to his office every weekday to "supervise"—the word the Vatican used—the daily affairs of the bank.

Somewhere in that tangled web—the CIA, Marcinkus money laundering, Polish intelligence, Mossad, and Maxwell—lay the answer to that question asked publicly by the distinguished Richard Pipes. Where did the $200 million for Solidarity go? The answer turned out to be staggeringly simple. Using Promis, the money had been intercepted by Mossad to finance its own black operations.

In the past, the intelligence service had used its doctored version of the software to access foreign bank accounts held by Israeli millionaires that they hoped had been discreetly transferred out of a country strapped for cash. Mossad had not only seized the sums, but had also summoned the hapless millionaires to a meeting. They were told that they would be levied a "fine" for their breach of the country's strict currency regulations. To refuse would mean a trial and certain imprisonment. "They all paid," Rafi Eitan said (to the author) with undisguised satisfaction.

In March 2004, William Hamilton, president of Inslaw, told the author that using Promis would "make it a relatively simple operation for Mossad to have stolen the money."

A copy of the software had also ended up in the hands of Osama bin Laden. It had been stolen by Robert Hanssen, a senior FBI computer specialist who was a longtime key spy in the bureau. He is now serving a life sentence for espionage. By then the KGB had sold it to bin Laden for a reported $2 million.

By the spring of 2004, Mossad had continued its hunt for bin Laden. Along the way Meir Dagan had acquired, through his field agents and analysts, a striking psychological profile of bin Laden that probably no other intelligence service could equal. It included how the world's most wanted man ran al-Qaeda.

If it were a multinational, bin Laden would have been its chief executive. There is a board: the close group of terrorists who had been with him from the foundation of al-Qaeda. It has, just like any corporation, divisions: one for finance, another for forward planning, a third for recruiting. There is even one division that handles the making and distribution of his audio- and videotapes. Al-Qaeda's sole reason for existing is to launch global holy war.

No other organization in living memory has changed the world as completely as al-Qaeda did when on September 11, 2001, the Twin Towers of the World Trade Center came crashing down and one side of the Pentagon burst into flames. Thousands of men, women, and children lost their lives in the most deadly terrorist attack on American soil. Never in its history had the mainland United States been the target of such a massive attack. The surprise bombing of Pearl Harbor by Japan was the only precedent in living memory—and that had been an assault against a distant military base on a Pacific island.

"The carnage of September 11 was deliberately aimed at civilians and struck at the principal symbols of American hegemony, commercial and financial power, military supremacy and political power. It was a seismic event with incalculable consequences. It exposed the fragility of the United States empire, exploded the myth of its invincibility, and called into question all the certainties and beliefs that had ensured the triumph of American civilization in the twentieth century. Many correctly feared it was only the first of many atrocities," wrote Professor Gilles Kepel of the respected Institute for Political Studies in Paris.

Since then, the world has watched numbed at the destruction in Bali and Istanbul, and the massacre in Madrid. The result has been a continual witnessing of the agony of the victims and their families, precipitate drops in stock markets, the threat of bankruptcy of several airlines, and a general upheaval in the world's economy.

Those are the inescapable truths about a fanatic who knew almost nothing about Western culture, Western thought, or Western ways. He was a man of the Word, and, as history shows, absolute adherents to the text—Hitler and Stalin being two examples—seldom have any imagination, or it is warped beyond comprehension.

Bin Laden was a slave to literal interpretations: the normal intellectual extrapolations upon which much European thinking depends is far beyond his power. For instance, in one of his rambling speeches, he once said he was certain that "a few attacks will see American states secede from the U.S."

"We must look with total revulsion at the way he has made al-Qaeda a brand name for terror. He has ensured that neither his death, nor a refutation of violence on his part—never likely—will halt Islamic terrorism. Instead, he will continue to release a toxin of poison on our world," said Dr. Ariel Merari, director of terrorist studies at the Jaffee Center in Tel Aviv.

Bin Laden resurrected his claim for the restoration into Arab hands of Andalusia, whose civilization marked the high point of Islamic pride. He began to rekindle across the Muslim world a reminder of that golden era in 1200, for instance, when the Spanish city of Córdoba had nine hundred public baths, and seventy libraries whose shelves were filled with the finest writings in the Muslim world. It had the finest doctors, the greatest restaurants, and, it is said, the most beautiful women. The Madrid bombing massacre has more to do with this dream than with the presence, and now withdrawal, of Spanish troops in Iraq. That is why al-Qaeda terrorists—having been efficiently located by Spanish security hiding in an apartment block in a Madrid suburb—blew themselves up even after the election of Jose Zapatero as the country's new prime minister in March 2004.

The nearest parallel in history of using violence to reclaim ancient lands was the Nazi dream of Aryan reclamation of those parts of Europe that had Germanic roots. The distinguished commentator Janet Daley has written that "the Wagnerian German romantic mythology of expulsion from homelands leading to a sacred Teutonic mission of rebirth has an uncannily similar ring to the new Islamic claims of Muslim displacement and injustice."

As bin Laden sat in his cave in the Tora Bora Mountains on the Afghanistan-Pakistan border, he was driven by the dream of creating a great caliphate that would stretch from Asia to southern Spain and beyond.

"That is the very real danger of this man. To try and achieve his aim, he will kill and slaughter on a scale that even the Mongols, Genghis Khan, the Crusaders, the Nazis, and the pogroms of Russia would pause to blink over," said Dr. Merari.

It is now estimated by the CIA that over $100 million has been spent in these past two years on satellite tracking and the use of state-of-the-art electronic tracking equipment to locate bin Laden.

Unlike Saddam Hussein, bin Laden has vowed he will die a "martyr's death" rather than face capture. His body is festooned with hand grenades, making him a pin pull away from eternity. At night he sleeps on a mat surrounded by explosives.

Al-Qaeda operatives—its suicide bombers who die on missions—do so knowing that the organization's Pensions Department will take care of their families. No one knows where or when the organization meets. It has no offices. Its turnover is measured by the number of deaths it achieves, the buildings it destroys. Its assets—the explosives and cash that keep it running—are hidden from even the most prying satellite camera.

Bin Laden's own personal assets—once estimated at £20 million from his share in the family construction business—were frozen in 2001. But he has managed to keep al-Qaeda fully funded from donations from Saudi Arabian princes, oil sheikhs, and wealthy Muslims in Asia.

"Bin Laden is the glue between terror groups that have little in common with each other but are united in a common hatred of the West," said a U.S. State Department analyst in Washington.

In 2003, perhaps sensing the net was closing on him, bin Laden appointed "twenty regional commanders" to run al-Qaeda operations. There have been persistent reports that their funding reaches them through the diplomatic bags of rogue states like Iran and, until recently, Libya. In Britain, MI5 has spent months trying to track money earmarked for al-Qaeda.

"So far we have had only our suspicions confirmed, but no hard evidence," said an MI5 source (to the author).

Whether he lives or dies is of little concern to bin Laden. To his millions of followers in the Muslim world he is a folk hero: the Saudi Arabian multimillionaire who feeds the poor, encourages their children to dance before him, and knows the verses of the Koran better than any Islamic preacher. To them all he is a living prophet come to cleanse the world of what he calls "Western decadence." With his high cheekbones, narrow face, and gold-fringed robe, he is the classic mountain warrior of the tribesmen who now hide him. His distinct pepper-and-salt beard and sharp, penetrating eyes are the most recognizable image on earth. But his smile is only for his followers, who see him as a hell-storming advocate, living a personal life of such frugality that even they find it hard to match. He is also a man steeped in personal violence, having once driven a captured tank over Russian prisoners in the Afghan war.

Ironically, in those days he was armed by the CIA, who gave him an arsenal of Stingers. When he had helped drive out the Soviet occupiers, he turned against America and its "hamburger and Coca-Cola values." He takes pride in being its most sought-after enemy. Everywhere he goes, so do his bodyguards: some fifty heavily bearded, taciturn figures. Every man is handpicked. Each is ready to die for him. Little is known about his private life: his four wives remain at home in Jeddah in Islamic purdah.

When he awakens, he will brush his teeth in the Arab fashion with a stick of *miswak* wood. Then he will pray for the strength to destroy his enemies. Like a cancer they consume him, burrowing into his mind, even capable at times of making him weep. Then, real tears will fall down his cheeks, the crying of an unforgiving fanatic who hates with a passion that is awesome. Though they far outnumber him, he continues to outwit their vast electronic and human resources—because the forces arrayed against him cannot agree on a strategy that will capture Osama bin Laden.

In Tel Aviv, a senior Mossad analyst said (to the author), "Part of the problem is the old one of the Americans thinking putting up more satellites and pouring in electronic surveillance equipment is the answer. We have told them that the best solution is human intelligence."

Rafi Eitan, who masterminded Mossad's capture of Adolf Eichmann, identified the problem of capturing bin Laden. "There is a need for patience. Satellites can only tell you what is happening *now*—not what could be happening in the future. That can only come from having men on the ground. The greatest successes Mossad has had are through 'humint'—human intelligence."

Long realizing that the United States has the capability to electronically eavesdrop on his discussions, bin Laden writes his orders in a neat hand, then distributes them to trusted aides. They travel to neighboring countries and transmit them from there to bin Laden's global network of some 2,500 terrorists. It was such an order that led to the Madrid massacre.

In 2003, via an Islamic Web site, bin Laden said, "We don't consider it a crime if we try to obtain nuclear, chemical, or biological weapons. Our holy land is occupied by Israeli and American forces. We have the right to defend and liberate our holy land."

Washington has doubled its bounty for bin Laden's capture to $50 million. Meir Amit, a former director general of Mossad, has said such a tactic often does not work. "Betrayal for money is a hard thing to induce in someone committed to a terrorist leader. Part of the reason is fear of someone discovering the treachery. Part of the reason is that the leader has picked his men with care. No promise of a bounty will make them think about turning bin Laden in."

However, in Tel Aviv a former Mossad *katsa*, Eli Cohen, said (to the author) that a weakness could be bin Laden's strong family ties to his four wives, seven children, and forty grandchildren. "We know where they live and their movements. If a wife and some of his children were kidnapped it would certainly focus bin Laden's mind. At minimum they could be held as hostages against him carrying out any further outrage. If he still did, then he should expect 'an eye for an eye, a tooth for a tooth' policy to exist. In other words, his family would be executed."

But no one knows if such a threat would be brushed aside by Osama bin Laden with the same indifference with which he treats all human life.

During the summer months of 2004, the world was shocked by the pictures and descriptions of Iraqi prisoners being abused by their U.S. military guards in Baghdad's Abu Ghraib jail. One of the most unpleasant images was of a naked Iraqi prisoner being held on a lead by a woman soldier. The consensus was that, horrific though the images were, they resulted from a toxic mixture of boredom, sadism, and a warped idea of entertainment by the guards. The Pentagon insisted it did not go beyond that. But action would be taken; severe punishment meted out to the guilty.

The prison commander, Brig. Gen. Janis Karpinski, was relieved of her post. A damning report, which effectively ended her career in the military, accused her of lack of leadership during her tenure as prison governor.

On July 4, Karpinski hit back. She publicly announced that among the interrogators at Abu Ghraib had been Mossad interrogators. Fluent Arab speakers, they had been given free access to the high-value prisoners.

Karpinski's claim had political implications that extended far beyond the walls of the prison. The Arab media used her claim to further inflame Muslim opinion. There were allegations that the Mossad interrogators had been responsible for the interrogation of Palestinian detainees in Iraq. Israel vehemently denied this. There was no way of independently confirming the claims. There may never be.

But soon there was an even more compelling moment to focus world attention. It was the appearance of Saddam Hussein in court in Baghdad in July to face an indictment for war crimes including genocide. Gone was the man who had emerged from a hole in the ground. His old arrogance had returned. He refused to recognize the court. He treated the prosecuting judge with indifference and at times, contempt. It was a chilling reminder of who Saddam had once been: a despot, a tyrant who held the fate of his people in his hands. It will be two years before his trial gets under way. In that time Saddam will, away from his court appearances, live the same daily routine.

Every morning at 4:30—an hour the many millions of Iraqis terrorized for years by Saddam Hussein call "the true dawn"—he will awaken. In the distance he will hear the call of the muezzins to prayer. But Saddam is only a lip-service follower. He will not prostrate himself toward Mecca—even though an arrow on the wall of his bedroom indicates the direction. Next door is his dayroom. The floor is covered with a carpet from his palace. It is the only visible reminder of his past.

For a moment he will blink owlishly in the bright wire-covered bedroom ceiling lights. Above the door, out of reach, is a security camera that provides a wide-angle view of the fifteen-by-fifteen foot room. It has a chair over which is draped the Arab robe he has taken to wearing. In a nearby control room, a bank of monitor screens and computers record his every movement, his occasional mumblings, his angry glares at the camera. Sometimes he shouts for the lights to be turned off. They never are.

Saddam is treated with the same vicelike grip that exists for any inmate on death row in America. Officially now under the legal authority of the new Iraqi interim government, he is in reality still a prisoner of the United States. But he has already won one tonsorial battle. His captors wanted to shave off his beard.

"Saddam convinced them his beard is a sign of mourning for his two sons. Tradition demands he must go unshaven for at least a year. Yasser Arafat, an old friend of Saddam's, maintains a close beard out of mourning for the Palestinian people," said Alice Baya'a, an expert on Saddam's life.

But they will control his every movement outside the time he meets with his defense team for his appearances in court. They will watch over him until the moment he is sentenced. But that would be at least two years away (it would finally open in 2006). Saddam also plans to delay matters by calling as witnesses presidents and prime ministers. The names of George Bush, Tony Blair, and Vladimir Putin appear on the list he has given his Iraqi prosecutors.

By July 2004, six hundred lawyers had already offered to defend him. For them it was a golden opportunity to showcase their talents. Twenty were selected by his family. None have been allowed to visit him in captivity—let alone enter his monastic quarters.

His iron bed is bolted to the floor. The bedding is standard U.S. military prison issue, a long way from the years Saddam slept between silk sheets purchased from Harrods of London. His pillows then were filled with the finest of feathers from rare birds shot by his guards in the marshlands of southern Iraq.

Saddam's quarters are in a storeroom. Once his retinue of servants used it to keep vats of fragrant oils for perfuming Saddam's bathwater. Other vats were reserved for masseuses to knead his body. Now his toiletries consist of a weekly bar of supermarket soap, a sponge, and a tube of toothpaste. But he has returned to the days of his childhood for his oral hygiene. He brushes his teeth in the Arab fashion with a stick of *miswak*, a hardwood.

In an alcove in his bathroom is a ceiling shower and a European-style toilet bolted across the original hole over which his servants once squatted. A metal washbasin and two towels complete the facilities. Like any cheap hotel, the towels are changed once a week. The toilet paper is the kind sold in any Baghdad marketplace.

When his breakfast arrives—his staple diet is yogurt, toast, and weak tea served on the same cheap plates his guards eat off—the guards treat him with respect. They call him "President Saddam," the only title he will respond to. While he uses airline-style plastic cutlery to eat with, they stand watch at the door. The guards are unarmed—a precaution in the unlikely event Saddam would attempt to grab a weapon. A high-ranking British intelligence officer who has firsthand knowledge of Saddam's conditions said (to the author): "The psychiatrists have ruled out that Saddam has suicidal tendencies. But he can be highly temperamental and abusive. And he can be very confrontational if his demands are not met."

Those demands have included international law books. There were growing signs that Saddam, like Slobodan Milošević, plans to star in his own defense.

"He is consumed by the idea he can cause huge damage to President Bush and Tony Blair. When he talks about them, his eyes mist over and he hates them with a passion which is awesome," said the British intelligence officer.

Each day follows the same pattern. Saddam has a noonday lunch—Arab-style food cooked by an Iraqi specially recruited by the Coalition.

There is a food taster who samples every dish before it is brought to Saddam. Drinking water comes from sealed bottles—part of consignments flown in from the United States for its troops.

Twice a day, after lunch and late afternoon, Saddam is taken out to a small courtyard to exercise. He often wears a T-shirt and a pair of military shorts—far from the days he had customized underwear of the finest Egyptian cotton. Those were bought by the boxload from a New York store. In a corner of the yard is a water tap. The first thing Saddam does is to turn on the tap. The sound of flowing water has always been a reminder for him that, in a land parched by nature, he could unfailingly command water. In his palaces there were magnificent tumbling waterfalls and the sound of water was pumped into his office. As he paces the courtyard, the water is a mere trickle. When his exercise time is up, the tap is turned off.

As the sky darkens into deep ebony, Saddam prepares for his night. His dinner will be fruit—dates and olives are a must on his menu—along with soup, possibly chicken and rice. The diet has led to Saddam shedding his potbelly. His shaggy salt-and-pepper beard is trimmed once a week, enhancing his sharp, penetrating eyes. After supper he will return to his law books, trying to fashion a defense for what the world thinks was indefensible. When his trial opened in January 2006, Saddam made good use of his studies, ranting at the trial judge and challenging court rulings.

Like his predecessors, Meir Dagan had come to accept the reality that intelligence is only occasionally successful and that the agency's best work is ignored, never makes it to the public domain. Coupled with this was the daily routine of giving unwelcome news to Mossad's political masters.

Increasingly, the sheer volume of intelligence reports meant politicians often had little time to digest what was being said. Dagan continued the system whereby only a few people—usually senior members of Sharon's cabinet—had access to all the intelligence information. It was not unique to Mossad; the CIA, Germany's BND, and even the two services Dagan most admired, MI6 and MI5, were careful about what they allowed to go beyond their own closed doors. All too often, the inquisitive media had increasingly ensured that no significant facts or operations could be kept totally secret for long.

Dagan continued to resist the way other agencies employed more specialists, called in to operate satellites and other technological intelligence. He still believed technology alone could not unravel secret plans. He was committed to show in the first decade of the twenty-first century that the number of good spies was in inverse proportion to the size of Mossad's support apparatus.

For him, Mossad's spies were more important than any piece of technology. He relished the thought that Mossad still remained a mysterious organization, where a small number of extraordinary individuals, armed with great courage, could achieve extraordinary results. That, for him, and his men and women, was a comforting assurance as they prepared to face the rapidly changing and frightening world ahead.

In the last week of October 2004, Yasser Arafat, the Palestinian leader who had once publicly embraced Saddam Hussein and brought upon himself further fury from Israel, sat down for dinner in his compound in Ramallah on the West Bank. For the past three years he had been confined to shell-pocked buildings on the orders of Israel's prime minister, Ariel Sharon. The decision to isolate him was in the hope that Arafat would call off the suicide bombers and the terror they had inflicted across Israel. Sharon felt Arafat had only paid lip service to stop the killing and mutilation.

Surrounded by Israeli tanks and his every word listened to by the surveillance experts of Mossad, Arafat's influence on peace in the Middle East remained strong. World leaders, like President Jacques Chirac of France, still telephoned him. His following among millions of radicals across the Arab world was constant. Sharon had said again publicly that until Yasser Arafat was removed from power there could be no lasting peace.

His own life had been a testimony to his ultimate failure to become president of a Palestinian state. He had seen his people demoralized by high unemployment through his failure to compromise, especially over the "right of return" of Palestinian refugees, a concession that would have sounded the knell of the Israeli state. His intransigeance was matched by his autocratic style of governing, highlighted by increasing sycophancy and corruption.

Now thinner and physically frailer than when he had first swept onto the world stage at the United Nations thirty years before as leader of his people, Yasser Arafat was now in his seventy-fifth year and, to ordinary Israelis, still a terrorist godfather whose complete annihilation of their state was a burning aim. To other previous U.S. administrations he was a Nobel Prize winner and the only Palestinian to do business with. To the Bush White House, he was a pariah.

But he sensed that soon, with the return of George W. Bush for another four-year term, Israel might finally decide to remove him. For twenty years he had been telling his doctor, Ashraf al-Kurdi, "They will do something."

" 'They,' was Mossad; 'something' was to kill him," Dr. al-Kurdi said (to the author).

On October 26 Arafat sat down for dinner. He began with a cream-based soup, the recipe for which he claimed had been handed down to him by his mother. Then came a fried piece of Saint Peter's fish from the lake of Galilee and named after the catch the apostle Peter was reputed to have made before Jesus converted him. All the fish bones had been carefully removed before Arafat ate. Next Arafat consumed roast chicken, hummus, bread, tomatoes, and a green salad. The ingredients were, as usual, from the local market in Ramallah. The food was set out on the long table in Arafat's workroom. There was also a non-alcoholic drink. Arafat had insisted it be prepared from homeopathic potions and herbs.

"He secretly chose them himself. The drink smelled awful. It made people unwell just sniffing it. But Arafat swallowed it as if it was champagne," Dr. al-Kurdi would tell Al-Jazeera Television.

The drink was based on homeopathic ingredients not available to the souks of Ramallah. But they could be obtained in one of the up-market alternative medicine outlets in Tel Aviv. Within hours Arafat was complaining of severe stomach pains. Dr. al-Kurdi diagnosed gastric flu. But when the prescription medicine did not help, the physician decided Arafat had a blood disorder, "perhaps one of the many types of leukemia." But again the symptoms did not confirm that. Just a few hours later, more expert medical aid was on the way to Ramallah. President Hosni Mubarak of Egypt dispatched his personal medical team, including a cancer specialist. King Abdullah of Jordan also sent the best doctor available in Amman. Both teams recommended that the increasingly ill Arafat, whose symptoms could not be firmly diagnosed, be sent to Europe. President Chirac was contacted. He said the Percy Military Hospital outside Paris would make its own renowned specialists available to treat Arafat.

On October 29 the still-conscious Arafat was helicoptered out of the

Ramallah compound. But by then the Arab world was already asking one question. Had Mossad's chemists obtained a sample of the contents of Arafat's homeopathic concoction? Had Meir Dagan done what his predecessors had resisted—out of the understandable fear of escalating the suicide bomber attacks—and taken charge of an audacious operation to assassinate Yasser Arafat?

Even as Arafat's plane was heading toward Paris, Dr. al-Kurdi added his medical guess to the souk rumors. He said, "Poisoning is a strong possibility." The other Arab doctors who had seen Arafat hinted darkly that they also did not rule out poisoning. In Paris, Arafat's wife, Suha, compounded the intrigue by saying she alone would reveal details of his medical condition—but only when she received "guarantees of my own personal position" regarding the whereabouts of $2 billion of Palestinian Authority funds, which the International Monetary Fund, having carried out an audit in 2003, said were still missing. A deal would later be made in which the Palestinian Authority agreed to pay her $2 million a year for the rest of her life "in recognition of her importance to the Palestinian movement and in her husband's life." She had, in fact, not seen him for four years before she visited his bedside at the Percy Military Hospital. She had traveled from her large suite at the deluxe Hotel Le Bristol in Paris; Arafat had also bequeathed her a magnificent villa on the city's elegant rue du Faubourg Saint-Honoré.

But by the time the deal was cemented, the medical mystery of Arafat's condition had deepened. He was variously reported as having liver failure, kidney failure, that he was brain dead, semiconscious, or unconscious. His French doctors refused to provide any details of scans, biopsies, or blood tests, which would have shown the condition of his vital organs. The information that dribbled out of the hospital came from Arafat's Palestinian aides. Apart from Dr. al-Kurdi, none of them were qualified and they had been denied further access to al-Kurdi's long-time patient. Arafat's aides announced on November 4 that Arafat was on a life-support system. Then abruptly the hospital spokesman said its doctors had found no trace of poisoning "having conducted two tests for a substance." He would not say what substance Arafat had been tested for.

In the Arab world speculation and anger raged. Somewhere in the innuendos and half-truths certain inescapable facts floated to the surface. Mossad had used a lethal chemical agent to kill newspaper tycoon Robert Maxwell when he'd threatened to expose Mossad's activities in his newspapers unless they agreed to help bail him out of his serious financial problems. Dr. Ian West, the Home Office pathologist who'd conducted Maxwell's autopsy, had written in his report (a copy of which the author possesses): "We cannot rule out homicide being the cause."

Mossad had used a drug to try and assassinate the Hamas leader on the streets of Amman, Jordan (see chapter 6, "Avengers"). Since the start of the new millennium, Mossad agents have been credited with poisoning over a dozen terrorists by using a variety of lethal drugs that can never be traced. Some were designed to act slowly. Others were fast acting so that by the time medical intervention came, it was too late—and the drug was no longer detectable in the victim's body. All these weapons had been created at Israel's Institute for Biological Research (see chapter 17, "Bunglegate," pp. 341–42).

As Arafat's condition further deteriorated, his aides said he had suffered a brain haemorrhage, a stroke caused by bleeding into the brain. Could that be true? The hospital spokesman would not say.

On Thursday, November 12, Yasser Arafat died in the early hours of the morning. The hospital spokesman told waiting reporters there would be no details released on tests of the cause of death. There would be no autopsy. And so Mossad's bête noire died mysteriously, surrounded by secrecy. He was brought back to his compound and buried in Ramallah the next day in a concrete coffin, which had been hastily constructed some days before. There were two reasons for this unusual casket, Dr. al-Kurdi said. Arafat's body would be preserved for an autopsy to be conducted and then he could be replaced in his concrete casket and one day be buried in the holiest of all mosques in the Muslim world—the one in Jerusalem.

When Meir Dagan heard this, he is said to have smiled. There was also a more important matter on his mind. The day before, hours after Arafat died, Mordechai Vanunu had been arrested in his rooms in St. George's Church in Jerusalem. He was charged with once more revealing classified information about Israel. Three months previously, Vanunu had said he would like to give up his Israeli citizenship and become a Palestinian. Vanunu said his one great wish was to be received by Yasser Arafat. The whistleblower's naïveté had not been tempered by his long sojourn in prison or his short months of freedom since his release. There can be little doubt that if the two men had ever been allowed to meet, Arafat would have exploited the occasion. He was a master of manipulation. In the end he had died as he had lived: amid confusion, intrigue, and farce. If he had been poisoned, no one now would ever know. If he had not, Arafat had left a legacy that would continue to promote the idea.

For years Arafat had operated according to the chaos theory of politics: as long as the Palestinians remained a festering problem for Israel, he would stoke the fires of not only his followers but the entire Muslim world. In his famous speech to the United Nations General Assembly that had marked his entry as a revolutionary icon, taking his place alongside Che Guevara and Fidel Castro, Arafat had declared, "I have come bearing an olive branch and a freedom fighter's gun. Do not let the olive branch fall from my hand. I repeat, do not let the olive branch fall from my hand."

On the day of Arafat's death, at a briefing later to his senior aides on what Arafat's death could foretell, Meir Dagan said that the only tragedy about Arafat's death was that it had not come sooner because Arafat had failed to ever let go of the gun.

CHAPTER 21

A NEW CALIPHATE
OF TERROR

The sixth floor of Mossad headquarters, with its olive-painted corridors and office doors that each bore a number in Hebrew but no name, housed the analysts, psychologists, behaviorists, and forward planners.

Collectively known as "the specialists," following Yasser Arafat's death they had combined their skills to evaluate and exploit how it was being perceived in the Arab world and beyond.

Their conclusions would guide Israel's future military and political moves in such key areas as Prime Minister Ariel Sharon's controversial plan to withdraw from the Gaza Strip and the relationship Israel should now have with the Palestinian Liberation Organization, the PLO.

The withdrawal was to take place in the high summer of 2005. It would be the first time that Israel had handed back settlements since its pullout from the Sinai in 1978 after the Camp David agreement had brought peace with Egypt. But already in the wake of Arafat's death, the withdrawal was being promoted by the PLO as the first step in finally creating a meaningful Palestine state that had been Arafat's abiding dream. But the Gaza Strip settlers saw their eviction as a betrayal of Israel's right to reclaim the land it had once occupied in biblical times. Their feelings of treachery were all the greater since the evacuation had been the work of Ariel Sharon, long regarded as the most powerful supporter of the settler movement.

The Mossad analysts shared the view of deputy prime minister Shimon Peres: "Zionism was built on geography but it lives on demography." They saw the *realpolitik* motives that had made Sharon order the razing of twenty-one Jewish settlements that lay along a stretch of the Mediterranean. To protect their eight thousand inhabitants from the surrounding 1.3 million Palestinians was a huge drain on Israel's resources.

To defend the settlements on the West Bank, Sharon had ordered the erection of a towering security barrier of reinforced concrete and razor wire that snaked down the length of the country; it meant Israel's effective border would be extended.

Like the majority of Israelis, the analysts were preoccupied by how soon Peres's prescient remark would become a reality. The forward planners on the sixth floor had calculated that by 2010 the number of Arabs living between the river Jordan and the Mediterranean would surpass the projected 5.2 million Jews living in Israel at the end of the decade.

In the months before his death, Arafat had predicted that not only would Gaza be "cleansed" of its Jewish settlers, but that the West Bank would also see the departure of its settlers from the ancient lands of Judea and Samaria.

The analysts had advised Meir Dagan that Arafat had left a legacy fraught with risk. They predicted that while the PLO would use the withdrawal from Gaza as a huge propaganda victory, Palestinian extremists like Hamas would defy calls by the PLO leadership to stop attacks on the settlements. It had turned out to be true.

The evacuation was conducted with overwhelming force by the Israeli army. Afterward synagogues left by the settlers were burned to the ground by Hamas militants. Following a short interval, the suicide bomb attacks on Israel resumed. Hamas justified them by presenting the Gaza withdrawal as no more than a maneuver by Israel to create more misery and frustration for the Palestinians. "Until the last Jew is removed from our land there can be no peace," Hamas said.

Throughout Arafat's life the PLO and Hamas had competed for control of the Intifadas of 1987 and 2000; each had aimed to persuade the *shebab*, the Arab youth, whose support was crucial in the direction the fight against Israel would take. By the second Intifada, when suicide bombings became the main symbol as Islamists and Fatah activists blew themselves up while killing as many as they could in Israeli pizzerias and restaurants, at bus stations and marketplaces—and Islamic religious leaders called for all-out jihad on the grounds that all Israelis, including women and children, were legitimate targets because Israel was a military society—Arafat was pressured into taking action against the terrorists, not only by Ariel Sharon, but also by moderate elements in the Arab world. Arafat still possessed a political legitimacy among them. But Hamas had the advantage of its Islamic extremism, a powerful drug to the dispossessed youth, epitomized further by the hero worship they bestowed on Osama bin Laden, who had repeatedly proclaimed, "There will be no solution to the Palestinian problem except through jihad." As the second Intifada continued to explode in a succession of fiery pyres, Arafat had seen his own infrastructure destroyed by Israel's sophisticated weapons, guided to their targets by the superb intelligence of Mossad and Shin Bet, the country's internal security service. In what Mossad analysts saw as a last desperate attempt to bolster his ailing leadership, Yasser Arafat had begun to claim that his way of carefully controlled political tension was the only means to pressure Israel into accepting his demand for the creation of a viable Palestinian state. By the time of his death, Arafat had attracted a considerable body of support among influential Palestinians. For Ariel Sharon the risk of Arafat being granted the martyrdom he was rapidly acquiring among moderate Palestinians, while at the same time Hamas continued its violence, was totally unacceptable.

The specialists had known from many years of listening to tapes recorded by the *yaholomin*, Mossad's communication unit, that Arafat had often spoken of his conviction that he had been chosen to lead the Arab world, a stepping stone to his assuming the mantle of a modern-day caliph; the position of leadership had been handed down from the time of the Prophet Muhammad's successors in the seventh century.

This fantasy had succoured Arafat during his darkest hours in exile and those turbulent years he had railed that the very existence of Israel was at the root of all problems, not only for the Arab nations but the entire Muslim world. In Washington and elsewhere it was long argued there was no point in listening to the rant of a demagogue whose sole message was one of violence.

But on the sixth floor the specialists knew it would be dangerous to ignore Arafat's words. While he and his associates no longer controlled terrorist operations, or at least very few, Arafat's ideology had inspired many young jihadists to see in his words that they had a sacred duty to somehow strike back at the West for actions in Muslim states. Following the emotional scenes at Arafat's funeral, Mossad *katsas* across the Middle East, in Kashmir and Chechnya, had all reported his death had stirred up passions.

A priority for the specialists was to show the billion-strong Islamic world that Yasser Arafat was never worthy of being a successor to Abdul Mejid II, the last caliph, who had gone into exile after Turkish nationalists, on March 3, 1924, had abolished the caliphate. Turkey's leader, Mustafa Kemal, or Atatürk, turned what remained of the Ottoman Empire, broken up at the end of the First World War, into a secular republic and forced through the wholesale adoption of European legal codes, writing, and a calendar. The seeds of jihad had been sewn.

In Egypt there followed agitation against British colonialism. The Muslim Brotherhood, founded in 1928, became a potent political force; and when Gamal Abdel Nasser staged a coup in 1952, he succeeded with their help. But Nasser soon saw the Brotherhood's extremism as a threat and banned the movement. Its members were exiled, jailed, or hanged. Many found refuge in monarchies such as Jordan and Saudi Arabia. It was then that Arafat and Osama bin Laden had become radicalized.

Both men, very different in their backgrounds, were influenced by a number of factors: Israel's defeat of Arab armies in 1967; Saudi Arabia's petrodollars, which gave Islamists the funds to proselytize around the Muslim world; and Ayatollah Khomeini's Islamic revolution, which overthrew the shah of Iran in 1979; and the Soviet invasion of Afghanistan that same year, a rallying call to wage jihad against the Soviet Union, funded by Saudi money and equipped with American weapons and with the full support of the Pakistan secret services.

The only blip in the ever-expanding militancy in the Islamic world was the assassination of Egypt's president Anwar Sadat in 1981 after he signed a peace treaty with Israel. Arab leaders incarcerated their own extremists.

"For the first time the West had become aware of what Israel had been saying for years about the danger of Islamic fundamentalism," said David Kimche, a former deputy director of Mossad (to the author).

But the radicalization, exploited by both bin Laden and Arafat, went unchecked. The United States became the Great Satan, the Infidel Empire. The deployment of American troops in Saudi Arabia to expel Iraqi forces from Kuwait in 1991 further radicalized the Muslim world.

It was at this stage that the specialists on the sixth floor had decided that Yasser Arafat and Osama bin Laden chose separate paths to achieve their aims, with bin Laden determining the way forward was to wage war against Israel's powerful ally, the United States. In 1993 came the bombing of the World Trade Center that brought terrorism home to America. In 1998, from the Taliban-ruled Afghanistan, bin Laden and Ayman al-Zawahiri, the leader of Egypt's Islamic Jihad, announced they were forming the "World Islamic Front for Jihad Against Jews and Crusaders." They issued a fatwa declaring that "it is the duty of every Muslim to kill Americans and Jews."

On October 12, 2000, suicide bombers rammed a dinghy packed with explosives into the side of the American warship, the USS *Cole*, in Aden, killing seventeen sailors. Two years later, on November 28, 2002, in Mombasa, three suicide bombers blew themselves up outside the Israeli-owned Paradise Hotel. Ten Kenyans and three Israeli tourists were killed. At the same time a surface-to-air missile narrowly missed an Israeli airliner taking off from Mombasa airport with two hundred tourists returning home to Tel Aviv.

Petro-Islamic terrorism had risen from the ruins of Arab nationalism. The "impious" precepts of the shah of Persia's regime had been replaced by the tenets of the Ayatollah Khomeini, which had spread beyond the borders of Iran to become the focus of hope in the greater Muslim world. The politicizing of Islam—until then largely seen in the West as a conservative faith losing its grip in the face of the growing influence of what bin Laden would call "the Coca-Cola society of the Great Satan"— had become a fully fledged revolution. Its first target, and never to lose that position, was Israel. Its defense against a stream of attacks fell upon Mossad. To destroy Arafat, his fedayeen, Hamas, and Hezbollah became prime objectives.

Syria had been quick to support these groups for a self-serving reason: it gave the regime credibility in the Arab world over its long-running enmity toward Israel. But it had become a double-edged sword. While Syrian-sponsored terrorist attacks had indeed finally persuaded Israel to negotiate over the Golan Heights—a precursor for what happened over the removal of the settlers from Gaza—its continued investment in terrorism had reinforced Israeli public opinion not to trust Damascus. Nevertheless, the removal of the Gaza settlements, as the promised precursor for a lasting peace for Israel, had resulted in growing resentment among a population that ironically began to echo the Hamas slogan that attacks would end only when every Jew was driven into the sea.

Mossad's analysts concluded that one way to win back support for the "road map" to peace was to carefully demolish Yasser Arafat's legacy. To do so, its Technical Services Department mobilized its skills in using the latest information technology. From the start of the second Palestinian Intifada in 2000, Arab terror groups, such as Al Aqsa Martyrs' Brigades, Hezbollah, Hamas, and Islamic Jihad, had used the Internet to promote their aims. Easy to set up, free to access, hard to censor, cyberspace had become an ideal place for issuing policy statements, claiming responsibility for terror attacks, appealing for funds, offering weapons and explosives training, and selling anything from suicide vests to the ingredients to create biological or germ warfare agents.

Mossad had been probably the first security service to monitor the Internet; as militants recognized that their mosques were almost certainly under surveillance, Web sites offered a new and relatively safe way to communicate with their followers. Mossad had created a large number of its own Web sites on which they posted carefully constructed disinformation in all the languages of the Middle East.

In the aftermath of Arafat's death, stories began to appear on the sites claiming Arafat had betrayed his own people for his own aggrandizement and noting his lack of moral probity. The sites claimed that vast sums of money intended to improve the lives of poverty-stricken Palestinians had ended up in Arafat's private portfolio.

The claims were the work of the dozen psychologists in LAP, Mossad's Department of Psychological Warfare. It had a long history of creating discord among Israel's enemies. Arafat's death had offered a further opportunity for LAP to show its skills.

Working with information from Mossad's twenty-four stations around the world, the psychologists had proved that Arafat controlled a financial portfolio estimated to be in the region of $6.5 billion. Yet the Palestinian Authority, which administered the PLO territories in the Gaza Strip and the West Bank, was close to bankruptcy.

LAP had planted a story in a Cairo-based newspaper, *Al-Ahram Weekly*, that Abdul Jawwad Saleh, a leading member of the Authority, wanted Arafat's financial adviser, Mohammed Rachid—who controlled the PLO portfolio—to be questioned. Soon newspapers and TV stations in the Gulf Straits, Jordan, Syria, and Lebanon found themselves in possession of copies of a highly secret PLO report that showed that for years the PLO had a deficit of over $95 million a month. The story became even more explosive when the IMF (International Monetary Fund) revealed Arafat had diverted "one billion U.S. dollars or more of PLO funds from 1995 to 2000."

The story swept like a desert storm through the Arab world. A Palestinian lawyer who had investigated PLO corruption said he knew of four Arafat loyalists who held secret Swiss bank accounts. The lawyer provided details of widespread corruption. He revealed (to the author on a guarantee of anonymity): "The deals involved the cement and building industries of the Palestinian territories. The corruption ran into millions of dollars, which Arafat covered up in return for the profiteers giving him a portion. He was the godfather of all the other godfathers."

The effect was to weaken the PLO at a time when, if it was to establish a bargaining position with Israel's prime minister Sharon, it needed to provide a strong and united front. By focusing on the undoubted murky world of Arafat's financial dealings, LAP had also effectively ended further speculation about any role Mossad had in his death. It was a textbook example of what Rafi Eitan had once said (to the author): "Well-placed words are often as effective as a bomb."

The deconstruction of Arafat's image was only part of Mossad's role in Israel's information warfare, infowar, which had become the hottest concept in the Kirya, the Israeli Defense Forces headquarters. Infowar was designed to exploit the ever-advancing technological concepts of the late twentieth century to allow Israel to launch swift, stealthy, widespread, and devastating assaults on an economic, military, and civilian infrastructure before an attack could be launched. Prime targets were Syria and Iran.

Powerful computer microprocessors and sophisticated sensors, and the training to use them, had been provided by the United States under yet another sweetheart deal Sharon had negotiated with the Bush administration.

IDF officers and several Mossad specialists had been sent to the National Defense University in Washington and the Naval War College at Newport, Rhode Island, to learn how to cripple enemy stock markets and morph images of a foreign leader. A favorite among the Israeli students was a tape of the ayatollahs appearing on Iranian television sipping whisky and carving slices from a ham, both forbidden in Islam. Before they had graduated, the students had flown on *Commando Solo*, the customized former USAF cargo plane that had been given a $70 million refit that enabled its crew to jam a country's TV and radio broadcasts and substitute messages—true or false—on any frequency. A version of the plane had been acquired by the IDF.

Mossad technicians were researching ways to infect enemy computer systems with a variety of virulent strains of software viruses. They would include the "logic bomb," designed to remain dormant in an enemy system until a predetermined time when it would be activated and begin to destroy stored data. Such a bomb could attack an enemy's air defense system or a central bank. The technicians had already created a program that could insert booby-trapped computer chips into weapons a foreign arms manufacturer planned to sell to a hostile country like Iran or Syria. Mossad *katsas* in key Eastern Europe arms manufacturing countries had also been briefed to find independent software contractors who wrote programs for such weapons systems. They would be offered substantial sums to slip viruses into the systems. An Israeli specializing in information technology said (to the author): "When the weapons system goes into attack mode, everything about it works, but the warhead doesn't explode."

Mossad agents were now equipped with a briefcase-size device that generated a high-powered electromagnetic pulse. Placed near a building, the pulse burned out all electronic components in the building. The device had its own built-in self-destruct mechanism that ensured its innards remained a secret. At the Institute for Biological Research, scientists were working to see if microbes could be bred to eat the electronics and insulating material inside computers in the same way that microorganisms consumed trash. Other scientists were working on aerosols that could be sprayed over enemy troops. Biosensors flying overhead would then track their movements from their breath or sweat.

On the other floors below, where the specialists created their Web site entries about Yasser Arafat, other equally skilled experts were going about their work.

The research and development laboratories on the second floor continued to create and update surveillance devices and adapt weapons. From there had come the matchbox-size camera, which could record and photograph a subject at over sixty yards' distance, and a variety of knives, including one that could slice through a spinal cord. These had been designed for the kidon, the unit specializing in assassination.

The third floor was occupied by the archives and the liaison offices with Shin Bet—Israel's equivalent of the FBI, with responsibility for Israel's internal security and foreign intelligence services that were deemed friendly. These included the CIA, Britain's MI6, French and German services, and the Russian Foreign Intelligence Service. Part of the floor was allocated to the Collections Department. This collated all incoming intelligence and distributed it to the appropriate departments on a need-to-know basis. The archives received everything; the data would be stored on high-speed Honeywell computers.

These included psychoprofiles of world leaders, terrorists, politicians, leading financiers—anyone who could be a help or hindrance to Israel. A typical profile contained personal details and close relationships. The one on President Bill Clinton listed the many transcripts from a *ya-holomin* surveillance of his conversations with Monica Lewinsky, some verging on phone-sex calls (see chapter 5, "Gideon's Nuclear Sword," pp. 103–5). The profile of Hillary Clinton contained a close analysis of her contact with Vince Foster, the Clinton White House deputy counsel. Mossad concluded that Foster did not commit suicide but, according to one Mossad officer who had read the file, "most likely was murdered to cover up what was a serious attempt by persons in the Clinton White House to keep secret material they would have preferred to keep quiet" (the author was told).

Osama bin Laden had an entire shelf of computer discs divided into his speeches, his sightings since 9/11, and the structure and restructure of al-Qaeda. In painstaking detail his profile explored how he had created the plans that had led to more innocent people being killed in the West than had died in Europe during any conflict since the Second World War. The analysis of his speeches showed bin Laden to be a slave to literal interpretations; the usual intellectual extrapolations upon which much European thinking depends appeared to be beyond his range. A late entry was the appointment of his eldest son, Saad, as his successor, and in the meantime the instructions were to concentrate on developing strategies for attacks on U.S. targets. The announcement had come from "the Jerusalem Force," the name bin Laden used when addressing his followers as a reminder of his ultimate ambition to ride in triumph through that city. A transcript of the message promised: "when that day comes our son Saad will ride at the head of our great cause." The Mossad analysts had concluded that the words were a further sign bin Laden did not expect to live long enough to see such an event. A separate file on Saad gave his age, twenty-six, and described him as the son of bin Laden's first wife and his favorite among the other twenty-three children he had fathered. The file described Saad as "the mirror image of his father, both physically and mentally." It revealed Saad had served with his father in Afghanistan and had fought against the Soviet occupiers. "Americans who met him there recall his readiness to kill." The last entry in the file said that Saad was on Mossad's list for assassination by kidon.

As Arafat lay dying in Paris, bin Laden had again resurrected his own demand to create a great caliphate of terror that would stretch from Asia to southern Spain. It was this claim that the specialists on the sixth floor had used for their own purposes. They had created documents, sourced to Hamas, that Osama bin Laden was set on "dishonouring" the memory of the PLO leader. In the Arab world, such a claim would create unease while, at the same time, would not diminish the impact of statements that Yasser Arafat had robbed the Palestinians of tens of millions of dollars. Setting one enemy of Israel against another was a tactic in which LAP was unrivaled.

One way of doing so had been to exploit the behavior of Libya's leader, Colonel Mu'ammar Gadhafi. Since he had seized power in 1969, as the twenty-seven-year-old head of a group of young officers, Gadhafi had been a prime target for assassination by Mossad. Having survived several attempts, it drove him to create a team of tall, muscular female bodyguards trained by the former KGB. LAP had focused on ridiculing him in the Arab world by using fake photographs created in the Mossad psychological warfare photo lab showing Gadhafi in sexual poses with the women. Meanwhile Gadhafi had backed terrorists, including arming the IRA and sponsoring attacks on airports in Vienna and Rome and in a Berlin discotheque, a favorite with U.S. servicemen based in the city. He had been linked to the Lockerbie bombing in 1998. At times his behavior seemed to drift beyond sanity. In 2001, he offered to buy all the bananas grown in the Caribbean to break the "stranglehold" of the World Trade Organization. Sartorially, he rivaled Michael Jackson, his favorite pop star; Gadhafi regularly wore orange robes, gold-braided military garb, and a powder blue jumpsuit.

In 2002, LAP scored another propaganda hit by planting a story Gadhafi had received a hair transplant. Later that year he arrived at an African summit with a container ship loaded with one thousand goat carcasses and distributed them to his fellow delegates. Afterward Jaafar Nimeiri, the former president of Sudan, described him as "a man with a split personality—both of them totally crazy." LAP was able to use this to great effect. It also focused on Gadhafi's sexual activities. Having fathered seven children by two wives, he had taken to offering interviews to foreign female journalists if they slept with him. That also became another item for LAP to promote around the world. More recently, in 2003, LAP planted stories that Gadhafi was terminally ill with cancer. But in mid-December 2004, his image as a buffoon who possessed a powerful nuclear arsenal, which he frequently threatened to unleash against Israel, was about to dramatically change.

Mossad's London Station was situated deep within the Israeli embassy in the fashionable district of Kensington. Accessed only by swipe cards that were changed regularly, and with a separate communications system from those of the main switchboard, the station was the most protected within a building where security was paramount. Each of the station's offices had a keypad door and a safe, the combination of which was known only to the office's occupant. Often a technician from Mossad's Internal Security Department, Autahat Paylut Medienit (APM), used a hand-operated scanner to check for any bugging devices; none had ever been detected. The half dozen intelligence officers and a support staff had been carefully selected for a key overseas posting in Mossad. The London Station now rivaled in importance that of the service's Washington base.

The staff worked under the direction of a man they all called Nathan. He had seen service in Asia and Africa before taking over as station chief. His formal duties included liaising with MI5 and MI6, Scotland Yard's antiterrorist squad, and foreign intelligence services based in the capital. He was a familiar face on the capital's diplomatic cocktail circuit and regularly dined at one of the city's members-only clubs alongside senior British politicians. It was one of those clubs, the Traveller's in Pall Mall, that focused Nathan's attention on that cold winter's day in December.

As Londoners made their way to another round of Christmas office parties, seven individuals arrived separately at the club, long a favorite meeting place for the senior officers of Britain's intelligence community. Situated within walking distance of the Ministry of Defence, Foreign Office, Home Office, and Downing Street, it was comfortable and discreet, a place where secrets could be shared over one of the finest steaks in clubland or a reputation gently questioned over a postdinner port in the club's lounge.

Six pinstripe-suited men and a woman in a black dress made their way past the club porter's lodge to a back room. It had been booked in the name of William Ehrman, the director general of defense and intelligence at the Foreign Office. A self-service buffet of tea, coffee, soft drinks, and the club's famed selection of sandwiches had been set up on a side table: the food did not include ham out of deference to the three men already waiting in the room with Ehrman. They were Musa Kusa, the head of Libyan intelligence, Ali Abdalate, the Libyan ambassador to Rome, and Mohammed Abul Qasim al-Zwai, the Libyan ambassador to London.

They were introduced by Ehrman to Eliza Manningham-Buller; John Scarlett, head of MI6; David Landeman, head of counterproliferation at the Foreign Office; and two high-ranking officials from Ehrman's department. He showed them all to opposite sides of a long mahogany table. At precisely twelve thirty on the mantle clock over the gas-fired Adams fireplace, Ehrman spoke.

"Gentlemen, we have come a long way. Let us now move to resolution."

So began a meeting that would last six hours to negotiate one of the most stunning breakthroughs in international diplomacy in decades. The meeting was to draft and approve every word of the text that would enable Colonel Gadhafi, the man President Reagan once called "the mad dog of the Middle East," to voluntarily give up Libya's weapons of mass destruction.

Over the years Gadhafi had created an arsenal that was the most powerful on the continent of Africa. Close to its southern border with Egypt was the Kufra biological and chemical factory. Concealed deep below the desert sands, it was beyond the bunker-buster bombs the United States had given to Israel's air force. The possibility of launching a successful sabotage attack had also been ruled out after a deep-cover Mossad agent managed to obtain a blueprint of the heavily guarded warren of laboratories where nuclear scientists from the former Soviet Union and former East Germany worked.

Sixty miles south of Tripoli, the country's capital, was a chemical weapons factory at Rabta that produced mustard gas, a First World War weapon, and more up-to-date nerve agents. These were also manufactured at the Tajura Nuclear Research Center, sited on the Mediterranean coast. In all, there were ten weapons of mass destruction facilities. All were guarded by long-range Scud missiles built with the help of North Korea.

On that December day the meeting in the Traveller's Club back room was the climax of efforts to end Gadhafi's thirty-five years of torrid relations with the West and allow Libya to be finally removed from the list of pariah nations.

The road to redemption had begun with the collapse of Soviet communism, which had erased Libya's hope that the continuous U.S. pressure would end. There had been the failure of a succession of economic programs that had made Gadhafi eager to attract foreign investment. Finally he had come to realize the ever-growing Islamic militancy was a threat of retaliation against his own regime and its long record of supporting terrorism. Even before Saddam had been captured, Libya had begun to ostracize the terrorist groups it had once embraced; at times Gadhafi had increasingly sounded almost like a moderate voice. In April 1999, Libya had agreed to allow two of its intelligence officers to stand trial under Scottish law for the destruction of the Pan Am 103 flight over Lockerbie. After the September 11 attacks, Gadhafi had secretly provided information to the CIA and FBI on al-Qaeda. In 2002, he had supported a Saudi initiative to offer Israel diplomatic recognition (yet to happen), and he had told Arafat not to declare a Palestinian state. All this had been summarized by his son Saif ul-Islam

Gadhafi: "If we have the backing of the West and the United States, we will achieve more in five years than we could achieve in another fifty years." The proof was the presence of his father's emissaries in the bastion of the English establishment.

During the meeting, Ehrman and Musa Kusa took turns using a telephone in an adjoining room to make calls. Ehrman's were to prime minister Tony Blair, who was on a visit to his Sedgefield constituency in the north of England. Using a second phone call, Blair kept President Bush in the White House updated on progress. Kusa's calls were to a phone in a Bedouin tent where Gadhafi was enjoying another of his desert sojourns.

In the preceding months, Kusa had, under Libyan diplomatic passport, traveled to London several times. As the man most trusted by Gadhafi, his mission was to agree to a text that would ensure the Libyan leader did not lose face and satisfy the British team that he could not renege. In an MI6 safe house near Gatwick airport, Kusa and document drafters from the Foreign Office agonized over every word. Time and again, when a breakthrough seemed to be close and a draft was sent to Libya on a secure fax, it came back with suggestions and amendments that were unacceptable to the Foreign Office.

A further complication was Kusa's suspicion of the need to involve Washington. Initially the Bush administration was also dubious about approving any deal with Libya. But as the secret meetings went on, the CIA asked to participate. Again Kusa was hesitant at their presence. He feared that Israel would learn of the plan from the CIA and possibly sabotage it. A Washington official involved in the negotiations said later: "Kusa was paranoid that the Israelis would want to torpedo the negotiations so that it could attack Gadhafi's weapons sites. The Brits were finding that trying to do a deal with Gadhafi involved a lot of walking on eggs without breaking one."

It had been like that from the August day in 2002 when Mike O'Brien, the Foreign Office minister, had visited Gadhafi in his desert tent. He was the first British envoy to do so. He was kept waiting for several hours before two female bodyguards finally ushered the gently perspiring minister into Gadhafi's presence.

"Gadhafi sat with dark glasses on and spoke through a translator, though I knew he had learned English at a course in England. When it became appropriate I raised the matter of his weapons of mass destruction. To my astonishment he did not deny he possessed them, adding that this was a serious issue. Time and again he emphasized he was genuinely interested to improve relations with the West and in particular to attract foreign investments to the Libyan oil and gas industries," O'Brien later recalled.

O'Brien returned to London convinced that Gadhafi was "genuinely ready to do a deal." But there was still a way to go. O'Brien made further visits to Libya. Though he was certain he had taken every possible precaution to maintain secrecy, the deep-cover Mossad agent in Libya had picked up his trail.

In Tel Aviv, Meir Dagan decided to fly to London. He arrived on the eve of the Iraqi war. During his visit Dagan managed to meet with Scarlett and Manningham-Buller and the man Scarlett was due to replace at MI6, Sir Richard Dearlove. Later it emerged that Dagan, in his usual blunt manner, had told the intelligence chiefs, according to one Israeli source (who spoke to the author): "Be assured that Israel will not impede your plans. But I do expect you not to try and hoodwink us."

In October 2003, with the initial Iraqi war offensive over, O'Brien was asked by Gadhafi to arrange for a team of British weapons experts and intelligence officers from MI6 and the CIA to inspect Libya's weapons of mass destruction sites. One expert had a close relationship with Mossad. His recall perfectly captured the atmosphere on the trip.

"The Libyans showed us everything. It was a case of: on your right, our famous chemical weapons; on your left, our secret uranium centrifuge; and tomorrow you'll see our biological weapons. At the end of our visit it was clear that while Libya had not yet acquired nuclear weapons capability, it was closer to having one than we had realized. It was also working on a variety of delivery systems, including ballistic missiles with a range capable of hitting any major city in Europe. The truth was that Gadhafi posed a far greater threat than Saddam did."

But with Saddam defeated, the negotiators in London decided to exert pressure on Gadhafi. A team of senior American negotiators from the State Department flew to London. They told Kusa they had "overwhelming" evidence that Libya could not have developed its programs on weapons of mass destruction without the help of Iran and North Korea.

"As a fully paid up member of the 'axis of evil' it was made clear to

Kusa that Libya remained very much on our target list," an official who attended the meetings said (to the author).

Nelson Mandela, the retired South African leader, was called upon to deliver a warning to Gadhafi that he must act—or face the consequences. Mandela called Bush and said that Gadhafi was "very serious about making an agreement."

But still the cautious fencing persisted between Libya and the negotiators. Finally it was made clear to Kusa that time was running out if Gadhafi continued to prevaricate. The deadline was January 1, 2005. The Traveller's Club meeting was convened.

The key part of the agreement was to be contained in the broadcast Gadhafi would make on Libyan television that evening. The text was sent to Tripoli for endorsement. A copy was faxed to Condoleezza Rice in Washington, whom Bush had asked to oversee the negotiations. She asked for minor changes to wording and emphasis. These were conveyed to Kusa.

The smiling intelligence chief said, "A woman's prerogative. But these are acceptable. We have a deal."

The historic announcement was to be made on Libyan television that night. The BBC monitoring unit at Caversham was sent a copy of the text and asked to monitor the broadcast. Shortly after the meeting at the Traveller's Club broke up, a copy of the text was handed to Nathan. In minutes it was on the desk of Ariel Sharon.

Having read the document, the Israeli prime minister told Dagan that as far as Libya went, Mossad was to maintain its close surveillance on the country. A copy of the document was sent to the third-floor archives and inserted in the Gadhafi psychoprofile. It contained a report that Musa Kusa had been one of the planners behind the bombing of the Pan Am jet over Lockerbie in which 270 people had died fifteen years before in the very week that Gadhafi was welcomed back from being a tyrant to a statesman.

In London, Jack Straw, the foreign secretary, praised Gadhafi's "huge statesmanship."

In Washington, the State Department announced that American companies with contracts on Libyan oilfields due to expire in 2005 were being allowed to open talks in Tripoli to extend their concessions.

In Paris, the French government confirmed that Kusa was still wanted in connection with the 1989 bombing of a French UTA airlines DC-10. But a spokesman admitted that given the spy chief's diplomatic status, it was "highly unlikely he will ever be questioned." In the French capital another long-running investigation was on the move again.

Mossad had continued to monitor events about the deaths of Princess Diana and Dodi al-Fayed. Faced with mounting public disquiet in Britain, the new Royal coroner, Dr. Michael Burgess, had overruled his predecessor's decision not to hold an inquest. He announced an inquiry, and the investigation would be headed by the former London Metropolitan police chief Lord Stevens. Stevens traveled to Paris to inspect the crash site. Among the media scrum that accompanied his every move was a Dutch-born *katsa*, Piet, a member of the Mossad Paris Station. Among those he had recruited was a *mahuab*, a non-Jewish informer, in the Paris police department. She was code-named Monique.

When the critically injured Diana arrived at the Salpêtrière Hospital, Monique was on duty in the emergency room to ensure no media entered. Shortly afterward, Diana was pronounced dead. She was draped in a clean gown and taken to a side room. Two nurses washed her body. One would later tell a reporter, "She looked so beautiful as if she was asleep."

The pathologist, Dominique Lecomte, arrived to find a scene of controlled chaos: "There were people around who you would not find in an operating room," she said later. They included two senior diplomats from the Paris British embassy, senior officials from the French Ministry of Justice, and the chief of the Paris police. The diplomats and the French officials stood in separate groups, whispering among themselves. Standing apart from the others was a member of the MI6 team in Paris who had been tracking Diana after her determined campaign against land mines. In London government circles, she had been called "a loose cannon." He was there to ensure there would be no obstacles to what Professor Lecomte was told "must be the swift transfer of Lady Di's body back to England. The order comes from high up in London."

Professor Lecomte asked for the body to be transferred to a side room adjoining the operating theater so she could conduct an autopsy. That was the moment the first conspiracy theory took root. The hospital had a fully equipped mortuary where an autopsy could have been performed. Had it not been used because transferring her there would delay matters? Alone with the body, Professor Lecomte began her "partial autopsy and partial embalming." Highly experienced though the pathologist was, even a "partial embalming" required time after she had performed a "partial autopsy." This would have required Professor Lecomte to remove a number of Diana's organs—probably including her heart and kidneys. She would also have removed organs from Diana's pelvic area. This would later further the speculation that Professor Lecomte had removed any evidence that Diana was pregnant. The pathologist then performed the "partial embalming," which French law requires before a body can leave the country. Even partial embalming is usually left to a mortician trained in the process. Skill is required in correctly diluting the formaldehyde so as not to discolor the skin or leave an unpleasant chemical odor.

In the years following the events in the early hours of that Sunday night, August 31, 1997, Professor Lecomte has refused to explain her crucial role. "The decision to embalm Diana's body would have tainted any samples taken at the postmortem in London. As a result the issue of pregnancy would have been covered up," insisted Mohamed al-Fayed, the father of Dodi, to the author.

Mossad's files on the deaths of Diana and Dodi contained detailed information on the role played by the CIA, MI6, MI5, and French intelligence. They answered speculation that Henri Paul was being used by MI6 to keep a discreet eye on Diana as her affair continued to attract world attention and contained details of the thirteen separate bank accounts held by Henri Paul for money he received from French intelligence. The former Israeli intelligence officer, Ari Ben-Menashe, had offered to provide Mohamed al-Fayed with copies of the files, claiming "they are the smoking gun that could reveal the full extent of the intelligence role in the deaths of Dodi and Diana," he stated to the author. He had asked for £750,000 for the files. Al-Fayed refused.

In Tel Aviv, Meir Dagan decided there would be no benefit to Mossad in providing Lord Stevens with access to the service's files. In that first week of 2005, he then had more important matters on which to focus.

Once more the specter that had haunted Dagan's predecessors had surfaced. The FBI had reopened its investigation to try and establish the identity of Mega, Mossad's deep-penetration agent high-level spy in Washington. He had originally been identified as working within the Clinton administration. But the FBI now believed he had successfully managed to conceal himself to secure a place in the Bush presidency. Like his predecessors, Dagan was probably the only spy chief in Israel who knew the true identity of his prized informer (see chapter 5, "Gideon's Nuclear Sword," pp. 100–2).

In the aftermath of George Bush being returned to the White House for another four-year term, FBI director Robert Mueller had briefed National Security adviser Condoleezza Rice—soon to become secretary of state—that Mega was the conduit through which highly sensitive policy documents on Iran had been passed to Israel. Mueller had told Rice that Mega would now be more important than ever for Israel as Bush began to formulate his policy toward the Middle East.

The FBI had already spent more than a year covertly investigating, using the latest electronic surveillance equipment, a Pentagon official, Larry Franklin, who was a senior analyst in a Pentagon office dealing with Middle East affairs. Franklin formerly worked for the Defense Intelligence Agency.

The Defense Department had confirmed the investigation, adding that Franklin worked in the office of defense undersecretary Douglas J. Feith, an influential aide to defense secretary Donald Rumsfeld.

The FBI had publicly said their investigation centered on whether Franklin passed classified U.S. material on Iran to the American-Israel Public Affairs Committee. The AIPAC is a highly influential Israeli lobby in Washington. Like Franklin, it had been swift to deny "any criminal conduct." In Israel, Ariel Sharon had taken the unusual step of issuing a similarly worded statement insisting: "Israel does not engage in intelligence activities in the United States."

Meir Dagan knew better. The United States had remained a prime target for Mossad operations after the 1985 conviction of navy analyst Jonathan Pollard on charges of passing secrets to Israel.

The FBI now believed Mossad had been responsible for how America's nuclear secrets, stored on computer drives, had been stolen from Los Alamos. The drives were each the size of a deck of playing cards and kept in the facility's most secure, password-protected vault in X-Division, twenty feet below the New Mexican mountains.

The theft was discovered after a massive forest fire threatened the area and scientists were ordered to enter the vault to remove the drives. But because of the intensity of the fire, Los Alamos was closed down for ten days, which meant a full-scale search for the drives was launched only after this period. The drives were designed to fit into laptop computers carried by members of the Nuclear Emergency Search Team (NEST) on permanent readiness to fly to the scene of any nuclear incident within the United States. NEST squads would use the highly detailed technical information on the drives to disarm and dismantle nuclear devices. The drives had been checked as all-present in an inventory taken in April 2002.

When the FBI finally arrived on the scene in May that year, their first suspicion was that a terrorist group had carried out the theft. But then, three months later, they discounted this when the drives were found behind a photocopier in another Los Alamos laboratory. In a report to Bill Richardson, then the energy secretary responsible for the lab, and its security chief, Eugene Habinger, the FBI concluded the theft was the work of a highly professional foreign intelligence service "like Mossad."

Now, three years later, the agency had not changed its view, Mueller told Condoleezza Rice. He also remained certain that somewhere within the Bush administration, Mega was securely entrenched. It was not a comfortable thought for the FBI director.

The Los Alamos theft had been prepared by the director general of CSIS, Qiao Shi. As well as being China's longest serving and most senior spy master, the eighty-two-year-old Qiao Shi was also chairman of the Chinese National Assembly since 1993 and the security chief of the Chinese Communist Party. It effectively made him overall intelligence supreme of the entire Chinese spying apparatus.

In the month preceding the Los Alamos operation, Qiao Shi had seen his power as vice-minister and overall co-coordinator of China's security services eroded in a series of internal struggles within the Politburo. Finally he was, effectively, demoted to be head of the Chinese Secret Intelligence Service's foreign intelligence branch. "The reason he was given was that the country's need in global intelligence gathering required more than one man to head up those requirements," a source told the author.

Qiao Shi was told that operations in place under his directions would remain his to control. He remained in post till June 2006.

The entire Los Alamos operation was given "total deniability" status by both Washington and Tel Aviv. The author was told in July 2006 by a former Canadian diplomat with knowledge of the operation "that publicity would have seriously damaged ongoing trade relations between both countries"!

Under Qiao Shi's direction, the Los Alamos theft had been prepared and carried out by PLA-2, the Second Intelligence Department of the

People's Liberation Army General Staff. Its multifunctions include tasking military attachés at Chinese embassies abroad and organizing clandestine operations. For months he had planned it in his office inside Zhonganhai, the government compound where the Chinese leadership lived in splendid isolation. As part of that planning, Qiao Shi had called upon CSIS's long-standing relationship with Mossad, which went back to their original collaboration in Africa (see chapter 13, "African Connections," pp. 250–2). For Mossad the chance to learn some of the secrets at Los Alamos was too good an opportunity to pass up. Mossad arranged for a team of LAKAM programmers and surveillance experts from its own *yaholomin* unit to travel to Beijing. They became part of the team that would electronically rob Los Alamos.

The fine-tuning of the operation had been placed in the hands of Wang Tomgye at the Science and Technology Department in the monolithic Ministry of Defense headquarters in Beijing's Dencheng District. In all, a hundred experts had been brought in to carry out the unprecedented heist. Many were experts in the difficult art of undetected computer hacking. Some of them had learned their skills while working for various companies in California's Silicon Valley. One by one they had been recalled to Beijing to take up their specialist work for the robbery.

The date was set for May 5, 2004. The target was the high security vault in what was itself Los Alamos's most secret facility. X-Division was a network of cramped offices on the third floor of the main laboratory building. Guarded by coded swipe cards whose entry numbers changed every day, the most sensitive of X-Division's data was stored in a strong room that had every device known to U.S. security experts. It was claimed to be more secure than Fort Knox's gold repositories. Inside the vault was a fireproof bag that could be opened only by using a special password. Inside that were the computer drives. Each disk contained detailed technical information, including how to dismantle the bomb designs created by rogue states like North Korea. They would provide anyone who obtained them with a massive advantage in knowing the nuclear secrets that the United States possessed.

Chinese and Israeli technicians had devised a hacking system that could electronically penetrate all the X-Division defenses. A replica of the Los Alamos vault was specially built in the basement of the Science and Technology Department. Inside the vault's steel walls was placed a fireproof bag. Inside the bag were put hard drives containing nonsecret information. The task of the hackers was to remove the information without revealing they had done so. They were to do so not from somewhere in Beijing, but at a considerable distance from the Chinese capital. The hackers were dispatched to Shanghai, several hundred miles away. They set to work. When the vault was later opened, there was no evidence the fireproof bag had been penetrated. The team of hackers returned to the basement. With them they brought true copies of the information electronically lifted from the hard drives stored in the bag.

The Chinese planners had worked on the premise that from time to time the hard drives in Los Alamos would be removed from their fireproof bag and placed in a computer they were certain would be inside the X-Division vault. This would either be done to check for a piece of information or to make sure the disks were in perfect working order. In Shanghai, the hackers had waited several days for the disks in the replica vault to be removed and inserted in a computer nearby.

The Chinese and Israeli team had also worked on the premise that at Los Alamos there was a good chance the hard drives would be left in the computer in an emergency. To create one, CSIS agents would light a brushfire that, given the prevailing wind direction, would sweep toward Los Alamos.

The next test took place in the Luzon Strait between Taiwan and the Philippine Islands. This time the hacking team was on board a Chinese nuclear-powered submarine of the blue-water fleet of the People's Liberation Army Navy. The submarine rose close to the surface, and the hackers went about their business. Once more they succeeded in electronically penetrating the replica vault in the Beijing basement. They returned to report their success to Qiao Shi.

Everything was ready. The team of hackers arrived in Puerto Penasco at the upper reaches of Mexico's Golfo de California. They were supplied with fishing equipment and boxes of tackle. Their journey to the port had been a long one. From Hong Kong they had flown into Mexico City and then driven to Puerto Penasco. Waiting for them was their rented fishing boat. Hidden on board, placed there by a CSIS agent in Mexico, was their equipment for hacking. They set to sea, ostensibly on a fishing trip.

With Los Alamos evacuated as the brushfire threatened to engulf the facility, the team set to work. Using the coordinates they had been provided with, the hackers had homed in on the X-Division vault at Los

Alamos. Just as they had waited in Shanghai for the right moment, so they had electronically lifted all the data from the hard drive disks in the fireproof bag. A week later, the team was back in Beijing.

No one would ever establish how the disks were subsequently found behind the photocopier. Was there a Mossad or CSIS agent inside Los Alamos? Late in November 2002, a meeting was held at Los Alamos to discuss the possibility. Gathered in a conference room in X-Division were George Tenet, then director general of the CIA; Britain's current MI6 chief, Dearlove; Director Freeh of the FBI (soon to lose his job); and Los Alamos security chief, Eugene Habinger. There was a consensus the theft had changed, almost certainly for the foreseeable future, the close intelligence links between Washington and London with Israel.

The sheer cold professionalism of the operation had placed CSIS, in Mossad's mind, as the one service it could rate as an equal. But in the past, the CIA had also worked with the Chinese. In 1984, William Casey, then head of the CIA, had secretly met Qiao Shi and persuaded him to act against the Triads who controlled over 60 percent of New York's heroin market. Every major American city had its Triad godfather, through whom an increasing amount of cocaine from Colombia and the Golden Triangle in Southeast Asia was marketed by dealers whose lineage went back to the opium dens of the 1800s. Casey had proposed a joint intelligence operation to combat the traffickers who had also started to target students on China's campuses. Mossad had monitored a meeting in the Mandarin Oriental Hotel in Hong Kong between senior CSIS officers and a team from the CIA, FBI, and the DEA in January 1985. It was another striking example of the hidden links and interdependencies between intelligence services.

CSIS had helped to produce some spectacular results in the drug war, including the now celebrated Golden Aquarium case in San Francisco. A million pounds of heroin had been discovered wrapped in cellophane and condoms inside fish imported from Asia. American federal agents had taken the credit for the bust. Privately they admitted they could not have succeeded without the CSIS team that had trailed the consignment across the Pacific. Later, after the Los Alamos theft, Qiao Shi had handed over to Mossad valuable information it possessed about the Triads. With an estimated million members scattered worldwide, the Triads were the largest drug traffickers on earth.

CHAPTER 22

OLD ENEMIES, NEW THREATS

In the three years since Meir Dagan had stood on a table in Mossad's

canteen on September 11, 2001, and had punched a clenched fist into

the palm of his other hand and told his staff that, metaphorically, he

expected them to eat the brains of their enemies, the number and ac-

tions of those enemies had dramatically increased.

Suicide bombers continued to strike; some were little more than

children. The supply of martyrs appeared to be inexhaustible.

Fissionable materials had been stolen from stockpiles in the former

Soviet Union; scientists at the European Transuranium Institute and

Karlsruhe in Germany, responsible for tracking all such material, had traced a small quantity of uranium-235 to the Paris apartment of three criminals known to broker arms deals with terror groups like al-Qaeda. The uranium was of weapons-grade quality. Two of the men—Sergei Salfati and Yves Ekwella—were traveling on Cameroon passports. The third, Raymond Loeb, possessed South African documents. The material came from a nuclear storage site at Chelyabisk-70, sited deep in the Ural Mountains. Tipped off by Mossad, French police had arrested the criminals.

Mossad had traced the route along which the uranium had been transported across the Ukraine, through Poland and Germany to Paris by employees of Semion Yukovich Mogilevich. Since the collapse of the Soviet Union, he had positioned himself to traffic not only in humans and arms but fissionable material as well. As with the site in the Urals, it had disappeared from other poorly guarded locations.

President Vladimir Putin had spoken darkly of a "new network of terror against which our forces are increasingly hard-pressed to overcome."

In Afghanistan and the near-lawless northern provinces of Pakistan, thousands of jihadists—holy war warriors—were being trained for what they were promised would be the endgame, the elimination of Israel from the face of the earth. Some of the graduates had returned to their homes in places like the Gaza Strip, the West Bank, the souks of Egypt, the Yemen, and, farther afield, the cities of Britain. All made no secret of their readiness to die in jihad, holy war, to perfect their newfound skills anywhere that could damage the financial and economic structure of Israel.

They were often financed by state-sponsored terrorism, either because of a shared ideology (Hezbollah and Iran), or calculated *realpolitik* (Hamas and Syria). Israel had worked tirelessly through the United Nations to get sponsors of terrorism to be stopped by sanctions or even military action. Mossad's department of psychological warfare had spun the story that Israel was ready to launch a preemptive strike should the ayatollahs continue to support Hezbollah and Islamic Jihad. The threat created fear among the Iranian population, even though its military tacticians briefed the country's rulers that geographically the Jewish state was sufficiently far away not to pose a serious and sustained threat. In the case of Libya it had played a background role in persuading Gadhafi that his interests would prosper by avoiding being the bagman for a number of terror groups.

As it did for every major Western intelligence service, al-Qaeda remained on top of Mossad's own threat list. Early on in Meir Dagan's tenure, two names had emerged to stand beside Osama bin Laden in the cause of Islamic extremism. One was Ayman al-Zawahiri, who increasingly performed the role as al-Qaeda's chief television propagandist. The Egyptian medical doctor, who had trained in London and Paris, had made over six video and audio broadcasts in 2005, earning himself the adulation of the Arab world as the organization's intellectual guiding force. Mossad analysts had postulated that bin Laden reserved his own appearances for major occasions, such as addressing the American people four days before the U.S. election, where he had sat at a desk like a newsreader and promised further attacks if Bush was reelected; and after the Madrid commuter train attacks that killed two hundred and injured almost two thousand, when he had repeated the warning. The other member of this trinity of evil was Abu Musab al-Zarqawi, the Jordanian ill-educated peasant responsible for some of the worst atrocities in Iraq. Before he had reached the age of thirty, he had beheaded a dozen Iraqis and foreigners and posted videos of their murders on Islamic Web sites around the world. He, too, had promised that the day would come when he would join bin Laden's son, Saad, at the head of a triumphal march into Jerusalem.

Now in the first weeks of 2005, it was not only terrorists that Meir Dagan found himself confronting. He had begun to have doubts about the new MI6 director-general, Sir John Scarlett. The roots of these reservations lay in what Dagan knew was seriously inaccurate MI6 intelligence that had led to the politicizing of information about Saddam's alleged weapons of mass destruction. It had confirmed Dagan's view that John Scarlett had a tendency to "shoot from the hip." Certainly for the crew-cropped Mossad chief with a liking for open-necked shirts, Scarlett was radically different as the quintessential English spymaster in his customized suits from Gieves, the Saville Row tailor, and hand-stitched cotton shirts, along with his buff-colored security files each bearing the red cross of Saint George. Over dinner at the Traveller's Club, Scarlett would display a taste for expensive claret and his gourmet's appetite for fine food. After his thirty-two years as an intelligence officer in Moscow, Kenya, and Paris, Scarlett had become chairman of the Joint Intelligence Committee (JIC) that monitored Britain's other intelligence services and reported directly to Tony Blair in Downing Street. It was a widely held view that Blair had exercised his prime minister's prerogative to appoint Scarlett to take over MI6. His appointment had brought Scarlett a knighthood to go with his CMG and OBE. It had also continued his close relationship with Blair, and Dagan was not the only foreign intelligence chief who sensed that Downing Street's hand could be detected in decisions made by Scarlett. It went against Dagan's own firm belief that an intelligence service should be independent of political influence.

Dagan's concern over this had turned to anger when Scarlett, with prime minister Tony Blair's approval, secretly sent a team of officers to Gaza to negotiate a cease-fire with Hamas, led by an experienced Middle East veteran intelligence officer, Alistair Cooke. For Dagan, the arrival of an uninvited foreign intelligence service on his doorstep contravened what he saw as a long-standing arrangement over the rules of cooperation. When Dagan had confronted Scarlett, he was reminded that MI6 had a long history of entering into negotiations with outlawed terror groups, notably the IRA in the 1980s, and that dialogue had ultimately led to the armed struggle in Northern Ireland giving way to political negotiation.

"Gaza is not Belfast," Dagan had said before ending the conversation. For him this signaled a low point in Mossad's working relationship with MI6. Not for the first time, he had been heard to say the English had never quite come to terms with not being spymasters to the world. It was a view he shared with Carlo de Stefano, director of Italy's antiterrorism unit; Manolo Navarette, the head of Guardia Civil Intelligence in Spain; and Porter Goss, who had replaced George Tenet as director of the CIA. Goss was no pushover. He was cut in the same no-holds-barred mold as Dagan, saying publicly that Tenet had ignored the agency's "hard core mission, and that it must return to the 'good old days of human intelligence' when information was gathered not by computers and satellites and other sophisticated eavesdropping, but by planting our agents within or behind enemy lines." Goss suddenly resigned in May 2006, after a turf battle with John Negroponte, the politically shrewd new director of national intelligence, a post created by President Bush to oversee intelligence gathering after 9/11. Goss was already unpopular with senior managers at the CIA, having forced half a dozen to resign. A high-ranking CIA officer told the author, "When Goss quit, there was more champagne drunk than on New Year's Eve."

Dagan's chagrin had increased over what he had learned about MI6's involvement in the critical intelligence that had clinched the case for Prime Minister Tony Blair and President George Bush going to war with Iraq. The intelligence service had produced what it insisted was "conclusive proof" that vast quantities of yellowcake, the iron ore from which enriched uranium is extracted, had been secretly shipped from the impoverished West African country of Niger. The evidence had hinged on documents MI6 insisted it had obtained from "a trusted source." Dagan knew it would be unthinkable to reveal such a high-value contact, providing that was who he or she was. Apart from MI6, no one else had seen the documents and there was a mounting suspicion they were not all that MI6 claimed. But if nothing else, Meir Dagan had come to the conclusion that the insistence of John Scarlett to continue to defend the veracity of the documents raised questions about his judgment.

The saga of how that happened would turn out to be a classic dirty tricks operation culminating in October 2005 with Lewis Libby, Vice President Dick Cheney's chief of staff, being indicted on perjury charges and Karl Rove, the White House senior adviser to President Bush, facing investigation by a grand jury. Their role centered in the unmasking of a CIA field officer, Valerie Plame, the wife of a former U.S. ambassador to Niger, Joseph Wilson. It is a criminal offense in America to identify an active secret agent. Mossad's role in the fiasco would remain untold until these pages.

The story had properly begun in the summer of 2004 with a former employee of SISMI, the Italian equivalent of the CIA. A year before he, "Giancomo" Martino, had resigned from the service to set himself up as an "intelligence analyst." In no time in Rome, a city well-stocked with journalists and spies, he became a source for, among others, Mossad's station, which was housed in a building near the Vatican.

In the world of spies and reporters eager for news, Giancomo was a useful contact able to peer through the keyhole of Italy's security apparatus. The tanned, bespectacled sixty-year-old, with a liking for sand-colored suits and whose English was spoken with an American twang, had from time to time provided snippets of information that, if not exactly earth-shattering, were nevertheless often intriguing. His most recent offering had been photocopies of SISMI documents that showed the agency had been involved in the notorious case of Roberto Calvi (see chapter 20, "God's Banker . . . ," pp. 413–20). The former head of Banco Ambrosiano had close contacts with the Vatican Bank, whose activities were of abiding interest to Mossad. Calvi had been found hanging beneath Blackfriar's Bridge in London in 1989. The documents Giancomo produced showed three senior SISMI officers had been closely involved with Calvi before his death.

On that summer day in Rome, Giancomo met his Mossad contact, Sammy-O (in the intelligence world aliases are often on a first-name basis, a piece of tradecraft used by most services). But as they sipped drinks in an open-air restaurant, it was not the murky connections between finance and intelligence that Giancomo had to divulge. The seventeen pages he had stored on his laptop came from a time when the CIA and MI6 had been tasked by their political masters to discover evidence that would bolster the claim in Washington that Saddam Hussein had obtained yellowcake ore from Niger. The rock was not only a key material in the process of producing enriched uranium but was also crucial to the Bush/Blair justification for going to war. Sammy-O's initial study of the documents showed some of them were encrypted, an indication they could be genuine. But there were also spelling mistakes and inconsistencies with dates. Were these the documents George W. Bush and Tony Blair had used to help recruit support for the invasion of Iraq? Giancomo had shrugged, a favorite gesture when he did not wish to commit himself.

Sammy-O had asked Giancomo to explain the spelling mistakes. The informer had again shrugged. Where had the documents originated? Giancomo had replied, according to the agent's later report submitted to Tel Aviv, that a contact in SISMI had introduced him to a woman official at the Niger embassy in Rome. After some discussion she had handed the documents over. Sammy-O had the usual questions: Who else had seen them? Why had the woman done that? What deal did Giancomo have with her? Giancomo had refused to answer. The documents indicated the yellowcake ore had been secretly sold to Iraq. They appeared to reinforce the claims of Bush and Blair that they had been right to go to war.

Niger's yellowcake came from two mines controlled by a French company, which operated within strict international laws governing the export of the ore. One document indicated the ore had come from "unofficial workings" whose product was sold on the black market. It was that market into which Saddam had supposedly tapped. Sammy-O had a final question: How much did Giancomo want for the documents? Fifty thousand Swiss francs was the instant response. The silence that followed was broken by Giancomo.

"The documents are forgeries. They were created by SISMI for the CIA and MI6 to support the claim of Blair and Bush that Saddam Hussein had obtained the ore. Don't you see what that means?"

Sammy-O saw. The forgeries had been the ones which MI6 had insisted were genuine and which Tony Blair and George Bush had used to defend going to war with Iraq. The documents reinforced the claim of the former ambassador to Niger, Joseph Wilson, who had been sent there by Bush in 2002 to check on their authenticity and had reported back that no yellowcake had gone to Iraq. President Bush had rejected his report and gone to war. When the initial conflict ended, Wilson had finally gone public on his findings and found himself discredited in a campaign orchestrated by Karl Rove and Lewis Libby, which had included them revealing the identity of Wilson's CIA secret agent wife, Valerie Plame.

What transpired under the café awning between Sammy-O and Giancomo came down to this: Mossad had paid the asking price for the forgeries. For the moment they would be used as a teaching tool at the service's training school, an example of an operation to seriously embarrass two world leaders. Who had asked SISMI to plant the fake documents would remain unknown, but Mossad knew that in the past the Italian service had bugged the country's presidential palace and the papal library as a favor to the CIA. And that agency had long fallen out with its Washington masters over the White House deliberately misrepresenting the truth about Saddam's nonexistent arsenal. Mossad believed Langley had set out to seriously embarrass the Bush administration, which had sidestepped the CIA's own intelligence-gathering apparatus before the Iraq war and after the conflict had condemned the agency for not providing sufficient intelligence. Using SISMI—and not for the first time—the CIA could expect its complicity to have remained undiscovered. That had happened before in black operations in Latin America. What the CIA had not calculated was Giancomo's greed for a sale. He knew that Mossad would pay for the documents, whether they were genuine or forgeries, once it realized they were the ones upon which Blair and Bush had largely based their case for going to war. Giancomo's refusal to say who else had seen them was a strong clue he had sold them to the MI6 station in Rome. All else had flowed from that.

As well as MI6's continued insistence the forged documents were genuine, there were other claims that concerned Mossad about the way the service was operating under Scarlett. He had claimed another "high-value source" had provided "good evidence" in the run-up to war that Saddam Hussein had portable chemical labs roaming in Iraq deserts ready to launch warheads with chemical and biological agents. U.S. secretary of state Colin Powell had endorsed the claim in his eve-of-war address to the United Nations, citing the source as MI6. Later, Mossad's deep-cover agents had established no mobile labs ever existed.

A senior Mossad analyst recalled (to the author): "MI6 was serving up, at best, speculation, at worst, baseless information as fact. It was the constant promise, underwritten by Scarlett, that the details were well sourced which made them acceptable. Only later, after the war was over, did we see that much of the data from London was often no better than the stuff the 'spy' in 'Our Man in Havana' dreamed up. He used drawings of a vacuum cleaner to support his reports. MI6 produced toy mobile labs for Powell to display before the United Nations."

Shortly before the enlargement of the European Union in May 2004, MI6 informed Mossad that the expansion could result in an influx of terrorists into Britain whose prime targets would be the Jewish business community. London Station failed to find any evidence to support this.

In May 2004, Dagan had sensed a sea of change happening in Langley, and he was determined that Mossad would benefit from it. He already knew Porter Goss's reputation from his eight years as the Republican chairman of the House Permanent Select Committee on Intelligence, during which he had openly declared the CIA had become too "gun-shy" after the 1998 terrorist bombings of the U.S. embassies in East Africa. Dagan had been further won over when Goss had publicly said he was not against assassinations. "I believe it is a concept most Americans are fairly comfortable with. If you have exhausted all other avenues then the possibility of lethal force is well understood," he had said after President Bush had nominated him to be the CIA's next director. His words had found considerable support among conservatives at a time when Osama bin Laden's freedom remained a major threat to America.

From their first meeting the two spy chiefs had formed an immediate bond. Goss had listened as Dagan had explained how he had inherited a Mossad where morale was low and its reputation seriously damaged, and how he revitalized it by the simple expedient of being a hands-on director. Since coming to office Dagan had made close to fifty trips overseas. Goss had spoken about his own stint with the CIA in the 1960s, the time of the Cuban missile crisis, and attempts to assassinate Fidel Castro with a poisoned cigar or a booby-trapped seashell when the Cuban leader went diving. Goss explained that ill health had finally made him give up a career with the Directorate of Operations that was responsible for all spying missions. He had entered politics, winning a seat for the Republicans in Florida. But he had never lost touch with the global intelligence world. In London, Paris, and other European capitals, he had kept alive a network that would serve him well in his new post.

As a practical step in their alliance, Goss and Dagan sent their spies into the badlands of Kazakstan, to the mountains of Kashmir, to the seaports of the Horn of Africa, into the highlands of Kenya and Ethiopia, and reinforced their presence in Saudi Arabia.

The kingdom's increasing volatility continued to provide a fertile recruiting ground for the jihadists and the seemingly unlimited funds available to finance them. Split by a power struggle, with the seventy-nine-year-old King Fahd clinging to life (he would finally die in August 2005) and many of the royal family's five thousand princes living in fear of the fundamentalist groups sprouting in their midst, the kingdom had provided them with billions of petrodollars in the hope they would be spared in any insurrection by the country's radicals. The most extreme spoke of the day when Osama bin Laden, himself a Saudi, would bring the royal family to its knees in much the way the Ayatollah Khomeini had returned to Iran in triumph. Already bin Laden had fulminated that Sharia law was not being implemented strictly enough in the Kingdom.

Supported by the Bush administration, the House of Saud had finally begun to crack down hard on the fundamentalists. Shoot-outs between the security forces and fundamentalists became routine. Captured jihadists were beheaded, and their heads displayed on spikes in public squares around the country. The displays had only increased the violence. In 2004, over 150 foreigners, agents of the security forces, and terrorists had died.

While the CIA worked closely with the Saudi secret service to locate the fundamentalists, Mossad's role was different. With Saudi Arabia having no Jewish economic interests to attack within its borders, Mossad agents were concerned with tracking jihadists coming out of the country and heading toward Israel. All too often before reaching its borders, they met their deaths at the hands of Mossad's most feared unit, kidon, its assassination squad.

Among the first decisions Meir Dagan had made was to increase its number from forty-eight to sixty; eight of them were women. All kidon had graduated from the Mossad training school at Herzliyya before undergoing specialist training at an army facility in the Negev Desert. On graduating, their average age was still in their midtwenties. They regularly underwent the same physical checks as a front-line pilot in the Israeli air force. Between them kidon were fluent in Arabic and the major European languages, English, Spanish, and French. Some had acquired a proficiency in Chinese.

In the $100 billion global intelligence industry, which engaged over a million people, kidon was regarded with respect. With an unpublished budget and no accounting for how it was spent, kidon was also the envy of other secret services. Only the Chinese Secret Intelligence Service (CSIS) had a similar freedom to kill.

In the past three years Dagan had sent kidon to seek out all those who had been condemned at a meeting he chaired in his office. The assassins had done so in countries across the Middle East, in Iran, Pakistan, and Afghanistan, striking in places where the souks and alleys had no names; in each case a killing had been swift and unexpected, using anything from a single bullet to the nape of the neck, to garrotting with a cheese-cutting wire or a knife thrust into the larynx. Kidon had also used nerve agents and a poisoner's arsenal of substances specially prepared for them. There were many ways of killing, and kidon knew them all.

To perfect their skill they watched some of Israel's leading forensic pathologists in Tel Aviv's Institute of Forensic Medical Research at work so as to better understand how to make an assassination appear to be an accident. They learned how a small blemish or a pinprick on a victim's skin would be a giveaway. Watching the pathologists cutting and dissecting a corpse, kidon were encouraged to ask questions. How had a pathologist decided exactly how a corpse had been murdered? What attempts had been made to disguise the method of killing? What was the significance of some small mark on the skin or damage to an internal organ the pathologist had discovered that had led him to a final conclusion? Later, back at their base, kidon would be closely questioned by an instructor on what they had seen and how it could be used for their own purposes. It was rare that a member of the unit failed the grilling, which would mean coming off the active duty roster for a spell of further intensive study of the pathologists at work.

Kidon routinely drove out to the Institute for Biological Research at Nez Ziona to consult with its scientists in their secure laboratories where they tested the efficacy of chemical and biological weapons prepared in labs in Iran, North Korea, and China. Some of the Institute's Jewish chemists had once worked for the KGB and the East German Stasi intelligence service. When these collapsed at the end of the cold war, the scientists were recruited by Mossad.

In a conference room reserved for the purpose, chemists and assassins would sit and discuss the merits and drawbacks of what was available for a specific assassination. Would the killing be at night or day? Some lethal pathogens did not work so well in daylight. Would an assassination be in an open or a closed space? Nerve gas often responded very differently in either situation. Would an aerosol be more effective than an injection? Where should either be aimed at the body? Behind an ear, the back of a hand, a jab into a calf or thigh? The questions required careful answers. A kidon's life could depend on them.

The choice of location was also important. Some nerve agents smelled of new-mown grass, others of spring flowers. To use them in desert surroundings would risk raising suspicion. Sometimes, however, it was important to leave evidence that kidon had struck to raise fear in others.

More recently, the desert tracks out of Saudi Arabia had been littered with the bodies of dead jihadists who had set off to wage terrorism against Israel—and had encountered kidon.

Mossad's African safari had been a high mark of its foreign adventures in the 1970s. The classic example of how Meir Amit had put together a textbook operation was part of the curriculum at the Mossad training school. When he came into office, he had studied how a very secret and deadly war had been successfully waged against the KGB and China's CSIS. Both intelligence services had been training African revolutionaries to mount guerrilla attacks against Western interests from the shores of the Indian Ocean to the Atlantic.

The prospect of thousands of well-trained and armed fighters within a few hours' striking distance of Israel had alarmed the country's politicians. Meir Amit had sent every available *katsa*—field officers—and kidon to Central Africa. For three years they waged a pitiless battle of attrition against Russian and Chinese agents. *Katsas* were killed with the same brutality. Their names were later engraved on one of the sandstone walls of the brain-shaped memorial at Glilot that commemorated Mossad's dead. In 2005 they numbered ninety-one.

Now this figure could increase as Dagan sent his agents into the jungles of Venezuela, the mountains of Colombia, the back streets of Mexico, the Amazon, and down into Chile and Argentina; in all those countries al-Qaeda was fomenting hatred against Israel. Once more the terror organization was helped by the CSIS Second Intelligence Department of the People's Liberation Army General Staff.

Both organizations had established a strong presence in El Salvador—part of their overall campaign to make Latin America both a powerful new player on the continent for China and to provide al-Qaeda with an operational presence that presented an increasing threat to Jewish interests in the region. San Salvador banks—including offshoots of Israeli, British, and U.S. financial institutions—became a routine stopover for the huge sums of money being laundered by both CSIS and al-Qaeda on cash-washing journeys around the world. These profits from drug running supplemented deals al-Qaeda had made with the drug cartels of Colombia.

Katsas and kidon, supported by CIA and DAS agents, ran a "kill or be killed" campaign in the dense jungles of Venezuela to stop al-Qaeda moving massive quantities of cocaine out of the country into the United States, Europe, and Israel. The dead of al-Qaeda were left to rot in the jungle, a warning to others. The bodies of the agents were airlifted out for burial in their homelands. In Israel there was no official acknowledgement where they had been or what they had done. Only the work of the stonemason at Glilot offered a clue as he carved each name with pride.

In al-Qaeda hideouts in the jungle, evidence had been found that over three thousand American-based companies, many in the high-tech industry, had been penetrated by the organization buying stocks. U.S. Treasury officials calculated that in 2004 the terror group had invested over a billion U.S. dollars. The shares had been acquired through investment brokerages in Asia, Malta, and Poland, payment having first been processed through banks in Saudi Arabia and Lebanon. FBI director Robert Mueller had assigned 167 senior agents to try and unravel the complicated financial structure that now gave al-Qaeda a growing presence in the global financial markets.

David Szady, the FBI assistant director for counterintelligence, had called the situation "a most grave and present danger. It could undermine the national security and economic advantage of the United States" (to the author).

At the center of al-Qaeda's money-laundering activities was the software program, Promis, developed by the Washington-based specialist company, Inslaw, and subsequently obtained by Israel. A copy of the software had later found its way into the hands of Osama bin Laden. It had originally been stolen from the FBI by Robert Hanssen, a longtime KGB spy in the agency. He had passed it on to the KGB, and its agents had then sold it to bin Laden.

While in Washington, al-Qaeda's tangled financial web was slowly being untangled, in Latin America Mossad had established how the terror group's operatives entered the continent through Honduras and Venezuela. The CSIS had high-speed trawlers based in Cuba capable of running the terrorists across the Caribbean to the virtually unguarded coastline of both countries.

When China's president, Hu Jinto, had visited Cuba in late 2005, he had agreed to provide Castro with the latest signals intelligence and electronic-warfare facilities. The complex was near Bejucal, twenty miles south of Havana. At the other end of the island, Chinese technicians had installed a surveillance system capable of eavesdropping on classified U.S. military communications by intercepting satellite signals. The presence of these powerful monitoring posts enabled China to conduct electronic surveillance of the southern United States and across Central America. They gave al-Qaeda cells on the continent vital foreknowledge of moves by Mossad and the CIA to attack them.

In Tel Aviv, Meir Dagan had told senior staff that he shared Porter Goss's frustration that there could be no preemptive strike against the Cuban sites.

"The memory of the Bay of Pigs fiasco still haunts Washington," Dagan was quoted as telling his staff.

On an afternoon in early February 2005, when even the air pollution was bearable, a Mossad agent, code-named Manuel, had arrived in Mexico City's international airport. He had flown from Florida on a Spanish passport; his base was in the city, a safe house in a neighborhood settled mostly by Jews who had retired.

In the past weeks he had visited the Bogotá headquarters of DAS, Colombia's intelligence service, and the security services of Peru, Bolivia, and the Dominican Republic. His hosts had described the extent of al-Qaeda's penetration of their countries. In Colombia, it had held meetings with FARC, the country's terror group, and with Shining Path, the Peruvian anarchists. Before he left, DAS had given Manuel copious documents showing how hard it was trying to cope with the terrorism al-Qaeda had brought within their borders and which they had little firsthand knowledge about. Manuel had promised he would arrange for key members of their security forces to come to Israel and receive firsthand briefing.

Mossad had been doing that for years in third world countries. It was another way to have its own contacts on the inside and work through them to fight terrorism.

In Mexico, Manuel was not yet certain he would find suitable contacts. Its law-enforcement agencies, especially its police, had a deserved reputation for bribery and corruption. Officers were involved in drug smuggling, kidnapping, extortion, and killings. But most alarming of all were the links between al-Qaeda and the country's Popular Revolutionary Army, EPR. They had been discovered in documents during antiterrorist operations by the CIA in Pakistan to try and locate Osama bin Laden. Copies had been passed on to Mossad at the instigation of Porter Goss. As well as confirming al-Qaeda ties with the substantial student population of Muslims on Dominica and the large number of Arabs living on Peru's border with Chile, the documents revealed that EPR had a key role in helping al-Qaeda operatives enter the United States through the busiest land crossing in the world, Tijuana.

Mossad analysts believed the documents were authored by Ayman al-Zawahiri, al-Qaeda's leading strategist. His psychoprofile in the Mossad archives included the observation that his few pleasures included watching videos of the attacks of 9/11. Since then he was reported to have made several visits to Latin America.

Manuel was eager to know if Mexico's Center for Investigation and National Security, CISEN, could provide further evidence of this. He would be unlucky. Its director, Eduardo Medina, insisted his service had no reason to believe al-Qaeda had any presence in Mexico. "Purely media speculation," he had said.

Next day Manuel caught a plane back to Florida. He had found no one in Mexican intelligence he would recommend should be invited to Israel. When he had made his report, he would then fly to Washington on a very different assignment.

At 10:00 a.m. EST, on a biting cold winter day, January 14, 2005, a war game chaired by POTUS—White House speak for the president of the United States—stand-in Madeleine Albright entered a hotel ballroom in midtown Washington, D.C., to preside over a summit of world leader stand-ins. They had convened in the expectation that they would discuss how best to handle the greatest natural disaster in modern history, the Indian Ocean tsunami, the death toll of which had climbed to over one hundred thousand and would eventually reach beyond three hundred thousand.

Instead, Manuel was among a select number of official observers invited to see how another and even more dangerous crisis would be handled. It posed a threat that successive Mossad directors, like intelligence chiefs everywhere, feared more than any other attack. What was about to be unveiled in the ballroom was a threat virtually impossible to detect in its creation or launch.

The CIA had learned that a breakaway faction of al-Qaeda had stolen a small quantity of smallpox virus from a biocontainment laboratory in Siberia. The lab was one of two places in the world where the virola was contained under stringent World Health Organization (WHO) protocols. The other was the Centers for Disease Control (CDC) in Atlanta, Georgia. The Siberian facility had a security system built by the Bechtel Group and paid for by the U.S. government to protect freezers containing 120 different smallpox samples. The CIA had still not established how the theft had happened or where the virus had been taken.

The president had been briefed that the virus was one of the most deadly diseases on earth; in the twentieth century alone it had killed

300 million people. It was not until 1980 that WHO announced smallpox had been eradicated. Now on that January morning, PO-TUS had summoned her fellow leaders to tell them it was once more a threat.

They sat in a U-shaped area of desks on which were phones, computers, and TV screens. Each desk bore a name: Prime Minister of United Kingdom; President of France; Chancellor of Federal Republic of Germany; Prime Minister of Canada; Prime Minister of Poland; President of European Commission; Prime Minister of Sweden; Director General of World Health Organization.

POTUS took a seat in their midst and began to outline the theft from the Siberia laboratory. She was still speaking when the television screens on the desks came alive. A masked man said he represented New Jihad, a group affiliated to al-Qaeda, and claimed responsibility for the theft of the virus. It would be used against the enemies of Islam.

The screens went blank and the stunned listeners looked at each other in disbelief. The ringing of their telephones broke the silence. The calls brought news that the first cases of smallpox had already been reported in the Netherlands; in Rotterdam over eight hundred people had become infected with the virola, which had been spread through the air ducts in the city's subways. Some victims were already displaying rash-like spots on their skin and lesions in their mouths, a sign victims were at their most infectious. Similar cases were being reported in Istanbul. Turkish doctors saw that papules, the rashlike dots of the disease, had begun to turn into pustules. This usually occurs on the fifth or sixth day. A few infected saliva droplets on the breath would bring a victim close to death.

The next report came from Frankfurt International Airport, where passengers were showing difficulty in eating and swallowing. Some of the travelers had flown in from Munich from where the first reports of the presence of smallpox in Germany had come: a family had manifested the symptoms after arriving from Turkey. By noon, two hours after the first telephone calls, the number of cases had risen to 3,320. Most were in Europe, but in the early afternoon reports came of infected passengers from Mexico arriving at Los Angeles International Airport.

Meantime, anti-Muslim riots had broken out in Rotterdam, and panic-driven Poles along their country's border with Germany had fought with border patrols trying to stop them entering the Federal

Republic. Poland's stockpile of smallpox vaccine was able to protect only some 5 percent of its population. The Federal Republic was only one of a handful of countries with sufficient stocks to vaccinate its entire population. The others were the United States, Great Britain, France, and Holland. The U.S. government had stopped mass vaccination of its population twenty years previously, when it was decided the risk of side effects from the vaccine outweighed the possibility of catching the disease. The death from side effects was calculated at 100 per 100 million vaccinated.

Five hours into the outbreak, just as in the wake of 9/11, the United States closed its borders. But it was too late. On Wall Street trading came to a halt, as it did in London, Tokyo, Frankfurt, and all the other financial centers around the world. It was the onset of global economic collapse.

As the crisis unfolded, so did the decisions. An appeal from Turkey—a NATO ally and a moderate Muslim country—for the United States to provide vaccine was rejected.

"The United States feels unappreciated now because of world condemnation of our position in Iraq. A lot of Americans are asking why should we help countries who do not support us," said POTUS.

The British prime minister reminded his fellow leaders that "the harsh economic climate following the collapse of the Soviet Union led to a brain drain of former laboratory scientists who had worked in the country's bioweapons programs. Leaving in droves, some made their way to Syria, Iran, and North Korea. The result is what we're confronting here."

By early afternoon, POTUS and the other world leaders had received projections on how the smallpox would spread. Within a month, there would be hundreds of thousands of deaths. Within a year the global number would have reached tens of millions. The computer projection showed that neither the medieval Black Death, the bubonic plague that had come close to destroying Europe, nor the influenza pandemic of 1918 would match the pandemic created by the smallpox disaster of 2005.

It was only then that POTUS looked around to her fellow leaders and spoke. "Gentlemen, we all know now what we face. We should all thank God this has not happened." There were murmurs of agreement from those present.

The events unfolded in that Washington ballroom, titled "Atlantic

Storm," were designed by the world's leading experts on bioterrorism. Former prime ministers and senior diplomats represented other countries. For five intense hours they had tried to cope with one emergency report after the other. Increasingly, their efforts to stop the spread of smallpox had faltered. Albright told her fellow "world leaders" that "the crisis we have failed to successfully cope with will face us, if not tomorrow then the day after tomorrow. But it will come . . ."

When Meir Dagan read her words, he echoed them. Then he and Porter Goss wrote a document that was circulated to European intelligence chiefs. Titled "The Future of Bioweapons," it concluded: "Al-Qaeda will soon be in a position to create artificially engineered biological agents which can spread disease on an unparalleled scale. The same science which is taught in universities can now be adapted to create the world's most frightening weapons. We must be aware that al-Qaeda is investing in postgraduate Muslim students on our campuses in the same way it invested in sending the 9/11 pilots to our flying schools."

There was no more than a polite response from other intelligence chiefs. The feeling was that once again Mossad and the CIA were combining to raise the level of the terrorist threat. This was particularly felt in London where MI5 and MI6 were still irritated by the constant demands from Israel that Britain should curb the activities of radical Muslim preachers allowed to remain in the country. In mosques in London and elsewhere in Britain they openly preached hatred against Israel and the United States.

On a Monday morning in the first week of March 2005, the heads of Israel's intelligence community drove down Tel Aviv's Rehov Shaul Hamaleku and turned into the Kirya, the headquarters of the Israeli Defense Forces. They included the director of Shin Bet, the service responsible for internal security; the heads of air force and naval intelligence; the commander of the Sholdag special forces battalion, and the chief of the Research and Political Center that advised the country's policy makers on long-term strategy. Meir Dagan, in his capacity as *menume*, which roughly translates from Hebrew as "first among equals," chaired the meeting. On the agenda was a subject never far from the minds who had assembled in the conference room: Iran.

Every man could recall the years of tension the Islamic Republic had brought to Israel since 1979. Over the ensuing twenty-six years, its policy had been articulated in a huge banner draped above the main entrance to the foreign ministry in Tehran. It bore the chilling words in Farsi: "Israel Must Burn."

For all those years Iran had been a terrorist-sponsoring nation, with particularly close ties to Hezbollah. Most of the weapons used by that group came from Iran. It was also currently engaged in undermining the fledgling democracy in Iraq by supporting its growing terrorism. Yet the diplomats of Washington's State Department and Britain's Foreign Office still clung to the belief that Iran was in a transition period toward democracy, and that there were moderates in the regime who could be persuaded to enter into an "accommodation" with the West and convince Hezbollah and other terror groups to cease their attacks on Israel. Mossad's eavesdroppers and informers in Gaza had overheard the MI6 team reiterating the claim.

John Scarlett's continued refusal to withdraw the team had led to an increasing coldness in Mossad's relationship with MI6. While important intelligence passed between both services on the usual need-to-know basis, Nathan, the London station chief, no longer took a regular cab ride from the Israeli embassy in Kensington to the glass-faced building overlooking the river Thames, known as "the wedding cake" for its tiered shape, to share a convivial hour with senior MI6 officers over drinks and sandwiches. The occasions were a chance to get to know the thinking within MI6 on a wide variety of issues, and there were lively discussions on what one MI6 officer had called "the current state of play" in Damascus, Riyadh, and Egypt. In that closed world in the hospitality suite on the fifth floor, what was not said was often as important as what was said. Scarlett had sometimes dropped in on those gatherings to inquire how things were in Tel Aviv.

But until the "Gaza business" was settled, contacts with MI6 were to be confined to essentials. Mossad's mood had not improved when Nathan's MI6 liaison officer had said that the Hamas team believed it was making good progress in persuading Hezbollah to end its attacks on Israel.

But for the moment the standoff with London was of less importance than the reason for the meeting. For the men around the conference table, who had helped Israel to survive wars and Intifadas, the high-resolution satellite photographs spread before them told a grim story. The images were of Iran's nuclear facilities, filmed only a week before by Israel's own satellite. They showed the six prime plants that were scattered across the country. Each facility was buried under thousands of tons of reinforced concrete, hard to penetrate with even the BLU-109 "bunker buster" bombs the United States had recently sold to Israel.

Accompanying the images were reports from Mossad's deep-penetration agents in the country. Their identities were a closely guarded secret between Dagan and his assistant director on the seventh floor of the headquarters building. One agent had revealed that the Natanz facility in southern Iran was working around the clock to enable its fifty thousand centrifuges to eventually produce huge quantities of enriched uranium in its three heavily fortified underground structures. Another report demonstrated how Russia had provided 150 technicians to upgrade the Bushehr nuclear power plant on the Persian Gulf, severely damaged in Iran's war with Iraq. A third report described the installation at the Sharif University of Technology of centrifuges capable of running a uranium-enrichment program. Yet another report highlighted the capability of the University of Tehran's nuclear reactor to come on stream in Iran's drive to build a nuclear bomb. One agent had pinpointed the entrances to underground facilities in the desert fastness of Yazd Province. The most detailed report described a plant on the outskirts of the ancient city of Esfahan. Sited close to the eastern suburbs, the cluster of modern buildings was near the towering Emam mosque and the magnificent eleventh-century bridge over the Zadaneh Rud River along which the carpet weavers of Esfahan have exported their wares for a millennium.

The men around the conference table saw the area around the uranium conversion facility had been recently reinforced, making it the most heavily guarded of all the facilities. A defense perimeter of anti-aircraft guns, razor wire, and thousands of heavily armed soldiers now surrounded the plant hewn into a hill. It was its capability to enrich uranium hexafluoride (UF6) gas that was reason enough for Israel's intelligence community to assemble in the room. The Mossad agent's report had ended with the revelation that Esfahan's uranium conversion facility had already produced three tons of UF6 gas. This was sufficient to enrich uranium for civilian nuclear power—which Iran claimed it would be used for—or for the fifty thousand centrifuges at Natanz ninety miles to the northwest to produce a nuclear weapon.

The agent's report listed other sites where missile production was underway. The largest was Darkhovin, south of the city of Ahvaz. The facility was heavily fortified with two battalions of the Revolutionary Guard. It employed three thousand scientists and engineers. Most of their work was underground building rocket motors. Mu-allimn Kalayeh was sited in the mountains near Qasvin, its uranium enrichment gas centrifuges produced the enriched weapons-grade material for warheads. Saghand was in the remote desert east of Tehran. It employed eight hundred technicians building casings for the rockets. Nekka, near the Caspian Sea, was buried underground; the complex employed over a thousand scientists. Its facilities included a neutron source reactor purchased from North Korea.

A separate report on the table before the intelligence chiefs was from Israel's own atomic experts. They estimated between fifteen hundred and two thousand centrifuges would create sufficient enriched uranium to manufacture one atomic bomb a year, and that could come as early as 2007, when the Natanz nuclear facility's centrifuges would all be fully operational.

Dagan revealed that Mossad had discovered Ali Shamkhani, Iran's defense minister, was in secret discussions with Syria to move eleven Iraqi nuclear scientists from Damascus to Tehran. They had arrived in Syria shortly before the collapse of the Saddam regime, bringing with them CDs of their research on Saddam Hussein's nuclear program. In Syria the scientists had been given new identities and hidden away in a military base north of Damascus. Syria's president, Bashar al-Assad, made one stipulation for the transfer to Iran: it must share its nuclear research with Syria. It could provide al-Qaeda with the basis to make a dirty bomb—yet another threat the men around the table had long feared.

Six years before, on April 21, 1999, over a hundred Israeli sailors had checked into small hotels and *Gasthäuser* in the German port city of Kiel. They wore casual clothes and, when asked, told their hosts they were members of a holiday club. Each was a member of Force 700, created to give Israel a crucial third pillar of its nuclear defense to equal their country's already powerful land- and air-strike capability.

Thirty-two years before, their predecessors had performed a similar function to smuggle seven gunboats out of Cherbourg, which had been paid for but which the French government of the day had embargoed after Israeli commandoes had destroyed thirteen Lebanese aircraft at Beirut airport—itself a reprisal for a PLO attack on an El Al 707 at Athens airport two days previously.

The decision to create Force 700 had come only much later, when Israel had placed an order with the Howaldtswerke Deutsche Werft shipyard for three Dolphin-class submarines, among the most modern afloat, each displacing 1,720 metric tons and costing $300 million apiece. The arrival of the sailors in Kiel on a warm spring day was surrounded with even more secrecy than Operation Noah had used to smuggle the gunboats out of France.

Critical to the Kiel operation had been keeping secret that among the thirty-five Israeli naval officers and ratings for each submarine were five specialist technicians who would be responsible for firing the nuclear weapons each submarine would carry if the order was given. These armaments would be fitted when the boats reached Haifa.

The three Dolphins left Kiel and headed for Haifa where specially prepared pens awaited them. For the next six weeks they were fitted with an adapted version of the Promis software that had been developed by Inslaw, the specialist Washington-based company. The software would allow each submarine to locate and destroy a target up to one thousand miles away. Promis was also programmed to probe defenses around a target and calculate the complex mathematics that would ensure a direct hit. After the software had been installed, each submarine was equipped with twenty-four cruise missiles. Fitted with nuclear warheads, each missile would have a destructive power greater than the Hiroshima bomb. Test firings, using dummy warheads, had been successfully carried out in the Indian Ocean.

Now, on that March day in 2005, the three Dolphins were directed to take up station on the seabed in the Persian Gulf and target Iran's nuclear facilities.

The matter of *if* and *when* to launch a preemptive strike against Iran would require Mossad to make a clear recommendation to Prime Minister Ariel Sharon. As the air in the Kirya conference room grew heavy with cigarette smoke, everyone knew that, depending on what the response would be, it could destroy President Bush's Middle East peace plan—already plagued with uncertainties—and trigger a powerful retaliation from Tehran against Israel and Jewish interests around the world. A preemptive strike against Iran could also draw fire from Syria and unleash the various terrorist groups in all-out jihad.

The head of the Research and Political Center raised other considerations. How would America, Britain, and the rest of the world react to such a strike? There were now powerful voices in the United States and Europe who would launch a verbal onslaught against Israel because an attack on Iran would create an environmental catastrophe on a par with the Chernobyl meltdown of 1986. Israel could find itself politically and economically isolated in the world.

But any attack would require a measure of coordination with American forces in the Gulf. Israeli warplanes would probably need to overfly Turkey and close to Iraqi airspace, which was under the complete control of the Pentagon. But that would present a further problem with Washington. The Arab world, and probably beyond, would see an air attack as part of a joint effort with the United States. Almost certainly it would be followed by new terrorist strikes on American soil.

Increasingly the feeling among the men in the Kirya conference room was to take all necessary precautions but not recommend a preemptive strike. In the meantime, Meir Dagan would send his already hard-pressed agents back into Kurdish Iraq, long a listening post close to Iran, and send other *katsas* into a country that had also become an area of mounting concern for the Mossad chief: Pakistan.

CHAPTER 23

THE PAKISTANI
NUCLEAR BLACK
MARKETEER

The mountain spring flowers of the Hindu Kush would have briefly

blossomed when the Mossad agent met his Pakistani informer. Both

were on the front line against terrorism, bound by a common cause.

Pakistan had become part of Mossad's front line against terrorism since

the arrival of al-Qaeda as the world's major terror group. To recruit

informers in the country was a priority. Jamal, the code name for the

Mossad agent, had encountered Horaj on his first trip to the region in

2001. Jamal had listened carefully to Horaj as Horaj expressed fears that

Pakistan would become a hotbed of Islamic fanaticism he was ready to

do anything to stop. Initially, Jamal wondered if Horaj's offer to inform for Israel had really been motivated by a desire to return respectability to his religion, which had been hijacked by the Taliban leaders and Osama bin Laden, who he believed had distorted the words of the Prophet to create hatred and fear. But Mossad psychologists had studied Jamal's background reports on Horaj and decided he could serve a useful role. Conspicuously excluded from the Washington list of states that sponsored terrorism was Pakistan. Indeed, after the September 11 attacks, the country had been regularly praised in the words of Condoleezza Rice as "our important ally in the war on terrorism." On the speed dial of her secure desk telephone was a button that enabled the secretary of state to reach Pakistan's president Pervez Musharraf. Another button was her direct link to President George Bush. Dr. Rice, a fifty-year-old former academic and Soviet specialist, was Bush's key adviser on foreign affairs and had guided his decision to keep Pakistan a partner, choosing to ignore that since 1989 the country had supported a number of Kashmiri terror groups in their war against India. They had carried out several mass killings on the subcontinent, helped by Pakistani intelligence agents to select targets and provide advance planning, which had included the attack on the Indian Parliament in 2001.

Mossad had become alarmed when Pakistan had developed its nuclear capability, which Musharraf had lauded as "our equalizer, which serves as a restraining influence on India." In Washington, Israel's fear that Pakistan had a weapon that could threaten the Jewish state was downplayed. A large number of officers in Pakistan's intelligence services were not only members of the country's radical religious groups but were also strong supporters of al-Qaeda. Would that terror group one day be able to acquire the means to make at least a "dirty bomb" or even obtain a fully fledged nuclear weapon? It was a question constantly debated within Mossad and which had once more brought Jamal on a long journey through icy ravines and past mountains shrouded in cloud to keep his appointment. Waiting for him was his informer, Horaj. The payment Horaj received each time he met Jamal may also have been a contributing factor to have brought him once more to this bleak vastness close to the roof of the world.

This was a land where Alexander the Great had lost an entire division one winter and, centuries later, where the Russians had fought, and lost, their war against the mujahideen tribesmen of Afghanistan. And here, against a mountain peak cloaked permanently in snow and deep fissures splitting the rocks, American Special Forces had lost some of their finest in their search for Osama bin Laden.

The most advanced technology in the world had been mobilized in that hunt. A hyperspectral satellite, the first of its kind, was geopositioned in the deep black of space, its hundreds of narrow wavelength bands designed to reflect energy from objects on the ground to detect specific terrain such as rock, vegetation, buildings, caves, and any human presence. Another satellite used the "spectral fingerprints" to take mono photos, each with a resolution of ten centimeters per pixel. Synthetic Aperture Radar (SAR) transmitted images at night in the often atrocious weather conditions of the area. Drones—unmanned aircraft—had constantly imaged an area the size of California every twenty-four hours from a cruising height of sixty-five thousand feet. Closer to ground, Predators—other radio-controlled unmanned aircraft—flying at heights of one hundred to twenty-five thousand feet had relayed data to where the Special Forces waited beside their helicopters, each fitted with "whispering technology," which made their approach virtually silent. They were armed with AGM-130 missiles that could be radar directed into the mouths of tunnels where bin Laden could be hiding. But the targets had been few and far between, and none of them had been the serpent's den of the most wanted man in the world.

Now in the spring of 2005, America's wonder weapons had gone to search elsewhere. Their departure had brought a wry smile from Meir Dagan when he had observed that technology still could not outsmart human intelligence. There is a saying in Mossad that information was only as good as its source. Jamal believed in Horaj he had the best. Jamal was not only fluent in Pakistan's official language, Urdu, but in several of the local dialects. But like all else about the two men, the dialect they conversed in was cloaked in the essential secrecy upon which their lives depended. Horaj's ethnic group—whether he was a Punjabi, a Sindhi, a Pushtu, a Baluchi, or a Muhajir—was known only to Jamal and his case officer in the Directorate of Operations. All other personal details, such as his age and marital status, were similarly restricted. Most protected of all was where Horaj worked and the level of access he had to information valuable to Israel. Consequently, none of his reports ever ended up in the Mossad archive's file on the individual whose actions had once more brought the two men to their clandestine meeting.

The man was Pakistan's leading nuclear scientist, Abdul Qadeer

Khan. Physically unremarkable, his lack of size was compensated with a winning smile for any woman who caught his eye—and many did—and matched by an overbearing arrogance toward those who dared to challenge him. He had easy access to Pakistan's leaders; lesser politicians spoke his name with awe. Those who refused to do his bidding found themselves banned from his inner circle; former prime minister Benazir Bhutto admitted that during her term of office even she was not allowed to visit Khan's research laboratories. It was there, in July 1976, he had used his years of research in Germany, Belgium, and Holland to understand the techniques for producing the enriched uranium needed to make a nuclear bomb. Eight years before, after neighboring India had tested its own nuclear bomb, Khan had been put in charge of Pakistan's nuclear program.

Mossad discovered that during his time in Holland on the staff of the Physical Dynamics Research Laboratory (FDO), Khan had access to the nearby URENCO uranium enrichment plant at Almelo. Established in 1970 by Britain, West Germany, and Holland, it provided a supply of enriched uranium for European nuclear reactors. To do so it used highly classified centrifuge technology to separate fissionable uranium-235 from U-238, spinning a mixture of the two isotopes at up to one hundred thousand revolutions a minute. Mossad established that successfully mastering the complexity of this technology had enabled Khan to create Pakistan's own nuclear arsenal in the utmost secrecy. After doing so, the country's newspapers front-paged his boast: "Our detractors who told the U.S. that Pakistan could never produce the bomb now know we have done it." For adoring millions of Pakistanis he became a revered figure, the genius who had provided a means to stop any preemptive strike by India.

Khan had remained a magical figure like no other in Pakistan, perhaps like no person in the Muslim world they had read about in their newspapers or heard of on radio or television. Fawned upon by the rich and famous, he was invited to sail on their luxury yachts on the French Riviera, flying there in their private jets.

Mossad knew there was another darker, and for Israel, far more dangerous side to Abdul Qadeer Khan. During one of his European jaunts, a Mossad agent had managed to gain entry to Khan's hotel suite and accessed his briefcase. Using a matchbox-sized camera, the agent had photographed documents that provided the first concrete evidence that Khan had recently bought five thousand specialized magnets from a government company in Beijing. The magnets were to speed up the process of uranium enrichment. Other documents showed that Khan had also made contact with other aspirant nuclear states, notably North Korea, Iraq, and Iran. In his book-lined office was a report from the John F. Kennedy School of Government at Harvard University. Khan liked to show visitors the passage he had highlighted: "A 10-kiloton bomb is smuggled into Manhattan and explodes at Grand Central. Some half-a-million people are killed and the United States suffers $1 trillion in direct economic damage." Khan would snap shut the book and replace it without comment on its shelf, no doubt secure in the knowledge he had created for Pakistan the weapon to achieve such a horrific scenario. Khan was the flawed genius, not only motivated by personal greed but also driven by a religious fanaticism and a contempt for Western values. As the Khan Research Laboratories became a mecca to which the scientists of third world nations came to seek his services for helping them acquire skills in the black art of nuclear bomb making, he had become rich and powerful. He had also become a target for Mossad's kidon. The unit had begun the slow, meticulous process of ascertaining all information its assassins needed when devising the most effective way of killing him.

Mossad had already dealt with one foreign scientist who had been identified as a threat, Gerald Bull. He had created, for Saddam Hussein, a supergun capable of launching nuclear warheads directly from Iraq into Israel. On March 20, 1990, three kidon had executed Bull on the doorstep of his luxury apartment in Brussels (see chapter 6, "Avengers," pp. 119–21). However, assassinating Khan was more complex. He was a national hero and the repercussions would extend beyond any direct retaliation against Israel. While Washington had imposed sanctions on both Pakistan and India for conducting nuclear tests, the United States wanted to maintain its support against the steady expansion of China; it would condemn Israel for the assassination. Nevertheless, kidon were asked to prepare a number of "options"—the detailed research that would be the prelude to any killing of Khan. Ari Ben-Menashe, who had tasked kidon to prepare "options" during his time with Mossad, said (to the author): "What they were doing was essential to their kind of operation. Their baseline is getting to know their target, his or her habits and style. How he or she reacts to a situation, what pushes his or her buttons. Only then could they construct an operational plan."

Footage of Khan's appearances on television and on cinema news-reels had been studied along with his endless newspaper interviews and magazine profiles. The names of his close associates were noted—fellow scientists in the nuclear program, secretive background men who worked directly with him. His journeys around Pakistan, Asia, and to Europe were carefully charted; how he liked his favorite seat when flying with Pakistan Airways—3A in first class—and that his accommodation choices in Europe's capitals were usually presidential suites. It was there that he had met diplomats from China, Iran, and Iraq. Many of these hotel suites were already on kidon computers so that if it were required to bug them it would be possible to do so. Details of his sexual preferences were investigated. Did he have a liking for a particular kind of woman? Could any of the companions he had been seen with in public be open to blackmail?

The profile of Abdul Khan had been painstakingly built from a wide range of sources. Part of that planning included the recruiting of Horaj. He and Jamal had met again after that momentous day, February 4, 2004, when Khan had sat in a television studio in Islamabad, faced the camera and made one of the most astonishing confessions in the long history of treachery.

"I am solely responsible for operating an international black market in nuclear weapons material," he intoned.

Before a stunned nation could adjust to the revelation, Pakistan's president, Pervez Musharraf, dressed in commando fatigues—he had been an army general—took Khan's place and announced that though "I was shocked by these revelations," he would nevertheless pardon Khan, whom he called "my hero," because of all his services to Pakistan. The excuse was less than the truth. Mossad knew that Musharraf could not afford to bring Khan to trial.

While the kidon continued preparing the ground for any decision to assassinate Khan, Meir Dagan and his analysts saw the scientist's confession and the equally extraordinary response by Musharraf as evidence of a massive cover-up to hide the full extent of Pakistan's complicity in nuclear proliferation. It was a cover-up buttressed by cynical political maneuvering. It had started when Pakistan won over China by supporting its border dispute with India. This led to a deepening relationship between Islamabad and Beijing. In the region's political jigsaw of alliances, it brought North Korea, an old ally of China, into friendly contact with Pakistan. At first it was only cultural and exploratory visits by diplomats. But in Islamabad, Khan was watching and waiting; his finely tuned political nose told him it would not be long before the way was open for nuclear deal making.

China had also been nurturing its relationship with Iran. It began in October 1984 when the first planeload of nuclear components had landed in Tehran. Since then Beijing had provided three sub-critical and zero-rated reactors and an electromagnetic isotope separation machine used in the process of creating enriched uranium. An 80-kilowatt thermal research reactor had followed. Each shipment had been monitored by Mossad's deep-cover agents in Iran.

Meantime Saddam Hussein, in the midst of his eight-year war with Iran, had turned to India for help to kick-start his nuclear arsenal. To encourage Delhi, he had publicly endorsed India's nuclear testing, and Iraq began to receive equipment to create a small amount of enriched uranium. It was all done in great secrecy, with the equipment described as "agricultural components." Mossad set out to expose what was happening. It dusted off a copy of a long-forgotten treaty of nuclear cooperation Iran had signed with India in 1974. The document was fed to the Iranian media. The revelation caused the furor in Tehran Mossad had intended.

Alarmed, the ayatollahs turned to China for assistance. But by then Beijing was already engaged, with the same secrecy it armed Iran, in providing Iraq with missiles to help Saddam fulfill his dream of reshaping the Middle East in his image and creating mayhem for the world's economic and political security. Beijing, ever ready to assist the rogue states, suggested the ayatollahs should invite Abdul Qadeer Khan to visit Tehran. Arrangements were quickly made. Khan was issued a false passport and papers describing him as a carpet salesman. In reality he was a carpetbagger, a scientist, with his country's blessing, off to market its most precious secrets for money.

He returned weeks later, cast by his hosts as the godfather of their nuclear hopes and with a substantial sum of money in a Swiss bank account. No doubt having enjoyed the favors bestowed by the ayatollahs, Khan had looked for other nations he could similarly service. To do so he enlisted the help of Pakistan's Inter-Service intelligence agency, ISI, the most powerful of the country's security apparatus. The service already had a large number of officers who were anti-Semitic, and Khan's verbal attacks on Israel made him a welcome guest in their midst. They readily devised the documentation needed for the scientist to carry out nuclear-technology transfers.

After Tehran, the tireless Khan's next port of call was to the closed world of North Korea. He did so on the back of Pakistan's deal for Pyongyang to supply a range of conventional military equipment. In return Khan agreed to provide blueprints and state-of-the-art P1 centrifuges for the country's nuclear program. What began as a deal based on North Korea's need for hard currency and Pakistan's requirement for conventional army equipment soon developed into a barter arrangement.

"One of Khan's blueprints appeared to be worth a container filled with North Korean field artillery," a Mossad analyst said (to the author).

Khan's activities had gained Pakistan increased influence as the Muslim world's first nuclear power; this was demonstrated by continued vast sums paid directly into Khan's bank accounts. By the time he had made his confessions on television, Mossad calculated he had acquired over $10 million. It made him one of the wealthiest men in Pakistan.

All these details had been passed by Mossad to the CIA at the time George Tenet was on the verge of resigning. But there was no sign the Bush administration had ever warned Musharraf to stop Khan's activities. Or an explanation why, eventually, Washington had only finally delivered a mild response to Khan's television admission. Indeed, Musharraf's pardon had earned praise from Richard Armitage, deputy secretary of state. Poker-faced, he said, "Pakistan's president is the right man in the right place."

Armitage's words were seen as further evidence that Washington's hunt for Osama bin Laden had become, said a Mossad officer with years of experience in counterterrorism (to the author), "that most dangerous of all in intelligence, a hunt driven by an obsession that overrides all else. For Bush, nailing bin Laden had become personal from 9/11. He would continue to sanction huge sums, men, and materials to capture him. Anyone who could help do that could ask for anything. Musharraf was in that category."

The president had seized power in a coup d'état in 1999. Despite the country's large Muslim majority, many of whom were fundamentalists, when 9/11 happened Musharraf offered unwavering support for Bush's war on terrorism. It was a huge gamble for a president who by then was already finding it hard to hold on to power. He had survived three assassination attempts and daily found himself confronting not only the country's religious leaders over their entrenched anti-American views but also the army and the ISI for his support in the war on terrorism. For many of them bin Laden was a folk hero. As he flitted through the mountains bordering Afghanistan with the peaks of the Northwest Frontier, always one step ahead of the U.S. Special Forces hunting him, he received help from members of the ISI.

At the time Khan was making his confession on television, the Special Forces near the northern provinces of Pakistan had once more picked up bin Laden's trail. The sightings were sent to the Joint Special Operations Command at Fort Bragg, North Carolina, on to the CIA, and finally to the Pentagon and State Department. Everyone recognized that this was a sensitive time. Only a week before, at the World Economic Forum in Davos, Switzerland, Musharraf had said he would not allow American troops to search for bin Laden inside Pakistan. Washington had gritted its teeth and said nothing.

Mossad's station in the capital had pieced together the understanding of what had transpired behind the scenes. Washington would not pressurize Musharraf to bring Khan for trial over nuclear arms trafficking. Instead, it would remain focused on Pakistan's continued support for the war on terrorism. In return the Pakistan army and the ISI would hunt for bin Laden inside the country. U.S. Special Forces would be allowed to participate but only under Pakistani command. It was a recipe for mutual suspicion in the field; and after four weeks, not surprisingly with no trace of bin Laden, the search was abandoned.

Bin Laden had issued several tapes since he had first exulted over the destruction of the Twin Towers and the Pentagon. The Mossad specialists—psychiatrists, psychologists, and behavioural scientists—determined that bin Laden continued to sound like a man who had created his own reality. Their conclusion (seen by the author) was: "At the core of his thinking is death. From his manner and his speech patterns, death is now an integral part of his life. It is not rage that drives him. There is a deeper and all-animating and all-emerging force. His voice is not simply that of the classic street demagogue. It displays what can be called 'the evil of the truly evil.' Hitler and Stalin possessed the same vocal traits. He is driven by masked violence. This allows him to operate in a completely detached manner against all those he does not accept have a right to live."

The arrival of his latest video in November 2004 had caused a frisson of excitement among the Mossad analysts. It had been made in a television studio with good quality sound and lighting. He had been filmed against a silk drape; its yellow color was known to be that of his favourite Afghan flower. But it was bin Laden himself who intrigued the analysts. His robes were no longer those of the mountain man but those worn by wealthy city dwellers. His stick and the Kalashnikov rifle slung over his shoulder—props he had always displayed on previous videos—had gone. His beard was neatly trimmed, his eyes clear, his skin healthy. He no longer looked the sick man of his previous videos. When he spoke, his delivery was calm and measured. In earlier videos his mumbling and hesitations had been marked. The latest video suggested he had received professional voice coaching. When he spoke, it was directly into the camera.

The Mossad analysts wondered if the video had been made either in Pakistan or even possibly in one of the northwest provinces of China, where several million Muslims lived in uneasy communion with the Beijing regime. Untold thousands were al-Qaeda supporters and worked in gangs smuggling humans or narcotics into the West. The analysts concluded that one of those gangs had been entrusted to bring the video to Al-Jazeera. As usual, the station publicly insisted it had no idea how the tape came into its hands.

But on that spring day in 2005, Jamal had met Horaj, not to receive further confirmation that, despite its angry denials, China *was* offering shelter to bin Laden, but to discover more about a secret underground route along which defectors from China and North Korea made their perilous way to freedom in the West. Of special interest to Mossad was the North Korean scientist who had been working on genetic weapons.

Since March 1984, when Saddam Hussein's pilots had dropped 100-liter canisters of biological agents on the Kurdish population in the township of Halabja, killing five thousand in minutes, the threat of a biowarfare attack on Israel had become a priority for Mossad.

Russian-speaking agents had tracked down scientists who had once worked for the secret Department 12 of the KGB's First Chief Directorate. Their work had been responsible for biological espionage, the planning and preparation of biological terrorism, and all-out biological war. The United States, Britain, and Israel had been among Department 12's prime targets. Its biologists had successfully genetically weaponized in their Moscow laboratories some of the world's most dangerous viruses: Ebola, anthrax, smallpox, and baculovirus. They had also been working on genes responsible for specific sex, race, and other anthropological features. Another weapon being researched included a toxin that would result in the corruption of human mental processes, induce uncontrollable fear, and lead to death. Substances had also been created to specifically poison reservoirs, food stocks, and pharmaceutical factories; and other Department 12 scientists had been developing sophisticated airborne delivery systems for the plague, the medieval Black Death, and the equally deadly botulinium. The Mossad agents discovered that when the Soviet Union collapsed, a number of the scientists were recruited to work in North Korea and China.

Links were also found between these countries and genetic weapons research, which had been carried out in the apartheid regime of South Africa; its Project Coast was specifically intended to create an ethnic bomb. The project's leader, Wouter Basson, was a gifted, totally ruthless, and amoral scientist whose ability to develop biological weapons had made him, in the later words of Archbishop Tutu, "the Devil's disciple working in the most diabolical aspect of apartheid." Using front companies that claimed to be conducting bona fide research, Project Coast gathered scientific information from around the world. Some of it came into a small, rented cottage near Ascot in Berkshire, England. Number 1 Faircloth Farm Cottage, Watersplash, was an unlikely address to receive germ warfare material from, among others, the scientists of North Korea. But for them—as isolated as South Africa was from the global scientific community in the days of apartheid—the cottage provided a means of exchanging data, one that escaped the surveillance of MI5. Later, scientists from Project Coast visited Iraq and Libya, and finally Iran.

At first the ayatollahs had refused to keep producing biological weapons as they were contrary to Islamic doctrine, a truth that Mossad's propagandists skillfully promoted across the Middle East. But after Iraq's massacre of the Kurds, the Tehran regime reversed the Koran teaching and the Majlis, Iran's parliament, voted unanimously that biological and chemical weapons should be mass produced. The document the South African scientists had left behind on their visit to Tehran were dusted off by the newly formed Quds Force—in the Arabic language *Quds* is Jerusalem—which was entrusted in providing Iran with a frontline capability until it had its nuclear arsenal. The South African blueprints ensured the work progressed rapidly.

Among the Project Coast documents was one (seen by the author) that claimed: "The key to creating a successful ethnic bomb lies in isolating the small but critical differences in the human genetic code. That difference consists of no more than 0.1 percent. But this minute amount, which accounts for 3 million letters of the genome code, makes it possible for a comparison between one individual and another. This also makes it possible to identify the differences between large ethnic groups. These differences make them exploitable as a military weapon." Project Coast's aim had been to isolate the DNA of certain genes so they could be attacked by deadly microorganisms its scientists were creating in their laboratories. Like Department 12, they also called it an "ethnic bomb," and it was designed to incapacitate, and even kill, the South African Black population. The work was still in its infancy when the apartheid regime collapsed.

Mossad discovered one colorful figure who had also worked with South Africa and North Korea, a Mormon gynecologist, Dr. Larry Ford, based on the faculty of the University of California, Los Angeles. With his cultivated bedside manner, casual clothes, and hightop basketball shoes, none of his patients suspected he was a villain from the pages of the thrillers he kept in his waiting room bookcase. Dr. Ford had built up a close relationship with Wouter Basson and, through him, had established contacts with the equally sinister scientists of North Korea. Not one of his patients suspected Dr. Ford regularly carried deadly toxins in his baggage on flights to South Africa. The mystery of where he had obtained them, who had authorized their transportation out of the United States, and the identity of the end user were also secrets Dr. Ford would carry to his grave. In the spring of 2000, he had committed suicide. When the police dealing with the case opened Dr. Ford's refrigerator in his home in Irvine, California, they found sufficient vials to poison, in the words of one officer, "pretty well the whole of the state. We knew then we were not dealing with some routine suicide." There were bottles containing cultures of cholera, botulism, and typhoid fever. It would remain an unresolved mystery how they got there.

In the aftermath of the Iraq war, Mossad had been allowed to interrogate Dr. Rihad Taha, the notorious "Dr. Germ," who directed Saddam Hussein's biowarfare program. Her total willingness to conduct terminal experiments on humans and her eagerness to find new ways to weaponize germs into even more effective armaments had made the slim, mousy-haired biologist a firm favorite with the Iraqi dictator. The daughter of one of the country's ruling Baath families, she had acquired her skills at the University of East Anglia in Norwich, England. She had gone there in 1979, arriving at Heathrow Airport on a first-class ticket with Iraqi Airlines from Baghdad. In her suitcases were designer suits from Paris. Taha took a $150 taxi to the campus. No one thought this was remarkable; foreign students were renowned free spenders. She had enrolled to study crop diseases. She was twenty-three years old, with an unattractive way of chewing flower stalks, a habit that had already turned her teeth yellow. While students found her arrogant, tutors were impressed by Taha's dedication and were sympathetic when her end-of-term results were disappointing. No one suspected this was a deliberate ploy to ensure she would remain at the university to continue her degree course.

The idea had been that of her Iraqi intelligence controller based at the Iraqi embassy in London and enabled her continued access to restricted papers on germ warfare, some of which came from Porton Down, Britain's own center for biowarfare research. The documents showed her how to weaponize anthrax, botulism, and other toxins. She learned how deadly germs could be sprayed in shopping malls and bomblets of pathogens distributed over a sports arena. All this could be achieved by using little more than the equipment in a school science lab. When Taha returned to Iraq in 1984, she had a degree in microbiology and joined a small team of other British-trained Iraqi graduates to spearhead Saddam's biological program. After she became its director in 1986, she abandoned her designer suits for the battle fatigues Saddam favored and hennaed her hair to the color of the Euphrates, which flowed past her mansion home. She set up her laboratories in the Al-Hasan ibn al-Hatham Institute outside Baghdad. It was there she started to kill her victims, the methods including how to inject babies with lethal doses of diarrhea. The babies were taken from women prisoners.

In the summer of 2004, Dr. Taha attempted to barter her freedom for the lives of American, British, and Irish hostages held by a fanatical Islamic terror group in Iraq. When the deal was rejected by the United States, the hostages were beheaded by the group's leader, Abu Musab al-Zarqawi.

In Tel Aviv, the Committee of the Heads of Services had met that year under Meir Dagan's chairmanship and agreed that after Iran the most serious threat posed to Israel by bioterrorism was from North Korea. The regime continued to threaten Israel with destruction by providing Iran with rockets capable of delivering warheads filled with germs. Mossad had established that a week before the meeting, the Pyongyang regime had been about to ship a container of warheads to Tehran. Using Mossad's "backdoor" channel with the CIA, Meir Dagan had asked Porter Goss to persuade the White House to ask the Beijing regime to halt the transfer. A phone call from Condoleezza Rice had produced the required result. But in Tel Aviv the intervention was seen as doing little to stop the deadly and illegal traffic between the two pariah states.

The meeting ended with the request that Dagan should send a small team of agents to South Korea to discover what was happening across the border with its northern neighbor. One of its members was Jamal. Under cover of being an Iranian businessman trading in artifacts, he had established a network of informers across South Asia. One had been Horaj, who had provided the first details of what became known in Mossad as New Exodus, the secret route refugees used to escape from the harsh regime of North Korea. For them it had become the equivalent to the biblical Exodus.

The route had a long and colorful history. Originally created by the CIA at the end of the Korean War, it had been used to smuggle its own agents and high-value informers out of North Korea and China. The informers were moved from one safe house to another and escorted by guides through China's towns and villages to the borders of Cambodia, Laos, and Hong Kong; the guides received little or no payment for this dangerous work. One guide probably spoke for many when he told his CIA controller, "I do this for democracy."

A journey could take weeks, even months. A CIA officer involved in running the operation recalled (to the author): "It was like traveling on a railway where you never knew when the signal would turn from green to red. Then everything shut down until there was another green light."

The route out of China was a tortuous one, often doubling back, and involved traveling by road, river, and train. Several of those who set out never reached safety; the risk of betrayal was a constant threat. China's Public Security spies and its formidable secret intelligence service were a fearsome duo. No one knows how many CIA agents or informers were captured and never heard of again. Eventually the Exodus route ceased to operate. Then during the 1990s, once more shocking accounts of the depravity of the North Korean regime began to emerge. Defectors all told the same story of a nation living increasingly in near starvation, of torture, and forced labor. Most horrifying of all were the reports of inhuman experiments on prisoners from relatives who managed to cross the 880-mile-long border into China. But those who had fled found little relief there. It had an estimated 5 million of its own prisoners in camps as grim as the gulags of North Korea. When caught, asylum seekers were swiftly transported back across the border to an inevitable fate of interrogation, torture, and death.

To save them, two remarkable human rights activists reopened the old CIA route. Their Mossad profiles paint ennobling pictures.

Douglas Shin and Norbert Vollertsen were both in their late forties and came from very different cultural backgrounds. Shin was a Korean-American church pastor who had been ordained after a career as a businessman and filmmaker, and he lived in a Los Angeles suburb as pastor of his church. He had the Asian's mannerisms of being polite and diffident; only when he spoke of the gross abuses of North Korea or its people was he aroused to quiet passion. Then his words filled with religious metaphors; the pain and anger in his eyes was there for all to see. There was about him then a sense that if you were not part of the answer he wanted, you were part of his many problems in rescuing people from the terror of Kim Jong Il's regime. He was one of the two "station masters" for New Exodus. The other was Vollertsen.

A tallish, stocky man, broad across the shoulders, Vollertsen looked and, at times, sounded like one of the hippy protestors who had taken to the streets against Vietnam and, later, the manufacture of nuclear weapons. Some people called him "a little crazy"; others said the world needed more men like him. Vollertsen accepted their plaudits the way he dealt with his detractors: with that same slow smile, the flick of a hairstyle rooted in a bygone generation. "It made him disarming even when he would continue to argue his point until there was no point left to argue," his Mossad file noted.

Vollertsen's student life in Düsseldorf had encompassed politics and journalism until he became a medical doctor, married, and fathered four sons. But on the eve of a new millennium all that was soon to change. He argued with the German health authorities how community care should be run. Ignored, he organized his patients to publicly demonstrate—the first time a doctor had done this in Germany. He was again ignored. He organized more patient marches. His medical association in the conservative city of Göttingen disowned him. Finally his wife divorced him, claiming he was "crazy." With his long blond hair and full moustache, he looked like an aging rock star. Finally he joined an organization called "German Emergency Doctors"; it sent physicians anywhere there was a need for humanitarian aid. Vollersten was offered either the baking Sahara of South Sudan or North Korea. He read several travel guidebooks about Sudan. But there was not one available for North Korea. He decided that was where he should go.

Shin had come from South Korea to California as a twenty-year-old. But the knowledge of what was happening in North Korea had followed him, and by the time he became a pastor, all he had read and heard made a decisive impact on him. He began to lay down the tracks for what became New Exodus and plugged into other human rights organizations around the world.

Meantime, in North Korea, Vollertsen had repeatedly encountered the terrified silence of patients asked about their lives. Leaving North Korea at the end of his contract, he mounted a ferocious campaign against the regime. He sought out North Korean refugees and retold their stories to anyone who would listen: journalists, politicians, other human rights workers. He traveled around Asia, lecturing, appealing; there was about him, he would admit, the angry passion of someone whose eyes had been opened. His battle cry of "inform, provoke, and mobilize" became his rallying call. He and Shin became two voices united in common cause to promote the plight of all those trapped in North Korea or who had fled their homeland into the hostile environment of China. New Exodus became the focus of all they wanted to achieve. By 2004, over three hundred thousand had traveled its length.

Along the invisible railway "platforms"—safe houses in China's cities, farms in its countryside, boats on its rivers—waited the intelligence agents and their informers. As usual, Jamal and the other Mossad agents worked alone. It was their way. Their brief was simple: to locate any defector who could provide the latest information about North Korea and its work on developing weapons of mass destruction. Then the spies and their informers all became united in common cause: to locate Dr. Ri Chae Woo. He was undoubtedly the most important escapee to be traveling along New Exodus.

Dr. Ri was a microbiologist and director of a project more secret than all the other secret projects in a country where secrecy itself was instilled from birth. Just as Department 12 and Project Coast had sought to create their ethnic bombs, Dr. Ri was employed at Institute 398, located at Sogram-ri in the south of Pyongyang Province to develop a similar weapon, this one designed to strike the white populations on earth. A sign of the institute's importance was being ring fenced by three battalions of troops. The first hint about Dr. Ri's work had come from a defector. Over the following months, details emerged from more defectors suggesting that Dr. Ri and his 250 geneticists could be further advanced than the South Africans and Russians had been. Now, many more months later, Horaj had sought a meeting with Jamal, bringing information that Mossad, like other intelligence services, had eagerly awaited. Dr. Ri was somewhere along the New Exodus route trying to make his perilous way to freedom. Norbert Vollertsen had learned Dr. Ri was carrying a dossier detailing human experiments used in North Korea's biological program. Western intelligence agents watched the moves of the CSIS and the country's Public Security as they tried to locate Dr. Ri. But amid a population of 1.3 billion people who were used to being constantly spied upon, the microbiologist had vanished into the air faster than the spent fireworks at Chinese New Year celebrations.

In Tel Aviv, Mossad's scientists consulted their own network of researchers at some of the world's leading science institutes. One recalled how, at the height of America's intervention in Nicaragua, the idea of creating a genetic bomb had occupied the CIA's geneticists. They had been ordered to locate what became known in the agency as "the Nicaraguan gene." Substantial sums of money were spent in obtaining blood samples of Nicaraguans and testing them in the CIA laboratories. No gene specific to Nicaragua was identified. The project was abandoned only to be later resurrected to select a "Cuban-only gene." This research also came to nothing.

But Dr. Ri's research showed that creating an ethnic bomb was no longer a fantasy. It had become what the Nobel Prize–winning scientist Joshua Lederberg had called the "monster in our backyard." Anthropologist John Moore, an acknowledged expert in the threat from an ethnic bomb, had predicted its creation would unleash genetic variations that could produce widespread contagion of the human population with rates of mortality like the fictional Andromeda Strain, sufficient to exterminate the whole species.

By the time Jamal and Horaj had separated after their meeting in the Hindu Kush, the Mossad agent had acquired a photograph of Dr. Ri. It showed he was physically the quintessential Korean, short and stocky with a pleasantly rounded face, eyes set wide apart behind his glasses. With the photo came a curriculum vitae that indicated his importance after graduating from the country's Hambung University of Chemical Industry, which produced scientists for North Korea's nuclear, chemical, and biological programs.

During the years that followed, Dr. Ri was transferred from one biotechnology center to another, and from time to time he would have encountered some of the thirty-eight thousand scientists and technicians from the Soviet Union who had been recruited to work in North Korea's biological warfare program. Others had gone to China, Syria, Libya, and Iran.

In 1999, he was appointed to work at Sogram-ri's Institute 398. NSA satellite images routinely passed to Mossad showed the compound was a half-mile square area, bordered by heavily patrolled roads. The featureless buildings included a headquarters block, a communications building, barracks, and fuel storage tanks. To one side were living quarters for officers and scientists close to a tunnel entrance. The photo analysts believed it led to the underground complex where Dr. Ri and his team worked.

The Institute was under the overall command of Dr. Yi Yong Su. Intelligence sources had established the fifty-one-year-old geneticist was widely respected and not a little feared by her fellow geneticists. She was known to have a close relationship with Kim Jong Il, who had succeeded his father in 1994 to become the country's supreme leader.

News that Dr. Ri planned to defect had alerted not only Mossad but the CIA, MI6, and the German, French, and Australian intelligence services. Then, as so often happens in the intelligence world, came a whisper: Dr. Ri was heading for Guangzhou, the chief city of Canton

Province in South China. With Hong Kong a short distance away, there was an opportunity to smuggle Dr. Ri on to one of the many foreign ships in the harbor. In the early hours of one morning—the day of the week or month would remain unknown—Dr. Ri, wearing a dark blue coverall, had appeared at one of the staff entrances to the Guangdong Hotel. Apart from its many fine facilities, the hotel also houses a number of foreign consulates on the fifteenth floor. Dr. Ri used a swipe card to access the building; how he obtained it would remain unknown. At some point inside the hotel, he was confronted by Chinese Public Security officers. Shortly afterward a police van drove him away from the hotel staff entrance.

In Tel Aviv, the file on Dr. Ri was closed and sent to the registry. Jamal and the other Mossad agents, who had hoped to find and persuade the scientist to work for Israel, were reassigned to other duties. They knew that by the very nature of their work, another "target of opportunity" would inevitably show up.

Early in May 2005, Jamal was tipped off by one of his informers in Rawalpindi that two men in the custody of the Pakistan Intelligence Service had revealed to their interrogators they had been asked to take part in an attack on London's subway system. The men were identified as Zeesham Hyder Siddiqui, who had been arrested by Pakistani agents in Peshawar, and Naeem Noor Khan, who had been arrested in Lahore.

On Mossad's computers they were both already listed as members of two of the forty-five extremist groups in Pakistan. Khan belonged to Jundullah, the Army of God; Siddiqui to Karkat-e-Jihad-e-Islami, the Movement for Islamic Jihad. Both groups were affiliated with al-Qaeda.

Scant though the details from Jamal were, nevertheless Meir Dagan sent an encrypted message to Eliza Manningham-Buller, the head of MI5. The months of frost between Mossad's and Britain's intelligence services, caused by MI6's presence in Gaza to try and broker a deal with Hamas, returned to normal after Meir Dagan had flown to meet with MI6 director John Scarlett. The two men and Eliza Manningham-Buller met in a private room in the Traveller's Club over lunch. Details of their discussion would remain secret. But shortly afterward, the MI6 agents left Gaza and Nathan, Mossad's London Station chief, received details of the interrogation by two MI5 officers who had flown to

Pakistan to question Siddiqui and Khan. Both admitted being close associates of two other young British Muslims who had launched a suicide bomb attack on a Tel Aviv nightclub two years before. They had also provided further details about the extent of al-Qaeda's network throughout Britain's Muslim community.

CHAPTER 24

WEB OF TERROR

Collecting the daily editions of the city's newspapers published in Arabic, Urdu, and other Middle East languages remained part of the daily routine for Mossad's London Station because the capital remained a center for radical Islamists to fulminate against Israel and the West.

After an initial assessment by the London Station analysts, the material was sent by the embassy's daily diplomatic bag to Tel Aviv. There it was cross-checked for published names against those on the growing list of captured al-Qaeda operatives who had been spirited away by the CIA to secret interrogation centers where the rules of the Geneva Convention and American law did not apply. Sometimes the relatives of the suspected terrorists gave the Arab-language newspapers details of where they had been captured, which helped the Mossad analysts build up a picture of the CIA's activities. It was doing so not because Mossad disapproved of torture—far from it—but for Israel's self-protection. For years Amnesty International, the International Red Cross, and other human rights organizations had condemned the Jewish state for its harsh interrogation methods and prison conditions. If the day should come when the United States would be forced to support an investigation into Israeli methods of coercive interrogation, then the file Mossad was accumulating would show that it was not alone in such methods.

Central to the CIA operation were two aircraft it had hired from a private company in Massachusetts, Premier Executive Transport Services. One was a fourteen-seater Gulfstream, with registration number N379P, the other a white-painted Boeing 737, with the registration number N313P (the company later declined to discuss the leasing with the author). Mossad had obtained both aircraft's flight logs detailing the journeys the planes had made to countries with poor human rights records; by October 2005, there had been forty-nine flights to Jordan, Uzbekistan, Egypt, and Guantánamo Bay. Rob Baer, a former CIA intelligence officer in the Middle East, would later claim (to *The Washington Post*): "If you want a strong interrogation you send prisoners to Jordan. If you want them to be seriously tortured fly them to Egypt, from where they never return. If you want them to be most severely tortured for information, send them to Uzbekistan." Craig Murray, the former British ambassador to Uzbekistan, was sacked in the autumn of 2004 for leaking a memo he wrote to foreign secretary Jack Straw, in which the diplomat alleged that some of the prisoners sent to Uzbekistan were "boiled alive. Its Soviet-trained interrogators carry out tortures watched by CIA officers stationed in the country, which is regarded as a close ally of the Bush administration."

An MI6 officer told the author, "I have personal knowledge that the prisoners are shackled to their seats and are often gagged and drugged during their flights."

Some of the flights had been cleared to overfly Israeli air space from the CIA secret interrogation center in Kabul known as "the Pit." It was part of a constellation of worldwide secret detention centers that were sometimes as small as shipping containers or as large as the complex at Guantánamo Bay. Majeed Nuaimi, a former justice minister of Qatar who represented the families of dozens of what he called "the disappeared," said (to the author), "No one will ever know how many have gone. But probably many thousands."

The conditions under which they were incarcerated were identified by the New York–based Human Rights Watch. "They are shackled continuously, intentionally kept awake for extended periods of time, and forced to kneel or stand in painful positions for extended periods."

Mossad had established that some of the techniques used at the secret interrogation centers were based on the notorious MK-ULTRA brainwashing program run by the CIA at the height of the cold war. The MI6 officer who had witnessed the shackled prisoners on their way to Uzbekistan claimed (to the author) that upon arrival they were subjected to "sensory deprivation for lengthy periods, mock executions, starvation, sexual violence, rape, immersion in water to the point of drowning, beatings, exposure to intense heat or cold, clamping off blood circulation by wire restraints, near strangulation, flesh burning with cigarettes, and the use of a variety of drugs to weaken a prisoner's resistance."

Meantime Mossad continued to identify names in Arabic newspapers of terrorists who had been sent to the torture chambers. The daily trawl also gathered up the latest pamphlets extolling as "heroes" the bombers of 9/11 and issued updated lists of addresses for Britain's synagogues and the homes of their rabbis. "They should be reminded of the crimes Jews have committed against Muslims," urged the London-based radical group, Al-Muhajiroun. The same kind of reminder was spelled out by another group, Abu Hafs al-Masri Brigades. It told its growing number of supporters in Britain it had "declared a bloody war against our non-Muslim neighbors. We will rase the cities of Europe to the ground. We will turn them into cities drenched with blood until its leaders withdraw their troops from Iraq."

Muslim clerics were regularly invited on to the BBC to justify the "martyrdom" of suicide bombers because, as Dr. Yusuf al-Qardawi told the corporation's current affairs flagship program, *Newsnight:* "It is an indication of the justice of Allah the Almighty." Many young British Muslims still carried with them the fatwa Osama bin Laden had issued in February 1998: "The ruling to kill the Americans and their allies— civilians and military—is an individual duty for every Muslim who can do it in any country in which it is possible to do it, in order to liberate the great Mosques of Mecca from their grip and in order for their armies to move out of the lands of Islam."

With the help of its sayanim network of Jewish volunteers throughout Britain, Mossad's London Station gathered mounting evidence on the extent of the threat Muslim extremism posed to the United Kingdom. There were now close to five thousand sayanim in Britain in 2005, who acted as "the eyes and ears" Meir Amit had envisaged when he created the network. They were no longer made up of relatives of European Jews who had arrived in the country in the 1930s, refugees from nazism. Now they included Jews from Lebanon, Syria, and, more recently, Iraq and Iran: shopkeepers, landlords, and café owners in Asian communities who provided a steady stream of information.

An Iraqi bookseller in the north London suburb of Wembley had provided proof that Islamic extremists had reached the heart of the Blair government. Ahmad Thomson, a Muslim barrister and a senior member of the Association of Muslim Lawyers, had been appointed to advise the prime minister on how to deal with the matter. Thomson was also the author of a fast-selling book in the Muslim community. Titled *The New World Order*, it claimed there was "a Zionist plan to shape world events" and predicted that events like 9/11 and the suicide bombings in Israel were "part of the coming confrontation between the *muminun* (those who accept Islam) and the *kaffirun* (nonbelievers)." Other Muslim advisers to the government had, before being appointed, described Osama bin Laden as a "holy warrior" and defended suicide bombers as "genuine martyrs."

Though the Blair government had finally promised that extremist preachers and scholars who promoted terrorism would be deported, those radical imams and teachers continued throughout the summer of 2005 to deliver their diatribes about holy war in their mosques and post inflammatory articles on their Web sites.

Mohammed al-Massari, a middle-aged Saudi militant who had fled that country to Britain and managed to convince the government he faced death if he was returned to the desert kingdom, still used his Web site in June 2005 to show videos of British and American hostages being beheaded in Iraq. He also ran an Internet radio station that called for holy war. Abu Qatada, who had fled to London from Jordan claiming he was being persecuted there for his religious beliefs, had been allowed to remain in Britain. He had repaid his host country by inciting his followers to go to Iraq and kill Coalition troops. Pakistan's Hizbol-Tahrir, the Party of Liberation, outlawed in its own country, used its London office to recruit young Muslims to go to Afghanistan to be trained to wage war against America. In other Muslim enclaves in the north and west suburbs of London, imams preached their invective as they did in the cities of Leicester, Manchester, Leeds, Bradford, and Glasgow; thousands of young, impressionable Muslims, many born in Britain, were being indoctrinated into hatred against their own country.

All this information had been stored on his computer by Nathan. Some of it had come from his MI5 liaison officer at the Joint Terrorism Analysis Centre (JTAC) in MI5's Millbank offices. Opened in 2003 as part of Britain's role in the war on terrorism, JTAC's one hundred staff were drawn from all areas of the intelligence community fighting international terrorism. They worked in a brightly lit, windowless room in the basement of the building; its unmarked door was opened only by swipe cards whose codes were changed regularly. From the workstations, equipped with state-of-the-art communications, came and went a continuous flow of information. Sensitive material, once shared only with the CIA, Mossad, and the French and German intelligence services, was now more widely distributed since the attacks on Bali and Madrid. The result had been a surge of high-value intelligence from sources like GROM, Poland's SAS-trained antiterrorist unit. They provided details about Jamal Zougam, who was implicated in the Madrid rail station bombings and who had planned a Christmas bombing campaign in Warsaw. Spanish intelligence had sent details of Zougam's visit to London, where he had visited the radical Finsbury Park mosque. Its imam, Abu Hamsa, had preached support for bin Laden and was now fighting extradition to the United States from his prison cell for his role in killing Americans in the Middle East. In 2006, Abu Hamsa was sentenced to seven years' imprisonment for "promoting and taking part in terrorist activities." After he served his sentence, he was deported to America and was found guilty of eleven counts relating to terrorism."

A French intelligence report estimated that as a result of a recruitment drive, al-Qaeda support in the country "stands at over 35,000, many of them are converts to Islam. They are organized into military-style units and meet regularly for training in the use of weapons and explosives, combat tactics, and indoctrination. They are controlled from local and district command centers under the al-Qaeda national command." In a further pooling of information, Germany's BND reported its estimate that there were, in June 2005, around thirty thousand al-Qaeda sympathizers in the Federal Republic. Nathan had told his liaison officer that Mossad believed the movement's leaders were based in the port city of Hamburg, from where several of the 9/11 bombers had come.

In June 2005, Nathan and his liaison officer had once more traveled to several cities in the north of England as part of an unprecedented security operation. Twenty of the world's security services had joined forces to help protect the G8 Summit at Gleneagles in Scotland in July.

Between them they had created a security ring, which included Germany's border with Poland, to intercept terrorists moving out of the Balkans. Spanish intelligence agents were linked through Britain's listening posts on Gibraltar and Cyprus to monitor the North African coast, long an established launchpad for al-Qaeda into Europe. SISMI, Italy's secret service, had deployed scores of agents to watch for terrorists coming out of the Islamic republics of the former Soviet Union. French and Dutch intelligence officers were stationed in the Channel ports.

At GCHQ, Britain's listening post in space, linguists, analysts, and technicians continued to track intercepts, seeking the first sign of a threat. Already its computers had deciphered "chatter" that indicated the Italian anarchists planned to enter Britain ahead of the summit. American satellites, controlled by the NSA base at Menwith Hill in the north of England, watched over an area from the deserts of Iraq in the west to the Ural Mountains in the east.

The DGSE, the French intelligence service charged with protecting President Chirac at the summit, discovered that European anarchists, including the Ya Basta group, had recently met with Class War, a notorious British anarchist group, at Calais. Both groups were known to advocate violent protest. Germany's BND secret service confirmed that German anarchists had also recently attended "a conference of anarchists" held outside Nottingham in England.

MI5, who would jointly coordinate the multinational security operation with MI6, were already hunting for an Italian terrorist nicknamed "The Raven" who was believed to have entered Britain and was known to have links to an al-Qaeda cell in Bologna, Italy, a well-known hotbed for terrorists. Details about him were discovered in a raid by

Italian agents that led to the arrest of eighty anarchists who had been planning to go to Gleneagles. The CIA had assigned two hundred agents and state-of-the-art electronic equipment to protect President Bush. Russia's three intelligence services, the GRU, the FCS, and the SVR, had provided MI5 with identikits of Chechnyan terrorists who could attempt an attack on the summit. The FCS, the Federal Counterintelligence Service, had warned JTAC (Joint Terrorism Analysis Center) that it should not discount a suicide bomber attacking during the summit.

Trying to avert that possibility had taken Nathan once more into the Muslim enclaves in the north of England. Not only did Mossad have its sayanim there, but it had also built up a network of informers within the Muslim communities. Mostly young, they risked their own lives and those of their families by providing information. They, too, had been alerted to watch for any signs that a suicide bomber attack was being planned.

In London, as part of the preparations for the G8 Summit, Mossad had already circulated a document to the police and security services on how Mossad had learned to identify a suicide bomber. In part the document read:

A suicide bomber will be young, at most in his late twenties. While he will usually be a male, remember there are an increasing number of female bombers. A bomber will either be carrying a ruck-sack filled with explosives or a bag, similarly equipped. A person about to undertake something so high risk will be perspiring. Look at hands; are they perspiring? Look at the eyes. Are they furtive? Does the person constantly look around? Are they making an obvious attempt not to make eye contact? A suicide bomber will usually wear a baseball cap or other headgear that will hide the face from closed-circuit television. If the bomb is in a bag, the bomber may constantly check it, especially on public transport. Look at physical shape. Average-sized legs usually mean an average-sized body. But if the person is bulkier than their legs, neck, or face suggest, that could be suspicious. Do not in any circumstances challenge the suspect. If you shout "it's a bomb!," you will most likely panic the bomber into detonating it. And remember: a suicide bomber has to live somewhere. His or her behaviour may have aroused suspicion in his community. Good intelligence will likely mean you have someone in that community to alert you. But also remember there is no precise science to spot a bomber. It depends on past experience and luck.

Mossad was not alone in its penetration of Muslim communities. MI5 had set up sophisticated surveillance sites in areas where Asian communities had become assimilated into British society, where the young held steady employment and made regular trips to see aunts and uncles in Pakistan and other places, where young men were never publicly seen mixing with angry militants after Friday prayers. These were the men that MI5 watched for. On those trips to Pakistan some had made contacts with al-Qaeda. Known as "Trojans," they had been recruited to become homegrown terrorists. Their cell phones were bugged, their conversations recorded and analyzed, their movements filmed, and their contacts subject to the same deep surveillance. Radio waves were bounced off windowpanes to monitor conversations in a room; the latest technology was used to screen e-mails and search for incriminating files on Web sites. Each MI5 surveillance unit had a lawyer from JTAC attached to it who oversaw the surveillance to ensure any evidence would be admissible in a court. The arrests had numbered few.

In part, this was because Islamic groups have been quick to embrace new information technology to achieve their goals. The Internet's full potential in the Arab world was first realized at the onset of the second Palestinian Intifada in 2000. The most successful Web site was Electronic Intifada, dubbed by Yasser Arafat "as our weapon of mass destruction." Its founding members were based in the Netherlands, Canada, Chicago, and Leicester in the English midlands. From there they waged asymmetric warfare using the latest technology to spread their message of hate across cyberspace.

Like MI5, Mossad's London Station collected the biweekly online magazine for all jihadists and, since 2001, a quarterly version for women mujahideen. The same Web sites were monitored by diplomats at the American embassy in Grosvenor Square, London. There was one significant difference. Mossad stations had staff able to instantly read what the Web site said; no such capability existed among those diplomats. They merely transmitted the material on to the State Department or the CIA. Their already hard-pressed translators and analysts played what one translator called "pick and choose" from the daily input of foreign language material. He told the author: "Lookit, not much has changed since the week before 9/11 when Mossad picked up a phone call from bin Laden to his mother—yes, *his mother*, for Chrissake!—that he couldn't come to her birthday party because he was too busy. The message was passed up the line to middle management at the CIA. It was deemed to be too vague to act upon."

From his contacts with sayanim and informers in Leeds, where Jews and Muslims lived cheek by jowl, Nathan had learned radicals had started to write messages on Hotmail or Yahoo e-mail accounts—but not sending them. Instead they left them stored in the "draft" folders of the accounts. Unsent, they could not be intercepted. However, any other radical who knew an account password could log on from anywhere in the world and read a message.

An informer had provided Nathan with a password. But there was nothing on the site to indicate an impending suicide bomber attack, or any form of assault, on the Gleneagles summit.

In the first week of July 2005, Nathan began each day began by listening to the BBC Radio-4 program *Today* as he drove to work. The program had long established itself as required listening for London's politicians, foreign diplomats, the mandarins of Whitehall, and the capital's intelligence community. All were expecting another clash with the Blair government and the BBC over the continuing fallout from its role in the Iraqi war. Though the initial war with Iraq had ended, the issue of Saddam's weapons of mass destruction had remained at the center of a political maelstrom that had threatened the governments of Prime Minister Tony Blair and President George W. Bush. At the core of the increasingly bitter storm was the original *Today* claim on air that Tony Blair had approved of the "sexing-up" of a dossier stating that Saddam had the capability of launching weapons of mass destruction against the West, the reason Blair had given for joining Bush in the war against Iraq. Dr. David Kelly had been publicly identified on the program as the scientist who had given one of its reporters evidence that the dossier had been "sexed up."

Dr. Kelly worked for the British government. He was a world-ranking expert on biological weapons at Britain's Chemical and Biological Defence Establishment at Porton Down and head of its Microbiology

Department. In the still largely secret world of how to combat the threat from biological weapons, Dr. Kelly became the voice of unchallengeable authority regularly consulted by officers on the counterproliferation desks in the Foreign Office, the Ministry of Defence, MI5 and MI6, and Mossad. For over a decade he had confronted the deceits, lies, and trickery of Saddam's biological weapons program. Into his office, room 2/35 in the Ministry of Defence Proliferation and Arms Control Secretariat in Whitehall, came daily e-mails and phone calls asking for his help.

Nathan had met him after Dr. Kelly had taken part in a joint Canadian/Mossad operation to interdict biological materials being shipped to Iraq from Montreal. Later, Nathan had accompanied the scientist to the Institute of Biological Research in Tel Aviv, one of the few outsiders allowed such a visit. When the second war against Iraq ended in 2003, Dr. Kelly returned to Baghdad. He had been told by the CIA and MI6 there were shells and missiles with warheads capable of delivering huge quantities of germs that had been secretly developed between the wars. He had found no such weapons. He had been urged by his superiors to go and look again. Still he had found nothing. The pressure continued. No one suspected the inner gyroscope that balanced Dr. Kelly's decision making had begun to slip out of kilter. Nathan had followed every twist and turn in the very public humiliation of Dr. Kelly that had followed his failure to find weapons of mass destruction: his appearance before a House of Commons Intelligence Oversight Committee, the leaking of his name as the source for the *Today* story that the government had "sexed up" its dossier, his subsequent hounding by the media. Finally, it had all become too much for Dr. Kelly.

At two thirty on the afternoon of Thursday, July 17, 2003, Detective Chief Inspector Alan Young sat down before his secure computer and began to create a highly restricted file. Across the top of his screen he typed a code name: *Operation Mason*. Beneath it he added: *Not for Release. Police Operational Information*. Below that he added the figures: *14.30* and *17.07.03*, indicating the file had been opened at two thirty p.m. on Thursday, July 17, 2003. Young's file had been created after a morning of tense discussions in various government offices in Whitehall. In his pastel-painted office suite in the Joint Intelligence Committee location, John Scarlett, its chairman for the past two years, had taken his share of the calls. Scarlett had a well-attuned nose for trouble and must have sensed Dr. Kelly's responses before the parliamentary committee and the continuing government row with the BBC were becoming a serious problem.

Scarlett had played a key part in producing the controversial dossier. In doing so, he had discarded the carefully judged input of Dr. Kelly in the early drafts. The original intelligence had come from MI6 and was approved by its then director general Sir Richard Dearlove before it had electronically made its way through the intelligence community, passing across the desk of the Defence Intelligence staff. None of them had supported Dr. Kelly's original assertion that Saddam had no weapons of mass destruction. He had become the lonely voice who had finally decided to speak to the BBC. What else could Kelly do, *would he do? And say?* These were the questions troubling Scarlett.

Dr. Kelly had received phone calls his wife, Janice Kelly, was certain came from MI6. She remembered her husband taking some calls behind the closed door of his study, fitted out with seven laptops and his high-security computer on his desks installed by MI5 along with his direct high-security line to Porton Down. It later emerged that when he had left the house, he received two more calls on his cell phone as he walked. The identity of the callers would never be traced.

Dr. Kelly's body was found in a woodland the next day. Two separate police teams gave different locations for where and how his corpse was positioned. By then, officers from the MI5 Technical Assessment Centre had removed from Dr. Kelly's study all his electronic equipment. The data on them would remain secret. However, three eminent British medical specialists took the highly unusual step of publicly saying Dr. Kelly could never have committed suicide based on the published forensic details. Their conclusions raised disturbing questions. What could account for the lack of blood from the small wrist slash? What part, if any, had the small number of painkillers he had swallowed played? Could the answers be linked to Dr. Kelly's own prediction made to a friend that he "would not be surprised if my body isn't one day found in the woods"?

There were a number of reasons for Mossad to pay more than a passing interest to those words. Dr. Kelly had triggered an unprecedented crisis for the Blair government after publicly questioning the validity of the now notorious "sexed-up" dossier. "Preposterous though it seems to outsiders, taking out a troublemaker is not unknown in the dark side of secret intelligence. Mossad does it with its kidon. Other services have their hit men available, contract killers who cannot be traced," claimed Ari Ben-Menashe (to the author).

There were persistent reports that Dr. Kelly had been targeted by Saddam Hussein's hit squads while he had been in Iraq probing the country's arsenal. His own MI5 contacts had warned him he was at risk. There were other possible threats to his safety. His work in unscrambling the Soviet Union's secret biological arsenal had angered many of its scientists when he refused to help them come to Britain to work. MI5 had warned Dr. Kelly that some of the scientists had maintained close contacts with the Russian foreign intelligence service, which currently had thirty agents working out of the Russian embassy. Dr. Kelly had been provided with a list of all the number plates of their cars. Only a week before his death, a Land Rover—bearing the diplomatic number plate prefix 248D, assigned to all Russian diplomatic vehicles—had been spotted less than twenty miles from Southmoor, the village where Dr. Kelly lived.

Meir Dagan had asked Nathan to prepare a report on the scientist's death. The London Station chief updated himself on the background to Dr. Kelly's death after he had been found on Harrowdown Hill, a beauty spot near his home. The technicians at the Tactical Assessment Center had deconstructed the computer disks recovered from Dr. Kelly's study, and calls to and from his cell phone found on his body had been analyzed. While most dealt with his daily workload at the Ministry of Defence and Porton Down, personal details had also emerged. They included two job offers he was considering to work in the private sector in America.

One offer was from the Washington-based company, Hadron Advanced Biosystems. It was run by a Soviet defector, Kamovtjan Alibekov, who had been the top scientist in that country's biowarfare program and the inventor of the world's most powerful genetically engineered anthrax. He had found a home in America's biodefense industry and changed his name to Ken Alibek. His company had close ties to the Pentagon and the CIA and described itself as "specializing in the development of technical solutions for the U.S. intelligence community." The other company was Regman Biotechnologies, one that Dr. Kelly had helped to set up in Britain. At the time of his death, the company had a contract with the U.S. Navy to "develop a diagnostic and therapeutic treatment for anthrax." It stated its prime function was to "research powerful alternatives to antibiotics." Both companies had offered Dr. Kelly remuneration double his present salary, sufficient to pay for private medical treatment that Janice urgently needed and for which there was a lengthy waiting list on Britain's National Health Service.

Nicholas Gardiner, the Oxfordshire coroner, concluded Dr. Kelly committed suicide by cutting his left wrist with a blunt penknife he used as a gardening tool. He had also ingested twenty-eight coproxamol tablets, a painkiller for arthritis. Dr. Kelly did not suffer from the condition. They would have been hard to swallow without water or crunching them with his teeth. A bizarre twist came when, an hour after his body was found, Dr. Kelly's dental records went missing from the local surgery. His dentist reported this to the police. Two days later the records reappeared in the surgery. Dr. Nicholas Hunt, the pathologist who carried out the autopsy, was sufficiently alarmed to ask the police to conduct a DNA test to "make sure the body was really Dr. Kelly's." The pathologist noted that there were "several superficial scratches on the wrist and one deep wound that had severed the ulnar artery but not the radial artery." He concluded this had led to a fatal hemorrhage.

The three experienced medical specialists, who had already questioned whether Dr. Kelly had committed suicide, again challenged the conclusion: Dr. David Halpin, a consultant in trauma injuries; Dr. Stephen Frost, a radiologist; and Dr. Martin Birstingi, a vascular surgeon, all said that in their combined clinical experience—numbering some fifty years—they had never come across a case where somebody had died from cutting their ulnar artery. "To die from hemorrhage Dr. Kelly would have had to lose about five pints of blood," stated Dr. Halpin. Dr. Frost said, "It is unlikely from the stated injury Dr. Kelly would have lost more than a pint of blood." In Dr. Berstingi's opinion, "When the ulnar artery is cut, there is a rapid fall in blood pressure and after a few further minutes the artery stops bleeding." None of these experts was asked to testify at the inquest.

Piece by piece Nathan had collected and analyzed the testimony of those involved in the scientist's death. He uncovered details of Dr. Kelly's hitherto unsuspected links to the biowarfare program of South Africa's apartheid regime—and that in the week before his death the scientist had been told he would be questioned by MI5 over bringing the program's head, Dr. Wouter Basson, to Porton Down. With all the other pressure he was facing, had the prospect of a grilling by security service interrogators finally been the last straw? Could his death possibly have any connection with the madcap schemes of Basson? Had he been killed to be silenced, another victim of the "dark side of intelligence" that Ari Ben-Menashe had identified? The questions would remain unanswered until Michael Shrimpton, a lawyer who has briefed the U.S. Senate Intelligence Committee on national security issues, made a bid to end the mystery.

He claimed to the London *Sunday Express* that "Dr. Kelly was most likely murdered by a team of assassins from the French DGSE security service and his body dressed up to look like a suicide. Within forty-eight hours of the Kelly death, I was contacted by a British intelligence officer who told me he had been murdered. Neither MI5 nor MI6 were involved and both services are unhappy over what happened. It is my opinion that well-placed persons in Whitehall considered Kelly to be a threat to the survival of the government and used a team from outside the country to take out Kelly. My information is that the French used Iraqi intelligence killers to carry out the killing." Shrimpton produced no ironclad evidence to support his claim. But they formed part of Nathan's report, which, in turn, would become part of the curriculum at the Mossad training school.

In that first week of July 2005, high summer had come to London, filling the city with optimism. A continuing heatwave had clothed the crowds in pretty dresses and open-necked shirts. Cafés had moved tables outside for al fresco dining. The stock market was still on the rise, and the shops were offering discounts on already bargain prices. The television images from Baghdad had faded from the screens.

Mossad had been among foreign intelligence services informed by the Home Office that the threat of a terrorist attack on Britain had been downgraded from "severe general" to the third highest alert, "substantial." That week Scotland Yard's commissioner, Sir Ian Blair, had briefed his senior staff that MI5 was "quietly confident" the battle against terrorism was under control.

Nathan had met, and liked, the commissioner. Since he had been appointed the previous January, Blair had started to run London's police force as a modern corporation based on the latest management techniques. With his calm, measured tones, the stocky uniformed figure, police cap clamped firmly on his head and jaw thrust forward, Blair radiated a bullish certainty. He had set out his stall in much the way Meir Dagan had done when taking over a dispirited Mossad. Blair had told his force of thirty thousand officers and fifteen thousand civilians that he intended to drag them away from what he saw as a sexist, homophobic, and often racist past. He had reminded them that he was a policeman who knew what it was like to extract a corpse from a train crash and had peppered his laying-down-the-rules-first speech to his senior officers with quotations from Voltaire. He raised a smile when he said that on his deathbed the great French thinker, asked to renounce the devil, replied this was not the time to make new enemies. He told the officers he didn't want them to treat him as their enemy, but he would not tolerate anyone who clung "to the old ways." From then on he slipped easily into the business jargon of "multitiered policing," "customer-shaped service," and "infrastructure connectivity." He used such unlikely police terms as "encapsulate," "ex cathedra," "antithesis," and "counsel of perfection."

Nathan had suspected those words would not sit easily with Meir Dagan's blunt language, nor the way Blair signed his memos with a gold-tipped fountain pen, nor how he had a Miró painting on his office wall and filled his bookshelf with copies of Tennyson and Yeats.

Satisfied that London was not at risk from an impending terrorist attack, Blair had ordered fifteen hundred Metropolitan police officers to the Gleneagles summit, where anarchists were among the protesters. The Yard's antiterrorist squad had also sent almost all its officers to Scotland. MI5 and MI6 had drawn tight its part of the net, which had been cast far and wide to catch terrorists. Not one had been spotted. Even the hunt for the "Raven" had petered out when Mossad said he had come and gone from Britain, disappearing somewhere into Europe. Around Gleneagles the massed ranks of police had overwhelmed protesters. The only moment of tension had come when President George W. Bush fell off his bicycle and grazed his hand.

Britain's capital awoke on July 6 to find the city had won the right to stage the 2012 Olympic Games, and driving to work that morning, tuned into the *Today* program, Nathan heard Commissioner Blair assuring Londoners that "we will cope with any terror threat to the games. Our police force is the envy of the policing world in relation to counterterrorism. We've upped our game."

That Wednesday afternoon a war game was winding down in JTAC (Joint Terrorism Analysis Centre). Predicting disaster scenarios on their computers was a regular part of the work of the specialists at their interlinked work stations. This one centered on two different types of attack on London. The first scenario predicted that terrorists would fly over the capital in a light plane leased from one of the private airfields to the west of the city and dump VX nerve gas to catch the prevailing wind. The specialists calculated 30 people would die at the point of release and another 250 downwind. The next scenario was based on terrorists spraying pneumonic plague in aerosol form at Heathrow. Not only would several thousand die in the chosen terminal, but the wind could carry the plague into London. The calculated death toll was put at 2 million as all the emergency services would be overwhelmed. To cope with the dead, JTAC had recommended that the London Strategic Disaster Mortuary Working Group, part of the UK Mass Fatalities Working Group, should set up mobile mortuaries on the outskirts of the city to provide "overflow capacity for hundreds of thousands of deaths."

That evening Mossad Station in London received its daily report from Tel Aviv that there was no evidence of any increase in "terrorist chatter" involving a threat to the United Kingdom. In MI5 headquarters, overlooking the river Thames in Westminster, the vast, open-plan operations room that stretched along most of one wing was in stand-down mode: its plasma screens were blank, the whiteboards empty, the maps of London streets rolled up, the scores of telephones silent.

Not one of the police and security services had picked up a hint of the atrocity about to happen.

On Thursday morning, July 7, Nathan was running a staff meeting in his office at the Israeli embassy when his MI5 liaison officer telephoned shortly after 9:00 A.M. He did not bother to hide the tension and anger in his voice. There had been three separate attacks on rush-hour trains on London's subway system and one on its famous double-decker buses. The death toll would be heavy (it turned out to be fifty-five dead and more than two hundred injured). The atrocity bore all the hallmarks of an al-Qaeda suicide attack. The MI5 officer concluded by asking Mossad to provide all possible assistance.

In the past three years MI5 had made several requests for Mossad's help over suspected plots to attack London's transport system, which the security service believed had Middle East links. They included poisoning the subway with sarin gas, planting cyanide in its air-conditioning system, placing the deadly poison ricin on the trains. Another plot had centered on exploding a car bomb in the city's Soho District, a favorite tourist area. Mossad had failed to find any evidence to support the MI5 claims that the plans had originated in the Middle East. Yet shortly before the London bombings, Lord Stevens, taking time out from his investigation into the death of Princess Diana, had publicly insisted MI5 had thwarted the plots. The claim had irritated Mossad.

Nathan knew that this time the request for help was being made to all foreign intelligence station chiefs in the capital. Within the hour they would have pulled back their own agents from the G8 Summit to help piece together the background on those who had carried out the worst terrorist attack Britain had ever experienced. Mossad would focus its own efforts on the Middle East and Africa, areas where its network of field agents and informers was unrivaled. Their information would be directed through Mossad headquarters for assessment and then routed by encoded e-mail to the London Station. It would receive a further assessment by Nathan and his own agents before being sent on to JTAC. A *katsa* based in Mogadishu, the capital of Somalia on the Horn of Africa, had been briefed to listen out for "chatter" that could link the London bombings with al-Qaeda terrorists who controlled the country through the local warlords. In the past three years more than thirty-five thousand Somalis had been granted asylum in Britain to escape the brutality. One or more of them might have become radicalized by Britain's imams.

By early afternoon Mossad Station in Cape Town, South Africa, had learned of a dispute between MI6 and CIA operatives over what to do with a British citizen of Indian descent, Haroon Rashid Aswat, who was under arrest in Zambia for an alleged connection with al-Qaeda. The CIA said he was wanted on an arrest warrant in the United States, which charged him with providing "material support to al-Qaeda and attempting to establish a terror training camp in Bly, Oregon, in 1999." The CIA had told MI6 they had a "strong supposition" that Aswat had made a number of phone calls to suspected Muslim radicals in Britain shortly before the bombings.

The CIA wanted Aswat to be collected by its Gulfstream and flown to a torture chamber in Uzbekistan. But while MI6 was ready to support having Aswat legally extradited to America over the Oregon charges, it would not allow a British citizen to be subjected to brutality.

It had also told the CIA that Aswat's phone calls did not link him to the London bombings.

While the hunt for the London suicide bombers continued, the relationship within the international intelligence community developed its first crack. The French and German security services told MI5 they had no evidence to support its claim that a senior al-Qaeda operative, identified as Mustafa, had traveled halfway across Europe and in and out of England shortly before the bombings. Yet Mustafa had continued to be listed as a "priority target" on the Anacapa charts, the specialist diagrams used in the MI5 operations center to try and build up a coherent picture from the information coming in. Nathan had been asked by his MI5 liaison officer to help establish whether Mustafa could still have been the mastermind behind the suicide bombers. Had he told them which targets to hit? Once more Mossad put out the word among its sayanim across Britain and informers in the Middle East. In the weeks to come the mysterious Mustafa would remain just that—a mystery.

London remained in a grip of fear when, on July 21, the city was subjected to a further suicide bomb attack. But this time the operation bore all the signs of amateur bungling: the homemade bombs failed to explode and the bombers were soon identified. Nevertheless hundreds of reports continued to reach Scotland Yard of people acting suspiciously. Each one had been checked and the suspect shown to have behaved, at most, foolishly. The police had warned that people who behaved like this in a time of high tension ran the risk of their behavior "being misunderstood."

And such was the case with Jean Charles de Menezes, a young Brazilian electrician, on his way by subway to fix a fire alarm in north London. Somewhere walking between his home and the nearby Stockwell underground station he had come to the attention of one of the many antiterrorist police teams on the streets. Each member was aware of the rule they could fire only if they believed a suspect was carrying a bomb. The order of shoot to kill, aiming at the head of a person, would come after a "gold commander" at Scotland Yard had given the order by radio phone to a team commander. The police did not have to shout a warning before they fired; to do so would negate the essential surprise. The rules of engagement were based on those drawn up by Israeli special forces to deal with the country's suicide bombers.

The unsuspecting de Menezes was tracked through the subway station, down an escalator, and onto the platform, where a train was about to depart. As he boarded, the police team moved. One wrestled de Menezes to the floor. Two others fired a total of seven bullets into his head and body. The details caused a growing public furor as it emerged Scotland Yard had lied in claims that de Menezes was "dressed like a suicide bomber." He had worn lightweight clothes. Police Commissioner Blair found himself progressively challenged over his statements that attempted to justify the shooting. Within his own police force, he was increasingly subjected to criticism by senior officers, who began to leak details to the media about unhappiness within the ranks over Blair's leadership. The criticism deepened when the early stages of the investigation into de Menezes's death showed a failure in communication between the team tracking de Menezes and their controllers at Scotland Yard. It transpired that one of the team had taken an unauthorised toilet break during a key part of the surveillance, and radio links between the team and Scotland Yard had temporarily broken down at a crucial stage. Later came the embarrassing news that Blair had authorized a small payment to be offered to the de Menezes family to help them with funeral expenses. The family rejected the offer.

Meantime, the death of the young electrician continued to fuel a huge outcry in Britain's media. Human rights organizations had seized upon the shooting to mount a campaign against police methods and demand a reassessment of its shoot-to-kill policy. In March 2006, Blair found himself mired in a new controversy. He admitted that he had secretly bugged his conversation with Britain's attorney general, Lord Goldsmith. They had been discussing telephone surveillance and the bugging of suspects at the time. The revelation brought new demands he should resign, the fifth call to do so since the death of de Menezes. He had brushed all those aside. But over the shooting he had one firm supporter. Nathan had told his MI5 liaison officer, "Those policemen thought they were acting in the best interests of everybody on the information they were given. Mistakes do happen."

In Tel Aviv for Meir Dagan one death had to be weighed against the loss of life suicide bombers had already carried out, not only in London and Israel, but all around the world. The one certainty, he had told his staff, was the further away the last attack, the closer was the next one.

In the early hours of the first Saturday in October 2005, the duty officer on the Asia Desk in Mossad headquarters received a "Flash" e-mail from the *katsa* based in Jakarta, the capital of Indonesia. It brought news that al-Qaeda's suicide bombers had struck again on the popular holiday resort of Bali, killing and injuring over fifty people. In 2002, other bombers had destroyed nightclubs on the island, killing dozens and wounding hundreds. The message ended with the chilling words: "All indications are this is the work of Husin."

The forty-eight-year-old graduate engineer from Reading University in England had been personally recruited by Osama bin Laden to become the organization's master bomber. As well as the previous Bali bombing, the Malaysian-born Azhari Husin had organized suicide bomb attacks on the American-owned Marriott Hotel in Jakarta in 2003 and the Australian embassy in the city in 2004. Thirty people had died in the attacks and over a hundred were injured.

A few days before, Mossad had finally confirmed the MI5 claim that the mysterious Mustafa had been Husin, who had planned and recruited volunteers for the London bombings. Meir Dagan had told Eliza Manningham-Buller that Husin had traveled to London before the attacks, using one of the many passports known to be in his possession and traveling under one of his disguises. He may even have been in the capital when the attacks occurred: one of his trademarks was to observe the effects of the destruction for which he was responsible. He had been spotted at previous locations each time escaping in the confusion to return to one of his hideouts, which Mossad believed were in the Toba Kakar range of mountains separating Pakistan's Northwest frontier from the equally inhospitable mountains of Afghanistan.

America's National Security Agency geopositioned a satellite over an area that extended from Murgha and Khanozai, small towns in the foothills of the Toba Kakar range. Pakistani troops, supported by U.S. Special Forces and Britain's SAS, began to prepare for another foray into the region. In the early hours of October 8, the entire region was devastated by an earthquake measuring 7.6 on the Richter scale. Millions of tons of rock and rubble buried the area. The Mossad analysts, who had been closely monitoring the area, decided that if Husin was buried beneath the debris it was unlikely his body would be found.

Then came reports that not only galvanized the analysts in Tel Aviv but also those in every major intelligence service; Osama bin Laden could be among the dead. Informers had told their intelligence controllers that he had been seen in the devastated area. One report said his face looked thinner. Could that be an indication his kidney condition had worsened? In recent weeks, Mossad had discovered that bin Laden had received from China a portable kidney dialysis machine. Drones, unmanned aircraft launched by U.S. Special Forces to overfly the search area, reported that all power supplies had been destroyed. In Islamabad, President Pervez Musharraf agreed to a CIA request to keep rescue teams looking for earthquake survivors from entering the search area for bin Laden and Husin. In Washington bin Laden watchers joined the speculation. Bruce Hoffman at the RAND Corporation, a think tank with good connections in the U.S. intelligence community, said that if bin Laden had survived he could have made his way back into Afghanistan. Milt Bearden, a CIA officer with hands-on experience of the search area, added: "If bin Laden is dead the world will never know. We just have to wait until somebody drags out his body, does the DNA checks, and says 'this is bin Laden.' My bet is that it won't happen."

Nevertheless the speculation continued. Donald Rumsfeld, the feisty U.S. secretary of defense, said it was now almost a year since bin Laden had made his last public appearance, and he could be dead; Nature's justice. "No longer the face of al Qaeda," Rumsfeld had mused. Certainly on the jihadist Web sites Mossad analysts noticed Abu Musab al-Zarqawi, the Jordanian responsible for some of the worst atrocities in Iraq, was increasingly labeled as a prime mover in the dream of restoring the Islamic caliphate.

On one of the Web sites appeared a chilling document titled: *The Nuclear Bomb of Jihad and the Way to Enrich Uranium*. Its eighty pages contained detailed instructions on how to "look for radium, an effective alternative to uranium and available on the market." Matti Steinberg, one of Mossad's experts on al-Qaeda's search for a nuclear weapon, said the manual was "dangerously impressive." While the author described himself as "Layth al-Islam," the Lion of Islam, it was to whom he had dedicated the manual that raised doubt that bin Laden was dead. "A gift to the commander of the jihad fighters, Sheikh Osama bin Laden, for the sake of jihad for the sake of Allah."

On October 18, a deep-cover Mossad agent in Tehran recorded a conversation between bin Laden's oldest son, Saad, and his siblings Mohammed and Othman. The three men were living in secure compounds in the city suburbs from where they ran terrorist operations rather than languishing under house arrest as the Iran government claimed. In the conversation, Saad reported he had spoken that day to his father, who wanted his sons to know he was alive and well. The recording was made ten days after the earthquake had struck.

Shortly afterward came the first clue for Mossad analysts that there was a shift of power in the upper echelons of al-Qaeda. In Afghanistan the CIA had intercepted a letter to be hand-couriered from Ayman al-Zawahiri, the long-time deputy to bin Laden and al-Qaeda's long-time strategist, to Abu Musab al-Zarqawi, whose ruthless bombing campaign in Iraq had brought a $25 million bounty on his head, posted by the United States. A copy of the letter was sent to Mossad to study. Its analysts were surprised: while the usual flowery Arabic remained, there was a sharpness to the tone over the deaths of many hundreds of Shias who had died in suicide bombings launched by al-Zarqawi. Zawahiri questioned "the wisdom of such a policy by you. Such action is not acceptable to our Shia supporters and will do nothing to achieve our aims. I have personally tasted the bitterness of American brutality when my family was killed in a bombing attack in Afghanistan. Despite that I say to you: we are in a battle and more than half of that battle is fought in the media. What you are doing is killing our Shia brothers and it will not help us win that battle."

Days later al-Zarqawi delivered his response. On a cold night in Amman, his suicide bombers lit the sky over the Jordanian capital with massive explosions that seriously damaged three hotels and a nightclub, which in the tourist season would be filled with foreign visitors. But on that night, the majority of the ninety-six dead and scores of wounded were Arabs, including a number of Shia families who had traveled over the border from Iraq to holiday after Ramadan.

The atrocity was seen by Mossad analysts as evidence al-Zarqawi was making a grim presentation to the al-Qaeda membership that he was their leader in waiting.

CHAPTER 25

CONFRONTING THE DRAGON

In the fading daylight of an October afternoon in 2005, an Israeli air force plane landed at a high security airport near Beijing. The flight had been specially arranged for Meir Dagan, the sole passenger on board. Only Prime Minister Sharon and members of the Committee of the Heads of Service knew the purpose of his long journey across Asia.

The Mossad station chief in Moscow had obtained evidence that former members of the Russian armed forces had supplied rocket technology to North Korea, enabling the pariah state to build missiles capable of striking not only Israel but all the capitals of Europe. Even more worrying was that the Pyongyang regime had secretly passed on the technology to Iran, immensely boosting its already formidable military capability. In the past month North Korea's state-owned Chongchengang Arms Corporation, which had brokered the deal with the Russians, had sent tanker planes to Iran loaded with liquid propellant needed to drive the rockets. Each missile was designed to carry a 1.2-ton payload, more than sufficient to reduce Tel Aviv to a wasteland. One of the rockets, the Taep'o-dong 2, could reach America's West Coast when launched in the Pacific from one of the Soviet SSN-6 submarines Moscow had sold to North Korea in 2003.

Even more disturbing was a later report from a Mossad undercover agent stationed in Seoul, the capital of South Korea. The city had long been a haven for spies from all over the world, who were on the constant lookout for refugees from the north who could provide inside information or, more important, who had worked in the secret military programs of North Korea. For weeks the agent had been cultivating a defector who had worked as a production manager at Factory 395 near the town of Jaijin in the far northeast of the country. He had not only provided details of the missile guidance systems being produced but also information about the scores of other factories in the regime's industry to manufacture weapons of mass destruction. All told, over two hundred thousand people were employed in producing nuclear materials, and chemical and biological weapons. The defector revealed that Factory 395's, missile guidance systems were capable of delivering warheads filled with chemical and biological agents. His duties had included buying electronic equipment made in a factory outside Nagasaki. Its salesmen regularly traveled to Factory 395. Their names had been passed to Mossad's Asia Desk and in turn to its station in Tokyo: the possibility of recruiting a salesman as an informer was an enticing one.

The defector had described the all-too-familiar story of the regime's oppression: dawn roundups, families set to spy on each other, starvation and abuses of power by those who were favored by the regime. The slightest indiscretion was severely punished. Men had been shot after defacing one of the portraits of the country's leader, which adorned every public place. Women had been taken by the police to their barracks and gang-raped. Some had committed suicide afterward. The names of some of those who had been brutalized and those of their torturers, along with the places where the brutality had occurred, had been recalled by the defector. At the factory he had witnessed a woman being roasted in an electric oven and a man being beaten to death with steel rods. Both had been caught trying to smuggle out food from the factory kitchen.

The Mossad agent's report had included details of how the Taep'o-dong 2 missile had been modified by North Korean technicians so it could fire the rocket from a land-based transporter. The vehicle had been dismantled and flown to Tehran. With it had gone a warhead designed to carry a biological weapon.

The details had been sent to Washington. Condoleezza Rice, the U.S. secretary of state, had flown to Moscow to protest to President Vladimir Putin about the situation that had resulted from the initial sale of Russian technology to North Korea. She had met with the cold response to direct her protest to North Korea. Dr. Rice had flown to London and discussed the matter with Prime Minister Tony Blair to see what diplomatic pressure could be jointly exerted by Britain and the United States on Iran. He had favored referring Iran to the United Nations Security Council. John Bolton, the U.S. ambassador to the UN, had publicly announced that he had evidence that Iran was determined to produce nuclear weapons which could be used to intimidate the Middle East and Europe and to "possibly supply terrorists" with the missiles. His statement was largely based on the Mossad report from Seoul.

Its content was later endorsed when Dr. Rice met MI6 director general John Scarlett. He told her the evidence had been "copper-bottomed" by Mossad, and that it was accepted North Korea could have acted only with the full knowledge of China. There was quick agreement that to avert the situation developing into a full-blown crisis, Beijing should be made fully aware of the intelligence Mossad had obtained and asked to exert its considerable influence over North Korea to withdraw its support from Iran. The overt diplomacy that had failed Condoleezza Rice was now about to go covert.

There were further discussions on how the request should be conveyed. It could be done at ambassadorial level, but there was no guarantee this would be perceived with sufficient seriousness by Beijing. But neither Dr. Rice nor Britain's foreign secretary, Jack Straw, could jump on the next plane to China; that would create a sense of panic Beijing could well exploit. Yet it was essential to convey to its leaders that North Korea must be stopped and that only Beijing could pressure a dangerously unstable regime to desist from helping Iran. After hours of consultation by advisers in London and Washington, and finally a secure-line conference call with Tel Aviv to Ariel Sharon, it had been decided that Mossad, which had provided so much of the detail, should once more use its connections with China's Secret Intelligence Service, CSIS, to convey the seriousness of the situation. "If it is not a full-blown crisis yet, then it will soon be," said John Bolton.

It was not the first time Mossad had played such a role. In the past it had paved the way for the diplomatic exchange of Egyptian prisoners captured during the Six-Day War; it had organized the bridge building that enabled Israeli diplomats to have working relations with Jordan and Lebanon.

All of Israel's political leaders had used Mossad for covert diplomacy. Some, like Yitzhak Shamir, Benjamin Netanyahu, and Ehud Barak, had exaggerated hopes of what Mossad could, or should, achieve; this was largely due to their own past connections with intelligence operations. In Ariel Sharon, Mossad had a political master who had both the temperament and experience to know how to handle the service. On more than one occasion he had tasked Meir Dagan to use the "backdoor" connection to the CIA to raise a politically sensitive matter and test the response in Washington before Sharon formally raised it with the White House. It was Dagan who told Porter Goss that Israel would continue to attack Hamas while still trying to negotiate with the Palestinian Authority. Sharon also well understood that in a high-tech world of intelligence gathering, the human factor remained critical when it came to covert diplomacy. The character of Meir Dagan was perfectly suited to the role and complemented Sharon's own rumbustious personality that had given him a keen interest in spies and their activities. For the prime minister, it was a natural progression to use Meir Dagan as his own secret diplomat.

"Our kind of diplomacy is based on contacts with other intelligence services. We tell their spymasters what our foreign service people would like to see happen. We know their intelligence people usually wield strong influence with the governments or regimes they work for. In more cases than not, it works very well. The diplomats get the public credit. We have the private satisfaction of a job well done," Meir Amit once told the author.

Setting up Mossad's latest venture into the dark side of diplomacy was something Meir Dagan had developed over his three years in office. On his personal computer were the updated names, direct-line phone numbers, and encrypted e-mail addresses of intelligence chiefs in over a hundred countries. His contacts also included diplomats, businessmen, and those who operated close to the edge of legality.

This would be Dagan's second visit to China. Eighteen months before he had been a member of a delegation that had included General Amos Yaron, the director general of the Israeli Defense Ministry, and a team of the country's top armaments salesmen. They had come to develop ties that had already produced for Israel over $4 billion in sales of arms and military equipment. Much of it had originally been sent to Israel by the United States, and when Washington had finally objected to Israel Aircraft Industries (IAI) selling an early warning system, AWACS, Israel had reluctantly paid $350 million compensation to cancel the deal. Diplomatic relations between Beijing and Tel Aviv, established in 1992, had become virtually frozen.

In Asia House in downtown Tel Aviv, the directors of IAI were furious after the years spent making Israel's arms industry its main export. They had brokered deals not only with China but South Africa and the nations of Latin America. IAI had become a home for former Mossad directors Zvi Zamir, Yitzhak Hofi, and Danny Yatom. Amos Manor, the first head of Shin Bet, the country's equivalent to the FBI, also had his office in IAI. It was a standing joke among them that the "big question is whether the state owns IAI or whether IAI owns the state of Israel." The corporation's unique position included being the only one in Israel that had total tax relief on all its income.

Dagan knew that when the time came for him to give up being the Mossad chief, he too would be offered a comfortable desk at IAI. How he performed on this mission to Beijing would be carefully watched.

For the previous sales trip to Beijing, the Israeli delegation had brought with them a number of enticing new weapons, many developed from their American originals. Among them was the latest version of Promis, the software program that could track the movements of literally untold numbers of people anywhere in the world (see chapter 10, "A Dangerous Liaison," pp. 195–202). China had been among the 142 countries to buy the software whose undetectable "trapdoor" had been installed by Israel's top programmers, enabling Mossad to monitor all those who used it. The new version could do that even better.

On that first visit, Dagan had seen that technology had become something China could not get enough of; more was spent on this than on food. Nowhere was it more evident than in surveillance. Ultrasonic detectors sensitive to noise or motion, electronic invisible beams that activated hidden cameras and silent alarms, bugging and debugging devices: Israel had the best and found a ready market in China. Some of the equipment the sales team had brought included gadgets developed by Mossad, such as voice analyzers that would monitor the tension in a person making a telephone call. IAI had created a new radar that emitted electromagnetic energy pulses that bounced off an enemy aircraft and betrayed its shape and size. Other Israeli companies had found a ready market for the kind of surveillance equipment that had become an integral part of the urban Chinese infrastructure: electronic monitors analyzed every minute of the working day, checked on performance rates, even toilet breaks and personal activities. Meir Dagan had seen that no building in Beijing appeared able to operate without its quota of Israeli microchips that constantly fed the banks of computers by which the government kept track of its citizens from birth to death.

At the banquets where the delegation had been feted, speaker after speaker had spoken of the Asian Century, that by the year 2005, of the thirteen cities with world populations in excess of 10 million, seven would be around the Pacific Rim. China's predicted economic growth of 8 percent a year would allow it to create the world's largest cybercity; its reserve of currency, by 2010, would exceed that of Japan; by that year one in ten of all corporations around the Pacific Rim would be under the virtual control of its Chinese investors; by the year 2015, countries like Thailand and the Philippines would be under the economic management of China. All this would be achieved, a banquet speaker had enthused, by China's ability to export technology it had bought from Israel. The irony was not lost on the guests.

At one banquet Meir Dagan had been introduced to Qiao Shi, once China's supreme intelligence chief. At over six feet, he was unusually tall for a Chinese man. Qiao's stoop, it was rumored, was from a childhood illness that had kept him bedridden for long periods during which he had pored over the written Chinese language. By the age of six he had mastered its radicals, strokes, phonetics, and recensions. The discipline of learning was good training for his future as China's spymaster, and he had become the longest-serving intelligence chief in the world. In their brief encounter, Meir Dagan had found Qiao polite yet distant, but ready to raise his glass of French cognac to toast the Israeli delegation and offer them Cuban cigars.

Now, eighteen months later on that October day in 2005, Dagan had come as an emissary to pass on the request to Qiao that Beijing must intervene to stop North Korea from arming Iran, an action that could not only precipitate a regional war but also might lead to a global conflict.

Their meeting came under the well-honed rule of Total Deniability. There would be no record kept of the secure-line phone calls to set up the meeting or its purpose. The flight plan and the passenger manifest were classified. Only Porter Goss and John Scarlett knew the purpose of the trip. Senior diplomats at the State Department in Washington and the Foreign Office in London had deliberately been kept out of the loop so that they could truthfully deny any knowledge of the mission.

Dagan had familiarized himself with Mossad's profile of Qiao Shi and the ultimate control he had over the activities of five spying organizations: ILD, the International Liaison Department, was engaged in covert activities primarily directed against the United States; MID, the Military Intelligence Department, targeted the military capabilities of America, Great Britain, and other member states of the European Union; MSS, the Ministry of State Security, handled all counterintelligence within China; STD, the Special Technical Department of the Ministry of State Security, which had helped carry out the theft from Los Alamos, also collated all signals traffic from Chinese embassies overseas; and NCNA, a news service reporting on Chinese affairs and also a cover for CSIS spies abroad.

CSIS had its own buildings in Beijing. Counterintelligence was housed in a four-story structure on West Qiananmen Street; foreign intelligence operated from a modern building near the city's main railway station. But the major activities of the several thousand men and women CSIS employed were coordinated from inside the compound at Zhongnanhai, where the Chinese leadership lived and worked. Next to the prime minister's office was a single-story, squarely built building with the traditional curved, red-tiled roof and a paved area containing a helicopter pad and parking space for cars. The building's roof was festooned with aerials. An American satellite's photograph revealed the building had an inner courtyard with an ornamental pond and a landscaped miniature garden. Qiao Shi's private office was the only one with direct access to the courtyard.

It was from there that he ran intelligence networks that extended across the Pacific into the United States and Europe, into the Middle East, Asia, Australia, and Japan. At his command was an army of spies and informers and an unrivaled budget to maintain them.

His entire career had been based on adroit, low-key moves, climbing up through one ministry's bureaucracy to another. His command of languages—he spoke French, Japanese, and Korean—had brought him to the Foreign Ministry. As a diplomat he had traveled widely before being recalled to a senior position in the Ministry. In 1980, he had been appointed by Deng Xiaoping as head of state security. Deng had died, but Qiao's power remained undimmed: he knew all the secrets, the peccadillos, and other personal shortcomings of the old men of Zhongnanhai, the last survivors of the Long March of 1934 when they had made an unforgettable two-year journey of six thousand miles across mountain ranges and provinces larger than most European nations; it had been not only a strategic military retreat from the terrible reality of brother killing brother but a major migration leading to eventual nationhood for a new China.

One of the first decisions of Mao Tse-tung after he proclaimed the birth of the Communist state on October 1, 1949, was to create a leadership compound in the lea of the Forbidden City, from where the emperors had ruled for seven hundred years. Qiao Shi had helped to turn it into one of the most fortified areas on earth. There were guard posts in the most unexpected places: cut into the trunks of trees with each niche just large enough for a man, or concealed within shrubbery. Sensors, tripwires, and body-heat-sensing cameras proliferated. No aircraft was permitted to overfly, and only helicopters, ferrying the old men to and from their summer palaces in the hills to the west of the city, came and went. In the compound they lived along the eastern shore of the lake in the center of the compound. Many of the homes were palaces, often with thirty or more bedrooms, magnificent salons, and indoor swimming pools. Furnished with artifacts removed from the Forbidden City, each mansion had its retinue of servants and guards who lived on the north side of the lake in several barracks screened by vegetation. There were over a hundred varieties of trees and shrubs planted around the compound as a reminder of those the old men had seen on the Long March. The lake itself was filled with carp. Mao had initially ordered a hundred thousand; over the years the number had increased, some said to several million. More certain was that the water was dark with their feces, and a team of gardeners were employed to constantly remove it. The few foreigners who had been admitted to Zhongnanhai had said there was an unpleasant smell from the lake.

Whether Meir Dagan's meeting with Qiao Shi took place in the compound would remain unknown, just as what was agreed between them. But twenty-four hours after his plane had landed it was in the air again heading back to Israel.

A few days later Mossad was among a number of Western intelligence services that discovered North Korea was weaponizing the bird flu virus. It added to the mounting concern that was already sweeping the world as the prospect grew of a repetition of the 1918 influenza pandemic that had killed 50 million. Then, as now, there was no ready vaccine to inoculate entire populations. Warnings from intelligence services said that in aerosol form the weaponized virus would be undetectable at border crossings, making it an ideal weapon for terrorists. In Washington, the Bush administration gave briefings classified "Top Secret/ Sensitive Compartmented Information" to members of Congress and the Senate, during which CIA Director Porter Goss and John Negroponte, the director of National Intelligence, revealed details of the terrorist threat.

The outbreak had originated in Asia and the intelligence chiefs explained it would be relatively easy for North Korean agents to obtain birds infected with the H5N1 strain from which the virus could be weaponized. Biopreperat's former director, Dr. Ken Alibek, who had defected from Russia and was now a senior adviser to the Bush administration on biodefense, said to the author, "The threat of a weaponized bird flu virus cannot be overemphasized. It would be the most terrible weapon in the hands of a terrorist. An aerosolized bird flu would be impossible to detect from one spread naturally by infected birds. But the lab-produced virus would be far more lethal and could be directed at specific targets."

Peter Openshaw, professor of virology at Imperial College, London, said, "It would be more terrifying than engineered smallpox. That would be relatively easy to contain because there is an existing vaccine." Hugh Pennington, professor of microbiology at Aberdeen University in Scotland, said North Korea's molecular biologists "could mix the bird flu virus with other flu viruses, making it easier to spread from personal contact."

Were the reports that North Korea was weaponizing bird flu an indication the regime had dismissed any approach by China to stop arming Iran? Had Qiao Shi simply politely listened to Dagan and done nothing? Or had he agreed with the old men of Zhongnanhai that it would not be in their own interest to put pressure on their unstable neighbor?

The one certainty was that a warhead filled with weaponized virus and launched against Tel Aviv would have disastrous consequences. But it was now not only the possibility of a weaponized bird flu virus that threatened Israel and the world beyond its borders. This one came from six nuclear scientists who had worked in the Pakistan nuclear industry and had left the country.

Mossad had discovered their activities before they had left Pakistan after having worked closely with Abdul Qadeer Khan, the father of the Islamic bomb and the godfather of nuclear proliferation. Their technical experience included the complex disciplines needed to use centrifuges to produce enriched uranium, the precursor for a nuclear bomb.

Their skills had been enhanced by South African nuclear experts secretly employed in Pakistan's nuclear program at the Khan Research Laboratories. South Africa's own space-age program had been dismantled after America had threatened trade sanctions in 1993. Overnight President Nelson Mandela had canceled his dream of putting an astronaut into space. And along with billions of rands being wasted, hundreds of highly skilled men and women found themselves out of work.

But the more talented did not have to wait long for offers. The first came from Dimona, Israel's nuclear facility. Its relationship with the South African program had prospered from the time Dimona know-how had fine-tuned South Africa's first intermediate-range missile, the Arniston, a carbon copy of Israel's own Jericho II rocket. A decade of close collaboration had finally ended in 1992, again with pressure from the United States. But the ties between the scientists had remained.

To those who had worked at Kempton Park, a facility outside Johannesburg developing high-resolution camera systems for satellites; at Somerset West, in the bushland of Eastern Cape, where rocket motors had been designed; at the systems engineering facility at Stellenbosch University near Cape Town, came attractive offers. No longer would they need to live in a country with the highest murder rate in the world and plagued with corruption scandals. In Israel they would earn salaries in a hard currency of their choice that far exceeded what they had previously earned. In no time they had begun to sell their homes near the missile test sites in KwaZulu-Natal and in the former nature reserve near Cape Town, and had flown north on the regular El Al flight to Tel Aviv, joining others from the nuclear warheads manufacturing plant out on the veldt beyond the country's capital, Pretoria. With all expenses paid and a substantial down payment in their bank accounts, they had settled into their new lives in the palm-fringed settlements that had been created for them in the Negev Desert. They found themselves working alongside a number of Russians who had also been headhunted after the collapse of the Soviet Union.

The recruiters from Pakistan had also been busy. Working with even more discretion than the Israelis had shown, they had offered other disaffected scientists salaries at even higher levels than those from Dimona. With them came the promise of a lifestyle in Pakistan that would match those the scientists had enjoyed during the high days of apartheid: servants they had to let go after the collapse of South Africa's space-age program would once more be plentiful in Pakistan, along with sundowners, the evening ritual of cocktails at sunset that had been an integral part of their South African life. They would live in homes even more lavish than those on the Cape; their children would be educated in private schools whose teachers came from the great universities of England, France, and the United States; and their private medical facilities would be staffed with the best doctors. Along with generous holidays, their income would be tax-free and deposited in any bank of their choice anywhere in the world. The offers were eagerly accepted and flights out of Johannesburg to Islamabad were filled with the scientists and their families.

Over the years, they helped to develop the skills of the six Pakistani nuclear scientists who had discretely slipped out of the country after they had been identified as being involved in what became known in Mossad, MI6, and the CIA as "America's Hiroshima." The intention was to smuggle into the United States a nuclear device that would be detonated in Washington. The bomb would be transported in one of the container ships that arrived at American East Coast ports every week. Few were subjected to a full search. Sleeper agents would collect the bomb, packed inside a container, take it to Washington, and detonate it, creating even more deaths and casualties than the September 11 attacks had achieved.

The operation had been devised by Osama bin Laden with an exactness that would have the same terrible synchronicity as the September 11 attacks. The intention was not only to terrorize and appall by the sheer number of victims, but at the same time provide an example of victory won by violence. Politically it was designed as a rallying call for global jihad, worldwide holy war. The leaders of Muslim nations who opposed it would be swept away in what bin Laden had likened to the creation of the new caliphate of which he had long dreamed. He envisaged how, barely a generation after many Muslim countries had won their independence, mostly from Britain, their world would enter a new religious era. Already the first phase was in place in Iran, where the 1979 Khomeini revolution had aroused the deprived masses. Next to fall in the aftermath of America's Hiroshima would be the Saudi royal family, who bin Laden had long accused of betraying their duties as custodians of the holy places of Mecca and Medina.

Details of the plan to detonate a nuclear device in America had emerged with the capture of Khalid Sheikh Mohammed, bin Laden's military operations chief, in an al-Qaeda safe house in Karachi on March 2, 2003. The arrest was made by Pakistani intelligence agents, allowing President Musharraf to offer further proof to Washington that he remained a staunch supporter of the war against terrorism. It continued to be less than the full truth. While Pakistan had indeed detained scores of al-Qaeda members, it still sponsored terrorist groups in the disputed state of Kashmir, funding, training, and arming them in their war of attrition against India. The Bush administration continued to regard Pakistan as its powerful ally in the war on terrorism espoused by bin Laden. "Kashmir is a side issue," a State Department official told the author.

The arrest of Mohammed earned further public gratitude from Washington. No mention would be made of the role played by the CIA and U.S. Special Forces, who had flown the high-value captive to their interrogation compound at the American base at Bagram in Afghanistan. They brought with them over a thousand documents and a hundred hard drives recovered from Mohammed's safe house in a Karachi back street; he had been betrayed for a thousand U.S. dollars. The documents and disks would later be deemed as "an operational gold mine" and served as the basis for Mohammed's interrogation.

Manacled and hooded in one of the compound's railroad freight trucks, subjected to sleep deprivation and long periods of amplified "white noise," denied air-conditioning during the intense heat of the day and warmth for the icy cold of the night, injected with drugs to weaken his resistance, coupled with physical violence and threats of summary execution—techniques later exposed by Amnesty International—Khalid Sheikh Mohammed began to reveal details of America's Hiroshima. It called for the detonation of seven tactical nuclear devices in seven cities simultaneously. The cities were New York, Washington, San Francisco, Los Angeles, Seattle, Chicago, and Boston. Each device would be capable of creating an explosion of ten kilotons. The planning for the multiple explosions was still in its early stages, and the operation would ultimately require smuggling into the United States the nuclear devices in seaborne cargo containers. Every year around eighteen thousand container ships arrive at U.S. ports; only a small percentage are thoroughly checked. To check all would require manpower far beyond what is available and would have serious consequences for America's commerce.

It was at this stage, in May 2003, that Mossad became directly involved.

A set of the captured documents and the first interrogation transcripts had been passed to Mossad as part of the close collaboration established between Porter Goss and Meir Dagan. In return Mossad had provided the CIA with electrifying news. Abdul Qadeer Khan had, in April 2003, met with bin Laden. The scientist had flown to Peshawar in the Northwest Province and had been driven through the towering mountains and across the Pakistan border into the hard, unforgiving, and desolate land of eastern Afghanistan. With Khan had gone one of the six nuclear scientists Mossad had been tracking. His name was Murad Qasim and he was the leading expert in the intricacies of centrifugal technology in the Khan Laboratories.

Now, a month later in mid-May, Qasim was among Khan's guests at his weekend house overlooking a lake outside Rawalpindi on the north plane of the Punjab. The area was a conservationist paradise.

Posing as fishermen, a Mossad *yaholomin* team had set up surveillance near the house. Direction mikes had been disguised as rods.

Five years had passed since Khan had successfully detonated Pakistan's first nuclear bomb at the test site beneath the Baluchistan Desert. In the intervening years he had continued to sell nuclear technology to Iran and North Korea. Besides Murad Qasim, Mossad had identified five of his colleagues who had also traveled there; Muhammad Zubair, Bashiruddin Mahmood, Saeed Akhther, Imtaz Baig, and Waheed Nasir. All were senior managers at the Khan Laboratories. On that weekend in May, they completed the guest list at Khan's retreat by the lake.

Like their host, Khan's guests were confirmed al-Qaeda supporters. Bashiruddin Mahmood, in addition, had held a meeting with bin Laden and the Taliban leader, Mullah Omar, in Kandahar, Afghanistan, earlier in the year. On his way back to Pakistan he had been briefly detained by U.S. forces in the town. Mahmood had claimed diplomatic immunity and insisted he was in the country on an "agricultural visit." Thanks to documents supporting his claim, he had been allowed to fly back to Islamabad. After being prompted by the CIA to interview him, Pakistan intelligence officers were astonished when Mahmood admitted he had indeed met the terrorists, who had asked him to devise a radiological bomb. It would be constructed from nuclear material wrapped in conventional high explosives, which bin Laden had obtained from a former Soviet Union nuclear site in Uzbekistan. Mahmood had insisted he had refused the request. The Pakistani government informed Washington that Mahmood was above suspicion. No mention was made of his meeting with bin Laden and Mullah Omar.

Now the eavesdropping Mossad team heard Mahmood tell Khan and his guests that his own contacts in Pakistan intelligence had warned him that the CIA knew about their own role in America's Hiroshima after their names had surfaced in the documents discovered with Khalid Sheikh Mohammed's capture. Mossad's long-rooted suspicions had been confirmed: Mahmood had gone to Kandahar not to discuss with bin Laden the making of a relatively simple "dirty bomb" but to pledge the services of himself and the five other scientists around Khan's table.

Next day, even as Meir Dagan was sending Porter Goss details of what the *yaholomin* unit had recorded, all six scientists had left Pakistan. Khan subsequently resolutely denied any knowledge of his staff being involved in the plot to launch nuclear strikes against America.

Their names had gone onto the Detain Lists of a number of security services. But like others with terrorist links, the scientists had vanished like proverbial thieves in the night. A year would pass before Mossad once more picked up their trail. They were in Saudi Arabia.

Almost a year after Abdul Qadeer Khan had made his televised confession of being a nuclear weapons black marketeer, a commercial flight from Cyprus landed at Tel Aviv airport. Among its passengers was Moshe Feinstein (a pseudonym). He was a Mossad *katsa* and its expert on nuclear proliferation. In Nicosia he had met with a member of Saudi Arabia's large foreign community. After months of careful cultivation and detailed checks into his background and that of his family, the foreigner had been recruited as a sayan and given the code name of The Salesman, a nod toward his business acumen. Meetings would be arranged through The Salesman placing a notice in the Lonely Hearts section of a London newspaper available in Riyadh. Two days after it appeared, Moshe would fly to keep the appointment.

The Salesman had developed strong connections with the House of Saud, exploiting the fact that its administration was highly personalized, often being no more than functionaries surrounding one individual, usually a prince of the kingdom. It was The Salesman's ability to target those key individuals that had made him important to Mossad. In an early briefing, The Salesman had explained to Moshe that the Ministry of Foreign Affairs revolved around Prince Saud al-Faisal; and no decision, however inconsequential, could be made without his approval. Other ministries were similarly run. The Salesman had summed up the situation as "if you give them a list of more than one item, they often don't get to the second. Negligence and incompetence are bywords."

In November 2008, five years after the lakeside meeting, Waheed Nasir chose to deny the Mossad report that he had been present or had gone to Iran. His tantalizing glimpses into the closed world of the kingdom came during his regular trips to Europe and vacations on Cyprus to escape the ferocious high temperature of summer in Riyadh. A contact in the Ministry of Information had revealed details of the increasing anti-Americanism in the country (in 2005, a regime-approved poll showed that 97 percent of the population held a negative view of the United States). Even more disturbing was the growing extent of the penetration of al-Qaeda into Saudi Arabia and how the ruling family had tried to avoid attacks on its members by allowing them to pay substantial sums to the organization—providing the money was used only to attack targets outside the country. The Salesman had provided details of how Saudi petrodollars had financed the September 11 massacre and the attack on the USS *Cole*. The Salesman's evidence enabled Dore Gold, a former Israeli ambassador with close ties to Mossad, to publicly warn: "Saudi Arabia is paying a ransom to be left alone. It does not care who else suffers. It will reap what it is sowing."

Within the House of Saud, a power struggle had persisted after the death of King Fahd and the appointment of Abdullah to rule over the desert kingdom. He was a half brother of a powerful faction within the royal family. It was comprised of Prince Sultan, the defense minister; Prince Nayef, the interior minister; Prince Turki, director of intelligence and now ambassador to the Court at St. James; and Prince Salman, governor of Riyadh. They were known as the Sudairi after their mother, Hassa bint Ahmad al-Sudairi, the favorite wife of King Ibn Saud, the founder of the kingdom. Abdullah, their half brother, since coming to power had antagonized the Sudairi by his constant rebukes for their profligate spending habits, which were also a cause of smouldering public resentment. This had led to a groundswell of religious fervor among the population, half of whom were under the age of eighteen. This had been compounded by the country's oil income fluctuations, leading to a decline in living standards. It had been a fertile breeding ground for al-Qaeda to exploit.

Moshe Feinstein had returned to Israel with important information from The Salesman. His ID card allowed him to bypass airport formalities and quickly reach the waiting car and driver. On the windscreen was a sticker bearing the motto of the Israel Tourist Office: two men carrying grapes and a pitcher, a reminder of the time Moses had sent Caleb and his men to seek the Promised Land and to find out if its people possessed poisons or disease-spreading germs that could be used with devastating effect on the Jews who had already endured much on their flight from Pharaoh's Egypt. Caleb had returned with news that the land, which later became Israel, "flowed with milk and honey." It was a running joke in Mossad that this was the first—and best—intelligence the country had received.

Thirty minutes later the car arrived at the gates of the Kirya, the headquarters of the Israeli Defense Forces. A sentry checked IDs, a hydraulic barrier was raised, and the car drove a short distance to halt before a featureless concrete building. Inside was the spartan conference room where the Committee of the Heads of Services met. With them was the director of military intelligence, Brigadier General Moshe Ya'alon. Within Israel he was a legend, a former paratrooper in the elite Saynet Maktal, the equivalent of Britain's SAS, who had served in all those trouble spots in the Middle East where the streets and souks often had no names and where it was kill or be killed. Beside him sat Meir Dagan.

Even allowing for the flat, emotionless tone in which Mossad encouraged its officers to deliver their reports, the men around the conference table could only have been galvanized when Moshe Feinstein revealed what The Salesman had told him. Abdul Qadeer Khan had secretly traveled to Riyadh and had met with Abdullah. The purpose of the meeting had been to activate the ultrasecret agreement on nuclear cooperation with Pakistan, which was designed to provide the House of Saud with nuclear weapons technology in exchange for cheap oil. Mossad had already discovered—through the network of informers its agent, Jamal, ran across Asia—that the pact also called for Pakistan to respond to any nuclear attack from Iran by launching its own nuclear arsenal. The pact had been signed during Abdullah's visit to Islamabad in 2003. Mossad's analysts had dismissed the promise to assist Saudi Arabia in such an event as little more than window dressing.

But the presence of Khan in Riyadh had heightened Israel's fear that if Saudi Arabia developed a nuclear weapons capability, its missiles posed a serious threat to the Jewish state.

Moshe Feinstein's briefing brought the possibility that much closer. The Salesman had told him that Saudi C-130 military transporters had started to make regular flights from their Dharan military base. It was from there that America had launched its first Iraqi war aerial onslaught on Iraq; the base was totally under the control of Riyadh after U.S. forces had now been pulled out of the country. The giant aircraft made round trips to Lahore and Karachi that had started after Khan's visit. The Salesman had discovered the aircraft returned with payloads of materials that had come from Pakistan's uranium enrichment factory at Kahuta.

Some of The Salesman's information dovetailed with what Mossad knew. In 1987, Saudi Arabia had bought CSS-2 missiles from China. Though their range brought Israel within reach, they were capable only of carrying conventional warheads and would prove no match for Israel's high-tech defenses. Saudi Arabia's first serious attempt to enter the nuclear arena was in 1990 when the House of Saud secretly transferred to Saddam Hussein $5 billion to build them a nuclear bomb. The transfer of the money was handled by Tiny Rowland, the London financier who was Saddam's bagman, hiding his massive fortune in banks around the world; it has remained undiscovered to this day (see chapter 19, "After Saddam," pp. 397–402). The bomb was never built, and the deal had surfaced only when Mohammed Khilevi, the first secretary at the Saudi mission to the United Nations, had defected in July 1994, taking with him over ten thousand documents that detailed the House of Saud's attempt to become a nuclear power. The International Atomic Energy Agency sent inspectors to the country to examine its nuclear facilities. They decided the kingdom had neither the technical capability nor the skilled manpower to handle a nuclear weapon.

Nevertheless the discovery of Riyadh's intentions had created international alarm, especially in Israel. This increased as evidence emerged of Saudi Arabia's support for jihadist causes in Kashmir, Uzbekistan, and Chechnya that were linked to bin Laden. It was the Saudi link with Kashmir that Mossad had focused on; Riyadh supported the Kashmir insurgents by funneling the funds through Pakistan; tens of millions of dollars were laundered through Islamabad's central bank. Vast sums were sent by the same route to support the Taliban in Afghanistan. Osama bin Laden, already lionized in Riyadh for his fight against the Soviet Union in Afghanistan, remained a heroic figure in the desert kingdom. Too late the House of Saud realized he was its mortal enemy. The September 11 attacks against the United States made the king and his thousands of princes realize the extent of the threat posed by al-Qaeda. With the American withdrawal of its protective military shield, the House of Saud found itself urgently needing a nuclear arsenal. Pakistan, still one of the world's leading sponsors of terrorism, had the capability of providing the weapons. It became the first port of call for the frightened rulers of the kingdom. The arrival of Abdul Qadeer Khan in Riyadh was further proof of Pakistan's readiness to satisfy their demands in return for unlimited oil at a bargain price.

Tel Aviv saw the real danger from a Saudi-Pakistan pact was that the House of Saud could be tempted to try and buy peace for itself by providing al-Qaeda with nuclear weapons.

The *katsa* had one final piece of information. The Salesman had identified the six Pakistani nuclear scientists who had vanished after being named in the America Hiroshima documents from photographs Mossad had obtained and had shown him.

It was then that the scientists had moved from Mossad's detain list to the separate and very secret one it kept for those it was tasked to assassinate.

Rules for an assassination had not changed. Each execution had to be approved by a committee chaired by the incumbent prime minister and was of a person, the evidence showed, who posed a clear and present danger to the state of Israel and who could not be brought to trial because he or she was protected within the borders of one of Israel's enemies. Among them were Saudi Arabia, North Korea, Iran, and the numerous Islamic republics of the former Soviet Bloc. In Mossad's eye view, the need for kidon had increased with the spread of Islamic fundamentalism in all its guises: Hamas, Hezbollah, Islamic Jihad, Solidarity Front, Palestinian Liberation Front, the terrorists of the Philippines; all were pledged to destroy the Jewish State. The kidon had killed in all those places, employing the many skills acquired through their extensive training under the precise guidelines they had learned and that had remained in force since Meir Amit, the most innovative and ruthless director general of Mossad before Meir Dagan had taken over, had written out the rules in his bold handwriting: "There will be no killing of heads of state however extreme they are. They will be dealt with politically. There will be no killing of a terrorist's family unless they are also proven to be implicated in terrorism. Each execution must be legally sanctioned by the prime minister of the day. It is therefore the ultimate judicial sanction of the state and the executioner is no different from a legally appointed hangman or any other lawfully appointed executioner of the state."

Part of what Amit once likened to a "theology of death" (to the author) is based on an eighty-page manual written in 1953 by a scientist, Dr. Sidney Gottlieb, who at the time was head of the CIA's Technical Services Division. The manual has remained to this day in the *midrasa*, the Mossad training school, and is used as part of the two-year course for its agents. From them came the kidon. Rafi Eitan, a former Mossad operation chief, told the author, "Only a handful show the requirements; a total coldness once committed, and afterwards no regrets."

Those requirements were imbued in the team who had begun to devise ways to assassinate the six Pakistani scientists the State of Israel had decided must die. Kidon assembled profiles of the scientists with the help of the Asia Desk, with information from The Salesman provided to Moshe Feinstein, from Jamal's informers in Pakistan and elsewhere. Ari Ben-Menashe articulated to the author: "They were getting to know their targets; background, family, and friends, any connection that could be useful. How they reacted in a situation; what pushes their buttons. Only then could an operational plan be constructed. They would study every inch of the country where they worked, its geography and climate. They would study videotapes, travel brochures, local newspapers. Their methodology was anchored in their well-honed ability to separate fact from conjecture and the plans they created were governed by the golden rule that facts could not always wait for certainty."

Late in October 2005, The Salesman gave Moshe Feinstein the news that the six scientists had flown from Riyadh to Tehran, a week after North Korea had delivered liquid propellant to power Iran's Shahab-3 rocket with its range of eight hundred miles and a capability of delivering a warhead that would obliterate Tel Aviv. On Tuesday, October 25, Iran's president Mahmoud Ahmadinejad addressed a Tehran conference called "The World Without Zionism." It was the last week of Ramadan, the time of prayer. Five months before, he had replaced a reformist president, Mohammad Khatami, who had advocated international dialogue and improving Iran's relationship with the West. With words reminiscent of Hitler, Ahmadinejad said, "Israel and the Jews must be wiped off the map. Anybody who recognizes Israel will burn in the fire of the Islamic nation's fury."

In the Kirya Israel's three nuclear submarines and their arsenal of missiles with nuclear warheads were brought to a level one stage below launch as they kept silent watch on the seabed in the Strait of Hormuz opposite the Iranian coast.

On November 2, 2005, a Mossad-inspired operation was moving to a climax in the Indonesian tropical city of Batu. A month had passed since a *katsa* in Delhi, the Indian capital, had learned that Azhari Husin, al-Qaeda's most experienced bomb maker, who had already been identified by Mossad as the mastermind behind the July bombers in London, had been in Delhi shortly before bombs had ripped through the city's Pahargani District. The attack was later earmarked as the work of an al-Qaeda group in Kashmir, Lashkar-e-Toiba, or Soldiers of Fortune. Over sixty people had died and over a hundred were seriously injured. Mossad's offer to help Indian intelligence track Husin was swiftly accepted.

For three weeks the search yielded no trace of one of the world's most wanted terrorists. Then a sayan on East Java, part of the Indonesian archipelago, told his *katsa* controller that a number of men had rented a house in a suburb of Batu, and two of them bore a resemblance to newspaper photographs of the terrorists suspected of being behind the previous month's attack on a restaurant in Bali in which twenty-three people had died. Within hours the *katsa* arrived in Batu. The newspaper photographs were of Azhari Husin and the leader of another militant group, Jamaah Islamiah, called Noordin Mohammed Top, a ruthless killer cast from the same pitiless mold as Musab al-Zarqawi in Iraq. The sayan reported that Top had left Batu the previous evening.

Working through a well-established rule that ensured Mossad's presence remained unknown, the *katsa* informed his station chief at the Israeli embassy in Dehli. The Indian Foreign Ministry was told. From there a call went to its counterpart in Jakarta, the Indonesian capital. Within an hour of the first call, a full-scale operation was underway in Batu. Led by Indonesia's elite antiterrorist unit, snipers were posted on neighboring roofs and a pitched battle began. From within the house, hand grenades were hurled and gunfire raked the street as the unit stormed the house. As they entered, Husin reached for the detonator on the explosive belt he was wearing, but was stopped from doing so when a police officer shot him in the chest and legs. But there was no time to stop another terrorist from detonating his own belt. The blast knocked the roof off the house. Azhari Husin ended his life like most of his victims, amid the devastation of a suicide bombing.

The bomb maker had been high on the list of terrorists to be "rendered" by the CIA Counterterrorist Intelligence Centers (CTIC) at Langley. Originally created in the mid-1990s by the Clinton administration, it had rapidly expanded after the 9/11 attacks to counter the threat of Islamic terrorism and overcome CIA difficulties in obtaining convictions against terrorists. Further expansion followed the end of the war with Iraq when a number of meetings took place in London and Washington, chaired by both countries' intelligence chiefs, to decide how to best deal with the large number of captured suspected terrorists. Mossad had a seat at the table. Out of those meetings came the creation of a purpose-built interrogation center at the U.S. base at Bagram in the charge of forty CTIC men and women, including doctors trained in the use of psychotropic drugs. Many were familiar with the use of mind-bending chemicals that had been developed for the notorious CIA MK-ULTRA program in the 1960s. Mossad's own interrogators were given full access to the captives. Intelligence they acquired was shared with CTIC.

Bagram quickly became crowded with captured Taliban and foreign mercenaries. In the first weeks, two died during interrogation and several were left permanently physically incapacitated. But the center was soon overflowing with prisoners. At a meeting in London in April 2002 chaired by John Scarlett at the offices of the Joint Intelligence Committee and attended by CTIC officers and at which Meir Dagan was also an observer, it was decided that Bagram was not able to operate efficiently under such conditions. Even when detainees were transferred on the so-called Guantánamo Express to Cuba, the freight car cells at Bagram quickly filled up with new prisoners. Could another site—possibly several—be found? Scarlett had served in Moscow as an MI6 officer and recalled the existence of interrogation centers throughout the Soviet Union: he said the worst had been those run by the KGB in Uzbekistan, Moldova, and Poland. They could well serve CTIC's purpose. Scarlett knew two senior officers of Polish military intelligence who had worked with GROM, a specialist Polish intelligence unit in Iraq. They were invited to London to meet senior members of MI6 who had worked in Eastern Europe. George Tenet, now in the dying months of his tenure, sent several senior officials to attend. The Poles confirmed the KGB interrogation centers remained intact and were used by local security services to question criminals.

Because of the considerable distance involved, the only way to transfer high-value al-Qaeda and Taliban terrorists from Bagram would be by air. CTIC already had its own aircraft, and its senior officer at the meeting said there would be no problem in arranging overflying and refueling rights in countries like Britain, Germany, and Spain. The Polish officers identified airfields within the old Warsaw Pact that could be used as stopovers; the air base at Tazar in south central Hungary, the Szczytno-Szymany air base in Poland, and the Markuleshti airfield in Moldova. During the cold war they had all been used for secret operations by Warsaw Pact Special Forces. Interrogations had also been conducted there by the KGB.

The operational plans sufficiently advanced, it was time for them to be politically rubber-stamped. Scarlett informed Prime Minister Tony Blair, and Tenet briefed President Bush. Both quickly endorsed them. Recognizing that Poland would have an important role to play as the refueling point for all flights going to Uzbekistan—selected by CTIC to be the prime interrogation center for the terrorists—it was essential to get the support of Leszek Miller, the country's soon to be ousted prime minister, who had staunchly supported the war on Iraq. He immediately agreed to allow the Szczytno-Szymany base to be used as CTIC's prime refueling point in Eastern Europe and would inform his cabinet colleagues of his decision. A London intelligence source told the author: "Miller may well have not known the ultimate fate of those who would be secretly flown in and out of his country. But he was also desperately wanting to remain a player in the post–Iraq war coalition."

The first flight began in May 2002. A Gulfstream V executive jet, registration N379P, landed at Northolt airport, a secure military airfield near London. It had a long history of being a staging post for CIA and MI6 officers en route to secret missions in Europe during the cold war. Under what the Ministry of Defence later called "standing regulations," the only details listed of the Gulfstream flight were the names of the pilot and the aircraft owner. No record was made of any passengers on board. The aircraft was registered to Premier Executive Transport Services. Subsequently, the *Mail on Sunday*, a mass-circulation newspaper in Britain, reported that the company's directors "appear to exist only on paper. Bryan P. Dyness, Steven E. Kent, and Audrey M. Taylor, appear to have no personal details or previous employment history. This is the kind of sterile identity the CIA uses to conceal involvement in clandestine operations."

On a sunny spring day the Gulfstream V and its unrecorded passengers flew across from Northolt to the Szczytno-Szymany base in northern Poland still blanketed by winter snow. After refueling, the aircraft flew south from there to Uzbekistan. Soon the executive jet was on a regular run, picking up detainees in Jakarta in Indonesia, Pakistan, and Bagram. One was the Yemeni microbiologist Jamil Qasim

Saeed Mohammed, wanted by CTIC "in connection with the bombing of the USS *Cole* while the warship was at anchor off Aden." He was flown to Uzbekistan and his fate remains unknown. Another passenger had been Muhammad Saad Iqbal Madni, an Egyptian suspect who had worked with the British "shoe bomber" Richard Reid. He was rendered from Jakarta to Egypt. His fate also remains unknown.

By December 2005, CTIC employed over one thousand people: field officers, analysts, translators, and liaison officers with foreign intelligence services. Their closest relationship remained with Mossad: its own *katsas* in Iran, Pakistan, Syria, and Afghanistan constantly provided updates of the movements of terrorist suspects on the CTIC list. The decision as to who would be rendered was made by CTIC in conjunction with CIA director Porter Goss.

The decision on how rendition would be carried out had been finetuned. CTIC officers were now stationed in twenty-two countries around the globe to handle the arrests and transportation of suspects. They were usually arrested by the local security service and held in solitary confinement until they could be flown out to a designated "black site"—the CTIC description of the interrogation centers. The decision as to which site a suspect should be sent was made by the senior CTIC officer on the spot.

"If a strong psychological interrogation with some physical force is required, a detainee is flown to Jordan. If a suspect is to be interrogated in between periods of strong physical force, he is sent to Egypt. For the most severe of torture for information, he is sent to Uzbekistan, where he is killed after he can reveal no more," a senior Mossad officer told the author.

Craig Murray, then a British ambassador in Uzbekistan, wrote in a memo to Jack Straw, Britain's foreign secretary, in November 2004 (a copy of which the author has seen): "The CIA chief in this country acknowledged to me that torture of those rendered includes the boiling in vats of prisoners." Murray was relieved of his post, labeled as "mentally unstable," and finally dismissed from the diplomatic service. By December 2005, he had become one of the first to publicly reveal details of the rendition process. As a result he said he was threatened by Britain's security services.

But the flights continued with CTIC's aircraft crisscrossing the world. The Gulfstream V had now been joined by a C-130 Hercules, a Casa

Turboprop, a Gulfstream, and a Boeing 737. All were painted white and bore no markings. Some were also leased from the Premier Executive Transport Service. When contacted by the author, it declined to discuss the planes or the purpose for which they were used. A glimpse of what happened on board the aircraft came from two intelligence sources—one in London, the other in Washington.

"The prisoners are shackled to their seats and are gagged and often drugged during their flights. CTIC officers travel with them to their interrogation country. The flight manifests contain no details of who they are. At a refueling stop, the aircraft window blinds are drawn. No local official is allowed on board. Fuel is paid for by a credit card the pilot carries. It is billed to CTIC," the London source told the author. The Washington source added: "In countries like Uzbekistan, Soviet-trained interrogators carry out the torturing. They have a list of 'information targets' to obtain. The answers are passed to the resident CTIC officer. He sends it to Washington."

From there the information was distributed within the U.S. intelligence community and sent to selected foreign intelligence services, including Mossad. In Tel Aviv it was carefully tested against other material gathered by the service's own network of agents and informers.

By late 2005, the "torture flights" (the description was coined by Amnesty International) had flown hundreds of suspects to the secret black sites far beyond the public eye and the U.S. justice system. In December, Swiss intelligence—a small but well-respected spying organization—intercepted a fax sent by Ahmed Abdul Gheit, Egypt's foreign minister, to its London embassy's intelligence chief. The minister wanted to know the fate of twenty-three detainees rendered from Afghanistan to a black site on Romania's Black Sea coast. Swiss intelligence, whose relationship with Mossad is close, sent a copy of the fax to Tel Aviv, where the authenticity of the fax was quickly established. In it the minister had referred to "similar interrogation centres in Ukraine, Kosovo, Macedonia, and in Bulgaria."

By late December 2005, the torture flights had made more than two hundred flights in and out of Britain and close to four hundred through German airspace. Other flights had passed through Spanish airports and Shannon, Ireland's international airport. The logs kept by air traffic controllers in those countries listed more than seven hundred flights of CTIC aircraft. One of those who survived a flight was Kuwait-born Khaled al-Masri, who had become a German citizen. He had gone on holiday to Macedonia in 2003 when the local police took him off a bus and held him for three weeks in a windowless cell. One night he had been taken to Skopje airport and handed over to CTIC officers. Al-Masri claims this is what happened to him then.

"I was taken to a room at the airport and injected with drugs. I was then put on an aircraft, it was a Gulfstream I think. On the flight I was told that I was going to a special place where no one would find me. I still have no real idea where it was. But after a long flight I was hooded and driven to a prison. I found myself among prisoners from Pakistan, Tanzania, Yemen, and Saudi Arabia. I was there for five months, regularly beaten, and told to confess I was a terrorist. Then one day I was dragged from my cell, put inside a closed truck, and driven to a plane. It was the same one that had brought me there. After a flight, I was taken from the plane. An American told me that a mistake had been made. He put me in a car with more Americans. They drove for a while, told me to get out, and drove off. I found out I was in Albania. I made my way back to Germany."

He reported his story to the police in Frankfurt. The details were passed on to the Bundeskriminalamt, the country's equivalent of the FBI. Al-Masri was interviewed by two agents. Satisfied, they informed the Bundesamt für Verfassungschutz, the Federal Office for the Protection of the Constitution. It contacted the CIA station chief in Berlin. He sent a report to Langley. He was told, according to a German police file on the case, there "was a mistake, a confusion of names." The German interior minister, Otto Schily, on a visit to Washington, raised the matter with Condoleezza Rice. She offered him the same response. Officially the matter ended. Al-Masri's attempts to obtain compensation have failed at the time of this writing and he has been told there is no point in pursuing it.

In Tel Aviv, senior members of Mossad began to view rendition as an embarrassing sideshow that was obstructing the CIA's real work and was unable to provide reliable intelligence. A veteran Mossad *katsa* said (to the author), "The danger with the torture flights is that they provide invaluable propaganda for our enemies. Where does harsh interrogation cross the borderline into torture? We are not averse to harsh questioning, but we draw the line at methods that allow prisoners to be severely beaten, sexually assaulted, and given repeated electric shocks and threats to their families. It is not that we are squeamish, but practical. That kind of interrogation does not produce credible intelligence."

But the torture flights continued in the closing days of 2005. At the time of this writing there were no plans to stop them. An intelligence source in Washington told the author, "They will continue as long as Bush's war on terrorism."

More certain, the flights were illegal and broke every United Nations convention against torture.

As New Year's Day, 2006, dawned over Tel Aviv, Mossad's specialists—its psychiatrists, psychologists, behavioral scientists, and psychoanalysts—continued to evaluate the mind-set of Iran's president Mahmoud Ahmadinejad. For weeks, often working from dawn until midnight seven days a week, they had studied his speeches and watched videos of his public appearances to get a fix on his personality and the world he had come from.

Born in a village in the shadow of the Alborz, the fourth of seven children, he was a year old when his father, Ahmed, had moved the family to Tehran to work as a blacksmith. The specialists had pondered how much the poverty that had plagued his formative years had influenced his future career and shaped his radical views. The youth who had ranked 130th in the nation's university entrance exam, sat by three thousand students, had become a committed campus activist during the reign of the shah and had gone underground from the regime's dreaded Savak security service. After the shah was deposed Ahmadinejad had welcomed the Ayatollah Khomeini as the country's new ruler.

The wiry, gaunt-faced, heavily bearded youth with piercing coal black eyes became a familiar figure at Tehran's University of Science and Technology (IUST) recruiting for his student organization, the Office for Strengthening. It became world famous when it held hostage American diplomats in their Tehran embassy in 1979 for 444 days. Ahmadinejad displayed unusual political skills in exploiting the situation to humiliate the United States. In 2006, Ahmadinejad became the focus of intense speculation when a photograph was published that claimed to identify him as the ringleader of the hostage takers and that he had personally ill-treated their captives. The CIA established there was no truth in the allegation. Long before then, he'd obtained a doctorate in engineering, joined the Revolutionary Guards, and seen action in the Iran-Iraq War. In quick succession he became vice governor of the remote province of Maku and then governor of the more important Ardabil Province. The mayor's office in Tehran was his next goal, and he was elected in 2003 with a 12 percent turnout. He canceled many re-forms introduced by his predecessor, emphasized the need for religious piety, and courted popularity by setting up soup kitchens for the city's poor. It was the platform for his campaign to become president, offer-ing "jobs for all and oil money on your tables." The incumbent presi-dent, seventy-year-old Ali Akbar Hashemi Rafsanjani, was swept from power. The world watched and hoped that the forty-nine-year-old Ah-madinejad would continue the dialogue with the West over its fears that Iran's quest for nuclear power was really a cover for producing nuclear weapons. Rafsanjani had indicated he was prepared to give the guar-antees Washington and London sought and which Israel insisted on. But the first hint that the new president would not be so malleable came when he told a Tehran rally in October 2005 that he would "develop the most powerful of forces to give us everlasting power and peace—nuclear power."

Since then every word Ahmadinejad had spoken, every diplomatic move he had made, every escalating threat against Israel he had deliv-ered in the harsh tones of his mountain village dialect had been care-fully studied by the Mossad specialists. His biography provided a useful means for them to explore what drove Mahmoud Ahmadine-jad. Part of it certainly was shrewd *realpolitik*, designed to win ap-proval at home and to spread fear abroad. He understood the power of Iran's oil resources on the global market and its rising price. He also saw America had been weakened by the insurgency in Iraq. He was equally as much an Islamic fanatic as Osama bin Laden and had latched on to the appeal for Muslim fundamentalists of demanding the elimination of Israel and being a Holocaust denier. In all this Ah-madinejad was not an original thinker; many of his ideas came from radical Islamic scholars who had long advocated jihad against Israel and the West. Ahmadinejad continued to use the Koran to reach out to pious Muslims yet maintained his appeal to Iran's militant youth. To them he emphasized the religious authority for all he said, none more so than invoking a lethal "Prophet's tradition" against all Jews and their motherland.

Increasingly the specialists saw an issue of major concern was whether Ahmadinejad *would* realize his idea of Armageddon across the Middle East—and possibly soon. On that New Year's Day they knew whether Israel would be forced to launch a preemptive attack against Iran's nu-clear facilities would depend on their analysis.

Plans had been finalized. Fifty Alsatian dogs would spearhead the attack on Natanz, the nuclear bomb-making complex ninety miles northeast of Tehran. The animals would be fitted with body belts of armor-piercing explosives able to penetrate the entrance to underground laboratories where Mossad's deep-cover agents had established thousands of centrifuges—the crucial device essential to produce weapons-grade uranium—were working around the clock. The dogs had been trained at an exact replica of the Natanz site constructed in the Negev Desert. Their handlers were part of the elite Oketz unit. The body belts would be detonated by remote control by their handlers. They had practiced mounting low-level helicopter attacks on the dummy site. Providing covering fire for any attack would be the Shaldag force modeled on the SAS. They would be supported by Israel's Air Force 69 Squadron, based at the Herzerim air base in the Negev. Over the New Year its pilots continued training for the long-haul flight to Iran and back without refueling. Each £60 million plane was equipped with the latest weaponry, including the "over the horizon" Promis software that could pinpoint a target forty miles away. The Dolphin submarines remained hidden in the depths of the Gulf of Oman. Their twenty missiles each would support the air attack.

While Mahmoud Ahmadinejad continued to threaten Israel would be "wiped from the map," Meir Dagan chaired a "crisis meeting" in the Kirya in early January to study the latest satellite pictures from Israel's own spy in the sky. The images showed the completed construction of a large new underground uranium enrichment plant at Natanz. Accompanying the images were new reports from Mossad deep-penetration agents in Iran and other Arab capitals. The meeting had been asked to assess the fallout from a preemptive strike against Iran. It was accepted that a wave of terrorism would follow. Hezbollah would launch rockets from Lebanon. Arab nations would publicly condemn. But Mossad chief Dagan said his intelligence predicted that Arab nations, while publicly condemning, would be "relieved that Iran's fangs had been drawn." The meeting was told that two more Chinese air force transport aircraft had landed at a military airfield near Natanz and unloaded crates of the state-of-the-art centrifuge known as P-2. It is designed to interconnect 164 centrifuges to form a "cascade." Gas is spun at high speed in a cascade to weaponize uranium 235 to the same capability as the Hiroshima bomb. Both China and North Korea in the past have provided Iran with nuclear-weapons technology.

Pa-kistan's maverick scientist, A. Q. Khan, the "father of the Islamic bomb," later sold designs and nuclear components to Iran and other rogue states.

Mossad chief Dagan told the defense chiefs at the Kirya meeting: "Our latest intelligence shows that scientists at Natanz have begun to produce weaponized uranium. That means our original estimate that Iran would go nuclear in five years has been cut in half. We are at three minutes to midnight." In May 2006, Dagan cut the estimate to possibly a year—one minute from midnight. Against this background the Mossad specialists continued their analysis of a man who had emerged from the shadows of Iranian politics to become a major threat to world peace. Increasingly Ahmadinejad appeared to believe he had a sense of divine mission. He had told his people he felt "the hand of God" continued to guide him after he had first threatened Israel. In December 2005, when an aircraft crashed in Tehran, killing 108 people, the president had thanked the dead "for they have shown the way to martyrdom which we must follow." He daily expressed his devotion to the Mahdi, the Messiah-like figure of Shia Islam, who would return to lead the Muslim world to freedom. All streams of Islam believe in a divine savior whose return would be preceded by cosmic chaos and widespread war. The vision is similar to the Christian version of Apocalypse. Mahmoud Ahmadinejad claimed the Mahdi would return in his own lifetime and that he had been given the task of creating chaos to hasten his arrival. He had opened the New Year with another virulent threat to destroy Israel and had exulted at the renewed fears across the world his words had generated. Was that why he had even welcomed a conflict with Israel and the United States—because he saw it as the launchpad for the Mahdi to appear? These were the questions the specialists studied but could as yet find no conclusive answers for.

As the meeting in the Kirya conference room came to an end, Meir Dagan reminded the others around the table of some of the last words Ariel Sharon had spoken before he had been rushed to hospital with a stroke: "Israel cannot, and will not, allow a nuclear-equipped Iran." Then the Mossad chief had left the room to update himself on the medical drama that had cast a great shadow over Israel's hopes for the New Year.

On January 4, with the setting sun low over the Judean Hills, Meir Dagan drove into the Negev Desert past the first of the guard posts which protected the perimeter of Ariel Sharon's most prized personal possessions, his Sycamore Ranch. Blending into the barren landscape, the building reflected its owner, strong and seemingly indestructible. On the seat beside Dagan was his briefcase containing the latest reports of Shaul Mofas, the soft-spoken minister of defense, and the abrasive General Dan Halutz, the chief of staff of the armed forces. Between them they had approved ten prime targets for any preemptive strike against Iran. Mofas had written: "Iran is now the greatest challenge facing us." The decision to launch an attack would be taken by the Committee of the Heads of Services. Dagan would provide the latest intelligence. There would be consultations with Benjamin "Bibi" Netanyahu, a former prime minister who had resigned from the Likud Party only to take over as its leader when Ariel Sharon had quit in December to form his own party, Kadima (Forward). His move had broken the mold of Israel's two-party system, Likud and Labor, to establish a powerful new force. A number of key Likud politicians had joined him, among them Shimon Peres, another former prime minister. While Israelis struggled to absorb the upheaval, Sharon suffered a ministroke, but in days he was back at his desk and, at the age of seventy-seven, was still working a twelve-hour day. It would be his final decision to attack Iran.

As Dagan drove toward the ranch, he knew the next time he would see the prime minister after this meeting would be following recovery from an operation to repair a small hole in his heart, which had been discovered when he was being treated for his stroke. Alongside the plans for a strike on Iran was Mossad's assessment of Hamas ending its "truce" of attacks on Israel. It came at a time when Sharon was still considering whether to allow Palestinians in East Jerusalem to vote in elections due later in the month; all the signs were that Hamas would make a good showing. But Dagan knew there were also personal troubles Sharon had to cope with. His son, Omri, had been forced to resign from the Knesset over a finance scandal that had led to criminal charges against him. The previous night's television news carried a report that the net was closing on a police investigation into $3 million secretly donated by an Austrian tycoon to help the prime minister repay expenses from his last election.

Dagan reached the ranch, built on the ruins of a Palestinian village and covering two thousand acres. As usual Sharon was waiting for his intelligence chief before sitting down to eat a meal prepared by his daughter-in-law, Inbal. The relationship between the two men had always been close, united by their common background of having fought in Lebanon. Then, Sharon had been as trim as Dagan had remained, but the prime minister, at 280 pounds, was now massively overweight for his five-foot-seven-inch height. To discuss the plan for the Iran attack, they sat in the ranch's spacious lounge. Afterward they had sipped coffee while Sharon reminisced; his eyes, restless and hard when he was younger, had now taken on an old man's softness, but his memory was as sharp as ever. He recalled in detail how he had captured a fortified zone in the Sinai by dropping paratroopers from helicopters, a tactic still studied in military academies in the U.S. and Britain. And how in the Yom Kippur War of 1973, when Mossad had been caught off guard, he had virtually single-handedly turned certain defeat into a brilliant victory. Dagan, as usual, listened intently as Sharon went on to explain how he had helped form the Likud Party after Labor had refused to accept him—and how he now intended to make Kadima live up to its name. He had spoken of his dislike for Netanyahu for his fierce opposition to the evacuation of the Jewish settlements. As the evening wore on, old friends dropped in to wish Sharon well for the next day's surgery. He told one, Reuven Adler, that he was worried about the general anaesthetic. Adler had joked, "What's the matter, Arik, you have turned into a coward all of a sudden?" When it came time for Dagan to leave, he noticed that Sharon looked more tired and pensive.

Shortly after Dagan had left, Sharon complained to his other son, Gilad, that he felt unwell and had some difficulty in focusing and had a strange feeling in the left side of his body. Soon he was finding difficulty in speaking at all. Schlomo Segev, Sharon's personal physician who was at the ranch, was summoned. By then Gilad had called one of the paramedics on standby duty with an ambulance and the head of Sharon's bodyguards. Gilad said his father should be moved to the nearest hospital, twenty minutes away. Segev overrode them, insisting the prime minister had suffered a major second stroke and should be taken directly to the Hadassah Hospital in Jerusalem. The journey took fifty-five minutes, during which Sharon's condition worsened. In the ambulance he suffered a cerebral hemorrhage caused by the rupture of an artery wall.

After seven hours of surgery, doctors put Sharon into a deep coma and onto a life-support machine. Meir Dagan was among those told that Ariel Sharon had suffered irreparable brain damage. He would never again make his mark on Israel's future. Mossad, whom Sharon admired, would never again have a political leader who had given it unprecedented freedom to operate. Emblematic of the gaping void left in Israeli politics by the loss of Sharon's leadership was the huge chair in the adjoining conference room to Dagan's office. It was where Ariel Sharon liked to sit when he came calling. Dagan told his senior aides that whoever rose to the daunting task of replacing Sharon would never sit in that chair. He had the piece of furniture removed.

In Gaza and beyond, extremists clamored for his death. From his mountain fastness in the Tora Bora range that divides North Pakistan from Afghanistan, Osama bin Laden called upon all Muslims to pray for Sharon's death to "be long and painful and that he should not die like our hero Azhari Husin, who went to Paradise like a true martyr."

CHAPTER 26

MISCALCULATIONS

Mossad's role in the elimination of Azhari Husin was not publicly acknowledged in the congratulations from countries where his suicide bombers had left a trail of death and destruction. It was ever so: compliments remained between intelligence services involved in a joint operation, along with commiserations over one that failed or led to loss of life. Rafi Eitan, the former director of operations for Mossad, once said to the author: "Herograms have no place in our business. We just do our job. If it works, fine. If not, we make sure it works next time."

Many of the still-unsung operations in which he and his successors have participated will remain forever secret; the only clue to their loss in lives are the growing number of names carved into the sandstone memorial at Glilot (see chapter 3, "Engravings of Glilot," p. 69).

"Gathering secret intelligence is not only dangerous, but a very imprecise art," Eitan once said. It is also very expensive. By 2004 the United States was spending $40 billion annually on acquiring it, Israel a small percentage of that; for both countries costs will inevitably rise in the coming years. But in Washington, Tel Aviv, and London, in all those nations with substantial intelligence services, information is power and the cost of obtaining it worthwhile.

Britain in 2005 had a £2 billion annual intelligence budget, half of it devoted to the Government Communications Headquarters (GCHQ) at Cheltenham in Gloucestershire. Costing £1.2 billion to build, contractors spent £50,000 of that to provide stainless-steel handrails to avoid marking by staff with rings on their fingers. Two electric trains circle the building's basement carrying boxes of files and sandwiches to the desks of its seven thousand staff on four floors. Shaped like a giant doughnut, the building has an inner courtyard the size of the Albert Hall. Eight-inch-thick black cladding is fitted to all the outer walls.

Its high-security computers handle strategic intelligence, the most important element of all modern intelligence gathering; it enables Britain's government and their advisers—civil servants, diplomats, and military chiefs—to be kept fully briefed on other countries and their future plans. Tactical intelligence, second, focuses on a potential enemy's battle plans, monitoring its training exercises to discern methods likely to be deployed in war. The third element is counterespionage, in Britain called "the defence of the realm." It focuses on uncovering foreign spying activities.

Mossad's brief includes all three elements, but it shares discoveries with "friendly" services on its long-established policy articulated to the author by its former director general David Kimche as "Israel, first, last—and always."

However, GCHQ maintains a "nothing held back" relationship with the most powerful intelligence-gathering organization on earth, whose activities are rooted in the deep black of space. From there America's National Security Agency (NSA) uses its armada of satellites to spy on the globe. The threat of terrorism has increased NSA's power; fresh targets are added to its electronic shopping lists by the CIA and other members of the U.S. intelligence community.

NSA cost more than $4 billion to run in 2005, employed twenty-seven thousand full-time experts, analysts, and technicians, plus a team of shredders to dispose of forty tons of paper a day; it also could call upon a hundred thousand U.S. servicemen and civilians scattered around the world. Part of its budget is spent on running highly secret listening posts in Britain: at Chicksands in Bedfordshire, Edzell in Scotland, Brawdy in Wales, and, the largest of all, at Menwith Hill near Harrogate in the north of England. All are linked to GCHQ and its own monitoring stations in Cyprus, West Germany, and Australia. It ensures nowhere is beyond surveillance.

Behind NSA's double-chain fence, topped by barbed wire interwoven with electric strands, its acres of computers vacuum the entire electromagnetic global spectrum, homing in on a dictionary of key words in scores of languages. Nothing politically, economically, or militarily significant in a telephone call, a conversation in the office of the secretary general of the United Nations, Kofi Annan, in a fax or an e-mail, escapes NSA's attention. While the UN headquarters in New York is sovereign territory and placing a bug there is illegal under international law, it is routinely done by NSA and GCHQ to spy on hostile countries and those deemed to be friendly to the United States and Britain; the latter are spied upon mainly for commercial reasons or to give London and Washington an edge on diplomatic negotiations. NATO allies are also under regular surveillance at the UN, and Mossad keeps a *yaholomin* unit in New York to spy on Arab and other missions.

The material finds its way through the electronic corridors of the intelligence community in Washington and London, and on to Tel Aviv. In turn, Mossad reveals intelligence to NSA and GCHQ on a need-to-know basis. Master copies of NSA data are stored in temperature-controlled vaults underground. Somewhere among the library of secrets are the 1,015 intercepts of surveillance it admits to carrying out on Princess Diana and Dodi al-Fayed in the weeks before their deaths in Paris. In 2005, NSA continued to resist all attempts by Dodi's father, Mohamed, to obtain copies of the intercepts, insisting they contained material of "national importance."

In the run-up to the war with Iraq, both agencies combined to provide their political masters—ultimately President George Bush and Prime Minister Tony Blair—with sensitive private conversations of at least one leader who had steadfastly pledged his support for the war.

On February 9, 2003, Sir Richard Dearlove, then the dapper, soft-spoken director general of Britain's MI6, had by early afternoon made several telephone calls about a surveillance operation to be mounted against Spain's prime minister, Jose Maria Aznar, Spain's ambassador at the United Nations, and senior officers at the Foreign Ministry in Madrid. Code-named Condor, the operation was marked "Beyond Secret," the highest classification MI6 shared with GCHQ and NSA.

Dearlove had spoken to George Tenet, the director of the CIA. Each had a high regard for the other; they were professionals at the top of the increasingly murky world intelligence gathering had become in the run-up to the war with Iraq. It was a world where, in the memorable words of Britain's former prime minister, Margaret Thatcher, "no one could surprise like a friend."

Deeply embattled over the coming war with Iraq, Tony Blair had secretly agreed for Aznar, a man he called a "trusted friend," to be spied upon. Britain and America—Blair and Bush—wanted to be absolutely certain that their Spanish ally in the imminent conflict remained as steadfast in his commitment behind the scenes as Aznar did in public. Over 95 percent of Spaniards either opposed going to war or were lukewarm about the idea. "There was an air of crisis, verging on panic in both Downing Street and the White House," recalled George Galloway, a maverick Labour MP—and later founder of the Respect Party—and regarded by Blair as a leader of the antiwar movement growing in Britain. "For Aznar to crack under pressure would be a disaster."

The first man Dearlove spoke to on that February day was John Scarlett. Tall, ramrod straight, with a domed head, the former MI6 spy was then the chairman of the Joint Intelligence Committee—the invisible footbridge over which crossed all MI6 intelligence for Downing Street. Scarlett's position as the overall monitor of Britain's intelligence services gave him a seat in Blair's Cabinet (later he would replace Dearlove as MI6 chief, a job Scarlett had long coveted). But as chairman of the Joint Intelligence Committee, his main task was to know what was happening in Iraq, to know what could be known about Saddam Hussein, and to predict what would happen as war drew closer. That included knowing, from January 2003, the real intentions of allies like Aznar.

In the previous two months, MI6, the CIA, and NSA had also been involved in bugging UN secretary general Kofi Annan and Hans Blix, the UN chief weapons inspector. Those operations finally surfaced when Clare Short, a former cabinet minister in the Blair government, claimed in February 2004 in Parliament that she knew "secret transcripts had been made of Annan's conversations by MI6 over the loom-ing war with Iraq." In the aftermath of Clare Short's revelations that Kofi Annan had been spied upon, Inocencio Arias, Spain's ambassador to the UN, said: "Everybody spies on everybody. And when there's a big crisis, big countries spy a lot. If your mission is not bugged, then you're really worth nothing." Details of how and why Aznar was bugged had remained secret until now revealed in this book.

In the weeks before the war, Blair had described Aznar as one of his "most frequent and trusted telephone callers," Alastair Campbell, the strategy director in Downing Street, would recall. Aznar knew and ac-cepted that his regular calls to Blair were listened into and a shorthand note taken. But he would never have expected—not for a moment—that his private briefings to his own aides were about to be spied upon on the orders of the prime minister.

Campbell, an astute judge of character, was among those in Down-ing Street genuinely puzzled at Blair's close relationship to the Span-ish prime minister. "Aznar was a man on the European right and it was as hard to explain his closeness to Tony Blair as it was the prime min-ister's closeness to George Bush," Campbell would later confide to Pe-ter Stothard, the former editor of *The Times*.

The fact was that Blair and Aznar were united over how weak their domestic support was for going to war with Iraq. Aznar's calls to Blair were taken in the prime minister's Downing Street den. It was a cozy room dominated by a small desk, on which stood a large framed por-trait of Nelson Mandela, a hero of Blair's. Next to it was a telephone. But the ringing came from an extension placed on a small table in the far corner of the room. It was where the note taker sat. The room was closed off from the rest of Downing Street by tall blue-leather doors. Blair always greeted Aznar with affection, saying, "Hullo Jose Maria." It was Blair at his telephonic best, transmitting his accomplished skills in making a person he was talking to feel like the only person who mat-ters. In these conversations Blair tried to convey his messianic view of the importance of removing Saddam Hussein; speaking of creating a United Nations being freed from its present helpless torpor; how the removal of the dictator would serve as a warning to other extremist na-tions that terror would be met with massive force. It would also be a message to Palestinians and Israelis that the present conditions of in-stability in the Middle East must cease.

Across the river Thames on that February day, Dearlove had

continued to make his own calls. Aznar now commanded less than 5 percent of the Spanish electorate to support his decision to back Britain and the United States in going to war with Iraq. "That's even less than the number of those who think Elvis Presley is still alive," Blair had joked to Alastair Campbell after another call from Madrid. It was that low electoral percentage that lay behind Dearlove's phone calls. Would Spain's prime minister remain committed to the ever-louder drumbeat of war, or would he waver and undergo a mind change that could wreck the military plans being finalized in London and Washington to invade Iraq and overthrow Saddam Hussein? The only way to find the answer was to bug Spain's ambassador to the United Nations, its key Foreign Ministry officials in Madrid, and the discussions Aznar had with them.

By the end of that cold February 9 day in London, the decision to bug Aznar had been taken. Those directly involved were Sir Richard Dearlove, George Tenet, John Scarlett, and the directors of GCHQ and NSA. The green light to do so had come from Downing Street after a lengthy conversation between Bush and Blair the previous day.

The decision to mount Operation Condor came when Frank Koza, a senior analyst in NSA, had sent his counterpart in GCHQ an e-mail asking for a surveillance "surge" against key members of the UN Security Council. Koza asked for "the whole gamut of information that could give U.S. policy makers an edge." His request was marked "Top Secret/COMINT/XI." The "XI" coding signified the request must never be declassified. It must stay Top Secret. However, a copy of the message somehow later found its way to GCHQ translator Katherine Gun. She passed it to an intermediary, who gave it to the British journalist Yvonne Ridley, who had achieved fame after being freed by the Taliban in Afghanistan and became a strong supporter of the antiwar movement. She, in turn, passed the memo to a journalist on London's *Observer*. Gun was arrested under Britain's Official Secrets Act; later, the case was dropped.

On that February day, the focus in GCHQ, NSA, MI6, and the CIA was spying on Aznar. The operation would be run out of Menwith Hill using NSA's ECHELON system's program called the Dictionary: its computers can target specific telephone numbers, words, and voiceprints, and includes "Tempest," which deciphers individual voices from laser beams directed at windows to read vibrations generated by people speaking. A segment of Aznar's voice was fed into the Dictionary computers, which were programmed to track every word Aznar and his key officials spoke in relation to Iraq anywhere in the world. Information obtained was downloaded to the Menwith Hill computers. Interlinked banks of computers decoded and analyzed the data and fed it down a secure line to GCHQ, where the material was turned into transcripts marked "Highly Classified." These were then sent to John Scarlett, chairman of the Joint Intelligence Committee. From there they were hand carried the short distance to Downing Street in buff-colored files each with the bold Cross of Saint George on their covers, an open indication of Scarlett's patriotism. To reach Blair, the intelligence supremo had to frequently step over the toys of Leo, the prime minister's youngest son, who often used the floor of Downing Street as a playground. Copies were sent via NSA to George Bush. For both politicians they became the prime source for judging the mood of Aznar and his officials. After the war it emerged that Aznar had remained consistent in his support. It would cost him his post as prime minister in Spain's next election.

In the closing weeks of 2005, Meir Dagan opened a staff meeting with what Sergei Kondrashov, a retired KGB chief of counterintelligence, had said, that if the KGB had been forced to chose between what a Russian mole in the U.S. administration reported and a subscription to *The New York Times*, he would believe the newspaper any day. Dagan reminded them that until Porter Goss became the CIA director, the agency evaluated intelligence reports on a simple scale: ABCD for the reliability of the source and 1234 for how accurate the information was. A1 meant the source was unchallengeable and the information unquestionably true. B2 indicated the source was good, and the intelligence was very probably true. Category D4 meant the source was totally unreliable and the information demonstrably false. Dagan had paused and said that Goss had spoken to a number of his deputy directors who admitted they had rarely seen A1 and only a small number of D4s. The great majority of reports crossing their desks were designated C3—the source had been reliable in the past and so his information was possibly true. Dagan had looked around the conference table and said that logically this meant a usually reliable source was sometimes also unreliable and the information described as possibly true could just as well be untrue. He reminded them that for Mossad good intelligence was always required to contain the caveat as Saint Paul glimpsed heaven—"through a glass, darkly." It was an indication of how Mossad must continue to face threats as the world became a global village and the demands made on an intelligence service grew daily. Gone were the clear divisions between the Soviet Union and the West. Terrorism, international money laundering, ruthless dictators, and ethnic conflicts had all changed the traditional role of spying and counterintelligence. In the desperate hunt for information to combat the new targets, intelligence services had been forced to operate in unfamiliar areas.

As 2005 drew to a close, the war on terrorism had not achieved many of its targets. While Saddam had been captured, Osama bin Laden and al-Qaeda remained a potent threat. Mossad's analysts had concluded that capturing or killing bin Laden would do nothing to eliminate al-Qaeda; it had a well-defined command structure ready to replace him, and the organization itself was increasingly focused on spreading its ideology to inspire others and imitate what had been achieved on September 11, 2001. Madrid, London, Bali, and Amman were all signposts on the road to further massacres. The analysts estimated al-Qaeda was now entrenched in sixty countries, truly a hydra-headed monster.

No one could have said what the effect would have been from the power play between Ayman al-Zawahiri, a fanatic with a scholar's beguiling mind, and the clinically insane Abu Musab al-Zarqawi. Both grasped the importance of using the Internet as a virtual base from which to proselytize and provide instruction. It meant that al-Qaeda training camps could attract jihadists who had already acquired the essential hatred of the United States, Britain, and, above all, Israel. The time recruits needed to be in the camps could be shortened, reducing the risk of them being caught in an air strike or a ground assault. Ironically, al-Zarqawi would be killed by a carefully planned air attack by the United States in Iraq in 2006.

Increasingly, state-sponsored terrorism had flourished and would continue to do so for the foreseeable future. Countries like Syria, North Korea, and Iran had calculated the risk of punishments they could face—and concluded they were worth the risk. In Damascus, Pyongyang, and Tehran the collective view was that not even the United States would contemplate starting a global war by launching a nuclear bomb against those states; neither would Israel, for all its posturing with nuclear submarines posted in the Gulf of Oman, be likely to launch a preemptive strike. So Islamic radicalism continued to grow, its sponsors knowing they would face, at most, no more than conventional military strikes. Sanctions, as Saddam Hussein's Iraq had demonstrated, did not work.

Al-Qaeda had also recognized that terrorism was war by another name, but was *not* treated as acts of war. Pakistan could arm Kashmiri terrorists to attack the Indian Parliament in 2001; Iranian-trained Saudis blew up the U.S. military base at Khobar in 1996; and Syrian-born members of Hamas bombed Israeli buses as they had done for years: yet none of these actions were treated as acts of war to be declared on the sponsoring states.

The danger of terrorism, as Meir Dagan had regularly lectured new members of Mossad, was its cost effectiveness. It cost little to produce a suicide bomber. One attack can create havoc, forcing a government to use its resources—manpower and technology—to try and capture the terrorists. A Mossad analyst had once calculated (for the author) that "one terrorist costs as much as a hundred expensively trained men to catch or capture him or her."

Into this already complex situation there was the ever-expanding role of the Chinese secret service, CSIS. China has a tradition of espionage that reaches back over twenty-five hundred years. But never had its activities been more far-reaching than today.

Since the theft of nuclear secrets from Los Alamos, CSIS had continued to expand its activities in the United States. Many of China's accredited diplomats in its Washington embassy, various consulates, and trade missions throughout the United States were either full-time intelligence officers or directly linked to the service. The FBI estimated that in 2005 the number of CSIS agents and informers was larger than any other foreign intelligence service operating within the country. Since Los Alamos they had between them obtained, either by theft or deception, an estimated $35 million worth of secrets, mostly from technology companies working in or for the defense industry. FBI Director Robert Mueller had ordered that all the firms be briefed on improving their security and that organizers of technology conferences, which had always attracted Chinese scientists, were instructed on "how to recognize a possible CSIS agent." Universities were asked to provide details of courses "and other interests" of the thirty thousand Chinese students on their campuses after the FBI established that CSIS had paid for an increasing number to study in America; many were attending postgraduate courses at universities like UCLA, Harvard,

Yale, and Stanford. After graduating, often in computer or science-related subjects, they had applied for jobs at companies with sensitive defense contracts. A former senior FBI officer, Ted Gunderson, who had worked on counterterrorism out of the Los Angeles field office, told the author: "The students are taught how to steal, photocopy, and return valuable blueprints and secret contracts and smuggle them out past the security guards. The material is often on microfilm inserted into a tooth cavity or swallowed to be excreted later in one of the many safe houses CSIS has around the country."

Meir Dagan's now-close relationship with Porter Goss enabled the backdoor channel to be used to provide details of what Mossad knew about CSIS activities in the United States. Both intelligence chiefs knew much of the material was too politically sensitive to pass on to the White House or the State Department until there was absolute proof of espionage.

In October 2005, a Los Angeles–based *katsa* informed Tel Aviv that a CSIS spy ring in California was about to courier to China disks containing ultrasecret details about U.S. weapons systems, which had been encrypted and hidden behind tracks of music CDs and the latest movie releases. A Mossad sayan who worked for the same high-security defense contractor, Power Paragon, in Anaheim, California, which employed a member of the spy ring, Chi Mak, had become suspicious and informed his *katsa*. The sayan was told to keep watch. In weeks, he had provided sufficient details for the *katsa* to alert Tel Aviv.

The details were passed by Meir Dagan to Porter Goss down the backdoor channel. A major FBI operation was mounted. On October 27, the day before Chi Mak was to fly out of Los Angeles with his wife, Rebecca, along with two other members of the spy ring—Chi Mak's brother, Tai Wang Mak, and his wife, Fuk Heung Li—the two couples were arrested at Chi Mak's home in Downey, California.

Federal officers discovered what one FBI agent, James E. Gaylord, described as "a house full of secrets." They would turn out to be the most damaging espionage operation against the United States since the theft at Los Alamos. Hundreds of thousands of documents and computer printouts were found in Chi Mak's home. Both he and his wife were naturalized American citizens who had arrived in the United States in May 2001. The CSIS spy ring was already in place. But Chi Mak set about upgrading its activities. He obtained a job as an engineer with Power Paragon. It gave him access to highly classified weapons systems, including blueprints of the new Virginia-class submarines and the Aegis battle-management systems, which are the core of U.S. Navy destroyers, cruisers, and aircraft carriers. Chi Mak, an electronics engineer with what the FBI called "advanced computer skills," had stolen material that would give China superiority if the United States went to the defense of Taiwan in any conflict with the Beijing regime.

Neighbors described Chi Mak and his wife as "polite but reserved" and "regular folk who lived quiet lives." Short of calling them "pillars of our society," they fitted the standard profiles of deep-cover agents, no different from the untold numbers who toiled every day in the dark and always dangerous world of secret intelligence. For them it was over. But how long before the next spy scandal came? When it did, Meir Dagan was determined it would not be Mossad caught pillaging secrets.

Arriving at work at his usual hour of 6:30 on the morning of Tuesday, January 24, 2006, Meir Dagan found on his desk the report he had eagerly awaited from Mossad's Research and Development Department. Its scientists, programmers, and technicians had finally succeeded in creating a new range of gadgets that would ensure the service remained at the forefront of intelligence gathering. Each item had been field-tested across Europe by *katsas*. In Paris and Brussels they had tried out the EDLB, the updated electronic dead-letter box, which used a state-of-the-art miniaturized computer system so that an agent could exchange information with other field agents or his controller at Mossad headquarters. Built into the EDLB was an encryptor that R & D programmers believed even the code breakers of the Chinese Secret Intelligence Service—acknowledged to be the best in the world—could not break. With it came a specially adapted mobile phone the size of a cigarette packet. Known as an "infinity device," it could hack into any cell phone, making it activate itself without triggering its display light. The device had been tested outside the European Union headquarters in Brussels, providing an eavesdropping conduit over a twenty-four-hour period and automatically transmitting, on the hour, every conversation it had downloaded. Another gadget known as "keystroke" was designed by the R & D team to be inserted into a target computer to download everything stored on its hard drive. This had been tested out on a dating agency in Madrid. Yet another device code-named "Tempest" was designed to scan all the computers in a building to discover the level of electronic protection each one had. The test site chosen was an unsuspecting Siemens Building in Munich. The R & D report indicated that Tempest had "provided a satisfactory result." Undoubtedly the greatest triumph had been creating a surveillance device known as "Smart Dust." These were ant-sized sensors that could be scattered in hostile territory—hidden in dust, grass, or soil—and their microdot microphones would pick up data transmitted to an EDLB designed to store several megabytes of information, which would then be automatically transferred to Mossad headquarters. The life of a sensor was a month before it would self-destruct.

Among the first to be equipped with this arsenal of gadgets were Mossad field agents in the Balkans, where al-Qaeda had set up a network that ran from Bosnia in the north down to Albania and where, under cover of mosques, Islamic fund-raising organizations and information centers operated. In the mountains behind the Adriatic Sea were the staging camps for jihadists from England, France, Spain, and Italy to be assessed before continuing their long journey east to Afghanistan, traveling along one of the many well-established heroin-smuggling trails. Later, their training completed in the mountains of Afghanistan—where bin Laden and his senior aides remained hidden—the jihadists made their way back across Iran into northern Turkey, through the south of Bulgaria, across Macedonia, and back into Albania. From there they either crossed the Adriatic into Italy or traveled north through Bosnia, Croatia, Slovenia, and into Austria. From there they made their way back home. Mossad called them "Trojan Horses," the silent, watchful, suicide bombers, the explosives makers, the terrorists trained in urban warfare ready to strike at the heart of Europe. Their prime target, Meir Dagan had told his *katsas*, was always going to be Jewish institutions—banks, synagogues, schools, and any organization in which Jews had invested. Then would come the American and British institutions. But those owned or partly controlled by Jews would be the first.

He had dispatched his finest operatives to interdict and kill the jihadists, ideally as they made their way to Afghanistan or on their return journey. Those who survived were hunted down as they made their way north back into Europe. Those who still managed to avoid death were brought to the notice of other security services. By 2006, Mossad had provided the Dutch security service, Algemene Inlichtingen- en Veiligheidsdienst (AIVD), the names of fifty jihadists who had arrived back in Holland in the past three years. In Belgium, Mossad had helped its intelligence service to uncover an al-Qaeda cell whose members had survived the long journey back from Afghanistan. In the cell's apartment in Brussels were discovered expertly forged passports and an al-Qaeda textbook on how to assemble a bomb. But once more Mossad had been frustrated to see that the much-vaunted security cooperation between Europe's own security services was not as close as its political leaders maintained. French intelligence continued to argue in 2006 that Holland was failing to extradite terrorist suspects wanted in France. The Dutch had rejected the accusation.

The suspects were members of Taqfir wal Hijra. Its founders had fled from Egypt to Algeria. There the organization had been absorbed into al-Qaeda. In 2003, it had arrived in The Hague. Operating in highly secret cells, its members set about recruiting jihadists to travel to Afghanistan for training. The bodies of those who did not return home lay along the trail to and from Afghanistan. As usual, Mossad arranged for their obituaries to appear in local Arab newspapers. Sometimes their families received flowers and a condolence card *before* a jihadist was killed. The gesture was designed to create panic among jihadists.

One who had escaped was Lionel Dumont, a native Frenchman from Roubaix, an industrial town in the north of France. In his early teens he had converted to Islam and later spent his military service with the French army in Somalia. The brutality of many of his fellow soldiers toward the Muslim population had a powerful and lasting effect on Dumont. During the war in the former Yugoslavia, he went to Bosnia to fight with al-Qaeda–sponsored mujahideen.

It was a time when Osama bin Laden was looking for new places to defeat the infidel. Almost simultaneously with the fighting in Bosnia, the conflict in Chechnya erupted. Then Albania provided another battlefield for al-Qaeda; chaos and anarchy already prevailed in the country, making it a fertile ground for arms traffickers and other terrorist-linked groups. Al-Qaeda welded them into a powerful force; unlimited funding was provided, along with humanitarian aid. Albania became a springboard into neighboring Kosovo. Dumont was among some five hundred mujahideen smuggled into the Albanian capital of Tirana. The operation was led by Osama bin Laden's deputy, Ayman al-Zawahiri. After a kill-or-be-killed conflict against government forces, the mujahideen swept on into Macedonia. Again money and aid won over impoverished villagers. In the end it would be NATO that drove them out. But by then al-Qaeda had scooped up hundreds more recruits. Many went to Afghanistan for specialist training.

When an uneasy peace came to the region, Dumont returned to Roubaix and formed his own group, which he trained and led to conduct a number of terrorist attacks. The French police tried, but failed, to arrest him, and Dumont fled to Bosnia. There he became a senior member of the rapidly expanding al-Qaeda organization. Finally captured, he escaped from prison and was spirited along the trail to Afghanistan. Twice Mossad *katsas* almost killed him before he reached the safety of the mountain fastness where al-Qaeda had its camps along the Afghanistan border with Pakistan. In January 2006, Mossad believed Dumont was still there, supervising the training of other French-born jihadists. The gadgets Mossad's R & D department had created would be used to track and kill them.

The budget of hundreds of millions of dollars to create the surveillance arsenal had been approved by Ariel Sharon. But on that morning of January 24, Meir Dagan knew that the one Israeli politician he revered above all others would never recover from the massive stroke that had left Sharon in an ever-deepening coma, paralyzed, and kept alive by a life-support system in his Jerusalem hospital. His medical team had indicated they could do no more. As often as he could Dagan had visited the seventh-floor suite where his old friend lay at death's door. Each time Dagan stood in the doorway, his sharply intelligent eyes watching Sharon's heartbeats continuing to move across the monitor positioned near the bed, the blips on the screen pulsing, reducing the old man's grasp on life to an endless trace. Sharon's family would be there, grouped around the bed, quiet, the emotions aroused by approaching death seeming to settle even more over them. Dagan could detect the sorrow, despair, and helplessness of the family and the barely concealed resignation of the doctors and nurses. He had wondered if Sharon sensed their presence. More certain was the family gathered around the bed were caught in some deep, primitive, and instinctive ritual, staring silently at the motionless figure, almost as if no words could communicate their inner feelings. Dagan well understood that; in his life as a soldier and head of Mossad, he had seen the effect of death on others many times.

He knew that the medical equipment surrounding Sharon, machines that clicked and pinged, would provide some confirmation for the family that all was not yet lost; that active measures were still being taken to keep the inevitable at bay. Close to the bed was a red-painted surgical trolley. This was the crash cart, the ultimate emergency aid with drugs to stimulate cardiac output, sponges, needles, tourniquets, probes, catheters, airway tubes, an aspirator, and a defibrillator capable of delivering through its paddles a powerful electric shock to start Sharon's heart if it stopped. The decision to resuscitate would come only when that moment arrived. Dagan had told aides that if it were his choice, he would not revive his friend to exist in a vegetative state.

After reviewing the R & D report, Dagan prepared for his first meeting of the day. It would be with two senior officers of France's Directorate for Surveillance of the Territory (DST). The largest of the Republic's six intelligence agencies, it employed several thousand staff and, over the years, had developed close ties with Mossad. These had been cemented when Mossad had helped the DST foil a terrorist plot to launch a jetliner into the Eiffel Tower. Since then both services had collaborated to thwart a number of al-Qaeda attacks in France. None of the details had subsequently emerged in public, but they had included a plan to assassinate President Chirac.

While France, like many European countries, publicly advocated a judicial approach to the war on terrorism, wherever possible arresting and trying terrorists; behind the scenes the DST was as ruthless as Mossad. This had followed a major overhaul in 1986 of the country's police and its intelligence-gathering apparatus. After the 9/11 attacks the cooperation with Mossad rapidly expanded. Both services had common ground in dealing with the effects of the jihad in Chechnya, Gaza, the West Bank, and Kashmir, which had led to a radicalization among Middle East Arabs who had arrived in Paris, Marseilles, and Lyon, cities where Jewish investment and influence were well established. The al-Qaeda network in France consisted largely of North African second-generation emigrants from working-class or middle-class families. The majority were still in their early twenties and had been seduced by the messianic preaching of Osama bin Laden on a video or persuaded to become a jihadist after listening to a radical preacher in a mosque. Hundreds had made their way to Afghanistan and, later, Iraq.

The closeness of Spain to North Africa made it an important conduit for al-Qaeda to smuggle operatives into France. A document that a Mossad analyst prepared in 2005 (which the author has seen) accuses the Moroccan police of receiving payment in return for smuggling terrorists into Spain. "Al-Qaeda controls criminal networks in Spain who deal in money laundering and trafficking in drugs and prostitutes from the Balkans. Spain is still considered a safe haven for Islamic extremists even after the Madrid bombings. The current estimate is that they are linked to eighteen radical groups that Spanish intelligence has not been able to successfully penetrate."

Information produced by Mossad's Spanish sayanim was passed on to the DST, together with al-Qaeda's growing presence on France's border with Germany. The Federal Republic had itself become a fertile ground for al-Qaeda to recruit jihadists in university cities like Hamburg, Berlin, Frankfurt, Wiesbaden, Duisburg, and Munich. Though Mossad had helped to destroy the most important al-Qaeda cell in Germany, the Meliani Kommando, as it was about to launch a terrorist attack in Strasbourg against the city's cathedral and its historic synagogue, al-Qaeda still had a sizeable network; many of its members had come from the Balkans.

To update themselves, DST officers regularly visited Tel Aviv and Mossad Station in Paris and had free access to the DST data bank. Central to this relationship was the joint monitoring of mosques and individuals across France. Warrants for wiretapping were easily granted and, since December 2005, surveillance had been extended to use video cameras in public areas and access to phone and e-mail communications of suspects. Again with the help of Mossad the DST had developed an unprecedented number of Muslim informers within the country's Muslim communities. For Mossad the value of its ties to the DST was that it served as an intelligence data clearinghouse from other French agencies, including the national police.

Through the DST Mossad could provide evidence to the country's judicial arm when it came to issuing arrest warrants, wiretaps, and subpoenas. These were served by a team of investigating judges who could also order the detention of suspects for an initial six days and even keep some of them imprisoned for years. In court, the suspects were judged by professional magistrates rather than under the jury system of Britain and the United States. Meir Dagan felt this approach could offer lessons to the Bush administration as it faced growing pressure and controversy over its own approach to fighting terrorism: its incarcerating suspects in its Guantánamo Bay camp, its continued rendition of suspects to secret prisons in Eastern Europe, and the doubtful legality of its military tribunals to try suspects.

The meeting with the two DST officers was conducted in Dagan's office and not in one of the small conference rooms where he usually met senior foreign intelligence officers; the choice of venue was a further indication of the closeness between the DST and Mossad. Like agents from British and European services, the DST regularly sent senior officers to the Palestinian Territories before traveling on to see Dagan. The visits were known as "pulse taking" by the Mossad director, who saw them as another way to check the strength of Palestinian fervor. On the surface it was a means to try and expunge decades of isolation that the removal of the Jewish settlers from Gaza had done little to diminish.

Dagan usually learned little from the visits by MI6 officers, Germany's BND, Spain, and the CIA. "Indeed some of their interpretations were wide of the mark," one of his aides told the author. But the DST usually provided well-informed judgments, helped by the ability of its agents to not only speak Arabic fluently but to understand its culture. It meant a DST evaluation could be trusted enough to be matched against what Mossad's own informers in Gaza and the West Bank reported. For Dagan it was essential to get the French view of the coming Palestinian elections and the influence wielded by Hamas at ground-roots level in its challenge to Fatah, the ruling party. Yasser Arafat had designed it to create a nationalist mythology using the symbols of his kaffiyeh, stubble, and gun, to fuel a revolutionary belief in which political struggle was heroic, fiery militance superior to mundane governance, vehement rejection better than compromise, all opponents—especially Israel—were evil, terrorism was cleansing, and the eventual victory would be all the better for it. But Arafat was gone and in the past year Fatah the organization had become increasingly inured to corruption. In the Palestinian Territories the despair among the young had grown by the day, along with unemployment, social chaos, and Fatah's seeming inability to recognize that governing required attention to the prosaic details.

Into this situation had emerged Hamas. The terrorist organization had also been founded on hatred, paranoia, and an apocalyptic vision of how Israel would be destroyed by a plentiful supply of suicide bombers and huge financial support from Iran. Hamas politics were rooted in absolutionist terms: vengeance was glorious and victory was achieved through martyrdom. Founded in December 1987 by Sheikh Ahmed Yassin, who became its spiritual leader, Hamas was cautiously encouraged by Israel as a means of balancing the extremists within Fatah. "Incredibly as it seems today, we thought the 'divide and rule' policy that had worked so well in the past would do so this time," recalled Rafi Eitan. In August 1988, Hamas published its "charter," calling on all Muslims to "destroy Israel and its people." The response was swift. Yassin was killed in his wheelchair by a fusillade of rockets from Israeli gunships. Abdel Aziz al-Rantisi, the organization's strategist, was killed by the same method shortly afterward. In 1997, Mossad failed to kill Khalid Meshal, the head of the organization's international branch in Amman (see chapter 17, "Bunglegate"). Salah Shehade, the architect of Hamas's suicide-bombing strategy, was killed by Israeli F-16 jets that precision-bombed his home in Gaza. His wife and children also died in the attack. By then more than three hundred suicide attacks had claimed four hundred Israelis, many of them women and children. But Hamas had continued to attract support among Palestinians with its pledge it would control the Palestinian Territories by 2027.

For Meir Dagan on that Tuesday morning the question was: How much closer would Hamas come to achieving its eventual aim through the coming Palestinian elections? Any success would be due largely to the failure of Yasser Arafat to leave Fatah a legacy of a properly functioning government after it had been given a monopoly on power by the Oslo peace accords of 1993. Thirteen years later, Fatah had still not been reinvigorated by promoting new young blood from within its ranks. Its leadership consisted of old men who clung to the past. The truth was that most Palestinians were worse off in 2006 than they were before the Oslo agreement. They lived inside a ring of Israeli military steel, and their economy, especially in the southern enclave of Gaza, was gradually being strangled by punitive restrictions on their movement. Would they awake in a few days' time to a green dawn—a mass of verdant Hamas flags heralding a victory?

The indications from Mossad's informers in Gaza and the West Bank, and its own analysts, were that Hamas would make a respectable showing at the polls—but that Fatah would be returned to office. This was echoed by the surveillance reports on Khalid Meshal in Damascus; his telephone calls to Hamas leaders in Gaza and the West Bank indicated their success in running hospitals, schools, and support agencies would, in the end, not be enough. What Dagan could not decide was whether Meshal, knowing he was being monitored, was indulging in skilled disinformation. Mossad's analysts thought not: that Meshal also saw the coming election as only the first step on the political ladder, that Hamas would not expect to have real political power for many years to come.

It later emerged the two DST officers had echoed this view to Dagan. On that note, the Mossad chief took his senior aides to see a film.

Meir Dagan had been a young conscript in the Israeli Defense Forces (IDF) when in the early hours of September 5, 1972, in the city of Munich, Germany, where the Olympic Games were being staged, eight Black September terrorists used a passkey to enter an apartment block where a number of Israeli athletes slept. Twenty-five minutes later two of the sportsmen were dead, murdered in cold blood. Nine others had been captured. They would also die in the days to come. The atrocity on that warm autumn night shocked the world. In Israel, even before the tears had dried, cold anger called for vengeance even as the terrorists demanded the release of 236 political prisoners. For twenty-four hours there was a tense standoff between the hostage takers and the German police. In mounting disbelief, Israelis, including Dagan, sat glued to their television sets as rescue operations were bungled. An attempt to storm the apartment block was aborted when the Munich police realized the terrorists were watching their preparations live on television. Two more attempts failed after the Black September group demanded a jet to fly them and their hostages out of Germany. The Germans swiftly agreed to provide two helicopters to fly them to Munich airport. Waiting near the getaway aircraft was an armed police team dressed as Lufthansa staff. But only moments before the helicopters landed, the team was told to abort the mission as it was too dangerous. Posted around the area were five German army snipers to deal with eight heavily armed terrorists. When the helicopters landed a firefight ensued as the snipers tried to hit their targets. The terrorists detonated a grenade in one helicopter and raked the inside of the other with gunfire. The snipers continued to shoot. In minutes all nine surviving hostages from the initial attack on the apartment were dead, along with five of the Black September group. Three were captured. But six weeks later, on October 29, 1972, a Frankfurt-bound Lufthansa jet was hijacked. The terrorists demanded the release of the captured trio. This was swiftly agreed to by the German government. The terrorists, smiling broadly, were flown to a Black September base in the Middle East and disappeared.

There was not a man, woman, or child in Israel who could not recount what followed. Mossad was given the task of hunting down not only the Munich killers, but all those who had planned the massacre. Every Mossad director general who had come into office had made it his business in the first days of his tenure to study the files of how Mossad had carried out its mission, one that Golda Meir, then the prime minister, had called the Wrath of God. Her successors, like Benjamin Netanyahu, Shimon Peres, Ehud Barak, and Ariel Sharon, had never tired of reading how Mossad's kidon had sown the seeds of fear in every terrorist heart. In Barak's later words (to the author): "The intention was to strike terror, to break the will of those who remained alive until there were none of them left."

For two years Mossad had carried out a carefully planned, clinically executed series of assassinations. The first was shot dead in the lobby of his Rome apartment eleven times—a bullet for each Israeli athlete he helped to murder. Another died when he answered a phone call in his Paris apartment; the bomb in the receiver blew off his head. The next to die was expertly pushed under a London bus at rush hour. In Nicosia, Cyprus, a bomb exploded in a bedside lamp. Hours before they died, each man's family received flowers and a condolence card bearing the same words: "A reminder we do not forget or forgive." After each kidon execution, a notice about the dead terrorist was published in Arab language newspapers across the Middle East. The flowers, cards, and notices had all been sent by LAP, Mossad's department of psychological warfare. While the kidon carried out the executions, it had required a team backup of some eight units. One group was responsible for tracking down each Black September killer. Technicians from *ya-holomin*, Mossad's vaunted communications unit, set up eavesdropping equipment to monitor each terrorist as he was located. Another team organized dead-letter boxes in a dozen European capitals to receive messages from informers. Safe houses were rented for secret meetings in London, Paris, and Madrid.

Thirty-four years later, Steven Spielberg, arguably one of the world's most successful moviemakers, had transposed the massacre into a $65 million film. When Dagan had heard of Spielberg's intentions, he had been surprised to learn that Spielberg had made no approach to

Mossad for, if not exactly seeking cooperation, at least asking for guidance on the accuracy of the screenplay. It was based on *Vengeance* by George Jonas, which had been published in 1984 to be quickly dismissed by Mossad as "mostly pure fantasy."

In the book Jonas claimed to "explore at first hand the feelings and revulsion and doubt that gradually came to haunt each member of the Mossad hit team and which, in the end, inexorably changed their view of the mission and themselves." He concluded that his story—the genesis of the Spielberg movie—"will inspire and horrify. For its subject is an act of revenge that goes to the very heart of the ancient biblical questions of good and evil, or right and wrong, which ultimately remain the deepest concerns of the Jewish people and which continue to haunt 'Avner' and his comrades on their mission."

But the book's mysterious "Avner"—who was the movie's leader of the hit team—had never worked for Mossad, let alone been selected to be a member of kidon. Even before Meir Dagan settled down for a private viewing of *Munich,* he knew that other members of Mossad had trashed the movie. David Kimche, the former deputy director, had castigated it "as a tragedy that a person of the stature of Steven Spielberg, who has made such fantastic films, should now have based *Munich* on a book that is a falsehood." Avi Dichter, a former head of Shin Bet, Israel's internal intelligence service, had dismissed the film as "a children's adventure story." From all over the world other retired members of Mossad had joined in the criticism.

In the film the kidon are portrayed as increasingly filled with doubts about the morality of the mission. Conversely the terrorists are given a platform to rationalize their murders, just as the apologists for suicide bombers today defend their atrocities. All this was done with the consummate skill of a great filmmaker. What angered the real-life members of the hit team, together with current members of kidon, was that like the book, the movie did not explain Israel's well-established justification for hunting down and executing terrorists who cannot be brought to trial by the usual means of arrest. In the movie the hit team is depicted as being isolated in the field for months. Two of its members are a forger and a bombmaker.

Rafi Eitan, the former Mossad operations chief who had played an important role in tracking down the Black September group, told the author: "It would have been unthinkable to expect a forger to produce documents under high-stress operational conditions. All the paperwork for the real operation was produced by Mossad's forgery department. There was no bomb maker as such on the team. The explosives were created in Tel Aviv and brought to the team in the field. The movie team did not include a woman. Yet female kidon have always been part of a hit squad. Having them there helps to get closer to a target. But where the film went totally wrong was the hit team members questioning the morality of their actions. It never happened. It could never happen. The real hit team chosen for the mission were handpicked for their mental stability. Like all kidon, they had undergone intense evaluation by Mossad psychologists. At the mission's conclusion, they were debriefed by the psychologists. The team showed not the slightest sign of personality disorders. For them it had been a mission that was legally supported by the State of Israel."

But Dagan wanted to judge for himself. He brought with him to the private viewing men who had been directly involved in the operational planning and execution of the Black September killers. His verdict at the end of the 145-minute movie was succinct: "Entertainment—maybe. Accurate—absolutely not."

It was a review Dagan doubted would ever appear in any Spielberg filmography.

On Thursday, January 26, 2006, a day that came to be known in Israel as Black Thursday, Meir Dagan watched in mounting disbelief the images on the television screen in a corner of his office. The pictures switched from Gaza City to the West Bank, to Nablus and Bethlehem, from Ramallah to East Jerusalem, from one Arab township to another, from villages that were mere dots on the map on Dagan's wall. Each image offered the same stunning sight of the green flag of Hamas raised in triumph. It fluttered from the minarets of mosques and the rooftops of buildings and moved through the streets in a great surge of green, held aloft by the chanting crowds. Hamas had won a sweeping, historic victory, one that had mocked all the pollsters, the foreign observers, and, most important for Dagan, the analysts of Mossad. How had everyone not foreseen what had happened? How had anyone not understood that Hamas had shown itself on poll day to be a disciplined organization able to turn out the faithful in huge numbers to vote? Why had no one discovered the preparation that had gone into creating the enormous green banners now being hung on public buildings? How had Hamas's Qassam Brigades, its military wing, marching across the television screen, firing their guns in the air, their usual masks discarded, been so well rehearsed without attracting suspicion? These were questions being asked of Dagan by Israel's cabinet ministers. He had no ready answers. Not a man to rush to judgment, he continued to sit and watch, as did all Israel.

One certainty was clear. The peace talks would remain frozen. The reason was in the one statistic that ticker taped across the bottom of the television screens. Hamas had won 132 seats, leaving Fatah to cling to 43, and some of those by the slimmest of majorities, ending more than forty years of its domination of Palestinian life. Dagan would not quarrel with an Israeli radio commentator, who likened the victory to "an earthquake or tsunami." It had changed for the foreseeable future Israel's own relationship with the Palestinians and the Arab world beyond its borders. For better or worse? He did not know. He doubted if anyone in Israel could answer the question.

By that Thursday afternoon, Dagan was receiving the first calls from foreign intelligence service chiefs. They wanted to know how Hamas, a terrorist organization that had continuously undercut every step toward peace, a desire sought by moderate Palestinians, had managed to persuade such a majority of them to overwhelmingly vote for Hamas. And having done so, would they ensure that Hamas would now cease to attack Israel and try to create a real Palestinian state that would come to live side by side at peace with its Jewish neighbors?

Dagan gave them all the same response. Hamas would focus initially on issues like education, health, and social affairs: these had been the cornerstone of its election success. But for that it would need funding, including $52 million the Palestinian Authority received from Israel. While Hamas had shown by entering the democratic process that it was already on the road from being an outlawed terrorist organization to a mainstream political force, to give any lasting meaning to its new status it must renounce the mainstay of its previous existence: the destruction of Israel. Until it did so, there could be no meaningful dialogue with Hamas. Dagan had reminded his callers that traditionally it had been Israel's hard-liners rather than the moderates who had made concessions. Menachem Begin, a terrorist turned peacemaker, had surrendered the Sinai in return for a peace treaty with Egypt. Another Israeli warrior, Yitzhak Rabin, had given his own life to try and broker peace with other Arab neighbors; in the end he had been assassinated by an Israeli extremist. More recently Ariel Sharon, once the hero of the Israeli Right, had earned their fury by ending the right of Israeli settlers to occupy Gaza.

Given Hamas's links to Iran and Syria, Israel would have to consider very carefully how far it could trust Hamas before relaxing its vigilance. And Hamas had swept to power with its pledge to uproot corruption. Yet some of the worst abuses were in the Palestinian security forces. Created by Yasser Arafat, it consisted of a dozen separate agencies that totaled 60,000 members, a large number to protect a total Palestinian population of less than 4 million in Gaza and the West Bank. Israel had accused the force of failing to prevent attacks on Jewish targets; Hamas had continued to proclaim during the election that the security forces were used by Israel to kill Hamas militants. The truth lay somewhere in the middle. Both Mossad and Shin Bet had its informers inside the security forces. They had been used to pinpoint targets for the Israeli air force to kill. Equally, Hamas supporters in the security forces had helped suicide bombers to be smuggled out of Gaza and the West Bank to strike inside Israel. For the majority of Palestinians, the security forces had done little to halt lawlessness in the territories. Meir Dagan believed the Hamas promise to reform the services and bring to trial its leaders, who had become multimillionaires by siphoning off millions of dollars, intended to improve security, into their numbered bank accounts in Switzerland and the Cayman Islands. He was prepared to use Mossad's resources to track down those accounts. But not yet. He wanted to see what else Hamas would do.

Mossad's analysts, who had miscalculated so badly the Hamas victory, were understandably cautious about predicting what the future would hold. Ever since the Oslo Accords, the Israeli and Palestinian leaderships had maintained a dialogue at some level, ranging from intense peace negotiations in 2000 to the limited contacts of the past three years due to the ongoing violence. In none of those contacts had Hamas been involved—except to send its suicide bombers from Gaza and rockets from the West Bank into Israel.

It was not only Hamas's electoral triumph that the analysts studied; it had come at a time when Israel itself was undergoing a political upheaval. Kadima, the centrist party that Ariel Sharon had created, continued to attract members. Was this in part a sympathy vote for its founder, or was it evidence that Israelis were growing tired of the hardline Likud Party and the indecisive Labor party? Ami Ayalon, the former head of Shin Bet and now a Labor parliamentary candidate for the coming elections in March, had said there could be no further "uni-lateral withdrawal from the Palestinian territories." But the acting Labor prime minister, Ehud Olmert, had insisted that if Labor won the next election, in March 2006, he would "relinquish parts of the West Bank and maintain a Jewish majority elsewhere, but I would prefer to do this in agreement with the Palestinians."

Did this mean he was willing to negotiate with Hamas? He refused to say "at this stage." But Dagan wondered if this was a piece of political doublespeak. (Kadima brokered a deal with Rafi Eitan and his Pensioners Party with its seven seats. They would join Kadima's coalition government to ensure Olmert was elected prime minister. Shortly afterward there were attacks on Israel by a suicide bomber followed by rockets. Hamas denied any complicity in the attacks. Dagan told his Monday morning conference, "Life as usual.")

The one certainty was that the Hamas victory had brought substantial gains by Islamic radicals in Egypt and Lebanon. In his own analysis, Meir Dagan had shown a political clarity that always surprised his people. He had told his senior staff at their Monday morning conference following the election: "There is a huge transition going on across the entire Middle East. It will be many months before we can see beyond the present unpredictability. That is the nature of big historic change. It's simply the way it is. We must be ready to accommodate it—whatever it brings. But the truth is that neither Israel, the United States, Britain, and the countries of Europe can ignore the popular will of the Palestinian voters. Their turnout was an impressive 78 percent. No other democratic country can claim to have recently achieved such a turnout. We should see it as a sign that democracy may well have taken root. We should take this into account when making decisions. That does not mean rushing to judgment. It means being realistic."

On May 14, 2006, Britain's Intelligence Security Committee issued its report on the London terrorist bombings of July 7, 2005. Dame Eliza Manningham-Buller was cited as saying: "Even with the wisdom of hindsight I doubt whether MI5 could have done much better than it did, given the resources available to us at the time and the other demands placed on us. Neither can we guarantee to stop future attacks."

While Meir Dagan admired her honesty, he also saw it as the inevitable result of MI5's failure to recognize the threat posed by Islamic terrorism from the end of the 1990s. It had taken what Dagan termed "the ultimate wake-up call of 9/11 to galvanize American intelligence." He found it depressing to read Dame Eliza's judgment that MI5 was still taking the attitude that attacks by Islamic extremists were unavoidable. "It may be realistic, but it also sounds complacent. Intelligence should not be touched by complacency," he told his aides. They were sentiments that would guide Mossad into the future.

CHAPTER 27

A Secret Channel and Hezbollah Rockets

On a cool morning in February 2006, eight middle-aged men were allowed to bypass the stringent security checks at Ben Gurion International Airport outside Tel Aviv. Four were Israelis, casually dressed. The Arabs wore dark suits and neatly knotted neckties. Little known outside their communities, the group had been given a pivotal role on the seesaw of Middle East politics. The Arabs were senior members of Fatah and were led by Jibril Rajoud, the party's hard-line national security adviser. The Israeli quartet was headed by Uri Saguy, a trim, quiet-spoken man who had once been head of Israeli army intelligence.

Only Meir Dagan and Ehud Olmert, soon to be prime minister of

Israel, and the Palestinian Authority president, Mahmoud Abbas, knew the purpose of the trip was to establish a "backdoor channel" between Israel and Fatah that would effectively sidetrack Hamas's overwhelming political dominance over the Palestinian parliament.

And, not for the first time, President George W. Bush had personally approved this secret intervention in the affairs of an elected government.

Each man carried a bulging briefcase which contained the details of their secret mission. Success would have a dramatic effect on Israel's relationship with Hamas and the new generation of Middle East political leaders. The men about to board the plane for their long flight to Houston, Texas, knew that any of those leaders would block what they hoped to achieve.

One leader was Bashar al-Assad, at thirty-four years old, the president of Syria for the past six years. He came to office after his elder brother, Basil al-Assad, had been groomed by their father, Hafez al-Assad, the country's long-serving tyrant, to take over. When Hafez died in June 2002, it should have been Basil who became president leaving Bashar to pursue his career as a London-trained eye surgeon where he had received his degree and met his wife. But one foggy night in January 1994, Basil crashed his Mercedes outside Damascus with fatal consequences and Bashar found himself lined up by his father to ensure the Assad dynasty continued.

Mossad analysts decided he could become one of the "potentially more open and progressive Arab leaders who might rule with a broader vision of the world." That hope steadily faded. On foreign policy issues above all, in his determination to cast Syria as the Arab champion of resistance to American and Israeli dominance, Bashar al-Assad had, in Meir Dagan's words, "clearly shown he has his father's political DNA." Bashar al-Assad had, it was broadly assumed, approved the Syrian-inspired assassination of the former Lebanese leader, Rafiq Hariri. The murder led to violence in Beirut and had forced Bashar to pull Syria's troops out of Lebanon. In a defiant speech in Damascus, the president made it clear the withdrawal was not permanent. His other ambition was to reoccupy the Golan Heights.

The men on the plane suspected Iran's president Ahmadinejad would have no hesitation in dispatching one of his death squads to murder the Fatah delegation as further proof he would do anything to ensure he remained on track for achieving his aim to "wipe Israel from the face of the earth." The Fatah quartet had taken great care to ensure that Hamas's volatile leader in Gaza, Mahmoud Zahhar, was unaware of what was afoot. The day before, each man had slipped quietly out of Gaza and through Ezez, the main Israeli checkpoint crossing from the Gaza Strip into Israel. Behind them they left men who smoked the *shisha* pipe, the water pipe smoked throughout the Middle East, and listened to the recordings of Umm Kulthoum, the region's iconic female Arab vocalist, and dreamed of the destruction of the Jewish state. Encouraged by the Hamas election victory, it had become a living, vibrant hope.

The Fatah group had been brought to Ben Gurion airport in a taxi provided by the Israeli government, who were aware there was one other powerful group who would violently oppose what they hoped to achieve with that "backdoor channel." It was Hezbollah. The organization represented the divide between two great branches of Islam that stretches back to the early history of the religion. While the Sunnis were the major branch throughout most of the Islamic world, the Shias had a larger number of followers in Iraq and south Lebanon and were dominant in Iran.

The division extended to the terror organizations. Osama bin Laden was a Sunni, al-Qaeda is predominantly Sunni and continues to be financed by Saudi Arabia, which is a Sunni society. Hezbollah is a Shia organization, which relies heavily on organizational support from Iran, which continues to supply it weapons. In the wake of Hamas's political victory, Iran had further fostered its common cause against Israel with Hezbollah. While Jibril Rajoud was secretly meeting with Uri Saguy in safe houses provided by Mossad, Mahmoud Zahhar met with Hezbollah's leader in Lebanon, Hassan Nasrallah, the chief power broker of the 1.4 million Shia community in the country. Intelligent, charismatic, and a born street orator, Nasrallah's entire career had been shaped by Israel's repeated interventions in Lebanon, from the civil war in the mid-1970s to when the Israeli Defense Force had unilaterally withdrawn from southern Lebanon after years of failing to subdue Hezbollah.

Just as his brother's death had led to Bashar al-Assad becoming Syria's president, it was an assassination that had paved the way for Nasrallah's rise to absolute power. In 1992 an Israeli gunship killed Nasrallah's mentor, his predecessor Abbas Moussawi. Since then Nasrallah has survived similar attempts by Mossad to kill him with explosives planted in both his home and his office in Beirut. Each failure to assassinate him has enhanced his status across the Arab world. Feted in Damascus and Tehran by its leaders, his photograph was displayed in the teeming streets as an example "of [my] being able to take the blows dished out by Israel and remain standing" (he told the author).

Born in August 1960, the eldest of nine children, Nasrallah aspired to be a cleric from an early age. In his teens he was sent to the great Shia theological center in Najaf in Iraq. During his two-year study he met Moussawi and became an early disciple. He returned to Lebanon during the Israeli invasion of the country in 1982 and became a commander in Hezbollah. He showed an aptitude for military tactics, which went with his by now well-honed political skills. When Israel withdrew in May 2002, Nasrallah was by then firmly established as Hezbollah's leader and was hailed in the Muslim world as the Arab warlord who had triumphed over Israel. In 2005, he orchestrated Hezbollah gaining twenty-nine seats in the Lebanese parliament following the departure of Syrian troops twenty-nine years after they had first arrived in the country.

Tehran launched a propaganda campaign to make him a living legend. Feature films, television "documentaries," and books were devoted with one simple message: while secular ideologies, from pan-Arabism to Arab socialism, had failed to liberate an inch of Arab territory, Islamism—in its Iranian Khomeinist version—working through Hezbollah, had achieved "total victory" over Israel in Lebanon.

Now, on that February day in 2006, Hezbollah, working with Hamas, was preparing to launch an even greater assault on the Jewish state. For the eight men ensconced in their first-class seats on the way to Houston, the hope was that they could thwart that attack.

The seating arrangement on the plane was a reminder of the deep divisions that divided their people and why they had agreed to make their long flight to Houston. The four Israelis sat on one side of the cabin, the Fatah group on the other. During meals and visits to the bathroom, they exchanged little more than polite conversation. But for the most part, they either dozed or studied the documents in their briefcases.

During the past weeks there had been discreet contacts with Edward P. Djerejian, the sixty-five-year-old former United States ambassador to Israel and Syria. He had been approved by Secretary of State Condoleezza Rice to act as moderator for the discussions that would take place at the James A. Baker Institute for Public Policy in Houston. It is widely regarded as one of the most secure think tanks within the

United States. The choice of Djerejian was also an astute one. An experienced Arabist and also trusted by Israel, he was calm and his authority was accompanied by a sense of humor. He had told Dr. Rice, to whom he would report progress, that "it's going to be like chairing the United Nations." One of Djerejian's first tasks would be to tell the two teams that he would be totally impartial. It was a necessary reminder: for the past several decades America's Middle East policy had revolved around its relationship with Israel. While there had been what former CIA director, George Tenet, had called "blips on the radar," the combination of Washington's unwavering support for Israel, and its own efforts to spread democracy throughout the region, had inflamed Islamic opinion. In Arab capitals the bond between the two countries was seen as based on shared strategic interests and the demands promoted by the powerful Jewish lobby within the United States. Even though other special-interest groups had some effect on aspects of U.S. foreign policy, none had managed to convince Americans, as the lobby had, that America's interests and those of Israel were essentially identical.

That fusing began after the October War in 1973 when Israel had been seriously threatened by superior Arab forces. To ensure that could never happen again, Washington had provided the Jewish state with a level of support far greater than it had given to any other nation. Since then, Israel had received over $3 billion in direct assistance—worth about $500 a year for every Israeli man, woman, and child. The largesse was particularly striking as Israel was, by the new millennium, a wealthy industrial country with a per capita income equal to that of Spain or South Korea. Other countries in receipt of U.S. foreign aid tend to receive the money in quarterly installments. Israel, on the other hand, gets its entire appropriation at the start of each fiscal year. This enables Israel to earn valuable interest on the stock markets of the world using money it will only later draw down.

There are other terms which give Israel "favored status." It is allowed to use 25 percent of its allocation to subsidize its own defense industry; again, no other nation is allowed to use U.S. funds for that purpose. Neither does Israel have to account for how the money is spent; this makes it hard for Washington to prevent the allocation being only partly used for purposes which it opposes, such as building settlements on the West Bank. Moreover, Washington has encouraged Israel's burgeoning defense industry to use a substantial amount of the annual budget it provides to develop the latest weapons systems. Some of these have been created from material stolen from the United States (see chapter 10, "A Dangerous Liaison"). The United States has also given Israel, at production costs, Black Hawk helicopters and F-16 jets. To top it all off, it has given the Jewish state vital intelligence it refuses to share with its NATO allies and has continued to allow Israel to increase its arsenal of nuclear weapons.

On the day their aircraft headed out from Ben Gurion airport, the men in their first-class armchairs would have seen on their left the distant outline of Dimona, the country's nuclear facility where over two hundred kinds of nuclear weapons were stored in 2006.

Equally important, successive U.S. administrations provided Israel with invaluable diplomatic support. Since 1982 the United States has vetoed more than thirty significant resolutions critical of Israel: this was more than all the numbers of vetoes cast by all the other Security Council members. U.S. diplomatic support had also included blocking the efforts to put Israel's nuclear arsenal on the International Atomic Energy Agency's agenda—which would have laid Dimona open to inspection. Time and again America supported Israel in time of war and used its influence when negotiating peace. Successive U.S. administrations had protected Israel against Soviet threats and later played a crucial role in the 1993 Oslo Accords. Meir Amit, the former Mossad chief and in 2006 still an "elder" of the intelligence community, recalled (to the author): "There may have been occasional bumps along the way, but Washington consistently supported our position." Rafi Eitan, Mossad's retired director of operations and in 2006 the head of a small political grouping of pensioners in the Knesset, remembered: "Time and again Israel has found Washington functioning as our unpaid lawyer on the world stage."

Eitan was among those who believed that Israel, for its part, had been a "valuable asset" to the United States during the cold war. "In many ways we had acted as Washington's proxy by helping to contain Soviet expansion in the region and inflicting heavy defeats on Soviet client states like Egypt and Syria. We had also helped to protect another U.S. ally, like Jordan, and, of course, we passed on important intelligence about Soviet intentions."

But Israel had also provided sensitive military technology, either sent directly from the United States to the Jewish state or developed within its own defense industry, to countries like China and South Africa. The

State Department's inspector general had described this as "a systematic, and continuing to grow, pattern of unauthorized transfers. Israel also remains the most aggressive in running operations against the U.S. of any ally."

Since 9/11 Israel and the United States has become even closer enjoined—"like identical twins" Meir Dagan said—due to the war against terrorism. Part of that relationship has been to allow Tel Aviv a free hand on how it would deal with Hamas in the Gaza Strip and with Hezbollah's threat on Israel's northern border.

It was against that background that the Houston discussions began. Much of the initial tension revolved around Uri Saguy. While he was seen in Israel as a hawk who had turned dove and the first to detect what he called "a sea of change in Damascus," it was a judgment which made him unpopular in Israel together with his argument that the Golan Heights must be surrendered. But to Fatah he was also the man who had approved Mossad assassinations including attempts on Yasser Arafat's life. Jibril Rajoud, for one, felt that "the jury is still out" on how Arafat had died. "Natural causes or murder, we may never now know," he said.

At the end of each meeting, using secure communication links provided by the U.S. State Department, Rajoud reported to President Mahmoud Abbas and Saguy briefed Ehud Olmert. That briefing, by agreement, had included Meir Dagan. It was in every sense Olmert's first real taste of international politics. The rise of the sixty-one-year-old lawyer had been meteoric as it was unexpected. Injured while serving in the Israeli Defense Forces as a combat officer, Olmert had completed his military service as a journalist on the Forces' *BaMahne* magazine. An untaxing position, it also had an unforeseen benefit. During the Yom Kippur War of 1973, Olmert joined General Ariel Sharon's headquarters as a military reporter. Sharon took a liking to the tall Olmert in his carefully pressed uniform and shoulder pip, which identified him as a lieutenant. Others saw him as "arrogant, cold, cunning, and unpleasant." That judgment, by Israeli's historian Tom Segev, would follow Olmert after he took a law degree at the Hebrew University in Jerusalem and opened a successful law partnership. From there it was but a step into political life. In 1973, at the age of twenty-eight, he became the youngest member of the Knesset. "I was often impetuous and wrong in the early years," he later admitted. He opposed

Israel's withdrawal from the Sinai land captured in the Six-Day War and had voted against the Camp David Peace Accords in 1978. The year before, he had also been embroiled in a political finance scandal involving Jerusalem businessmen, organized crime, and corrupt legislators. Though he was later acquitted, he was unable to shake off his image of a fat-cat lawyer tainted by sleaze.

On the February day the negotiators had flown out to Houston, an inquiry was announced into the 1999 sale and leaseback of Olmert's Jerusalem house in allegedly questionable circumstances. But soon events brewing in Lebanon would see the investigation firmly placed on the back burner of Israel's legal system. In the meantime, Olmert had become a rising but colorless politician, holding portfolios that included health, communications, and finance until, in 2003, he became Sharon's deputy prime minister. By then he learned to control his temper with reporters and had cultivated an air of being shrewd. Benjamin Netanyahu, the new leader of Likud, the party Sharon had left to form Kadima, said that Olmert is "a very clever guy." Certainly, while withdrawal went against Olmert's hawkish views, he also now believed it was the only response to the changing demographics of a growing Palestinian population which could eventually outvote Israelis.

Olmert's political position was one of the few times he found favor among his own family. His wife, Aliza, a left-wing playwright and a painter whom he had met at college, publicly admitted she had been at odds with his right-wing politics for much of their thirty-five-year marriage. Their children shared her dovish views. His daughter, Danna, a lesbian who lived openly with her girlfriend in Tel Aviv, was an active member of Machson Watch, a group monitoring Palestinian rights in Gaza and the West Bank. She had barely spoken to her father since he withdrew funding for an annual gay parade in the city in 2006. His eldest son, Shaul, had signed a petition refusing to serve in the Israeli army when he was ordered to duty in the occupied Palestinian territories. His brother, Ariel, named from Olmert's admiration of Sharon, had avoided his military service by moving to Paris.

Just as with Syria's Bashar al-Assad and Hassan Nasrallah, circumstances had intervened to change Ehud Olmert's future. When Sharon announced he was leaving Likud to implement his plans for radical political adjustment that would take into account the demographic changes of a growing Palestinian population, Olmert had been one of the first to join him. When Sharon had collapsed from a massive stroke in January 2006, a month before the joint Israeli-Fatah team flew to Houston, Olmert became acting prime minister. When Kadima won the election, Olmert became head of a coalition government with the Labour party.

Weeks before then, the secret "backdoor channel" that came into operation after a series of meetings in Houston had—like so many other expectations involving the Middle East—achieved little. Saguy commented, "It's really a question of whether we both saw the glass as being half full or half empty."

Mossad analysts had already decided the Houston meetings were doomed to failure after Mahmoud Abbas had made it clear that underpinning them was his plan to solve his own mounting internal crisis in Gaza. Daily the plan brought closer the possibility of a civil war involving Fatah and Hamas as gun battles spread across the Gaza Strip between the two organizations. Hamas was determined to hang on to political power. Abbas saw resolution in what he called the "prisoners' covenant," a document worked out by Hamas and Fatah prisoners in Israeli jails and designed to be "a platform for national reconciliation." Abbas had seized upon the covenant as a solution to the crisis erupting all around him. What he had failed to take into account was that his search for an internal solution in Gaza had reduced his "already desperately narrow space for compromise in future peace negotiations with Israel," one analyst wrote.

Shlomo Ben-Ami, a former foreign minister of Israel, had echoed that view. "It is one thing to work out a platform for an internal peace with Hamas and quite another to ask Israel to subscribe to such a platform. Referenda are supposed to approve peace deals; they are not made in advance of peace negotiations to tie the hands of the negotiators."

The flaws in Abbas's initiative arose from the wrong assumption that he could reconcile his domestic crisis and use a united Hamas Fatah alliance to strong-arm Israel into reopening peace talks or face the consequence of renewed attacks. There was much more in the covenant that the Mossad analysts knew would be rejected. One example was its repetitive demand for Palestinian refugees to return to their former lands in Israel, the mystical "right of return." The document also represented a clear departure from Fatah's willingness to consider compromises on border adjustments and the controversial position of Jerusalem. All these had been stumbling blocks in the past. Now the document made it clear that they were non-negotiable. Legitimized by

Abbas's endorsement, it led to further radicalization of Fatah and the growing fear in Israel that it did not have a negotiating partner on the Palestinian side, regardless of who was in office in Gaza and the West Bank. The expectations of Houston, never high, were now dead.

As the first quarter of 2006 drew to a close, for part of what was called "the education of Ehud Olmert," Mossad continued, on the sixth floor of its headquarters, to supply the new prime minister with only carefully selected intelligence. The mood within Mossad was that Olmert was still struggling to shake off the shadow of his illustrious predecessor, Ariel Sharon. With tensions mounting in Gaza and the West Bank, and farther north on the border with Lebanon and in the Beka'a Valley, the fear was that Olmert did not yet have Ariel Sharon's capability to see what Meir Dagan called "the big picture." Israelis continued to have deep reservations about Olmert's political decisions, though few would deny they could count on "Arik"—the nickname that the comatose Sharon had enjoyed all his political life—to fight in their corner. And unlike other flamboyant characters who had occupied the prime minister's office—including the iconic Yitzhak Rabin and the driven "Bibi" Netanyahu—Ehud Olmert gave the impression of being the backroom, career politician who had risen, almost without trace, to implement Sharon's plan to complete Israel's unilateral withdrawal from the Palestinian territories it had occupied since the Six-Day War in 1967. While Israelis were open to persuasion by Ariel Sharon, they increasingly wondered if Olmert had the skills to ensure that Israel would not be drawn into conflict. In a martial nation like Israel, whose voters have traditionally been reassured by the presence of a battle-hardened veteran at the political helm, Meir Dagan knew that Olmert faced a massive task in trying to convince his countrymen that their security was as safe in his hands as it had been under Ariel Sharon.

With Mahmoud Abbas's power base in Gaza almost daily being further eroded and Hamas's continued rhetoric against its near neighbor, Ehud Olmert became more belligerent. While Israeli prime ministers have rarely been inclined to demonstrate restraint when responding to Arab provocation because the eye-for-an-eye ethos is far too deeply ingrained in the national psyche, the language coming from the new prime minister raised the question: Just how serious was his government in coming to a negotiated settlement with the Palestinians?

Mossad analysts increasingly felt that irrespective of the pledges Ehud Olmert had given President Bush and Prime Minister Blair about adhering to the principles of the much-maligned "road map" for a permanent Arab/Israeli peace deal, Olmert would welcome the chance for a military resolution with Hamas and Hezbollah, a view his generals also encouraged. They saw it as one way to deal with the "plight of the Palestinians," the potent propaganda tool for radical Islamic groups in the Middle East and beyond—a tool which would remain as long as the Palestinian aspirations for statehood remained unfulfilled. There was a feeling in Mossad that Ehud Olmert wanted an opportunity to show he was as rough as Ariel Sharon, both as politician and as a military leader. That feeling had been reinforced by what Meir Dagan described at his weekly senior staff meeting in early May 2006, as "a Shia expansion." He asked them to "join the dots" and find answers to pressing questions. What was the exact nature of the current link between Hezbollah and Hamas after Iran's President Ahmadinejad had publicly embraced the Sunni organization? What was the involvement of Iran in Gaza and the West Bank? Was there evidence of a shift of power between Syria and Iran, which could change the geopolitics of the region for the foreseeable future?

The answers were not reassuring. The signs were that the doctrinal, cultural, and political differences between the Sunni Hamas and the Shia Hezbollah were being buried in the common cause to destroy Israel. Bashar al-Assad, who has a powerful resemblance to his father— the same high forehead and piercing eyes—had begun to try and steer Syria clear of the theocratic militancy of Iran his father had supported, but in the complex religious map of the region, the al-Assads are members of a minority Shia sect in a predominantly Sunni majority Syria. But increasingly the new power of the Iraqi Shia—65 percent of the population—had allowed Iran to profit enormously from their dominant role in that chaotic country. A Mossad report revealed: "Iraq's Shia leaders regularly visit Tehran to settle issues such as border security and developing joint energy projects. Iranian businessmen are investing heavily in Iraq's overwhelmingly Shia southern regions and Iran's highly skilled intelligence operatives are embedded in Iraq's nascent security forces and within the Shia militias who rule the streets of Basra."

Even more worrying for Israel, Mossad undercover agents reported the growing presence of those spies in the Hezbollah strongholds in the Beka'a Valley. It was there that the organization was believed to have stockpiled its growing supply of missiles and rockets supplied by Iran. One Mossad report put the figure at 18,000. This number included the Katyusha rockets made in Russia, which have a range of fifteen kilometers. More powerful were the Iranian-built Fajr-3 missiles, almost six meters long, which have a range of almost forty kilometers. Most powerful of all was Iran's version of a Scud missile, the Shabtai-1. They could reach any Israeli city. When Iraqi Scuds rained down on Haifa and Tel Aviv during the Desert Storm conflict in 1991 (see chapter 16, "Spies in the Sand"), hundreds of buildings were destroyed and scores of civilians injured. One of Mossad's *yaholomin*, the electronic surveillance units, had picked up conversations between Mahmoud Ahmadinejad and Khalid Meshal in his fortress-like villa in a suburb in the north of Damascus. Meshal, who had survived a Mossad assassination attempt in Amman, Jordan, was now the overall strategist for Hamas and a respected figure within Hezbollah.

Meir Dagan was a good example that much intelligence is anti-historical because it uses stratagems to frustrate the truth as well as unearth it. Facts are often directed toward some distant, unwritten goal, and it is the highest purpose of any intelligence to leave complicity hidden and ambiguous. At the Mossad training school, the Sources and Methods class reminds students that they cannot simply adhere to the historian's discipline; that a perfect historian must possess an imagination sufficiently powerful to make his narrative affecting and picturesque, but he must control it so absolutely to work only with the material on hand and refrain from supplementing deficiencies with additions of his own. But the class instructor explained that in intelligence work the deficiencies are precisely what is expected to be supplied. "Action cannot wait for certainty. Motive deception will be at the center of their endeavors. They will create situations to draw fact out of the darkness. The art of informed conjecture will be part of their skills, but always to be used within the range of probability. Their writ will confine them to the realm of surmise," one of the instructors told the author.

Those finely-honed skills had served Meir Dagan well. Now they went into overdrive after Mohammad Khatami, a senior member of the Iranian leadership, in the second week of May described Hezbollah as "the sun of Islam who will soon shine even brighter." A few days later President Ahmadinejad ended another of his anti-Semitic harangues to a Tehran crowd with the promise: "We shall very soon witness the elimination of the Zionist state of shame." Was this merely more rabble-rousing rhetoric? Or was it finally the precursor of what Dagan had long predicted: an attack on Israel on two fronts—Hamas in Gaza and Hezbollah coming out of the olive and banana groves of south Lebanon and the Beka'a Valley? And would that be the moment Iran would mobilize its Revolutionary Guards and would al-Qaeda seize the opportunity to marshal its untold numbers of jihadists throughout the Muslim worlds? To try and find answers Meir Dagan had sent encoded priority signals to Mossad stations across the Middle East to report signs of mobilization. Then he refreshed himself on Hezbollah and its previous methods.

Throughout the 1980s the organization, having adopted the name of the "Party of God," kidnapped more than two hundred nationals in Lebanon—mainly American or western Europeans, including Terry Waite, the Archbishop of Canterbury's envoy. It had organized the highjacking of civilian aircrafts and had more or less pioneered the idea of suicide bombings against American and French targets—killing almost 1,000 people—including 241 U.S. Marines in Beirut and 58 French paratroopers.

By the time the Iran-Iraq War was over, Tehran saw the "Party of God" as a trump card it could play in the Middle East by using it to influence the broader course of regional politics and to wage a low-intensity war against Israel. The emergence of Hassan Nasrallah led to Hezbollah controlling southern Lebanon. Financially it cost Iran very little—no more than one day's profit from its oil revenue at €50 million a year—to maintain Hezbollah. However, Hezbollah was also funded by income from businesses set up by the movement. These included a bank, a mortgage cooperative, an insurance company, six hotels, a chain of supermarkets across south Lebanon and the Beka'a Valley, a dozen urban bus and taxi companies, and a travel agency that sends tens of thousands of pilgrims to Mecca and other Muslim holy places. Between them they provide Hezbollah with €300 million a year.

The Beka'a Valley had become its power base, centered on the historic city of Balbeck, with its own modern hospital and staffed by Syrian and Iranian doctors and nurses. It also ran clinics, a social welfare system, centers for orphans and widows, and schools—where the syllabus was identical to the one taught in Iran. It collected its own taxes with a 20 percent levy, called *khoms*, on all incomes. All this contributed to the image of Hezbollah being an independent state within the state of Lebanon. To emphasize its status, it had a number of "embassies"; the one in Tehran is the largest; others are situated in Yemen, Damascus, and Beirut.

Its relationship with the rest of Lebanon was complex. In May 2006, it still held 14 seats in the 128-seat national assembly, including 2 portfolios in the council of ministers. But Hezbollah also insisted it was primarily "a people-based movement fighting on behalf of the Muslim world." To reinforce that idea, it has a powerful media department, including its satellite television channel, al-Manar (the lighthouse), which transmitted to the entire Arab world and was regarded by many viewers as better than al-Jazeera. Supporting its rolling news channel were four radio stations, two newspapers, several magazines, and a book publishing house. Its own police force worked within Sharia law and Hezbollah courts sent the convicted to its own prisons in the Beka'a Valley.

Mossad estimated its militia numbered nine thousand in May 2006: the well-equipped fighters were backed by an estimated three hundred thousand reservists. It was a more powerful force than the Lebanese armed forces that were supposed to have disarmed it under the United Nations Resolution 1559. That was unlikely to happen, given the majority of the army were Shi'ites and would refuse to fight their own.

Within Iran, Hezbollah's support bridged the political divides within the ruling establishment. The country's mullahs, whether "reformist" or "hardliner," regarded Hezbollah as a reminder of their own revolutionary youth. In the same week that Mohammad Khatami and President Ahmadinejad had delivered their chilling words, the Majlis, the Iranian Parliament, had temporarily set aside their arguments to unite in demanding that the Revolutionary Guards should be ready to fight alongside Hezbollah should Hassan Nasrallah call upon them. The deputies had also agreed to send Hamas an "emergency grant as a gift" to counter the freeze imposed by the European Union and other international donations intended for the new Palestinian government. It was Iran's first move to marginalize Mahmoud Abbas and make Hamas the only legitimate representative of the Palestinian people. In Lebanon, Hezbollah had begun to lean on the new pro-American coalition government led by Fouad Siniora and Walid Jumblatt, the Druze leader.

For Meir Dagan the situation was starkly clear. Iran was positioning itself to expand its influence through what could be a pincer movement by Hamas and Hezbollah—the war on two fronts the intelligence chief had long feared. Success for Tehran would mean for the first time since the seventh century its direct power would have extended to the shores of the Mediterranean. If Israel were to launch a preemptive strike—under the guise of being the regional champion of Western democracy at the frontline in the fight against political Islam—it might earn the approval of the Bush administration, but it would leave Israel exposed to fierce criticism elsewhere. Meir Dagan's advice to Olmert was that Israel should continue to "wait and see." In the meantime, two of his predecessors, Efraim Halevy and Meir Amit, also started to sound a warning.

After four years at the helm, Efraim Halevy had departed as Mossad's spymaster as quietly as he had arrived. Within Mossad ranks, the memory of his studious presence—his thin lips pursed before speaking, his eyes impassive behind his spectacles—had been largely forgotten. Those who did remember him on the upper floors spoke of Halevy as the man who spectacularly failed to lead the service into the new millennium and failed to make it a force to be reckoned with. In 2008 he published his memoir of those days, *Man in the Shadows*. It was an unsuccessful attempt to tell his side of the criticism that had dogged him throughout most of his tenure. But it also provided a platform for him to issue a warning: the further Israel is from the last attack, and for that matter, the countries of Europe and the United States, the closer it is to the next one. "Much of what lies ahead can only be achieved in a clandestine manner. In order to triumph we shall have to understand that diplomacy is the art of the possible, that intelligence is the craft of the impossible. And life is fast becoming more impossible than ever in human history," he said (to the author).

In between time spent in London to launch his book and talking to Nathan, the Mossad station chief, he spoke to the author about his belief that the United States and Britain would have to "make fateful decisions" concerning their Middle East policies. "In Iran and Iraq they cannot simply gather their troops and head for home. They must adopt a firm exit strategy, one that will need a positive contribution from Israel. That will mean being sensitive to our interests and visions." He concluded by delivering a grim warning: "We are looking down the barrel of World War Three unless the world wakes up."

Shortly afterward, Meir Amit, now a member of Israel's leading think-tank, spoke out (to the author): "Israel must continue to take strong measures to defend itself. Terrorism is like a cancer, spreading silently and effectively. No nation can fight it alone. Saddam Hussein is yesterday's monster. But we have a new one in Iran, whipping up the Shia revolutionary hurricane that will soon engulf Israel and, left unchecked, will engulf the world beyond our borders."

The first breeze of that hurricane was already starting to blow across the Gaza Strip.

A reminder of the constant terrorist threat to Israel came when Swiss intelligence, working closely with a Mossad agent in the country and officers of France's DGSE, disrupted a well-prepared plot to shoot down an El-Al passenger plane with a rocket propelled grenade as it flew in to land at Geneva airport. Documents recovered from the seven Algerians responsible showed the plot had been masterminded from Madrid. Shortly before the attack, its two al-Qaeda operators returned to North Africa.

But cooperation did not always run so smoothly. Meir Dagan received a report from his Mossad agent in New York of a closed-door discussion between foreign ministers after intelligence predictions. These suggested that Iran was, in May 2006, "possibly only a year away from producing a nuclear device." Tension erupted at the meeting when Russia's foreign minister, Sergey Lavrov, verbally attacked the U.S. State Department official, Nicholas Burns, who was the senior adviser to the meeting's host, Condoleezza Rice. Lavrov accused Burns of "seeking to undermine our efforts to resolve the crisis with Iran." Ministers from Britain, France, Germany, and China, all members of the United Nations Security Council, were stunned at Lavrov's outburst in the Waldorf-Astoria Hotel suite where they had gathered. The Mossad agent's report offered a revealing insight into the backroom disagreement of high-level diplomacy.

It was British foreign minister Margaret Beckett's first day in her post and she was taken aback by how bad-tempered the discussion had become. Lavrov had arrived late and was still furious about a speech U.S. Vice President Cheney had just made in Lithuania in which he had criticized Kremlin policies. Lavrov castigated Dr. Rice and her team using the kind of language, Minister Beckett was heard to say, that was more in line with Cold War rhetoric. At one point, Lavrov threatened to veto a security council resolution that Britain and France had drafted and which Washington supported. It was a new attempt to persuade Iran to give up its uranium enrichment program.

Despite efforts by John Sawers, the British Foreign Office political director, to calm matters, Lavrov continued to rage. At another point, he attacked Israel claiming its policies were "designed to drag us all into conflict." Dr. Rice intervened by telling Lavrov he was "not being helpful." During dinner the row rumbled on until Lavrov abruptly left. The next day over breakfast John Sawers sat down with senior delegates from China, France, the United States, and Germany to find a proposal to put before the foreign ministers at their lunch. It would give Iran a new trade deal with the West, security guarantees against any attack from Israel, and nuclear technology "which will only be used for non-aggressive purposes" on condition Iran would halt all production of weapons-grade uranium.

Over lunch—salmon and California Chablis, which the French delegation barely touched—Dr. Rice emphasized the proposal was "a major shift in our policy." However, Margaret Beckett had been briefed that it was doubtful Iran would accept it. The meal broke up with the decision to put the matter on hold for further discussion—diplomatic-speak meaning that it had little chance of success. At a summit of Islamic heads of state in Indonesia a few days later, President Ahmadinejad said, "I will consider negotiating with anyone except Israel. It has no place on this earth."

The Mossad agent monitoring the conference had more disturbing news. Russian officials attending the conference as "observers" had secretly offered to sell Iran technology that could help protect its nuclear secrets from international scrutiny. The equipment would include state-of-the-art security encryption technology developed by Atlas Elektronik, a Russian government-controlled defense company.

As May drew to a close, the Israeli Defense Forces (IDF) found themselves increasingly responding to Hamas rocket attacks on settlements. Encouragement for Hamas to continue its guerrilla warfare grew more vociferous from Tehran. A Mossad deep-cover agent in the Iranian capital sent the first details of a hitherto unknown nuclear underground site in northern Iran at Abe-e Ali. The report revealed that over three hundred Chinese and North Korean nuclear experts were working to produce a new centrifuge to enable the high-speed purification of uranium to achieve the 90 percent level required for weapons-grade. Ehud Olmert agreed with Meir Dagan that the evidence was of such great importance the Mossad chief and Nathan should fly to London, and then on to Washington.

For several hours over orange juice, coffee, and sandwiches the two men showed John Scarlett and other MI6 officers the evidence acquired from inside Iran. It included close-up photographs of the Abe-e Ali complex and two new workshops at the Natanz uranium enrichment plant. Dagan's briefing formed a key part of a meeting of Britain's defense chiefs after Condoleezza Rice told Prime Minister Blair that "if all else fails on the diplomatic front, we are prepared to go it alone, or with the assistance of our good friend, Israel." An official who was at the meeting told the author, "She made it plain that going it alone meant military action."

The meeting was held in the monolithic Ministry of Defence building in Whitehall and was chaired by General Sir Michael Walker, the chief of Britain's defense staff. The Foreign Office team was led by William Ehrman, director general of the defense office, and David Landman, head of the nuclear proliferation department. Both had played an important role in bringing Libya out of the political wilderness. John Scarlett and Eliza Manningham-Buller were on hand to brief the meeting on Israel's position. For the first time the Pentagon battle plans for an all-out assault on Iran were on the table. Tactical Tomahawk cruise missiles would be launched from U.S. navy ships and submarines in the Gulf to target Iran's air defense systems at the nuclear installations. The updated Tomahawks had an onboard facility that allowed them to be reprogrammed while in flight to attack an alternative target once the initial one was destroyed. Each missile also had a "loitering" capability over a target area to provide damage assessment through its on-board TV camera. U.S. Air Force B2 stealth bombers, each equipped with eight 4,500-pound bunker-busting bombs, would fly from Diego Garcia, the isolated U.S. navy base in the Indian Ocean, the Whiteman USAF base in Missouri, and the USAF base at Fairford in Gloucestershire, England. Each meter-long bomb of hardened steel could penetrate six meters of concrete. There would be no ground-force follow-up attacks.

The meeting attendees then went on to discuss the risks associated with such an attack. The details were subsequently obtained by the author and are published here for the first time. The meeting attendees were told that an American-led attack could trigger "devastating repri-sals" against the 8,500 British troops based in Iraq and the 4,000 Brit-ish soldiers who had arrived in Afghanistan. Ehrman reminded them that both countries had strong religious and political ties to Iran. Walker predicted the attack might be preceded by Washington reorganizing its plan to withdraw a substantial number of troops from Iraq. It would also certainly lead to confrontation with China and Russia—whose sup-port would lead to Iran cutting off its oil supplies to the West. Scarlett cited Meir Dagan's view that the offensive on Iran would see a dramatic increase in suicide bomber attacks against Israel. The intelligence chief added that MI6 intelligence could provide no guarantee that an aerial assault on Iran would destroy the eight identified targets the Pentagon designated. These targets were:

- Saghand, a mining operation set to begin later this year, yielding fifty-to-sixty tons of uranium annually.
- Ardkan, where ore is purified to produce uranium ore concen-trate known as yellowcake.
- Gehine, a mining and milling facility.
- Esfahan, where yellowcake is cleansed of impurities and con-verted to uranium hexafluoride gas.
- Natanz, an enrichment site, which can be used to produce weapons-grade uranium.
- Tehran, a research reactor and radioactive waste storage facility.
- Bushehr, a Russian-built light water reactor.
- Arak, a heavy water research reactor.
- Anarak, a nuclear waste storage site.

No date had yet been fixed for an air attack, but if Iran continued its bellicose attitude and ignored demands made by the UN, the Bush ad-ministration could launch military action in 2007, but possibly not later than the run-up to Bush's final year in office in 2008. The present mis-sion plans were two-phased. Cruise missiles would destroy defenses around the targets, then B2 stealth bombers would strike their plants with bunker-busting bombs. The Pentagon estimated the total mission time in the target areas at probably eight hours. Submarines would simultaneously launch rockets.

The meeting studied the latest intelligence on Iran's current ballis-tic missile capability: a total of eighty-five S-300 air defense missiles.

Provided by China, they would be effective against U.S. fighter-bombers, less so against the multi-defense systems of the Tactical Tomahawks. There were also forty X-55 cruise missiles, each with an estimated range of over one thousand miles. They were based close to the border with Turkmenistan. Less than thirty Shabtai-3 rockets provided by China were based in sites in southern Iran, bringing them well within range of Israel. The Shahab-4 rocket was currently being developed near Natanz, south of Tehran. Present intelligence estimates said it would not come on line until 2008. Each would have a range of eight thousand miles—able to strike anywhere in Europe and the United States. The present missiles could be adapted to fire from Iran's twenty-five missile crafts and its three frigates. None, however, could be launched from Iran's air force of two hundred aging aircraft: Tomcats, MiG-29 Fulcrums, and Phantoms. Iran's five hundred thousand army of regulars and conscripts were poorly led and trained. Most of their equipment comes from the former Soviet Union.

The meeting then turned to a lengthy discussion of who, apart from the Blair government and Israel, would support a U.S. attack. The conclusion was that diplomatic support within the European Union would probably only come from Poland.

What the meeting did not know, and which would only emerge in August 2006 (through Seymour Hersh, an investigative journalist), was that President Bush and Vice President Cheney had proposed using nuclear weapons to destroy the uranium enrichment plant at Natanz. The plan had been fiercely opposed by the Chairman of the Joint Chiefs of Staff, marine general Peter Pace. He and other Pentagon commanders, at an equally secret meeting, warned Bush and Cheney of what they saw as "the serious economic, political, and military consequences. A military strike on Natanz would vent fatal radiation for three hundred kilometers." This would include Tehran and its multimillion inhabitants. The Pentagon chiefs argued for dropping the "largest possible bunker bombs available in a multi-drop attack which would generate sufficient force to accomplish what a nuclear warhead would achieve, but without provoking an outcry over what would be the first use of a nuclear weapon in conflict since Nagasaki."

The chance of success by such an attack was challenged. A Pentagon adviser argued that such an attack "would be like bombing water, with its currents and eddies. The bombs would likely be diverted." More certain was that such an attack would be seen throughout the Muslim world as another example of American imperialism and would lead to unprecedented retaliation. Already the growing prospect of such retaliation had come to preoccupy the intelligence services of Britain, Mossad, the CIA, and the Pakistan intelligence service. The threat was centered on a plot, that if successful, would lead to the greatest terrorist outrage the world had ever known.

Since March 2006, Operation Overt had become the largest, most secret and widespread surveillance and intelligence operation ever mounted in Britain, post-WW II. It had quickly widened to include Scotland Yard's antiterrorism squad and its special branch, GCHQ, Britain's spy in the sky; NSA, its counterpart in the United States; the CIA and the FBI, the DGSE in France, Germany's BND, the Pakistani intelligence service and Mossad.

In all some five hundred of the world's most experienced spies were involved in an operation aimed at two British-based cells of suspected Islamic militants who were believed to be plotting a massive terrorist attack. How it would be carried out, the target, and its time and place were still unclear in late May 2006.

For weeks the intelligence teams had been patiently gathering the tentacles that had emerged from suspects uncovered in the "concentric circles" which materialized after the London bombings in July 2005. The first cell had been pinpointed after one suspect had returned from an al-Qaeda training camp in the "badlands" of northern Pakistan. The second cell had been identified as operating out of the Muslim community in the suburbs of south London. Both cells were placed under intense monitoring. All public meetings in both areas were infiltrated by MI5 officers. Telephone contacts by those who attended the gatherings were traced to Paris, Frankfurt, and, as one antiterrorist officer later said, "to all points East and West." E-mails were intercepted by GCHQ and NSA. From listening posts on the island of Cyprus to the deserts of Afghanistan, the mountains of Iran, and the northwest border of Pakistan, the words of cell members and their associates were plucked out of the air, recorded, and sent to the Joint Terrorism Analysis Centre (JTAC) in London's Millbank. Its Anacapa wall charts—specialist diagrams to create a coherent picture from all the incoming information—were constantly updated.

In the world outside, other stories came and went in the headlines. One was the assassination of Abu Musab al-Zarqawi, the murderous leader of al-Qaeda in Iraq. In late June 2006 his hideout near Baghdad was devastated by a laser-bomb attack. He had tried to crawl to safety, but had been shot by U.S. Special Forces. They were led to al-Zarqawi by a whistleblower in his midst. The man received "a very substantial payment" and was given a new identity in a country of his choice. He was assured its whereabouts would forever remain a secret.

Also in late June 2006, Hamas militants in Gaza kidnapped an Israeli soldier, Corporal Gilad Shalit. Israel promptly launched a massive offensive against targets in the territory. Ostensibly it was to recover Shalit. In reality it was the precursor of the war in Lebanon that started in July 2006. That was confirmed by Ehud Olmert on July 12 when Hezbollah guerrillas killed eight Israeli soldiers and kidnapped two more on the border of south Lebanon. Ehud Olmert called it "an act of war." Two days later, with strong support from Israel, the U.S. and British missions at the United Nations opposed a motion on a ceasefire. By then, the first Hezbollah rockets rained down on Haifa and other towns in northern Israel. Israel's powerful air force had made its first strikes on south Lebanon and Beirut. The dead were left where they lay, soon numbering a hundred a day. Meir Dagan found himself at the cutting edge of the conflict, deploying his agents into hostile territory.

On October 12, 2011, the abduction of Gilad Shalit (see page 696) ended after five years with the news that Israel had agreed to a "historic deal" for his freedom in exchange for the release of almost one thousand Palestinian prisoners from Israeli jails. The deal involved Mossad chief Tamir Pardo, who for weeks had held secret meetings with Hamas leaders in Gaza. With elections due to be held in Israel and the Palestinian territories in 2012, both sides knew they could make capital from a successful exchange. Pardo, a shrewd tactician, had told hardline prime minister Netanyahu that the return of Shalit would pave the way for further direct political negotiations with Hamas—a prelude to possible peace in the region.

CHAPTER 28

FIGHTING THE FIRES OF SATAN

Every morning before the sun rose over the Judean hills, Israeli Prime

Minister Olmert, who was barely three months into office, routinely

slipped out of the bed he shared with his wife, Aliza. In no time he had

shaved, showered, and dressed in another of his lightweight suits, which

nevertheless would leave him slightly perspiring in the fierce midday

heat. A consolation, he told an aide, was that it was nowhere near as

unbearable as the temperature inside the tanks he had sent across the

border to fight in south Lebanon. By 5 A.M. each day Olmert was read-

ing the overnight intelligence summary left for him on a table. No more

than two foolscap pages long, the document had been prepared by Meir

Dagan and faxed to Olmert. It consisted of little more than bullet points listing the latest number of overnight rocket attacks on Israel's northern cities, the current body count, the number of injured, the number of missions flown by Israeli air force jets, the assessment from Mossad stations around the world of the criticism of Israel, and the mounting demand for a ceasefire.

In those first weeks of July after the war had started, the summary could only have brought little comfort to the man whom Efraim Halevy had dismissed as "just happening to be in the right place when he could make or break his career." Already his domestic critics were asking if Olmert's limited experience of military tactics meant he was the wrong man to lead the war to a successful conclusion for Israel. As July drew to a close and the first body bags with IDF soldiers were brought back for burial, the war showed all the signs of becoming a widespread conflagration. It had all seemed a long way from only two weeks before when President George W. Bush had pronounced at the G-8 summit in Saint Petersburg on July 16, four days into the conflict, that "this is a moment of clarification. It is now clear why we don't have peace in the Middle East and that Iran and Syria are the root causes of instability in the region." Two days later calls came from several governments for the United States to lead the negotiations to end the fighting. But Secretary of State Condoleezza Rice insisted that any ceasefire was not possible "until the conditions are conducive." She never explained what "conducive" meant, brushing aside media requests to do so.

Ehud Olmert had been told by Meir Dagan that Mossad's intelligence from Washington was that the Bush administration believed that a swift war against Hezbollah would serve as a prelude to the eagerly anticipated preemptive attack that the president and his vice president, Dick Cheney, were still convinced was their solution to "why we don't have peace in the Middle East." In the meantime, Mossad agents had uncovered another reason. Al-Qaeda had asked an estimated million-plus jihadists to fight alongside Hezbollah. By mid-July the agents were reporting that from the snow-capped mountains of Afghanistan to the scorching deserts of Saudi Arabia, the call to join the "Holy War" was being answered.

In Washington, however, Olmert knew he could continue to have the support of an impressive number of organizations and individuals who included a number of influential Christian evangelicals—preachers like Jerry Falwell, Gary Bauer, and Marion "Pat" Robertson—as well as Tom DeLay and Dick Armey, who had been majority leaders in the House of Representatives. They were all united in a common belief that Israel's existence was the fulfillment of a biblical prophecy and was "God's will." In their support of Israel, they could count on the support of powerful neoconservative gentiles like John Bolton, now America's ambassador to the United Nations; Robert Bartley, the former editor of the highly respected *Wall Street Journal*; William John Bennett, the former secretary of education; Jeane Kirkpatrick, the former UN ambassador. Between them they had established that in Congress, Israel would remain virtually free of criticism. No nation in the Middle East had gone to war knowing it had such powerful backing.

This must have been a comfort to Ehud Olmert as he was driven in his armor-plated car from his official residence in a Tel Aviv suburb for his first appointment of the day with his generals.

Once hostilities had started, critics—especially those in Europe—found themselves under familiar attack for condemning Israel. The specter of anti-Semitism, never far from the surface, was given a fresh outing. Most of it came from Muslims in Germany and France, which has the largest Muslim population of any European nation. The attacks portrayed Israel in Nazi-like terms, ignoring the incident when a French Jew was murdered in France before the fighting broke out in Lebanon and tens of thousands of demonstrators had filled the city streets to condemn anti-Semitism. Even Jacques Chirac and Dominique de Villepin had attended the victim's funeral service to show their solidarity. The attacks in the Arab press had predictably been more inflammatory. From Tehran to Cairo they had been united in calling Israel's actions "war crimes." Equally predictable, the powerful pro-Israeli elements in the America media had sprung to its defense. One commentator saw it as "a two-word message to be delivered to other hostile regimes: you're next." In case there was any doubt who "next" should be, a radio pundit said: "It is time to turn the screws on Syria." It was described as "terror friendly" by the New York *Daily News*, and "a serious threat to the United States" in *The New Republic*.

The reality was that the Bush administration was now divided over attacking the Damascus regime. While Donald Rumsfeld and Dick Cheney were in favor, both the new head of the CIA, General Michael Hayden, and Condoleezza Rice strongly opposed the idea. Hayden pointed out that Syria continued to provide the CIA with important intelligence about al-Qaeda—the "backdoor channel" had been created when George Tenet had met with Syrian intelligence chiefs after 9/11. The CIA had been given secret access to Mohammed Haydar Zammar who had been identified as one of the recruiters of the hijackers that had flown their planes into the Twin Towers and the Pentagon. Hayden had argued that to attack Syria, either directly or to allow Israel to act as Washington's surrogate, would almost certainly end Damascus's cooperation. Dr. Rice had reminded the president that Syria posed no direct threat to the United States and that an attack would encourage it to foment trouble in neighboring Iraq. "Before any dealings with Syria, it would be sensible to finish our work in Iraq," she was reported as saying to an aide.

Now, on that July morning as Ehud Olmert was driven from his home for his first early morning meeting with his generals, he was fully aware of how much Washington depended on his promise to destroy Hezbollah and its heavily defended interlocked web of bunkers in south Lebanon and the Beka'a Valley. Mission reports on the relentless bombing raids conducted by the Israeli air force were being routed to the American embassy in Tel Aviv and then on to the Pentagon where they were further analyzed. While the State Department saw the bombing campaign as a means to reinforce their encouragement of the Lebanese government to deal more firmly with Hezbollah—a forlorn hope—the Pentagon strategists saw the round-the-clock aerial assault on Hezbollah redoubts as what one former Pentagon official told the author "was a test run for Iran." The official had added, "the only real on-the-ground intelligence we have was from Mossad's undercover agents in Iran. While it confirmed much of what we suspected, and had helped us to devise a proper bombing strategy against Iran's nuclear facilities, we still needed to know how it would play out. The air attacks on south Lebanon and the Beka'a Valley provided such an opportunity."

A hint of that had surfaced when Shabtai Shavit, a former Mossad director and, in 2006, a national security adviser to the Knesset said, "we do what we think is best for us, and it happens to meet America's requirements. That's just part of a relationship between two friends." This would explain why a small team of U.S. Air Force strategists had been in Israel for weeks and had held several meetings with Lieutenant General Dan Halutz, the chief of staff of the Israeli Defense Forces, who during his time in the Israeli air force had helped to prepare the attack plan for an aerial assault on Iran. It was that plan which had been used to launch the air assault on south Lebanon. The effect would once more form the core of the morning meeting in Israel's war room.

The size of a Hezbollah rocket crater—forty by twenty feet—the war room was deep inside the Kirya, the Tel Aviv headquarters of the Israeli Defense Forces. It was accessed by swipe cards whose codes were as closely guarded as the life-or-death decisions made within the feature-less concrete building. Tacked to the olive-green walls were maps and charts showing the progress in the war: the number of IDF air strikes and their targets, bombardment by Israeli warships of the towns and vil-lages around the port city of Tyre, ground advances by the crack Galilee and Nahal divisions into south Lebanon. On a separate chart were the latest figures of rockets launched against northern Israel and the precise location where each Katyusha BM-24 and Fajr-3 rocket had landed. An-other chart listed the armaments Hezbollah still possessed, but had not yet fully used. The Fajr-5 rocket with its range of 55 miles and the dead-liest of them all: the Zelzal-2 Iranian missile with a range of 150 miles. It brought Tel Aviv and the Kirya within its range.

Against one wall was a bank of screens. They brought into the war room unedited footage from IDF cameramen on the frontline: advanc-ing with troops into Arab villages, perched on mine-sweeping bulldoz-ers clearing the way for tanks, or on the hull of the tanks as they ground their way forward, firing as they advanced.

In the center of the room was a conference table made from cedar wood from Galilee. There were twenty chairs around the table. With the sun already high over the Judean hills, they were all occupied by 6:25 A.M. each morning by the men who would direct the war against Hezbollah. The fanaticism and ruthlessness of their opponents had sur-prised them. Their faces showed the strain of long days and shortened hours of often disturbed sleep. They knew before they left the room each morning they would make more life-or-death decisions which, when they were implemented, would draw further harsh criticism from not only around the world, but from within Israel.

A great deal of criticism had been directed against Ehud Olmert from an increasingly bewildered public that had begun to ask what was be-ing gained from a war where the number of Israeli dead rose by the day and tens of thousands cowered in bomb shelters and protected rooms in the north of the country. Hezbollah, far from being crippled, ap-peared to have a limitless supply of rockets and antitank missiles that had destroyed the pride of the IDF army—its latest American-built tanks.

Every morning Israeli Army Radio carried the anguished words to the people that the prime minister had promised to teach Hezbollah a lesson it would never forget—and from which it would never again threaten Israel. And it was not only Hezbollah who would be dealt with. Hamas had continued to attack the Jewish state, creating an effective war on two fronts. Olmert in one of his regular broadcasts had promised the day of reckoning would also soon be upon Hamas. But there was a growing number of Israelis who felt the prime minister not only looked increasingly tired, but sounded ever more uncertain. That would have been noted by his waiting generals in the war room.

Pinned to one wall was a blow-up of an Israeli newspaper editorial: "If Israel fails in this war, it will be impossible to continue to live in the Middle East. What is it about us, the Jews, the few and persecuted? We are not hesitating, apologizing, or relenting. The Jewish state will no longer be trampled underfoot."

By 6:30 A.M. the last cup of coffee had been cleared from the table. Olmert opened proceedings with a political update on the view from Washington. He did not have to remind his listeners there was now only a limited time left to crush Hezbollah. On that July morning Ehud Olmert returned to a question raised previously in the war room. Where did the "hawk of hawks"—U.S. secretary of defense Donald Rumsfeld—stand? Could his virtual silence be no more than a reminder of Rumsfeld's age, that for him this was just another war in a career that dated back to Vietnam in 1975, when Rumsfeld had been a junior White House aide as American troops had withdrawn? Washington's Israeli ambassador had been reassuring—his latest inquiries showed "Rummy remained as enthusiastic as ever over what Israel was doing," Olmert assured the battle-hardened men around the table.

Olmert's preamble done, he handed over the meeting to Meir Dagan, who sat across the table from the prime minister. He, too, had news from Washington. While there was no evident split within the Bush administration, his station chief in the capital had picked up that Condoleezza Rice had modified her position over whether it was not yet "conducive" to formally intervene in the conflict. The Mossad man had learned from his own sources within the State Department that Rice had redefined her role to that "of a mediator waiting to intervene." It was still too early for her to resume her shuttle diplomacy, but she hoped that day was coming soon. In Dagan's judgment this could be interpreted as the secretary of state, for the moment, continuing to take a backseat in the crisis while the neoconservatives around Bush maintained their position of all-out support for military action. It was the latest steps in that action which preoccupied Major General Elyezer Shkedy, commander of the Israeli air force, and Major General David Ben Ba'ashat, commander of the Israeli navy. Sitting around the table were the other men charged with running the war. Lieutenant General Dan Halutz as chief of staff sat next to Olmert. He was the highest ranking officer in the room; the minister of defense had, since 1976, held overall command of the IDF. He was represented by Colonel Yaakov Toran, director general of the ministry. Olmert's cabinet was also asked to approve all military policies and operations. In reality, this was done by the Foreign Affairs and Security Committee, but the decisions taken in the war room had so far not been challenged—and were unlikely to be.

Next to Halutz sat his deputy, Major General Moshe Kaplinsky, and Amos Yedlin, director of military intelligence. Others around the table included the three key field commanders, Major General Yair Naveh of Central Command, Major General Yoav Gallant of the southern command, with responsibility for watching over the Sinai, and Major General "Udi" Adam, who was the northern field commander at the cutting edge of the conflict with daily responsibility for running the war in south Lebanon. Toughened by years of fighting, the three officers gave their reports in the clipped language of seasoned military briefers. Another important member of the gathering was Major General Avichi Mendelblit, the IDF's military advocate general. Among his many responsibilities was to ensure that the air attacks would avoid being labeled as war crimes. Brigadier General Moshe Lipel, the IDF's financial adviser, was present to give the daily cost of running the war. Down to the last tank-shell fired and the sticks of bombs dropped, all was accounted for.

Miri Regev, the articulate chief spokesman for the IDF from 2002–2007, sat down-table. He would later be responsible for trying to convince an increasingly skeptical world that Israel had no alternative but to continue to strike hard. Others around the table guarded their anonymity. They included the head of Special Forces, whose recent commando raid deep into the Beka'a Valley had echoes of the raid on Entebbe. Then it was to rescue civilians held by another terror group.

The Beka'a raid came after Dagan's deep-cover agents in the valley reported that the two Israeli soldiers captured by Hezbollah and its leader, Hassan Nasrallah, were hiding there. Neither the soldiers nor Nasrallah were found.

Every morning, in his precise tones, Meir Dagan updated those around the table on the hunt for both the soldiers and Nasrallah. For ninety minutes the daily briefing on the next steps to be taken ranged from providing targets for the advance into south Lebanon by the IDF's six brigades to identifying renewed air strikes to be made on the Beirut suburbs. Then came what Meir Dagan has called "the wider picture." Would Syria once more increase Hezbollah's rocket arsenal? Fifteen hundred had been fired so far, another fifteen hundred destroyed. That left ten thousand. What would be the next step that Syria's president, Bashar al-Assad, could take? His palace at Ladekye, outside Damascus, had already been buzzed by Israeli warplanes. It was Dagan's idea. He called it "a little warning." And Iran—what would President Ahmadinejad do? The wiry, gaunt-faced, heavily bearded president had once more said, "We will wipe Israel from the face of the earth." An idle boast or a serious threat? Meir Dagan's answers to those troubling questions would remain—at least for the moment—inside the war room. By 8:00 A.M. the men around the table had left to carry out their daily orders. The first the world would learn about them would be on the news bulletins.

Two thousand miles to the west of the Kirya war room, the analysts in Britain's Joint Terrorism Analysis Centre (JTAC) continued to explore the latest ramifications of Operation Overt, the multinational terrorist operation. Their suspicions had hardened when the FBI sent MI5 an urgent bulletin—copied to all the other intelligence services engaged in the operation—that suicide bombers had been recruited to hijack transatlantic aircraft by smuggling individual explosive ingredients past airport security and then assembling them as bombs on board. The FBI warning (a copy of which the author has seen) was entitled: "Possible Hijacking Tactic for Using Aircraft as Weapons." In part it read: "Components of improvised explosive devices can be smuggled onto an aircraft, concealed in either clothing or personal carry-on items such as shampoo and medicine bottles, and assembled on board. To avoid cases of suspicious passenger activity, this will most likely take place in an aircraft's lavatory."

Another piece of information had come from an al-Qaeda Web site believed to be operating out of Yemen. Though protected by a secret password, it had been interdicted by GCHQ specialists and had yielded valuable clues. It gave detailed instructions on how to create new types of miniature bombs by using the flash mechanism on a digital camera as an electronic detonator. Various ways of powering the detonator were suggested, including personal music players. What focused the attention of the analysts was that the instructions were written in English as well as Arabic. This raised the strong possibility that the planned attack would require the services of the two cells under surveillance by Operation Overt.

Then, a few days later, a third GCHQ intercept came from another al-Qaeda Web site, this one in Uzbekistan. It discussed the qualities of using an explosive it called "The Mother of Satan" and indicated it had been tried out by Hezbollah. Mossad's London station chief confirmed the explosive was made from triacetone triperoxide (TATP) and was made from combining four ingredients: two harmless domestic liquids, hair bleach, and nail varnish remover. The Web site promised that "when care is taken to mix the ingredients, the result will be a powerful explosion similar to that produced by a military grenade." TATP had been the choice of explosive used by suicide bombers in the July 7, 2005, attacks on London. TATP could be carried on board in containers such as bottles of soft drinks or even a feeding bottle for a baby. The two chemicals to create TATP would normally have to be mixed at low temperatures to make the explosive more stable. But for a suicide bomber this would not be necessary. The only problem the terrorists would face would be to ensure the mixture was sufficiently solid before it became a lethal explosive, otherwise it would be difficult to detonate as shown by the failure of the second London suicide attacks on July 21, 2005.

But there was still no time frame for the attack Operation Overt was monitoring, only that it would most likely originate with flights taking off from Heathrow, London, heading for the United States. As July drew to a bloody close in south Lebanon and Israel, Eliza Manningham-Buller reminded the hunters that "we will not stop them all—but we will have a damned good try."

By the first week of August 2006, the war had become a grim parade of military funerals and television interviews with grieving families. With each death the unease within Israel deepened over the conduct of the fighting. Retired military experts—known as "the armchair brigade" among Ehud Olmert's aides—called for an increase in ground forces and bombing raids on Hezbollah's rocket launchers and for the razing of villages where Hezbollah was suspected of hiding. This had already led to tragedy roundly condemned around the world when Israeli bombs destroyed an apartment block in the south Lebanon city of Cana, killing some fifty women and children. Journalists had reminded readers that Cana was where Jesus had changed water into wine "and now the water of Cana is red with the blood of the innocent," wrote one reporter. And for the first time since hostilities started, Mossad came under criticism. Why hadn't its agents located the bunkers and tunnels which, over the past six years, Hezbollah had been using to stockpile rockets supplied by Syria and Iran? The question had led to angry discussions in the Knesset. But there was no response from Meir Dagan. It had been left to Shabtai Shavit to defend his old service, pointing out that the public perception of intelligence gathering does not take into account the "bigger picture below the surface."

An example of this came on August 3, 2006, when Dagan received a message from an agent in Balbeck, the historic city in the Beka'a Valley that Hezbollah had turned into a stronghold. The message said that Hassan Nasrallah, the head of Hezbollah, would be traveling overnight to meet with Saad bin Laden, the eldest son of Osama bin Laden and his appointed successor. Days before another Mossad agent in Damascus had reported that the scion of the al-Qaeda leader was in the city and had held meetings with Syrian intelligence officers. That night Israeli Black Hawk helicopters swept IDF commandos ninety miles into Lebanon. With them were several Arab-speaking Mossad officers. While the commandos hunted for their human targets, the officers headed for the Hezbollah-operated hospital in the center of Balbeck. They found it deserted; patients, doctors, and nurses had all fled. Using a floor plan provided by a Mossad informer, the team found what they had come for: computers. One was in the medical records office. Another in a consultant's suite. A third in a nurse's station. The computers were unplugged and rushed to a waiting helicopter. Two hours later the disks were being studied in Mossad's Tel Aviv headquarters.

Some information on the disks set out details of Hezbollah "sleeper cells" in Britain. By the time the commandos returned to their base to report they had not found Nasrallah or Saad bin Laden, details of the cells had been transmitted to London. They found their place on the Anacapa wall charts inside the Joint Terrorism Analysis Center.

U.S. secretary of state Condoleezza Rice was once more back in Tel Aviv, flying in on Air Force One. The Boeing 747-200B was not a particular aircraft, but the call sign for any of the small fleet of aircraft reserved for the president or his senior aides. In all there were seven in the fleet. The aircraft Dr. Rice was using comprised a crew of twenty-six to pilot and look after her needs and seventeen secret agents to protect her on the ground.

The Air Force One fleet had undergone a $50 million upgrade since 9/11 to enable the president to rule the United States from the air. The chaos surrounding his movements after the attack on the Twin Towers and the Pentagon was a painful reminder of communications shortcomings.

Dr. Rice's aircraft had a mobile command center with encrypted communication links with all of the national security networks in the United States. The state-of-the-art telephone system had a total of eighty-five separate lines and scrambled handsets. Plasma screens positioned around the aircraft showed, in real time, the live satellite news channels. The plane's extensive defense system was intended to detect and deflect any missile attacks. Secretary of State Rice had an executive suite behind the flight deck that included a stateroom, which was a duplicate of her Washington office. Behind it was a dressing room, toilet, and shower that only she was allowed to use. Her own bedroom was wood paneled with a queen-sized bed. The suite also had a dining room. On board were two galleys, each capable of providing meals for two hundred passengers; the larders stocked with enough supplies for two thousand meals. The nonstop flight from Washington had cost $40,243 an hour. At the back of the plane sat her officials and carefully vetted members of the press.

Known as the "Warrior Princess" to her staff, but never to her face, Dr. Rice brought with her an alarm clock that played the opening bars of a Mozart symphony and she kept her watch on Eastern Standard Time. The two pieces were gifts from President Bush, visible signs of the esteem in which he held her. At 5 A.M. EST she awoke and spent the next hour working out on the weights and a rowing machine installed in the suite at her request. Physical fitness was an important part of her life; it had given Dr. Rice the figure of a catwalk model and the stride of an athlete. At some time during the flight she had used her phone—code-named POTUS (for President of the United States)—to call President Bush; they spoke several times each day. Fifty-two years old, Dr. Rice was the most powerful person in his administration. Its other members knew she was perhaps one step away from her ultimate ambition of becoming the first woman to be president of the United States, and the first African American to hold the office.

The Mossad profile revealed that if Dr. Rice had a weakness, "it is shoes. She is known to have splashed out on eight pairs of Ferragamos and regularly sends her personal shopper into Washington fashion boutiques to see what's new from Paris, Milan, or London." The profile had contained other personal details—how as a student she had her hair curls ironed out and "has taken to wearing her hair in a style that suggests a headmistress at a Swiss finishing school." It described her upbringing in the midfifties in the still segregated deep South, how her parents had christened her after the Italian musical term *Condoleezza*—"with sweetness." How she had taken piano lessons at the age of three and studied Spanish and French until she became fluent. When she was eight years old, her hometown of Birmingham, Alabama, was torn apart by civil rights agitation and a bomb planted by a white extremist had exploded in her local Baptist school, killing four black girls, one of whom was her closest friend. Her father, John, patrolled the city streets with a shotgun to keep white racists at bay.

Afterward the family moved to Colorado where Condoleezza was enrolled in an integrated Catholic school. In her teens she learned Russian and at college wrote her dissertation on the Czechoslovak Army. Her most notable achievement came when she became provost of one of America's top universities, Stanford. She was the youngest to do so, at the age of thirty-eight, and the first African American to hold the post. Her next climb up the ladder came when the then secretary of state, George Shultz, nominated her to the board of the oil giant Chevron. One of its million-barrel oil tankers was named after her. That tanker still sails the high seas even in the most turbulent weather.

The Mossad profile pointed out that "turbulence has continued to surround Dr. Rice"—not least because of the surprise caused when George Bush asked her to join his presidential campaign in 1998. They quickly bonded through their common zeal for physical fitness. "She gave him a pedometer to check how many steps he took during his coast-to-coast campaign. Their faith also plays an important role in their association; both are devout Sunday church-goers." Bush made no secret of his dependency on her. "She explains the subtleties of foreign policy in a way I understand," he once said. When Bush took over the presidency in January 2001, he made her his national security adviser. Dick Cheney tried to block the appointment. She dealt with his opposition in a closed-door meeting. Since then the "Warrior Princess"—a nickname given to her by Donald Rumsfeld—has translated the president's impulses into foreign policy. Never married, she relaxes by "playing her Steinway grand piano and watching American football on television," revealed the profile.

It also explained why she had two mirrors in her offices to check the back of her hair was in place down to the last brush stroke. "If she is having a 'bad hair day,' it is like a weather vane warning." There had been many of those times: her confrontation with Germany and France over the war with Iraq; her determination to maintain Spain's resolve to support the war. All this made her an admired figure in Israel.

Now, on that July day in 2006, as the giant aircraft made its long journey to Israel, Mossad's station chief in Washington had sent Meir Dagan the latest denials by both Hillary Clinton and Condoleezza Rice that they intended to run in the 2008 presidential campaign. Of more immediate interest to the Mossad chief were the details of a most secret plan Dr. Rice had reluctantly helped to create with President Bush and Vice President Cheney. The plan was the underlying reason for her visit. On the surface it was to once more explore the prospects of a ceasefire. In reality it was to discover if the Israeli air force attacks on Hezbollah had been so successful they could serve as a blueprint for an attack on Iran. Dr. Rice had initially been nervous about launching such an assault. Did she now feel the same? Meir Dagan had become convinced—and told Prime Minister Ehud Olmert as much—that the secretary of state was not merely nervous, but had started, according to the Mossad station chief in Washington, to "agitate inside the administration" to be allowed to go to Syria to try and persuade President Bashar al-Assad to order Hezbollah to stop its onslaught. But a Mossad agent in Damascus had, shortly before the 747 aircraft touched down at Ben Gurion airport, discovered that President al-Assad refused to meet her.

A further indication of President Bush's hard-line thinking had come from Richard Armitage, who had been deputy secretary of state in Bush's first term. Armitage had described Hezbollah as "maybe the A-team of terrorists. Israel's campaign on Lebanon, which has faced unexpected difficulties and widespread criticism, may, in the end, serve as a warning to the White House about Iran. If the most dominant military force in the region, the Israeli Defense Forces, cannot pacify a country like Lebanon, you should think carefully about taking the template to Iran with its population of seventy million. The only effect that the Israeli bombing has achieved is to unite the Muslim world against the Israelis."

Condoleezza Rice had come to explore again what she thought, according to one source, "could be a solution. It was to form a Sunni-Arab coalition with Saudi Arabia, Jordan, and Egypt that would win the support of Britain and Europe to unite and bring pressure on the Shia mullahs in Iran." But to achieve that, the source acknowledged, would require the removal of Hezbollah as a threat to Israel. Dr. Rice knew the hope of such plan for a coalition of what she called "like-minded Arab states" had been dented when the Saudi foreign minister, Prince Saudi al-Faisal, had come to Washington early in the war and told President Bush to "intervene immediately to end this conflict." Predictably, Bush had demurred.

All these issues formed a backdrop to Dr. Rice's discussions in Israel. Those who attended, including Meir Dagan, listened intently to a woman who combined elegance—her weekly hairdo in her apartment in Washington's Watergate Center cost $500—with a steely determination. "Her smile never quite reached her eyes. We remembered that when, for instance, it came to push and shove between Blair and Rice, Bush always chose her view. With Blair now a lame-duck prime minister, her mood was that he didn't really matter anymore," recalled one of those who attended the meetings.

While those discussions went on, so did the war. The dead and the dying, the homeless and the bereaved in northern Israel and up through southern Lebanon to the suburbs of Beirut continued to grow. And elsewhere, other developments required Meir Dagan to shift the focus of Mossad's attention.

A Mossad undercover agent in Tehran had established that Provisional Republican Irish Army (PIRA), the extreme Irish terror group, was providing Hezbollah and Iran's Revolutionary Guard with expertise on how to make ultra-sophisticated roadside bombs. The agent tracked the Irish bomb makers to three factories in the Lavizān suburb in northern Tehran. Adapted to be fired from antitank missiles, the bombs were made from concave steel or copperplate. When fired at 2280 km an hour one could penetrate ten centimeters of armor at a distance of one hundred meters. The missiles had already destroyed several Israeli tanks in Lebanon.

Earlier in 2006 the six-man PIRA team had traveled from Dublin to Frankfurt and onward to Damascus. From there they were brought in an Iranian military aircraft to Tehran. The bomb makers had been recruited to provide expertise in how to make and disguise infrared triggering devices. During the conflict in Northern Ireland, the success of roadside bombs had left dozens of British soldiers dead or injured. The bombs were also used to topple buildings and bring terror to the streets of Belfast and other cities in the province.

The weapons were attached to explosively formed projectiles (EFPs). Since June, EFP weapons have been transported out of Iran into Iraq and Damascus, Syria. From there they were smuggled down into the Beka'a Valley. In Tehran the PIRA team was divided between the three ordinance factories that were working around the clock mass-producing the sophisticated roadside bombs. This was not the first time that PIRA had sold its bomb-making experience to a terror group. Four years ago, three of its members went to Colombia to train that country's terror group, the Revolutionary Armed Forces of Colombia (FARC). Colombian intelligence, on a tip from Mossad, arrested the trio. They were sentenced to long terms of imprisonment in a Bogotá court, but escaped with the help of the terror group and eventually were smuggled back to Ireland. Despite attempts by the Colombian government to have them extradited to serve out their sentences, the Dublin government refused to return them to Colombia.

The membership of the PIRA was estimated by Mossad at "no more than two hundred." They had never recognized the terms of the Good Friday Agreement that finally brought peace to Northern Ireland. Since the ratification of the protocol, the IRA has been selling its expertise to other groups associated with al-Qaeda.

"The Islamic terrorists are well financed and expanding their operations. But they lack the skills of the PIRA. Its members have become 'guns for hire.' Following the ceasefire in Northern Ireland they are out of work and in need of money," a Mossad analyst told the author.

Mossad also learned that the PIRA members had met with members of a South African terror group called People Against Gangsterism and Drugs (PAGAD). The meetings took place in a favorite holiday resort for Irish tourists, Sotto Grande, near Malaga in southern Spain. PAGAD wanted to recruit them to come to South Africa to work in their terror camps in the hinterland beyond Durban. PAGAD was originally formed in 1995 to rid the streets of South Africa of drug dealers, but its ideology changed due to the strong influence of the million-plus Muslims in the country. In the past year, intelligence services like Mossad and MI6 have established that PAGAD had strong links to the Tehran regime. Meetings with the regime have taken place in Beirut and Damascus.

A Mossad analyst on South African terror groups told the author: "Since the bombings in London last year, PAGAD has become more militant. No country is safe from the global terror network that is growing, it is highly organized and extends across the world. Its patron and ultimate beneficiary is Iran."

That July in London, Nathan learned that the investigation surrounding the death of Dr. David Christopher Kelly, the microbiologist who had been Britain's foremost expert on biological and chemical warfare, had been reopened three years after his body had been found in an area of woodlands near his home in Oxfordshire. An inquest pronounced the scientist had taken his own life shortly after he was identified as passing classified information about Iraq's weapons of mass destruction to the BBC. The weapons had proven to be nonexistent. But as Operation Overt continued to move forward, Mossad found itself feeding into what would eventually turn out to be the biggest intelligence operation ever mounted in post-war Britain, whose focus had narrowed down to the possibility that two Islamic terror cells in London had been working on bombs made from liquid explosives.

Against this background two members of parliament announced they wanted a new inquiry into Dr. Kelly's death. One was the Liberal Democrat Member of Parliament Norman Baker, who revealed that for the past six months he had been investigating the Kelly death and had concluded there was "strong evidence he had not committed suicide but may have been murdered." Another Member of Parliament, Andrew MacKinlay, a Labour member of the Foreign Affairs Select Committee, had tabled questions to the defence secretary, Des Browne, about the connections between Dr. Kelly and Wouter Basson, who had run a team of scientists in apartheid South Africa whose work allegedly had included attempts to produce a drug that would affect black fertility and darken the skin of white spies so they could infiltrate anti-apartheid groups.

In April 2002, Basson, a heart specialist once the personal physician of the former South African leader, P. W. Botha, had been cleared by a court in Pretoria on forty-six charges. They included fraud, drug-trafficking, and eight counts of murder committed when he had been in charge of Project Coast, the country's secret apartheid-era germ warfare program. After the verdict, Dr. Basson had been smuggled out of the court by South African intelligence agents. The judge had earlier ruled that cases involving alleged assassinations of apartheid opponents outside South Africa were beyond his jurisdiction. During the trial, Wouter Basson had revealed that the South African government had given him "unlimited power and money to devise defenses against chemical or germ attacks on the country."

Now, in July 2006, MI5 had begun to investigate whether those defenses had included using the expertise of Dr. Kelly and two other sinister figures in the secret world of biological warfare. One was a Mormon gynecologist, Dr. Larry Ford. Attached to the University of California campus in Los Angeles, Ford had a secret life none of his patients suspected. He had built up a close relationship with Wouter Basson and, through him, established contacts with the biowarfare scientists of North Korea—and Dr. Kelly. The two men had met in a safe house Basson had rented for such meetings. It was at number one, Faircloth Farm Cottage, Watersplash, near Ascot, Berkshire. There, MI5 now believed, Dr. Kelly and Dr. Ford regularly met until the gynecologist committed suicide in 2000 at his home in Irvine, California. When police dealing with the case opened Dr. Ford's refrigerator, they found bottles containing cultures of cholera, botulism, and typhoid fever. All three toxins were among those Dr. Kelly had been working with during his time as head of the microbiology department at Porton Down, the chemical warfare research establishment in England. Had he provided them to Dr. Ford? If so, why? Did Ford or Basson intend to pass them on to North Korea? These were some of the questions for which MI5 wanted answers.

Since October 1989, Dr. Kelly had also established contact with another sinister figure in the world of germ warfare. He was Dr. Vladimir Pasechnik, the former top scientist in the Soviet Union's biowarfare program, Biopreparat. In one of those classic spy novel moments, the fifty-three-year-old Russian microbiologist had strolled out of a drug industry fair in Paris. Telling his colleagues he was going to buy souvenirs for his wife and children back home in St. Petersburg, Pasechnik had instead hailed a taxi to the British embassy in the city. He had been brought by MI6 agents on the next EuroStar train to London. Dr. Kelly was appointed "to open the Pandora's Box of biological secrets the Soviet Union had kept concealed from the world," he later admitted to the author. Assisting Dr. Kelly was Dr. Christopher Davis, a member of the Ministry of Defence Intelligence staff. Over weeks of questioning Dr. Pasechnik revealed, among much else, how the Soviet Union had planned to spread the plague—the medieval Black Death—across Europe.

Later, Dr. Kelly, now a close friend of the Russian scientist, helped him to start Regma Biotechnologies Company and became a regular visitor to the company's offices in Wiltshire, England, located Porton Down, Britain's secret biodefense establishment. He also arranged for Pasechnik to have his own office and laboratory in the same building where Dr. Kelly worked at Porton Down. On November 21, 2001, Dr. Pasechnik left his office at Regma Biotechnologies. Staff later remembered he seemed happy and in good health. At home he cooked dinner, washed up, and went to sleep. He was found dead in bed the next day. Initially police said the death was "inexplicable." The coroner, however, accepted the pathologist's report that Pasechnik had died from a stroke. No details of the autopsy were made public. No reporter covered the coroner's inquest. The funeral, which normally would have attracted media attention given who Pasechnik was, went unreported. A full month later the briefest announcement of his death was released by Dr. Christopher Davis, by then retired from the Ministry of Defence and living outside Washington, DC.

By July 2006, Nathan learned that MI5 had discovered Dr. Kelly had assisted Mossad on a number of occasions and that in his diary there was an indication he planned to contact the Mossad London station chief shortly before his death. There was no mention of the reason why and Nathan had set up an appointment. But had he learned that the MI5 inquiries included seeking answers as to whether the suicides of both Dr. Kelly and Dr. Ford were merely a coincidence—or something more sinister. Were all Dr. Kelly's contacts with Mossad fully authorized— and if so, by whom? Who had given Dr. Kelly clearance to help Dr. Pasechnik to set up his company? And had the Russian's death really been from a cerebral stroke—or had it been induced by some other method? It was no secret the Russians and other intelligence services had created fast-acting drugs that could mimic a stroke or heart attack—and leave no trace.

Nathan had been told to maintain a watching brief on developments. There was no more that Meir Dagan would, or could, do.

On August 11, 2006, the UN Security Council finally agreed to the text of a Lebanese ceasefire resolution. Even as the details were being sent to Tel Aviv, in the Israeli Defense Forces war room the men around the table were about to launch a full-scale land offensive into Lebanon using thirty thousand troops and massive air strikes. Their objective, the Litani River, had finally been approved by Prime Minister Olmert. Then, despite furious criticism from his military chiefs around the table, Olmert had decided to wait and see for himself what the exact wording of the UN resolution contained. The generals had accused him of wavering and said that, no matter what the resolution said, this was the time to strike a decisive blow against Hezbollah. Olmert caved in. The IDF would launch its massive assault, bombard Beirut and other cities in south Lebanon, and send its soldiers deep into Hezbollah-held territory.

Within hours, an air armada of fifty-five helicopters, hugging the hills of southern Lebanon for protection, dropped paratroopers near the Litani River. Simultaneously an aerial bombardment fired twenty missiles into the Beirut suburbs. Hezbollah shot down an Israeli transport aircraft killing all five crew members including the woman copilot. They were among twenty-four IDF soldiers to die on that day. The IDF claimed it had killed forty Hezbollah fighters during that period. But over 250 rockets had rained down on northern Israel.

In the war room in the Kirya, the arguments carried on as to whether the UN resolution met Israel's requirements. It called for Hezbollah "to cease all its attacks" while ordering Israel to end "only its offensive operations." Chief of Staff General Dan Halutz insisted that after the ceasefire his forces should be allowed to remain in their present positions in south Lebanon. It was finally agreed that Ehud Olmert could issue the briefest of statements that his government would accept the UN resolution.

Meir Dagan left the meeting knowing that Olmert failed to achieve his two reasons for launching the war: to crush Hezbollah and recover the two captured soldiers, Ehud (Udi) Goldwasser and Eldad Regev. Both had been the reasons given for Israel to go to war. The Mossad chief believed the two captured Israeli soldiers had been moved to the Beka'a Valley and he began to make preparations for another raid into the area. It would not be until 2008 that their bodies would be returned to Israel by Syria in exchange for the release of two hundred Hezbollah prisoners from Israeli jails. In the next few days Dagan's agents, accompanied by IDF commandos, once more flew to the Beka'a Valley. After a fierce hand-to-hand battle with Hezbollah fighters, the Israelis withdrew having failed to find the two soldiers. It was also a predictable paradox of the thirty-four days of war that the fire fight would come after both sides had theoretically agreed to halt hostilities. The truth was, Meir Dagan told his senior staff at their weekly meeting, no one had won the war.

The biggest loser was Lebanon. Over one thousand of its people had been killed, fifteen thousand homes and other buildings had been destroyed, tourism and the economy had been decimated. Tourism had generated 15 percent of the Lebanese national economy and the economy had shrunk by 3 percent. Mossad analysts said it would require $2.5 billion to rebuild the country. Israel had lost 144 lives and hundreds more were injured. Israel had also spent $1.6 billion waging the war—equalling 1 percent of its GDP. Its all-important tourist industry had fallen by 50 percent—and would remain like that for some time. President Bush and Prime Minister Blair had both suffered a humiliating defeat in accepting Olmert's insistence at the outset of hostilities that it would be a short conflict. And, even when that had looked unlikely, they had still done nothing to halt the fighting. Their stance had reinforced the view in the Muslim world that Britain and the United States would always side with Israel.

As Israeli troops trudged back from Lebanon, many of them were bitter and angry. They spoke of how they had gone to war in the stifling summer heat without even sufficient water to drink and how they had to take canteens from the bodies of dead Hezbollah fighters. By the time they reached Israel, many signed a petition claiming incompetence "at all levels" in the way the war was run. Others pitched tents outside government buildings in Jerusalem to protest, charging that Ehud Olmert and his security advisers provided incoherent leadership and must be held accountable. It was a view shared by the Mossad analysts. On the top floor of Mossad headquarters there was also anger that Ehud Olmert had asked an old friend, Ofer Dekel, a former head of Shin Bet, the country's internal security service, to try and open discussions with Hezbollah to return the two captured soldiers. Meir Dagan told his senior staff that it was too soon to contemplate such a move.

In the streets of Israel's cities the anger grew. Brigadier Yossi Hyman, the senior paratroop officer, accused the IDF of "the sin of arrogance," while expressing his own regret that he had not better prepared his own soldiers for war. A group of reservists sent a devastating indictment of IDF commanders to the country's defense minister, Amir Peretz. The document accused IDF officers of "chronic indecisiveness and displaying under-preparation, insincerity, and an inability to make rational decisions." Never before had there been such an attack on Israel's military elite.

Meir Dagan was not alone in recognizing that if Israel was to survive in an Islamic world grown more determined to remove it, it must urgently learn from its mistakes and adapt. There was a growing public demand that Olmert should resign along with some of his generals. Among those who did resign was Chief of Staff of the Israeli Defense Forces General Dan Halutz. But the prime minister clung to office. It was only when he became the target of a criminal investigation, alleging he had been involved in corrupt financial deals, that he finally announced he would leave office in October 2008 and fight to clear his name.

As an uneasy truce settled over Lebanon, Operation Overt, to which Mossad was one of half-a-dozen security services making a contribution, began to move to resolution. MI5 was checking all Britain's universities and technical schools for Middle East students who had come to Britain to study thermochemistry, the science which includes creating liquid explosives. The search also extended to all British firms that had employed foreign students since 9/11. The fear was that any of them could have been recruited by one of the two terror cells now under intense surveillance in London that were now known to MI5 to be linked to al-Qaeda. MI5 was certain the plot centered on destroying transatlantic flights from Heathrow to the United States.

Mossad's own scientists had already told MI5 the most effective way of smuggling explosive liquids onto an aircraft would be by using two stable fluids which could be mixed in an aircraft lavatory to create a powerful bomb. Research by the chemists showed that nitroglycerine hidden inside a tub of hair gel or a shampoo bottle, with a detonator hidden inside a cell phone, would be one effective method. Another was to use two bottles of clear chemicals hidden inside cans of soft drinks or toiletries. A prime candidate for this method would be triacetone triperoxide (TATP), a crystalline white powder. The July 7, 2005, bombers in London had used this method to create the explosions on the city's underground system. On board an aircraft the two chemicals would be mixed to create TATP.

Ehud Keinan, a member of the Technical Institute in Tel Aviv, whose expertise was invaluable to Mossad, said (to the author):

> There are a number of ways to make liquid explosives. My guess is that terrorists would use one based on the peroxide family. This is because it is relatively easy to initiate such explosives. There is no need for a detonator and a booster. A burning cigarette or a match would be enough to set them off. The basic materials to achieve this are readily available in unlimited quantities in hardware stores, pharmacies, agricultural suppliers, and supermarkets. Sadly, most airports are not yet equipped with the appropriate means to detect those explosives. The truth is that there is no efficient way to stop a suicide bomber who carries a peroxide-based explosive on his body or in his carry-on luggage.

The Mossad chemists concluded that while it would be difficult to destroy an aircraft with one liquid-based bomb, it could be achieved by combining several bombs on one aircraft and placing them near windows or escape hatches. But even a small device could sever an aircraft's hydraulic control cables. MI5 chemists had studied the precedents for such attacks on board an aircraft. In June 1985, Sikh militants had obliterated an Air India aircraft over the Atlantic Ocean, killing all 329 passengers. Pan Am Flight 103 had been similarly destroyed on December 21, 1988, over the Scottish town of Lockerbie. In 1995, al-Qaeda operatives planned to attack a number of passenger planes over the Pacific Ocean. One aircraft owned by Philippine Airlines was attacked with a nitrocellulose bomb, which killed one passenger and injured ten others. On December 22, 2001, Richard Reid, a British-born follower of Osama bin Laden, tried to destroy American Airlines Flight 63 as it flew from Paris to Miami. He had explosives stuffed in his shoes.

The details of all these acts were on the screens in the Joint Terrorism Analysis Centre in London. At 10:30 on a warm Sunday night in

August, the red light on the senior duty officer's desk blinked. The caller was Eliza Manningham-Buller, head of MI5. Moments earlier she had been told that four months of a patient and top-secret investigation by MI5, MI6, the CIA, Mossad, and Pakistan's intelligence service was about to reach its climax. John Scarlett, the head of MI6, had just received a "flash" encrypted e-mail from a field agent in Karachi. Pakistan intelligence had confirmed that al-Qaeda was about to launch a series of attacks on British and American transatlantic flights from Heathrow. It was the moment the greatest terrorist threat Britain had ever faced brought JTAC to "full operational mode." In rapid succession, Tony Blair was alerted. He contacted President Bush. By then key officials in Cobra, the government crisis team, were being briefed. So was Sir Ian Blair, Britain's top policeman. Airline chiefs and other authorities, including the director of security for the Channel Tunnel, were also alerted. All the heads of foreign intelligence were told. By then the Anacapa charts were filling, the center's plasma screens were alive with data, and the phones blinking furiously. Over the next six days, into and out of the work stations—each equipped with state-of-the-art communications systems—information flowed. Intelligence—once only shared with the CIA, French, and German security services—was exchanged with other services. The question all urgently needed to answer was: had they picked up even "a whisper in the wind" of when the plot to destroy the airliners would happen? From Rome came the first hint. SISMI, the Italian secret service, said they had a large number of terror suspects under surveillance. One had admitted the attack would come "very soon."

Porton Down's experts were called upon to decide what kind of liquid explosive would be used. Around the clock, surveillance reports continued to come to the work stations. In between long days and nights, men and women catnapped in a nearby dormitory in the basement. One report was from an MI5 undercover team near a house in High Wycombe in Buckinghamshire. Other teams reported from south London and Birmingham. GCHQ specialists analyzed phone intercepts from suspect houses. In communities where the suspects lived, MI5 had set up other sophisticated surveillance sites. Some of the suspects had become assimilated into British society, but had made regular trips to relatives in Pakistan and elsewhere. Pakistan's intelligence service had provided JTAC with details. The suspects were known as "Trojans," JTAC-speak for those who may have been recruited to become home-grown terrorists. Their cell phones were bugged. Their every movement noted. Radio waves bounced off windowpanes to monitor conversations in a room they occupied. The latest technology filtered through thousands of e-mails. The surveillance teams' information was studied by a JTAC lawyer to ensure their findings would be admissible in court.

Seventy-two hours later sufficient information had been gathered for arrests to go ahead. Twenty-two people were taken into custody. They included a convert to Islam and a seventeen-year-old youth. But in JTAC the work continued to establish the full extent of the plot. Scotland Yard predicted it could possibly be a year before the suspects were brought to trial.

In Tel Aviv, Meir Dagan received a thank you call from Eliza Manningham-Buller. At the end she said, "We may not have caught them all, but it's a start." For the intelligence chief it was a good result to justify what Mossad tries to do.

In September 2006, the arrival once more of the first cooling breezes was a time to which the Jews of Israel and the Muslims of Lebanon and the Gaza Strip would look forward. A time when Jewish mothers prepared borscht, beetroot soup, and young lovers walked down the Cardo, the covered street in the Jewish quarter of Old Jerusalem and, nearby, the Muslim faithful worshipped within the cool of Haram al-Sharif, the enclosure in the Muslim quarter of Old Jerusalem which contained the al-Aqsa Mosque and the Dome of the Rock, the third holiest site of the Islamic world. This, too, all went on as it had for many centuries, rituals as ancient as wearing the tallith, the Jewish prayer shawl, and the checkered Arab headdress.

But now there were other matters to preoccupy the people of the Holy Land. In Gaza the fighting continued with guerrilla attacks by Hamas and counterassaults by Israel. The Israeli air force launched precision-bombing raids across the Strip. Shin Bet, the internal security force, rounded up more legally elected members of the Hamas-dominated parliament on the grounds they belonged to an organization whose military wing was responsible for the continued kidnappings, rocket attacks, and suicide bombers.

In Israel, the fallout from the war in Lebanon continued and calls came every day for the resignation of those deemed to be responsible for the country's failure. Early on in the conflict, Dan Halutz, after his air force had destroyed fifty-four Hezbollah rocket launchers, had announced "we have won the war." Now, on the streets of Israeli cities, the words were publicly mocked as it gradually became clear after five weeks of fighting that the last of the optimism had evaporated, and with it, the invincible reputation of the Israeli armed forces. Instead of celebrations, which had greeted other victories, the air was filled with anger over the soldiers' poor training and outdated equipment. Despite individual acts of bravery, some of the men of the IDF had been pushed to the point of mutiny. A humiliated Halutz wrote a contrite letter to all his soldiers in which he admitted "there were mistakes and these will be corrected." But as the days of September passed, it became far from clear whether the fifty-eight-year-old fighter pilot, who had flown with distinction in the 1973 Arab-Israeli War, would survive. A poll revealed that 54 percent wanted Halutz to resign.

Even though Ehud Olmert had announced he would set up a public inquiry into the conduct of the war, it did little to reduce the national anger Israelis directed at him. Sixty-three percent of the electorate polled said he should resign at once; his defense minister, Amir Peretz, fared even worse: 74 percent demanded he should leave office as soon as possible. Both politicians had been overwhelmingly dominated by Halutz and his dependence on air power, which had brought swift victory in previous conflicts. Mossad analysts, who had been monitoring public attitudes, also saw a consensus forming among IDF veterans that Halutz had failed to understand air power was only there to assist ground forces and could never win a modern-day war. It was a view Meir Dagan had put forward in those initial meetings in the war room. He had argued, in the calm, cogent matter which had been his hallmark since taking over Mossad, that air power should have been supported by ground forces capable of driving Hezbollah back from the border area. But now the first murmurs had also surfaced in the street as to why the intelligence—always a critical factor in any past war Israel fought—had been so inept. Why had Mossad not discovered well before battle commenced the exact whereabouts of the Hezbollah rocket sites? Why had its agents not pinpointed the fallback positions of the launchers? Why had they not been able to more effectively track the movements of Hassan Nasrallah?

In Lebanon, Hezbollah, despite parading through the streets of Beirut in triumph, also had suffered heavy casualties. Those who had survived watched fifty French army engineers come ashore, the vanguard of the seven thousand UN troops promised by the European Union states as peacemakers. The UN had also received offers of soldiers from several Muslim countries, some of which did not even recognize Israel. It did not augur well for the future—particularly as President Bashar al-Assad of Syria again began to make threatening announcements that the time "will once more come when we have to retake the Golan Heights by force."

But the real threat came from Iran. Not only had it been the real beneficiary of the conflict, it had united the Sunnis and the Shias in common agreement to fight the detested infidels. From having its back to the wall only three years before, when the invasion of Iraq had intimidated the ayatollahs next door, Iran had emerged as the influential power in the region's Muslim world. It had achieved this position by shrewd opportunism and the miscalculations of its enemies. It had either ignored or played subtle politics against the threats of the UN Security Council to punish it with economic sanctions for consistently refusing to stop producing enriched uranium, a process for making material for nuclear bombs. In that first week of September, Iran's contempt continued to be demonstrated when it announced "a new phase" in its heavy water construction, ignoring the opposition of the International Atomic Energy Agency, the world's nuclear inspectorate. Mossad had already discovered the plant had been operational since mid-August. In a memo to Olmert, Meir Dagan reminded the embattled prime minister that India, Pakistan, and North Korea had all opened similar plants to convert uranium into plutonium for bombs.

Mossad analysts believed Iran's mercurial president, Mahmoud Ahmadinejad, was counting on the disunity of the Security Council and the continued support of China and Russia to block any UN sanctions. John Bolton, America's ambassador to the United Nations, had spoken of imposing them through a "coalition of the willing." But would they include Jacques Chirac and Tony Blair? Both were leaders in the twilight of their political power.

In a prophetic memo, a Mossad analyst wrote in late August: "The world must face that Iran is determined to become a nuclear military power. Inevitably that would lead to a nuclear arms race. Syria will feel emboldened to go for 'the nuclear option.' Saudi Arabia might well want to do the same. Egypt might also consider 'going nuclear.' We would then face a new and most dangerous situation."

It was against this background that Olmert appointed his air force chief, Major General Elyezer Shkedy, to be overall commander for a new department within the IDF. It was to be called "The Iran Front." Its task was two-fold. First, to task Mossad in obtaining "all possible intelligence from within Iran by all possible means." In turn that information would form part of a working battle plan. On Shkedy's appointment, his first visitor had been Meir Dagan. For several hours, Shkedy, the forty-nine-year-old son of Holocaust survivors—whose prized possession was a picture of an Israel F-15 flying over Auschwitz—spelled out his requirements. Dagan asked what was the time frame. Shkedy replied, "the list of options is becoming shorter. But on present calculations there may be a year before we have to decide." That decision, of course, would not be finally made in Israel. It would ultimately come from Washington, made by the Pentagon and delivered from the Oval Office by President George W. Bush. He had already told his inner cabinet—Rumsfeld, Cheney, and Rice—that Israel was "singing from the same hymn sheet as we are. We have no argument about Iran's intentions. It's going to do all it can to go nuclear."

In the meantime in Tehran, Mohammed-Reza Bahonar, the deputy speaker of Iran's parliament and a staunch ultraconservative supporter of President Ahmadinejad, warned that Iran would pull out of the Nuclear Non-Proliferation Treaty "if our patience finally runs out with the international community, our country may have to produce nuclear weapons as a defense measure."

In Tel Aviv, Meir Dagan told his own senior staff that "once more the clock is moving closer to midnight."

In London another clock had stopped, at least for the moment: the long-awaited report into the death of Princess Diana nine years before had gone into limbo. The Royal Coroner, Dr. Michael Burgess, who knew the contents of the report by Lord Stevens, had astonishingly resigned, deciding he was "too busy" to preside over the most significant and high-profile case of his or any coroner's life. In a letter to interested parties, including Prince Charles and Mohamed al-Fayed, the mild-mannered Burgess had written about "my heavy and constant workload." As the ninth anniversary of Dodi al-Fayed and the princess's death were marked by the annual surge of visitors to the midnight car crash location in Paris, the questions continued to be asked and the speculation was rampant. Had Dr. Burgess refused to continue because there was pressure upon him to declare the crash had been nothing more than a tragic accident? Or had he resigned because he would not discount that murder had been committed—and that powerful figures in the intelligence world and in Britain's royal family had exerted their combined influence to dismiss any suspicion of foul play? More certain is that if there was finally to be an inquest it would require months of searching for a replacement for the sixty-year-old Burgess. By August 2006, it had appeared that Lord Falconer, the Lord Chancellor, had been unable to find one. Lord Stevens, who had headed the inquiry into the two deaths, knew that any new coroner would have to read a massive dossier to familiarize himself with its myriad contents numbering ten thousand pages. That would take many months. The experienced Stevens knew that the moment any fresh legal figure examined the results of his team's two-and-a-half-year investigation he would be "bound to want supplementary inquiries to be made." That would, one of his handpicked detectives told the author, "add another year or even more to our work." Privately Lord Stevens told friends that the inquiry "could go on for years."

In September 2006, a date for when the inquest might take place was put at the earliest 2007, possibly 2008. Even then, asked the conspiracy theorists, would *everything* be disclosed? How "routine" had Diana's "partial embalming" been? Why didn't the National Security Agency in Washington release the surveillance tapes of Diana and Dodi it had made in the last weeks of their lives? Did the tapes add anything of value to the investigation? Even if the couple had fastened their seatbelts as the Mercedes hurtled them to their deaths, would that have saved their lives? Was Diana pregnant? Her close friend, Rosa Monckton, had told the Stevens investigators that on August 20, 1997, when she said good-bye to Diana eleven days before her death, Diana's menstrual cycle had started. But even then questions had been asked: How long was her menstrual bleeding? Had she been able to bear a child by the time her menstrual cycle stopped? And finally, what had the investigators discovered about the role of the intelligence services—not least Mossad?

In one of those surprise statements which had become a hallmark of the Blair government, it was announced after the ninth anniversary of Diana's death that a replacement for the Royal Coroner had been found. She was Baroness Elizabeth Butler-Sloss, a retired High Court judge. She had agreed to come out of retirement to preside over the inquest into Diana's death. An indication of the formidable reading task she faced came when Lord Stevens announced his detectives had so far taken 1,500 witness statements, many more than the previous figure.

On the day of the Butler-Sloss appointment, Diana's former butler, Paul Burrell, published his latest revelations about her death. It included a confidential police report about the items recovered from the crash scene. The inventory was prepared by Captain Christophe Boucharin of the Paris Criminal Brigade, marked BC No 288/97. It listed fourteen personal effects, including a pair of black Versace shoes size 40, a Ralph Lauren belt, a Motorola mobile phone, a Jaeger-Lecoultre gold watch, a Bulgari seed-pearl bracelet held at each end with diamond-encrusted drags, and a gold ring. In a footnote Captain Boucharin wrote: "The funeral directors took responsibility for all the artifacts. They put the bracelet on Diana's right wrist and the ring on her right finger." Burrell wrote that "she had agreed on my advice when she received the ring from Dodi to wear the ring on her right hand as a friendship ring—not on her left hand denoting an engagement."

The position of the ring would contradict Mohamed al-Fayed's persistent claim that his son and Diana were engaged to be married. The veracity of this would be one of the many factors that Baroness Butler-Sloss would have to consider when she eventually presided over the inquest.

In Tel Aviv the latest developments were carefully filed in the Mossad library. Meir Dagan had made his decision about not involving Mossad in the investigation. He had heard nothing to change his mind.

Being driven to his appointment through Washington in a government car, Meir Dagan saw that across the Potomac the headstones as usual stood proudly in ranks on the slopes of Arlington Cemetery. The graveyard was so different from the smooth sandstone, brain-shaped monument at Glilot, north of Tel Aviv, and its engravings of the dead of Mossad. Ahead, the Washington Monument's long shadow gave the last reading of the day before fading into darkness. Along the sidewalk people still pounded along as the lights blinked out in the buildings and flags dropped down poles to be swiftly gathered up. If there was a time he had to come to Washington, Meir Dagan preferred September. Until then the summer would be without a breeze and the atmosphere filled with fumes and ozone, often covering the city with a haze. Visitors said it was the result of car exhaust smoke and the swampy location. Cynical locals knew better, claiming it was a noxious mixture of wasted breath and oxidized hopes that turned to poison when the sun broke through. The cause, of course, was government.

It was its secret side, the CIA, which had once more brought the Mossad chief to Washington. He had arrived at the time for Washington's powerful pretenders to lock away their documents and to ignore, until the morning, the telephone calls they had not returned. Those without a future headed home to their families. The ambitious, the Mossad chief knew, had further duties. A late drink at an embassy and later still, dinner with friends and enemies, a time when a secret could be quietly shared or a reputation tarnished.

Before leaving Tel Aviv, Meir Dagan had learned that Rafi Eitan, once Mossad's director of operations and now the pensioners minister in the coalition that Ehud Olmert hoped would allow him to continue governing, had called for the readying of bomb shelters and reinforced rooms to be established in advance of a possible conflict with Iran. Eitan, once so secretive, had become adept at sound-bites on television.

Staging through London, Dagan learned that MI5 had discovered al-Qaeda had supplied its estimated 2,000 sleeper agents in Britain with what Eliza Manningham-Buller described as "the most sophisticated terror manual ever found in this country." The document gave information on how to create liquid explosions far more powerful than those planned to be used to destroy ten passenger planes over the Atlantic in August 2006. The precise steps to produce the bombs were set out in chilling detail on an al-Qaeda DVD. On one part of the disk were instructions that mimicked the style of a cookbook—only its pages provided recipes for unparalleled carnage. An example shown to the author reads:

> First obtain the raw ingredients. Where possible, always shop in supermarkets to avoid the staff remembering your visit. An ideal base liquid is nitromethane. This is used to propel the engine of a model aircraft. It should be mixed with a suitable sensitizing chemical. Gloves must be worn at all times when mixing the chemicals so as to avoid generating heat which could produce a premature explosion. The mixing should also be done in a cool room. The final result will be a crystalline white powder. The technical name for this is triacetone triperoxide. The powder can be suitably concealed in containers in common use.

Sidney Alford, chairman of Alford Technologies, a leading British explosives company, said (to the author): "Everyone in the business knows that nitromethane is an explosive, but many people, including some in the police and security services, have yet to cotton on to that." And in Tel Aviv, Ehud Keinan, a world-ranking authority on liquid explosives whose expertise was prized by Mossad, confirmed that the details discovered on the al-Qaeda DVD were "of major importance in the fight against terrorism. It is very easy to produce such explosives once the know-how is explained. The raw materials are readily available in unlimited quantities on any main street."

Meir Dagan learned the DVD was discovered during the climax of an MI5 surveillance operation that had begun in Dublin, Ireland, and ended on the road to Chester in the north of England when intelligence officers swooped on a 2000-reg Lancia, which had come from Dublin on the car ferry to Holyhead in North Wales. At the wheel of the vehicle was a middle-aged English woman who had driven to the Welsh port from the Midlands. Beside her sat an Algerian-born man, also middle-aged, who lived in a fashionable Dublin suburb. Both had been under surveillance as part of Operation Overt, which led to the arrests of twenty-four terrorists in March 2007. The couple and their car were driven to an MI5 safe house near London. Waiting were senior interrogation officers. While they questioned the couple in separate rooms, MI5 forensic experts conducted a search of the car. It was then that the DVD was found.

Dagan also learned that MI5 officers had reopened the case of another Algerian terrorist who had lived for four years in Lucan, another Dublin suburb. In December 2005 he was convicted under the name of Abbas Boutrab for conspiracy to blow up aircraft and sentenced to six years at Belfast Crown Court. However, it subsequently emerged that Boutrab was not his real name—but one of nine different aliases on passports found in an al-Qaeda safe house in Ireland.

The Republic had increasingly become a concern for Mossad since it had emerged in the aftermath of 9/11 that al-Qaeda had infiltrated the thriving Muslim community in Dublin. Ireland's small security service had gratefully accepted help from Mossad, MI5, and European intelligence services to mount various surveillance operations and GCHQ, Britain's "spy in the sky," had monitored the e-mails and phone calls of suspects. One result had been to thwart the plan of Abu Hamsa, the radical cleric, to seek political asylum in Ireland before he could be arrested on an extradition warrant to face terrorist-related charges in the United States. Hamsa was now in Belmarsh, one of Britain's high-security prisons, serving a sentence for his involvement in terrorism. Hamsa believed, wrongly, that the long history of the IRA's political wing, Sinn Féin, in successfully opposing extradition from the United States of IRA suspects to face trial in Northern Ireland would ensure he would not be extradited to America. He was counting on the Dublin government facing legal problems; like other European countries, Ireland has strict laws about extradition. In 2008, the Irish government had still refused to return the three Provisional IRA members to Colombia. They continue to live quite close to the Irish border with Northern Ireland.

In the past year al-Qaeda had started an intensive recruitment drive among Ireland's young Muslims to become jihadists. MI5 agents had established that one-and-a-half tons of ammonium-based nitrate fertilizer, which had been found in London, had been smuggled into Britain from Ireland. If it exploded, it could have killed more than had died in the Madrid train massacre. The agents had discovered that every year 150,000 tons of the lethal material were shipped annually from Russia and there were few controls at any of the Republic's docks as to who collected it. An MI5 agent had then established that a terrorist could buy half a ton of the fertilizer at any of the Republic's agricultural merchants. The fertilizer had lain in plastic sacks in the yard the agent visited. To weaponize it, all a terrorist had to do was separate the potash from the ammonium nitrate, then douse the nitrate with domestic fuel oil and add a detonator.

The deep concern this had caused was reinforced (to the author) by Northern Ireland's leading antiterrorist chief, Detective Superintendent Andy Sproule of the Serious and Organized Crimes Unit: "There are increasingly large amounts of this fertilizer coming into Ireland and it is not even what it claims to be. The levels of ammonium nitrate are too high and it is dangerous." The ban in Northern Ireland since 1996 to stop it being sold to the IRA has led to a dramatic increase in the import figures of the deadly fertilizer into the Republic. It arrives in container ships from Russian plants near the Ural Mountains. Before 2001 the Republic had imported hardly any artificial fertilizer containing high levels of potash and ammonium nitrate. Sensing a market opening, the Irish Fertilizer Manufacturers Association (IFMA) began to import the Russian fertilizer. In 2003 the amount was 120,000 tons. A year later it reached 150,000 tons. The figure continued to grow.

It was one matter Meir Dagan could raise with General Michael Hayden, who had been appointed to replace Tenet in 2006. Their meeting in Washington would be their first face-to-face encounter. The agenda would include the ongoing roundup by Hezbollah's security service of informers in the Beka'a Valley and south Lebanon, several of whom had risked their lives and those of their families by identifying for Mossad the locations of missiles. Hassan Nasrallah had made the capture of the informers a priority. For discussion would also be the failure of Israeli intelligence to locate and capture the Hezbollah leader and his senior aides.

The two spy chiefs would also update each other on the identity of a mysterious name—Rakan Ben Williams. Was he who he claimed to be, an American convert to Islam? Al-Qaeda now claimed to have hundreds of such members. Or was it a code name for a cell or even a group? In London, MI5 analysts were trying to discover if the name fit one of the men arrested in Operation Overt. In the meantime, "Williams" had continued to utilize the Internet for his threats. Each was signed as "al-Qaeda undercover soldier in the USA." But the style suggested the writer could be a woman. Or it might simply have been a hoaxer of either sex. Long ago, Meir Dagan had realized counterterrorism was plagued with often well-constructed nonsense. But no matter how outlandish it appeared, it had to be tracked down. At the Mossad training school, instructors reminded students that from the moment man established himself as a new species unique among all animals, it was the moment when he first used his primitive language to lie; the world became his to create and destroy. It would ever be so.

CHAPTER 29

FOR THE
MOMENT . . .

Mossad, like other intelligence services around the world, braced itself

for the fifth anniversary of September 11, and the attacks on the Twin

Towers and the Pentagon. Since the discovery of the London-based plot

to bring down ten American and British airliners over the Atlantic, the

intelligence analysts had listened closely to what one called "the whis-

pers in the wind" for the first hint that the fifth anniversary would be

marked by another massive atrocity. The analysts of Mossad focused

on the latest threat al-Qaeda had issued—that it would soon strike

against Israel with a ferocity never seen before. The Jewish state was

still reeling from its failure to defeat Hezbollah and the increased fighting in the Gaza Strip. The threat from Tehran continued. Islam, the giver of many lasting benefits to mankind and the proud possessor of a thrilling history, had been transformed into a rabid form of Islamism by its devotees who called for the elimination of all those who opposed them. "Death to the infidel" had become a call that closed anti-West rallies across the Muslim world.

The trumpet call followed those seventy-one minutes which began at 8:46 A.M. on September 11, 2001, in the blue sky over New York. That was the moment when American Flight 11 gouged into the North Tower, and ended at 9:57 A.M. when the doomed passengers on United Flight 93 tried, but failed, to regain control over their plane before it crashed into the Pennsylvania soil. After 9/11 the calumny took root, nurtured by the new freedom of the Internet and ironically supported by the words of then U.S. Secretary of State Donald Rumsfeld: "We know what we know; we know there are things we do not know; and there are things we know we know we don't know." That classic Rumsfeldism—which had actually referred to the need for a regime change in Iraq—was seized upon by the extremists as proof America had something to hide over 9/11.

The official 9/11 Commission said there was no evidence that office equipment in the towers had been "pulverized down to the last computer microchip." Lee Hamilton, the former vice chairman of the Commission, felt compelled to say (to the author): "A lot of people I have encountered believe the U.S. government was involved. Many say the government planned the whole thing. Of course the evidence does not lead that way at all."

So why is it that many millions of people in the United States and Europe continue to embrace the accusation of a vast conspiracy? Is it possible—as a Mossad psychologist told the author—that what he called "the reality of terror" had become "dulled by the constant replaying of the television images so people saw it subconsciously as another kind of computer-generated game?"

The apologists for al-Qaeda filled the airwaves across the Arab world with claims that the 9/11 attacks had been a gigantic conspiracy by the Bush administration as an excuse to attack Afghanistan and Iraq. In 2006, five years after they had first surfaced while smoke from the Twin Towers rose from the world's largest funeral pyre, those claims had been given a new legitimacy. Seventy-five American academics, who called themselves Scholars for 9/11 Truth, claimed things were not as officially presented. Some go so for as to speculate that a shadowy group of neo-conservatives, many of them embedded in the Bush administration, knew of the attack in advance and conspired with the CIA to topple the World Trade Center and the Pentagon in the hope such unprecedented attacks would gain overwhelming support for a U.S.-led war in the Middle East. The last time such an attack had aroused the collective fury of Americans had been Pearl Harbor, when Japan had launched its assault on the U.S. fleet. The decision to do this had been to give Tokyo a clear geopolitical advantage in the Pacific and pave the way for an attack on the United States. That dream had finally died in the ashes of Hiroshima and Nagasaki. Then, sixty-one years later, the Scholars for 9/11 Truth—professors, lecturers, and academics of all kinds—claimed the decision to secretly launch 9/11 was also rooted in geopolitics, its objective to give the Bush administration control over the oil fields of Iraq.

A founder and leader of the group, Steven E. Jones, a physics professor at Brigham Young University in Utah, has said: "There is the clear possibility of thermite-based arson and demolition. The planes seen crashing into the Twin Towers were just a distraction. We don't believe that nineteen hijackers and a few others in a cave with bin Laden pulled this off acting alone. We challenge this official theory and, by God, we're going to get to the bottom of this," he said.

His case, presented with all the scholarly language of academia, has given some credence to the hundreds of books and tens of thousands of Web pages devoted to 9/11 that argue the Bush administration had encouraged the attacks. Central to the argument is Professor Jones's thesis that there is no official explanation for the speed with which the Twin Towers collapsed; each of the 1,400-foot towers had taken 10 seconds to topple; another building in the complex, a 47-story structure, had taken only 7 seconds to do so, of that there is no dispute. But for the Scholars for 9/11 Truth this was a phenomenon that contravened "the physical law of conservation of momentum and offers no credible explanation of how the towers fell at near terminal velocity into their own footprint. For some reason ninety percent of the building material was converted into 'flour,' creating a massive volume of sub-one-hundred-fifty-micron dust across southern Manhattan. By comparison with the destruction of other high-rise buildings, which have also spontaneously collapsed, either through mudslides or earthquakes, they fell to the side, largely intact or reduced to only large pieces of rubble and minimal dust amounts. The physical energy required to collapse the World Trade Center buildings and pulverize all office contents including computer chips to their basic elements clearly indicates a quantity of energy far beyond the gravitational energy potential of each tower; this is further evidence that the weight of a tower is insufficient to produce the energy required to pulverize its contents to such an extent."

A poll conducted by Ohio University revealed that one-third of the American public believed the federal government assisted in the World Trade Center attacks or took no action to stop them. The poll offered one clue as to why millions accepted this. The pollsters found that the people most likely to believe "are those who regularly use the Internet but who do not regularly read, watch, or listen to 'mainstream' media. Alone before a computer, linked to their cyber friends as their only company, they can easily begin to accept all sorts of bizarre notions, especially when trying to make sense of an event as grotesque as the collapse of two skyscrapers," reported the London *Daily Telegraph*, two days after the fifth anniversary.

So who is Professor Jones, who many see as an exposer of what would be undoubtedly the world's greatest conspiracy—one that left the news that Princess Diana's inquest was to open in January 2007 as little more than a passing footnote? The soft-spoken professor is the same man who is also convinced that Jesus wandered through ancient Mexico around AD 600, paying calls on various Mayan villagers, and has published "evidence that the Mayans [were] well aware of the resurrected Lord" centuries before the Spanish priests brought them the good news. Professor Jones has also, for the past ten years, promoted in Third World countries a solar funnel cooker based on the highly disputed scientific theory of cold fusion. But despite this colorful background for a physics professor, Professor Jones has gathered like-minded academics to support his claim of a 9/11 conspiracy. However, in checking the author found that many of the Scholars for 9/11 Truth are not scientists with proven expertise in relevant fields like aviation, air defense, air traffic control, civil engineering, firefighting, metallurgy, and geology—all essential skills to come to an informed conclusion about how the Twin Towers were felled. Many are academics who have devoted a great deal of their careers tilting at various windmills. Professor James H. Fetzer, who teaches in Minnesota and is head of a splinter group, is convinced that President John F. Kennedy was killed by several shooters and that the moon landing in 1969 was likely a hoax. More recently he has been quoted as urging that Americans "arm themselves and lend support to a military coup that will replace the Bush government with a new regime."

Just as the Holocaust has increasingly attracted its deniers, so the tragedy of 9/11 is indeed so shocking and incomprehensible that it has attracted a growing number of people to reject the simple truth: that al-Qaeda had announced its coming, weeks before—and that the clear warnings from Mossad had been largely discounted. In Tel Aviv a senior Mossad analyst told the author in September 2006:

> The Bush administration has given groups like the Scholars for [9/11] Truth credibility by doing so much of its work in secret and by giving the public so many fake stories. A good example is that President Bush finally admitted in September, nine months after he had solemnly denied it, terrorist suspects were being secretly held in interrogation centers outside the jurisdiction of the United States. The result is the paranoia of groups like the Scholars for Truth are fed by the arrogance of those around President Bush.

More certain is that those members of the Bush administration in power on that September 11, 2001, overreacted to the destruction. The official exaggeration began with the initial reports of casualties estimated as high as twenty thousand. The number, thankfully, would turn out to be under three thousand. In the weeks after 9/11 dozens of innocent "terrorist suspects" were imprisoned without charge. The administration did nothing to deny rumors that Iraq was preparing to launch an arsenal of weapons of mass destruction. Saddam Hussein became the new Hitler. President Bush, like his father, was cast in the role of the fighter pilot ready to lead his nation to victory against the evil forces of al-Qaeda. No wonder the president readily admitted that the Hollywood movie *Independence Day* was one he never tired of watching.

A Mossad analyst, a veteran of many years of cool and careful judgments, said to the author:

> The best argument against a conspiracy within the Bush administration is the profound incompetence of what followed. The same people who are now making a mess of Iraq and Afghanistan simply do not possess the skills, and deviousness, to stage a complex

assault on two narrow towers of steel and glass standing along-side the Hudson River. The truth is that the attacks were the work of desperate men ready to die and with a goal that was clear. It was Osama bin Laden, an engineer of standing, and his brightest pupil, Mohamed Atta, who understood the best way to collapse the World Trade Center was not by targeting the base, but by un-dermining the upper levels of each structure. But this has all been discounted in the search for something more sinister at the very heart of American democracy. The very real danger is that the conspiracies will encourage the world to take its eye off the real-ity that the further we are away from the last catastrophic terror-ist attack, the closer we are to the next.

As the last quarter of 2007 waxed, in Tel Aviv Meir Dagan briefed Gen-eral Elyezer Shkedy, the country's air force chief, on the latest intelli-gence from his deeper agents inside Iran. Israel's embattled prime minister had told Shkedy to prepare for a full-scale aerial assault on Iran's nuclear facilities. Mossad's former director of operations, Rafi Ei-tan, now a key member of Olmert's shaky coalition, had publicly warned the population to update their bomb shelters against an attack from Teh-ran's missiles. Israel's decision to ratchet up its preparations for an air assault came after Tehran had ignored the UN deadline to stop its nuclear enrichment program to create atomic weapons. General Shkedy, the forty-nine-year-old son of Holocaust survivors whose office is dom-inated by a photo of an Israeli F-15 flying over Auschwitz, described the concern over Iran as "a serious threat to Israel and the rest of the world. My job is to maximize our capabilities in every respect. Beyond that, the less said the better." Giora Eiland, Israel's former national security adviser, added: "Trying to negotiate with Iran is going nowhere. Teh-ran is now a major threat to Israel. President Mahmoud Ahmadinejad is ready to sacrifice half of his people to eliminate us."

A special Israeli Defense Forces unit, "Iran Force," had been created under Shkedy. Several Pentagon strategic bombing specialists were at-tached to work alongside Israeli military planners. The unit has real-time access to American satellite images taken over Iran's ten nuclear facilities. Israel's air force, equipped with the latest American bunker-busting bombs, was the only means the country had to attack Iran. Dis-tance ruled out a ground force assault. Uri Dromi, a former air force colonel, told the author: "Dates and time frames are under close scrutiny. No formal date has yet been set. But the options for an attack are shortening." Much would depend on information from Mossad spies in Iran.

In London Nathan, the Mossad station chief, had been fully briefed on an MI5 antiterrorism operation that had discovered Britain's first Islamic "school for terror." It followed the arrests across London of fourteen radical Muslim extremists. They included Abu Abdullah, who was detained after he preached at a London mosque that he would "love to see our jihadists go to Iraq to kill British and American soldiers." Abdullah had been a regular visitor to the Jameah Islamiyah Faith School. The tall, gothic building stood in fifty-four acres on the edge of a beautiful English village and had long been a brooding presence even in its days as a Roman Catholic seminary. It was to the school that Abu Hamsa, the hook-handed extremist preacher, "brought young Muslims to be indoctrinated in jihad," confirmed a senior MI5 officer. After serving seven years for incitement to murder Hamsa was deported to the United States where he was convicted on terrorist charges in May 2014.

The discovery of the school for terror reveals how extensive al-Qaeda's influence was within Britain's Muslim community. Peter Clarke, head of Scotland Yard's antiterrorist squad, said that Britain now had "a secret army of thousands of well-trained guerrilla fighters ready to kill in the name of religion." Over two hundred MI5 and antiterrorist officers had surrounded the school at Mark Cross near Crowborough in East Sussex. The raid followed the latest admission by a prisoner held at Guantánamo Bay that he had attended a summer training camp at the school. It had been conducted by Abu Hamsa shortly before he was jailed in February 2006. The school was run by Bilal Patel, the school imam. He claimed (to the author) the school "welcomes all groups to enjoy camping in an Islamic environment in our grounds." Mr. Patel ran the private school "as a charity." But he admitted he had received donations from wealthy Muslims to buy the property for £800,000 from the previous owners, a ballet school.

A senior MI5 officer said: "We have long feared that Britain has become a sanctuary for terrorists from the battlegrounds of Chechnya, Kashmir, and Afghanistan. They pose as asylum seekers. What we are now discovering is a nightmare scenario coming true." He revealed that al-Qaeda has developed a one-week basic jihad training course to be taught at "foundation camps set up in rural UK locations." The course is available through al-Qaeda Web sites. A British government report published last May revealed their number was "somewhere between five thousand and ten thousand." The report also said there were an estimated 16,000 people in the United Kingdom who "are supportive of al-Qaeda."

The news didn't surprise Meir Dagan. He had long felt that in one of their meetings, Eliza Manningham-Buller, the head of MI5, had shown commendable reality when she had said: "We can catch some of them, but not all of them."

The early morning sun caught the rust-stained hull of the 1,700-ton cargo ship as it slowly steamed into the busy Mediterranean port of Tartus in Syria on September 3, 2007. From its mast flew the flag of South Korea and the stern plate identified the *al-Hamed* as being registered in Inchon, one of the country's major ports.

Watching the ship maneuvering into its berth from a distance was a man with the swarthy skin of a Kurd or one of the marsh Arabs of Iraq. He was fluent in both their languages as well as some of the dialects of Afghanistan. He was, in fact, a Turkish-born Jew who had eschewed the life of a carpet seller in the family business in Istanbul to go to Israel, serve in its army as a translator, and finally achieve his life's ambition to work in Mossad. Fifteen years later, he was recognized as one of its most brilliant operatives. In that time, he had operated in a dozen countries under as many aliases, using his linguistic skills and chameleon-like characteristics to observe and be absorbed into whichever community he had been sent.

Now, for the moment, he was code-named Kamal with a perfectly faked Iranian passport in his pocket. Meir Dagan had stressed to him the importance of his mission: to confirm the role of *al-Hamed* in the dangerous relationship which the Syrian regime of Bashar al-Assad had formed with North Korea.

Kamal had known before he left Tel Aviv the ship had sailed from Namp'o, a North Korean port in the high security area south of the capital, Pyongyang. An NSA satellite image had shown it steaming out into the Yellow Sea on a journey which had taken it across the Indian Ocean, around the Cape of Good Hope, up the Atlantic and through the Strait of Gibraltar into the Mediterranean, and finally into Tartus harbor. At some stage of its voyage, it had reflagged itself at sea and the crew had painted on the stern plate the port of registration as Inchon. The newness of their work was still apparent against the drab gray of the rest of the hull.

Through a contact in the Tartus harbormaster's office, Kamal had managed to check the *al-Hamed*'s manifest and all day had watched trucks being loaded with the cement it listed. Then, as the sun began to set, military trucks arrived at the dockside and from the ship's hold cranes lifted crates covered in heavy tarpaulin, which soldiers guided into the trucks. Using a high-resolution camera no bigger than the palm of his hand, Kamal photographed the transfer. When he finished, he pressed a button on the camera to transmit the images to a receiving station inside the Israeli border with Lebanon. In an hour, they were in Mossad headquarters.

Kamal knew then his trip had achieved all Meir Dagan had hoped. Though he could not see inside the crates, the spy intuitively knew the steel-cased containers were holding weapons-grade plutonium, the element which had fueled the American atomic attack that destroyed the Japanese city of Nagasaki on August 9, 1945. In his mission briefing, Kamal had been told by Professor Uzi Even, who had helped to create Israel's own nuclear facility at Dimona, that the plutonium would, in its raw form, be easily transported as nuggets in lead protective drums and the shaping and casting of the material would be done in Syria.

On that warm September day almost fifty-two years after Nagasaki had been destroyed, sufficient plutonium had been delivered to Syria to devastate an entire country, its neighbor, Israel.

Shortly before noon on September 4, 2007, a number of cars drove past the concert hall of the Israeli Philharmonic Orchestra in Tel Aviv and entered the heavily guarded headquarters of Major General Elyezer Shkedy, the country's air force commander. As a fighter pilot he had won a deserved reputation for daredevil tactics coupled with a cool analytical mind. His speciality had been flying dangerously close to the ground, maneuvering past peaks and rocky outcrops, then hurtling skyward to ten thousand feet, nearing the speed of sound, before diving on the target, his weapon system switched on, his eyes flitting between the coordinates projected on his hood screen to the bombsight and the target. Weapons released, he would turn radically, the screech from the strain on the airframe like a banshee wail, and he would once more hurtle skyward. From dive attack to his second climb, it would take him only seconds.

For the past week Shkedy had prepared for an unprecedented operation, which would require those tactics to be carried out by pilots he had handpicked because their flying skills matched his own. But they would be flying not the F-16 fighter plane he had once commanded, but Israel's latest jet, the F-151. Flying at almost twice the speed of sound and capable of delivering a five-hundred-pound bunker-busting bomb, it was the most formidable fighter plane in the Israeli air force.

For weeks the pilots had practiced the flesh-flattening G-force of right-angle turns, diving and evading, to hit a small circle, carrying out bombing runs at an angled dive of thirty degrees. They had practiced all this in the pitch black of night in the Negev Desert. At first many of the dummy bombs had fallen wide of the circle, but soon they were landing inside, a number scoring the required bull's-eye. Shkedy called them "my Top Guns"—though they were far removed from the Hollywood version of *Top Gun* pilots. His fliers were sobersided, led quiet lives, rarely partied, and had trained day and night for when they would finally be given the order to fly tactical strikes against Iran. Those attacks, they had been told, would take place at dawn or dusk. But all they knew so far about the mission they were spending weeks training for was that it would take place in the dead of night. No one had yet told them when or where, and they were content it should remain so. Curiosity was not one of their traits.

While F-151 twin afterburners glowed over the desolate night landscape and the pilots dropped their dummy bombs, which exploded white phosphorous smoke on the ground to determine the accuracy of the drops, in Shkedy's Tel Aviv complex his staff studied the approach to the target and discussed the precautions each F-151 must take from the moment its pilot pressed the red button on the control stick to release his bomb. The time they would spend over the actual target, TOT, would have to be between two and four seconds. Immediately after releasing its bomb, an F-151 would sink dangerously toward the ground, giving the pilot a second to fire his afterburner to climb and avoid the "frag pattern," the deadly metal fragments of spent explosive, which would follow the detonation. A bomb's shrapnel would rise to three thousand feet in seven seconds and unless the aircraft was clear of the target area, it could be blown up and other pilots already at various stages of their bomb runs would fly into a curtain of lethal fragments, which could destroy them. To avoid this, each pilot would have to endure body-crushing pressure of eight Gs while negotiating a radical ninety degree turn away from the target after bombing and climb to thirty thousand feet from the target zone to avoid ground missiles.

To calculate the precise distance from takeoff to target and the exact angle for the attack, the planners pored over computer graphs, satellite images, and physics tables to check and recheck figures. The targeters calculated that because the bombs would pierce the target roof before exploding inside, the roof would momentarily serve as a shield, reducing the frag pattern by between 30 and 40 percent. To help further protect the lead aircraft over the target, it would have its laser-guided bomb fitted with a delay fuse, providing a precious two-second lead time before the detonation.

Given the distance to the target, it was clear the F-151s would each have to carry two external fuel tanks, one under each wing. Filled with five hundred gallons of fuel, each tank added three thousand pounds to the aircraft weight. That required further complex calculations to be made: the exact point at which the bombing dive would start and the altitude at which the ordnance would be dropped.

In late August, while the *al-Hamed* was entering the Strait of Gibraltar, General Shkedy flew to the base of the Sixty-ninth Squadron in the Negev; the squadron was the air force's frontline air assault force trained to attack Iran. Waiting for Shkedy in the airfield briefing room were the five pilots whom he had selected to carry out the raid. With an average age of twenty-six, many came from families who were Holocaust survivors, like Shkedy himself.

For him the pilots had a kind of nobility to their youth; behind their relaxed and open manner was steel. Once before, he had flown to speak to them at the start of their special training and had begun by saying they had been selected for an air-to-ground mission, military speak for bombing a ground target. He had looked into their faces, glad to see they showed no emotion. No one had looked at the huge wall map of the Middle East. Nevertheless he anticipated each would be creating in his mind the potential mission profile: a low-level flight to the target, then a high-level return very possibly into headwinds. It could be Iran. But they had not asked him then and they did not do so on that late August morning when Shkedy once more met them in the briefing room.

Standing before a plasma screen, he used a remote control to illuminate it. For the first time the pilots saw the target: a complex deep inside Syria almost one hundred miles northeast of Damascus. He explained there was "good and sufficient intelligence" to destroy the complex, which the Syrians were using to build nuclear bombs. He waited for the flicker of response, then continued. Under the cover of being an agricultural research center, the complex was already engaged in extracting uranium from phosphates. Soon it would have weapons-enriched plutonium coming from North Korea. He told them the Israeli satellite Ofek-7, which had been launched only two months before, had been geo-positioned to watch the activities at the complex near the small Syrian city of Dayr az-Zawr. He indicated its position on the screen. No bombs must fall on civilians.

Shkedy then turned to the route in and out of the target area. The aircraft would fly up along the Syrian coast and enter its airspace at the last moment north at the port town of Samadogi and then follow the border with Turkey. At the point where the River Euphrates began its long journey south into Iraq, the attack force would swing south to the Syrian desert town of ar-Raqqah beyond which they would begin the bombing run. The way out would be a high-altitude straight run between the Syrian towns of Hims and Hamah to the Mediterranean. Over the coast of Lebanon they would turn south and return to base. The total mission time would be eighty minutes. In the event of an emergency, navy rescue launches would be positioned off the Syrian coast.

He ended the briefing by saying the attack would be in the early hours of the morning and would take place "soon." For a moment longer the air force commander looked at the small group of pilots. Perhaps sensing their one concern, he added that every step would be taken to ensure Syria's vaunted air defenses would be jammed. He did not say how and no one asked. It was a mark of the trust and respect they had for General Elyezer Shkedy.

The genesis for the operation ensued three years prior when a massive explosion on a North Korean freight train heading for the port of Namp'o occurred on April 22, 2004. Mossad agents had learned that in a compartment adjoining a sealed wagon were a dozen Syrian nuclear technicians who had worked in the Iranian nuclear program at Natanz, near Tehran, and had arrived in North Korea to collect the fissionable material stored in the wagon. The technicians died in the train explosion, and their bodies were flown home in lead-encased coffins aboard a Syrian military plane. By then a wide area around the explosion site had been cordoned off and scores of North Korean soldiers in anti-contamination suits had spent days recovering wreckage and spraying the entire area. Mossad analysts suspected they were recovering some of the estimated fifty-five kilos of weapons-grade plutonium North Korea possessed. Since the explosion—its cause never established—the intelligence service had tracked Syrian military officers and scientists on a dozen trips to Pyongyang, where they met with high-ranking officials in the regime. The most recent meeting was shortly before the *al-Hamed* had left Namp'o.

It was Kamal's report and photographic evidence of the arrival and unloading of the ship that was the focus of the meeting in General Shkedy's headquarters on September 4, 2007. The air force commander's briefing room was dominated by large plasma screens on two walls. One contained a blowup of the ship and the covered crates being off-loaded and driven away. A second screen showed the town of Dayr az-Zawr. A third screen displayed a satellite image of a large square building surrounded by several smaller ones and a security fence. The area was identified by the word: "Target."

Seated around the conference table with Prime Minister Ehud Olmert were the other key players in the operation, code-named Sunburst. For Olmert, it was further proof of his powers of survival. A year ago he had been close to being driven out of office after the debacle of the war in Lebanon, when he was vilified as the most incompetent leader Israel had ever had. He had fought back, appointing Ehud Barak as his new defense minister and Tzipi Livni as foreign minister. Both now flanked him at the table, giving Olmert the political support he needed for "Sunburst." Beside them sat Benjamin Netanyahu, a former prime minister and now leader of the Likud Party. Like Barak, Netanyahu was experienced in the complexities of "black" operations. Barak had been a leader in Sayeret Matkal, Israel's elite commando force, which bore the same motto as Britain's SAS: "Who Dares Wins." Netanyahu had approved several Mossad missions while in office.

The lynchpin of "Sunburst" was Meir Dagan. Early in the summer, he had presented Olmert with evidence that what he called "the nuclear connection" between Syria and North Korea had reached a dangerous level. Syria already possessed sixty Scud-C missiles, which it had bought from North Korea, and on August 14, when the freighter *al-Hamed* was already bound for Syria, North Korea's foreign trade minister, Rim Kyung Man, was in Damascus to sign a protocol on "cooperation and trade in science and technology." Afterward the minister had flown to Tehran, furthering the triangular relationship between North Korea, Syria, and Iran.

Mossad's analysts had concluded that Syria was not only a conduit for the transport to Iran of an estimated £50 million of missiles, but also could serve as "a hideout" for North Korea's own nuclear weapons, particularly its plutonium, while the regime continued to promise it would give up its nuclear program in exchange for the massive security guarantees and financial aid the West had promised.

Until recently, Meir Dagan had remained uncertain whether this was the case. Now, the latest intelligence from his agents in the country showed that Syria was determined to create its own nuclear weapons.

The meeting had been called to discuss the matter. Dagan began by saying the crates unloaded from the *al-Hamed* had been tracked by Israel's satellite to the complex. Dagan continued the meeting with his usual succinct analysis. The large square building was now almost certainly to be where the crates had been delivered. Inside its main structure was the machinery to cast the warheads for housing the weaponized plutonium. Scientists at Dimona had concluded that a small quantity of polonium and beryllium would be used to create the chain reaction for the plutonium, after the pellets were machined in "glove boxes," sealed containers accessed only by special laboratory gloves to protect the technicians at the site. Dagan had concluded with a final warning: the longer Israel waited to destroy the site, the closer the technicians in the building would come to creating their weapons.

Within minutes the decision was taken to eliminate the complex.

In the late evening of September 5, 2007, Israeli commandos from the Sayeret Matkal dressed in Syrian army uniform crossed into Syria over its northern border with Iraq. They were equipped with a laser guidance system designed to guide aircraft to the target. With them were specialists from the Israeli Defense Forces. In their backpacks was equipment linked to IDF electronic countermeasure jamming technology designed to disrupt Syria's formidable air defenses. When they were forty miles from the target the men hid and waited.

At their airfield in the Negev, the five mission pilots sat down to a large dinner. Even though they were not hungry, they knew they would need all the nutrients for the sheer physical energy and mental skills they would expend in the coming hours. Afterward they went to the briefing room where Shkedy was waiting with other senior officers. The briefing officer once more ran through the mission procedure: radio frequencies, radio silence protocols, and individual call signs. Takeoff time would be at 23:59 with twenty seconds separating each plane. There would be a dogleg out to sea at five hundred knots, over eight miles a minute, then, with Haifa to their right, they would drop to sea level and head up the coast of Lebanon past Beirut and continue into Syrian airspace. From there it was on to the target.

When the briefing ended, Shkedy walked to the front of the room and paused to look at each pilot.

"You all know the importance of your target. It must be destroyed at all costs. This is the most important mission any of you have taken or probably will ever take. Every step has been taken to protect you. But if anything does happen, we will do everything to rescue you. That I promise you. But I am confident that surprise is on our side. You will be in and out before the Syrians realize what has happened," said General Shkedy.

No one in the room doubted him. They all knew the mission was a pivotal point in the protection of Israel. The silence was broken by Shkedy's final words: "God be with you!" Then he stepped forward and shook the hand of each pilot.

By 11:45 in the evening, the ordnance technicians had checked the bombs, ensuring each was securely positioned in its release clip beneath the wings of each F-151. After his check, the technician removed the metal safety pin from each bomb.

A minute later, the runway crew reported the strip was clear of small stones or any other obstruction that could be sucked into the engine and destroy it.

From the twin tailpipes of the first aircraft, followed by the others, came the scalding heat from the afterburners.

In each cockpit the pilots had gone through the same drill: activating the computerized checks of the navigation, mechanical, communications, and finally the firing systems.

Each pilot wore two suits: his flight suit and, over it, the G-suit, a torso harness, survival gear, and a helmet. Clipped to each harness was a small gadget that would send a homing signal if he was forced to abandon the mission.

At one minute to midnight the first F-151, with a roar and a plume of exhaust marking its progress, sped down the runway. Shortly after midnight the last of the planes had retracted its wheels. Sunrise had started.

The mission was a total success. Satellite images showed the complete destruction of the complex and, the next day, Syrian bulldozers covering the blitzed area with earth to avoid the spread of radiation. It would be ten days before the country's vice president, Farouk al-Sharaa, would only say: "Our military and political echelon is looking into the matter." In Tel Aviv Ehud Olmert, not quite able to conceal his smile, said: "You will understand we naturally cannot always show the public our cards." But to play them, in the early hours of the morning of September 6, 2007, those pilots had carried out one of the most daring air strikes ever.

In January 2008, three days after President Bush had left Israel, where he had been privately briefed on the mission, the Israeli Defense Force released a satellite image that showed Syria had commenced rebuilding the destroyed site.

On Saturday morning, February 2, 2008, a man emerged from the U-Bahn, Berlin's railway system, and stood outside the subway exit on the Kurfürstendamm, the city's elegant shopping quarter. He had started his journey in one of the eastern suburbs of the city and its purpose was contained in the briefcase he carried. A car pulled up, the driver opened the passenger door, and together they drove off.

Who the man was and what he had been asked to do was known, apart from the driver, to only Meir Dagan and a handful of senior Mossad officers in Tel Aviv. They had patiently waited for the car's passenger to obtain what they wanted.

Six months before, the driver introduced himself to the man as Reuben. It was not his real name: like all other details about his identity, that remained in a secure room where the names of all current *katsas*, field agents, were kept in Mossad headquarters. A few days ago, the man had left a message at one of the agreed dead-letter boxes, which Reuben regularly checked, that he was ready to deliver what he had been asked to provide in return for a substantial sum of euros, half as a down payment, the balance on delivery of what was now in his briefcase.

They were photos of Imad Mughniyeh. Next to Osama bin Laden, he was the world's most wanted terrorist.

Long before the al-Qaeda leader had launched his pilots against New York's Twin Towers and the Pentagon in Washington, Mughniyeh had introduced suicide bombers into the Middle East. The Hezbollah terrorist mastermind had read an account of the WWII Japanese kamikaze pilots in Hezbollah's own newspapers, *Al Sabia* and *Al Abd*, which had praised the pilots for their sacrifices. In the alleys and souks of Beirut, Mughniyeh had persuaded families it was a matter of honor to provide a son, or sometimes even a daughter, for similar sacrifices. They had remained the human weapons of choice against Israel, Iraq, and Afghanistan. Those who had chosen to die were remembered in Friday prayers in the shadowy coolness of the mosques, after the rhetoric of the muezzin calling for the destruction of all those who opposed Hezbollah.

The deaths of the young bombers were lauded and their memories kept alive. Mughniyeh told their families the souls of their children needed no more, that their suicide bombings would be remembered forever and assured them a place in Hezbollah's version of Heaven.

Like bin Laden, Mughniyeh had been hunted across the Middle East and beyond by Mossad, the CIA, and every other Western intelligence service. But each time he came close to capture, he escaped, the trail gone cold. Until now.

On that cold winter day in February 2008, with a bitterly harsh wind from the Polish steppes whistling through the streets of Berlin, Reuben drove along past the smoke-blackened ruins of the Gedächtniskirche, the church that was a memorial to the Allied bombing raids of WWII, a grim contrast to all the other buildings, which made the city look like any other European capital.

At some point the man produced a file from his briefcase and, in return, replaced it with an envelope Reuben handed over containing the balance of the fee for the images in the file.

The cover of the gray-colored document bore the stamp of what was once one of the most powerful agencies in the German Democratic Republic, the GDR, itself at one time the most important satellite nation in the former Soviet Union. The stamp identified the file had once belonged to the Stasi, the GDR's Ministry of State Security.

In the forty years of its existence it had employed 600,000 full-time spies and informers, roughly 1 secret policeman for every 320 East Germans. The Stasi had its own imposing headquarters in East Berlin, interrogation centers around the city, its own hotels and restaurants in the countryside, and clinics where only Stasi staff and their families could be treated. One clinic, close to the River Spree, had facilities to perform plastic surgery including facial reconstruction for Stasi agents and sometimes carefully selected members of terror groups with which the Stasi had close connections.

With bewildering speed, the citizens of East Germany awoke in November 1989 to find the collapse of the Berlin Wall, the resignation of the GDR's Politburo, and the official end of the Stasi's reign of terror. But not everything had ended. The clinic near the Spree had remained in business, offering its skills to those with the funding to pay for plastic surgery.

The file now in Reuben's possession contained photos of Imad Mughniyeh, which had been taken at the clinic after post-operative surgery. His face looked very different from the one which had last filled the pages of newspapers and magazines after he had been photographed at a Hezbollah rally before disappearing almost a quarter of a century previously. Subsequently he had established an even more murderous reputation than any other terrorist of the 1980s.

It was an era when the Venezuelan-born Marxist Carlos the Jackal's claim to notoriety had begun with taking forty-two OPEC oil ministers hostage in Vienna in 1975. He had then embarked on a reign of terror before Mossad had tipped off French intelligence so they could grab Carlos in Sudan and bring him to trial in Paris for his crimes on French soil, where he continues to serve a life sentence. Like Carlos, Abu Nidal had become another headline-grabbing terrorist after he ordered the gunning down of innocent men and women as they waited to board their Christmas flights in Rome and Vienna airports in 1985. Nidal had finally been killed by a Mossad kidon team. For a quarter of a century Imad Mughniyeh had dodged assassination.

On that February morning, the file in Reuben's possession could bring Mughniyeh's death closer for some of the worst crimes committed on Israel's doorstep—Lebanon. His history of violent attacks was appalling. In 1983, he had plotted the attack against the American embassy in Beirut. Among the sixty-three dead were eight members of the CIA, including its station chief in the Middle East. In the same year,

Mughniyeh arranged for the kidnapping of William Buckley, the CIA replacement station chief in battered Beirut.

Next he arranged the bombing of the U.S. Marines' barracks near the city's airport, killing 241 people. In between, he had carried out sky-jackings and organized the kidnapping of Western hostages, including Terry Waite, who had gone to Beirut to try to negotiate with Hezbollah's spiritual leader, Sheikh Muhammad Hussein Fadlallah, to free the hostages Hezbollah already held. Along with Buckley, Waite—the emissary of the Archbishop of Canterbury—had been incarcerated in what became known as the Beirut Hilton, the underground prison beneath the city.

Imad Mughniyeh had been responsible for the murder of over four hundred people and the torture of even more. America had placed a bounty of $25 million (£12.5 million) on his head.

One by one Mossad's *menume*, the Hebrew title by which each director general is known, plotted Mughniyeh's downfall. Men like the cool Nahum Admoni (1982–1990), the quiet-voiced Shabtai Shavit (1990–1996), the relentless Danny Yatom (1996–1998), and Efraim Halevy (1998–2002), the *menume* his staff called the "grandfather of spies," had all chaired endless secret meetings to plan the assassination of Imad Mughniyeh.

Their agents had tracked him to Paris only for him to once more slip away, as he had done in Rome and Madrid. For a while the trail led to Minsk in Belarus and then to the Islamic republics of the former Soviet Union. There were reports he was in Tehran, living under the protection of the fundamentalist regime. But each time the hunt had petered out.

In 2002, Meir Dagan took over Mossad. He did what all his predecessors had done and studied the growing number of files that listed how close Mossad agents had come to capturing Mughniyeh. At times they had been close, very close. But somehow he had still wriggled free. The suicide bombings had continued. For Dagan it became an article of faith that, as the tenth *menume*, he would finally terminate Mughniyeh's reign of terror.

Dagan had asked Mossad's psychiatrists, psychologists, behavioral scientists, psychoanalysts, and the profilers—collectively known as "the specialists"—to focus on where Imad Mughniyeh could be and the best way to kill him. There was a consensus the ideal means of doing so was with a car bomb. "It would be poetic justice," one specialist said.

Using the only photograph of him published in a newspaper and a handful of biographical details, they set to work.

Born in a south Lebanese village, the son of a fruit seller, Imad Mughniyeh had joined Force 17, Yasser Arafat's personal bodyguards, at the age of fifteen. He was sixteen years old when he had killed his first Israeli, a settler in the Golan Heights. After Arafat's Palestinian Liberation Organization (PLO) was forced to leave Lebanon in 1982, Mughniyeh stayed behind in Beirut and joined Hezbollah, the organization which had already established itself as the prime militant force resisting Israel. He came to the notice of Sheikh Fadlallah, who arranged for Mughniyeh to rise quickly in the Hezbollah ranks. By the age of twenty, Mughniyeh was a full-fledged terrorist after a spell of training in Tehran under the auspices of Iran's Revolutionary Guard.

The newspaper snapshot, showing an exultant Mughniyeh addressing a Hezbollah rally in Beirut, was studied under computer analysis. Various shapes of beard were superimposed to suggest how he might look now as the specialists tried to create an image of him and to seek clues to his mindset. Using a technique which they called "remote in-depth analysis," but referred to among themselves as RIDA, they continued the task of mapping out his personality. They evoked a great deal in their analysis: Allah and the devil and the role each might play in his life. Much of what they posited was intended to remain only between them, verbal signposts along the road of trying to discover Imad Mughniyeh's thinking as well as his physical appearance.

Other specialists worked to discover the psychological forces which motivated Mughniyeh. He was a mass murderer, certainly, yet he did not fit the typology of fanatics, those who were driven by anger. It would be satisfying—at least for the behaviorists—to conclude that at the root of his evil was all-consuming rage. It was there of course, but was it an all-animating and life-energizing force? The psychologists wondered if he was what they deemed "inhabited by a strong streak of masked violence?" This would have allowed him to go about his work in a businesslike manner, whether he was recruiting little more than children to be suicide bombers or ordering the bomb makers to make even more powerful explosives. But again there was no clear answer—no more than there was to the question of how he maintained order within his own immediate psychological universe so he could equate his unspeakable actions to his own belief he was right to kill and destroy. Was he the man who had been psychologically shaped by all he had done over the past twenty-five years?

In the photo that had been taken in the 1980s at that Hezbollah rally, a full beard covered his chin and the peaked cap he wore covered his hair. Rimless spectacles hid his eyes. One by one the facial analysts used their computer skills to remove his beard, spectacles, and hat, and aged him to his present forty-five years. The specialists concluded there was evidence that at some point Mughniyeh's face had undergone some surgical work. But the traces of scar tissue indicated it had been done at least five years ago when he had first disappeared after the spate of suicide bomb attacks on Israel.

The Chinese were the acknowledged leaders in the field of facial surgery. But the Beijing regime had turned its back on Hezbollah. The Russians were a possibility, but again the Mossad medical experts ruled out plastic surgeons that had once worked for the KGB. Others who operated on what the experts called "close to the wind" were checked in Romania, Serbia, and North African countries. But Mossad agents did not discover any evidence Mughniyeh had undergone plastic surgery in any of these countries.

Then, in June 2007, came the break. Since the end of the war with Hezbollah in south Lebanon, Mossad had been steadily recruiting Israeli Arabs in the West Bank who were opposed to Hezbollah. One of the informers had a relative in a village near Mughniyeh's birthplace. The cousin had told him that a friend of her family had heard Mughniyeh had traveled to Europe from the safe house the Syrian regime had provided. He had sent postcards from Paris, Frankfurt, Munich, and finally Berlin. It was little to go on, but it was a start.

First a Mossad agent, a fluent Arab speaker, had traveled to south Lebanon and had met the informer's cousin. The agent had posed as an old friend of Mughniyeh. Little more had emerged except that the cousin was certain Mughniyeh was back in Damascus, but according to her friend's family, he now looked different.

Within hours, Reuben had been ordered to investigate the possibility that Mughniyeh had visited Berlin to undergo further plastic surgery. Now, six months later, the *katsa* had the proof in the file his informer had handed over.

On Sunday afternoon, February 3, 2008, Meir Dagan chaired a meeting in the conference room adjoining his office. On the table were jugs of water and pots of coffee for those seated around it. They were the head of Shin Bet, the country's internal security force; the government's national security adviser; the political adviser to Prime Minister Ehud Olmert; and the military advocate-general to the Israeli Defense Forces, IDF. Among them sat a brigadier general, the head of kidon, Mossad's unique unit that conducted legally approved assassinations. Beside Dagan sat his director of operations. In a corner of the room was the table and chair usually occupied by the notetaker to record decisions and other discussions. Now it was empty. There would be no record of this meeting.

Over the past six years, similar meetings had been held by Dagan since coming to office in August 2002. The first had been four months later in December of that year to discuss the case of Ramzi Nahara, a Mossad informer Dagan had known personally, who had defected to Hezbollah. Was it for money? A skewed belief in the group's cause? Had he fallen for one of the Arab women Hezbollah used to try and entrap a foreigner? There were no answers. But the meeting was short and unanimous. Nahara had to be located. He was tracked to an Arab village and killed with a car bomb planted by a former colleague in the service he betrayed.

In March 2003, another meeting discussed Abu Mohammed Al-Masri, who had been sent by al-Qaeda from Pakistan to create a cell to target Israeli villages on the border with Lebanon using rockets. He, too, died in a car bomb as he drove around south Lebanon seeking recruits and suitable sites to launch the weapons. The next target the meeting had discussed, in August 2003, was Al Hussein Salah, Hezbollah's explosives expert, who had begun rebuilding the organization's arsenal in the Beirut suburbs. He was on his way to meet his bomb makers when he died in yet another car bomb planted by the Mossad.

A full year had passed before Dagan once more summoned the men in his conference room. The decision had been taken in the stifling heat of July 2004 that Ghaleb Awali, the Hezbollah liaison between Damascus and the activists in the Gaza Strip, should be killed by a car bomb as he headed south to meet the activists. The bomb was planted under his seat. In Awali's place came Izz El-Deen Sheikh Khalil, a senior Hezbollah official in Damascus who had been given responsibility by Syria to liaise between Damascus and Hamas and Hezbollah units in Gaza and the West Bank. Even as he drove to his first appointment, Khalil was killed by a Mossad car bomb in a Damascus suburb. In May

2006, Mahmoud Majzoub, a senior member of the Islamic jihad committee through which Hezbollah liaised with Tehran, was killed by a car bomb as he drove to lunch in a south Lebanon restaurant.

Each of the targets had been carefully selected and placed under surveillance; the moment of their deaths was the result of the planning that would once more occupy the men in the conference room on that Sunday afternoon. It was there that the fate of Imad Mughniyeh would be settled. His death warrant was in the folder beside Dagan on the table. It had originally been signed by the then prime minister, Ariel Sharon (in 2008 still in a coma) and ratified by Ehud Olmert. The question the meeting was asked to decide was: How could the warrant be executed?

On the table before each man was a copy of the file that Reuben had transmitted on a high-security line from his Berlin office. Inside the file was a series of still prints from a video, in all thirty-four images. They showed the various stages of the plastic surgery Imad Mughniyeh had undergone. First his beard had been shaved and the previous scar tissue carefully removed. A note attached to the print contained the original observation in German, now translated into Hebrew, that the scar tissue on the cheeks, jaw, and the temples dated from 1993 following surgery at a clinic in Tripoli, Libya. Close-up images revealed further details of the surgeon's work at the East German clinic. The eyes had been reshaped by tightening the skin on Mughniyeh's temples. His lower jaw had been expertly cut, a piece of bone removed and then re-sewn to provide a narrower jaw line, which gave the face a leaner look. A number of front teeth had been removed and replaced with others of a different shape. His hair had been colored a distinguished-looking gray and, instead of his spectacles, he now wore contact lenses. Compared to the original newspaper photograph, Imad Mughniyeh looked radically different.

Those around the table decided a car bomb would once more be the most effective way to carry out the assassination. But there were problems. Mossad's previous car bombing of Mughniyeh's associates would undoubtedly have made him cautious about traveling anywhere in his own car. There was a possibility he would use the vehicle of one of his bodyguards. But there was no firm intelligence of who they were or what type of cars they used. The information the Mossad agent had acquired that Mughniyeh was back in Damascus looking "very different" would need time to be checked so a plan could be properly developed.

It was Meir Dagan who brought the discussion to a halt. He reminded others that in nine days' time, February 12, a historic event would be taking place in Tehran and other Arab countries. It would mark the twenty-ninth anniversary of Ayatollah Khomeini's Iranian Revolution. In Syria a day of celebration would be marked by a reception at the city's Iranian Cultural Center, given by the newly appointed Iranian ambassador to Syria, Hojatoleslam Ahmad Musavi. It would be a fitting time for him to be introduced to Imad Mughniyeh. In Dagan's view there was more than "a good chance" Mughniyeh, if he were back in Damascus, would attend the function. To refuse such an invitation would not only offend his Syrian hosts, who had given him shelter, but also the Tehran mullahs and their ambassador, who would bask in the reflected glory of being in the presence of such an exalted figure who had done so much damage to the West.

Meir Dagan had spoken the words he had used before at other meetings to order an assassination.

"We do it."

By Monday, February 4, 2008, the kidon brigadier general had chosen the three operatives he would use for the assassination. Each had been assigned a code name, which matched the one-off passport he would have. The documents would be specially prepared by the Mossad travel department from the stock of passports in storage. Other documents provided details of their home addresses and occupations. Pierre, the French passport holder, had an address in Montpelier, France, and was identified as a car mechanic. Manuel, the holder of the Spanish passport, had a home in Malaga and was described as a tour guide; Ludwig's German passport described him as living in Munich where he worked as an electrician.

The names, addresses, and job backgrounds were genuine, those of sayanim, the Jewish volunteers upon whom Mossad often depended on for its more dangerous operations. Among the tasks the volunteers fulfilled was that of providing cover for agents by allowing them to assume their identities.

While the documents were being prepared by the forgers working in the basement of Mossad headquarters, in the Negev Desert the three kidon memorized their "legends"—the stories they would tell if challenged by immigration, police, or the security officers of Syria. Each story was kept as simple as possible: Pierre could talk knowledgably about car engines; Manuel about his work escorting tourists around the south of Spain; Ludwig memorized the intricacies of being an electrician.

In the meantime the travel department checked the flights into Damascus. In his briefing, the brigadier general had told the head of the department the kidon should travel separately and arrive at different times in the Syrian capital, and the flights should be on Air France, Jordanian, and Alitalia airlines. Each ticket should have a selection of return flights booked. All the seats should be in economy. Pierre should arrive first and have a prepaid hired car waiting for him at Damascus. Like the other two, the purpose of his visit should be given as "holiday."

In the next week a Mossad sayan in Beirut, a man who had made the journey several times, drove north to Damascus. His familiar figure and the reason for his journey—to explore with the Syrian Ministry of Tourism the possibility of creating twin holidays to Lebanon and the historic ruins of Syria—aroused no suspicion. The sayan visited the ministry, made his pitch, and drove around Damascus. Among the many photographs he took were several of the Iranian Cultural Center and the surrounding streets. By nightfall he was back in Beirut. That evening the photos had been transferred onto a disk and transmitted to a travel agency, a front for Mossad in downtown Tel Aviv. From there it was couriered to their headquarters in the city.

Day after day the planning for the assassination continued. Instructors at their desert base checked every detail with the kidon: the language they would speak, the clothes they would wear, the reason why they had come to Syria out of season. The answer to that, given in different ways, was they each wanted a quiet holiday and one they could afford. Like the rest of their cover stories, it was believable from the way they dressed and spoke.

In between, the three men still had much to study and memorize: the roads to the Iranian Cultural Center, the routes from across the city, the area where they could find a lock-up garage, the location of the dead-letter box where the explosives had been left for them to kill Imad Mughniyeh. The material would be placed there by the Beirut sayanim. How and when he did so would remain one of the secrets of the operation moving to its climax.

Meir Dagan had tasked Israel's own spy satellite, Trescas, to mount surveillance in the area of Damascus where the Iranian Cultural Center was situated. Mossad had priority over all the country's military agencies for such an operation.

Day by day, images were downloaded and studied by photo interpreters in the Kirya, the IDF headquarters in Tel Aviv, looking for any sign of Mughniyeh. There were several "possibles," but none that matched the photo in the file Reuben had sent. The silent search from outer space continued. Dagan had "a gut feeling" the terrorist would be going to the Iranian celebration at the cocktail party, he told his director of operations.

On Saturday, February 9, 2008, the three kidon made their way to Tel Aviv airport to catch their flights to Vienna, Paris, and Frankfurt. A week before, Reuben had received the file from his informer and transmitted it to Tel Aviv. By nightfall, the three kidon were in their airport hotels waiting for their flights to Damascus the following day.

On their cell phones was a close-up of Mughniyeh's face, which had been altered in that former Stasi clinic near the River Spree.

On Sunday morning, February 10, 2008, Pierre boarded Air France Flight AF 1519 at Charles De Gaulle airport for the journey to Damascus. The sun was setting over the city when he arrived. From Madrid, Manuel had flown on Jordanian Airways Flight RJ 110 to Amman and then on to the Syrian capital. An hour later, Ludwig's Alitalia Flight AZ 7353 had left Milan's Malpensa airport in mid-afternoon and arrived in Damascus at 6:30 P.M. local time.

Shortly after, the three men—untroubled by Syrian immigration and customs officers—stowed their carry-on bags in the trunk of the hired car and, with Pierre at the wheel, drove into the city. By late evening they had driven past the dead-letter box and located the lock-up garage which the Beirut sayanim had said would suit their purpose. Satisfied that neither the dead-letter box nor the garage were under surveillance, they picked up the explosives, the small portable radio, and the key to the lock-up garage left in the box. Behind the door of the garage, they worked to prepare the bomb, which would be concealed inside the radio and placed in the car's headrest on the passenger side. By dawn they had finished.

Taking turns to stand watch, the three kidon slept in the car for most of the day. Late that afternoon, they drove around the city, finally passing the Iranian Cultural Center. It was bigger than the sayan's photographs had suggested. It stood on a road with exit routes close by. The plan they had devised would work. Satisfied, the team returned to the lock-up garage. There was no sign that anyone had disturbed its door by dislodging the piece of cigarette paper placed at the bottom.

What they did for the next twenty hours would remain a mystery.

At 7 P.M. on Tuesday, February 12, the team was back outside the Iranian Cultural Center. Ludwig took up position at one street corner, Manuel another. Pierre drove the hired car farther down the street from where the oncoming traffic was approaching. He activated the bomb placed in the headrest. Inside the radio, the timer began to tick. It had a four-hour clock. It was now 7:30.

Guests for the Iranian celebration of the Khomeini Revolution were steadily making their way into the Center. At 8 P.M., the Iranian ambassador arrived and hurried inside. None of the guests resembled the face on the cell phones of the three kidon.

At 9 P.M. a silver Mitsubishi Pajero turned into the street and parked close to where Ludwig and Manuel were standing on opposite sides. For a moment the driver and his passenger sat checking the street.

Then the passenger door opened and Imad Mughniyeh emerged. He wore a dark suit and his beard had been neatly trimmed. He started to walk up the street toward where the hired car was parked. He was level with the vehicle when there was a huge explosion, which blew the car into pieces and beheaded Mughniyeh. Later, some of his body parts were found twenty meters away.

Which of the kidon was the first to trigger the bomb would remain unknown. But before the first screaming guests ran from the Iranian Cultural Center reception, and the police and ambulances arrived, the three assassins had vanished.

It would later be suggested in some reports that a car had been left for them in a nearby side street and Pierre had driven the team to a predetermined pickup point in the south of Syria for an Israeli air force helicopter to collect them. Eyewitnesses would claim they saw a helicopter flying out to sea. Another report said they had left Damascus airport on night flights to Europe. But nobody would ever know.

On the Friday, February 15, following his assassination, Mughniyeh was buried at a huge Hezbollah funeral in Beirut, from where he had first launched his terrorist activities. His mother, Um-Imad, sat amid a sea of black chadors, a somber old woman who wailed that her son had planned to visit her on what had turned out to be the day after he died.

A few days later, she received an envelope. Inside was a copy of one of the pictures taken of Mughniyeh's face when he had undergone his successful plastic surgery. He had been her third son to die in a Mossad car bombing.

CHAPTER 30

NATHAN'S WORLD

In December 2009, Nathan—the code name for Mossad's long-serving station chief in London—had sat for two days listening to Sir John Sawers giving evidence to the Chilcot Inquiry into the Iraq War. As Mossad's senior intelligence officer in the United Kingdom, Nathan had relished his first opportunity to see Sawers performing publicly as the new head of MI6. In June that year Gordon Brown, the incumbent prime minister, had announced that Sawers would replace Sir John Scarlett as head of the Secret Intelligence Service (SIS). The outgoing chief had been a controversial and often unpopular head of the intelligence service, frequently attacked in the media and Parliament for his role in the run-up to the Iraq War. Nevertheless, Scarlett had sidestepped the inquiry's probing questions and disappeared back into his hobbies of collecting history books, visiting medieval churches, and engaging in fine dining.

Would Sawers also escape lightly from the inquiry? At the time of the war he had been the foreign affairs adviser to Prime Minister Tony Blair. Having left office, Blair had taken with him all the worthwhile secrets of the war. Would Sawers keep those he knew? He had been in his new office barely a month.

To Nathan, Sawers looked paler and thinner than in the photo in his entry on Facebook, the social networking site. In the photo he was in his swim trunks, posing like a James Bond look-alike; his interests were listed as going to first nights, hiking, tennis, cycling, and ballroom dancing.

"Too much information," Meir Dagan grunted when Nathan had alerted him to the entry. It was removed on the order of the foreign secretary, David Miliband.

Nathan knew that Sawers was no mere "pinup of the spy world," as one tabloid had called him. Sawers had worked at MI6 stations in Yemen and Syria before going to spy in South Africa during its transition from apartheid. Later he had been Britain's ambassador in Cairo (2001–2003), then its special representative in Baghdad after the Iraq War before serving as Her Majesty's ambassador to the United Nations (2007–2009).

In the hours Nathan had sat among the spectators in the Queen Elizabeth Hall listening to Sawers testifying, the new chief—the title given to a century of heads of MI6—had certainly protected the cloistered world of British intelligence. Nathan had sensed the relief of the senior MI6 officers at the back of the hall listening to Sawers's evidence.

Nathan knew why he had been asked by Meir Dagan to assess Sawers. The relationship between the Mossad and MI6 was mutually important, especially over Iran. But in the past weeks the station chief had also been aware that his counterpart in the British embassy in Tel Aviv had been reporting to London that Meir Dagan had shown signs that the threat posed by the Tehran leadership was becoming too much for the Mossad to handle. For years under Dagan the Mossad had been credited with an unprecedented success rate in eliminating and assassinating terrorists; keeping Syria on a tight rein; being the most respected intelligence service not only in the region but also in the world.

But increasingly Nathan had heard rumors from inside the Mossad of anger over Meir Dagan's management style: his blunt treatment of senior staff, abusing them at meetings before sacking some, and the sudden changes he made in the way the service operated.

In a stopover in London, one Mossad officer had told Nathan that Meir Dagan had also begun to show a lack of decisiveness in who to promote and who to demote. A divisional director had been accused of leaking details to an Israeli newspaper and frog-marched from his office to his car; his place had been taken by an officer who while close to Meir Dagan was regarded by many of the field agents as having insufficient operational experience. There was increasing talk that Dagan's relationship with Prime Minister Netanyahu, once close, was deteriorating. There were further embarrassing leaks from inside the Mossad that Dagan was no longer a hero but a bullyboy.

Increasingly, his visitor had told Nathan, the question being asked was: how long could Dagan survive? Dagan's plan to assassinate the Iranian ambassador to Syria, Hojatoleslam Ahmad Musavi, for his support of the Hezbollah terror group had been firmly rejected by the Mossad strategists. Others had suggested that Dagan was looking for an opening to reestablish himself as the golden boy of Israeli intelligence, in the hopes that Yuval Diskin, the head of Shin Bet, the country's internal security force, and the Israeli Defense Forces chief of staff, Lieutenant General Gabi Ashkenazi, would once more support instead of challenging Dagan at staff meetings.

Under Dagan the Mossad had been tasked with halting Iran's nuclear ambitions. In Washington the new president, Barack Obama, had made it clear he did not want Israel to pursue a military option—a position the Pentagon supported. Meir Dagan had, not for the first time, flown to London to see John Scarlett to discuss the matter. MI6's support would be crucial in gaining the support of Britain's government under Prime Minister Gordon Brown. Nathan had gone with him to the meeting.

It was soon clear that the outgoing MI6 chief did not see an Israeli air force strike as the solution. That should be seen only as a last resort, Scarlett had urged. In Scarlett's view, the counter to Iran's posturing would be diplomacy, using solid information from the Mossad and MI6 agents on the ground. Israel would then have the support not only of the British government but also of Europe's leaders and the White House. But launching a preemptive attack would leave Israel isolated, a position that could well make it an even stronger target for terrorism by Hezbollah and Hamas, Scarlett had concluded.

Meir Dagan was still angry when Nathan had driven him to catch the El Al flight to Tel Aviv.

When Scarlett's retirement was announced, Nathan had been ordered to find out if Sawers was more malleable. After watching Sawers deftly deflect difficult questions at the Chilcot Inquiry, Nathan had concluded that the bull-in-a-china-shop manner that nowadays was typical of Meir Dagan would not work with the new head of the Secret Intelligence Service.

Nathan's role as a diplomat at the Israeli embassy in London provided cover that made his work easier, allowing him to meet with British government officials in the course of his duties. His was a familiar face on the city's cocktail circuit, and he was also a member of several of the most exclusive clubs in and around Whitehall where he met other foreign diplomats. He knew that some of these diplomats were also spies. However, unlike him, they had often not been "declared" to the Foreign Office as being intelligence officers. Israel had decided to declare Nathan; listing him as a diplomat would also help him obtain access to potential sources unlikely to be always informed of his real status. Israel itself was categorized by the Foreign Office as a friendly country. If Nathan overstepped his boundaries as a spy, he would simply be expelled as a diplomat, his intelligence background protected.

The most dangerous of the nondeclared were the spies of Russia and China. In 2010, the Russians had thirty-five nondeclared intelligence officers working under diplomatic cover at their embassy and trade mission in London. In addition, Harry Ferguson, a former MI6 officer, claimed there were an estimated twenty "illegals," deep-cover agents. In the *Sunday Express*, Ferguson wrote: "the targets for both the nondeclared spies and illegals remained the same: military and nuclear secrets; new links between Britain, the United States and NATO; cultivating Labour politicians and trade union leaders with access to Downing Street."

The illegals also tried to obtain commercial and economic secrets without compromising their own cover. The bullion and metal markets of the Bank of England and the City of London were key targets.

Urgent information was sent to Moscow Center, the SVR foreign intelligence service headquarters on the ring road around the Russian capital, using a science known as steganography, the embedding of secret messages in Web sites. Nathan knew that despite MI5's own ultrasophisticated tracking system, steganography was almost impossible to detect.

In 2010, according to Ferguson, the Chinese Secret Intelligence Service had even more spies in Britain than the Russians. Among their tasks was to discover how strong Britain's defenses were against cyberwarfare. MI6 had increased its specialist staff to deal with the cyberwarfare launched by the latest generation of China's computer systems. In 2009 there had been over 40,000 intrusions into Ministry of Defence computers and those of its defense contractors. Sawers had predicted within five years the figures would double.

In 2010 there were over two million Muslims in Britain. Nathan spoke several of their dialects, read their newspapers, and understood the cultural differences within their world. In previous postings he had perfected the skill of being taken for a well-spoken businessman, perhaps from Cairo or Beirut, who had traveled widely before settling in London. He was able to move within the city's multiethnic groups without arousing suspicion. One of his priorities was to learn all he could about how these communities viewed the conflict between Prime Minister Benjamin Netanyahu and the new administration of President Barack Obama.

The rift between Washington and Tel Aviv had begun over Israel's expansion of its settlements in the West Bank and East Jerusalem and was widening at a time when Israel needed all the support it could muster from the United States, Britain, and Europe to oppose Iran's nuclear policy. Netanyahu reluctantly agreed to a moratorium on future building pending "peace talks" hosted by U.S. Secretary of State Hillary Clinton in Washington between himself and Palestine president Mahmoud Abbas. When the talks opened on September 3, 2010, Israel's prime minister had called Abbas "my partner in peace," though the Palestinian had smiled uncertainly when Netanyahu added: "I see a framework deal in twelve months and a phased-in-stage-by-stage agreement over thirty years."

Hamas, the elected ruler of Gaza, which Israel saw as a terror group, was not invited. As the delegates assembled, Hamas continued to attack its neighbors, killing four Israeli settlers.

"Nothing has changed. Nothing will change," wrote one of the many reporters covering the talks. Other journalists at the conference noted that the relationship between Obama and Netanyahu was as distant as ever.

Increasingly the developing crisis had led Britain's Muslims to finance young men to be trained as jihadists, holy warriors to fight for an Islamic coalition of Iran, Hezbollah, and Hamas. Hundreds of Muslims had traveled to training camps set up by al-Qaeda in Pakistan and Yemen. Friday prayers had become more pronounced in their attacks on the Jewish state. The calls for money to support jihad had become more demanding. Iran's leader, Mahmoud Ahmadinejad, Hezbollah's Hassan Nasrallah, and Hamas's Khalid Meshal were extolled as heroic figures.

Nathan knew that Obama's deliberate coldness toward Netanyahu had not been lost on community leaders. Shortly after President Obama had been elected he had gone to Cairo to address the Muslim world but had not made a "balancing" visit to Jerusalem. The slight was greeted by cheers from worshippers in hundreds of British mosques. Nathan knew that the Mossad analysts were uncertain whether Obama's snub was simply personal—his dislike of Netanyahu was well known—or whether it reflected a deeper dislike of Israel itself.

Increasingly those Nathan spoke to in the British intelligence world felt that Netanyahu, not for the first time, had mishandled his relationship with an American president. The Israeli prime minister's relations with President Clinton during his tenure in the White House had been similarly poor.

London had long been a port of call for intelligence chiefs on their way to and from the Middle East. On their must-visit list were the heads of MI5 and MI6 and Nathan.

In January 2010, Leon Edward Panetta, the seventy-one-year-old former chief of staff of the Clinton White House, became the nineteenth director of central intelligence. A Washington insider, he had no hands-on experience with running a global foreign intelligence service. Nathan had been told that Meir Dagan had dismissed Panetta's appointment as "another softie takes over."

Panetta was a wealthy California-born lawyer with a degree in political science and a predilection for striped business suits. Perhaps to avoid being perceived as an unwelcome outsider running the agency, he was on a trip to familiarize himself with key intelligence organizations.

Panetta had already attracted his first headlines. On Christmas Day 2009, a London student, Nigerian-born Umar Farouk Abdulmutallab, failed to bring down a passenger plane over Detroit with a bomb concealed in his underpants. Panetta had publicly predicted that al-Qaeda would try "another attack against the United States in the next three to six months." Nathan had wondered what the new CIA director would prophesy next. Nathan and Panetta's meeting was to review the CIA's relationship with Israel. The discussion had centered on Iran's nuclear capability. Panetta said his staff on the Iran Desk had concluded that Israel could "well be right" that Iran would produce sufficient highly enriched uranium for a bomb within a year to eighteen months, but that the agency's scientists had also told him it would take three to four years before Tehran had "a deliverable weapon."

Nathan had pointed out that even then the United States would most likely still be beyond the range of any nuclear bomb Iran could launch. Israel, on the other hand, was already in the range of Iranian rockets. A nuclear nose cap was all that would be needed to destroy Tel Aviv. Panetta had replied that if Nathan's statement was a warning that Israel would launch a preemptive strike, this action would never be supported by the Obama administration. Nathan had replied that as far as he knew a preemptive strike was not on the table.

Days later Egypt's intelligence chief, General Omar Suleiman, had called on Nathan. Suleiman ran EGIS, the Egyptian General Intelligence Service. All of the Middle East's most critical issues landed on his desk in Cairo. His handsomely furnished office was a long way from the mud-walled home where he was born in Qena, an impoverished town on the Nile in Upper Egypt. He had been a skinny nineteen-year-old dressed in his father's old clothes when he had arrived in Cairo after passing an entrance examination to the country's prestigious military academy in 1954. Two years later Egypt's president, Gamal Abdel Nasser, had struck at the last pillar of Britain's fading empire by nationalizing the Suez Canal.

When Hosni Mubarak became Egypt's president in 1981, Suleiman was a career army officer rapidly moving up the promotion ladder. In 1986 he became deputy head of military intelligence and came to Mubarak's notice over the way he destroyed two powerful terrorist groups. In 1993 Suleiman took over EGIS. He became known in the global intelligence community, and he became lauded for his ruthless ways; his skill at intelligence gathering was matched by his ability to solve intractable problems.

The tall, balding spymaster, seventy-five years old when he visited Nathan, had an iron-gray mustache and a clipped English accent. Some members of the Mubarak administration argued that when the president retired—in 2010 he was eighty-one years old—Suleiman was his logical successor. But at this point Suleiman still ran EGIS with a firm hand. Nathan's visit to its Cairo headquarters had cemented Mossad's relationship with EGIS.

Nathan knew why Suleiman had come to see him. Suleiman was trying to broker a deal over Gaza, which required he win the trust of both Israel and Hamas; though both were sworn enemies, they would negotiate with General Suleiman. In the past week, before coming to London, the Egyptian spymaster had gone to Gaza City, Damascus, Libya, and Saudi Arabia. In London he had already seen Sir John Sawers. But the visit would not be complete unless he called on Nathan.

Suleiman made clear the concern in Cairo over the deteriorating relationship between Netanyahu and Barack Obama. In the Egyptian's view the rift would inevitably add to Egypt's own domestic problems with terrorists, who would seize the opportunity to reinforce the Hamas-ruled enclave of Gaza. Terrorist groups had already bored tunnels under the Sinai desert sands to smuggle explosives into Gaza. In the past year Hamas had fired thousands of rockets on southern Israel. While these were lacking in aim and power, they had nevertheless increased the fears of the Jewish population. Israel had finally retaliated with belligerence. The Egyptian media, like newspapers everywhere, had called Israel's Operation Cast Lead a war crime, citing the civilian casualties, especially the deaths of children buried in the rubble. Nathan had found it hard to deny Suleiman's categorization of Israel's actions as an atrocity. Nathan knew Suleiman had always supported Israel's right to survive in what he had once called a "crucible of hatred." In fact Egypt was then the Jewish state's only friend in the region.

The Egyptian spymaster had told Nathan that Netanyahu should support the new American president in trying to reengage with the Islamic world. Obama's own words had convinced Suleiman, who had met the president on his visit to Cairo, that America wanted to be an honest broker in the Middle East, a powerful country that saw its role as the vanquisher of jihadism.

However, if Netanyahu continued to defy Obama, Iran would be the beneficiary. Suleiman urged Nathan to convey to Tel Aviv that Netanyahu should suspend further construction of the illegal settlements in the West Bank and East Jerusalem. Suleiman said that on his own visit to Washington, he found nobody supported the expansion of the settlements, while their very presence was a source of anger and distrust in the Arab world.

At times like these, Nathan felt he was as much a diplomat as a spy; the professions overlapped and he had to juggle them simultaneously. He had found Panetta sensitive to criticism of American policies, especially those concerning the Middle East; meanwhile Suleiman was expert at clouding the issues.

Nathan had enjoyed his meeting with the Egyptian far more than his meeting with Panetta. Nathan, who himself had been born in Beersheba, a town in the Negev, felt a sense of kinship with Suleiman. Panetta was the quintessential product of the Washington political machine, eager to prove himself as an intellectual sparring partner in any discussion; the politician in him was never far from the surface, subtle diplomacy less so. Nathan had wondered how the brusque CIA chief would get on with the even more aggressive Meir Dagan.

Both MI5 and MI6 shared with Nathan, as a declared spy, what they called "mutually beneficial information." In 2010 it included such details that both services were recruiting more spies—four hundred for MI6 and a further six hundred to join MI5. The Secret Intelligence Service was also expanding its activities in East Africa and the Gulf, where its officers were already based in Dubai. The focus of these spies would be Iran.

Nathan had provided both services with the Mossad's latest list of terrorists and their last known whereabouts: from Damascus to the Yemen and along the Afghanistan-Pakistan border. Some may have returned from training to Europe or Britain. MI5 would send a copy of the list to immigration officers at Britain's airports and seaports; MI6 would transmit the details to its stations on routes along which terrorists traveled. Everyone knew the chance of locating them was not high. But it had to be done. If the phrase President Bush had coined—"war on terror"—had been phased out, the conflict remained as deadly as ever.

Jihad terrorism had lost none of its luster among many of the world's 1.5 billion Muslims. The image of Osama bin Laden had been refurbished by al-Qaeda to attract more followers from Algeria to Indonesia. The Gaza Strip, twenty-eight miles long and three to eight miles wide, served as a launching pad to attack Israel. Suicide bombing had developed its own twisted logic for those chosen to deliver it.

In 2010 there were over 250 unsuccessful suicide bombers in Israeli prisons, caught when their bombs had failed. Some were as young as thirteen. All were motivated to kill Jews. Some were young women, who saw joining a terrorist group as an opportunity to meet men without parental supervision. All were guaranteed martyrdom: their name would be called out at Friday prayers in the mosques, and their photo would hang in a golden frame in their home. Every suicide bomber knew that his or her parents would receive death benefits—up to $10,000—and gifts such as a clock, a rug for the earthen floor, and a television to watch the video their loved one had made before death.

After the killing of Imad Mughniyeh the Mossad had placed Mahmoud Abdel Rauf al-Mabhouh at the top of the kidon list for assassination. As Hamas's senior military commander and head of the organization's suicide bomber operations, al-Mabhouh was also its liaison with Iran's Revolutionary Guards. The Mossad had established that he had organized the smuggling of explosives and weapons into Gaza. In a photograph al-Mabhouh stares unblinking into the camera, his face that of a man born and raised in the Jabaliya refugee camp in Gaza on February 14, 1960. He was the oldest of thirteen brothers and sisters. At seventeen he married a teenager from the camp and fathered four children in quick succession. From boyhood he had worked in one of the camp's garages, and when the owner of that garage died, al-Mabhouh had bought the business. People in the camp sometimes whispered that al-Mabhouh had killed his employer, but never to his face. Al-Mabhouh had become a Hamas fighter; at night the garage was a bombmaking factory.

Al-Mabhouh would watch them preparing their bombs to launch against Israel, admiring the way they worked, like the alchemists of old, using experience and instinct, their language rich with words of death: oxidizers, desensitizers, plasticizers, and freezing points. The craftsmen knew the exact quantity of hexogen—which they differentiated, like all explosive experts, as either RDX or PETN.

These people, *his* people, had fired him with determination to destroy Jews. It filled him as he answered the call of the muezzin crackling through the minaret loudspeaker summoning the faithful to prayer; it was there in the shadowy coolness of the mosque as he prostrated himself among the bomb makers. He admired them because they were at the peak of their skills, men with the sharpest eyes and steadiest hands, creating booby traps from pieces of piping they found in his garage.

In May 1989, he had led a small group to abduct and murder two Israeli soldiers on border patrol, the murders of which he had celebrated by standing on one of the corpses. From then on in the rubble of Gaza, people stepped out of his way, a sign of the respect for a figure who had spoken directly to the enemy.

A day after the murders the Israeli Defense Force had sent soldiers to capture al-Mabhouh. He had fled to Beirut. There his murders had made him a hero. The Grand Ayatollah Muhammad Hussein Fadlallah, the founder of Hezbollah, had singled out al-Mabhouh's "heroic action" in one of his sermons.

In June 2010, Fadlallah died at the age of seventy-four. In his eulogy for Fadlallah, Britain's ambassador to Lebanon, Frances Guy, had said that the ayatollah was a decent man who ranked as the person she most admired out of all those she had met: "The world needs more men like him willing to reach out across faiths, acknowledging the reality of the modern world and daring to confront old constraints." In London the Foreign Office had said the ambassador had expressed only her personal view. CNN's Middle East correspondent, Octavia Nasr, was fired by the U.S. network for describing Fadlallah as "one of Hezbollah's giants I respect a lot."

On that January day, as Nathan prepared to fly to Tel Aviv to address the Mossad training school, al-Mabhouh continued to evade capture.

Like all Mossad recruits, Nathan had spent two years learning his spycraft in the dun-colored buildings inside the high security fence. Days in the classroom had been followed by long nights on field exercises: learning how to make brush passes, exchanging documents on a busy Tel Aviv street; mounting surveillance on an Arab village outside Haifa;

writing reports for his instructors, men who once they made a decision had no patience for further discussions.

His instructors included technical officers and scientists along with veteran field officers. Between them they trained students in espionage and counterintelligence. Nathan had learned forms of secret writing; the use of miniature cameras; the encoding of messages. Planting audio bugs and tapping telephones were part of the curriculum. Other classes were devoted to tracking devices and sensors; disguises and forged documents; and psychological assessments of targets. Spies were trained to do a job that would provide cover while they engaged in clandestine work.

Nathan remembered the weekly meetings with a school psychologist to assess his level of commitment. Every six months there would be a review of a student's progress: his understanding of how and when to use the techniques, gadgets, and tricks he had been taught. There were also term papers to write on such diverse subjects as the difference between the CIA and KGB, or the political significance of Britain's MI6 or MI5 and their relationship with the Mossad.

Before each half-yearly review he had to submit a list of books he had read and what he had learned from them. One of Nathan's favorites was by Colonel William "Wild Bill" Donovan, the founder of the U.S. Office of Strategic Services (OSS) and America's first spymaster. It was a textbook introduction to what Rudyard Kipling had called the Great Game.

The theme of Nathan's lecture was how far the Great Game had come since he had joined Mossad.

For an hour he had stood describing Mossad's role in helping to foil a conspiracy as dastardly as that perpetrated on 9/11. The aim of the plot was to kill thousands of people flying on more than half a dozen aircrafts across the Atlantic in the autumn of 2006. The Mossad had been called in by MI6 and MI5 to help with Operation Overt, an effort to trace the background of the plotters.

Well educated, the would-be terrorists had made good use of advances in telecommunications and data processing. The spread of terrorism around the world had made it easier for the group to plan and harder for the intelligence services to establish an effective surveillance method against them.

Knowing the Middle Eastern cultural background of the plotters,

Mossad had focused on their support group, sympathizers who provided essential financial and logistic backup. In that manner, slowly but surely, the UK-based terrorists had been penetrated and the plot uncovered. It had still taken almost two years before Operation Overt had concluded with the arrest and imprisonment of the last of the terrorists in 2010.

Nathan studied his audience while he spoke. They were all in their final year. In a few weeks they would face the school director and his senior staff on the assessment board. A number would fail and be returned to one of the units in the Israeli Defense Force's military intelligence or be placed with private sector companies as bodyguards or investigators. They were all guaranteed a good job. Those who passed would be assigned to work either at the headquarters or in one of the Mossad stations abroad. There were now a dozen more stations since Nathan had his first overseas posting, as head of mission in Bangkok. A few who had passed near the top of their course would be asked to join kidon (see chapter 6).

Nathan noticed that the number of women in the audience had increased since his last lecture. He had long supported the need for women in the service. He believed they had much to offer in the digital intelligence world. A fully trained female counterintelligence operative was often more expert at information gathering than a man. The school director had told Nathan that women recruits showed more aptitude in learning how to spot a person's alcohol dependency, drug habit, poor credit reports, or spotty job record. Yet women in the Mossad were still not being promoted or paid in accordance with their abilities.

In contrast, MI5, MI6, and the CIA paid their senior staff substantial salaries. A line manager with proven experience in the field could earn $250,000 a year in any of those services. In British Intelligence the domination of men had been broken by Dame Stella Rimington (1992–1996) and Baroness Eliza Manningham-Buller (2002–2007). Both women had been director-general of MI5 at a salary of $450,000 a year and had promoted women to become heads of departments, including counterterrorism. Sir John Scarlett in MI6 included many women on his staff. In 2010 there were fifty women employed in the war against terrorism. One woman agent described her job as "working in those alleys which have no names."

But in 2010 no top positions in the Mossad were held by women. That decision had been made by Meir Dagan.

Tzipporah "Tzipi" Livni had been one of the Mossad's few female high fliers. She had graduated top of her year at the training school and was posted to Paris as a kidon. Her targets were Carlos the Jackal's gang and the killers of Abu Nidal. For Efraim Halevy (1998–2002), Dagan's predecessor, "Tzipi was ready to take substantial risks to get her target." Livni had resigned to launch a political career and became the country's foreign minister, a position that gave her more authority over Mossad than she had ever had while in the service.

After his lecture Nathan sat with some of the students in a nearby bar, doing what he always did on his visits to the training school: looking for a potential officer for his team at the London embassy.

On his return to London from Tel Aviv in February Nathan had used his diplomatic passport to pass unchallenged through Heathrow airport. In 2010 the UK terrorist threat level had remained at "substantial" since set the previous July by the Home Office on the advice of MI5's director-general, Jonathan Evans. This meant an attack was a strong possibility. Britain has a system of five threat levels: "critical" was two levels above the current status, and indicated an attack was expected immediately.

Before flying back to London Nathan had his usual meeting with Meir Dagan. The Mossad chief was thoroughly frustrated. The leaks about his management style continued to find their way to journalists and politicians. There was talk in the corridors of the Knesset, Israel's parliament, that the Mossad should come under closer supervision and operate within a legal framework.

This discussion was the outcome of the kidon-attempted assassination of Khalid Meshal in Amman in 1998. The Hamas leader now lived in a fortress-like building in a northern suburb of Damascus and remained the overall strategist of the organization. Danny Yatom (1996–1998) had run Mossad during that period, and the failure of the attempt to kill Meshal had led to Yatom's dismissal by Netanyahu, then the incumbent prime minister. Following the debacle there had been two reports, one by the Knesset subcommittee overseeing Israel's secret services and the other by a Foreign Office committee. Both had recommended that the Mossad should operate under legal constraints, which had yet to be defined.

Dagan maintained he would not be answerable to politicians who had little idea of the secret world in which the Mossad operated. To make Mossad operate under the same conditions as Shin Bet was, in Dagan's view, unworkable. Even those in government had no grasp of how the Mossad functioned. Dagan reminded Nathan of the number of times he had told the Knesset subcommittee when he appeared before them that the Mossad operated overseas and did not meet the rule of law of those countries. More than once he had left the committee room feeling he had wasted his time trying to explain how the Mossad couldn't work by rules drawn up by men with no experience of secret operations. Dagan had grumbled that even now there were complaints about the fact that the Mossad would not be assigned a mission for the purpose of advancing partisan political interests.

Nathan knew the tone of Meir Dagan's directorship was set by a photograph on the wall of his office in the Tel Aviv headquarters. It showed an SS officer aiming his rifle at an old man's head. At their first meeting Dagan had explained to Nathan what that picture meant to him. "The old Jew was my grandfather. He represents my own philosophy of Jewish self-defense and survival. We should be strong, use our brain, and defend ourselves so that the Holocaust will never happen again."

He told Nathan on that cold February day that he was not going to walk away from his obligations to his staff or to Israel and its people. Hunching his shoulders, he shook Nathan's hand and wished him a good flight.

On January 17, 2010, an MI6 officer stationed in Dubai, one of the seven nations in the United Arab Emirates, was carrying out his daily routine in his office on Al Maktoum Road, a thoroughfare that leads to the international airport bearing the same name. This airport handles fifty million passengers a year, mostly tourists come to vacation in some of the most luxurious hotels on earth or passengers on a stopover before heading further east. But increasingly realtors, financiers, and other dealmakers had turned Dubai into a global business hub.

A small contingent of these travelers interested the officer, who sat before a computer that MI6 technicians had created for his work watching a flow of images taped by CCTV cameras at the airport. This computer was searching for matches he had asked it to look for: details about arms dealers, drug runners, diamond smugglers, and the terrorists known to have gone to al-Qaeda training camps along the borders of Pakistan and Afghanistan. Once an identification was made, the computer would tell the officer where a person had flown from and where he was going to.

This computer was programmed to check passenger manifests of all flights. After 9/11, the Dubai police force allowed MI6 to have access to all the information from the airport cameras and computers. The data included passport photographs; where a passenger's flight had originated; where and how the ticket had been booked. America's Homeland Security had a similar system.

All the MI6 officer in Dubai had to do was to watch his computer screen and wait for a flashing light signaling it had found a match. Some time on that January day the screen revealed that a return ticket had been bought for a first-class seat on Emirates flight EK 912 from Damascus. The passenger was named as Mahmoud Abdel Rauf al-Mabhouh. The officer had passed the details to the MI6 Communication Centre in London, which in turn sent this information on to those in the intelligence community in Britain. Thus Nathan learned that the most wanted man on the Mossad kidon list had been located.

In the afternoon of January 17, a black Audi A6 limousine drove to the Mossad headquarters. In the backseat, protected behind bulletproof glass, sat Benjamin Netanyahu. Usually he met Meir Dagan in his own office, but there had been urgency in the Mossad chief's voice. For a moment, the prime minister told an aide, he had wondered whether Dagan had decided to resign in the face of mounting criticism about the Mossad's methods.

Only recently a sharp-eyed woman had spotted a young man attaching what looked suspiciously like a bomb to the underside of a car parked in a quiet street in Tel Aviv. When the police arrested him, he had shown them his Mossad ID. He was a student from the training school on an exercise. Though the bomb was a fake, newspapers had called the prime minister's office for comment and the story had made the evening news. Arriving at Mossad headquarters, Netanyahu speculated that there had been another bungled operation he was going to be asked to explain away.

Meir Dagan was waiting in the entrance. With him was the head of kidon, who had driven from the unit's base in the Negev Desert. After Dagan had given the prime minister the news about al-Mabhouh, Netanyahu relaxed. Dagan told the prime minister he intended to have the Hamas leader assassinated. A source "with knowledge of Mossad" would later tell Uzi Mahnaimi, the Tel Aviv correspondent of the London *Sunday Times:* "Inside the briefing room were some members of the hit squad. As the man who gave authorisation for such operations, Netanyahu was briefed on plans to kill Mahmoud al-Mabhouh. The mission was not regarded as unduly complicated or risky and Netanyahu gave his authorisation, in effect signing al-Mabhouh's death warrant. 'The people of Israel trust you. Good luck,' he said."

Netanyahu's role in the assassination was over. He left Meir Dagan, the kidon director, and the hit squad to continue making their plans.

While the news of al-Mabhouh's impending arrival in Dubai had given little time for preparation, the backup units had swung into action. Over the years the department responsible for providing passports had acquired thousands of travel documents, either buying them through the underworld—after they had been reported lost by their original owners—or copying them when visitors arrived in Israel. Expert forgers studied them and decided how they could be adapted to pass scrutiny at international ports. Passports of the United Kingdom, Canada, Ireland, France, Germany, and New Zealand were the most prized: long experience had shown the Mossad agents they were the least checked. U.S. passports were less desirable; U.S. immigration checks were regarded as the most thorough.

For the Dubai operation, British, Irish, German, and French passports would be used by the hit squad. Care was taken to ensure there were no previous entry stamps for the emirate. The photograph in each passport was replaced by that of a team member, who would travel under the name of the original owner.

One passport had been specially created for the only woman in the team, who was tall and leggy with a winsome smile and shoulder-length auburn hair. The passport identified the woman as Gail Folliard, a citizen of the Republic of Ireland, born on April 16, 1976. A document accompanying the forged passport gave her address as a fashionable Dublin suburb and her marital status as single. The role of this woman was similar to that of Cheryl Ben-Tov, who twenty-four years earlier had entrapped Mordechai Vanunu in London and persuaded him to go with her to Rome. Waiting there had been six Mossad agents who had drugged the hapless technician and spirited him back to Israel to face trial for betraying its top-secret nuclear facility at Dimona (see chapter 9).

In the hours before their departure, the team members were updated. An informant in Gaza had learned that al-Mabhouh was going to Dubai to meet an Iranian arms dealer. The Hamas leader had booked a suite in one of the city's most luxurious hotels, the Al Bustan Rotana.

The Mossad agents were told to book into hotels nearby. They would pay for their rooms with the U.S. dollars they were given to avoid leaving a paper trail.

The assassins would be led by "Peter Elvinger," who was traveling on a stolen British passport. He had been an instructor at the kidon base. Uzi Mahnaimi would later claim that after being fully briefed the team had rehearsed the assassination plan, "using a hotel in Tel Aviv as a training ground."

The Mossad travel unit had booked flights for the team; they would arrive in Dubai hours before al-Mabhouh. The assassins started their journey to Dubai from Paris, Frankfurt, Geneva, and Madrid. To make their connections they flew to the cities of origination on January 18.

On the morning of January 19, a Mossad sayan employed as a cleaner at Damascus International Airport saw Mahmoud al-Mabhouh arrive. Al-Mabhouh wore a brown-striped suit and a white shirt, the perfect image of a Middle Eastern businessman. With him was a bodyguard of sorts, almost certainly an officer of the Idarat al-Amn al-Amm, the Syrian General Security Directorate. He would have brought al-Mabhouh from his home and would remain with him until he boarded. Syria has long provided such protection for guests who were targets for the Mossad.

Both men arrived at the airline check-in desk for the flight to Dubai. Al-Mabhouh handed over his small suitcase, keeping his briefcase. His escort ushered him through the departure formalities to the Emirate VIP lounge. When the flight was called, al-Mabhouh made his way to the departure gate.

At 10:05 A.M. the A330 Airbus rose into the wintery sky and headed south. The news of al-Mabhouh's departure reached the Mossad communications center minutes later. A message had already gone to Elvinger that al-Mabhouh was to travel from Dubai to the Iran port of Bandar-Abbas to conclude arrangements with the Revolutionary Guards for a shipment of arms to Gaza.

Gail Folliard had arrived in Dubai on a night flight. She wore a long-sleeved blue dress and knee-length boots. The CCTV cameras captured her as she pulled a suitcase through the customs halls. She took a taxi from the airport to a hotel near the Al Bustan Rotana.

She gave her address on her hotel registration form as 6, Elgin Road, Ballsbridge, Dublin. This house—owned by James Reynolds, the brother of Albert Reynolds, a former taoiseach (prime minister) of Ireland—had stood empty for ten years. Gail Folliard went to her room and changed into a summer dress and shoes. She wore sunglasses when she left the hotel to walk the short distance to the more impressive Rotana.

During the final briefing in Tel Aviv, the kidon team had discussed how they would carry out the assassination. There were a number of choices: pushing al-Mabhouh off his hotel balcony or under a car; drowning him in his bath; poisoning him with a drink spiked with a poison provided by the Mossad's scientists. Another possibility was to place a bomb in his hotel bedside telephone. When one of the kidon rang the room, the bomb would blow al-Mabhouh's head off. Another method to kill him was for one of the agents to pose as a room service waiter.

They had discussed what to do if al-Mabhouh had someone in the room with him. There was also the question of whether he had hired a bodyguard to protect him in Dubai. This was a real possibility, given a Syrian security officer had escorted him to the plane. In the end the team agreed that they could decide on a method only after Gail had made her check of the hotel. The mission was now officially under way, so al-Mabhouh would be referred to only as the target; this was standard operating procedure for the kidon.

One of the Rotana's security cameras caught Gail among the guests going into the hotel.

The rest of the kidon team had arrived at irregular intervals at the Dubai airport. British passport holder "James Leonard Clarke" and German passport holder "Michael Bodenheimer" had traveled on a flight from Frankfurt. A CCTV camera in terminal three captured them in their business suits—blue for the bespectacled Clarke and black for Bodenheimer—standing and discussing some paperwork. British passport holders "Melvyn Mildiner" and "Michael Barney" had flown in from Paris and were filmed leaving the airport. "Kevin Daverson" had arrived on a flight from Madrid and was caught on camera approaching the immigration area. He told an officer there he had come to Dubai for a tennis tournament.

None of the team caused the MI6 computer to flash a warning light.

Gail Folliard found the Rotana facilities all she would expect in any deluxe hotel. She was standing near the reception desk when Mahmoud al-Mabhouh arrived and heard a clerk call for a bellboy to take the guest to room 230. The clerk set the room's billing account for extras—room service, telephone calls, laundry, and so on—to commence at 3:30 P.M. According to the Dubai police chief, Dahi Khalfan Tamim, the clerk later recalled that a woman had asked if any rooms were available, explaining that her employer was about to arrive from Paris and she needed to make a reservation for him. She gave his name as Peter Elvinger and was assigned room 237, just across the corridor from al-Mabhouh. The clerk would later identify the woman as Gail Folliard, remembering her as "the lady who paid cash." Elvinger had checked in with Daverson. They both went to room 237.

The hotel's automatic billing system recorded that soon after 4:00 P.M. a series of short local calls to nearby hotels were made from room 237. Basic police work—using the images from CCTV footage—later established they had been to the kidon team staying in these places.

Meanwhile Gail Folliard kept watch in the hotel lobby. Al-Mabhouh, carrying his briefcase, emerged from an elevator, walked to the entrance, and went off in a taxi. Folliard had called room 237 on a house phone. Moments later Daverson and Elvinger arrived in the lobby. They had spoken briefly and then returned to the room.

Where al-Mabhouh went is still unknown. Dubai taxi drivers do not keep worksheets showing where they have taken passengers. But by seven o'clock that evening he was back in the hotel with his briefcase. The bellboy who had taken al-Mabhouh to his suite earlier remembered his return.

By late afternoon the rest of the kidon squad had assembled in the hotel lobby, ordering soft drinks and keeping watch. Several were dressed in tennis gear. They told waiters they were taking part in a local tournament.

Al-Mabhouh's return galvanized the group. Daverson followed him into the elevator.

There are two differing accounts of what happened next; the two versions are derived from separate police sources. Both accounts agree that the CCTV cameras on the bedroom floors did not cover the full length of the corridors. Guests in 230 and 237 could come and go without being filmed. The night maid assigned to freshen up rooms and turn down beds did not come on duty until 8:00 P.M. The only staff likely to visit the rooms before then would be room-service waiters.

But from that point on, the accounts differ. In one version a guest was already in the elevator when al-Mabhouh was suddenly joined by Daverson. Two experienced journalists, Duncan Gardham and Gordon Rayner, working for the London *Daily Telegraph*, give this account of what happened when the elevator reached al-Mabhouh's floor: "As the male guest stepped out of the lift, Daverson, wearing wig and glasses and holding a clipboard, stopped him from entering the corridor by pretending to be a member of staff. He held the man up for several minutes as he politely asked to see his room key card, then continued chatting until the coast was clear and let him go on his way."

By then al-Mabhouh had reached his room and the corridor was empty.

In the *Daily Telegraph* article the reporters claim that after al-Mabhouh's earlier departure from the hotel, members of the hit squad tried to reprogram the lock to his room: "The police believed that the assassins had to abandon their original plan, probably involving lying in wait for Mr. al-Mabhouh inside the room—and decided to fool him into opening the door when he returned."

Uzi Mahnaimi, the *Sunday Times* reporter, suggested how that deception could have been arranged and gives a plausible reason why Daverson had delayed the guest at the elevator. Certainly it would have given a kidon time to cross the corridor to room 230 to have "lured him into opening his door." This reporter suggested that "perhaps a woman, posing as a member of the hotel staff, had knocked at the door." Had it been Gail Folliard?

Neither version of how the hit squad gained access to al-Mabhouh's room has yet to be fully substantiated. More certain is that he was overpowered by the assassins and smothered with a pillow, a quick death.

His body was arranged in the bed so that he appeared to be asleep.

One of the assassins took the briefcase with him. As they left the room, a DO NOT DISTURB sign was placed on the door handle of room 230.

Within hours the team had flown out of Dubai to different destinations: Paris, Hong Kong, and South Africa. Mossad appeared to have gotten away with another lethal mission.

That evening the night service maid, noting the sign hanging from the door handle, pushed her cart of fresh towels past room 230. She moved on to the next room, intending to return to room 230 later. When she did return, the sign was still there. This time she used her passkey to open the door. The curtains were drawn, the room in near darkness. The maid left the room undisturbed. Often guests who had arrived after a long flight retired early. The body lay undisturbed through the night.

By the time Meir Dagan sat down to his usual vegetarian breakfast in Tel Aviv the next morning he had learned the operation had been a success. Later he planned to call Ariel Sharon's wife to inquire about a report on the radio that the former prime minister was breathing for short periods without the aid of a life-support machine, which had kept him alive since his stroke four years earlier. Known for his fierce loyalty to his friends, Meir Dagan had never forgotten that Sharon had put him in charge of the Mossad. Though Sharon had once been described as "one of the living dead, kept alive by the wonder of modern medicine," Dagan was sure the radio report would give hope to Sharon's devoted family.

On the morning of January 20, 2010, the daytime routine in the Rotana was under way. The first room service orders were being delivered. A housekeeper noted that the guest in room 237 had checked out. Room 230 still had the DO NOT DISTURB sign on its door. She knocked. Getting no reply she used her passkey to enter room 230. The curtains were drawn. She asked the figure in the bed if he wished to have the room made up. There was no response. She inquired if he was all right. There was no reply. Sensing there was something wrong, the housekeeper switched on the bedside light. The bedding was not rumpled, as would normally be the case after a night's sleep. The housekeeper called again. Still getting no reply, she dialed the duty manager on the bedside phone.

When the manager entered the room, he drew back the curtains and went to the bed. He could see that al-Mabhouh was dead. His face was peaceful and there was no indication that he had made any attempt to use the bedside phone to call for help. The duty manager called the hotel doctor.

Al-Mabhouh had hung his clothes in the closet and left his shoes next to the bed before he had climbed into bed, naked. When the doctor arrived he estimated the time of death as anywhere between eight and twelve hours before, from a heart attack.

The manager began to carry out the normal procedure for a sudden unexplained death in a hotel. The room was locked and the DO NOT DISTURB sign left on the door. The housekeeper was instructed to allow no staff to enter the room. As al-Mabhouh had traveled on a Syrian passport, the authorities in Damascus would have to be informed. That would be done by the Dubai police department. Within an hour details of the death had reached the desk of the chief of police in Dubai, Dahi Khalfan Tamim.

He knew he had a problem. He already had a photo of al-Mabhouh, the one the Mossad had circulated with its list of terrorists; it had been passed on by the MI6 station in Dubai. Dahi Khalfan ordered an autopsy of the body. He also assigned a team of detectives to view the relevant CCTV footage. Meantime he also contacted various foreign embassies in Dubai to alert them as to what had happened.

The body was removed from room 230 inside a sheet-covered trunk the hotel kept for this purpose and taken down to a waiting coroner's ambulance. Detectives then examined al-Mabhouh's clothes and his suitcase and searched the room. Nothing suspicious was found. The bellboy remembered that al-Mabhouh had carried a briefcase. A further careful search of the room, including its guest safe, failed to turn this up.

Police questioned the staff and guests at the Rotana and employees of the other hotels in which the kidon were now known to have stayed. In the malls, restaurants, coffee shops, and beach cafés, employees were shown photos taken off the CCTV cameras. Had they seen any of these people? A few waiters and shopkeepers thought they could recall some faces. But no one was positive.

Nevertheless, Dahi Khalfan had meetings with foreign intelligence officers based in the city, including operatives from the CIA and MI6. In Gaza Hamas attempted to find out why al-Mabhouh had not returned. But telephone callers to the Rotana were told only that the hotel did not have a registered guest in his name. In Damascus the Syrian security service, Idarat al-Amn al-Amm, having received the news that al-Mabhouh was dead, may well have suspected he had been murdered by the Mossad. If so, from past experience, the Syrians knew the kidon would have covered its tracks. In Dubai, Dahi Khalfan impatiently awaited the autopsy report.

CHAPTER 31

FAREWELL

On January 29, the police chief received the results of the postmortem

examination carried out by pathologist Dr. Fawzi Benomran, the di-

rector of the Dubai police forensic medicine department. During the

autopsy and dental charting, photographs and X-rays had been taken,

and the proceedings had been video recorded. A histological examina-

tion of the heart had ruled out a heart attack. "The deceased did not

suffer from any cardiac disease or any other degenerative disease which

could have resulted in myocardial infarct." An examination of al-

Mabhouh's brain showed only what would be consistent with a man of

his age: a mild edema with slight congestion of the cerebral vessels. An examination of his lungs showed no evidence of bronchial obstruction, bronchitis, or emphysema.

The final conclusion in the report was death by smothering. Dahi Khalfan concluded that the killing of al-Mabhouh had been carried out by the one organization he knew had the expertise to handle such an operation: the Mossad. That conclusion was supported by the CCTV evidence. Images of the kidon squad arriving at the airport matched those taken by the Rotana cameras. Further checks had confirmed the departure of the hit squad. They had spent no more than nineteen hours in Dubai.

The police chief called a press conference. With him was Dr. Ben-omran. The London-trained pathologist told the crowded room that this was the most difficult postmortem he had ever conducted. "In the end I concluded that the killers had put his body in the bed and covered it, to make it appear he had died in his sleep. Death was caused by suffocation by smothering, most probably with a pillow." Passport photographs of and details about the hit squad were issued to the reporters. The story filled the front pages of the world.

The web of intrigue around the assassination grew. Dahi Khalfan issued international arrest warrants through Interpol for "assassins who traveled on forged British, Irish, French, and German passports." In Gaza, Hamas announced that al-Mabhouh had been "murdered by a Mossad electric weapon which had been inserted in his ear." In Brussels the European Union protested against the use of forged passports. Soon the number of assassins identified on the Dubai Interpol warrant had risen to twenty-six. The sheer number produced mounting astonishment among the global intelligence community. No service, let alone the Mossad, had previously used anywhere that number of agents to assassinate someone. Was the Dubai police chief not only exaggerating, but in danger of destroying the credibility of his case against the Mossad? By early February Dahi Khalfan had issued Interpol warrants for thirty-two names.

A possible explanation for his claim was that the Mossad had used the murder as an exercise for final-year students at the training school. Israeli passport holders or those with documents showing the bearer to have entered Israel were refused entry into Dubai, a practice common in most Arab countries. But in the past year the Mossad had recognized the need to increase its own deep-cover presence in countries like Iran, Yemen, and Somalia. Had its future spies been sent to Dubai on false passports to test their skills? Were they ordered to leave Dubai before the kidon squad arrived? There was no way Dahi Khalfan could check that possibility.

In London the British foreign secretary, David Miliband, flatly denied Britain had any foreknowledge of the assassination. But he called "the seeming use of cloned British passports outrageous."

In Israel, Avi Issacharoff, writing in the *Haaretz* newspaper, described al-Mabhouh as "a central cog in the weapons smuggling trail from Iran to Gaza. The assassination is a mortal blow to Hamas."

Prime Minister Netanyahu stoically refused to comment.

Miliband had summoned MI6 chief Sir John Sawers to a meeting. The *Daily Mail*, known to have good contacts in the intelligence community, had published a ten-page article under the sensational headline: "Did Britain know about the Mossad hit? Israeli agent claims MI6 was tipped off." The story detailed how a Mossad agent told the Secret Intelligence Service in a "courtesy call that a situation might blow up." He was quoted as saying the British authorities will have "to slap us on the wrist, as the British government has to be seen to be going through the motions."

Miliband had taken Sawers line by line through the newspaper story. Each sentence was robustly denied by the intelligence chief. The Foreign Office rushed out a strong denial. But the damage had been done.

In the Israeli embassy, a dismayed Nathan recognized that within the intelligence community he could be seen as the source of the story. The *Mail* article quoted the Mossad agent as saying the "British government was told very, very briefly before the operation that these people were travelling on UK passports."

Israel's ambassador Ron Prosor was called to the British Foreign Office and was questioned by a senior diplomat; he left with the demand that Israel provide the assurance that it would never again sanction the use of UK documents in operations by the Mossad. Prosor was also warned that Prime Minister Gordon Brown was considering what further actions Britain would take.

Nathan wondered if this would be "just another bump in the road" in the ever-rocky British–Israeli relations. For years there had been a group hostile to Israel in the Foreign Office. On Nathan's own visits there under his declared cover as a diplomat, the station chief had occasionally heard remnants of that hostility, a reminder of the time Prime Minister Edward Heath had been persuaded to slap an arms embargo on Israel in the 1973 war, resulting in Tel Aviv's relying on the United States ever since for weapons. The Foreign Office had tried over the years to balance its support for Israel with sympathy for the Palestinians as a people. But it needed little for relations to turn cold.

In 1987 Prime Minister Margaret Thatcher ordered the closure of the Mossad station in London after the kidnapping of the nuclear whistle-blower Mordechai Vanunu. That same year eight British passports had been found by MI6 in a bag in a West German telephone booth that the Secret Intelligence Service knew was a pickup point for the Mossad. The then Israeli ambassador in London, Yehuda Avner, was on the receiving end of the British protest. Nahum Admoni, the incumbent Mossad director-general, sent a conciliatory message to MI6 chief Sir Christopher Curwen, stating that in the future British passports would not be used in secret operations. The Mossad station in London was soon fully operational after Admoni's guarantee.

Nathan doubted whether Meir Dagan would offer such assurances; this was not his style.

Across the Arab world the assassination led to huge protest marches. In Damascus, Khalid Meshal, the leader of Hamas and a survivor of an earlier assassination attempt by the Mossad, called for "the blood of our brother to be avenged" (see chapter 6). In Tehran a senior member of the Revolutionary Guard, Abdollah Araghi, said that Iran had new missiles ready to strike "at the killers of our beloved brother." In Beirut, Yemen, and the Horn of Africa, terrorist groups promised they would attack Israel and its allies. British and U.S. embassies throughout the Middle East were placed on high alert.

In Gaza City al-Mabhouh's relatives called for revenge and were lauded at Friday prayers by the clerics, who provided the faithful with a violent criticism of all things non-Islamic. Al-Mabhouh's death had entered the folklore of Gaza. It ensured that many more Gazans needed no encouragement to attack Israel. At night, armed with antitank grenades and automatic rifles, weaponry smuggled in from Iran via Syria, Hamas terrorists had gone in search of targets on the other side of their fence. To do so, they had dug underground tunnels, some more than a quarter mile long, into the Jewish state.

On June 25, 2006, a group from Gaza had emerged from such a tunnel near the kibbutz Kerem Shalom, the Vineyard of Peace, in the southernmost corner of the Israeli border with Egypt and Gaza. This is a place as desolate as it had been when Moses had led the Israelites into the Promised Land.

Israeli Defense Forces soldier Gilad Shalit was on patrol when the terrorists struck. Two soldiers lay dead and three more were seriously injured. Troops who rushed to the scene found no trace of Shalit except his bloodstained flak jacket, a piece of evidence that indicated he had been shot in the back. A search of the area suggested the slim nineteen-year-old conscript with the toothy smile and close-cropped dark hair had been taken into Gaza.

Within hours three groups had claimed responsibility for the attack. One was the al-Assam Brigade, the military wing of Hamas. Another was the Army of Islam, loosely linked to al-Qaeda. The third claim came from the Doghmush clan, Gaza's most powerful crime family.

Tel Aviv newspapers published their first photo of Shalit. At his family home near the Lebanon border, Gilad's parents waited for news.

Three days after his capture, having demanded Shalit's unconditional release and receiving no reply, Israel launched a full-scale invasion of Gaza a year after it had left the Strip. The invasion team failed to locate Shalit. More than a hundred Palestinians died in the assault along with one Israeli soldier. The senior UN representative in the area condemned the attack as a "disproportionate use of force."

Gilad Shalit remained a prisoner in a land of twisted metal and rubble that had come to epitomize the heart of darkness in the Middle East. In the streets Gazans greeted each other with the catchphrase: "Gaza is a good place to be—from."

For the Hamas leadership Shalit was simply a pawn, a bargaining chip to secure freedom for the 9,000 Palestinians in Israeli jails. In Tel Aviv Meir Dagan was among government officials who tried to calculate what Hamas could be offered in return for Shalit's release.

Refusing to negotiate directly with Hamas, the Israeli government of Ehud Olmert agreed to Meir Dagan's proposal to use Omar Suleiman as a mediator. Egypt's intelligence chief shuttled between Gaza and Damascus—to speak with Khalid Meshal—before going to Tel Aviv to brief Meir Dagan. "It would help if we knew that Shalit was alive," the

Mossad chief had told Suleiman. In September 2009 Suleiman delivered a package to Dagan that he had brought back from Gaza. It contained an audiotape on which Shalit said, "My health is deteriorating daily. I am especially struggling emotionally and it is causing me much depression." Dagan asked whether the words had been dictated by his kidnappers. Suleiman said it was possible.

From Tel Aviv Suleiman flew to New York to speak with former U.S. president Jimmy Carter. Carter agreed to become involved in the negotiations to free Shalit and added it would be a good idea to bring Germany on board. "Berlin has good connections in the part of the world we need to influence," the Egyptian spymaster recalled Carter saying.

In Tel Aviv Mossad's specialists analyzed the audiotape. They concluded that Shalit felt stupid both for allowing himself to be snatched and for his behavior in captivity. His health was failing and he was depressed and afraid. The Mossad experts knew that if his captors were sufficiently clever they would exploit his mood swings. A psychologist later explained: "Those shifts were part of an inner void the captors were trying to create. What was fundamentally his guilt—failing to avoid being captured—would be easier to exploit." What the specialists needed was a video of Shalit to study.

Returning to Tel Aviv, Suleiman told Meir Dagan Israel would have to give Hamas something in return for a tape. Prime Minister Olmert agreed to free twenty women prisoners taken from Gaza in exchange for the video, which was two minutes forty seconds long. It showed Shalit in civilian clothes standing against a banner emblazoned with the logo of Hamas's military wing; he held up a Gaza newspaper dated Monday, September 14. It was the first confirmation of a long-held assumption that he was still in Gaza.

Technicians enlarged selected frames of the video to try to establish the background against which the soldier had been filmed. In the end they decided it was rough-plastered stone, suggesting the filming had taken place in a cellar. More than that they could not establish. Other experts took over.

They decided Shalit's gaze was of someone who had been deprived of daylight; he blinked as if he'd had difficulty adjusting to what appeared to have been a not very powerful light used to illuminate him for filming. A careful study of what skin was visible, enhanced section by section, indicated his wrists bore chafe marks, either from a rope or possibly chains. There were no marks on his face.

The audiotape was played against the images on the video. The guilt evident in Shalit's voice from the audiotape was there in his eyes, and the overall impression was that he had been drugged.

In March 2009, Suleiman's negotiations with Hamas ended. He told Dagan he felt there was no more he could achieve in his shuttle diplomacy. Six months later the uneasy truce between Hamas and Israel broke down, and in December that year, Israel launched its twenty-two day operation in Gaza until it reluctantly agreed to withdraw.

In the years since Shalit's capture, Mossad informers in Gaza had risked their lives in attempts to establish the fate of the soldier. One informer was caught sifting through the bin outside a doctor's office, seeking clues the doctor might have treated Shalit. The hapless youth was executed by Hamas. Shortly afterward Hamas issued a statement that Shalit had been "according to our religion well treated and has made a good recovery." This press release ended with the warning that any attempt to rescue Shalit would lead to his death. From time to time news filtered from Gaza into Israeli newspapers. He was described as "enjoying watching football and basketball on the TV he has been provided with."

Prime Minister Ehud Olmert—embroiled in a corruption scandal and close to resigning—announced the immediate release of 199 Palestinian prisoners from Israeli jails. Olmert said the prisoner release was a clear message that diplomacy, not violence, was the way to win concessions from Israel. In Gaza, the Hamas leadership condemned the move as no more than an attempt to exploit the embattled Palestinian president, Mahmoud Abbas, Yasser Arafat's heir as leader of Fatah, who since Hamas had seized control of the Gaza Strip in 2007 had increasingly been sidelined by Hamas. Among the prisoners freed were two of the longest-serving terrorists. Most of the others were members of Fatah; none were Hamas supporters from Gaza.

Hamas reacted swiftly. "If this attitude continues to free none of our people, our enemy should consider Gilad Shalit as Ron Arad number two." Arad had been a lieutenant colonel in the Israeli air force who had parachuted out of his damaged fighter jet on a mission over Lebanon and was captured by the Lebanese Shi'ite Amal militia. After two years of intense negotiations for his release as part of a prisoner exchange, the Mossad learned that Arad's usefulness to his captors as a bargaining tool had failed. There were reports he had been "sold" to Iran.

Two months before Shalit had been captured, images of Arad had appeared in the Israeli media. In the photos, Arad was pajama-clad, bearded, hollow-eyed, and visibly injured. Were his injuries the result of the crash or from torture by his interrogators?

Meir Dagan knew that inevitably in Gaza the assassination of Mahmoud al-Mabhouh would be measured against the continued incarceration of Gilad Shalit. Asked by a reporter how his son could cope in captivity, his father had replied: "We hope he is strong. But he was very young when he was kidnapped. How can we know? How can anyone know how they would react in such a situation?"

Dagan continued to wonder how Hamas would use Shalit to exploit al-Mabhouh's death.

A week after Mahmoud al-Mabhouh's body had been returned to his family, Khalid Meshal traveled from Damascus to a memorial rally in the small northern town in Gaza, Beit Lahiya. Hemmed in by bodyguards Meshal moved slowly through the crowd, accepting their applause with an occasional wave of his hand, pausing only to pat the head of a child or nod to a face he recognized.

Over three thousand followers were crowded into the town square, where a huge portrait of al-Mabhouh framed with red roses covered one wall of the largest building. Beneath it an honor guard of militants in the red-and-white-checked headdress of Hamas stood on an Israeli flag, which they continually stamped. On the rooftops around the square, lookouts scanned the sky for any sign of Israeli attack.

Meshal was escorted to a platform on which sat the leaders of Hamas, men who had made their way to the rally separately to avoid being attacked by an Israeli aircraft. It had happened many times before. But even if they escaped attack, they suspected their presence would be reported to Tel Aviv by an informer in the crowd. Nowadays there was always one. Before Meshal addressed the crowd, four militants marched to the platform, each holding aloft a framed photograph of an IDF soldier Hamas had killed. A fifth carried a photo of Gilad Shalit, now in his fourth year in captivity.

The soldiers held the photos up to the crowd while Meshal addressed them. Frail though he looked, his voice was strong. He reminded his listeners that al-Mabhouh had been a founding member of Hamas and was "the bravest of the bravest, a hero who died before he could see his dream come true—the destruction of our enemy." He waited for the clapping to die down before continuing. "We will continue to capture our enemy's soldiers until we free all our prisoners in their prisons." Another round of applause swept the square. Once more Meshal raised his hand for silence before continuing. "Israel is the terrorist. We must appeal again to countries to recognize that we are the victims." The applause continued while he kissed in turn the cheek of each Gaza leader on the platform. With a final wave to the crowd he stepped into his waiting car and was driven away.

In the Israeli embassy where Nathan waited to learn what further sanctions the Foreign Office would take over what the media called the passport identity theft, the case of Ashraf Marwan preoccupied the station chief. Nathan had been asked to study the case file that could result in the Mossad being implicated in a cold-blooded crime of even greater magnitude than the Dubai assassination.

Three years earlier, shortly after 1:30 P.M. on June 26, 2007, the broken body of sixty-three-year-old Ashraf Marwan had been found on the pavement below his fourth-floor luxury apartment in Carlton House Terrace, an exclusive address in London's Mayfair. When the police arrived they noticed that Marwan wore no shoes. The patrolmen sent for the detectives, who arrived with forensic experts. While the detectives searched the apartment, the experts focused on its balcony. They concluded that if Marwan had committed suicide he would have had to have stepped over a large potted plant and then climbed past an air-conditioning unit to jump over the meter-high balcony rail. But there there were no footprints in the pot's soil and its plants were undisturbed. Logically Marwan should have left some visible traces in the soil and on the air-conditioner.

They also found no shoes on the balcony. Had Marwan for some reason removed them before throwing himself off? Or was there a more sinister possibility? Was Marwan tipped over the balcony rail by someone grabbing him by his feet, who, fearing he had left his own fingerprints on the shoes, had taken them with him when he fled the scene? The detectives assumed the perpetrator was a man because Marwan was too tall—six feet three inches—for a woman to have easily dropped him off the balcony. The missing shoes were the first of the unresolved mysteries about his death.

A search of the apartment revealed Marwan was taking medicine for a severe nerve condition affecting his feet. Mona, Marwan's wife, told detectives that her husband had difficulty even stepping into his bath and also had a history of heart problems.

At the time of Marwan's death, Mona had been abroad visiting relatives in Cairo. On her return she explained that Marwan had stayed home to complete a book he was writing. She told detectives that the subject matter was so explosive he had told her "on three separate occasions that the contents could lead to his murder."

The police had asked to see the manuscript. When Mona opened the wall safe in her husband's home office, she found no trace of it. There was no evidence of a file for it on Marwan's computer. Mona told the police her husband "would go at night and check the locks on the front door and was becoming more suspicious. This was not his behavior of the previous thirty-eight years. He was suspicious that he would be killed, that somebody would be after him, but it was not paranoia. He was brave, but being cautious."

There was no evidence in the apartment of a break-in. But a neighbor had told the police "I saw two men standing on a balcony above Mr. Marwan's. They were doing nothing, just looking down." The neighbor said the intruders "looked Mediterranean," but this was no help in tracing them. The police spoke to Marwan's doctor, who revealed that his patient had been "under considerable stress of late and was low, frustrated and had lost interest in things." The Home Office pathologist who performed the autopsy found traces of an antidepressant in Marwan's blood. There was no sign a weapon had contributed to his death.

The local detectives were baffled. Had Marwan committed suicide, or was it murder? The case was handed over to Scotland Yard's Specialist Crime Directorate. A spokeswoman for the Metropolitan Police admitted Marwan's missing shoes are "deemed to be critical in what is a complex case."

From the moment Nathan had first heard about Ashraf Marwan's death on that June afternoon he had realized how important it was for the Mossad to ensure it could not be linked to the death.

Ashraf Marwan's father-in-law had been Egypt's president, Gamal Abdel Nasser, whose daughter Mona had married Marwan in 1966.

Marwan had become Nasser's personal adviser on security, making this son of one of Egypt's wealthiest families the most important person in the president's entourage. He was cultivated by foreign intelligence services, including the KGB, MI6, and the CIA. All hoped he would bring them closer to the imperious Nasser. But others also sought Marwan's help. Among them were Adnan Khashoggi, the Saudi arms dealer; the Libyan leader, Colonel Mu'ammar Gadhafi; the unscrupulous Tiny Rowland, the City of London financier who numbered Saddam Hussein as a friend. They had all paid generously for Marwan's advice. Already wealthy, the handsome Egyptian moved from millionaire to billionaire. Soon his portfolio of holdings included a percentage of one of Britain's top football clubs, Chelsea, and property development companies across the globe.

In Tel Aviv, Meir Amit, head of the Mossad (1963–1968), had closely followed Marwan's career. He was a man, Amit would later describe, "of high interest to us." After Nasser's death, Marwan became special adviser to Egypt's new president, Anwar Sadat, and continued to be privy to the vitally important decisions Sadat and his senior officials made about going to war with Israel.

It was then that the Mossad decided to recruit him. Thirty-eight years later, Marwan's death brought to an end the secret career of one of Mossad's most effective spies.

Marwan's career as a spy had begun on a spring day in 1969 when he had flown to London to consult a Harley Street doctor about a stomach ailment. Along with a set of X-rays from a private hospital in Cairo he brought a folder containing secret state documents. By then Marwan had already made contact with the Mossad. How and where that was made has remained secret.

The consultation had been arranged by the Mossad. The doctor was a sayan, one of the "helpers" Meir Amit had originally created as backup for its operations. He would confine himself to saying before he died that "I did have some dealings with Marwan at an early stage." Those contacts were confirmed by Eli Zeira, a former head of Israeli military intelligence, who said Marwan was "my key informant in the run-up to the Yom Kippur War in 1973."

It had been arranged that Marwan would hand over the documents to the sayan, who would then deliver them to the Israeli embassy in London. Marwan had been told not to go near the building. The possibility of his being identified by the surveillance MI5 ran on foreign missions would have blown any chance to use him. Instead he was told to wait in London for a week to hear the results of the medical tests the sayan had carried out.

Marwan's documents were hand-carried by an embassy employee to Tel Aviv. They were judged to be genuine. Zvi Zamir, who had replaced Meir Amit as head of the Mossad, decided it was time to recruit Marwan.

The sayan called the hotel where Marwan was staying and said the test results were all clear. The doctor suggested Marwan would like to celebrate by buying his wife a gift and recommended a visit to Harrods. This was the signal to Marwan that the Mossad wished to pursue matters.

After contact had been made in the London department store, Marwan was taken to a Mossad safe house near the Dorchester. It had been wired to record every conversation.

Nathan knew that time and again Marwan had delivered top-secret Egyptian documents and had been given several code names including, Angel, Babylon, and most frequently, the In-Law. After each meeting with his Mossad handler, he received £50,000 in cash. Over his years of spying Marwan had supposedly received £10 million. If this is true, no spy in the history of the Mossad had been paid such a sum.

In his regular visits to London to visit his Harley Street consultant, Marwan continued to hand over at the Mossad safe house high-grade highly classified data. Any lingering suspicion that he could be a brilliant double agent sent to penetrate the Mossad faded after Zvi Zamir came to London to question Marwan. Zamir was regarded as the best among the service's interrogators. He was satisfied that Marwan wanted to forestall a war with Israel. Israel's military and political leaders believed that Marwan was giving them access not only to Egyptian intelligence but also to sensitive material passed to Cairo from the Syrian and Jordanian security services. This access made Israel not only the most powerfully armed nation in the region, but one with intelligence that the CIA and MI6 realized was invaluable. London and Washington both asked who this Israeli source was. Knowing that the Mossad would never share such an asset, both services wondered how they could get to him. In Moscow the KGB was soon asking a similar question.

On each of Marwan's trips to London he had more invaluable information to impart. But these visits had also given him and Mona a taste for English life. It was one thing to be a member of the Gezira Sporting Club in the fashionable Cairo suburb of Zamalek, where Egyptian society gathered; it was quite another to mingle with the aristocrats of London. Marwan decided that while a suite in the Dorchester was fine, they needed a permanent home in London. When the apartment on Carlton House Terrace became available, they bought and furnished it lavishly.

By then Egypt and Israel had developed a cordial relationship, drawn together by the specter of Islamic extremism, and after Omar Suleiman had taken over EGIS, Egyptian intelligence began to work with the Mossad in dealing with the threat. Marwan's information became less valuable to Tel Aviv.

Suleiman could provide better, more up-to-date information. While Marwan remained an asset, his visits to the London safe house became infrequent and finally stopped, and he decided to retire from spying.

Marwan set himself up as an international business consultant, moving between London, New York, and the capitals of Europe, providing advice on investing in the Middle East. His business acumen made him a billionaire. But sitting in a boardroom with financier Tiny Rowland, or cementing a deal with Adnan Khashoggi over dinner, or eating couscous in the Libyan desert with Colonel Gadhafi paled in comparison with those dangerous and exciting years of being at the center of a major intelligence operation. His time working for Mossad was something that his new associates and their deals could not equal.

Ashraf Marwan began writing a book, telling his wife, Mona, that he expected it "would send shock waves across the Middle East." Of course others had written about the intelligence services in which they had served, but no one could reveal the inside workings of Mossad as he could. He also had much to tell from his unique position alongside his father-in-law, Gamal Abdel Nasser, and later with Anwar Sadat. He had been there when attempts to assassinate both presidents had taken place.

Marwan had worked with the Mossad long enough to know that secrecy was its stock-in-trade and its most precious asset. Indeed, writing a book about the Mossad placed Marwan, and perhaps his family, in mortal danger.

On the morning of his death Marwan had asked his chauffeur to drive him to a meeting at the Marriott Hotel in London. Marwan had gone to the Marriott the previous day as well. Both visits had lasted no more than ten minutes. No one—including the hotel staff, Mona, and the chauffeur—knew just who Marwan had met either time. A later police check of the hotel's guest list produced no clues. But the Scotland Yard Specialist Crime Directorate discovered that Marwan had booked a flight to New York after that second meeting to meet with his lawyer.

Had those meetings or the one he planned to have with his lawyer anything to do with his book? Perhaps Marwan had finished the manuscript and planned to publish it in America, the way other whistleblowers from the intelligence world had done. That could explain why he had turned down an offer from Dr. Ahron Bregman, an Israeli historian based in London, to coauthor the text. In Tel Aviv, Dr. Uri Bar-Yosef, another reputable historian, said he was "convinced that Marwan was one of Israel's best spies."

Scotland Yard detective inspector Kevin Naido, who headed what had become a worldwide investigation, concluded "that my understanding, depending on the individual person I speak to, is that the manuscript was taken at the time of his death. I am unable to conclude exactly where the document was specifically kept or how it could have been moved. Or for that matter, who had stolen it."

Egypt's President Hosni Mubarak described Ashraf Marwan's death as "that of a man who had carried out patriotic acts which it is not yet time to reveal." But Nathan had found nothing in Marwan's file to reveal who had assassinated the Mossad's spy to keep those "patriotic acts" secret.

In the early hours of a March day in 2010 the leaders of Hamas met somewhere in Gaza. A messenger had brought instructions from Khalid Meshal in Damascus as to how to exploit an astonishing development.

Mahmoud al-Mabhouh's assassination continued to attract unprecedented coverage of conditions in Gaza, now widely described in the media as an "Israeli prison camp." The media praised Hamas for its effort to keep Gaza's 1.5 million inmates from starving. These reports had brought the Hamas leaders together to act on Meshal's orders to exploit the media condemnation of Israel for denying Gaza food, medicine, and building materials. In some stories al-Mabhouh was portrayed as a hero who had been murdered on a mercy mission to Dubai to arrange for help. The al-Jazeera rolling news channel and the Tehran-financed Press-TV network had given Hamas an opportunity to support thousands of Web sites in their public relations attack on Israel. In turn these reports were picked up by the BBC, European, and U.S. networks.

In Tel Aviv Mark Regev, the articulate Israeli government spokesman, found himself spending a great deal of time standing before the world's television cameras trying to justify Israel's actions. But the images of the ruined landscape of Gaza were too powerful. Hamas supporters across the Arab world seized upon every television and radio report. When Gilad Shalit's name came up, a Hamas spokesman would counter that Shalit was a prisoner of war treated under the Geneva Convention unlike Palestinians in Israeli jails.

A new discourse about the way Israel was handling Gaza was developing. Even moderate Jews across the Diaspora began to write that while Israel was justified in trying to stop arms from reaching Hamas and in killing a merciless terrorist like al-Mabhouh, starving women and children—"the damned and the dying," one blogger called them—to death was not acceptable. Until that point newspapers in Washington had almost all been pro-Israel. But now papers such as the *Washington Post* and neoconservative organs such as *The New Republic* and *The Weekly Standard* found their support for Israel under attack over Gaza by a generation of gifted young writers on their Internet blogs.

Khalid Meshal and the Hamas leaders in Gaza saw the attacks had damaged Israel's "special relationship" with the United States. By the end of their meeting the Hamas leaders had endorsed Meshal's plan to continue to focus world attention on the Strip. To do so, it would ask its militant Islamic supporters in the West to send a flotilla of ships filled with essential supplies to Gaza. The ships would sail under the banner of Insan Hak ve Hürriyetleri, the IHH (the Foundation of Human Rights and Humanitarian Relief). In the words of Khalid Meshal, "to stop IHH would be like stopping the Red Cross." From its headquarters in Istanbul, the Islamic militants of IHH prepared both to deliver food and medicines to Gaza and to launch a propaganda coup against Israel.

On the morning of Wednesday, March 23, 2010, Foreign Secretary David Miliband called the Israeli ambassador, Ron Prosor. That afternoon Miliband was to be one of the guests of honor—the other was the chief rabbi, Lord Sacks—at the ceremony to mark the reopening of the embassy after months of refurbishment. Miliband said he could not attend because he had "pressing business" in the House of Commons. He did not hint what it was, but the ambassador may well have guessed it was related to the cloning of the British passports. The newspapers continued to discuss the "crisis" this had caused in Anglo-Israeli relations.

That afternoon when Miliband addressed Parliament he left no doubt how serious he viewed the cloning. He told MPs that Scotland Yard's Serious Organised Crime Agency (SOCA) had sent officers to Israel and Dubai before concluding that the owners of the passports had been "the unwitting and innocent victims of official identity fraud." The House remained silent as the foreign secretary continued: "This was a very sophisticated operation, in which high-quality forgeries were used. We have concluded there are compelling reasons to believe that Israel was responsible for the misuse of the British passports. The fact that this was done by a country which is a friend, with significant diplomatic, cultural, business and personal ties to the UK, only adds insult to injury."

Miliband's tone became even more measured. "Israel's intolerable misuse of British passports shows a profound disregard for the UK's sovereignty. No country or government could stand by in such a situation. I have asked that a member of the embassy of Israel be withdrawn from the UK as a result of this affair." Shortly before the ceremony, Ambassador Prosor took Nathan aside and told him he was being expelled.

Next day in the *Daily Telegraph* Stephen Pollard, the editor of *The Jewish Chronicle*, wrote: "The notion that Israel is uniquely guilty—the only country that uses subterfuge and underground activities to defend itself from terror—is risible. Is there anyone in the know who could maintain with a straight face the line that the UK's intelligence and defence services have never cloned a passport or stolen an identity as part of their undercover operations?"

In Tel Aviv Meir Dagan met with the resident MI6 head of station at the British embassy. The two worked well together, able to handle intelligence and its associated diplomacy. They understood the undercurrents Nathan's expulsion had created. The relationship between Benjamin Netanyahu and Gordon Brown, fighting for his political future as Britain's prime minister, had long been a minefield for both Meir Dagan and the MI6 officer to negotiate. These two politicians were different in temperament and politics, which they often tried to impose on their intelligence services.

The latest request Netanyahu had made was that the British government allow Nathan to be replaced "at once" by another spy. Dagan had asked the MI6 station chief to encourage Sir John Sawers to lobby Downing Street to agree. Dagan reminded his visitor that Nathan's expulsion came at a time when Britain's intelligence services were more than ever conjoined with the Mossad in dealing with the threats from Hamas and Hezbollah along with the increasing belligerent attitude of Syria and the most dangerous threat of all, Iran. The Mossad was also now working alongside MI6 in Afghanistan and had provided the British army with guidelines on how to handle suicide bombers.

The MI6 officer reassured Dagan that Nathan's removal would not damage the close working relationship between the Mossad and British intelligence. However, he explained that the British Foreign Office had requested "a formal guarantee there would be no repeat of the passport cloning." Meir Dagan said Netanyahu had ordered no such guarantee should be given.

On the eve of Britain's general election in May 2010 the Foreign Office announced: "We look to Israel to rebuild the trust we believe is required for the full and open relationship we would like. We have asked for specific assurances from Israel, which would clearly be a positive step towards rebuilding that trust."

The election of Prime Minister David Cameron and his coalition government produced no change in Israel's refusal to provide the guarantee. The stalemate continued.

In mid-May 2010, one of the financial investigators in the Terrorist Finance Tracking Program (TFTP) of the U.S. Department of the Treasury spotted an interesting development on SWIFT, the worldwide international financial telecommunication network. SWIFT links 8,500 banks and financial institutions across the United States, Europe, Asia, and the Middle East and is TFTP's key tool in tracing funds for terror groups.

The investigator noticed transfers of substantial sums from banks in Brussels and Madrid to one in the Fatih district in Istanbul. This bank was where IHH (Insan Hak ve Hürriyetleri) had its account. The investigator knew the transfers came from accounts operated by front companies for Hamas.

The possibility that a political strategic attack was being financed was relayed by TFTP to a number of intelligence services, including CIA, MI6, and the Mossad. The information was passed from Tel Aviv to the Mossad station in Turkey. MIT, Turkey's military intelligence service, had long had a good relationship with the Mossad and regularly exchanged information. With the growing threat posed by Iran, the Mossad used its station in Turkey to "sniff at the mullahs through the back door."

Mossad's operations directorate in Tel Aviv asked one of those doorkeepers, a Turkish-born Jew code-named Omar, to find out what lay behind the money transfers. Omar made his way through the narrow streets of Fatih. The suburb was close to Istanbul's famous tourist attraction, the Blue Mosque, but few tourists ventured there. Fatih was filled with chador-covered women and swarthy-faced men from the countryside who had added to the city's already overcrowded population of fourteen million. From their shacks in the shantytowns on the outskirts these people walked to Fatih to visit Islamic radical groups and listen to the recruiters asking them to join other jihadists.

Omar had learned how to blend into this hostile world. He would stop at one of the open-air street cafés to sip coffee and read one of the paperbacks or magazines printed in Fatih. Dressed like any other young man, he understood the customs of the area and spoke the local dialect. This made it easier to listen to the gossip drifting around him.

Investigative Magistrate Jean-Louis Bruguière, a product of France's complex legal system, had a track record of exposing terror organizations before the European Union appointed him to work with TFTP. Working with French intelligence, DGSE, he had discovered that forged Moroccan passports were being distributed by the IHH to Islamic militants, and that the organization had bases in Bosnia and Afghanistan. Within a year he had built a case strong enough for Turkish police to raid the IHH headquarters in Fatih, where an arsenal of weapons and explosives was found together with forged documents. IHH was closed down and its organizers arrested. It had been reopened with the support of the Turkish government, who described it as an "Islamic charity with no connection to terrorism."

But details of the money transfers had alerted Bruguière that IHH was back in business. He soon found out that while it was not planning to finance a terrorist attack, it was organizing an operation that would not only seriously damage the relationship between Israel and Turkey—an essential connection in the global war against terrorism—but would also inflame world opinion against the Jewish state.

IHH was going to fund a "peace flotilla" to bring 10,000 tons of food, medicine, and building supplies to Gaza. On board would be some of the world's leading peace activists to add to IHH's claim that the ships—six in all, led by the passenger ship *Mavi Marmara*—were on a mission to save lives. There had been previous such voyages, but none on this scale. The Israeli navy had successfully intercepted those ships. But this time IHH had assured the activists that the flotilla would not stop until it reached Gaza. On board the *Mavi Marmara*, the command ship, were several freelance photographers and Andre Abou Khalil, a cameraman from the al-Jazeera network.

An upper-deck salon had been set aside for the media under the supervision of an IHH spokeswoman. She provided the reporters with handouts giving background details of the "peace mission" and promised that by the end of the "adventure" there would be a "global story" to report. Most of the reporters were from Arab newspapers and radio stations. IHH had its own TV crew. The spokeswoman insisted no weapons had been brought on board by the forty IHH staffers traveling on the ship.

Nevertheless, through the windows of the salon reporters could see that several of the IHH men carried machetes and knives with long blades. Several of them had chain saws. Once clear of the harbor of Istanbul they began to use the chain saws to cut through deck rails to form batons and staves. These were distributed among the IHH members. In a re-creation of the event by the BBC *Panorama* program one of the staffers would argue that "we had to protect ourselves against the expected attack we knew would come by Israel."

Omar had discovered that the peace activists included Henning Mankell, an acclaimed Swedish author; Sarah Colborne, the London-based director of the Palestinian Solidarity Campaign; Theresa McDermott, a member of the Free Gaza Movement; and Hanin Zoabi, an Arab politician in Israel's Knesset. Most of the activists had asked IHH to keep their identities secret. Some had been on previous blockade-running voyages to supply Gaza and had been taken prisoner by Israeli gunboats; in the words of one, "we were scared out of our skins."

Altogether six hundred activists were assigned to the six ships in the flotilla. Like those on board the *Mavi Marmara*, each boat had a crew of tough young Turks selected by IHH. Some had come from Hamas training camps. Omar suspected their role was to defend the ships against any attempt to board them. A destroyer of the Turkish navy accompanied the flotilla as it headed south into the Mediterranean Sea.

In Tel Aviv, Omar's latest intelligence report confirmed that the flotilla had the full support of the government. Various ministers appeared on radio and television programs endorsing what one called "the peaceful intentions of these people." But the attitude toward Israel had hardened; several commentators demanded that the ships be allowed to land their supplies at Gaza. Israel was reminded that the request was made by a NATO partner and should be considered in that light.

Nevertheless, Meir Dagan did not feel cause for undue alarm in Omar's report. He was more interested in how Netanyahu, who was in Canada, would handle his upcoming meeting with President Obama in the White House. "The relationship between them has become even cooler. It could be make-or-break time for the prime minister," one correspondent predicted.

Netanyahu was discussing tactics with his aides when he took a call from his defense minister, Ehud Barak. The two men were close and respected each other. Barak wasted no time in advising the prime minister that the flotilla was still in international waters but drawing close to Gaza.

The prime minister ordered that the ships be stopped by Flotilla 13, Israel's highly respected seaborne commando unit. The Israeli special forces would be commanded by Vice-Admiral Eli Marom, a veteran of heavy-duty missions. An operations room was established in the hotel to link him to the Kirya, the IFF headquarters in Tel Aviv. Netanyahu had donned his favorite mantle of the warrior prime minister. Plans on how he would deal with President Obama were put aside.

At the briefing the commandos were told they should expect minor resistance from the peace activists, and paint guns and laser-type weapons would be sufficient to subdue them. But they were also to carry their usual sidearms. An IDF psychologist described how to deal with the peace activists: be firm and keep violence to a minimum.

On Sunday, May 29, 2010, an Israeli air force reconnaissance plane spotted the *Mavi Marmara* rendezvousing with the other blockade runners south of Cyprus. The commandos assigned to fly to the attack boarded their Black Hawk helicopters. One said later: "Usually before an operation we sit in the helicopter, silent like the grave. Now we were in high spirits, talking and cracking jokes."

A similar mood prevailed among the commandos in their Morenas, the unit's fast gunboats, at Ashod Navy base. There were two women among the attack group. At 1:00 A.M. Israeli time on Monday, May 31, Netanyahu called the Kirya operations room. Barak told him that everything was ready. "Then let's go," Netanyahu said.

The gunboats roared out of the base. Above them in the moonlit sky flew the Black Hawks. Their onboard radars showed the blips of the peace flotilla were still in international waters.

Operation Sky Winds had begun.

On the *Mavi Marmara* Sarah Colborne recalled, "I could see the gunboats and a decision was made to move further back into international waters." In the ship's radio room the operator was broadcasting that the ship was on a humanitarian mission, responding to a UN call for supplies to be sent to Gaza. On the upper deck the IHH men had taken up position, each brandishing a stave cut from the deck rails or holding a knife.

On deck Theresa McDermott, who had helped to set up a medical emergency room onboard, heard over the ship's public address system that everyone was to put on life jackets and prepare for an attack.

Challenger 1, the smallest boat in the flotilla, had come alongside *Mavi Marmara*. The passenger ship's radio operator continued to broadcast his message.

Theresa recalled that "the gunboats were shadowing us all the way. At 2:00 A.M. we realized one of the boats had come right up the back of the flotilla, but then it dropped back again. They were trying to make us feel very nervous. Then it went very quiet and we could hear people starting to say their prayers."

The flotilla was still in international waters. Suddenly the gunboats raced through the flotilla, firing smoke bombs and noise grenades onto the *Mavi Marmara*. Above the ship a Black Hawk hovered and their commandos rappeled onto the upper deck. They were grabbed, beaten, and hustled away to a lower deck by some of the crew. More commandos landed and suffered the same fate. The sound of gunfire filled the air. Someone screamed in Hebrew into his com radio: "They are shooting at us!"

In his command speedboat Vice-Admiral Marom was fifty yards from the *Mavi Marmara* hearing in his com set the shouts from the deck. These were being relayed to the Kirya operations room. From a monitor screen came Marom's voice: "They are using real arms. I repeat, they are using real arms. Request permission to use handguns."

Standing beside Barak was Lieutenant General Gabi Ashkenazi, head of the IDF. The defense minister called out: "Finish this at once."

The phone satellite link to Netanyahu in Canada blinked. His call was ignored. All eyes were on the monitor screen.

On board *Mavi Marmara* Sarah Colborne saw the first fatality. "He was shot in the head. He was obviously in a very bad way and he subsequently died. There were bullets flying all over the place. I couldn't believe the Israelis were doing this. We were still in international waters."

Abdul Razzaq Maqri, a former Algerian parliamentarian on board as an observer, heard "a shot and a fellow Algerian activist fell bleeding from an eye. Overhead was the whirl of helicopter blades and more commandos abseiling onto the ship to fire at unarmed civilians."

The other gunboats closed in on the *Mavi Marmara*. Their crews used scaling ladders to climb on board. Pieces of wood and metal were hurled at them. The flash of knife blades accompanied hand-to-hand fighting across the deck as the commandos sought to gain a foothold. Several of them were thrown back into the sea. Shouts and screams of pain filled the night. "The sound of gunfire and the sight of metal poles flailing at bodies created an unforgettable horror," recalled Sarah Colborne.

From his vantage point in the gathering dawn, Vice-Admiral Marom saw his commandos storm the wheelhouse. The crash of the door being kicked open carried clearly. The ship came to a stop. "We have control!" shouted an exultant voice.

In the Kirya, Barak asked to be connected to Netanyahu. "Everything is under control," he told the prime minister. Barak did not add that this had been achieved while still in international waters. A moment later Marom reported that three commandos were missing. "Find them," ordered Barak.

On board the *Mavi Marmara*, commandos rushed down through the ship. Following them filming as he went, was Andre Abou Khalil, the al-Jazeera cameraman. "Over the public address system a voice said the Israelis would only be freed after medical help was provided for the badly wounded. The Israelis continued to shoot. One of the IHH men got a bullet in the head. Another was shot in the neck," recalled the cameraman.

The commandos burst into the engine room, killing a militant guarding it. They found a wounded commando chained to a pipe. He was cut free, had his wounds treated, and was carried back on deck, where he was lowered into one of the gunboats. The other two captured commandos had jumped into the sea and were picked up by a gunboat.

The helicopters and gunboats withdrew. Behind them they left nine dead Turks and a number of wounded peace activists. On board the *Mavi Marmara*, commandos ordered the captain to lead the flotilla into Ashdod harbor.

Henning Mankell, the Swedish writer, said he spoke to the two women commandos. "They were very disciplined, but when I looked into their eyes they looked as if they really felt like—shit, what the hell are we doing here? I asked one why they had done this and she said we had weapons on board. We didn't. She said they had searched the ship and produced a razor and a little knife. I laughed at this point. What else could you do?"

Waiting for the flotilla at Ashdod were detachments of IDF troops. They escorted the activists away to be interrogated. In Canada Netanyahu cut short his trip and returned to Israel. On the flight he was told about the start of the worldwide condemnation of operation Sky Winds.

The international fallout over the al-Mabhouh assassination was further reinforced by the mounting worldwide criticism of the attack on the flotilla. Tension between Turkey and Israel reached a new high. There was public pressure for the Ankara government to break off diplomatic relations with the Jewish state. The fury spread as the first of the freed activists returned home to give their stories to the media. By then the Mossad intelligence station in Turkey had been closed down on the order of the Turkish government.

In Israel there was the mounting belief that the entire operation had failed because the Mossad had not provided adequate intelligence. Questions were asked and never answered. Had Dagan briefed Netanyahu on the operation before he had left for Canada? At what stage had Barak become involved? Only months later did the defense minister accept that the responsibility for the failure rested on him. By then Meir Dagan had been singled out as the figure primarily responsible for the debacle. The Israeli media wasted no time in lambasting the intelligence chief.

For Meir Dagan it was another humiliation and added to the tension within Mossad. Three of the deputies he had appointed, one to be the head of operations, resigned. One of Israel's television stations announced that Dagan was to be fired. In June 2010, the government press office, after refusing to comment, finally stated: "The prime minister decided last year to extend the head of the Mossad's tenure by a year. Since then no additional decision has been made."

Many within the Mossad and elsewhere saw the words as marking the end of Meir Dagan's eight years of running the service. An article in *Haaretz*, Israel's most respected newspaper, appeared under the headline "Mossad Is Supposed to Gather Intelligence, Not Sow Death." In the accompanying article, Gideon Levy put into words the mood of many of the paper's readers. The gifted writer asked if people wanted to live in a country "that has death squads" and send its secret agents to "suffocate people with pillows in hotel rooms." Dagan was attacked as "a man who craves adventurous actions" and Netanyahu as "the man who approves them." In the history of the Mossad never had its *kidon* been so savagely attacked. The cold ferocity of Levy's words outweighed all previous favorable judgments of the Mossad.

In early August 2010, Meir Dagan let it be known that if Netanyahu demanded his resignation he could have it. Perhaps recognizing the effect the loss of the Mossad chief would have on his political future, the embattled prime minister bluntly told the world that Turkey should never have allowed the peace flotilla to set sail. He would not allow the commandos who had taken part in the attack to give evidence to the inquiry he had agreed the United Nations should hold. And of course he was not going to have the role of the Mossad publicly examined.

During June 2010, having rejected calls for an investigation into the Gaza-bound flotilla from the United Nations and governments around the world, Israel set up a domestic inquiry approved by the cabinet of the Netanyahu government to investigate the legality of the attack. The committee held closed-door sessions under the chairmanship of Jacob Turkel, a retired judge of the Supreme Court. Sitting with him were Shabtai Rosenne, a professor of international law, and Amos Horev, a military expert. Two international observers, David Trimble, a former First Minister of Northern Ireland, and Ken Watkin, a Canadian military judge, completed the committee.

Critics of the committee seized upon their age—an average of eighty-five—complaining that the group was too old to assess the evidence. Jurists challenged its mandate as too limited. There were calls in the media for "at least one woman" to serve to give the committee "a wider spectrum."

The UN Secretary-General Ban Ki-moon said that in its present form the committee would not have "international credibility." His view was ignored, though Judge Turkel threatened to resign unless the powers of the inquiry were expanded. Prime Minister Netanyahu finally agreed that the inquiry would have powers of subpoena to call witnesses. Nevertheless, it would not be allowed to take evidence from the commandos, who had carried out the raid that had killed nine persons and had left many more wounded. Increasingly Meir Dagan became a specific target over the way Mossad had failed to handle the intelligence relating to the flotilla attack. For his part Dagan let it be known, through his own media contacts, that he regarded the inquiry as "a waste of time and we are not going to give them anything about our intelligence."

Letters between the committee and the intelligence chief became more angry, with Judge Turkel insisting that, as he was conducting an inquiry sponsored by the government, Dagan was bound by law to respond to all requests. Dagan insisted secret intelligence came under national security. Judge Turkel finally responded with a warning that he was empowered to take legal action against Dagan. Dagan brushed the threat aside. On September 13, the Mossad handed unspecified material over to the committee.

One by one, in the searing heat of high summer, the witnesses involved in planning the raid began to appear before the committee. What they were asked and how they responded remained behind closed doors. It didn't stop the speculation that more than one witness had criticized the Mossad. Others were said to have blamed the attack on the flotilla as "a political shambles that was typical Netanyahu." The prime minister was among the first to testify, followed by the justice minister, Yaakov Neeman, and the defense minister, Ehud Barak. According to journalists covering the hearing, Bibi Netanyahu was dismissive of many of the questions put to him, while Neeman and Barak used their experience in appearing before various committees and tribunals to give what one reporter called "smooth answers that answered nothing."

Israel's military chief of staff, Lieutenant General Gabi Ashkenazi, was the quintessential soldier, upright and brusque, his answers short. His commandos had been forced to defend themselves; they had done so with courage and a minimum of force. He marched from the room as briskly as he had entered. It was a bravura performance from "a veteran who didn't know what all the fuss was about," observed one reporter.

Judge Turkel announced he was going to write to the Turkish ambassador to Israel asking him to invite the Turkish captain of the flotilla, Khalid Tariq, to testify. Tariq had claimed in an Istanbul newspaper that he had seen some of the activists firing on the commandos before throwing their weapons overboard.

The news enlivened life for the reporters. There came more excitement: the arrival of Meir Dagan. Unsmiling, he strolled into the inquiry carrying a briefcase. Did it contain the documents Judge Turkel had asked for?

This session of the inquiry, as Dagan had insisted, was closed and lasted over two hours. Dagan left the room as he had arrived, with an uncompromising look in his eyes, brushing aside reporters' questions. He rode away in the back of his armor-plated car, knowing that the rumors of his departure from office continued to spread. But no one could be sure if he was going to resign or be sacked.

In late September 2010, Turkey's president Abdullah Gui told the United Nations he was still waiting for an apology from Israel, along with monetary compensation to the families of those killed or injured in the raid.

On Friday, September 24, the UN Human Rights Council announced the attack on the flotilla had been "disproportionate and brutal. The conduct of the Israeli military and other personnel toward the flotilla passengers demonstrated levels of total unnecessary and incredible violence. There is clear evidence to support prosecution."

In Tel Aviv, Netanyahu dismissed the report as "biased and distorted.

It has a politicized and extremist approach." The council is based in Geneva and was established in 2006 following accusations that its predecessor, the UN Commission on Human Rights, had openly discriminated against Israel. The council has itself over the years passed several resolutions condemning Israel over its actions in Palestinian territories.

On December 4, 2010, after a month of planning, two kidon assassinated a key Iranian scientist in the country's nuclear bomb program as he was driven to work through the Tehran morning rush-hour traffic. One kidon maneuvered a high-powered motorcycle through the traffic. His pillion passenger clutched a small but powerful bomb fitted with a suction pad. As the motorcycle drew alongside the car of Majid Shahriari, Iran's expert in building switches for a nuclear bomb, the pillion passenger stuck the bomb on Shahriari's side of the windshield. Even as the driver tried to swerve away, the bomb exploded. By then the motorcycle had roared away into the traffic.

Next day the assassins were back at their base in Israel, having traveled out of Iran on the long-established secret route established by the Mossad and operated by its Kurdish allies.

On December 6, Meir Dagan called his department heads to a meeting in his office and told them he would resign on New Year's Eve, after eight eventful years. No one questioned the decision. For weeks the media attacks on Dagan had continued. He told them that the Tehran operation was proof that "we haven't lost our teeth."

He then pointed to his deputy, Tamir Pardo, and said Pardo would take over Mossad. This appointment had been agreed to by Prime Minister Benjamin Netanyahu.

Pardo, a squat figure with crinkly gray hair, said, "I have big shoes to fill and lots of work to do." At fifty-seven, he had spent thirty years in the Mossad, serving in various overseas postings.

Dagan led the applause over his appointment. After a round of handshakes, the change of command of the Mossad was accomplished.

In January 2011 Pardo made his plans clear in a series of telephone calls to various intelligence chiefs around the world. It would be business as usual. Iran would remain the prime target. The Mossad would increase its presence in Yemen and Somalia and spearhead the hunt for al-Qaeda's new chief of military operations, Saif al-Adel. More agents would be sent to Egypt and other unstable countries in North Africa.

For thirty years Mossad had maintained a close relationship with EGIS, the Egyptian General Intelligence Service. In February 2011, its director Omar Suleiman was made the country's first vice-president by President Hosni Mubarak as he faced revolution. After eighteen days Mubarak was deposed. Suleiman had announced he had no intention of standing for the presidency in elections due in September 2011. In a telephone call Pardo urged him to resume his position as intelligence chief. Suleiman was noncommittal. Israel's main ally in the region, and the first to sign a peace treaty with the Jewish State, faced an uncertain future. At his first staff meeting following the departure of Mubarak, Pardo asked: who will be next?

CHAPTER 32

A New Spymaster

On the first Friday in March 2011 Tamir Pardo, the eleventh director

of Mossad, studied the satellite photo on the cedar-wood conference

table in his office. A man of middle height with a tight suntanned skin,

he held himself with the bearing of the professional soldier he had been.

He looked about fifty, ten years younger than he was, but whereas other

soldiers of his age often carried traces of the skirmishes and battles they

had survived for Israel, he seemed scarred by something else other than

bullets and shrapnel. His many battles nowadays were quiet affairs,

weighing the intelligence he received. Then the questions would start in his mind, ones that physical combat did not have to ask. So it was with the satellite image.

The image showed a missile base in Saudi Arabia's Empty Quarter, the Rub' al Khali. The missiles were powerful surface-to-surface DF-3 rockets with a range of 2,000 miles. Each carried the distinctive emblem of Saudi Arabia: two scimitars beneath a palm tree. Circled on the photo were two targets: Teheran and Tel Aviv.

Seated around the table were Mossad's division chiefs. Some of them wore a yarmulke. The younger ones looked like men who delighted in secrets. Five were new to their post, Pardo's first promotions for division chiefs. For years Pardo had been one himself. Now he was the oldest man in the room, his hair beginning to gray, the first lines etched on his oval face, brown eyes reflecting a long-established cynicism. Over the years he had developed an air of formality and held his dignity close. He had developed such characteristics during those years he had helped Mossad face the challenges of global terrorism and threats from Israel's neighbors, especially Iran, in the sensitive area of weapons of mass destruction.

He had attended similar meetings and was used to taking his turn to speak. Now he was conscious that he was the decision maker; that anything he said would be registered by the others around the table. They would judge him by any demand he made that would require the fresh collection of operational data. Pardo was certain that from the day he was appointed there wasn't a man among them who had not boned up on his background; it was part of the way of life in the upper echelon of Mossad to assess the new chief following the premature resignation of his predecessor.

Pardo was the son of a family of Turkish and Serbian origins who had emigrated to what was then called Palestine. They were observant Jews who dutifully kept Sabbath. He had gone to shul on Friday evening and when he came home he found his mother had always prepared the table, the wine and the challah loaves in their appointed place, and she had lit the candles with the same words, "light in darkness." He had grown up to understand that the Jewish people were born in the land of Israel, which it had ruled, on and off, for thirteen centuries between 1200 BCE and the second century CE. It became a foundation for the history of the Arab-Israel conflict of 1948 that he absorbed.

Pardo had completed his education at Tel Aviv University, and spoke several languages in time to serve his compulsory military service in the Israel Defense Force. At the age of twenty-two he graduated from an officer's course in communications and was posted to the elite special forces unit, Shaldag. He took part in several classified operations and was three times awarded an Israel Security Prize. In July, 1976, he was selected to take part in Operation Entebbe (see chapter 7, "The Gentleman Spy," pp. 143–45). He came back one of its publicly acclaimed heroes. Shortly afterward he married a childhood sweetheart, fathered a son and daughter, and later became a grandfather. His home life in a Tel Aviv suburb remained as little known as when the family had first moved there.

In 1980 he joined Mossad, and two years later graduated from its training school and was assigned to its Keshet department, one of the most sought-after postings in the service. Its technicians gathered electronic intelligence, supported operations, and were often sent to any part of the world. If it called for concealing a camera or a microphone in the office of a target or installing a phone tap in a particular building, a technician would do it. Pardo had soon become praised for his ingenuity, experience, and tradecraft. He saw the importance for Mossad to communicate with its informers in the Arab world and studied existing methods for the exchange of information that the CIA called a *dead drop*, the KGB *taynik*, and MI6 a *dead-letter box*. As he worked his way up to become head of Keshet he devised new ways for informers to communicate with their handlers.

In 1982 the Israeli army moved into Lebanon to eliminate the Palestine Liberation Organiation (PLO). Pardo was in charge of the unit monitoring electronic signals from Syrian tanks and SAM rocket batteries in the Bekáa Valley. The signals were swiftly analyzed and Pardo's team was able to determine the operational characteristics of the SAM radars and pinpoint their location. Within hours the Israeli air force had destroyed all the SAM batteries. It gained Israel total control of the sky over Lebanon and eliminated any serious possibility that Syria would enter the battle on the side of the PLO.

Pardo recognized that the skills, tools, and the culture of tradecraft were expanding. Specialized subminiature cameras he first used during the Cold War had become obsolescent. Microphones and transmitters now had minute batteries with a far longer operational life. Video cameras were small enough to be sent crawling through an air-conditioning vent shaft or up inside a drain pipe to record an image or sound that was then encrypted and transmitted to a nearby receiver.

Unmanned aerial vehicles with wingspans of under half an inch could carry a camera or audio sensor into a building as a flying bug. Gadgets like those had become critical components in Mossad operations against terrorists.

The need for information increasingly took on an urgency. A new terror group had arrived to create even more deadly havoc alongside Hamas and Hezbollah. It called itself the al-Aqsa Martyrs' Brigades. A Mossad informer in the Gaza Strip had told his handler that the brigade was recruiting suicide bombers to attack Israel. It soon emerged that it was also seeking recruits with physical appearances and skin tones that would allow them to pass as white and avoid arousing suspicion as they went on missions. A Mossad agent in Amsterdam reported an informer had told him "the whiter a recruit looked the greater would be his financial reward. The money, of course, would be paid to his family after his suicide."

In the early hours of April 26, 1986, Pardo had been night duty officer in the Mossad communications room when a message arrived from its agent in Kiev, Ukraine. Until then it had been a quiet night with reports from agents. Pardo routed them to the desks in headquarters responsible for dealing with them. The Kiev agent had been posted to keep track of terrorists or arms traffickers making their way into the Balkans and along the Mediterranean to attack Israel.

The message from the agent revealed there had been a nuclear disaster at the reactor plant at Chernobyl, south of Kiev. The entire area had been quarantined for several miles around the plant, including a new "workers city" for fifty thousand workers and their families.

Two months after the Chernobyl disaster its extent became clear. Over two hundred workers who had been working in the plant when the reactor exploded were diagnosed with acute radiation syndrome, ARS, and had died. A further two hundred thousand had been drafted from all over the Soviet Union to help with the cleanup; many received huge doses of radiation in the months that followed. A large number died.

Reports from Mossad informers claimed that the al-Aqsa Martyrs' Brigade was were willing to pay huge sums of money to families with a relative who was a victim of the Chernobyl catastrophe and willing to be a suicide bomber. Each would be provided with travel documents to enter Israel and spread their radiation sickness. But the number of those who may have been approached by the terrorist group remains unknown.

On that first Friday morning in March 2011, the department chiefs had delivered their briefings on how the latest developments could impinge on Israel. One by one the regions' trouble spots were reviewed across the table where Pardo sat. He asked questions, nodded approval, and guided the conversation forward, pinpointing the weakness of a proposal as well as its potential.

Behind his eyes a quick intelligence weighed the information he received. When a speaker had finished he turned to the next man. Those who knew him well had come to know it was the energy of someone who knew how much he should consume before he needed to act. When he did, it would be decisive.

Several of them who had worked with Pardo for years knew that once he had made a decision he had no time for further discussion. There were other reminders he would deliver from time to time: the words of Cicero. "To be ignorant of what happened is to remain ignorant" and the saying of G. K. Chesterton: "The disadvantage of men not knowing the past is that they do not know the present." That morning Pardo reminded his division chiefs that areas of the Middle East were collapsing beyond Israel's borders as their rulers struggled to retain control over their population.

Arab dictators who had ruled brutally over hundreds of millions of people—Hosni Mubarak of Egypt and Ben Ali of Tunisia had been driven out of office—while Mu'ammar Gadhafi in Lybia and Bashar al-Assad in Syria were fighting to avoid the fate of Saddam Hussein in Iraq. For decades they had played their power games across the Middle East, using the rules they had borrowed from their scripture and to plot the removal of Israel from their midst.

When Pardo became Mossad's deputy director, Meir Dagan had appointed him to oversee what was happening in the Arab world, especially to analyze what could follow after the Palestine people voted to return representatives for the Palestine Authority to govern them. The expectation was that the Fatah party of Mahmoud Abbas would lead his party to victory and become the Authority's president. It was a hope shared in Washington by George W. Bush and his secretary of state, Condoleezza Rice. Both believed it would give credibility to the "roadmap" the Saudis had drawn up that promised full Arab recognition for Israel if it went back to its 1967 borders. Pardo had forecast "it was an expectation that belongs in Disneyland."

On January 26, 2006 (see chapter 26, "Miscalculations," pp. 580–83),

Hamas had swept to victory on a platform of a social-support system modeled on the Muslim Brotherhood.

Pardo's report had not only impressed Dagan but had found its way into military and political arenas in Israel. Mossad was told to report what else could unexpectedly happen in those Arab countries whose rulers had been propped up by the American dollar and had fled into exile with bank vaults of foreign cash, leaving behind what Pardo called "a stagnant pond of retardation in which their people had toiled fantastically under the yoke of tyranny across North Africa to the Gulf."

During the time he had worked in operations, Pardo had contributed to planning missions to send Mossad agents into Syria, on which the al-Assad family's grip had increasingly tightened since they had seized control in 1970.

The Syrians had fifteen separate intelligence organizations, the largest number in any Arab country. They are controlled by the Presidential Security Council, which has a global reach with spies in all its embassies. In Damascus other organizations monitored all political activity and supervised "discussion clubs," censored all publications, and reported the activities of all foreigners.

The most powerful of the organizations was the Shu'bat al-Mukhabarat al-Askariya, Military Intelligence (MI). Its role included the protection of the president and his family and providing him with strategic and tactical intelligence and the loyalty of his armed forces including its powerful air force. MI had a brief to carry out assassinations against the regime's opponents in Lebanon and Europe. The head of MI, like those in charge of the other intelligence organizations, was a member of the Alawite sect, from where the al-Assad family had sprung.

Like other dictatorships, Syria had informers who in return for money deposited in European banks would provide valuable information to Mossad. One had provided details of the regime's arsenal of chemical weapons. These included mustard gas, a weapon first used in the Great War in 1916 by the Germans. Sarin was a nerve agent that swiftly produces paralysis and death. Equally deadly was Novichok, a gas that renders useless protective suits and gas masks. The weapons had been supplied to Syria by Iran in barrels along with rockets that could be used to launch the chemicals into Israel.

Mossad had established that the poisons were stored in underground bunkers across the country. Two were near Aleppo, in the north, close to the Turkish border. Another site was at Latakia on the Mediterranean coast. Inland at Homs and al-Safira were four other storage bunkers. And near Damascus were five more. Each bunker was protected by Scud missiles, part of one of the largest missile arsenals in the Middle East. Close to each site were airfields, guarded by Syria's air defence system provided by Russia.

In his last days in office Meir Dagan had passed the information to Air Force headquarters in the center of Tel Aviv. A report had also been sent to the Kirya, the IDF headquarters where the committee of the Heads of Services had their offices. They would ultimately have to decide whether the threat posed by Syria's chemical arsenal would require an air strike.

Pardo's elegant language had enhanced the files he had brought with him to his new office. They held the latest information on Iran and the Lebanese Hezbollah; Syria and President Bashar al-Assad, who had inherited the murderous methods of his father to launch a sectarian civil war that threatened to spread on down to Yemen and across the Red Sea into Africa. Other files contained reports from agents Pardo had sent into Eritrea, across the Blue Nile into Sudan and Chad and on into Niger, Mali, Mauritania, and up to Algeria and Tunisia.

It was in those places that the seeds of revolution had been born, created from what an UNESCO report in one of the files called "the massive youth bulge." Half of the Arab population was under the age of twenty-five. They had begun to march through the streets chanting they wanted a chance to be educated, to be trained in some skill that would give them a place in the workforce. They wanted to be like the few graduates their governments boasted they were training. They wanted to be understood: "We live like Third World People, but we are First World People."

Pardo's analysis continued to be in demand from Prime Minister Netanyahu. The intelligence chief accompanied him to Washington to brief the Obama administration.

Pardo had found that in Langley and the State Department there was little grasp of the latest situation in the Middle East. He had decided that in the minds of American diplomats and intelligence officers there were often two groups: those to be trusted, those not to be. Egypt, Saudi Arabia, and the Gulf States were on the okay-to-trust list. Syria, Libya, Hezbollah, Hamas, and the Muslim Brotherhood were on the not-to-talk-to list.

The Mossad chief had spent hours explaining what changes were under way in the region and that they must be taken into account. Saudi Arabia's relationship with Syria had been a frosty one since the First Persian Gulf War, 1980–88, when Saudi Arabia supported Iran against Iraq. After the war Teheran and Damascus drew closer—an alliance that increasingly concerned Israel as Syria became the base for the Hezbollah terror organization. Syria, never a friendly neighbor, became a threat to Israel. Russia, whose role in the region had faded, was once more making a determined attempt to rebuild its old power in the Middle East, promoting the idea that America, like Britain after the Suez Crisis, would continue to disengage itself from the region.

One of Pardo's hosts, a CIA officer, had reminded him of what had happened in 1982 when Ronald Reagan had sent an 1,800-strong force of U.S. Marines to Lebanon in response to an international outcry over the killing of hundreds of innocent men, women, and children in the Sabra and Shatila Palestine refugee camps. Reagan had ordered the marines to stop the massacres and bring an end to Lebanon's brutal civil war. Within a year the mission had ended in tragedy when 241 marines were killed after Iranian-backed terrorists had driven two truck bombs into the building where the Americans were housed. It was the deadliest single loss suffered by the United States since the Second World War.

The CIA officer had said the only Israeli action he would support would be that of Israeli special forces deployed to ensure that any air attacks on biological weapons targets in Syria would hit their targets.

The officer had leaned across the table where they had sat over dinner in Georgetown and said he well understood that thousands of Israelis had been dusting off the gas masks they first wore during the Gulf War against Iraq in 1991. But if they expected President Obama to order air strikes against those thousand tons of chemical weapons in Syria, they should think again. Pardo had reminded him of Goethe's words: "Coming events cast a long shadow."

He had concluded his briefing in Washington with this blunt judgment. The Middle East was steadily showing signs that America would have to rethink its foreign policy.

On the flight home to Tel Aviv, Pardo had told Netanyahu he had felt at times "I was talking in the dark." The prime minister smiled and replied it was often how he had felt after trips to Washington.

On that Friday morning briefing in March 2011 Pardo had told his division chiefs he saw satellite photos of the Chinese rockets as further evidence that the United States, which had been the only great power remaining in the region, was steadily being replaced by the People's Republic of China. There was not a country in the Middle East where the red flag of China did not fly over one of its banks. Chinese diplomats spoke fluent Arabic and placed great store on the relationships they established with Arab clients. It became increasingly clear that Beijing anticipated using its influence in the region with substantial sums of money to nourish the seeds of the Arab Spring. The phrase had been adopted from Prague in 1968 to describe its uprising at the height of the cold war. Fast moving as it was, the Arab Spring was being used as an event that would climax in democracy in a new Middle East, so was the expectation in London, Washington, Paris, and elsewhere on the international stage. It was one not shared by Pardo.

He believed the latest surge of Arab nationalism would peter out as it had done in the 1950s. Then, its leaders had believed the West would support them. This time the rebels had failed to recognize China would not support their call that human rights should be introduced in kingdoms whose ruthless rulers had been overthrown.

The Arab Spring had also presented Mossad with a close-to-home problem. Would it spill over into the Gaza Strip? Hamas after a period of silence had begun to show its revolutionary credentials by firing rockets into Israel. The casings had been hammered into shape in one of the workshops in the Strip, the ammunition smuggled through tunnels dug deep under Sinai's border with Egypt. Through them came food and medical supplies that circumvented the blockade Israel maintained, insisting that "most Western governments must consider Hamas to be a terrorist organization because it kills our people." The smuggled food was sold by vendors on Omar Mukhtar Street, Gaza's main thoroughfare, and the rocket components assembled in backstreet courtyards before being launched.

On that Friday, Pardo had a report that the rockets had neither the power nor range of the Chinese rockets. He also knew from another report that those rockets had a very different purpose.

Pardo had been among the Israeli delegation in 1991 at the Madrid conference. Jointly sponsored by the United States and the Soviet Union, its purpose was to agree on guidelines to resolve the Israeli-Arab conflict. His role as the Mossad observer was to gather background information. It had been an opportunity to mingle with the spies of America, Russia, France, and China as well as those from Arab countries. Egypt's intelligence chief, General Omar Suleiman, had introduced Pardo to Prince Bandar bin Sultan, who would soon become Saudi Arabia's intelligence chief. They had found common ground that had developed into a friendship.

While the conference had produced little to justify the optimism in the closing statement, Pardo had returned to his office in Tel Aviv with a number of other valuable contacts he had made. In the years to come he had found himself increasingly in discussions with several of them. By the time he took over Mossad he knew they regarded him as "a source" on developments in the Middle East, in turn he saw them as hinting at the intentions of their governments in the political turmoil in the region. His analysis of that had been another step up the promotion ladder that had finally led to him studying the satellite photo of those Chinese rockets in Saudi Arabia.

Pardo had reminded his department chiefs at their Friday briefing that the rockets were part of a larger question: When would Israel attack Iran's network of nuclear facilities? He knew there was not a Western or Middle Eastern intelligence service that did not ponder the question.

It had driven them to redefine their own missions and mandates and some had found new rationales to increase their institutional and budgetary resources. However, none could match Mossad, whose funding was more than spent by Israel on its domestic requirements. Mossad had the latest eavesdropping equipment and satellites technology and had trained its agents to switch from espionage to counterterror with a speed that had impressed the other standard-bearers of intelligence, the CIA and MI6.

Outwardly Mossad's old enemies had ceased to pose a threat: Ronald Reagan's "evil empire" of the Soviet Union; the East German Stasi; the State Security, BOSS, of South Africa's apartheid regime. Pardo knew they had all once made life difficult in his formative years in Mossad. Nevertheless, new threats had emerged. Al-Qaeda remained a deadly force, as were the chemical and biological weapons of Syria and the arrival of cyberwarfare. They all defined his daily life, together with that question: When would Israel attack Iran?

The matter had intensified since 2001, when one of Israel's leading newspapers, *Haaretz*, published its story that the country had signed "intelligence collaboration agreements" with thirty-nine countries, including China. Each pact called for a signatory state to work together in joint operations with Israel.

The relationship between Israel and China had already become a matter of growing concern in Washington since the first Egyptian revolution in 1952. In its aftermath Beijing had started to become not only involved in Arab countries but had developed links with Israel.

Diplomats were exchanged and Chinese trade delegations appeared in Tel Aviv. Over lavish hospitality they told their hosts they were happy to invest in Israel's high-tech industries and agricultural programs and help to sell their products to other Arab countries.

In the wake of Chinese businessmen and politicians came the agents of the Ministry of State Security, MSS, traveling on diplomatic passports and in many cases speaking passable Hebrew, or Arabic and English.

They reported to the Central External Liaison Department in Beijing. It has no equivalent in any other intelligence organization. Unique not only in size, estimated by the CIA to have over a thousand employees, it supervised China's international security and conducted espionage on a worldwide scale. It also processed every visa application, carried out all checks on applicants, and assigned MSS agents to watch a visitor while he was in China.

A Mossad briefing document given to each Israeli businessman going to China started: "Chinese intelligence operates within a legal framework especially in teams of a male. A MSS woman often is selected to seduce a foreign businessman once he is registered in a hotel room fitted with a bugging device. The Chinese approach is subtle and invariably highly motivated and totally incorruptible."

Some of the MSS agents, Pardo believed, had been present when Chinese diplomats had explored Israel's predisposition toward the United States. The State Department had cautioned the Tel Aviv government that this mutual wooing was a danger and that China was looking for details of the military help that the United States provided to Israel. The first opportunity came when Israel sold the People's Republic details of America's advanced avionics for the LAVI night fighter Israel had jointly developed with funds from America.

The intelligence pact between China and Israel had also raised more concern in the Pentagon and State Department. In a dozen and more meetings the question was asked: Would Israel once more cause a problem by providing China with details of U.S. nuclear weapons? It had first happened in the 1980s, at a time when Israel was beginning to create its own nuclear arsenal, and Jonathan Pollard, a key member in one of the U.S. Navy's most secret establishments, with access to thousands of documents, had stolen them in a Mossad operation that had allowed Israel to become the first nuclear power in the Middle East (see chapter 4, "The Spy in the Iron Mask," pp. 83–87).

There had been reports that both countries continued to draw closer to each other as America armed Iraq in the run-up to the Iran-Iraq war.

In the end it had been against Iraq that Israel launched its first attack in the nuclear arms race in the Middle East.

On September 30, 1980, the eighth day of the Gulf War between Iran and Iraq, the radio in the Mossad training school canteen, where Tamir Pardo was breakfasting, announced that overnight Iranian MiGs, bought from Russia, had destroyed an Iraqi oil refinery at Basra and a pumping station at Abadan. On the stock markets of London, Paris, and New York oil shares dropped. However, the excited voices around the table were from the students who had been told by their tutors that they had passed their semester exam.

Pardo was one of forty students in the exam room who had sat for the exam designed to test their skills as future operatives, spies, and saboteurs. There had been questions to discover how much they had learned about ciphers, deciphering, and coding messages. The graduation field exercise had included being dropped in Tel Aviv and coming back with as much information as possible to support their cover stories. They were told they had to bluff their way into a hotel without paying as part of the intelligence and aptitude tests designed to test ingenuity, creativity, leadership, personality, and even patience. A final term paper had required each student to produce an analysis of an operation that had involved Mossad either with the Israeli air force or its navy. Particular attention had to be given to its political ramifications. It was a challenge Pardo had met and overcome in his essays at university.

Among the features of the training school was a well-stocked library with bound copies of speeches in the Knesset and extracts of debates on Israel in U.S. Congress and the House of Commons in London, where politicians had spoken about issues arising from that day in May 1948 when Israel's foreign ministry had been established. It was an area of its foreign diplomacy that Pardo had decided to use for his term paper. It dealt with Mossad's discovery in 1977 that the French government, which had provided Israel with the blueprint for its nuclear reactor at Dimona, had also secretly given Iraq "technical assistance" and nuclear materials to build a reactor. The facility was at Al-Tuweitha, north of Baghdad (see chapter 8, "ORA and the Monster," pp. 158–60).

The more he read in the library's files about the Iraq reactor, the firmer grew Pardo's belief that it would provide the material he needed for his term paper.

He began to quote from documents written by Israel's chief of army intelligence, Uri Saguy, a regular lecturer at the training school, who had once told the students that "if I was an Iranian I would be worried knowing that Iraq would soon be a nuclear power." Pardo had used the words as an example of how LAP, Mossad's Department of Psychological Warfare, spread the warning the threat Iraq posed. In London, the United States, and Europe LAP planted stories how the nuclear reactor was also an attempt to obstruct scientific and technological developments in the Arab world.

While the presence of the reactor only a short distance from Israel continued to provide LAP with a skilfully managed propaganda campaign against France and Iraq, Israel's own diplomatic efforts in Paris, London, and Washington to stop the reactor from being built increasingly failed. French intelligence, which had its own anti-Israeli axe to grind, planted stories that there was not a strand of evidence to show that the reactor was a threat. *The Sunday Times* in London was told that the Israeli air force, in the time of Reza Pahlavi, the shah, had trained Iran's air force and provided its pilots with targeting information "including a comprehensive survey of Baghdad's air defences and principal targets."

Meantime Mossad's incumbent chief, Yitzhak Hofi (1974–1982), had briefed Brigadier General Ephraim Poran, the military adviser to Prime Minister Menachem Begin, on reports from Mossad undercover agents in Iraq on the progress the French technicians were making in constructing the reactor.

Their latest reports included photographs of a large circular structure that rose above the other buildings standing in an area of sixteen miles of irrigated desert to the east of Baghdad. The experts at Dimona, Israel's nuclear facility, decided that the large, brown concrete dome was intended to house the nuclear reactor, evidence that the project was reaching the stage when it would be able to produce the Arab world's first atomic bomb.

On June 6, 1981, the anniversary of D-day in Europe, a succession of military cars drove along Tel Aviv's longest road, Rehov Shaul Hamaleku, to a guarded entrance set in a high concrete wall topped with barbed wire. Saluted through the gate by the guards, the cars drove into the grounds of the Israeli Defense Forces, the Kirya, known to all the Hebrew speakers who worked there as "the place."

In three of the vehicles were the commanders of the army, navy, and air force. In the other cars were the head of Shin Bet, the domestic intelligence service, and the chief of the military intelligence service, Aman. A division of the Ministry of Defense, it had been formed in 1961 to secure intelligence and weapons technology. Its head was the Labor politician, Shimon Peres. He was in the last car to enter the Kirya.

Yitzhak Hofi waited for them in a conference room on the ground floor of a tower visible from the Judean Hills. The towering edifice was the electronic hub of all Israeli military, diplomatic, and intelligence communications traffic. With the Mossad chief was General Uri Saguy and Brigadier Ephraim Poran. They would later report to Prime Minister Begin on the outcome of a meeting requested to approve the targeting of Iraq's nuclear reactor. Not since August 1945, with the bombing of Hiroshima and Nagasaki, had any nation chosen to destroy the element that had given birth to the military Atomic Age.

Once everyone was seated around the conference table Hofi opened the meeting. The ebb and flow of the discussion was there for Tamir Pardo to read in the training school library documents.

France had a new president, François Mitterrand, long known for his sympathies for Israel. He had appointed a similar-minded foreign minister, Claude Cheysson, who immediately began conducting a review of France's contracts to supply the Iraqi reactor. His first move had been to cancel the previous government's deal to supply Iraq with highly enriched uranium fuel that would provide the Iraqis with atomic bombs.

Others around the table had discussed what effect an attack on the reactor would have on Israel's relationship with France and its effect on the Republic's trade with Iraq. A quarter of French oil was supplied by Iraq's oil fields and its other imports from Iraq amounted to a stunning twenty-four billion Francs ($4 billion) a year. In turn, the reactor deal had given France an international position as Iraq's major supplier of Mirage aircraft, squadrons of tanks and armored personal carriers, and high-powered patrol boats to protect its coasts. Furthermore, French salesmen had made deals to build Iraqi petrochemical plants, roads, and a telecommunication system. To lose those contracts would seriously affect France's trade balance.

During the afternoon a thirty-three-page personality profile of the Iraqi leader, Saddam Hussein, had been passed around the table. It had been prepared by Mossad. It posed two questions. Would Saddam Hussein use an atomic bomb against Israel? Or would he use the reactor as a propaganda tool to arouse fear in the region? Several Mossad analysts, including two psychiatrists, had contributed to the document. The consensus was that Saddam was a "complex person, both cunning and sophisticated, as well as cruel." The document would become one of the most read in the training school library, where it remains to this day.

On that June day in 1981 it had been left to Uri Saguy to read aloud one conclusion. "If in Saddam's estimation the use of atomic weapons would give him the chance to strike against Israel and gain for himself at the same time a leadership position in the Arab world, he would not hesitate to use the bomb. And he would use it even if it would cost him similar retaliation from Israel that would create damage and loss of life in Iraq itself."

Saguy would remember (during the making of *The Spy Machine*, the film by the author) "there was a sudden silence in the room then a feeling of urgency from my colleagues of the need to take action against Iraq."

Brigadier Ephriam Poran had said he would support an attack on the reactor. Shimon Peres was to recall, "I added my voice and I sensed it was not mine alone, that some of the others shared my view and I said not to attack the reactor, not in the present time and in the present circumstances."

The air force chief had produced maps from his briefcase and began to indicate the key elements for any attack on the reactor. The route to the target was a round trip of 1,800 miles. There were seven Iraqi airfields between Israel and the reactor at Al-Tuweitha. They all either had the latest French Mirage 4000s or Soviet 18s aircraft. Given that the airfields were defended it should be assumed the reactor would also have a similar defense.

The mission would require a total of fourteen aircraft: eight of the new American-built F-16s and six F-15 fighter-interceptors. The F-16s would take off from their airfield at Etzion in the south of the country. They would be fitted with extra fuel tanks to increase their range and special bomb racks for the 2,000-pound Mark 84 bombs each would carry. The F-15s would also have extra fuel tanks and would intercept any Iraqi aircraft on the flight route.

The two forces would rendezvous over the desert where Jordan forms its border into an arrowhead with Israel. From there they would fly east across its borders into Iraq to the target.

The air force chief had fought in the Six-Day War in 1967 and said the attack force would follow similar tactics, flying in close formation and keeping well clear of the American Advanced Warning (AWACS) aircraft stationed in Saudi Arabia to warn of any attack on its oil fields. The chief explained his own intelligence officers had produced details of all commercial flights passing through the attack route to and from the Far and Near East. The bombing force would fly in close formation to fool any Arab radar into believing a large commercial plane was flying through the area. The Israeli aircraft would be approaching the target area with the setting sun behind. The F-15s would then take up interception positions and the F-16s would attack. Their aiming point would be the reactor dome.

The technical briefing over, there was one more matter. Brigadier Poran, in his position as the prime minister's military adviser, called for a vote he could take to Begin. All but Shimon Peres favored an attack.

Poran left the room and drove with General Uri Saguy to the Tel Aviv suburb of Bnei Brak where the prime minister lived in his official residence at the end of an avenue of trees. Both were members of the government's Ministerial Defence Committee. Waiting with Begin were its other members: Foreign Minister Yitzhak Shamir; Ariel Sharon, the former war hero and now agricultural minister; General Rafael Eitan, the chief of staff of the IDF. They had listened as Poran briefed them on the vote in the Kirya conference room. Begin had shrugged at the mention of Peres, saying, "he is always a dove when it comes to military action." He turned to the others in his library. "I want your votes." The five men said in turn they supported an attack. Begin had one more question. "When do we go?"

Sunday, June 7, 1981, was the holiday weekend of Shavuot, the Jewish festivity to mark Moses receiving the Torah in Sinai. The beaches of Israel were filled with sunbathers, when on that afternoon they saw a formation of Israeli aircraft heading toward the border with Jordan and disappearing over the horizon.

Miranda Hayun was down by the Red Sea with her sister Maria and her husband, a soldier home on leave, when they saw the planes. He told them it was probably a training exercise.

Gabriel Raphael and his wife, Murit, were in their garden outside Jerusalem as the formation shrank to a speck on the horizon. The elderly couple had paused to watch them fly out of sight then resumed preparing the evening cookout for their family. Gabriel was a retired diplomat in the Israeli foreign service and he had wondered if the aircraft were on their way to deal with the Syrians who had recently threatened to place missiles in southern Lebanon. Gabriel had told Murit that would be typical of the Syrian regime. Maybe the aircraft were going to fly along the border as a warning.

In the newspaper office of *Ma'ariv*, the afternoon shift was facing what Alex Doron, its science editor, would call "a slow news day. Holidays were always like that. Even the wire tapes had little to report."

In her dress shop across town Gilah Bronstein was totaling up the week's take in the back office. Earlier her son had called to say that the air base where he worked as an aircraft mechanic was still in lockdown. The air base was at Etzion.

The Kirya had been in lockdown since General Rafael Eitan had received the radio signal that the attack force was airborne. There would be no break in radio silence until the coded signal from the F-16 leader confirmed the attack had been carried out.

Mossad chief Hofi chose to spend the waiting hours in his office. Meanwhile Mossad staff in the communications unit were monitoring Arab radio stations across the region, especially those in Baghdad. Every ten minutes Hofi was called on his desk phone to say there was nothing to report.

In his library Prime Minister Begin waited by his phone reading a book. All over Tel Aviv men sat and waited.

From the Israeli pilots' altitude the desert looked like Sinai, where they had prepared for the mission. The air force had mocked up the target site, including the dome, made from canvas stretched over a wooden frame. In rehearsal the aircraft had swept out of the sun and, racing across the sand, dumped their dummy bombs. Some of the casings had buried themselves in the earthworks around the dome. Back in the Etzion operation room the crews had studied the photos taken by their aircraft cameras. The team of mechanics and engineers who serviced the F-16s made suggestions and adjustments. The pilots had flown another rehearsal. Air force officers in their observation shelters out in the desert noted improvement. After a few more rehearsals the bombers were dropping their dummy bomb casings all around the few low-slung buildings around the dome and marked on the pilots maps as workshops and storage warehouses. Meantime the F-15s had practiced their role to provide a protective umbrella for the bombers.

When the two forces rendezvoused, the earth was well into its daily journey around the sun. Their target was beyond the banks of the Euphrates. A distance to go yet, above narrow gorges and mesa-like terrain. The hills were already in shadow and forbidding. There wasn't a pilot who didn't know that to crash there would be fatal. And so they pressed on.

Suddenly the target was there. The leading F-16 pilot waggled its wing. A number of rehearsed moves followed. The other bombers formed up for their bombing run. The F-15s stationed on either side of the bombers rose in the sky ready to deal with any Iraqi attack.

Away in the distance Baghdad was lost in a heat haze.

Two F-15 fighters swept out of the sky toward the target, passing over the compound where the French technicians working on the reactor lived with their families. Most of the hundred French technicians who had originally lived there in two-room bungalows had gone back to France, leaving behind a small team of technicians to complete the work on the reactor.

One was Jean-François Masciola, a thirty-year-old specialist electrician who was completing the wiring of the reactor. He had just returned home from his morning shift when the two Israeli fighters roared over the compound. He rushed outside to see the planes had fired rockets into two of the antiaircraft guns positioned around the reactor area and were zooming away from the burning gun emplacements.

Masciola ran back into the bungalow, picked up his small son, and led his wife to a sandbagged shelter outside the front door. Inside, the family huddled as the first F-16 swooped down out of the sun and raced toward the reactor complex half a mile away.

Crouching in the shelter entrance Masciola saw that the reactor dome had been hit. By now other planes were dropping bombs on the complex. Workshops were on fire and the dome seemed to be exploding like a firecracker.

"In less than a minute it was over. The planes had gone and the sky was darkening. The whole complex was burning. The only noise was the antiaircraft guns firing. But there was nothing to hit. All I could see in the flames were huge pieces of concrete flying off the dome that was leaning like the tower of Pisa before it collapsed," Masciola recalled.

Several of his French colleagues who were working inside the dome's reactor installing its cooling system could have been killed. But his first duty was to his young family. He helped his wife pack their belongings and headed in his car for Baghdad. Next morning they caught the first flight to Paris.

While the family was fleeing, somewhere above them in the dusk the mission commander in his F-16 broke radio silence to transmit "*Mazel tov.*"

Shortly afterward the telephone rang in Prime Minister Begin's library in Tel Aviv. The caller was General Rafael Eitan in the Kyria. He told Begin "the strike was a hundred percent success."

Begin summoned his press secretary who had been waiting in an adjoining room and dictated a statement: "On Sunday, June 7, 1981, the Israeli Air Force launched a raid on the atomic reactor near Baghdad. Our pilots carried out their mission fully. The reactor was destroyed. All our aircraft returned safely to base."

The words concluded Tamir Pardo's term paper.

Before his meeting with the departments chiefs on that Friday morning in March 11, 2011, Pardo had long known that Israel faced a far greater danger than Iraq.

Years before Iran had joined the nuclear arms race. In the mid-1960s 114 nations had signed the Nuclear Non-Proliferation Treaty, sponsored by the United States, the United Kingdom, and the Soviet Union. Israel, Pakistan, and India had all refused to sign the agreement. Israel had continued to develop its nuclear arsenal and the other two abstaining countries soon became the possessor of the atomic bomb. Unlike Israel both nations openly posed a threat to each other's own people, one that could engulf the entire region. The history of conflict between India and Pakistan stretched back over fifty years and full-scale wars had erupted on three occasions. They each created intelligence services while in pursuit of the latest nuclear developments in the United States. Mossad had established relationships with both.

From the coast of Morocco to the shores of Indonesia, Islam is the dominant faith, not only as a religion but as a culture that regulates every aspect of millions of lives. It is a way of life in which prayer and power are interlocked, never so much as in Iran of the Ayatollah Khomeini. For his followers Israel was the one target to be "wiped off the face of the earth." At Friday prayers his imams prayed that the day was soon coming when the Islamic bomb would be a reality.

For years Iran had insisted that it needed nuclear energy despite its large gas and oil resources, but had failed to convince the International Atomic Energy Agency, IAEA, that it would only be used for "domestic purposes."

Mossad had sent deep-cover agents into Iran to spy (see chapter 22, "Old Enemies, New Threats," pp. 478–79). Pardo had studied their reports with the same concentration he used on the documents Jonathan Pollard had stolen from the United States that had given Israel a head start in developing its nuclear arsenal. Pardo had also read Pollard's file, filled with Prime Minister Netanyahu's efforts to have him set free from his high-security jail in America. He suspected that no amount of pleading argument with an incumbent U.S. president would ever result in Pollard being released.

Pardo had discussed the case with Ehud Barak, Netanyahu's deputy prime minister and defense minister. His response was "Thank God Pollard was working for us and not Iran."

He had touched on an issue that was still hardly out of the headlines: Would Israel finally attack Iran? The matter had been ignited again by the words of Gabi Ashkenazi, a former IDF chief of staff. On a morning radio breakfast show he had pronounced "Iran is not a threat."

Asked for a comment Barak had responded to the show host. "It's good to have a diversity of opinions. But when a military man looks up he sees the minister of defense and the prime minister. But when we look up we see nothing but the sky from where the missiles will come raining down."

Into the controversy had stepped Meir Dagan. In his last week as Mossad's chief he met with Netanyahu in the prime minister's office. The meeting had been "polite but cool," Dagan would recall, and it ended with him saying he had accepted the post of chairman of Gulliver Energy Ltd., which would be exploring the Sinai for precious minerals.

Returning to his office he had handed his secretary a short list of names and asked her to call them. Each was a journalist who, over the years, he had occasionally briefed on the outcome of various operations.

The arrangements Dagan told her to make had all the drama of a spy arranging a secret meeting with his informers. Each journalist was to make his way to a parking lot of a movie theater in the north of Tel Aviv. They were to bring no laptops, tape recorders, cell phones, only a notebook. They were each given a time to arrive in the afternoon.

Waiting in the parking lot were cars with shaded windows and a black jeep. As each journalist arrived he was bodily searched by one of the car drivers. Led by the jeep the cars drove to a building. One of the reporters later wrote: "We knew it was not marked on any map." It was the Mossad headquarters. Escorted into the building the reporters were taken to a conference room on the ground floor and told to sit around the table with their notebooks and pens ready.

Suddenly Meir Dagan strode into the room. Ronen Bergmann, a veteran defense correspondent, would recall: "Dagan's opening words were 'there are advantages to be wounded in the back. You have a doctor's certificate that you have a backbone.'"

Smiles greeted the words. They knew they were a reminder of the anger Dagan felt at his departure from office. Stories had already appeared in some newspapers that he had been "stabbed in the back." Pausing only to clear his throat, Dagan launched at dictation speed into an attack on Netanyahu and Barak. "For even contemplating the foolish idea of attacking Iran," he said.

Some of the reporters exchanged looks. "Was that on the record?" asked one. Dagan nodded and continued: "The assumption that it is possible to totally halt the Iranian nuclear project by means of a military attack is incorrect. There is no such military capability. It is only possible to cause delay, but even that would only be for a limited period."

In the silence Dagan continued: "Attacking Iran would start an unwanted war with Hezbollah and Hamas and I am not convinced that Syria will not be drawn in. While the Syrians won't charge at us in tanks, we will see a massive offensive of missiles against our home front. Civilians will be on the front lines. What is Israel's defensive capability against such an offensive? I know of no solution that we have for this problem."

A reporter asked if he had shared his views with Israel's decision makers. Dagan nodded: "I have expressed my opinion to them with the same emphasis as I have here. Sometimes I raised my voice, because I lose my temper easily and am overcome with zeal when I speak."

Dagan nodded and strode from the room.

The most astonishing briefing any Mossad intelligence chief had ever given was over.

Shortly after Meir Dagan's words found their way into print, he addressed an audience at Hebrew University to repeat his criticism of the prime minister and his defense secretary. With him was Rafi Eitan, eighty-five-years-old, who was given a sustained round of applause, led by Dagan, who reminded the audience that Eitan had been Mossad's director of operations and had captured Adolf Eichmann.

Standing shoulder to shoulder beside Dagan, Eitan told the audience if any of them wanted Israel to launch a preemptive attack on Iran they "should just think of two missiles a day, no more than that, falling on Tel Aviv, and what will you do then? Besides, our attack would not cause the Ayatollah's significant damage. Far from delaying them for three years, as our experts say, it won't stop Iran for even three months. They have already scattered their facilities all over the country and underground."

From the body of the hall came a question: "How could Iran be stopped from becoming a nuclear power?" Over his microphone Eitan boomed. "In the end if they want a bomb they'll get it. That's reality. The way to stop them is by encouraging a change of regime in Iran. So far we have really failed there. There are opposition groups who have turned to us time and again to ask for our help and instead we sent them away empty-handed."

At the back of the hall, Tamir Pardo slipped out before the reporters who were starting to move among the audience could have spotted him.

In the days that followed Dagan found himself in the vanguard of public opinion that any attack on Iran would be catastrophic. Once more

Ehud Barak's voice could be heard over the morning radio show. "The prime minister and myself are responsible in a very direct way for the continued existence of the State of Israel. Indeed for the future of the Jewish people."

While Eitan had quietly withdrawn from the arguments, Dagan had continued to not only rail against attacking Iran but had widened his criticism of Netanyahu for his failure to resolve the conflict with the Palestinians. He, too, had found a ready platform on the morning radio show. "The absence of any workable plan has left Israel in a hopeless position if the Palestinians push at the United Nations to be recognized as a state," Dagan warned.

Suddenly the mood changed. Newspapers that had supported Mossad began to remind readers that operations Dagan had authorized in Lebanon, Dubai, and on a suspected nuclear reactor in Syria had brought international pressure to bear on Israel. Now he had endorsed Saudi Arabia's peace plan to offer normal relations with all Arab countries if Israel would make a peace agreement with the Palestinians. The attacks on radio and television against the former Mossad chief grew.

Dagan's behavior had led to a split within Mossad ranks. There were those who echoed the words of his predecessor, Efraim Halevy (1998–2002), that the chief "had been cruelly treated by the knights of purity and ethics who have stuck their swords deep into his back."

Others said Netanyahu had treated Dagan fairly to the point of agreeing that he could present his resignation as his own decision. But in the end the prime minister had become fed up with Dagan's public pronouncements and Netanyahu's office had started to tell reporters that he was "just bitter at losing his office." However, Dagan had found a new supporter in Yuval Diskin, the head of Shin Bet, Israel's internal security service. He told *The Jerusalem Post*, "I don't believe in a political leadership that makes decisions out of messianic feelings."

In the corridors of Mossad others spoke of their relief over Dagan's departure. His cold fury was renowned when an operation had gone wrong because of a failure to understand the mechanics of what he called "the trade of intelligence." Those would be the times when Dagan would spend hours with a department head going over every step of an operation's planning that had failed before asking for the resignation of a field officer, a *katsa*.

When the day had finally come for Dagan to leave Mossad he had shown little emotion to his staff; a word of thanks, a handshake to a desk officer before he had walked out to the parking lot where his driver waited with the car door open. Pardo accompanied Dagan, who said, "You were a great support. I will not forget that." Pardo watched the car drive out of the parking space Dagan would never use again.

The end of the Dagan era made front-page news around the world. Those who had known him well George Tenet of the CIA, Jonathan Evans, head of MI5, and Sir John Scarlett, chief of MI6, all of whom would fall foul of their politician masters, commiserated with Dagan over his fate. Their replacements in Washington and London began to reflect on how Dagan's departure would affect the interplay between intelligence and politics in Israel, where he had been a permanent feature of the scene ever since the country had become independent in 1948.

Taking over Mossad, Pardo knew he would introduce changes. Some would be among the division heads, including those in operational units. He would also want to appoint new heads for overseas stations; there would be a need to review their sources and methods. Some veterans would find it hard to adjust and they would begin to count down to their retirement. He had made a list of their names.

There was a new department to absorb, the cyberwarfare unit. He had already handpicked the Mossad officer who would be in charge. He had been one of several officers who had undergone training at America's National Security Agency and had taken part in some "soft" espionage missions including hacking into Iran's version of Facebook and other social network sites.

Pardo knew that cyberwar against Iran would be a major goal and would be warfare without boundaries, using tactics that would dictate how future conflicts would be fought. Already graduate software engineers, mathematicians, and communication specialists were being recruited by Mossad from the university campuses of Israel.

In those first weeks in office Pardo had kept to himself his views on Dagan, a position he would maintain to this day. But early on he made it clear to Prime Minister Netanyahu and the Defence and Foreign Relations Committee of the Knesset he would mould Mossad in his own way.

It was his decision that first week in March 2011 that gave him an opportunity to make that clear.

CHAPTER 33

Arab Spring Time in Winter

In January 2011, Israel had received its first squadron of unmanned aircraft, drones from the United States, Hellfire missiles, and 500-pound bombs. The drones were a weapon that had already proved itself in the American hunt for terrorists in the border lands of Pakistan and Afghanistan. Israeli F-16 pilots had been sent for training to the United States to learn how to operate the drones.

They had yet to be given a target when the satellite image of the Chinese rockets base in the Saudi Arabian desert arrived on Pardo's desk. An analyst in the Assessment Department had traced on the image two targets: Tehran and Tel Aviv. Beneath them he had attached his evaluation.

It concluded Saudi Arabia had purchased the rockets to enhance its defense against two threats. The first involved Iran. The Saudis' own intelligence would have decided that if Tehran launched a nuclear weapon against Israel the fallout would spill over into Saudi Arabia, carrying radiation fallout on the wind. The second threat involved Israel. Just as it had destroyed Iraq's nuclear reactor it could still unleash a preemptive strike against Iran's nuclear facilities. While that would also create a radiation threat to Saudi Arabia, the attack would need an Israeli air strike far more powerful than the one on the Iraqi reactor. To achieve that would require their aircraft to fly down the Red Sea and inevitably violate Saudi airspace on its way to attack Iran's nuclear facilities. The analyst had concluded that Saudi Arabia had deliberately pointed the rockets at Israel as a warning to choose another route if it intended to attack Iran.

Pardo had taken the satellite photo to his staff meeting on a Friday morning. He told them that in his meeting with Netanyahu and Barak they had stressed that no decision had yet been made to attack Iran.

Putting aside the satellite photo, Pardo told his division chiefs around the conference table that he nevertheless intended to strike against one threat to Israel as soon as possible.

Accompanied by Lieutenant General Benny Gantz, the army chief of staff, Tamir Pardo drove to air force headquarters in Tel Aviv. Waiting at the entrance to a bunker was the commander of the drone squadron, Amir Eshel. He took them inside the air-conditioned bunker.

In Pardo's briefcase was the death sentence he had collected from Netanyahu's office after the prime minister had signed it. The two air force officers, pilots who had once flown F-16 fighters and would execute the sentence, sat before their computer screen.

Visible on their screen was a desert highway and its traffic: cars, trucks, and an occasional caravan of loping camels. The highway linked Port Sudan airport and Khartoum, the country's capital.

Suddenly a Hyundai Sonata limousine emerged heading out of the airport. One of the officers called out that the target was located. Both pilots began to tap on their keyboards. The image of the car came closer, almost filling the screens. Inside was a passenger, sitting beside the driver. He was Abdel Latif al-Ashkar, at the top of Mossad's list of assassination targets after he had been identified as the Hamas procurer of weapons.

Al-Ashkar was forty-four years old, married with three children. He had come first to Mossad's attention five years ago when he had been involved in the kidnap of Gilad Shalit, the Israeli soldier (see chapter 31, "Farewell," pp. 697–700). Since then al-Ashkar had been hunted, moving from one safe house to another in Gaza until an informer had revealed he had gone to Khartoum to negotiate a deal with an Iranian arms dealer.

Another well-paid informer had passed the details to the Mossad undercover agent in the city. Hours later the information had reached Pardo. The drone attack had been authorized at his request.

It had been launched earlier that morning from its secret base in the Negev Desert and, guided by the officers in the bunker, had flown south over the Red Sea to take up its position. Now, fifteen thousand feet above the speeding car the drone hovered above the road to the Sudanese capital.

In the bunker Amir Eshel called out, "How long"?

The drone operator replied, "Thirty seconds. Locking-on."

The weapon chosen to kill al-Ashkar was one of three types attached to the Israeli air force squadron of silent killers. The largest was the MQ-9 Reaper with a payload of four Hellfire missiles and a range of 1,150 miles. The RQ-170 Sentinel had a cruise speed of 440 mph and was used for surveillance with its 550-mile range. An MQ-1 Predator had been selected for that morning's mission. Its two Hellfire missiles cost $60,000 apiece and were each equipped with a laser beam that reflected off a target once it was locked on.

In the silence Amir spoke, "Kill the bastard." In turn each operator pressed a button on his keyboard. Seconds later a Hellfire air-to-ground missile was fired from the drone.

On the screen the limousine became engulfed in a fireball.

Pardo said, "Good shooting." He shook hands with both operators and left the bunker.

Later firefighters found the charred bodies of al-Ashkar and his driver in the twisted heap of burnt metal.

In Mossad the summer of 2011 had an increasingly ominous feeling as the civil war in Syria threatened to spill over its borders with Jordan and Lebanon. While that posed a problem to Israel, the real threat remained Iran. Meir Dagan's outbursts after his departure from Mossad had once more raised the question of whether a preemptive attack on Iran could soon be on Netanyahu's desk. This was fueled by Tehran's constant reminder that it was ready to deal with any attack: its high-speed gunboats would repel any invasion force from the Gulf, while batteries of Fateh-110 missiles had been upgraded and positioned to strike any part of Israel.

Those words were accompanied by the irrational hatred of Israel by Iran's leaders. The Supreme Leader, Ayatollah Ali Khamenei, usually ended his Friday prayers radio broadcast with a promise that "soon the Jews will disappear." President Mahmoud Ahmadinejad had constantly called Israel "a cancerous tumor that we must remove." A cleverly re-searched story planted by Mossad's Department of Psychological War-fare, that Ahmadinejad had Jewish ancestry, had been widely published in Arab and other countries, but had not halted the sustained flow of threats from Teheran.

Mossad agents had established that Iranian freight carriers had started to land at a military airfield near Damascus with cargos of Scud and other missiles. These were being trucked into southern Lebanon to re-inforce the arsenal of Hezbollah, the Shi'ite terror organization backed by Iran. It was estimated 50,000 rockets of all varieties were now hid-den in fortified villages along the border with Israel.

The level of anxiety rose among its population as they were issued gas masks and heard the air raid wail across the cities and villages from Haifa to Hebron even after the radio warned it was only a test. Crews manned the "Iron Dome," the antimissile shield against short-range rockets and mortars. The government assured the nation that radar-guided missiles would destroy any incoming Iranian rocket.

Pardo knew the logistics of a preemptive attack on Iran's nuclear fa-cilities was formidable and different from destroying the Iraq reactor in 1981. Israel's fighter-bombers would have to fly three hours to reach even the first target in Iran and would require air refueling aircraft to be positioned along the flight path. To bomb all the nuclear facilities in Iran would need repeated operations. By then the farthest Iran sites could have moved their equipment so far underground that it would require American "bunker-busting" bombs. In his meetings with Prime Minister Netanyahu and Defense Minister Ehud Barak both had made it clear that an ineffective attack against Iran would only spur the mul-lahs to acquire a nuclear weapon. Both men had appeared to share the view that Israel could become an international pariah if it launched a preemptive strike.

There was also another matter that demanded all their attention.

Mohammed Bouazizi had light brown skin high cheekbones and a thin face. He was like the hundreds of desperate, downtrodden young men in the small town of Sidi Bouzid in Tunisia, on the edge of the Sahara. He was, however, luckier than most in that he at least earned an income as a street peddler selling fruit and vegetables, work he had done for seven years. He had no license to do so because he could not afford the bribe needed to obtain the document. Bouazizi was twenty-six years old and the breadwinner of his family of eight.

On December 17, 2010, his livelihood was threatened when a policewoman confiscated his unlicensed vegetable cart and its goods. It wasn't the first time it happened, but it would be the last. Not satisfied with accepting the ten-dinar fine that Bouazizi tried to pay, the policewoman slapped the scrawny young man, spat in his face, and insulted his dead father. Humiliated and dejected, Bouazizi went to the provincial headquarters, hoping to complain to local municipal officials, but they refused to see him. Less than an hour after his confrontation with the policewoman he returned to the provincial headquarter, an elegant white building with arched shutters, shouting he had come to protest the regime of the most powerful and hated man in Tunisia, President Zine El Abidine Ben Ali. Bouazizi poured fuel over himself and set himself on fire. His act of self-immolation was protest against the humiliations he had received from the officials inside the building, the representatives of the country's dictator.

Buckets of water were doused over Mohammed and he was rushed to the hospital. Ninety percent of his body had been charred. All that was visible of his face was his mouth, into which a doctor had inserted a breathing tube. There was so much outrage over his ordeal that even President Zine El Abidine Ben Ali visited Bouazizi on December 28, to try to blunt the anger. Surrounded by his family Mohammed existed for a few days, a living deadman. When he finally died on January 4, 2011, the old Middle East died with him.

Bouazizi's suicide had struck a chord first with the town people, then across Tunisia, and finally around the region. Mohammed was seen as the template for so many million lives, an act of self-desperation that represented their own lives in countless villages, towns, and cities.

Like him, day after day, generation after generation, men and women, struggled to make a living. Mohammed had given a voice to those with no voice. The outcry in Tunisia could not be suppressed and, on January 14, just ten days after Bouazizi died, Ben Ali's twenty-three-year rule over Tunisia was over. He was forced to flee to Saudi Arabia with his wife, Leïla Ben Ali, and his three children. The rise of the Arab people against their tormentors had begun. The Arab Spring had bloomed.

Twenty-one days after the body of Bouazizi was buried in a shroud under the sands, on January 25, Egypt's capital, Cairo, suddenly found itself in the grip of demonstrations protesting his death. Within days the demonstrators had grown to over a million people, not only mourning a suicide, but using it as a reason to make known their own demand. They wanted their own hated president, Hosni Mubarak, to be dismissed from office for his brutality against them.

In the West, the demonstrators were seen as an inspired outbreak of "people power" and applauded as the Arab equivalent of the Berlin Wall demonstrators, who had called for freedom and democracy. Those two words became the battle cry of the Cairo demonstrators.

The base of their demonstration—a canvas town of tents and kitchens—was Tahrir Square, the vast open space in the noisy chaos of midtown Cairo. Day and night it echoed with their demand that Mubarak must go. They called him the last Pharaoh and chanted his list of abuses during his three decades of dictatorial rule over the most populous and important Arab country. While a suicide in Tunisia had triggered their mourning, what was now happening was their seminal moment, one they assured each other would define their own futures.

Seventeen days after the mass demonstrations started, on February 11, Omar Suleiman, head of the country's intelligence service and new vice president, came on the state radio to announce that Mubarak has resigned. Mubarak was arrested to stand trial for not giving orders to stop the police from killing peaceful protesters and being involved in the assassination of his predecessor, Anwar Sadat, which had brought Mubarak to power thirty years before. Suleiman ended by saying the country was now under the control of the Supreme Council of the Armed Forces.

Within hours army tanks and trucks had surrounded the square, not to attack the demonstrators but to drive out the police, a move greeted with tumultuous cheers. The crews were lifted off their tanks onto the crowd's shoulders and paraded around the square through a sea of flags. One chant dominated all others: "The people and the army are one." The tanks and the trucks were decked with flowers and fireworks rose into the air, exploding overhead.

Foreign ambassadors who had been in the square rushed back to their embassies to cable their ministers that it was only a matter of time before the army chose the people over the dictator. More than one envoy posited that other despots would soon be swept from power.

After his broadcast announcing the end of Mubarak's reign Omar Suleiman had slipped out of the back entrance of State Television and was driven to his office near the square from where the sounds of crowds still cheering filled the night air on that Friday. He had never known the army to have received such a welcome. He knew their behavior had been ordered by the old men of the Supreme Council. They had deployed the soldiers, almost the total strength of the Cairo garrison, not to save the demonstrators from the violence of the police but to protect the generals, admirals, and field marshals who had sat in their open-top cars, their medals and sashes gleaming in the sunlight during the military parades that had turned the city into a replica of the march-pasts on Moscow's Red Square.

Since 1979 the United States gave Egypt an average of $2 billion a year in military aid. It made the country the second-largest recipient of American aid after Israel. Suleiman knew that millions of that money was siphoned off to support the business ventures of those who sat on the Supreme Council. Many of Cairo's luxury hotels and the seaside resorts were owned by the old men. A number were paid a percentage of the fees for ships to use the Suez Canal. Others kept private jets at Cairo International Airport to fly their wives or mistresses on shopping sprees to London and Paris.

Nevertheless there were some in Tahrir Square who also wondered about the presence of the army who had sacrificed Mubarak. They were members of the Muslim Brotherhood. Still banned after eighty years from working within the framework of a system that Mubarak had manipulated, they were not a revolutionary organization. They were there to reinforce the foundation stone of the Arab Spring: the first call for a democratic and free election for a head of state in the five-thousand-year history of Egypt.

In the early hours of that Friday morning, with the sun rising over the Nile beyond his window, Omar Suleiman had turned to a leather-bound book on his desk. It was a copy of the Camp David agreement signed in 1978 that had guaranteed peace between Egypt and Israel. The treaty had never been broken and had led to the Madrid Convention in 1991, the first time that Israel had sat down with all its Arab neighbors to discuss a continued peace. Suleiman had found common ground with Mossad on the need to share joint intelligence that would be important to both countries. The Egyptian wondered how the Arab Spring would affect that relationship.

The Tahrir protesters had yet to fully grasp the long-term implication of overthrowing Mubarak. In those first weeks of occupying the square even the better-educated demonstrators showed little sign of being able to convert their achievements into political power. They were using their mobile phones to send messages and pictures to the global media.

That suited the Muslim Brotherhood. Its members on the square continued to discreetly move among the growing crowds: vendors, vagabonds, and pickpockets who had been drawn to the square that was turning into a huge rubbish dump. The Brotherhood spread the word that there must be an election for a new president. Increasingly they urged the ideal candidate was Mohamed Morsi. His name and photo began to be waved. Morsi was a longtime member of the Brotherhood.

Omar Suleiman, as vice president, had been approached by Farouk Sultan, the president of the Presidential Election Commission and president of the Supreme Constitutional Court, to ask if he would consider running for office. The intelligence chief had politely refused.

In due course Morsi was duly elected as the fifth president of the Egyptian Republic. The Muslim Brotherhood had its first voice in the Presidential Palace.

In Tel Aviv one question was asked: how would the Brotherhood use their power in relation to Israel? Egypt was still the first Arab country that had signed a peace treaty with the Jewish State. Meantime Mossad had come to recognize that its neighbor, Jordan, had an excellent intelligence service, Deirat al-Mukhabarat al-Ammah, its General Intelligence Directorate, GID. It had a long relationship with Britain's MI6. Mossad had made a discreet overture to GID to collaborate in keeping track of Yasser Arafat.

Since 1969 Arafat had led the Palestinian Liberation Organization, PLO, after it was driven out of Jordan by King Hussein, and he had taken the PLO to Beirut to continue his war of attrition against Israel. General Ehud Barak had led the IDF into Lebanon to expel the PLO to Tunisia. Arafat had left behind the families of his fighters in refugee camps near Beirut. Israel's soldiers had stood by and watched the families slaughtered in a frenzy of rape and murder by a Lebanese militant group. Outrage across the world followed, including in Israel. Arafat not only became a figure of anger around the Arab world for the way he sent the PLO on suicide bomber missions in Israel but became a prime target for Mossad assassination.

Israel signed a defence treaty with Jordan in 1994. Mossad and the GID found themselves working together with Egypt's General Intelligence Service, EGIS. In all three services the abiding question was: what would the Muslim Brotherhood do about the two peace treaties?

Tamir Pardo met with his department heads to discuss the one clause in the Egyptian treaty with Israel that concerned Mossad. It had given Egypt back the Sinai Peninsula. Though its military presence on the border was strictly limited, a loophole had increasingly developed. It was the border crossing at Rafah into Gaza from Egypt. Originally it had been used to smuggle drugs into the Gaza Strip from the hash market in Cairo. Since Hamas gained control of Gaza on what became known in Israel as its Black Thursday in 2006—a sweeping election victory that gave the terror organization a base from which to attack its near neighbor—the Rafah crossing had become a prime concern for Israel.

One of the most powerful men in Gaza, Sheik Ahmed Ismail Hassan Yassin, the cofounder of Hamas, had discovered a new way to increase both its arsenal and his own income. He had purchased tents, shovels, and picks in Cairo to dig tunnels that led from Gaza into the Sinai Desert. Through the tunnels came food, medical supplies, and weapons, many of which had been flown from Iran to Sudan to be smuggled across Sinai into Gaza to use against Israel.

The traffic had also caused trouble for Omar Suleiman. The mountains of Sinai were havens for militants opposed to Egypt and he feared that some of the smuggled weapons were being sold to them. Suleiman had proposed to Mubarak before his arrest that the Egyptian air force should bomb the area around the crossing to destroy the tunnels. The idea had been put on hold with the start of the Arab Spring.

Egypt's new president, Morsi, had told the ailing intelligence chief that he would inform Israel that the tunnels "are a matter for them." The matter was never raised again in Cairo or Tel Aviv. Within days of Morsi's election Omar Suleiman retired from public life. He was suffering from heart failure and flew to the United States for treatment in a Cleveland clinic where he died on July 19, 2012. His body was flown home for a military funeral. The mourners were led by the Supreme Council and included the Israeli ambassador to Egypt. There were reports that Meir Dagan and Tamir Pardo had sent their condolences.

Ehud Barak often spent Sabbath evening in his spacious library in his comfortable home in north Tel Aviv and read the latest reports he had brought home. Their sensitive contents were proof of the high standing the former Special Forces commando and tank commander held in the political and military communities in Israel. In Washington he had been seen by the Obama administration as a calming influence on Netanyahu as the prime minister had continued warning about the threat Iran increasingly posed.

Netanyahu had finally sent Barak to Washington in his dual position as deputy prime minister and defense minister to reinforce his own view of the threat. Barak had received a cool welcome in the White House and returned to Tel Aviv with a blunt Obama message: Iran is not a danger that cannot be contained in good time.

A furious Netanyahu had said the words echoed Meir Dagan. It had been reported that the former Mossad chief had met America's ambassador to Israel before Barak went to Washington. Shortly afterward, Barak was replaced as deputy prime minister and defense minister. That position was given to Moshe Ya'alon, a hard-line supporter of Netanyahu.

Before he read his reports Barak would neatly stack them on a side table alongside his coffee percolator. The files contained updates on the current situation in the Golan Heights, Nablus, the West Bank, and Gaza, towns and villages he knew so well from the days he had commanded an armored tank division in the 1967 Six-Day War and the 1973 Yom Kippur War. He had served on the southern front and in the north on the borders with Syria and Lebanon. Later he had led IDF forces into Lebanon. In 1987 he became the deputy chief of the General Staff.

He served as chief of the General Staff from 1991 to 1995. The photos of those times hung on the library walls, a collection of thousands of books he suspected few homes had, ranging from philosophy, history, and military strategy to poetry.

More than once Barak would break off his reading to find a notation he had made in the margin of a book to refresh his memory of what was in a report. He would go and stand at the window of the library and gaze out at the lights of Tel Aviv, lost in thought before returning to his armchair to resume reading. It would often be long after midnight before he left the library to go to bed.

That happened frequently when he read reports from Pardo. Barak had played his role in convincing Netanyahu and the other twelve members of Israel's inner security group that Tamir Pardo had been the ideal choice to replace Meir Dagan. It was a view Barak had never changed.

In the aftermath of Hosni Mubarak's arrest and before the election of his successor, President Mohamed Morsi, relations between Israel and Egypt reached their lowest point since the 1979 peace treaty. The Sinai border became an area of conflict and anti-Israel sentiment was expressed in protest by masses of Egyptians in the streets of Giza and in Greater Cairo, where the Israeli embassy was.

On August 18, 2011, Egyptian militants crossed the border into southern Israel, leaving eight Israelis dead. IDF soldiers launched a counterterrorist operation, killing several Egyptian soldiers. Egyptian troops guarding the border crossing at Gaza burned the Israeli flag. In Cairo the Supreme Council of the Armed Forces announced it was considering recalling the Egyptian ambassador in Tel Aviv. A diplomatic schism was eventually avoided when Israel's Foreign Ministry apologized for the death of the Egyptian soldiers. The apology was dismissed as "insufficient."

After the protests on Tahrir Square had started, Mossad posted another agent to Cairo. Slim and dark-skinned, he looked like anyone else in the crowds. He spoke fluent Arabic with a Lebanese accent and his visa identified his profession as a businessman from Beirut. His mission was to evaluate the demonstrations and any threat they posed to Israel. He rented a room in a hotel that catered to travelers and was close to the square. Over several weeks he got to know a number of demonstrators. Some were members of the Muslim Brotherhood and had told him that the army was driving the nation to the "edge of a preci-pice." Some were from Qatar and supported the Brotherhood. Others expressed views that Israel was the enemy of Islam as it had shown in Gaza and against the PLO. He nodded politely when one had expressed the view: "The Jews will find in the end that their tanks, bombers, and soldiers will not be enough in the confrontation which is coming with the entire Islam nation, the Ummah."

Once a week, usually on a Friday afternoon, the agent went to the Israeli embassy to transmit his report. The embassy compound was pro-tected by a high wall, recently constructed following intense protests in August, and a gated entrance was guarded by Egyptian policemen from a nearby police station.

Ambassador Yitzhak Levanon had a total staff of eighty-five, mostly diplomats and their families. The mission was housed in a building on its twentieth and twenty-first floors and was only accessed by an eleva-tor in the spacious lobby where embassy security staff checked all visi-tors. The ambassador and his staff and families were accommodated on the lower floors of the building.

Early on Friday afternoon, September 9, 2011, as the embassy staff prepared to mark the start of the Sabbath, Ambassador Levanon re-ceived a call on his direct line from the Mossad agent in Tahrir Square. Members of the Muslim Brotherhood were urging protesters to march on the Israeli embassy and occupy it as a protest over attacks on Gaza and Israel's refusal to support the PLO search for a homeland. Thou-sands of protesters were already chanting they would occupy the em-bassy.

Levanon reacted immediately. All the staff were to remain in the em-bassy, which would go into lockdown.

Throughout the afternoon Ambassador Levanon had telephoned Egyptian Prime Minister Essam Sharaf and several ministers. In a po-lite but firm voice he had reminded them that Egypt was committed under its international treaty with Israel to protect the safety of all dip-lomats and staff residing in the embassy. By midafternoon trucks with soldiers and riot police began to arrive to erect barricades outside the embassy compound wall.

At 4:00 P.M. the Supreme Council declared over Cairo radio a "state of alert" and all demonstrations around the Israeli embassy were banned. Three miles away demonstrators carrying banners with slo-gans attacking Israel were marching through the streets toward

Giza, jeering at the warning that had come over their transistor radios.

In Washington, where it was midmorning in the Pentagon, secretary of defense Leon Panetta received a call from Levanon to update him on the situation developing in Cairo. They had met when the former director of the CIA had visited Cairo a year ago to familiarize himself with the Middle East. Panetta ordered the American embassy in Cairo to "take all steps to protect the Israeli embassy personal." The platoon of U.S. Marines guarding the embassy was ordered to be ready to go to the Israeli mission to assist in their safe evacuation.

At 6:00 P.M. the embassy staff had completed filling diplomatic bags with secret files and papers and sealing them. Families had packed their personal belongings and placed them inside the embassy entrance. They had been told to either stay in their apartments or go to the embassy café to wait further instructions. In the lobby the security men had barricaded the building entrance with furniture.

The Mossad agent had taken a taxi from Tahrir Square. He reported to Ambassador Levanon that when he had left there were signs of trouble brewing and the taxi driver had insisted on taking short detours to the embassy to avoid the angry demonstrators marching toward it.

At 6:30 P.M. they began to arrive. The security cameras on the outside walls of the embassy showed on the screen in Lavanon's office that many demonstrators were equipped with sledgehammers and battering rams. There appeared to be thousands of people in the crowd gathering outside the embassy.

In the communications room an operator relayed the closed-circuit images to Tel Aviv, where they were seen in a secret bunker by the most powerful man in Israel, who had been urgently summoned to deal with what was happening in Cairo. Created after the signing of the peace treaty between Israel and Egypt, the bunker was intended to be used as a special link with the embassy in a communication breakdown. It had not been used since the Iran hostage crisis, when U.S. diplomats had been held captive for 444 days after an Islamic mob had stormed the American mission in Tehran. Both Mossad and the Egyptian intelligence service were involved in helping to have the diplomats freed.

As the evening wore on the surveillance cameras installed inside the embassy showed the demonstrators using their sledgehammers to attack the embassy's perimeter wall. There was no sign of soldiers or riot police making any effort to stop them.

In the early hours of Saturday morning, the wall was breached. What followed was recorded by both those in the Tel Aviv bunker and the Mossad agent in the embassy. His report described how: "By 1:00 A.M. the demonstrators had entered the lobby and proceeded through the rest of the building. They ransacked the embassy and threw items, including documents, some marked 'confidential,' from the windows. By then the number of protesters had grown to about 3,000 still attacking the perimeter wall. The ransacking of the building continued into the early hours. Outside the compound protesters burnt cars as the police tried to disperse them with tear gas and soldiers fired warning shots into the air."

As dawn broke squads of Egyptian army commandos arrived in half-tracks and buses outside the embassy. They were in response to the state of emergency the Supreme Council of the Armed Forces had declared. The commandos stormed through breaches in the wall and began driving the demonstrators out of the embassy, using their guns as clubs.

During the night Ambassador Levanon, the diplomats, and their families had sheltered in the embassy strong room. The Mossad agent and the lobby guards had drawn their guns, prepared for a last stand outside the strong room. The commandos assured them that the embassy staff was safe.

In the Tel Aviv bunker the crisis team continued to brief foreign governments. In Washington, President Barack Obama expressed "grave concern." In London, Prime Minister David Cameron issued a statement that he had reminded the Egyptian government to honor their responsibilities under the Vienna Convention. One of the London tabloids claimed that Britain's SAS unit based in Cyprus was ready to rescue the embassy staff. Germany, Canada, and Bahrain foreign missions issued various levels of support. Iran's parliament expressed "full support for the ransacking of the Israeli spy nest in Cairo."

By then the decision had been made by the crisis team that the embassy staff must be evacuated as soon as possible. Later that night a chartered passenger plane was en route to Cairo.

At 2:40 A.M. that Saturday two buses arrived at the international airport carrying the ambassador and his staff. Guarded by the Egyptian commandos, they were escorted to the aircraft. The last to board was the Mossad agent.

Waiting on the tarmac at Tel Aviv airport was Prime Minister Netanyahu. When the plane was clear of Egyptian air space he had been told that Prime Minister Essam Sharaf had ordered Egypt's information minister Osama Heikal to issue a statement: "This country is fully committed to our international peace treaty with the State of Israel and the safety of all its diplomats. Those who have breached our undertaking will be fully punished."

Eleven months later, in August 2012, seventy-six Egyptians were charged with partaking in the embassy attack. Each was sentenced to one year's imprisonment.

The Mossad agent from Cairo had served Africa where the black emblem of al-Qaeda continued to be hoisted in the listless air over Niger, Chad, South Somalia, and had started to appear across the border with Kenya.

Pardo had visited Nairobi when Mossad had opened a station a few blocks from the city's venerable Norfolk Hotel after Kenya's intelligence service helped in Israel's rescue of Jewish airline passengers who had been hijacked to Uganda by terrorists (see chapter 7, "The Gentleman Spy," pp. 142–45). Over the years the Kenyan spies had benefited from visits to Israel for further training with Mossad.

Both services now collaborated in monitoring al-Qaeda. A swath of land five times the size of Great Britain had been renamed the Islamic Maghreb (AQIM for al-Qaeda in the Islamic Maghreb) by Ayman al-Zawahiri, the Cairo-born doctor who became head of al-Qaeda after Osama bin Laden was killed in Pakistan by U.S. Special Forces in May 2011.

Al-Zawahiri intended the Maghreb to become the foundation for the restoration of a New Caliph. He had designated its capital to be the ancient city of Timbuktu, once a route to the ports of Mauritania, Senegal, and Sierra Leone from where the slaves of Central Africa had been shipped to North America.

For centuries Timbuktu was known as the city of 333 Muslim saints until al-Zawahiri ordered their two remaining mausoleums to be destroyed. Timbuktu was also placed under Sharia law. Western music was banned from its local radio station. Women were publicly beaten for leaving their heads uncovered in public. Husbands were beheaded after Friday prayers when caught trying to flee the city with their families.

The adobe architecture of Timbuktu's three great mosques–Sankore, Sidi Yahia, and Djingareyber–was venerated in the Islamic world as symbolic of Arab culture. They had become storage areas for the al-Qaeda trans-Saharan smuggling route out of South America to run cocaine into Algeria, Morocco, and on into Europe. Al-Zawahiri had also brought fighters from Pakistan to run the network of training camps scattered across the Maghreb.

Mossad agents and their Kenyan colleagues had discovered that each camp was stocked with military equipment provided by the United States to the Mali army to defend its country against terrorists.

The main training camp was on the Somalia border with Kenya, under the command of Ahmed Abdi Godane. He had been asked by al-Zawahiri to bring his group al-Shabaab into Maghreb where he was given a position in its top command tier.

The tall thirty-six-year-old bachelor with a passion for expensive sunglasses had already imposed a Taliban-style rule across much of Somalia, venting his hatred of the West through his poetry, a mode of political expression long a tradition in Somalia. His broadcasts were downloaded by his followers to be played in training camps. They were also being recorded by Mossad and other intelligence services.

Godane's background as a child prodigy had led to scholarships to study in Sudan's and Pakistan's Islamic schools. He first met al-Zawahiri when he spent time in a training camp in the northwest mountains in Pakistan and later boasted he had met Osama bin Laden after the 9/11 attack. Godane returned to Somalia fired by what he had been told and formed al-Shabaab. He showed his taste for terror by murdering several Western aid workers helping refugees. By the time he absorbed his group into Maghreb he had hundreds of fighters, motivated, like him, by the hatred he filled his poetry with. On visits to Nairobi he had discovered that Israel businessmen were investing in developing the city, including its largest supermarket complex. It was a target he had discussed with al-Zawahiri.

The Maghreb training camps were linked by a sophisticated electronic network that used a variety of service providers to transmit messages in a number of coded languages. Its operators were certain that the vast electronic forest of words they used ensured they would never be discovered. They had no way of knowing Mossad was silently stalking them.

Mossad's cyberwar unit had its own slogan: "Tomorrow is zero hour." The words were an intercepted phone message by the American National Security Agency, NSA, which had turned out to allude to the 9/11 attack on the World Trade Center and the Pentagon. The warning had come too late.

Day and night the unit's experts data mined, using their computers to comb through huge amounts of information looking for patterns and clues to fight cyberterrorism on an invisible battlefield. From there, Israel's enemies tried to target its government, industry, military, power, communications, water, fuel, and transportation infrastructure, all of which would be vulnerable to destruction

When he visited the unit, Prime Minister Netanyahu told them that their electronic battles against cyberattacks were regarded as Israel's most important defense. He had come to thank them for the software program they had helped to design to attack the centrifuges at Iran's nuclear enrichment facility at Natanz. A field officer, a *katsa* with a science background, had been trained in how to insert the malware before the Iranian scientists at the nuclear enrichment plant had spotted its presence. The unit called the malware Stuxnet, to reflect the many months needed to create the malicious software program that had, in Netanyahu's words, slowed "Iran's race to create a bomb by up to three years.".

In that time their war would continue to be fought from a ground floor high-security area in Mossad headquarters behind a soundproof door that could only be opened by a key code.

The successful Stuxnet operation increased the profile of cyberwarfare. Sir Iain Lobban, the head of Britain's Government Headquarters, GCHQ, revealed the country's Ministry of Defence was targeted over a thousand times a year. He identified the attacks were mostly coming from the Tenth Bureau, the highly secret department of China's People's Liberation Army responsible for science and technology. In the United States General Keith B. Alexander, the head of the Pentagon's Cyber Command, confirmed that "our targets are enemy military command centers that we can reach from cyberspace. We know China's cyber spies are under strict orders to target any of our organizations, from government to hedge funds, whose secrets may be of benefit to Beijing."

Barack Obama and Vladimir Putin agreed to install a secret cyberwar hotline "to provide a direct voice communication between the U.S.

cyberwar coordinator and the Russian deputy secretary of the security council should there be a need to directly manage a crisis situation arising from a security incident." The existence of this link was first revealed by the White House in June 2013.

A number of the most skilled cryptologists in the Mossad unit had become its code breakers and code makers. They had mastered steganography, how to conceal secret information within a digital file. They discovered that al-Qaeda used the technique, encrypting its messages in goods offered for sale on eBay. Several other Mossad operatives spent their time tracking the Internet message board Reddit. More than once this had led an operator to a terrorist using hexadecimal characters and prime numbers. Decoded they sometimes indicated an attack was being planned or even about to happen.

The information was passed to Mossad operations for circulation to its field agents. When it appeared the attack could take place in a certain country, details were sent to its intelligence service's cyber command. America's Air Force Cyber Command was based at Fort Meade in Maryland and Britain's GCHQ, in its doughnut-shaped headquarters. Both centers were securely linked to Mossad's cyberwar unit.

Its most experienced cryptologists were chosen for their skill in accessing an area inaccessible to the search engines of Google, Yahoo, and Bing. Called the Dark Side, it contained billions of Web pages and is estimated to be five thousand times larger than any other on the Internet. The Dark Side is where the Mossad has continued to fight a keyboard war like no other.

In the meantime, Tamir Pardo reinforced Mossad's presence in those Middle East countries where the last of the surviving dictators still ruled.

The mass demonstrations in Tahrir Square had steadily faded away as the Egyptian army, which had removed Mubarak, strengthened its grip on the nation. Arbitrary arrests and reports of torture increased. More people were tried before military courts over a few weeks than in the thirty years of Mubarak's ruthless regime. The Muslim Brotherhood was allowed a degree of lenience to participate in the country's political life. But their candidate for the presidency, Mohamed Morsi, had become a lackey to the army. One quarter of voters had joined the hard-line Salafist Party, the party whose strain of extremism had given birth to Egypt's al-Qaeda. Democracy became an enemy for the Islamists. The concerns of women's groups and human rights activists were driven back into the shadows with their dreams fading memories. Theirs was a life where the economy was worsening, unemployment rising, and living standards falling.

Tunisia, once the most progressive country in North Africa, had voted for the country to once more become in effect a Muslim caliphate, a form of rule that had not been seen since the Middle Ages. In the street where Mohamed Bouazizi had set fire to himself vendors once again paid bribes to peddle their wares.

In Libya, Sharia law had legalized polygamy. The black flag of al-Qaeda flew over the offices of the new government within a year after Mu'ammar Gadhafi had been assassinated. His rule of fear and torture had finally led to his people launching their version of the Arab Spring: they called it "Day of Rage" that led to a war endorsed by a United Nation Security Council Resolution to "protect civilians in populated areas under threat of attack." The protection was provided by NATO, using British and French bombers. The United States had a lesser role.

For months Gadhafi managed to avoid capture, until October 20, 2011, when he had led a convoy of cars and trucks with his supporters from Tripoli, where he had been hiding. French bombers and British Typhoons fighters that were conducting a surveillance flight over the already bombed city swooped down on the convoy of fifty vehicles as it headed into the desert. All but ten of the vehicles were destroyed. From the lead car Gadhafi had leaped with his bodyguards and dived into a large irrigation drainpipe alongside the road. They were spotted by rebel troops close by who rushed to the pipe, firing into the opening and killing most of the bodyguards.

Blood streaming from his head, Gadhafi had emerged from inside the pipe. One of the rebels hauled Gadhafi to his feet and peered into his face. The rebel suddenly shouted.

"It's him!" The other rebels started to run forward. "It's Gadhafi!"

The rebel holding Gadhafi shot him in his chest. Gadhafi dropped to the ground. Another rebel shot him in the forehead.

In the days to come the body was publicly displayed. On October 25, at dawn it was taken in a truck and buried in the desert at a place that to this day remains secret.

Elsewhere the Arab Spring was still alive in Jordan, Morocco, and Bahrain; its supporters were bought off with promises of symbolic reforms by rulers who recognized that despite all their soldiers it could still become difficult to rule an angry people. They also saw what had happened in Eastern Europe and South America where brutal regimes had fallen. Though some of their foreign allies, the United States and Great Britain, were still active in the Middle East, new and influential players had emerged, none more so than China. All sat back and watched if the Arab Spring would flower. Many of its original supporters in Tunisia and Egypt had seen what Islamism had done. In countries like Jordan and the Gulf Emirates there was a growing feeling that it was one thing to call for political reform but equally important to recognize that what was happening in Syria would rekindle the Arab Spring and sweep beyond Syria, where President Bashar al-Assad had become the most brutal of the region's dictators.

Increasingly a full-scale war in Syria was a possibility.

Early in the morning of January 1, 2013, the day that marked the start of Tamir Pardo's third year as head of Mossad, he had gone on a secret mission to Amman, the capital of Jordan. He was the only passenger on the Israeli government Learjet. In his briefcase was a recording: its contents were the reason for his trip. In his time in office he had made a number of visits to the desert kingdom to discuss joint intelligence matters with General Faisal Al Shoubaki, the chief of the Jordanian intelligence agency. But never had he gone on such an important mission.

Israel had continued to experience rocket attacks from Gaza, launched by Hamas in the past weeks. But it now faced an even more terrifying threat. The recording contained evidence that Hamas had approached Syria to provide chemical and biological weapons to be launched from inside the Jordanian border into Israel.

The evidence was the result of weeks of work by a deep-cover Mossad agent in Damascus. He had been cultivating a Syrian member of President Bashar al-Assad's entourage who had gradually indicated he wanted to defect. A month ago, in December, the agent and defector had crossed the border into Lebanon. Bypassing Beirut they had made their way south to the Israeli border post. A car waited to drive them south to a Mossad safe house. Two experienced officers had been sent to interview the defector. It was agreed he would be named Hassan bin Ali and would be given the right papers to remain in the West Bank. He had revealed all he knew, which had been recorded and later listened to by Pardo. He had shown it to Netanyahu and it was agreed that Pardo would take it to Faisal Al Shoubaki. A meeting had been immediately agreed by the Jordanian intelligence chief and clearance for the flight to Amman arranged.

Hassan's duties had included eavesdropping on conversations in one of the waiting rooms outside the president's office and reporting all he had heard while visitors had waited to see al-Assad.

They had included a Hamas delegation from Gaza who had discussed among themselves how they would approach the president to provide Hamas with chemical weapons. They would launch them from inside the Jordanian border into Israel, either after being inserted in rocket warheads or dropped in barrels into the Dead Sea and floated across to the Israeli shore. Either way, the delegation had agreed, it would be an effective way to attack Israel. Hassan bin Ali had said on the recording that when the Hamas men had emerged from the president's office they had "looked very satisfied." Despite close questioning by the two Mossad officers, they were satisfied with his story.

In Amman, Pardo played the interview disc to General Al Shoubaki. They agreed it should be taken to Nasser Judheh, Jordan's foreign minister. He had listened to the recording and said that Syria "is undoubtedly ruled by a war criminal willing to support terrorists." Nevertheless, he added, the risk of taking military action against Syria would be highly dangerous, at least for Jordan. Al-Assad would look to both Russia and Iran for support at the United Nations.

While Jordan would reinforce its northern border patrols to intercept any attempt by Hamas to smuggle chemical weapons from Syria and the Jordanian air force would maintain air surveillance along its border down to the Dead Sea, Judheh had said there was nothing more Jordan could do.

On the flight back to Tel Aviv the Mossad chief may well have considered what was possible. There were, after all, a number of options.

On February 20, 2013, two military trucks entered the naval base in Haifa and drove to the submarine pen where Israel's three Dolphin-class submarines were docked. From the first truck climbed frogmen from Flotilla 13, Israel's elite naval commandos. They removed several large rocks from the second truck that they had dug up weeks before from a group of uninhabited isles two miles off the coast of Syria's port city of Latakia. It had been one of the cities that Hassan bin Ali had identified as housing a chemical storage bunker.

In the past weeks the rocks had been hollowed out and fitted with tracking devices and surveillance systems by Mossad technicians in their laboratories. Once the rocks were stowed on board the submarine the submarine set course north back to the rocky mound off the Syrian coast.

As darkness fell the submarine surfaced. The frogmen came on deck and loaded the rocks on dinghies equipped with silent outboard motors and sent off for the rocky outcrop to replace the rocks where they had been dug up. The submarine dropped below the surface.

In the radio room one of the technicians who had worked on their creation used equipment he had brought on board to tune into the devices concealed in the rocks. In the small hours of that February morning he began to receive signals from inside the rocks as they transmitted images to an Israeli satellite in space. From there they were being downloaded to a control command center near the Israeli side of the Dead Sea.

A week later people living on the eastern outskirts of Latakia were awoken at night by a sudden explosion near the village of Al-Samiyah. The London-based Human Rights Organization, Amnesty International, announced that the explosion had "completely destroyed a mysterious bunker" near the village. Colonel Qasim Saad al-Din, the head of the Free Syrian Army fighting the regime, said that the bunker had been "a storage facility for chemical weapons." The London-based Arabic newspaper, *Al-Hayat*, speculated that the missile that destroyed the bunker had been launched from an "Israeli submarine with the agreement of the United States." In Tel Aviv, Israel's defense minister, Moshe Ya'alon, said, "Israel is forced to defend its vital national interests. We have a set of red lines in regard to our national interest and we keep to them."

Since May 2013, Mossad analysts had followed the progress of Iran's election campaign to replace the incumbent president, Mahmoud Ahmadinejad. The eight candidates in what would be Iran's eleventh election would each have a total of 405 minutes broadcast time on national radio and television to present their case.

They had been summoned before General Masoud Jazayeri, the formidable deputy chief of the armed forces. He read them the electoral laws: "A candidate will become instantly imprisoned if they spread untrue information or a black portrait of the regime to obtain votes. Any campaign worker they employ who is caught distributing propaganda against the State will also be arrested. If guilty he will be executed. The only enemy that can be attacked is the State of Israel. Any attempt to influence the Iran Electronic Tracking System, the government polling organization, IETS, will result in a candidate being disqualified and his votes distributed among other candidates."

During the previous election, which had returned Ahmadinejad, three candidates had been imprisoned for the offenses General Jazayeri had listed. One still remained in jail awaiting the outcome of his appeal.

On the eve of the start of the election the Ministry of Interior announced that 50,483,192 persons were eligible to vote at one of 66,000 voting stations.

Two of the candidates had withdrawn by the first week of campaigning and urged their supporters to vote for one of the other three of the remaining six candidates. By the end of the second week the poll showed that Mohammad Bagher Ghalibaf was in front with his slogan plastered over Tehran: "Change, Life, People: A Glorious Iran." He was the city mayor and the commander of the air force.

Mohsen Rezaee, in second place, was the commander of the Revolutionary Guards and had twice run for the presidency under the same optimistic slogan: "Say hello to life." In the third place was Hassan Rouhani, head of the Moderation and Development Party and a deputy speaker of the Iran Parliament. He was also the country's chief nuclear negotiator and had continued to gather support in the countryside with the assurance Iran would not be attacked.

After the third of the television debates support for Rouhani increased dramatically. By the first week of June the other campaigners had all dropped behind. By June 12, the bespectacled Hassan Rouhani in his white turban had attracted 38 percent of the vote. On election day, June 15, he was victorious and was elected in the first round of voting with 50.88 percent of the vote. At 8:30 P.M. local time, the ministry announced Rouhani as the new president.

In Tel Aviv, Prime Minister Netanyahu had told Tamir Prado that "one of the most dangerous things to do after an Iranian election is to believe that it will lead to a reforming moderate we can do business with."

From early September 2013 Mossad cryptologists monitoring the Dark Side of the Internet had begun to pick up messages that indicated that al-Shabaab was preparing an attack somewhere along the border with Kenya. Mossad's Nairobi station was alerted. The information was passed to Kenya's intelligence service. By the middle of the month, the possibility of an attack had been raised to an "ongoing risk." Nearly half a million Somalis who had fled from their country in a sprawling refugee camp in a Nairobi suburb. Since 1998 they had been subjected to regular police checks after al-Qaeda had bombed Nairobi's U.S. embassy, killing approximately two hundred people and injuring thousands.

At midday on September 21, four al-Shabaab militants stormed Nairobi's Westgate premier shopping mall, which had been financed with Israeli investments, throwing grenades and indiscriminately shooting shoppers, resulting in seventy deaths. Four of the terrorists were killed by special forces. A fifth man, fitting the description of Ahmed Abdi Godane, was seen fleeing from the scene before the attack started. He appeared to have gone to the northwest border area of Kenya where he disappeared back into Somalia. Days later he used the Internet to broadcast his "complete satisfaction" with the al-Shabaab mall attack.

Pardo had steadily built up his contacts with the region's spy chiefs after Omar Suleiman had brokered them. The Mossad chief had become a bridge builder with Turkey. Since Arab commandos had blockaded the Turkish *Mavi Marmara* ship on its way to Gaza with food and medical supplies (see chapter 31, "Farewell," pp. 711–715), Ankara had withdrawn its ambassador. Pardo became Netanyahu's "backdoor," using Hakan Fidan, the head of Turkish intelligence, Milli Istihbarat Teskilati, MIT, to reopen relationships.

His voice, like his hair, was thin and he had sad brown eyes. He had begun his career in antiterrorism, fighting Kurdish terrorists. Pardo made several flights to Ankara to discuss the growing war in Syria and its spillover into both countries. Turkey had accepted over three hundred thousand refugees from Syria by July 2013 and Iran's new president, Hassan Rouhani, had put aside his campaign slogan, "Moderation and Wisdom" and replaced it with his warning there would be "no overnight solution to problems unless Israel changed its policies."

On Pardo's last visit to Ankara the two intelligence chiefs had discussed the possibility of Iran and Syria being behind the summer riots on Istanbul's Taksim Square against the government.

Turkey was a NATO member and they had discussed how the United States would deal with the new regime in Tehran. Was the answer in the words of President Obama in January 2013? "I am more mindful than most people of our incredible strength and capabilities. In a situation like Syria I have to ask, can we make a difference in that situation? Would a military intervention have an impact? What would be the aftermath of our involvement on the ground? Could it trigger even worse violence or the use of chemical weapons? What offers the best prospect of a stable post-Assad regime?"

Before he had flown back to Tel Aviv, Fidan had told Pardo. "Obama is good at asking questions. It's answers we need."

Shortly after he returned to Israel a document arrived in Mossad headquarters from its station chief in Washington. It contained details of the new bunker-busting bomb that the United States Air Force had successfully tested. Code-named GBU-57B, the bomb weighed three tons and could penetrate two hundred feet of rock.

At Pardo's weekly senior staff meeting there was agreement that Washington would hold off delivering the bomb to Israel until it became clear what Iran's new leader would do at the forthcoming meeting in Geneva to discuss a deal with Iran on its nuclear program.

The first signs were not encouraging. The Supreme Leader, Ayatollah Ali Khamenei, had announced that "Iran will not step back from our nuclear rights and I also welcome Britain's parliament vote against an air strike on Syria's chemical bunkers."

On the day the talks opened in Geneva between Iran and the P5+1 countries—the United States, Great Britain, France, Germany, China, and Russia—Netanyahu had flown to Moscow to see Vladimir Putin, the fifth time they had met. He intended to show Putin that "I have to care for the survival of my country and Iran threatens that unless there is a big change at Geneva."

In late October 2013, Pardo had received an invitation from General Al Shoubaki to travel to Dubai and meet with Arab intelligence chiefs. He had expected that the meeting would deal primarily with the current situation about terrorist activities in the region, including drug smuggling and human trafficking. The Dubai meeting turned out to have greater significance. The Saudi Arabia intelligence chief, Prince Bandar bin Sultan, had been accompanied by Crown Prince Salman bin Abdulaziz Al Saud, the deputy prime minister and minister of defense. They had asked for a private meeting with Pardo, at which he was offered the reassurance that the Chinese rockets in Saudi's desert were only there to protect their country from an enemy they both shared the Republic of Iran. Prince Bandar added they both knew that their countries shared concerns that at times put them at odds with the United States. The Crown Prince felt the threat of Iran had reached a stage where it must be handled.

That began the start of several meetings that had taken Pardo to Riyadh and Amman to meet with both the royal princes and senior Saudi military officers. By November it had been agreed that Israel could use Saudi air space to launch air attacks on Iran's nuclear facilities and for Israeli drones, rescue helicopters, and tanker planes to be positioned over Saudi Arabia and the Red Sea and have refuel facilities at various Saudi airfields.

The arrangements would come into operation in the event of the Geneva talks failing to satisfy both sides.

In November, President Rouhani announced after the Geneva talks that a preliminary deal had been struck with the West on Iran's nuclear program, under which Teheran agreed to stop enriching stockpiles of uranium beyond the 5 percent level required for civilian nuclear power. In return, the West had agreed to begin lifting the international sanctions that had gripped the Iranian economy.

Six months had been given to Iran to bring the deal into force, and would expire in May 2014.

On December 8, 2013 *The Jerusalem Post*, known for its contacts in Mossad, had summarized the weeks of meetings over the past weeks between Pardo and the Saudi princes. "They were to contain Iran by all possible means and at the same time exercise strong control over the Iran sponsored Jihadist forces in Syria and to continue to sideline the Muslim Brotherhood and blow away the last breeze of the Arab Spring."

At one of the meetings in the Jordanian port of Aqaba the spy chiefs had each brought their cyber specialists to discuss the production of a malware more devastating than Israel's Stuxnet to spy on and destroy the latest software structure of Iran's nuclear program. The Saudi delegation had indicated it was ready to finance further research. Crown Prince Bandar had told Pardo there would be "no limit to cost."

By the first week of December 2013 suspicion of the deal, negotiated by John Kerry, the U.S. secretary of state and his counterparts from

Britain, Russia, France, Germany, and China had led to Benjamin Netanyahu ordering Mossad to gather all evidence of Iran violating the deal.

Netanyahu told Tamir Pardo, "By the coming May Israel may well have to look for delivery of those bunker-busting bombs from America for what will have been a historic mistake in believing another Iranian president."

On Saturday morning, January 11, 2014, Pardo received a telephone call at home he had expected. Prime Minister Netanyahu told him that after eight years in a medically induced coma the eighty-five-year-old Ariel Sharon, long known to his people as the "Lion of God," who had cheated death for so long after suffering a massive stroke and cerebral hemorrhage, was dead.

Since his stroke in January 2006 surgery had failed and had left him in a vegetative state. Surgeons had urged his family to allow him to die. Instead they had told them to keep him alive, insisting that brain scans indicated a response when he was shown photographs and listened to their recorded voices. But on that Saturday morning all intervention came to an end (see chapter 25, "Confronting the Dragon," pp. 554–57).

Pardo had served as Sharon's electronic officer in the Lebanon invasion in 1982, when Sharon had stamped himself indelibly on the face of the Jewish State. He epitomized the Israeli military ethic of personal courage and boldness. When he had entered the political arena he turned out to be a determined pragmatist, ready to undermine his own political colleagues within the right-wing Likud party. He formed Kadima, a centrist movement, strong on security but anti-settlements. He had closed those on the West Bank knowing the risk to his own life from Israeli extremists. One had already assassinated Yitzhak Rabin after signing the Oslo Accords between Israel and the Palestine Liberation Organization.

"My life has been spent defending Jews. Now I have to guard against Jews and Arabs," Sharon said as he came to dominate the air waves. With a booming voice, a lisp, and a nasal twitch he became the most vivid figure of any Israeli since his mentor, Moshe Dayan.

Even in death he had remained a controversial figure. "Hope you are looking forward to hell, Ariel. You were our evil. Every bit as bad as Arafat," an Israeli wrote. His two sons, Omri and Gilad, refused to comment to the newspapers on such recent comments.

Prime Minister Benjamin Netanyahu, who had once replaced Sharon as prime minister, ordered that the state funeral should "be appropriate to his significance in Israeli history."

Sharon lay in state for a day outside Israel's parliament, the Knesset, in Jerusalem. The funeral was attended by leaders from all over the world. Afterward Sharon was laid to rest beside the grave of his late wife, Lily, at his beloved ranch in the Negev Desert.

In his own tribute to Sharon, Tamir Pardo told the family that with his passing he would be remembered as the warrior statesman who had fought so hard to shape the map of the Middle East.

NOTES ON SOURCES

I have had access at a sufficiently high level within the Israeli intelligence community to have made this an authoritative account. As with my previous books, I came to the subject of Mossad with no baggage. I have used information its members provided in the way any writer does when dealing with an intelligence service: checked it, checked it, checked it.

Some eighty hours of taped recollections were made, including repeated interviews with persons connected directly or indirectly with Mossad. Others were with persons Mossad had tried to kill. They included Leila Khaled, who came to notoriety during the spate of aircraft hijackings by the PLO in the 1970s, and Abu Al-Abbas, who masterminded the hijacking of the *Achille Lauro* in which a crippled American Jewish passenger was hurled over the side of the cruise liner to his death. I met them in May 1996 in Gaza City, where they had been permitted to visit Israel as part of its rapprochement with the PLO. I also spoke to Yasser Arafat, himself once a prime target for Mossad assassination.

I was introduced to the business of writing on intelligence matters in 1960 when I worked with Chapman Pincher, then Britain's foremost writer on the subject. We were both employed by the *Daily Express* in London. A number of our stories—notably the Burgess and Maclean debacle for British intelligence—helped to change the perception of how such matters should be reported. It is a position I have tried to maintain with such books as *Journey into Madness*, *Pontiff*, and *Chaos Under Heaven*. *The Black Book of the CIA*, *Secrets & Lies*, and *Secret Wars*; the latter title published by the publisher of this book.

I have reported on the secret intelligence wars being waged against Iran, Iraq, Syria, and Afghanistan, areas in which Mossad remains directly involved. I have also written extensively on Mossad's relationship with the Vatican. My own contacts with the Holy See were useful in conducting further background interviews for this book.

In 1989 I was in China at the height of the student unrest. Once more I witnessed the machinations of intelligence agencies and detected the hand of Mossad over its concern that China's exporting of weapons to both Iran and Iraq could pose a serious threat to Israel. I went on to write about the role of Mossad in the Persian Iraqi War and in the aftermath of Soviet Communism.

In August 1994 I received a call from Zvi Spielmann. Spielmann is something of a legend in Israel: he fought with distinction in its War of Independence and went on to create Israel's United Film Studios. He has produced a raft of films, many of them Hollywood coproductions. Spielmann asked if I would write and present a documentary on Mossad. He assured me I would have a completely free hand, that the only restriction on the information I obtained would be the questions I asked to obtain it; the more I asked, the more I would learn.

I discovered that, apart from Victor Ostrovsky's books, and the work of Ari Ben-Menashe, there was precious little to read about Mossad in the way of hard information. This was in marked contrast to the CIA, which has some two hundred books devoted to its work. The British Secret Intelligence Service has close to fifty, and similar numbers are in print for the KGB and the German and French intelligence agencies. But a check on their contents showed where there were gaps in the secret wars they had waged. It became clear that Mossad could fill many of these.

On trips to Israel, some on behalf of Britain's Channel 4, the process of interviewing was like any other. The time frame of the story my interviewees had to tell initially encompassed a strange period, somewhere between recent history and fading memory. Gradually, as we came to know each other and their accounts moved closer to the present time, they became more specific, better able to remember the minutiae—who said what, when, and where.

It became clear that even those who had helped found Mossad had vivid recollections of a period that was part of their living history—and that had never been recounted from their perspective. Most important, they could relate those earlier times to the present day. For example, when they identified Mossad's role in the closing days of the shah of Iran, they translated it as the root of the current scourge of Islamic fundamentalism. When they revealed Mossad's involvement with South Africa, they were able to juxtapose it with that country's situation today. Time and again they showed how the past was part of Israel's present; how Mossad had bridged the gap between then and now.

They showed that legends attributed to Mossad paled into insignificance when placed against what really had happened. I remember

Rafael Eitan chuckling and saying, "Almost every published fact about the capture of Eichmann is pure bullshit. I know because I personally am the man who captured him."

In many ways Eitan and his colleagues turned myths into a compelling reality. They asked I should do no less.

Listening to Eitan, his achievements seemed to be as inexhaustible as his energy. He had fought a great secret war. A man of endless vision, all he asked was to live long enough to see the day when Israel would truly be at peace. In October 2008, Eitan told a German magazine that Iran's President Ahmadinejad should be kidnapped and brought to trial at the Hague War Crimes Tribunal. Eitan was then the head of the Pensioners Party in the Israeli Knesset.

I learned quickly that there were distinct and acrimonious camps among my interviewees. There were the "Isser Harel" people and the "Meir Amit" people, and the contempt each had for the other was undimmed by the years. I sensed there will never be a mellowing on either side.

This led to an additional problem: weighing the emphasis to be put on their information. My interviewees are also in a race with time. Men like Meir Amit are in the twilight of their lives. It was to his credit that he was willing to endure lengthy interviews and repetitive questions. He granted his last one shortly after he had returned from Vietnam, where he had gone to learn firsthand about how the Vietcong had often outsmarted U.S. intelligence in the Vietnam War.

One of the most fascinating interviews was with Uri Saguy. He sat in Zvi Spielmann's office and spoke candidly on such diverse subjects as the need for Israel to come to an accommodation with Syria and the problem he sometimes had with "tasking" Mossad when he had been Israel's overall intelligence supremo.

David Kimche rarely let down his guard, insisting on seeing all questions beforehand. Nevertheless, he did impart important insights regarding his personal attitude toward people and events. My enduring memory of him was watching him feed his dog while elegantly destroying the credibility of those who did not measure up to his own standards.

Yaakov Cohen opened his home—and his heart and mind to me. We sat for many hours in the kibbutz where he now lives as he remembered what he had said and felt at the time. As an example, he alone could recall the fear and remorse he had experienced when killing his first man. His reaction was in marked contrast to Rafi Eitan's feelings about killing.

Yoel Ben Porat had the mentality of the lawyer's lawyer, dealing only with the facts and slow to conjecture. In many cases he was able to fill in gaps that had been left open by history. Reuven Merhav was a font of information about Mossad's position in the framework of Israeli politics.

Among the Israeli journalists I spoke with, two need special mention. Alex Doron was ready to sound off about Israeli intelligence in a way that was candid and refreshing. His support was valuable. On the other hand, Ran Edelist, who had been engaged as a researcher by Channel 4 for the TV film I was to present on Mossad, often paced an office in Zvi Spielmann's studio complex, insisting it would not be "proper" to give "full details" in many cases. At times he seemed more concerned with what should not be in the program than with what should. In some of the interviews he attended, he frequently interrupted interviewees to caution them to "be careful." Thankfully, few took his advice. Independently of Ran Edelist, I met with other Israeli intelligence operatives who were able to be open on the understanding they would not be directly quoted.

They invited me to their homes; I met their families and came to know something of their private lives; it was a reminder that spies do not live in one dimension. I still remember completing a long interview with a former *katsa* who provided an account of how he had killed. Suddenly he looked around at the comfortable living room with its views of a biblical landscape and sighed deeply and said, "This world is not this world."

The words have stayed with me. I think that what he meant was that, compared to his former work, beneath ordinary rhythms and appearances of life, a darkness and menace had never left him. I found that with several of the others with whom I spoke.

It was a sobering reminder that the world of intelligence is, as Saint Paul glimpsed heaven, all too often indeed "seen through a glass, darkly."

PRIMARY INTERVIEWEES

Meir Amit	Edward Kimbel
Haim Cohen	David Kimche
Nadia Cohen	Otto Kormek

Yaakov Cohen   Henry McConnachie
William Casey   Ariel Merari
William Colby   Reuven Merhav
Rafael Eitan   Danny Nagier
Zvi Spielmann   Yoel Ben Porat
Isser Harel   Uri Saguy
Emery Kabongo   Simon Wiesenthal

Newspapers and Journals

Daily Express, London   *Los Angeles Times*
Daily Mail, London   *The Jerusalem Post*
Daily Telegraph, London   *The Sunday Times*, London
The New York Times

Organizations

Palmach Archive, Israel   The Press Association Library,
                                 London
Public Record Office, London   The Library, Trinity College,
                                 Dublin
National Archive, Washington   The Secret Archives, Vatican
                                 City State
The New York Public Library   The Archive, Glilot, Israel

SELECT BIBLIOGRAPHY

Agee, Philip. *Inside the Company: CIA Diary*. Harmondsworth, England: Penguin Books, 1975.

Allon, Yigal. *Shield of David*. London: Weidenfeld & Nicolson, 1970.

Bainerman, Joel. *Inside the Covert Operations of the CIA and Israel's Mossad*. New York: SPI Books, 1991.

Bamford, James. *The Puzzle Palace: A Report on America's Most Secret Agency*. Boston: Houghton Mifflin, 1982.

Bar-Zohar, Michel. *Ben-Gurion, A Biography*. London: Weidenfeld & Nicolson, 1977.

———. *Spies in the Promised Land*. London: Davis-Poynter, 1972.

Ben-Porat, Yeshayahu, et al. *Entebbe Rescue*. New York: Delacorte Press, 1977.

Ben-Shaul, Moshe, ed. *Generals of Israel*. Tel Aviv: Hadar, 1968.

Black, Ian and Benny Morris. *Israel's Secret Wars*. London. Hamish Hamilton, 1991.

Blumenthal, Sid, and Harvey Yazijian, eds. *Government by Gunplay: Assassination Conspiracy Theories from Dallas to Today*. New York: Signet, 1976.

Brzezinski, Zbigniew. *Power and Principle: Memoirs of the National Security Adviser, 1977–1981*. New York: Farrar, Straus & Giroux, 1983.

The CIA's Nicaragua Manual: Psychological Operations in Guerrilla Warfare. New York: Vintage Books, 1985.

Cline, Ray S. *The CIA Under Reagan, Bush and Casey*. Washington, D.C.: Acropolis Books, 1981.

———. *Secrets, Spies and Scholars: Blueprint of the Essential CIA*. Washington, D.C.: Acropolis Books, 1976.

Cline, Ray S., and Yonah Alexander. *Terrorism: The Soviet Connection*. New York: Crane Russak, 1984.

Constantinides, George C. *Intelligence and Espionage: An Analytical Bibliography*. Boulder, Colo.: Westview Press, 1983.

Copeland, Miles. *The Game of Nations*. New York: Simon & Schuster, 1969.

———. *The Real Spy World*. London: Sphere Books, 1978.

Deacon, Richard. *"C"—A Biography of Sir Maurice Oldfield*. London: Macdonald, 1985.

Dekel, Efraim. *Shai: The Exploits of Hagana Intelligence*. Tel Aviv: Yoseleff, 1959.

———. *A History of British Secret Service*. London: Granada, 1980.

De Silva, Peer. *Sub Rosa: The CIA and the Uses of Intelligence*. New York: Times Books, 1978.

Dobson, Christopher, and Ronald Payne. *The Dictionary of Espionage*. London: Harrap, 1984.

Dulles, Allen. *The Craft of Intelligence*. Westport, Conn.: Greenwood Press, 1977.

Eisenberg, Dennis, Uri Dan, and Eli Landau. *Meyer Lansky: Mogul of the Mob*. London: Corgi Books, 1980.

———. *The Mossad: Israel's Secret Intelligence Service Inside Stories*. New York: Signet, 1979.

Elon, Amos. *The Israelis: Founders and Sons*. London: Weidenfeld & Nicolson, 1971.

Farago, Ladislas. *Burn after Reading*. New York: Macfadden, 1963.

Gilbert, Martin. *The Arab-Israeli Conflict.* London: Weidenfeld & Nicolson, 1974.

Golan, Aviezer, and Danny Pinkas. *Shula, Code Name the Pearl.* New York: Delacorte Press, 1980.

Groussard, Serge. *The Blood of Israel.* New York: William Morrow, 1973.

Gulley, Bill, with Mary Ellen Reese. *Breaking Cover.* New York: Warner Books, 1981.

Haig, Alexander M. Jr. *Caveat: Realism, Reagan, and Foreign Policy.* London: Weidenfeld & Nicolson, 1984.

Harel, Isser. *The House on Garibaldi Street.* London: Andre Deutsch, 1975.

Harris, Robert, and Jeremy Paxman. *A Higher Form of Killing.* London: Triad/Granada, 1983.

Haswell, Jock. *Spies and Spymasters: A Concise History of Intelligence.* London: Thames & Hudson, 1977.

Henze, Paul B. *The Plot to Kill the Pope.* London: Croom Helm, 1984.

Laqueur, Walter, ed. *The Israel-Arab Reader.* New York: Bantam, 1969.

———. *The Struggle for the Middle East: The Soviet Union & the Middle East 1948–1968.* London: Routledge & Kegan Paul, 1969.

Lotz, Wolfgang. *The Champagne Spy.* London: Vallentine Mitchell, 1972.

McGehee, Ralph W. *Deadly Deceits: My 25 Years in the CIA.* New York: Sheridan Square Publications, 1983.

McGhee, George. *Envoy to the Middle World: Adventures in Diplomacy.* New York: Harper & Row, 1983.

Meir, Golda. *My Life.* London: Weidenfeld & Nicolson, 1975.

Moses, Hans. *The Clandestine Service of the Central Intelligence Agency.* Mclean, Va.: Association of Former Intelligence Officers, 1983.

Neff, Donald. *Warriors at Suez: Eisenhower Takes America into the Middle East.* New York: Linden Press, 1981.

Offer, Yehuda. *Operation Thunder: The Entebbe Raid, the Israelis' Own Story.* Harmondsworth, England: Penguin Books, 1976.

Ostrovsky, Victor. *By Way of Deception.* New York: St. Martin's Press, 1990.

———. *The Other Side of Deception.* New York: HarperCollins, 1994.

Powers, Thomas. *The Man Who Kept the Secrets: Richard Helms and the CIA.* New York: Knopf, 1979.

Rabin, Yitzhak. *The Rabin Memoirs.* London: Weidenfeld & Nicolson, 1979.

Richelson, Jeffrey T. *The U.S. Intelligence Community.* Cambridge, Mass.: Ballinger, 1985.

Seth, Ronald. *The Executioners: The Story of Smersh.* New York: Tempo Books, 1970.

Smith, Colin. *Portrait of a Terrorist.* New York: Holt, Rinehart and Winston, 1976.

Sterling, Claire. *The Terror Network: The Secret War of International Terrorism.* London: Weidenfeld & Nicolson, 1981.

Stevens, Stewart. *The Spymasters of Israel.* London: Hodder & Stoughton, 1981.

Stevenson, William. *90 Minutes at Entebbe.* London: Bantam Books, 1976.

Stockwell, John. *In Search of Enemies: A CIA Story.* New York: W. W. Norton, 1978.

Tinnin, David B. *The Hit Team.* Boston: Little, Brown and Company, 1976.

Tully, Andrew. *CIA: The Inside Story.* New York: William Morrow, 1961.

———. *The Super Spies: More Secrets, More Powerful than the CIA.* New York: William Morrow, 1969.

West, Nigel. *A Matter of Trust: MI5 1945–72*. London: Weidenfeld & Nicolson, 1982.

———. *MI5: British Security Service Operations 1909–1945*. London: Triad/Granada, 1983.

———. *MI6: British Secret Intelligence Service Operations 1909–1945*. London: Weidenfeld & Nicolson, 1983.

Wiesenthal, Simon. *The Murderers Among Us*. London: William Heinemann, 1967.

INDEX